POPULAR
MECHANICS

COMPLETE BOOK OF

HOME REPAIR

and

IMPROVEMENTS

$$\left[\begin{array}{l}\textit{Complete Encyclopedia for}\\\textit{Home, Workshop and Garden}\end{array}\right]$$

GREYSTONE PRESS

NEW YORK, N.Y.

PRINTED IN THE UNITED STATES OF AMERICA
BY THE J. J. LITTLE & IVES COMPANY, NEW YORK

ABOUT THIS BOOK

THIS BOOK is the answer to a million written and unwritten letters. Every year the editors of *Popular Mechanics* receive thousands of letters from home owners all over the world asking for help with their problems. Is there any way to stop a fireplace from smoking? What do you do about a leaky basement? Should you paint over wallpaper? How do you install fluorescent lights? Have you any instructions for building kitchen wall cabinets? How do you take care of old paint brushes? Is there any cure for a leaky faucet? How do you build a garden fireplace? There are those seeking advice on how to fire a coal-burning furnace, or how to get the most out of an oil burner. Craftsmen want help in building everything from a birdhouse to a seven-room home.

The editors of *Popular Mechanics* reasoned that what the world handyman and his wife needed was a book which had the answers—a book that would stand by on its shelf in readiness to meet almost any householding emergency.

The Popular Mechanics Complete Book of Home Repair and Improvements is such a book. It contains the answers to most of the help-seeking letters we have ever received, and additional answers to written and unwritten letters of the future. It was aimed at complete coverage of the field in text "written so you can understand it" and backed up by plenty of photographs, diagrams and drawings.

The material has been organized and indexed so that you can find the answer to any home problem in a jiffy. The section called "Inside Home Maintenance and Improvements" tells how to build a home freezer unit, how to frame and hang a door, lay linoleum, install a hardwood floor or make an air filter for your windows. "Painting, Decorating, and Finishing" presents a thorough coverage of this important field. "Electricity and Plumbing" includes everything electrical from care of the vacuum cleaner to tricks for converting an electric clock to a time switch. "Heating and Insulation" holds many hints for cutting down ever-rising fuel costs. "Outside Home Maintenance, Lawn and Garden" covers the home exterior field from the curb to the back fence. The section on "Woodworking" is divided into techniques and projects for your convenience. "Furniture" includes tips on upholstering, the use of foam rubber, and instructions for building, repairing and finishing furniture. "The Home Workshop" section contributes power tool shortcuts, instructions for tool grinding and drilling, tricks in using tools, an array of work benches you can build yourself, and scores of other items which the home workshop owner cannot afford to miss.

Any single item in *The Popular Mechanics Complete Book of Home Repair and Improvements* should save a homeowner the price he paid for the book. That assurance is a source of pride to

THE EDITORS OF POPULAR MECHANICS

CONTENTS

PART 1

INSIDE HOME MAINTENANCE AND IMPROVEMENTS

PART 2

PAINTING, DECORATING AND FINISHING

PART 3

ELECTRICITY AND PLUMBING

PART 4

HEATING AND INSULATION

PART 8

THE HOME WORKSHOP

Part 1

INSIDE HOME MAINTENANCE
AND IMPROVEMENTS

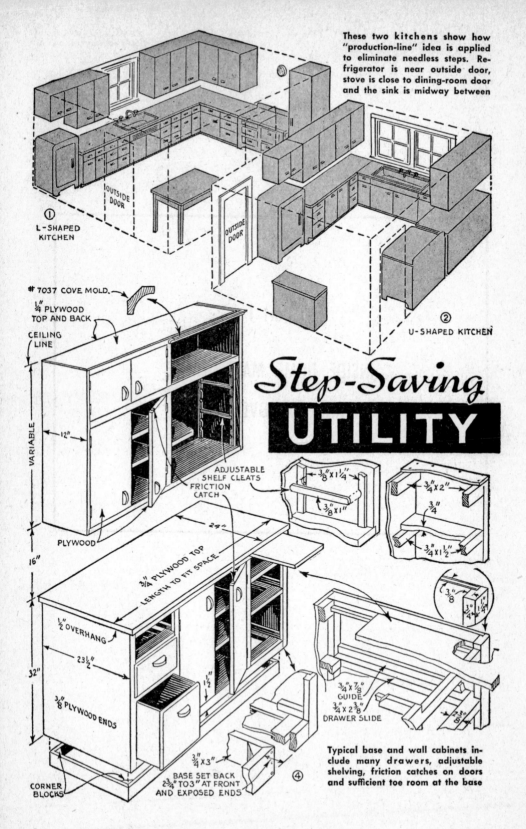

These two kitchens show how "production-line" idea is applied to eliminate needless steps. Refrigerator is near outside door, stove is close to dining-room door and the sink is midway between

① OUTSIDE DOOR

① L-SHAPED KITCHEN

OUTSIDE DOOR

② U-SHAPED KITCHEN

7037 COVE MOLD.

¼ PLYWOOD TOP AND BACK

CEILING LINE

VARIABLE

12"

PLYWOOD

ADJUSTABLE SHELF CLEATS
FRICTION CATCH

16"

Step-Saving
UTILITY

24"

¾ PLYWOOD TOP LENGTH TO FIT SPACE

½" OVERHANG

23½"

32"

⅜ PLYWOOD ENDS

1½"

CORNER BLOCKS

¾" X 3"
BASE SET BACK 2¾" TO 3" AT FRONT AND EXPOSED ENDS

④

⅜" X 1¼"
⅜" X 1"

¾" X 2"
¾"
¾" X 1½"

⅜"
¾" ¼"

¾" X ⅞"
GUIDE
¾" X 2⅜"
DRAWER SLIDE

2⅜"

Typical base and wall cabinets include many drawers, adjustable shelving, friction catches on doors and sufficient toe room at the base

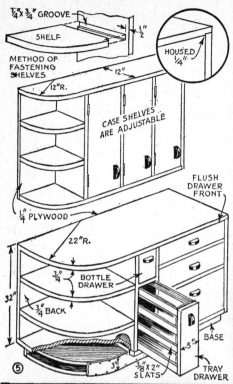

1/4″ x 3/4″ GROOVE

SHELF

1/2″

METHOD OF
FASTENING
SHELVES

HOUSED
1/4″

12″

12″R.

CASE SHELVES
ARE ADJUSTABLE

FLUSH
DRAWER
FRONT

1/4″ PLYWOOD

22″R.

3/4″ BOTTLE
DRAWER

32″

3/4″ BACK

BASE

5″

3″

3/8″ x 2″
SLATS

TRAY
DRAWER

⑤

Photo courtesy Pittsburgh Plate Glass Co.

KITCHENS

CABINETS AND BENCHES ARRANGED TO AVOID NEEDLESS WORK IN HOME

MODERN kitchens are designed not only for appearance but also for the purpose of effectively reducing unnecessary movements and needless steps in storing delivered food; in preparing it for the table; in having dishes, cutlery and utensils arranged within easy reach from the place they are used and also within easy reach from the place they are cleaned. It's surprising how much less tiresome it is to anyone who has a kitchen in which work can be accomplished efficiently with minimum effort. In a well planned kitchen the basic idea of arrangement is somewhat similar to the idea of a production line in modern industry—the raw material comes in at one end and the prepared food goes out at the other. With this in view, the ideal kitchen has the refrigerator near the outside entrance, with a counter or table near by on which delivered foods may be placed before storing them in the refrigerator or cabinets. The stove should be located near the dining-room door for convenience in serving, and the sink should be set about midway between refrigerator and stove. Figs. 1 and 2 show two layouts of efficient kitchens. Although the shape of your kitchen, the location of doors and windows, etc., may not conform to either of these examples, the basic "triangle" arrangement between refrigerator, sink and stove should be maintained.

Most kitchen cabinets consist of base units provided with counters and wall units spaced from 15 to 18 in. above the counters. Wall units may extend clear to the ceiling and the upper sections are used for storing articles seldom needed. In case the wall units do not extend to the ceiling, the space above them is often boxed in for appearance. Dimensions of cabinets depend to a great extent upon the space you have available although the basic construction is shown in Fig. 4. The details in Fig. 3 show adjustable shelf cleats and

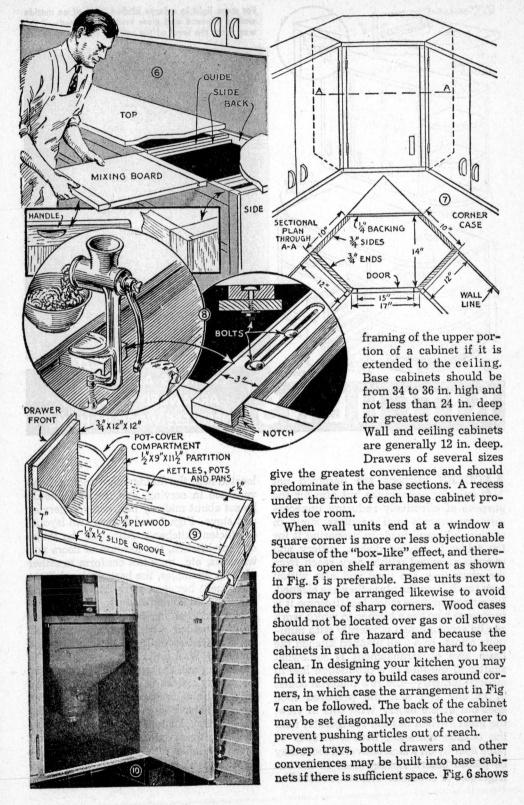

⑥ GUIDE SLIDE BACK

TOP

MIXING BOARD

SIDE

HANDLE

⑧ BOLTS

← 3″ →

NOTCH

DRAWER FRONT

¾″ x 12″ x 12″

POT-COVER COMPARTMENT

1½″ x 9″ x 11½″ PARTITION

KETTLES, POTS AND PANS

1½″

¼″ PLYWOOD

7″

¼″ x ½″ SLIDE GROOVE

⑨

⑦ CORNER CASE

A — — A

SECTIONAL PLAN THROUGH A-A

10″ ¼″ BACKING

¾″ SIDES

¾″ ENDS

12″ DOOR

15″

17″

10″

14″

12″

WALL LINE

⑩

framing of the upper portion of a cabinet if it is extended to the ceiling. Base cabinets should be from 34 to 36 in. high and not less than 24 in. deep for greatest convenience. Wall and ceiling cabinets are generally 12 in. deep. Drawers of several sizes give the greatest convenience and should predominate in the base sections. A recess under the front of each base cabinet provides toe room.

When wall units end at a window a square corner is more or less objectionable because of the "box-like" effect, and therefore an open shelf arrangement as shown in Fig. 5 is preferable. Base units next to doors may be arranged likewise to avoid the menace of sharp corners. Wood cases should not be located over gas or oil stoves because of fire hazard and because the cabinets in such a location are hard to keep clean. In designing your kitchen you may find it necessary to build cases around corners, in which case the arrangement in Fig. 7 can be followed. The back of the cabinet may be set diagonally across the corner to prevent pushing articles out of reach.

Deep trays, bottle drawers and other conveniences may be built into base cabinets if there is sufficient space. Fig. 6 shows

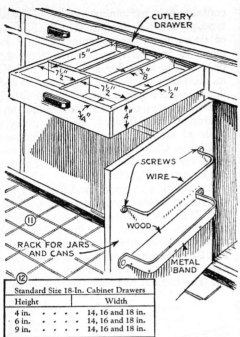

CUTLERY DRAWER

15″

7½″

3″⁄8

7½″

½″

¾″

4″

⑪

SCREWS

WIRE

WOOD

RACK FOR JARS AND CANS

METAL BAND

⑬

Standard Size 18-In. Cabinet Drawers	
Height	Width
4 in. · · · ·	14, 16 and 18 in.
6 in. · · · ·	14, 16 and 18 in.
9 in. · · · ·	14, 16 and 18 in.

⑫

how mixing and cutting boards may be made to slide under the top and Fig. 8 pictures a convenient slide for clamping a food chopper or other similar equipment. A deep drawer for pots and pans is shown in Fig. 9. The partition provides a separate compartment for covers. Racks to hold jars, cans, and many other articles may be attached to the inside of cabinet doors as in Fig. 11. This drawing also shows how cutlery drawers are divided with partitions. Articles placed in deep cabinets are often difficult to reach without kneeling, but this is avoided if shelves are made to slide as in Fig. 16. For many small articles, such as spices, an intermediate, half-width shelf is convenient. A special metal bin may be installed for flour as shown in Fig. 10. Such a bin slides on metal strips fastened to the underside of a shelf so that it can be removed for filling. Space on counters under wall cabinets may be utilized for keeping motor-driven mixers and juicers as shown in Fig. 13.

Types of cabinet doors are shown in Fig. 14. The flush type is popular because of the ease with which it can be cleaned, although many people prefer the panel type. If you do not care to make your own doors, you can purchase them from millwork dealers. Standard sizes of panel-type cabinet doors are given in Fig. 15, which also

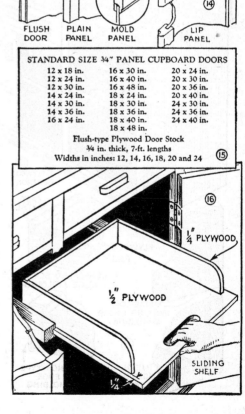

PLYWOOD

PANELS

FLUSH DOOR

PLAIN PANEL

MOLD PANEL

LIP PANEL

⑭

STANDARD SIZE ¾″ PANEL CUPBOARD DOORS		
12 x 18 in.	16 x 30 in.	20 x 24 in.
12 x 24 in.	16 x 40 in.	20 x 30 in.
12 x 30 in.	16 x 48 in.	20 x 36 in.
14 x 24 in.	18 x 24 in.	20 x 40 in.
14 x 30 in.	18 x 30 in.	24 x 30 in.
14 x 36 in.	18 x 36 in.	24 x 36 in.
16 x 24 in.	18 x 40 in.	24 x 40 in.
	18 x 48 in.	

Flush-type Plywood Door Stock
¾ in. thick, 7-ft. lengths
Widths in inches: 12, 14, 16, 18, 20 and 24

⑮

⑯

¼″ PLYWOOD

½″ PLYWOOD

SLIDING SHELF

¼″

contains data pertaining to sizes of flush-type, plywood-door stock. For the lip type of doors your case openings should be made ⅝ in. smaller each way than the door size to allow for a ¼-in. lip and 1/16 in. clearance all around. Lip drawers and doors require less accuracy in the fitting but do not give quite the "streamline" appearance often desired. Fig. 12 gives a table of standard size drawers that are available. Chromium-plated hinges of various types are obtainable, some of which are shown in Fig. 20.

An old sink in good condition and not too badly located, may often be utilized. Fig. 22 shows how a cabinet may be built under an old sink. The framework for such a cabinet is shown in Fig. 21, and Fig. 23 gives details of construction. However, in most cases a new sink is suggested. The cabinet to house the sink is built

Cabinet-type sink sizes are: 14 x 20, 16 x 24, 18 x 18, 20 x 24, 20 x 30, 20 x 32, 18 x 42 and 22 x 48 inches. Last two are double sinks

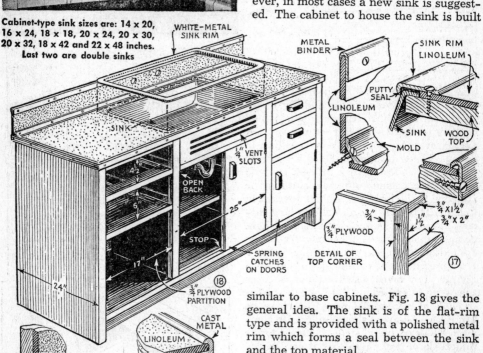

similar to base cabinets. Fig. 18 gives the general idea. The sink is of the flat-rim type and is provided with a polished metal rim which forms a seal between the sink and the top material.

The top or counter surface of base cabinets and the top of the sink cabinet may be covered with linoleum or other hard-wearing, waterproof covering material. Stainless metal moldings shown in Figs. 17 and 19 are used to give the finishing touch to counter and sink tops.

As walls around sinks, stoves and counters are subjected to splattering of water and grease, they should be protected with tile board, linoleum or a suitable wall covering. On the floor you can use linoleum

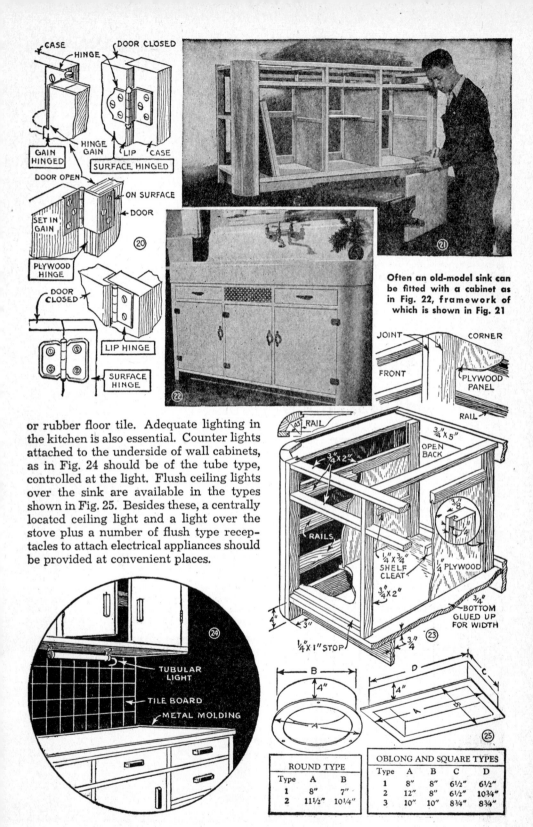

Often an old-model sink can be fitted with a cabinet as in Fig. 22, framework of which is shown in Fig. 21

or rubber floor tile. Adequate lighting in the kitchen is also essential. Counter lights attached to the underside of wall cabinets, as in Fig. 24 should be of the tube type, controlled at the light. Flush ceiling lights over the sink are available in the types shown in Fig. 25. Besides these, a centrally located ceiling light and a light over the stove plus a number of flush type receptacles to attach electrical appliances should be provided at convenient places.

ROUND TYPE		
Type	A	B
1	8″	7″
2	11½″	10¼″

OBLONG AND SQUARE TYPES				
Type	A	B	C	D
1	8″	8″	6½″	6½″
2	12″	8″	6½″	10¾″
3	10″	10″	8¾″	8¾″

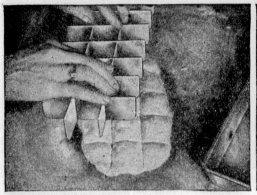

To cut biscuits in a hurry, use the divider from an ice-cube tray. After mixing the dough, roll it to the right shape and cut with the divider. When baked, separate the biscuits at the dividing lines

Tired of using rubber pads, metal plates and other unsightly objects to keep the feet of kitchen furniture off the linoleum, one housewife cut circular pieces of thick celluloid and placed them under the feet

PRACTICAL

HOUSEHOLD

HINTS

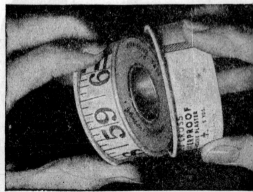

An old toothbrush will provide excellent service as a comb cleaner. Trim it to the correct size by cutting off all bristles except the three end rows

When storing or drying boots, use this converted clothes hanger to keep them off the floor. The hanger is cut and bent as shown, the space between the eyes being governed by the width of the sole

If a tape measure is wound on the spool of an adhesive tape container, it will not kink and become limp. Stored in this way, it's ready for use and will not become entangled in the workbasket

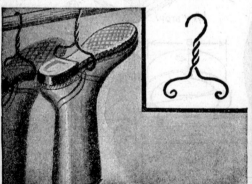

Wrap a piece of onion skin around the broken stalk or branch of a house plant to hold it securely until it has healed. This makes an inconspicuous patch and one that may save your favorite plant

Made with a built-in drawer, this cutting block will hold most of your knives and other cutlery. The drawer is lined and spacers are provided to separate the knives so the edges are not dulled

One way to keep a clothesline taut is to suspend the wire between crossarms that screw into a tee fitting. The wire is wound around the pipe before it is pulled up. Tightening it will remove the slack

In rainy weather, place a large desk blotter inside the front door so that wet rubbers and galoshes can be dried on it. When not in use, the blotter can be rolled up and kept in a hall closet

Brushing that steel soap dish with colorless nail polish will prevent unsightly rust spots from appearing where the protective coating has worn off. These spots cause the soap to stick to the dish

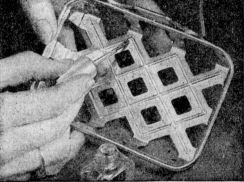

Squeegee Increases Efficiency When Cleaning Floors

TUBING

RUBBER

CUT FROM BARREL HOOPS

This squeegee will eliminate much of the labor of cleaning and drying floors. The curved pieces that hold the rubber are two equal lengths of barrel hoop with holes for 3/16-in. stove bolts drilled on 3-in. centers. A broomstick is used for the handle with a 9-in. length of thin-wall tubing as a yoke. The tubing is split for a distance of 3 in. and bent and drilled as shown to attach the handle to the squeegee. Stove bolts of the same size are used throughout.

Safe Way to Wash Lace Collars

When laundering lace collars, crocheted doilies and similar articles, you can avoid stretching them out of shape by washing them in a jar of soap suds. Just fill a quart fruit jar with water and soap, put in the articles, replace the lid and shake the jar up and down several times. After washing, rinse the articles thoroughly with clear water in the same way.

◖Sawdust used with soap and water makes a good hand cleaner to remove grease.

Removing Ink Spots from Upholstered Furniture and Rugs

If the ink spots on furniture or rugs are still wet, remove as much ink as possible with the repeated application of blotting paper. Then outline the spot with white basting thread so the exact area to be further treated is shown. Soak clean cloths in a weak solution of oxalic acid and remove the balance of the ink, working outward from the center of the spot. Following this step, mix fuller's earth

Pad Sweeps Dust Off Records

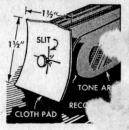

SLIT

TONE AR

CLOTH PAD

REC

Scraps of velvet, velour and similar fabrics can be used to make a "sweep" that will brush dust off a record as it is being played. The squares of cloth have cross slits in the center to slip over the needle tig' ing screw on the tone arm. The should be adjusted to clean the record in the path of the needle as the disk is rotating. It may be necessary to use cellulose tape to hold the cloth in the desired position.

Removing Stains from Furniture

Dishwater, grease and ink stains are removed easily from a piece of furniture when the mark is on top of the varnish. A light oil and pumice stone, mixed to a putty-like consistency, is rubbed briskly with a cloth in the direction of the grain until the mark disappears. If the grease or ink has penetrated the varnish into the wood, repeat applications of oxalic-acid solution. The solution is made by dis solving one tablespoon of oxalic granul in a pint of water.

Easy Way to Clean Plaster Objects

After a time almost all plaster objects, such as statuettes, plaques, etc., collect dust that cannot be removed with a cloth. To clean such bric-a-brac, make a thick paste of white powdered starch and hot water. Brush the paste over the plaster and allow it to dry. Then scale the sta from the object and the dirt will be removed with it. Before using this starch paste, make sure it will not mar the finish of the plaster by applying a small amount on a test area.

Common Bleach Removes Ink

Common bleaching solutio laundry variety can be used as cator that will remove inks of all kind except indelible. It is convenient to place the remover in an empty bottle with a glass rod attached to the cork.

with the oxalic acid until a putty-like consistency is obtained. Apply and allow it to dry. Then clean with a brush having stiff bristles. It may be necessary to apply oxalic acid several times. Other dark spots caused by chimney soot are cleaned by applying salt or corn meal. Spread large quantities over the soiled area and then brush it up. Repeated applications will be necessary.

Silencing SQUEAKY FLOORS

WAYNE C. LECKEY

HAVE you annoying squeaks in your floors? There are several ways to cure the trouble, but as each squeak presents an individual problem, no one treatment can be given that will guarantee results in all cases. Where floors cannot be reached from below you will have to work from above as is shown in Figs. 1, 2, and 3. Squeaks in lower floors that are accessible from a basement can be stopped usually by one of the methods indicated in Figs. 4, 5 and 6. Before proceeding in any case have someone stand or walk on the spot while you carefully check the action taking place and the exact location where the squeak is most noticeable. If the joints seem to be nailed inadequately, toenailing, as in Fig. 1, will often silence the squeak by drawing down the hardwood strips securely to the subfloor. Finishing nails, 1½ in. long are driven at a tangent along the joint, in both directions, and the heads set below the surface and filled flush with wood putty.

Where movement is detected at the butt ends of the strips, a screw at the joint will pull both down solidly as in Fig. 2. Use a ⅞-in., No. 10 wood screw in a counterbored hole centered on the joint. Take care not to counterbore completely through the hardwood strip, but just enough to allow the screw head to be hidden with an oak plug, which is pared off flush and touched up with a little varnish to match the floor as closely as possible.

In the event rubbing is noticed along an open joint, penetrating oil mixed with powdered graphite has been found effective in relieving the

Toenailing

NAIL HEAD SUNK AND PUTTIED OVER
HARDWOOD FLOOR
1½" FINISHING NAILS
SUBFLOOR
SECTION

Screws at joints

COUNTER-BORED HOLE
OAK PLUG GLUED
END JOINT
⅞" NO.10 SCREW
FLOORING

Lubricating with powdered graphite

17

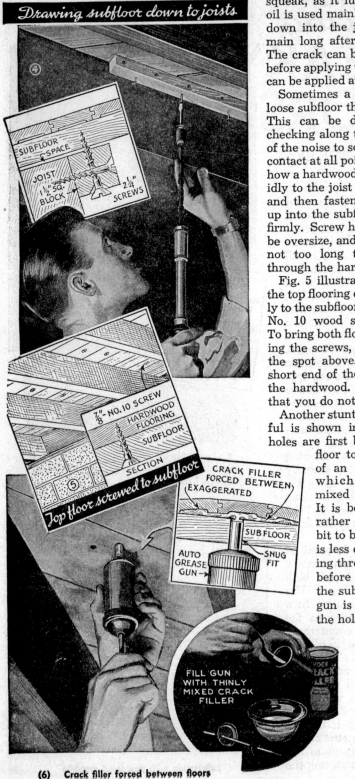

④

SUBFLOOR
SPACE
JOIST
1 1/2" SQ. BLOCK
2 1/4" SCREWS

7/8"-NO. 10 SCREW
HARDWOOD FLOORING
SUBFLOOR
SECTION
⑤

Top floor screwed to subfloor

CRACK FILLER FORCED BETWEEN
(EXAGGERATED)
SUBFLOOR
AUTO GREASE GUN
SNUG FIT

FILL GUN WITH THINLY MIXED CRACK FILLER

(6) Crack filler forced between floors

squeak, as it lubricates the joint. **The** oil is used mainly to carry the graphite down into the joint, where it will remain long after the oil has dried out. The crack can be packed with graphite before applying the oil, Fig. 3, or the two can be applied at once with an oilcan.

Sometimes a squeak is caused by a loose subfloor that has become buckled. This can be determined quickly by checking along the joists in the vicinity of the noise to see that the subfloor is in contact at all points. If not, Fig. 4 shows how a hardwood strip, first screwed solidly to the joist even with the top edge, and then fastened with screws driven up into the subfloor, will draw it down firmly. Screw holes in the block should be oversize, and be sure the screws are not too long to pierce completely through the hardwood flooring.

Fig. 5 illustrates a manner in which the top flooring can be anchored securely to the subfloor by driving short 7/8-in., No. 10 wood screws up from below. To bring both floors together while driving the screws, have someone stand on the spot above. This will permit the short end of the screw to take hold in the hardwood. Again it is important that you do not drive them too deeply.

Another stunt you might find successful is shown in Fig. 6. Here several holes are first bored through the subfloor to take snugly the spout of an automobile grease gun which is filled with thinly mixed crack-filler compound. It is best to use a twist drill rather than an ordinary wood bit to bore these holes, as there is less chance of the spur coming through the hardwood floor before a clean hole is made in the subfloor. The spout of the gun is pressed tightly up into the hole and the filler is forced between the two floors. Be sure to plug each hole as soon as it is filled to prevent the crack filler from being forced out when pressure is applied to adjacent holes. When the filler becomes hard, it will bind the two floors together.

Steel Wool Cleans Stove Burners

Aluminum burners in domestic gas ranges are kept clean and bright by using steel wool to polish them at weekly intervals. Pipe cleaners will remove steel-wool waste that is caught in the burner holes. Any small bits of steel that may drop into cracks or on flat surfaces of the stove can be picked up with a magnet.

Washing Rugs Without a Machine

When you do not have a washing machine in which to clean such heavy articles as rag rugs or chenille and crocheted bedspreads, soak them overnight in the bathtub in thick soap suds. The next morning dip them up and down several times and, without wringing, hang them on the clothesline. Turn the hose on them until all the soap is rinsed out.

Washing Flat-Painted Walls

If your flat-painted walls streak or spot when they are cleaned, try the following method: First, mix washing soda, ¼ lb., commercial size, ½ lb., with water, 1½ gals. Brush this solution onto the wall, working the solution into the dirt. Then rinse well with a sponge. You will find that the solution cleans the walls without leaving streaks or dark spots.

POT SCOURER

DOWEL

Scraps of Paper Swept from Floor by "Broom" of Wire Mesh

Small scraps of paper can be removed from a floor by using an improvised "broom" made by attaching a pot scourer or piece of wire mesh to a length of dowel. Used with a sweeping motion, the mesh will grip the paper scraps so that they can be brushed into a dustpan.

Removable Crosspiece on Ladder Simplifies Window Washing

When second-story windows are washed on the outside from an ordinary ladder, the job is both difficult and dangerous because the ladder has to be placed at one side of the window or rest on the sill. From either position it is not easy to reach all parts of the window pane. However, if two pieces of flat iron are bolted over the ends of the ladder and a wood crosspiece inserted, the ladder can be placed directly over the window.

Eggshells Clean Narrow Vases

When narrow-neck crystal vases and bottles need cleaning and a bottle brush won't do the work, break several eggshells into the bottle or vase, add a little water and shake until all film and dust disappear from the glass. After rinsing, the vase will be crystal clear.

Chemical Test for Hard Water

A simple test to determine whether water is hard or soft is to use a solution made by dissolving chemically pure mercurous nitrate crystals in distilled water. A tablespoonful of the crystals is dissolved in a cup of water to make the test solution. If the water to be tested is hard, it will become cloudy when a small amount of the solution is poured into it, but if it is soft it will remain clear. The unused solution may be stored in any nonmetallic container for future use.

Ammonia Removes Oven Scorch

Ovens scorched when pie or other confections run over may be cleaned by leaving a cloth saturated with ordinary household ammonia over the spot for a couple of hours, after which the scorched material will wipe off.

Chalk Paste Removes Grease

To remove a grease spot from wallpaper, French chalk is mixed with dry-cleaning fluid to the consistency of a thick paste and applied to the spot. After remaining overnight, it then is brushed off carefully. The process can be repeated if the spot is still visible.

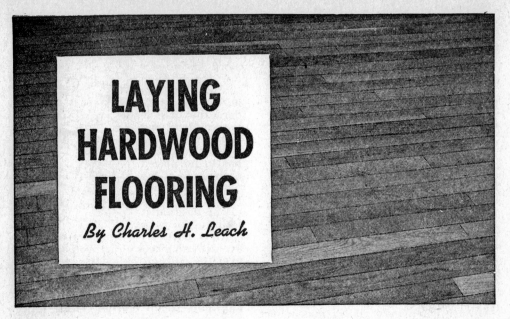

LAYING HARDWOOD FLOORING

By Charles H. Leach

Photos by Roger Williams

This article shows the homeowner and builder the step-by-step process of laying a hardwood floor. Complete instructions on how to finish it are given in an article, "Finishing Floors," which begins on page 26. These instructions also apply to finishing an old floor.

IF YOU are one of many homeowners who have purchased an old-type house and are remodeling it yourself, few improvements will increase its value and improve its interior appearance more than beautiful hardwood floors. Whether the condition of present floors is beyond refinishing and requires resurfacing with thin flooring, or whether an old softwood floor is to be covered, almost anyone who is handy with a hammer and saw can do the job with excellent results. Most of the

tools required are common ones. Besides a hammer, you'll need handsaws for ripping and crosscutting, a nailset, a pair of dividers or a compass and a can of plastic wood putty to cover exposed nailheads where the flooring must be surface-nailed.

Types of flooring: The attractive grain of quarter-sawed flooring makes a beautiful job when waxed or varnished and, when available, is to be preferred to the plain or "flash sawed" type shown in Fig. 3. Quarter-sawed flooring is recognized by the wavy pattern of surface grain and by the slant of the growth rings in the end grain. It is somewhat more expensive than plain-sawed flooring, but has less tendency to curl and surface splinter. Flooring usually is sold in bundles of strips ranging in length from 2 to 12 ft. or more and end-

This is how the last strip of each row is marked for length with a try square by placing it end for end against the wall and parallel with adjoining strip

Flooring is sold in bundles of strips of random lengths up to 12 ft., which are end and edge-matched with a tongue and groove, and cup-molded on the underside

1

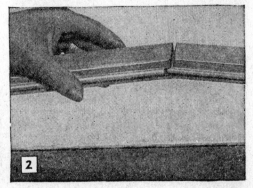

2

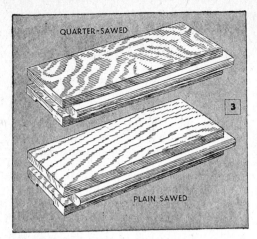

matched, Fig. 2, as well as edge-matched by a tongue and groove in the edge. The underside face of the strips is hollowed or cupped so that any unevenness of the subfloor will not interfere with their lying flat. Flooring can be had in four hard woods: oak (white and red), maple, beech and birch. Oak flooring is available in strips of two standard widths and thicknesses. One measures ⅜ by 1½ in., the other 1³⁄₁₆ by 2¼ in. The condition of the subfloor or nailing base determines largely the size and type of flooring to use. Some homeowners prefer a floor laid of narrow strips which are used in resurfacing an old hardwood floor and when the nailing base is solid. The 1³⁄₁₆-in. flooring generally is used over a rough subfloor or one that is not thick enough or properly reinforced to give adequate support to thin-type flooring.

Ready-finished flooring recently has been introduced which saves the work of finishing and the inconvenience encountered in waiting for the floor to dry. This feature is especially desirable when laying a new floor in an occupied house. It differs from regular flooring in that it has

a V-joint instead of a tongue and groove and, of course, it is stained, sealed or otherwise finished, ready for use as soon as it is laid. However, being prefinished, it requires great care in laying to avoid marring. To help reduce possible damage from hammer marks, the flooring is factory drilled for nails and is packaged for further protection. It naturally is considerably more expensive, as in addition to being finished, it is specially selected for straightness and uniform grain.

Keep flooring dry: Due to its low moisture content when kiln dried, flooring is highly subject to dampness and, until it is laid and completely finished, it is very important that it be kept *dry* at all times. This is especially so if the flooring is stored for any length of time prior to laying. It also is important that if laid during damp weather, the building be heated. If allowed to absorb moisture, a tightly laid floor will shrink when it dries out, leaving objectionable openings between the strips. In new construction, flooring should not be laid until the plaster has dried completely as it will absorb moisture from the walls.

Preliminary steps: The first step in laying a new floor is to inspect the old floor, or subfloor if it is new construction, for loose boards, ridges and any other high places that might prevent the new flooring from lying flat. Nail such places thoroughly to pull the boards down flush. This is important to assure a squeakless floor and prevent movement in the finished floor. In resurfacing a previously laid hard or softwood floor, it is advisable to remove the baseboard. This can be done without damaging the baseboard by locating the nails and driving them completely through and into the studs with a pin punch. Following this, the floor should be swept clean

Starting strip should be laid at right angles to side walls. If corners of room are not square, mark grooved edge of strip with compass to match wall

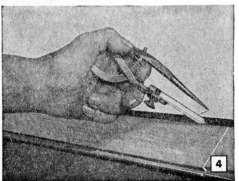

and covered with a good grade of building paper, lapped at the sides and ends. Old softwood floors that are worn badly sometimes are covered first with plywood and special long nails used to apply the flooring. On new floors, the paper liner serves as a dust-and-draft barrier between the subfloor and finish floor, while on an old floor, which without doubt was originally laid over a paper covering, the new paper simply provides a smooth, clean, working surface.

How flooring is nailed: Flooring is nailed blind, in other words toenailed, so that the nailheads are hidden. This is done by driving the nails into the angle between the tongue and front edge of the strip as shown in Fig. 6. Use 8-penny wire flooring nails or special cut-steel flooring nails and drive them at an angle of 45 deg. Experience will enable you to drive the nails practically all the way with a hammer, as in Fig. 9. However, it is advisable at first to drive them part way and finish with a nailset to avoid the possibility of accidentally damaging the edge of the flooring. If cut nails

are used, they can be driven home by using the side of the head of another nail as shown in Fig. 7. The important thing is to drive the head flush or slightly below the surface so that it will not interfere with drawing up the subsequent strip. In the case of very hard woods, such as maple or birch, it may be necessary to first drill holes for the nails to avoid splitting, especially if wire nails are used. The blunt nose of cut nails will not split the wood as readily, as they punch through the wood. The nails should be spaced about 8 in. in laying ⅜-in. flooring and from 10 to 16 in. for thick flooring. It pays to nail a floor well to avoid later squeaks and loose boards.

Laying the starting strip: If you are covering a badly worn hardwood floor, the new flooring is laid at right angles to the old. The first strip is selected for straightness and is laid with the grooved edge facing the wall and close enough so that the baseboard, if used, will cover any small opening. If the corners of the room are not square, the starting strip should be placed at a 90-deg. angle to the side wall, marked

When waste portion of the last strip in each row is a foot or more in length it is used to start next row

Blind-nail each strip by nailing in angle of tongue and edge. Use 8-penny nails driven at 45-deg. angle

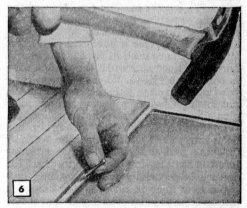

Each nailhead must be set flush or slightly below surface. Side of cut nail or regular nailset will do

Pencil compass is handy for marking strips when fitting flooring neatly around or under a doorcasing

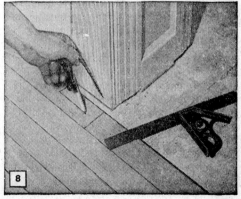

22

with a compass as in Fig. 4 and ripped to conform to the adjacent wall. This starting strip generally is face-nailed along the rear edge and sometimes it also is toenailed in the tongue. While it is best to have the starting strip in one piece, the size of the room may require several pieces laid end to end. In the latter case, if the piece cut off is greater than a foot in length, it usually is used to start the next row, Fig. 5. The last strip in each row is marked for length with a try square as in Fig. 1, after placing it end for end and against the wall. From here on it is a case of drawing the flooring strips of each row tightly against those of the preceding row to assure tight-fitting joints. For this purpose cut a scrap of flooring and use it to drive against. This will prevent damaging the tongue and will be found helpful in drawing up stubborn joints. Strips of flooring that are slightly bowed can be forced tightly against the preceding row by prying with a wooden block placed against a 2 by 4-in. lever and block temporarily nailed to the floor. The joints in each subsequent row always

Abutting strips are placed crosswise to the door opening when ending the floor at bathroom or kitchen

9

Practice will enable you to drive nails rapidly from standing position. Heads are set later with nailset

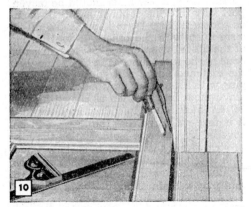

10

Final fill-in strip is marked to conform to wall by wedging full-width strip and marking with compass

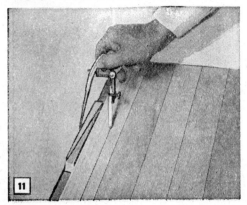

11

should be staggered at least 6 in. or more.

Notching around doorcasing: When you must fit the flooring around or under the casing of a doorway leading to an adjacent room or closet, a pair of dividers or a compass is used to mark the depth of the required notch. Fig. 8 illustrates how this is done, the flooring in this case being fitted to butt against the casing. If you are resurfacing an old floor and wish the flooring to run under the casing and jamb, it will be necessary to saw off these two pieces to allow for the extra thickness. As shown in Fig. 8, the strip to be marked is not nailed but is simply tapped temporarily in position and butted against the end of the adjoining strip in the same row. Note that the joint of the adjoining strip ends flush with the face of the jamb. Now, measure the space between the loose strip and the face of the casing and set the compass so that this distance is marked on the strip when one leg of the compass is held in contact with the casing. Any slight cant or irregularity of the casing will be transferred to the strip assuring a perfect-fitting butt joint. The loose strip is removed and replaced with a full-width strip, the two strips being laid at the same time to enable wedging snugly in place. When the direction of the flooring runs through a doorway and you wish the new floor to end in

23

12

13

Drive nails part way and bend them over to support narrow fill-in strip flush with the rest of the flooring

Bowed fill-in strip is forced in place tightly for marking by prying against wall with board and block

the center of the opening as in Fig. 10, the compass method is used as before to mark the strip to fit the jamb. Note here that one or two strips of flooring are first nailed down parallel with the opening and serve as header strips against which the flooring is butted. This generally applies when a hardwood floor is butted against a bathroom or kitchen floor which is to be built up flush and covered with linoleum.

Fitting final strips: If no baseboards are to be used and only a shoe mold, the steps in fitting the last remaining strips are shown in Figs. 11 to 15 inclusive. When the space remaining along the wall is less than a full width of flooring, the strip next to

the final one is set in place temporarily and wedged either with tapered blocks as shown in Fig. 11, or forced in place by prying as shown in Fig. 12. After this it is marked, as before, with a compass to transfer the contour of the wall, then ripped and used as a fill-in strip. Due to the fact that flooring is cupped or hollowed on the underside and ripping removes one supporting edge, a few nails should be driven part way into the subfloor and bent over, as shown in Fig. 13, to support the fill-in strip flush with the others. Actual laying of the fill-in strip and the last few strips is done at the same time, as in Fig. 14, so that the matched edges will go in place. Tapping with a hammer and wooden block will drive them into position as shown in Fig. 15. As the fill-in strip cannot be toenailed, it is face-nailed so that the heads will be covered by the shoe mold. Fitting the fill-in strip tightly is not so important when both baseboard and shoe mold are used, as together they will cover any slight gap that may remain along the wall.

To permit inserting the fill-in strip, last few strips are laid at same time to engage the matched edges

Fill-in strips and others are gradually forced down with hammer and block. Then the strip is face-nailed

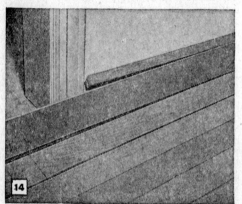

14

15

Drop Shelf Near Refrigerator Saves Many Steps

A drop shelf near the refrigerator will come in handy when taking out foods. Many different items can be taken out at one time, which eliminates opening and closing the door repeatedly. For example, if milk, eggs, butter, meat and salad dressing are needed, this usually means two or three trips to the refrigerator, but with this shelf all can be handled at one time. The shelf is made 18 in. wide so that the supports can be screwed into studding. The manner in which the brace fits into the cleat is indicated in the circular detail. The shelf can be painted white and decorated with decals

Handy Shoe-Shining Foot Rest Folds Into Dresser Drawer

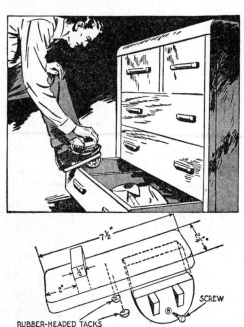

Pivot this simple foot rest to one side of the lower drawer in your bedroom dresser and it will always be handy to shine your shoes. When not in use, the foot rest folds down inside the drawer out of sight.

Novel Drawer Lock on Dresser Keeps Children from Prying

Children are naturally curious, and a dresser or chest of drawers is a fertile field for exploration. To keep youngsters out of the drawers, one parent connected a series of latches in such a manner that no lower drawer could be opened unless the top one, which the children could not reach, was first pulled out. The latches, as shown in the detail, were connected to a screw eye in the top drawer with a cord. Pulling out this drawer lifted all the latches.

FINISHING

Although floor finishing on old or new work is one of the simplest wood-finishing jobs, the process calls for careful attention to details. Here are ways of making old floors new, and new floors better

By Charles H. Leach

FINISHING either old or new hardwood floors requires the same procedure except that on an old floor you sometimes add one more step, that of removing the old finish. Some finishers take off the old varnish first with a paint and varnish remover. This will save time when sanding floors which have been varnished several coats. However, in most cases where the floor has been finished in the usual way, removal of the varnish before sanding is not necessary. The first step on either old or new floors is to smooth and fill the bare wood. On new floors this should be done before the floor has been walked on or exposed too long to changes of temperature and humidity. Dust, which settles and becomes embedded in the open grain of the wood by the action of moisture darkens the surface.

Sanding: On both new and old floors the edges of the boards will be slightly raised, due to shrinkage and also the clearance in the joints. This wavy surface

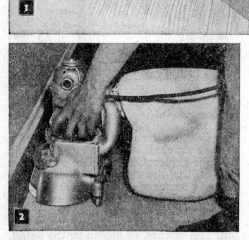

With an edger like this one you can sand the floor clear to the baseboard. Machines of this type are available at most hardware stores on a rental basis

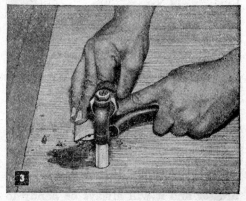

On nearly every floor there will be some spots you cannot reach with the sander, near drain pipes and in corners. Finish such places by hand with a scraper

FLOORS

can be noted by passing the palm of your hand over the floor. Although these raised places can be removed with a hand scraper as was the regular practice in older methods, a much faster way is to go over the floor with a sanding machine.

There are several types of sanding machines available on a rental basis and you will need two of them. The drum-type machine, Fig. 1, is used for preparing the open area of the floor to within 2 or 3 in. of the baseboards, while the disk-type edger, Fig. 2, is designed to finish this remaining strip. It is best to remove the shoe mold before using this machine. If there are radiators in the room, these also should be taken out. Remove the finish from an old floor with a coarse abrasive on the sanding drum. Then use a medium grit for smoothing out the scratches left by the first abrasive and finally finish with a fine-grit abrasive. On a new floor in good condition, the coarse sanding is not necessary.

In the operation of these machines, it is essential to keep them in motion while the abrasive is in contact with the floor. Otherwise the abrasive will dig in. Speed of movement over the floor is not as important as uniformity. When operating the drum-type machine keep it in motion and raise the drum from the floor when you reach the baseboard. Roughing (first sanding) can be done in any direction, with the grain or across the grain. Most floor finishers run the machine at an angle of 45 deg. for the first sanding, as shown in Fig. 1. The rough sanding removes the old finish and evens up the individual floor boards. When finishing with the medium and fine abrasives, sanding is always done with the grain. Use coarse, medium and fine disks on the edger also, so that you get the same uniformity of finish all the way to the baseboards.

Scraping: There are always some spots you cannot reach even with both sanding machines, such as around radiator pipes, sink drains, and a small area in each corner of the room that the shoe mold will not cover. Here the old finish must be removed and the wood smoothed with a hand scraper, Fig. 3. Care must be taken when scraping around water pipes, as the wood is nearly always discolored. It's important to remove all this discoloration as otherwise it will show up with greater emphasis when the floor is finished.

Dusting: When the floor has been thoroughly sanded and scraped, dust off all window stools and frames, all doorframes,

The filler should be reduced with turpentine to a light, creamy consistency. Stir thoroughly to dissolve all lumps, and stir the mixture occasionally while using

Some finishers apply the filler with the grain as shown; others insist that it is better to apply it across the grain, as this method promotes greater absorption

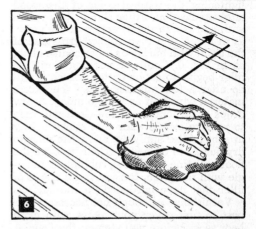

Filler should always be rubbed in across the grain with a coarse cloth. Double the cloth several times to make a soft pad which will pick up excess material

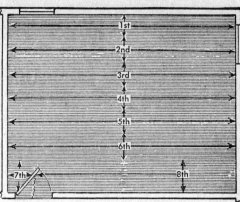

Above and left, apply sealers and varnish with long strokes, using a wide, well-filled brush. Begin in the corner farthest from the door and apply a strip about 2 ft. wide all the way across the room. Finish to the door with successive varnished strips of equal width

doors and baseboards. Use a painter's tack rag for this as it picks up dust without scattering it about. Dust the floor thoroughly with the same cloth. Frequent dusting while the finishing process is going on is important. If light dust accumulates in the room air movement may dislodge it. Floating dust particles always settle on the freshly varnished surface, and cause flecking and spotting of the finish.

Filling: All porous woods must be filled. Some finishers prefer to apply a light oil stain before filling, to give the floor an even color tone. Others mix the stain with the filler. On a new floor this latter method is faster and gives good results, but on either old or new work, the former method generally is considered the best practice. In either case, a small quantity of stain is added to the filler, Fig. 4, to prevent it from lightening the natural color of the wood after application. Filler should be applied with a brush, in the direction of the grain, as in Fig. 5, and then rubbed crosswise of the grain with burlap or other coarse cloth, as in Fig. 6. Continue rubbing until the filler begins to set or flatten, which it will do after a few minutes. Keep the excess material wiped off as you go along. A few drops of turpentine on the cloth will help to remove excess filler that sticks tightly in spots. After applying, allow the filler to dry for 24 to 36 hours. Then go over the floor with fine steel wool, rubbing at an angle with the grain, to remove all traces of filler that have hardened on the surface.

Varnishing: Although not necessary, it's best to first cover your shoes with cloth boot socks before you step on the floor. A smudge from a rubber heel is difficult to remove. Next, apply a floor sealer with a wide brush. Start in a corner and work a strip from one side of the room to the other, Fig. 7, laying on the material with a full brush and with the grain of the wood. After allowing this coat to dry in a temperature of 68 to 70 deg., smooth with fine steel wool and dust thoroughly. Follow with one coat of high-grade floor varnish. Flow on the varnish coat with a full brush, covering narrow strips successively, as in the detail at the right of Fig. 7. Finish up at the door. Allow this coat to dry for a longer period than the first, and then smooth again with fine steel wool. If, after drying, the floor shows a dull spot here and there where the wood grain has taken up the finish, you will need to apply a third coat. Usually, however, one coat of sealer and one of varnish are ample on a well-filled floor.

Waxing: Wax protects against scratches because it provides a "slip" surface. Grit, shoe nails, toys or other sharp objects tend to slide over a waxed surface without gouging or scratching. However, a rubbed and polished wax coating is slippery and rugs placed on such a floor may be the cause of injury to someone from falling. Avoid this danger by using a "self-polishing" wax which gives a pleasing gloss without being slippery.

Don't wax the floor immediately after the varnish is dry. Allow at least two weeks, although more time is better. If a paste wax is used, apply it to the sealed floor in thin applications with a cloth pad. Two light coats of wax are easier to polish than one heavy coat. Like sanding machines, wax-polishing machines are available on a rental basis. Some polish with a rotating brush, others with a cloth belt.

BUCKET OF SAND

WEIGHT OF LADDER KEEPS TRAP CLOSED

WHEN TRAP DOOR CLEARS THIS POINT, LADDER SLIDES DOWN

Disappearing
ATTIC LADDER

Critically counterbalanced and riding on ball-bearing skate wheels, this lightweight attic ladder is easy to raise or lower. By using a pail filled with sand as a counterweight, it's a simple matter to find the exact balancing point of the ladder. From the detail below you can see how sides are added to the trap door to which sets of skate wheels are fastened to engage hardwood cleats screwed to the sides of the ladder. The pulleys should be located high enough overhead to keep the pail of sand from touching the attic floor when the ladder is drawn up.

JOIST

HINGE

1" X 1¼" HARDWOOD

LADDER

4½"

CLEAT

TRAP DOOR

HINGE

TRAP DOOR

SKATE WHEELS

RABBETED ⅛"

¾" TREAD

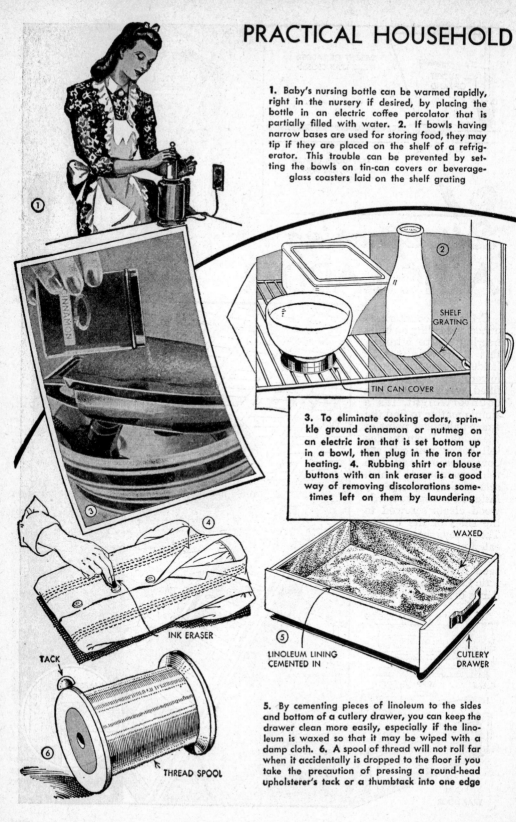

PRACTICAL HOUSEHOLD

1. Baby's nursing bottle can be warmed rapidly, right in the nursery if desired, by placing the bottle in an electric coffee percolator that is partially filled with water. **2.** If bowls having narrow bases are used for storing food, they may tip if they are placed on the shelf of a refrigerator. This trouble can be prevented by setting the bowls on tin-can covers or beverage-glass coasters laid on the shelf grating

①

②

SHELF GRATING

TIN CAN COVER

3. To eliminate cooking odors, sprinkle ground cinnamon or nutmeg on an electric iron that is set bottom up in a bowl, then plug in the iron for heating. **4.** Rubbing shirt or blouse buttons with an ink eraser is a good way of removing discolorations sometimes left on them by laundering

③

④

INK ERASER

WAXED

⑤

LINOLEUM LINING CEMENTED IN

CUTLERY DRAWER

TACK

⑥

THREAD SPOOL

5. By cementing pieces of linoleum to the sides and bottom of a cutlery drawer, you can keep the drawer clean more easily, especially if the linoleum is waxed so that it may be wiped with a damp cloth. **6.** A spool of thread will not roll far when it accidentally is dropped to the floor if you take the precaution of pressing a round-head upholsterer's tack or a thumbtack into one edge

HINTS

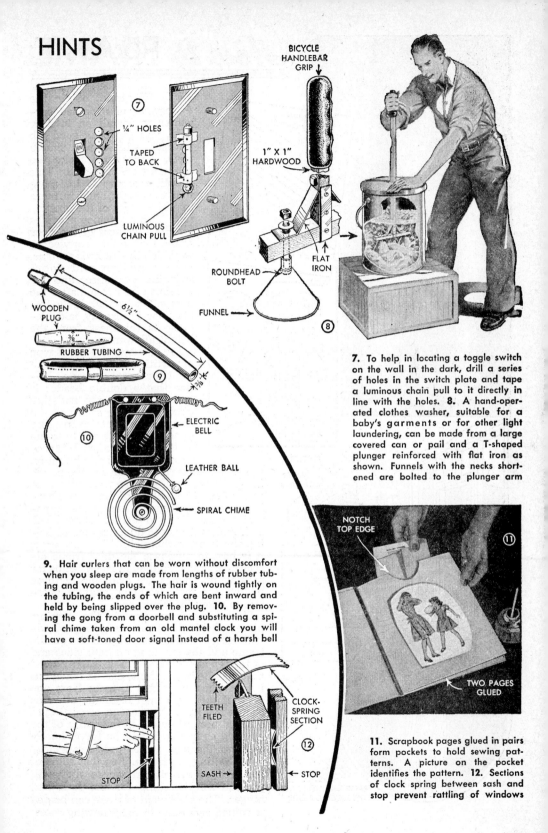

BICYCLE HANDLEBAR GRIP

⑦

¼" HOLES

TAPED TO BACK

1" X 1" HARDWOOD

LUMINOUS CHAIN PULL

ROUNDHEAD BOLT

FUNNEL

FLAT IRON

⑧

WOODEN PLUG

6½"

3/8"

RUBBER TUBING

3/8"

⑨

ELECTRIC BELL

⑩

LEATHER BALL

SPIRAL CHIME

NOTCH TOP EDGE

⑪

TWO PAGES GLUED

7. To help in locating a toggle switch on the wall in the dark, drill a series of holes in the switch plate and tape a luminous chain pull to it directly in line with the holes. **8.** A hand-operated clothes washer, suitable for a baby's garments or for other light laundering, can be made from a large covered can or pail and a T-shaped plunger reinforced with flat iron as shown. Funnels with the necks shortened are bolted to the plunger arm

9. Hair curlers that can be worn without discomfort when you sleep are made from lengths of rubber tubing and wooden plugs. The hair is wound tightly on the tubing, the ends of which are bent inward and held by being slipped over the plug. **10.** By removing the gong from a doorbell and substituting a spiral chime taken from an old mantel clock you will have a soft-toned door signal instead of a harsh bell

TEETH FILED

CLOCK-SPRING SECTION

⑫

STOP

SASH

STOP

11. Scrapbook pages glued in pairs form pockets to hold sewing patterns. A picture on the pocket identifies the pattern. **12.** Sections of clock spring between sash and stop prevent rattling of windows

How to FRAME

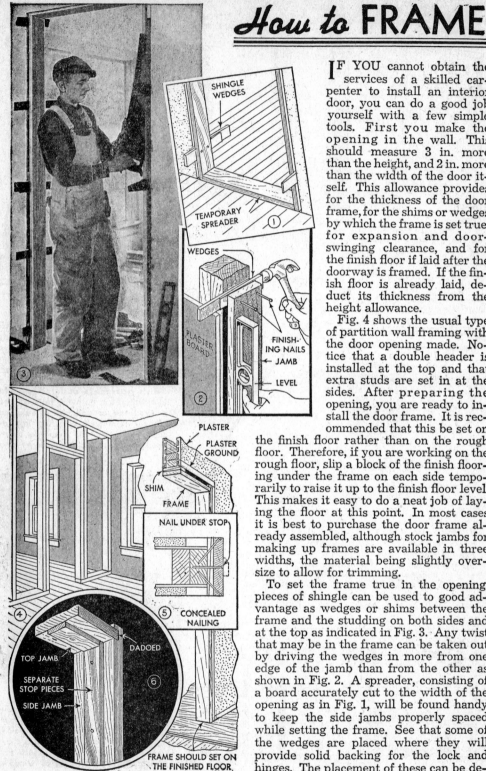

SHINGLE WEDGES

TEMPORARY SPREADER ①

WEDGES

PLASTER BOARD

FINISH-ING NAILS
JAMB
LEVEL ②

③

PLASTER
PLASTER GROUND
SHIM
FRAME

NAIL UNDER STOP

④

⑤ **CONCEALED NAILING**

DADOED

TOP JAMB
SEPARATE STOP PIECES
SIDE JAMB

⑥

FRAME SHOULD SET ON THE FINISHED FLOOR.

IF YOU cannot obtain the services of a skilled carpenter to install an interior door, you can do a good job yourself with a few simple tools. First you make the opening in the wall. This should measure 3 in. more than the height, and 2 in. more than the width of the door itself. This allowance provides for the thickness of the door frame, for the shims or wedges by which the frame is set true, for expansion and doorswinging clearance, and for the finish floor if laid after the doorway is framed. If the finish floor is already laid, deduct its thickness from the height allowance.

Fig. 4 shows the usual type of partition wall framing with the door opening made. Notice that a double header is installed at the top and that extra studs are set in at the sides. After preparing the opening, you are ready to install the door frame. It is recommended that this be set on the finish floor rather than on the rough floor. Therefore, if you are working on the rough floor, slip a block of the finish flooring under the frame on each side temporarily to raise it up to the finish floor level. This makes it easy to do a neat job of laying the floor at this point. In most cases it is best to purchase the door frame already assembled, although stock jambs for making up frames are available in three widths, the material being slightly oversize to allow for trimming.

To set the frame true in the opening, pieces of shingle can be used to good advantage as wedges or shims between the frame and the studding on both sides and at the top as indicated in Fig. 3. Any twist that may be in the frame can be taken out by driving the wedges in more from one edge of the jamb than from the other as shown in Fig. 2. A spreader, consisting of a board accurately cut to the width of the opening as in Fig. 1, will be found handy to keep the side jambs properly spaced while setting the frame. See that some of the wedges are placed where they will provide solid backing for the lock and hinges. The placement of these can be determined according to the following rules:

and HANG a Door

Place the top of the upper hinge about 5 in. from the top of the door, or in line with the top door rail, and the bottom of the lower hinge 10 in. from the bottom of the door, or in line with the bottom rail, as in Fig. 8. The height of the door knob, which determines the placement of the lock, should be 3 ft. from the floor.

Naturally, the nails through the jambs to secure the frame must be driven where they will not interfere with installing the hardware. Therefore, mark the approximate positions of the lock and hinges on the jambs before you begin to nail. The nails can be driven as in Fig. 2, or you can conceal them by driving them as in Fig. 5. After the frame has been nailed securely, nail on the casing, setting it back ¼ in. from the edge of the jamb to allow room for the hinges. See Fig. 15. Then tack on the stops temporarily with nails driven in part way. Fig. 9 shows a section of one side of a completed door frame.

Before hanging a new door, cut off the horns as in Fig. 7, and plane just enough of the excess material off the sides to permit it to be slipped snugly into the frame, Fig. 10. Then, with dividers or a scriber, mark a line on the door true with the top jamb as shown in Fig. 11, and cut off the top of the door. Now, before you do any further trimming, you must decide on the clearance to be allowed between door and frame. The proper clearance for the door you are hanging is based on two factors: First, the weather conditions of your locality, and second, the kind of finish that will be applied to the wood. In a dry locality, a clearance of 1/16 in. is about average for a door that is to be stained and varnished, or 3/32 in. if it is to be painted. In a damp locality a clearance of 3/32 in. is

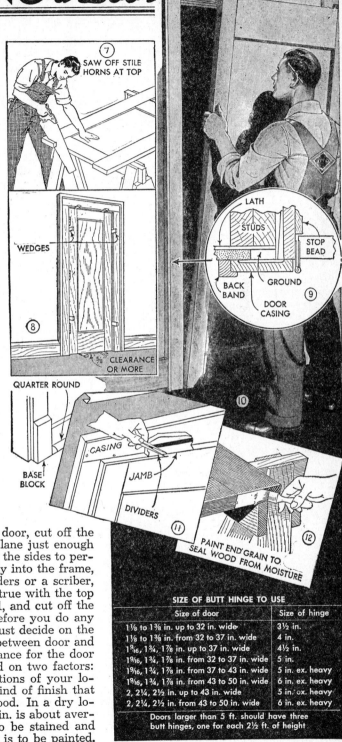

SIZE OF BUTT HINGE TO USE

Size of door	Size of hinge
1⅛ to 1⅜ in. up to 32 in. wide	3½ in.
1⅛ to 1⅜ in. from 32 to 37 in. wide	4 in.
1 9/16, 1¾, 1⅞ in. up to 37 in. wide	4½ in.
1 9/16, 1¾, 1⅞ in. from 32 to 37 in. wide	5 in.
1 9/16, 1¾, 1⅞ in. from 37 to 43 in. wide	5 in. ex. heavy
1 9/16, 1¾, 1⅞ in. from 43 to 50 in. wide	6 in. ex. heavy
2, 2¼, 2½ in. up to 43 in. wide	5 in. ex. heavy
2, 2¼, 2½ in. from 43 to 50 in. wide	6 in. ex. heavy
Doors larger than 5 ft. should have three butt hinges, one for each 2½ ft. of height	

HINGE JAMB · DOOR · 13 · NARROW CHISEL

14 · SCRIBING HINGE GAIN · ¼" · BUTT GAGE

case, note the way in which the temporarily mounted half of the hinge adjusts itself to the movement. Then take down the door, unscrew the hinge from the jamb and recut its mortise to close up or spread the hinge, whichever is required, Figs. 16 and 17. It may be necessary to shim up one side of the hinge with a strip of cardboard if too much wood has been cut away. Be sure to get the hinges out far enough to prevent the door, when wide open, from binding on the casing trim or striking the base block, if base blocks are installed. See

recommended for a door to be varnished or ⅛ in. if painted. The customary clearance between the bottom of a door and the top of the finish floor is ⅝ in., which allows for carpeting or for a threshold if used. Additional clearance in the form of a bevel must also be given the lock edge of a door to permit the inner corner to clear the jamb when the door is swung in or out as indicated in Fig. 15. The edges of a newly hung door should be painted as soon as the door has been trimmed and fitted, Fig. 12, as a safeguard against moisture or dryness which causes the wood to warp. This is especially important in the case of the top and bottom edges, where the porous endgrain invites penetration of moisture if left unsealed.

To mount the hinges, first set the door in the frame with the lock edge flat against the lock jamb and propped up to its correct hanging height, as in Fig. 8. Locate the position of the top hinge and mark its top edge on the jamb. Then make a corresponding mark on the frame. This can be done accurately by wedging a narrow chisel between the door and the jamb, using the edge to make the transfer as shown in Fig. 13. Mark the placement of the bottom hinge in the same way. Break the hinges apart by pulling out the pins, scribe the hinge gains or mortises, Fig. 14, cut them in the door and screw the hinge halves permanently in place. Then cut in the jamb gains or mortises, but fasten the hinge halves with only one screw in each one. Now hang the door and observe the behavior of the hinge pins as you open and close the door. If a pin moves, it means the hinge is improperly set. In this

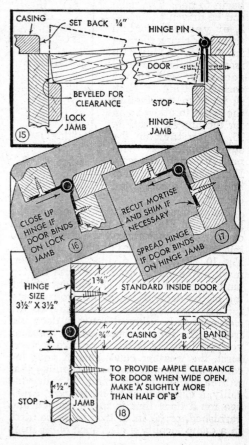

CASING · SET BACK ¼" · HINGE PIN · DOOR · BEVELED FOR CLEARANCE · STOP · LOCK JAMB · HINGE JAMB · 15

CLOSE UP HINGE IF DOOR BINDS ON LOCK JAMB · 16 · RECUT MORTISE AND SHIM IF NECESSARY · SPREAD HINGE IF DOOR BINDS ON HINGE JAMB · 17

HINGE SIZE 3½" X 3½" · 1⅜" · STANDARD INSIDE DOOR · A · ¾" · CASING · B · BAND · STOP · JAMB · ½" · TO PROVIDE AMPLE CLEARANCE FOR DOOR WHEN WIDE OPEN, MAKE 'A' SLIGHTLY MORE THAN HALF OF 'B' · 18

34

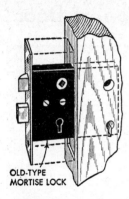

OLD-TYPE MORTISE LOCK

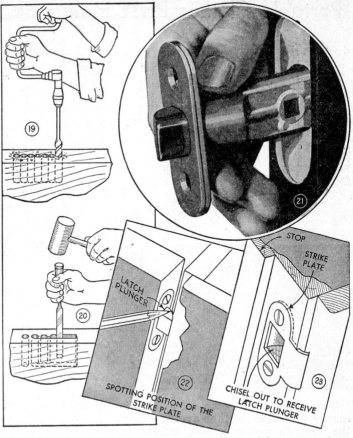

SPOTTING POSITION OF THE STRIKE PLATE

CHISEL OUT TO RECEIVE LATCH PLUNGER

STOP

STRIKE PLATE

detail below Fig. 8. By making distance A in Fig. 18 slightly greater than one half of distance B, ample clearance will be assured.

Next, install the lock or latch set by cutting the body mortise into the lock stile of the door. In the older type of sets, this entails drilling holes and then chiseling out the wood as shown in Figs. 19 and 20. Very little chiseling is required in the installation of the type shown in Fig. 21. Cutting it in is simply a matter of drilling holes. Careful placement of the strike plate is essential if a latch or lock is to operate smoothly without causing the door to bind or allowing it to rattle. Spot the position of the plate by hanging the door, closing it and turning out the latch plunger so that it touches the jamb as shown in Fig. 22. Do the same with the lock plunger if the set is a combination. Mark the location of the plunger, top and bottom, and carry these marks squarely across the jamb to a point corresponding to the depth at which the plunger is set back from the face of the door. Then

place the plate in position over these marks and, with a scratch awl, outline the mortise and then spot the screw holes. Cut out the mortise and screw the plate in place as in Fig. 23.

Finally, adjust the stops to the latched door, allowing clearance for the paint or varnish finish, and nail them permanently in place, Fig. 6. Oil the hinge pins and latch to make the door work smoothly. Later on, if the door should bind due to swelling, do not attempt to trim off the lock edge, which would entail moving the lock. It will be easier to dress off the hinge edge and resink the hinges accordingly.

Mass-Producing Slotted Dowels with Simple Jig

This simple jig has increased production many times in mass-producing slotted dowels in the home workshop. The jig is made by slotting a piece of wood to clear the saw blade when it is set for the desired depth. Then drill a hole, having a diameter slightly larger than that of the dowels, through the top of the block, so that when the jig is in place, the hole is centered directly over the saw blade. The jig is held to the saw table with C-clamps. With the blade rotating, merely press the dowels down through the hole.

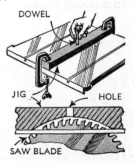

DOWEL

JIG

HOLE

SAW BLADE

35

Portable Clothes Rack Hangs on Top of Door

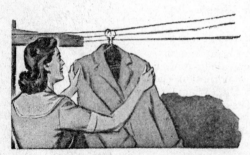

This clothes rack was designed primarily to take care of the overflow from the average clothes closet, but in an emergency it provides additional hanger space for the coats and hats of guests on party nights and also serves as a special rack for choice garments on ironing days. When not in use, it takes very little storage space. All parts except the spacer blocks at the top of the hanger hooks are cut from ½ by 2-in. hardwood. Join the parts with flathead screws and glue. Sand the wood smooth and round all corners and ends. Finish in the natural color of the wood or with enamel. Then attach the metal coat hooks with screws, spacing them on 7-in. centers.

Garments Held on Clothesline by Crossing Hangers

When airing garments on a clothesline, hang each one on two hangers hooked over the line with the hooks pointing in opposite directions as shown in the detail. If buttoned or pinned closed, the garments will not blow off the line even in a strong wind.

Heavy Rugs Held on Clothesline by Two Trouser Hangers

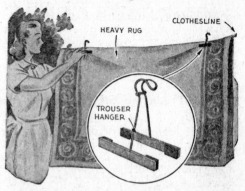

If you have found common clothespins too small for holding heavy rugs on the clothesline, try a couple of trouser hangers of the type shown.

AIR FILTERS for your windows

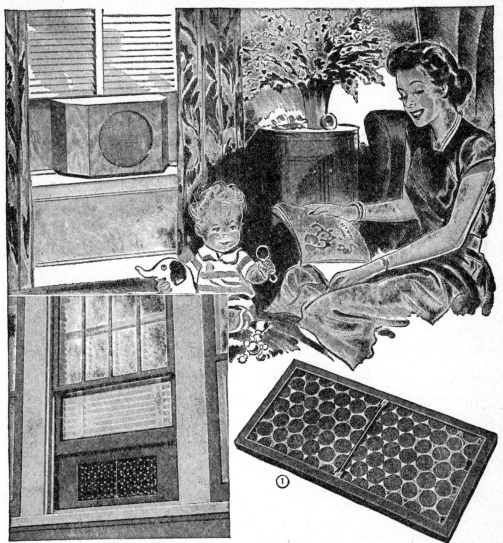

①

NO matter where you live, an open window anywhere in the house lets in all kinds of airborne dust, soot and plant pollens. Homemakers, always beset with the dust problem, and especially hay-fever sufferers and those confined to the sickroom will appreciate these efficient air filters which use filtering units of the spun-glass and honeycombed fiber type. They are easily made to fit in any double-hung window. The first type, detailed in Figs. 1 to 4 inclusive, is fitted with an electric fan and three spun-glass filter units of the type used in warm-air heating plants equipped with circulators. The fan is hooded for greater efficiency and is housed in a neat cabinet which projects only a few inches

beyond the window stool inside the room. Since the filter units come in standard sizes it's a good idea to have these at hand before you make the cabinet. Width of the filter units must be less than the width of the window. Also, it should be noted that dimensions given in Fig. 3 are only suggestions. They must be altered to suit the window frame and the fan and filter units at hand. The cabinet should be made of material that can be finished to match the woodwork. Birch plywood in ½-in. thickness is a good choice as it can be painted or stained and varnished to match almost any interior finish. However, for a painted finish, ½-in. fir plywood will do very well.

First, measure the window to determine

37

½" STOCK

12"

10½"
14⅜"

1"

20½"

3⅝"

2"

3¾"

9¼"

TO SUIT WINDOW FRAME

③

FILTER UNITS

THICKNESS OF WINDOW SASH

④

FAN MOTOR

LIGHT SOCKET

②

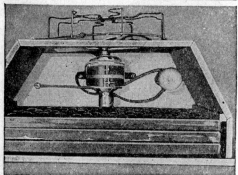

the length of the panel that fits under the raised sash. This measurement should be the same as the width of the lower sash. Note that this panel is made in two parts with a width adjustment so that it can be set in the opening between the inside sash stops and then widened to fit snugly in the sash grooves and against the pulley stiles. The extension piece, Fig. 3, is held in place with three small bolts which pass through slots cut in both members as shown. Wing nuts are used to provide a quick and easy adjustment. The outer ends of both members are built out to the thickness of the sash with cleats so that they fit snugly in

the sash grooves. The panel should be about 4 in. wider than the filter unit, and the opening should be about 1 in. smaller each way than the overall size of the unit. This provides a ledge or stop against which the outer unit fits when the cabinet is assembled. See Fig. 3.

Building the five-sided fan housing is mostly a matter of getting the angle joints cut to fit properly. If you don't have a circular saw, the best way to do this is to make the cuts outside the dimension lines with a handsaw and then finish with a plane to a perfect fit. The circular opening in the front member should be about ½ in. larger in diameter than the circle described by the fan blades. The opening can be covered by a fine-meshed wire grille or with the wire guard which is removed from the fan. Usually the guard is just about the right size and makes an attractive finishing detail as well as affording protection from the whirling fan blades. Generally it is necessary to alter the fan unit by removing the regular base and substituting another sawed from hardwood as in Fig. 4. Two sheet-metal compression bands, tightened with stove bolts, are used to hold the motor in place on the wooden base. This is anchored to the bottom of the cabinet with

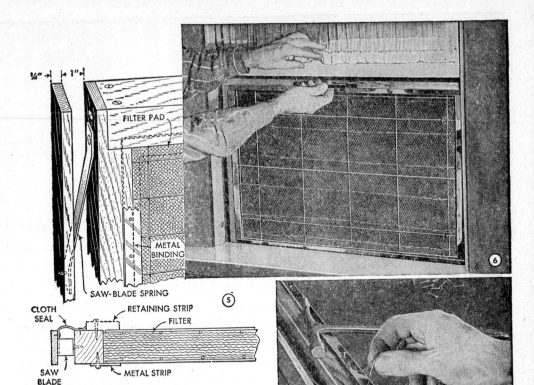

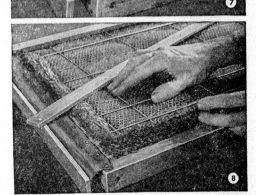

two small steel angles as indicated. If a heavy rubber band cut from an inner tube is slipped over the motor frame before clamping it in place, the fan will be practically noiseless, and if you want a constant-speed fan to run slower than its normal speed, you can connect a porcelain light socket in the motor circuit as in Fig. 2. A 60-watt lamp in the socket will reduce the speed of a universal-type fan motor sufficiently for the purpose. The completed cabinet should have a snug-fitting cover.

Another type of air filter, detailed in Figs. 5 to 8 inclusive, utilizes the less expensive honeycombed fiber filter unit or pad. This comes in standard sizes, usually 2 by 16 by 20 in., 2 by 16 by 25 in. and 2 by 20 by 20 in. overall. The 25-in. length can be framed to fit nicely in the average window frame. Fig. 5 suggests one way of framing the filter unit so that it will be dust-tight yet can be removed easily. Note in Figs. 5 and 8 that a strip of cloth covers the space between the spring-mounted strips and the frame, thus forming an effective seal. The spring-mounted strip allows the assembled unit to be telescoped slightly so that it can be inserted in the window frame past the inside sash stops. The springs can be made from hacksaw blades, although any flat spring of sufficient strength will do. The inside of the frame is finished with linoleum seam binding as in Fig. 7. The

filter unit bears against a retaining strip screwed to the outside of the wood frame as in the lower detail, Fig. 5. A small metal handle attached to the top of the unit aids in removal. Where the unit is left in the window throughout the season it's a good idea to provide a cover to prevent driving rain from entering the filters. A strip of sheet metal screwed to the top member of the frame will serve this purpose. It should be about 4 in. wide and 1 in. shorter than the frame and should be bent down at an angle so that it sheds the water. Paint the metal strip to match the trim color.

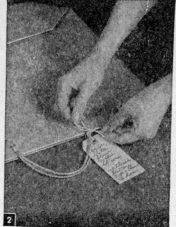

Practical Household Hints

1 If you have a wood or coal-burning stove, and it's necessary to store fuel in your kitchen, this bin is ideal for wood, coal and kindling

2 You won't have to waste much time hunting for a shopping list if you write it on a tag and then tie it to the handle of your shopping bag

3 Cut from an inner tube and slipped over the small end of an ironing board, a rubber band will hold the legs of the board securely

4 When new, reinforce the finger tips of rubber gloves with adhesive tape to make them last longer. Reinforcing is done on the inside

5 Toothpicks are easier to remove from a flat-bottom holder if a shallow paper cone is placed in the base of the container as indicated

6 Where the walls of a room are finished in a light color, extension cords will harmonize if painted with white-sidewall-tire coating

7 Keep embroidery floss between notebook pages. Glue edges together, bring ends through top sheet. Put identifying label on same page

8 Long seams can be ripped easily if the material is held under the presser foot of a sewing machine. This will serve as a third hand

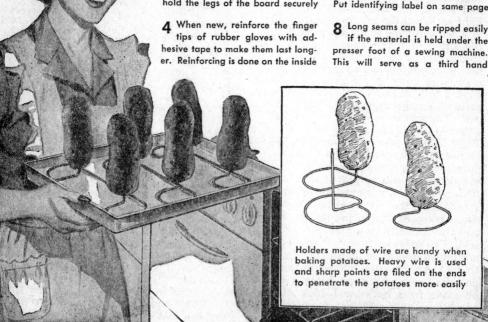

Holders made of wire are handy when baking potatoes. Heavy wire is used and sharp points are filed on the ends to penetrate the potatoes more easily

Trouser hangers may lose their grip after continued **use**. When this occurs spread the legs of the hanger as above to restore the proper tension

WHITE RUBBER TIRE COATING

Fireplace

By J. B. Temple

THERE'S no need to worry about chilly evenings at your cottage or camp if you have this circulating fireplace. It's also equally effective in your home for cool evenings during late spring and early fall so you won't have to start the heating plant. And during the winter it will lessen the load on your furnace considerably on extremely cold days. Because it recirculates the air instead of sending most of the heat up the chimney, this fireplace is an efficient unit. The path which the air follows is shown in Fig. 2; it enters the cold-air intake, passes through the space formed by the metal shell and the masonry, where it is heated, and finally is discharged through the hot-air outlet.

Details of the steel shell are given in Fig. 4 and the assembled unit appears in Fig. 3. Plate E, Fig. 4, which is the main part of the unit, is formed from a 36 by 60-in. piece of No. 12-gauge sheet metal. No lap is required if the unit is assembled by welding. However, if it is riveted or bolted, the lap indicated by the dotted lines should be followed. These joints must be

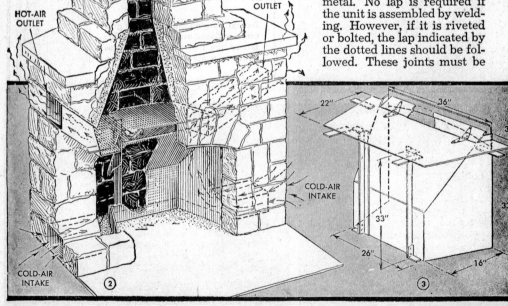

Fig. 1

ALTERNATE COLD-AIR INTAKE AT FLOOR LINE
HOT-AIR OUTLET PLACED HIGH AS POSSIBLE AT SMOKE SHELF
14″ 44″ 14″
10″
4″
16″
4″
24″
26″
ALTERNATE HOT-AIR OUTLET FOR ROOM BEHIND FIREPLACE
72″
HEIGHT TO SUIT
9″ X 14″ FLUE
9″ 14″ 9″
CLEANOUT
24″
HOT-AIR OUTLET
SMOKE CHAMBER
18″
54″
½″ X 3″ FLAT IRON
33″
DAMPER
COLD-AIR INTAKE
SMOKE SHELF
14″
29″
AIR HEATING CHAMBER
4″ 16″ 4″ 10″
4″ 36″ 4″
18″ 18″
72″
34″

Fig. 2
HOT-AIR OUTLET
HOT-AIR OUTLET
COLD-AIR INTAKE
COLD-AIR INTAKE

Fig. 3
22″
36″
3′
COLD-AIR INTAKE
33″
33″
26″
16″

CIRCULATES WARM AIR

smoketight and may require the use of furnace cement. Plate A, Fig. 4, is used as an apron at the top of the front shell. The curvature of the lower edge conforms with that of the arch support in Plate B. The smoke shelf, Plate D, is a piece of No. 10-gauge metal 22 by 48 in. This is welded or bolted to the shell, Fig. 3, and supported at the rear by two ¼ by 1½ by 1½-in. angles cut and assembled as shown in Plate C, Fig. 4. The edges of this plate are set into the masonry about 1½ in. Flat-iron lugs are welded to the underside of the shelf.

The damper control, lower right-hand detail, Fig. 1, is a piece of flat iron cut in the shape of a gooseneck and hinged to the damper. Adjustment of the damper is obtained by engaging notches in the gooseneck with a catch set in the masonry. A ½ by 3 by 48-in. bar is used to make the arch, Plate B, Fig. 4.

A stone, rubble and concrete foundation is carried to solid ground below the frost line. If the house has a basement, break the floor up and carry the foundation down the same way. When the foun-

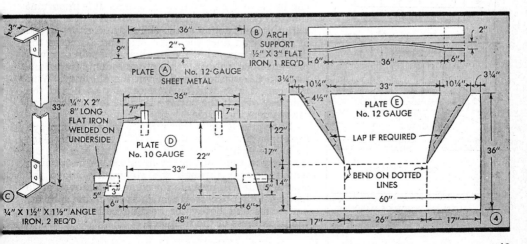

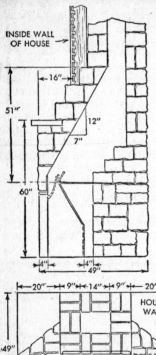

INSIDE WALL OF HOUSE →

16"

51"

12"

7"

60"

4" 4"
49"

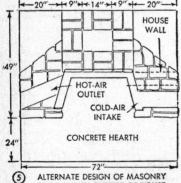

20" 9" 14" 9" 20"

HOUSE WALL

49"

HOT-AIR OUTLET

COLD-AIR INTAKE

CONCRETE HEARTH

24"

72"

⑤ ALTERNATE DESIGN OF MASONRY FOR CHIMNEY OUTSIDE OF HOUSE

dation has been completed to the level of the hearth, the steel shell is set in place. The masonry is built up 4 in. away from the sides and the back of the shell, with the smoke shelf, as mentioned previously, sealed into the stonework. When building the masonry, allow for cold-air intakes at the bottom, Fig. 2. The hot-air outlets are slanted upward, beginning under the smoke shelf. These are either standard 6 by 8-in. ductwork or 7-in. stovepipes. Besides the outlets shown in Fig. 2, additional outlets are suggested in the upper right-hand detail of Fig. 1. This would apply when the fireplace is not against an outside wall and it is desirable to heat a room at the rear of the unit. For every outlet installed there is a cold-air intake.

However, before the outlets are completed, the arch bar, Plate B, Fig. 4, is installed. This is done when the masonry has been carried to the height of the damper. The smoke chamber part of the flue has a slope of about 60 degrees. It is built around a wooden frame which is knocked down and removed before the chimney is built. No attempt should be made to burn the frame out. The inside dimensions of the flue are given as 9 by 14 in., but these dimensions can be varied somewhat as long as the cross sectional area is over 100 sq. in.

Fig. 5 shows an alternate masonry design when it is desirable to have the chimney outside the house. This avoids cutting out a portion of the wall and roof of the house, but requires wider and heavier masonry at the base and a higher smoke chamber to obtain the proper bevels. In this case, since the chimney is not seen from inside the house, it can be built of brick.

There are many refinements and conveniences that may be added to this basic fireplace. A cleanout door can be located above the smoke shelf at the back of the fireplace so that accumulations of soot can be cleaned out from time to time. It is important that this door be a tight fit; otherwise it will interfere with the draft action of the chimney. A short length of galvanized duct the same size and shape as the flue, with a conical or pyramid-shaped rain cap, will prevent mice, squirrels and other rodents from running up the masonry and down the chimney. With this cap it also will be unnecessary to board the chimney over if the cottage is to be left unoccupied for any length of time.

Other attachments that may be added to improve the appearance and add to the utility of the fireplace include a swinging arm or crane. This is set in the masonry at the front of the fireplace. A metal oven which extends through the stonework above the smoke shelf will provide for some Dutch oven style baking. Other accessories such as revolving spits for barbecues and hot-water heating coils will add to the usefulness of the fireplace.

Easy Ways to Cure SMOKY FIREPLACES

Also, simple tricks of starting and keeping cozy fires

HAVE you a fireplace that occasionally smokes? If so, there's no need of letting this condition go on. In most cases you can apply an effective cure yourself. Some fireplaces smoke because of a slanting smoke shelf as shown in detail A of Fig. 1. Note how a descending column of cold air in the chimney rolls down the shelf and forces the fumes and smoke from the fireplace out into the room. The builder of such a fireplace thought only of the column of hot fumes from the fire but overlooked the fact that the chimney must also accommodate a heavy column of descending cold air. A modern horizontal smoke shelf is shown in detail B. From this you will see that the cold air descending along the back of the chimney strikes the shelf, is retarded, and is heated by the hot front part of the shelf and also the fumes from the fire, causing it to turn back up the chimney. Of course, it may not be possible in your case to change a slanting shelf to a horizontal one like this, but the same results can be gained by the simple alteration shown in Fig. 2. Here a row of bricks

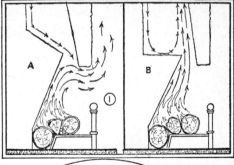

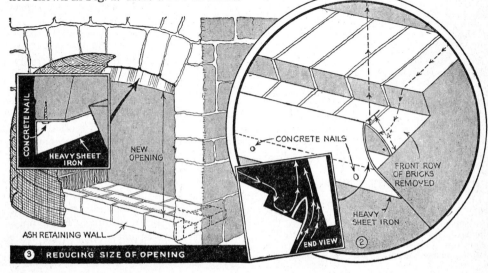

CONCRETE NAIL

HEAVY SHEET IRON

NEW OPENING

ASH RETAINING WALL

③ REDUCING SIZE OF OPENING

CONCRETE NAILS

FRONT ROW OF BRICKS REMOVED

HEAVY SHEET IRON

END VIEW ②

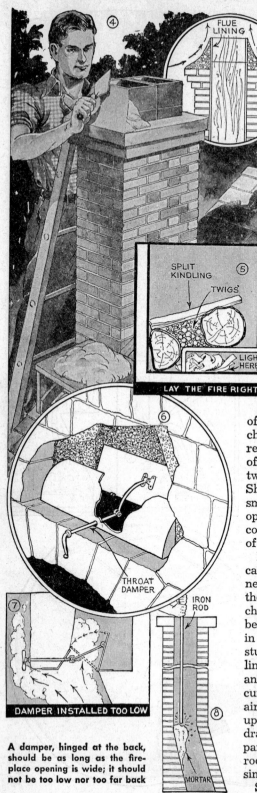

FLUE LINING

④

SPLIT KINDLING ⑤

TWIGS

LIGHT HERE

LAY THE FIRE RIGHT

⑥

THROAT DAMPER

⑦

DAMPER INSTALLED TOO LOW

IRON ROD

⑧

MORTAR

A damper, hinged at the back, should be as long as the fireplace opening is wide; it should not be too low nor too far back

has been removed and a heavy sheet-iron "fence" has been attached to project upward from the lower edge of the slanting shelf, which warms and turns the descending column of cold air. Iron heats up rapidly and transfers heat to the cold air coming down against it. Another method of overcoming this trouble is to install a throat damper which should be just as long as the width of the fireplace opening. It should be hinged at the back of the smoke chamber as shown in Fig. 6, and must not be installed too low as in Fig. 7, nor too far back, which would leave insufficient space for an effective smoke shelf. Also be sure that there is an adequate smoke chamber between the damper and the fireplace opening. When raised, the damper will have the same effect as the sheet-iron "fence" shown in Fig. 2, and besides, such a damper gives adequate draft control.

Another common cause of smoky fireplaces is that the size of the fireplace opening and the size of the chimney are not of correct proportions. It is recommended that the cross-sectional area of the chimney should not be less than one-twelfth of the area of the fireplace opening. Should you find that your chimney is too small you can reduce the size of the fireplace opening by either raising the hearth with a course or two of bricks, or by adding a piece of heavy sheet metal at the top, Fig. 3.

Many well designed fireplaces smoke because of chimney faults. The top of a chimney should project no less than 3 ft. above the highest point of the roof. The higher the chimney, the better will be the draft. But, before extending your chimney or investing in a rotating chimney top, try the simple stunt shown in Fig. 4. Set a section of flue lining on top of the lining in the chimney and build around it a cement shoulder curved as shown. This deflects horizontal air currents upward and results in positive upward draft in the chimney. Insufficient draft may also result from mortar or debris partially clogging the chimney. Ramming a rod against the obstruction as in Fig. 8, is a simple method of dislodging it.

Some other causes of smoky fireplaces

are as follows: Double use of a flue for two fireplaces—as for instance, a basement fireplace below one in the living room—or the use of a single flue for both a fireplace and a furnace or a kitchen stove. Off-center flues above the fireplace smoke chamber cause eddy currents and consequent slow exit of smoke. Sometimes gas-vent pipes from a hot-water heater or gas furnace project too far into the chimney and reduce the cross-sectional area of the chimney. Also, the same effect comes from a chimney top of smaller size than the chimney itself. Flue linings that are not joined flush, but in which one length of lining is allowed to overlap the one below it, where the chimney is slightly slanted, are likely to cause trouble by reducing chimney capacity. Joints of flue linings may be leaky because of disintegration and falling away of the mortar between them, allowing cold air to enter and interfere with chimney draft. If smoke seems to come from a crack between the mantel and the wall, find out whether a crack extends from the smoke chamber to the mantel.

Laying a good fire is an art. Burning a large heap of crumpled newspapers on the hearth will produce more fumes in a few moments than most ordinary fireplaces can dispose of. Fig. 5 shows how to lay a fire. A heavy log is placed on the hearth against the back wall—not on the andirons. This is the traditional "backlog," one purpose of which is to protect the back brickwork. Then, a smaller log of long-burning wood—not a split piece —is placed across the andirons about 6 in. from the backlog. On the floor and in the space between the logs, a few crumpled newspapers, some very small pieces of wood and possibly pine cones or dried bark, are inserted, extending forward under the front log. Finally, small twigs and a dozen pieces of kindling are piled loosely between the logs. Now, all that is needed to start the fire is a match. As the kindling ignites, knock it down between the logs and add some fresh pieces until the front log is burning, after which it is pulled forward to make room for a fresh log. A good material to take the place of kindling is sawdust moistened with kerosene. This is kept nearby in a can and is thrown under and about the logs. Where a fireplace does not have a damper, you can prevent the fire from burning too fast by piling ashes under and on all sides of the logs.

Adhesive Tape Will Muffle Bell

For the benefit of those who retire early or for any other reason wish to muffle the noise of a doorbell, this solution should be satisfactory. Paste a piece of adhesive tape on the gong so the clapper will s t r i k e the tape and not the metal. When the full tone of the bell is desired, rotate the bell to a point where the clapper will hit the metal. Be careful that the m e t a l doesn't become loose.

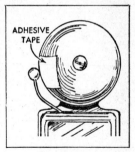

Repairing Cracked Glass Jar

All that's needed to repair a cracked glass jar or other g l a s s container are a saucer, candle, w a t e r - c o l o r paintbrush and a small quantity of sodium silicate (water glass).

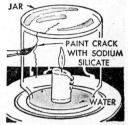

Fasten the candle to the saucer by setting it in melted wax, and pour a little water into the dish. Invert the glass over the lighted candle and allow it to burn until it goes out. Then, immediately paint the outside of the crack in the jar with sodium silicate. The vacuum created inside the container as the heated air cools will draw water glass into the crack and make the repair leakproof. Purpose of the water is to keep air from entering the jar through the space between it and the saucer and breaking the vacuum.

Electric Heater from Headlight

An efficient and beautiful chrome - plated electric h e a t e r can be made at very little cost by using an old auto headlight. J u s t install a porcelain lamp socket

inside the headlight shell to take a heating element, which can be purchased from electrical supply stores. The headlight reflector can be cut to fit behind the socket. A suitable handle can be had from an old electric flatiron, and a base can be found around most homes. In many cases, a scrolled iron base from an old floor or table lamp can be used. The headlight lens is replaced with screen wire, which is held in place by the lens rim.

BUILT-IN SHELVES
utilize waste

NEED for additional closets, cupboards and shelving often can be met by making effective use of dead wall space. For instance, ironing facilities can be provided by building an ironing-board compartment on a door as in Fig. 1, or a separate wall cabinet can be installed for this purpose. Also, a telephone niche, Fig. 2, may be built in a wall or partition of standard thickness if sufficient base space for the instrument is provided by letting the shelf project. Sometimes hot-air furnace ducts and plumbing are spaciously enclosed in extra wide partitions which offer available wall space for cabinets, Fig. 7, or other small compartments. Waste corner space in rooms can be put to good use by installing corner cabinets for linens, books or dishes, as in Fig. 8. Corner cabinets are available ready-made in a variety of sizes and shapes

STIFF WIRE

FLASH-LIGHT

16"

STUDDING

SECTION TO BE CUT OUT

STARTING HOLES

STUD

INSERT HEADERS

and CABINETS
wall space

⑧

⑨

⑩ EXTEND FRAMING AND PANELING
— INSTALL SHELVING —

⑪

if you prefer not to build your own.

Among other places where dead wall space may be found are the enclosures surrounding the masonry of fireplaces and chimney stacks, which are commonly blocked off with straight and square-cut walls for the sake of appearance and to cut framing costs. The size and shape of such spaces can be determined without doing any appreciable damage to the surrounding walls by probing behind them through peep holes, using a flashlight and a length of stiff wire as illustrated in Fig. 4. After such a survey, the holes can be plugged with patching plaster.

A simple method of installing shelving between the studs of a wall is shown in Figs. 3, 5 and 6. Begin by drilling four straight holes through the wall surface between studs. Then, using an old keyhole saw, cut down each side, holding the blade snugly against the stud while sawing. After sawing across the top and bottom, remove the cut section. Insert headers at the top and bottom, toenailing these to the studs. Take

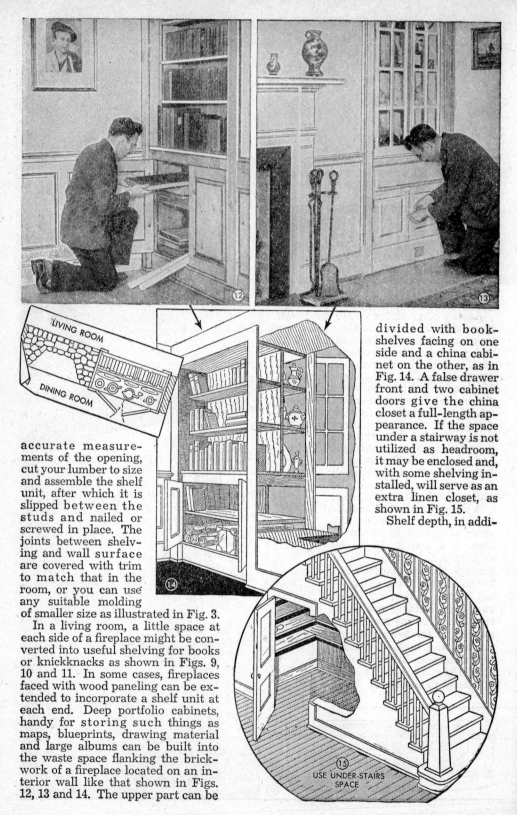

accurate measurements of the opening, cut your lumber to size and assemble the shelf unit, after which it is slipped between the studs and nailed or screwed in place. The joints between shelving and wall surface are covered with trim to match that in the room, or you can use any suitable molding of smaller size as illustrated in Fig. 3.

In a living room, a little space at each side of a fireplace might be converted into useful shelving for books or knickknacks as shown in Figs. 9, 10 and 11. In some cases, fireplaces faced with wood paneling can be extended to incorporate a shelf unit at each end. Deep portfolio cabinets, handy for storing such things as maps, blueprints, drawing material and large albums can be built into the waste space flanking the brickwork of a fireplace located on an interior wall like that shown in Figs. 12, 13 and 14. The upper part can be

divided with bookshelves facing on one side and a china cabinet on the other, as in Fig. 14. A false drawer front and two cabinet doors give the china closet a full-length appearance. If the space under a stairway is not utilized as headroom, it may be enclosed and, with some shelving installed, will serve as an extra linen closet, as shown in Fig. 15.

Shelf depth, in addi-

USE UNDER-STAIRS SPACE

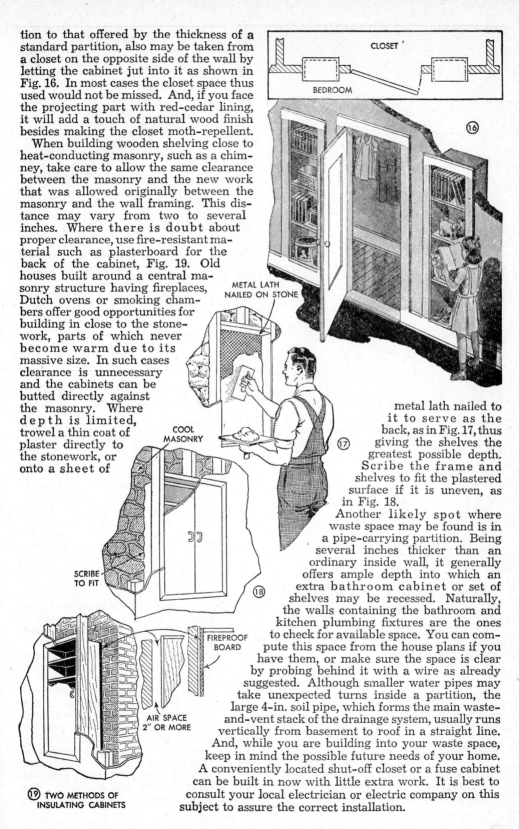

tion to that offered by the thickness of a standard partition, also may be taken from a closet on the opposite side of the wall by letting the cabinet jut into it as shown in Fig. 16. In most cases the closet space thus used would not be missed. And, if you face the projecting part with red-cedar lining, it will add a touch of natural wood finish besides making the closet moth-repellent.

When building wooden shelving close to heat-conducting masonry, such as a chimney, take care to allow the same clearance between the masonry and the new work that was allowed originally between the masonry and the wall framing. This distance may vary from two to several inches. Where there is doubt about proper clearance, use fire-resistant material such as plasterboard for the back of the cabinet, Fig. 19. Old houses built around a central masonry structure having fireplaces, Dutch ovens or smoking chambers offer good opportunities for building in close to the stonework, parts of which never become warm due to its massive size. In such cases clearance is unnecessary and the cabinets can be butted directly against the masonry. Where depth is limited, trowel a thin coat of plaster directly to the stonework, or onto a sheet of

CLOSET

BEDROOM

16

METAL LATH NAILED ON STONE

17

COOL MASONRY

SCRIBE TO FIT

18

FIREPROOF BOARD

AIR SPACE 2" OR MORE

19 TWO METHODS OF INSULATING CABINETS

metal lath nailed to it to serve as the back, as in Fig. 17, thus giving the shelves the greatest possible depth. Scribe the frame and shelves to fit the plastered surface if it is uneven, as in Fig. 18.

Another likely spot where waste space may be found is in a pipe-carrying partition. Being several inches thicker than an ordinary inside wall, it generally offers ample depth into which an extra bathroom cabinet or set of shelves may be recessed. Naturally, the walls containing the bathroom and kitchen plumbing fixtures are the ones to check for available space. You can compute this space from the house plans if you have them, or make sure the space is clear by probing behind it with a wire as already suggested. Although smaller water pipes may take unexpected turns inside a partition, the large 4-in. soil pipe, which forms the main waste-and-vent stack of the drainage system, usually runs vertically from basement to roof in a straight line. And, while you are building into your waste space, keep in mind the possible future needs of your home. A conveniently located shut-off closet or a fuse cabinet can be built in now with little extra work. It is best to consult your local electrician or electric company on this subject to assure the correct installation.

Above, stair rails of the type shown consist of a number of precut parts made from selected hardwoods. Below, layout of stair is based on normal length of step on a level floor

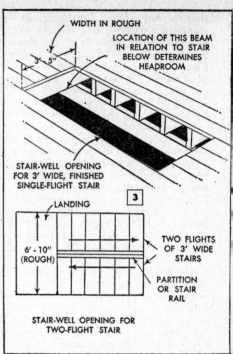

WIDTH IN ROUGH

3'-5"

LOCATION OF THIS BEAM IN RELATION TO STAIR BELOW DETERMINES HEADROOM

STAIR-WELL OPENING FOR 3' WIDE, FINISHED SINGLE-FLIGHT STAIR

3

LANDING

6'-10" (ROUGH)

TWO FLIGHTS OF 3' WIDE STAIRS

PARTITION OR STAIR RAIL

STAIR-WELL OPENING FOR TWO-FLIGHT STAIR

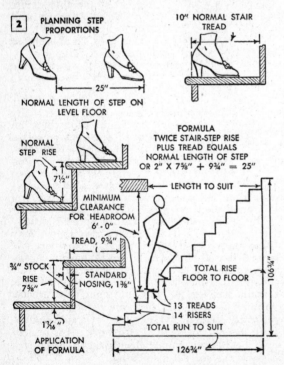

2 PLANNING STEP PROPORTIONS

10" NORMAL STAIR TREAD

25"

NORMAL LENGTH OF STEP ON LEVEL FLOOR

NORMAL STEP RISE

7½"

FORMULA
TWICE STAIR-STEP RISE PLUS TREAD EQUALS NORMAL LENGTH OF STEP OR 2" X 7⅝" + 9¾" = 25"

LENGTH TO SUIT

MINIMUM CLEARANCE FOR HEADROOM 6'-0"

TREAD, 9¾"

¾" STOCK

RISE 7⅝"

STANDARD NOSING, 1⅜"

TOTAL RISE FLOOR TO FLOOR

106¾"

13 TREADS
14 RISERS

1¹⁄₁₆"

TOTAL RUN TO SUIT

APPLICATION OF FORMULA

126¾"

STEPS IN

INSTALLATION of a safe, attractive stair in either old or new homes is one of the most important details in the interior construction. Stairs that pitch too steeply, or those with abnormal treads and risers and insufficient headroom are a constant accident hazard. For safety, the stair must include all of the basic construction features detailed in Figs. 2 and 3. In the construction or remodeling of small and average-size homes in which stair space usually is limited, the two or three-directional, open-string stair with landings or winder treads often is best as it generally can be placed at the end of a room. In remodeling older homes it sometimes is necessary to use a single-directional closed-string stair, especially in large rooms.

In determining the step proportions for an average stair, use measurements of the typical step shown in Fig. 2. These dimensions should not be varied more than ½ in. either way, except in some special cases, such as on long flights made possible by ample space in large homes and buildings. On these stairs, a rise as low as 6 in.

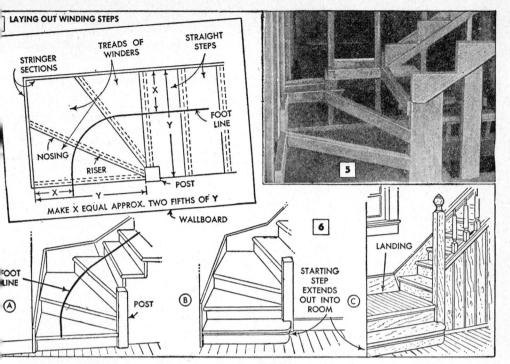

STRINGER SECTIONS

TREADS OF WINDERS

STRAIGHT STEPS

X

Y

FOOT LINE

NOSING

RISER

POST

X

Y

MAKE X EQUAL APPROX. TWO FIFTHS OF Y

WALLBOARD

5

6

FOOT LINE

A

POST

B

STARTING STEP EXTENDS OUT INTO ROOM

C

LANDING

STAIR BUILDING

By John Modroch

and a tread as wide as 11½ in. may be used. Actual measurements will depend to some extent on how many steps of this proportion can be fitted into the stair space. To determine the number of risers for a given stair, first divide the total rise by the step rise, or a figure close to it that will give an even result. Then to get tread measurement divide the total run by the number of treads, which is always one less than the number of risers.

The stair opening, or well, should be cut wide enough and long enough to provide adequate headroom, Fig. 3. Remember also that dimensions of the opening must allow for the finish stringer, upper-floor nosing, and space for a rail. For example, the total finish allowance for the ordinary 36-in. single-flight open-string stair ordinarily would come to 5 in. These figures are based on ¾-in.-thick plaster wall and a standard 2⅜-in.-wide rail, plus 1 in. minimum finger room between the rail and wall. Always check walls of the stair well with a level and straightedge to determine beforehand the allowances for out-of-plumb walls, corners and other irregularities.

In planning the installation of a stair in a new location, which often is done in making alterations in old houses, obstacles that interfere with the placement of the stair well may be encountered. These may be supporting main beams or joists, chimneys or other installations that cannot be moved. If the obstacle is at one end of the proposed opening, the loss in length sometimes can be compensated for by shifting the location of the stair in the opposite direction. If this cannot be done, then winding steps or landings, Figs. 4, 5 and 6, sometimes can be installed. However, there is a definite minimum total run as well as a minimum headroom. Built to any dimension under these limits, the stair is not only difficult to ascend or descend but actually may be dangerous in some locations. Fig. 6, A, B and C, detail the commonly used methods of building approaches to both open and closed stair flights. In detail A, three winder treads are used. Winders are tapered steps which pivot at the newel post. Here the nosing of the winder starting step is flush with the stair wall. Better construction is shown in detail B where the starting step is straight and extends its width into the room. Somewhat simpler construction of the open-string stair employing a landing is indicated in detail C. In laying out winders, the plan should be drawn full size as in Fig. 4. The tread width of winders is gauged by intersecting the foot line, which represents the normal path of travel on winding steps, with a compass set to the tread width of the straight steps.

53

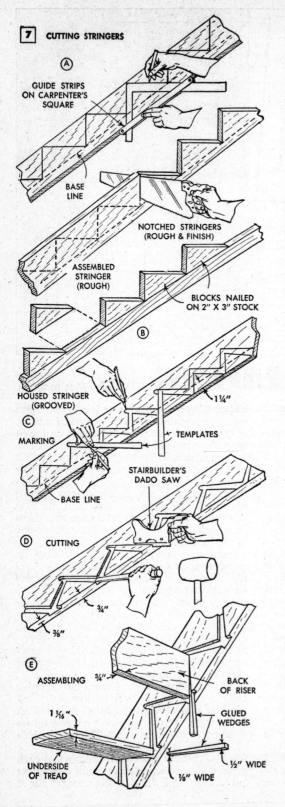

7 CUTTING STRINGERS

A

GUIDE STRIPS
ON CARPENTER'S
SQUARE

BASE
LINE

NOTCHED STRINGERS
(ROUGH & FINISH)

ASSEMBLED
STRINGER
(ROUGH)

BLOCKS NAILED
ON 2" X 3" STOCK

B

HOUSED STRINGER
(GROOVED)

1¼"

C

MARKING

TEMPLATES

STAIRBUILDER'S
DADO SAW

BASE LINE

D CUTTING

¾"

⅜"

E

ASSEMBLING ¾"

BACK
OF RISER

1 1⁄16"

GLUED
WEDGES

UNDERSIDE
OF TREAD

⅛" WIDE

½" WIDE

Only thoroughly seasoned lumber should be used in building a stair. Treads and risers in standard lengths and widths may be purchased. Treads preferably should be oak, dressed to 1 1⁄16-in. thickness. Risers usually are cut from pine, ¾ in. thick. Starting steps, built with curved ends to match standard rails and newel posts, nosing returns and cove moldings, also are stock items. Clear ¾-in. pine boards commonly are used for making finish stringers. Rough stringers are cut from 2-in. stock.

In building a stair, make the stringers first. They may be the open or notched type, details A and B, Fig. 7, or the housed type, detail C, depending on the method of stair installation. On either type, begin by laying out the rise and run of each step as in detail A. On a notched stringer make the saw cuts shown. On a housed stringer, locate and pencil the outlines of the grooves with the aid of two templates, one for the tread grooves and one for the riser grooves, as in detail C. Both templates must include an allowance for wedges, Fig. 7, E. When the layout is completed cut the grooves as in detail D. Be careful when chiseling out the waste to bring the grooves to a uniform depth. At this stage, cut risers and treads to width, but not to length unless the stair is to be assembled beforehand and installed as a unit.

To avoid damage resulting from exposure to moisture in a new-house installation, the stair should not be installed until after the rooms have been plastered and have had time to dry out. However, where the rough-stringer method of construction is used, the stringers may be put in beforehand and temporary tread boards nailed on so that the stair can be put into immediate use. Finish the stair after the plastering is completed and thoroughly dried.

To install a closed-string stair in a plastered stair well, fasten the stringers to the walls by nailing through the plaster into the studding. Next, cut the treads and risers to length and wedge them in the grooves as at E in Fig. 7. Set the wedges in glue and be especially careful to drive them to a uniform tension. Where it is practical to support a notched wall stringer away from the wall, E in Fig. 8, a plain board can be used as the finish stringer, thus eliminating the need for notching or grooving. Slip the board down into the space between the notched stringer and the wall and fasten with finishing nails driven through the plaster into the studding. Then install the risers and treads by butting them against the finish stringer instead of the plaster. Other methods of installing notched stringers are shown in Fig. 8, details A, B, C and D. A method of miter-joining the risers to notched stringers is shown at A, Fig. 9. The use of decorative brackets, detail B in Fig. 9, simplifies the miter-joining of risers and finish stringers on the open side of the stair, making it somewhat easier to produce neatly finished edges, and affording a simple means of correcting open joints caused by errors or inequalities of lumber. Anchor newel posts to the stair structure as shown in Fig. 9, detail C. If the installation permits working under the stair, the groove-and-wedge method as used with housed stringers may be employed for anchoring steps to posts, instead of the cleat-and-nail method shown at C. Wedges produce a tighter job. When installing a stair on subflooring, which is common practice, be sure to allow for the thickness of finish flooring by making corresponding increases in the width of the bottom riser and the length of the stringers and newel post.

An attractive stair rail not only is of decorative value, but it's an essential part of every stair as it reduces the accident hazard to the minimum. The rail must be rigidly mounted on newel posts that have been firmly anchored in the stair structure, and it should be capable of withstanding more than normal strain. To aid stairbuilders in doing good rail jobs at reasonable cost and with a minimum of hand work, ready-made rails are preferable for use on stairs of common measurements. These come in sections that are assembled on the job. Matching newel posts and balusters should be obtained with the rail. If the stair follows a normal layout with average run-and-rise measurements, it is easy to fit these standard parts. To determine the dimensions of parts needed, draw full-size plan and elevation layouts. A typical layout of the balustrade is shown in Fig. 11, the parts lettered A to E inclusive, Fig. 10, being shown in position in the plan view, Fig. 11. A common procedure is to assemble the rail in flight units, beginning at the lower, or starting, newel. First bolt the easement section of the rail to the starting newel cap. Join the gooseneck section of the

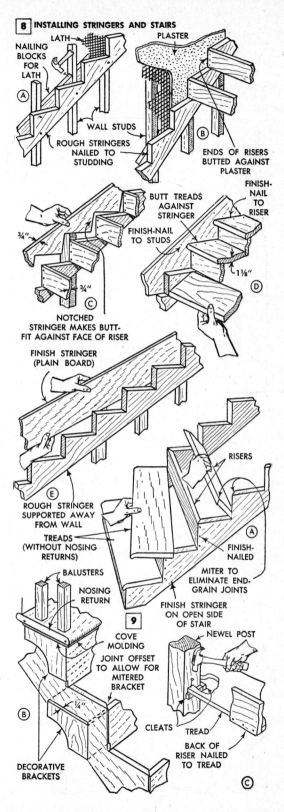

8 INSTALLING STRINGERS AND STAIRS

LATH
PLASTER
NAILING BLOCKS FOR LATH
A
WALL STUDS
ROUGH STRINGERS NAILED TO STUDDING
B
ENDS OF RISERS BUTTED AGAINST PLASTER

BUTT TREADS AGAINST STRINGER
FINISH-NAIL TO RISER
FINISH-NAIL TO STUDS
3/4"
3/4"
C
1 1/8"
D
NOTCHED STRINGER MAKES BUTT-FIT AGAINST FACE OF RISER

FINISH STRINGER (PLAIN BOARD)

RISERS

E
ROUGH STRINGER SUPPORTED AWAY FROM WALL
TREADS (WITHOUT NOSING RETURNS)
A
FINISH-NAILED
MITER TO ELIMINATE END-GRAIN JOINTS
FINISH STRINGER ON OPEN SIDE OF STAIR

BALUSTERS
NOSING RETURN
9
NEWEL POST
COVE MOLDING
JOINT OFFSET TO ALLOW FOR MITERED BRACKET
B
1/4"
CLEATS
TREAD
DECORATIVE BRACKETS
BACK OF RISER NAILED TO TREAD
C

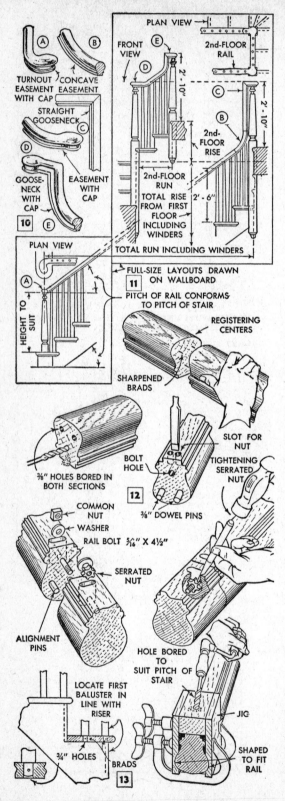

TURNOUT EASEMENT WITH CAP

CONCAVE EASEMENT

STRAIGHT GOOSENECK

GOOSENECK WITH CAP

EASEMENT WITH CAP

10

PLAN VIEW

FRONT VIEW

2nd-FLOOR RAIL

2nd-FLOOR RISE

2' - 10"

2' - 10"

2nd-FLOOR RUN

TOTAL RISE FROM FIRST FLOOR INCLUDING WINDERS

2' - 6"

TOTAL RUN INCLUDING WINDERS

PLAN VIEW

HEIGHT TO SUIT

11

FULL-SIZE LAYOUTS DRAWN ON WALLBOARD

PITCH OF RAIL CONFORMS TO PITCH OF STAIR

REGISTERING CENTERS

SHARPENED BRADS

SLOT FOR NUT

BOLT HOLE

TIGHTENING SERRATED NUT

3/8" HOLES BORED IN BOTH SECTIONS

12

3/8" DOWEL PINS

COMMON NUT

WASHER

RAIL BOLT 5/16" X 4½"

SERRATED NUT

ALIGNMENT PINS

HOLE BORED TO SUIT PITCH OF STAIR

LOCATE FIRST BALUSTER IN LINE WITH RISER

¾" HOLES

BRADS

13

JIG

SHAPED TO FIT RAIL

rail to the landing-newel cap. Then bolt the cap-and-easement units temporarily to the straight rail section, hold the assembly on the newel posts as in Fig. 1, and check the rail for length. Straight sections are joined with dowels and special stair-rail bolts as in the five steps shown in Fig. 12. Finally, complete the flight assembly by bolting on the cap-and-gooseneck unit. Assemble any succeeding flight units in the same way. In those styles where easements and goosenecks are not employed or in cases where factory-joined units are used, some of these special operations are unnecessary, of course. After the parts have been fitted and bolted together, fill openings and screw holes either with wooden plugs glued in, or with wood putty.

Balusters are fastened to rails in either of two ways, depending on the style employed. Square balusters, made to fit grooved rails, are held in position by means of spacers, or fillet strips, which are inserted between the balusters. Turned balusters are designed to fit into holes bored in the rails as shown in Fig. 11. Balusters of three different lengths are required for each step except the step directly under an easement, which takes a fourth size of extra length. To locate baluster holes on the rail, set it in place on the posts. Then raise plumb lines from the baluster holes in the step treads up to the rail, using a carpenter's level. Boring the holes at the required angle can be done accurately on the straight sections of the rail with the aid of the simple boring jig shown in the right-hand detail in Fig. 13. Holes in the curved sections of the rail must be bored freehand. In spacing balusters, locate the first one on each step in line with the riser as shown in the left-hand detail in Fig. 13.

Before preparing a newly built stair for painting or varnishing, allow time for the wood to become adjusted to the atmospheric conditions in the house. Otherwise, slight shrinkage may loosen the filling in the joints and spoil the paint job. For this reason, it is best to do all other decorating work in the house first, leaving the stair to the last. Meanwhile, protect the treads from dirt and scuff marks by covering them with heavy paper held in place with cellulose tape. In painting the stair well do not get paint on the stair parts as it will be difficult to remove.

DRY WALLS

Moisture condensation in any part of the house can result in rotted framing, ruined paint jobs and damaged walls

By W. Clyde Lammey

WHEN water vapor comes in contact with a cold surface it condenses to form either frost or water droplets, depending on the temperature of the surface. In older homes having porous, uninsulated walls and ceilings, the space within the walls or ceilings is constantly warmed by passage of heat. Ordinarily, there is no condensation except on the windows, for the warm, moist air passes directly through both walls and ceilings and the vapor does not condense within the structure. One occasional exception is when uninsulated walls are painted on the room side with several coats of oil paint. This acts as a vapor barrier and to some extent as insulation, allowing cold air to penetrate the wall from the outside. When the air in the house is excessively humid and the structure is in an exposed location, moisture will condense on the room side of the wall as in Fig. 2, detail B.

Condensation troubles usually begin when weather stripping, storm sash, calking and insulation are used,

To avoid condensation troubles in homes under construction, vapor barriers are installed between the plaster and studding. The barrier prevents moisture from air in the room penetrating to inner wall space

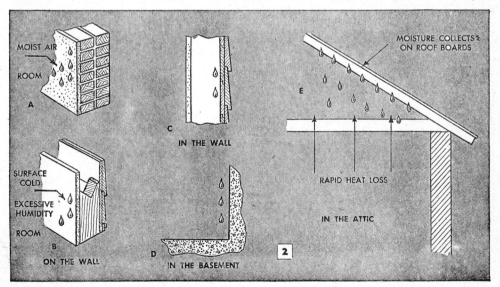

as leakage of moist, warm air through the walls is greatly reduced. Certain of these weatherproofing materials are more or less porous but at the same time they reduce heat loss to the minimum. This greatly reduced heat loss allows cold air to penetrate the walls from the outside. Warm, moisture-laden air from the inside meets this dry, cold air and vapor in the warm air condenses within the wall, Fig. 2, detail C.

In winter, moisture condensation usually will be evident as damp spots on the ceilings and room-side surfaces of exterior walls, water and ice on inside surfaces of windows and loose particles of ice on the attic floor. If the attic is not fully insulated or if the insulation of the attic floor is not adequate, the heat loss is correspondingly more rapid, Fig. 2, detail E. Moisture will condense on the underside of the roof boards, particularly on nail points which project through them. The beads of ice which form on the nail points eventually loosen and drop to the attic floor. When these melt the water is likely to cause damage to the plastered ceiling underneath.

Blistering and peeling of the paint on the outside of the exterior walls, Fig. 3, are more often due to condensation than to any other common cause. The paint acts temporarily as a vapor barrier and as a result moisture coming from inside the house gathers underneath it and forms blisters, eventually causing the paint to peel and expose the bare wood.

3 Blistering and peeling of paint are more often due to dampness within the walls than to any other common cause

4

■ - Average Jan. Temperature 35° F. or Less

5	PLACE	CAUSES
WINDOWS (Inside surfaces of windows.)		Excessive condensation on the windows may cause: • Paint to peel from sash. • Water to run down frame causing dampness around frame and perhaps paint-peeling on outside of building.
EXTERIOR WALLS 1. Condensation on exterior walls and ceilings of room.		Moisture may condense directly on cold surfaces of room. This occurs in certain uninsulated homes.
2. Condensation within ceilings and walls (inside of exterior wall).		Unobserved condensation may also occur within wall. Probability depends on humidity of inside air, outside temperature, and vapor permeabilities of wall.
CLOSET WALLS (Problem similar to that of exterior walls.)		Condensation on or within such walls is caused by closet being unheated. The inner surface temperature of the wall becomes lower than the temperature at which moisture in inside air condenses.
ATTICS (Problem is essentially the same as condensation within walls.)		Condensation in attics may occur when: • Insulation is applied without vapor barriers in the upper ceiling or attic floor. (Roof boards become very cold as a result.) • Attic doors are poorly fitted. (Large volumes of high-humidity air pass from living quarters to attic.) • Vapor penetrates the side walls and passes to attic.
FLOORS (First floor in basementless house.)		Concrete floors laid on ground present condensation problem.
BATHROOM		Vapor from running bath water or shower condenses.
KITCHENS AND LAUNDRIES		Humidities are high because of cooking, washing and drying processes.

In homes under construction, vapor barriers to prevent wall condensation should be used wherever the average January temperature is 35 deg. F. or colder, Fig. 4. In new homes various types of vapor barriers are available for application to inside walls under the plaster or other finishing material, as in Fig. 1. To be fully effective the vapor barrier should be continuous and unbroken, with joints lapped and securely tacked.

In homes already built, oil paint applied to walls and ceilings, as in Fig. 6, has proven value as a vapor barrier. Usually two coats of interior oil paint will be required to obtain best results. As a rule, water-emulsion paints are not good barriers. Condensation on the room side of uninsulated masonry walls above and below grade, Fig. 2, details A and D, often can be prevented, or at least minimized, by some means of ventilation. This can be a window fan, in the case of a basement, or an outside cold-air intake in a warm-air heating system which brings fresh, dry air into the house continuously. This arrangement has proved effective in homes having solid masonry walls where visible condensation and frost sometimes occur on the room side of the walls. In basementless homes built over a shallow excavation or "crawl space," ample ventilation under the floor, plus insulation between the floor joists, will minimize any tendency toward condensation. Fig. 5 gives causes and cures in more detail, although the causes and cures given will not apply fully in every instance. Much depends on peculiarities of the individual structural design.

Oil-base paints and also varnishes applied to the room side of walls and ceilings form effective vapor barriers in homes already built. Usually two coats of paint will be required for best results. As a rule the water-emulsion paints are not good barriers to moisture

CURES	NOTES

• Install:
    Double windows
      or
    Storm sash.
	Double windows permit about 33% relative humidity at 70° without condensation, compared to 14% with single window.

• Insulate walls.	Insulation keeps inner surface temperature of the wall warm enough to prevent condensation.
• Use vapor barriers.	

• For condensation on walls:
    Insulate, if house is uninsulated.
 • For condensation within walls:
    Use vapor barriers.
	A vapor barrier must be continuous and unbroken.

• Ventilate attic.
 • Prevent moisture from reaching attic by:
    Weather-stripping attic door.
    Using vapor barriers to prevent moisture from penetrating side walls, and ceilings under attics. Seal off basement air from stud space.
	Excessive humidities can be reduced most effectively by proper ventilation.
	 Water found in attics is more often caused by condensation than by leaky roofs.

• Insulate by using gravel, cinders, crushed stone or other insulating material underneath floor.	Install insulation at edges of slab.
• Install mixing faucets for hot and cold water. • Avoid running excessively hot water. • Install ventilator to bring in outside air. (Cold drafts are avoided by careful installation.) • Decorate bathroom walls with vapor-resisting material (oil paint, linoleum, tile, etc.).	
• Ventilate (exhaust fan). • Decorate kitchen walls with vapor-resisting material (oil paint, linoleum, tile, etc.). • Avoid excessive evaporation of water.	

Courtesy University of Illinois Small Homes Council

PRACTICAL
HOUSEHOLD
HINTS

To avoid soiling a recipe and to keep it handy while preparing food, use a celluloid "envelope" with a cardboard support bracket into which the recipe can be slipped

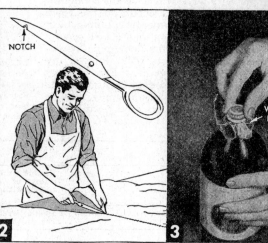

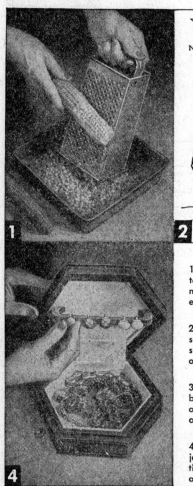

1. Shelling popcorn with bare hands is apt to result in sore and tender palms. However, this trouble can be avoided if an ordinary grater is used and the corn is shelled into a cake pan. Shell enough for several "poppings" and store in a sealed paper bag

2. One of the blades salvaged from a broken or discarded pair of scissors makes an excellent seam-ripping tool for home upholsterers. Grind a shallow notch in the cutting edge near the tip of the blade and sharpen both sides so seams can be ripped easily

3. Because of the nature of their chemical composition, many bleaching compounds have a corrosive action on the metal cap of the bottle that serves as a container. This corrosion can be avoided if a waxed-paper lining is used under the cap as shown

4. A scrollsawed strip of wood across the inside of the top of a jewel box makes an ideal rack for holding earrings. It will save time when hunting for them; keep pairs properly matched and guard against damage which might occur if they were left loose in the box

Above: If you have rusty spots on the refrigerator racks, remove them with fine steel wool and then wash in soapy water. After the racks have dried, cover the rusted spots with colorless nail polish to prevent any further spread. Right: To keep a youngster from cluttering up his room, use a vegetable bin for toy storage

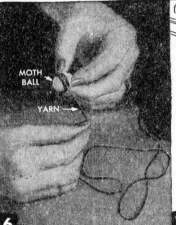

5. To avoid getting scratched by the ends of tiny feathers that work through a pillow, remove the feathers and turn the ticking inside out. Go over the ticking carefully, pulling out all feathers that may be sticking through. Then press with a hot iron coated with beeswax

6. When winding yarn from a hank into a ball, use a moth ball as the core. This will protect the yarn against damage when it is stored or not used for some time. If considerable yarn is kept in one box, it's also a good idea to scatter moth balls in the box

7. Sew a horizontal seam, with both ends open, at the lower end of an apron. This should be of a size to accommodate several kneeling pads. When scrubbing a floor or performing some other task that requires working on your knees, the apron will come in handy

8. An easy way to clean venetian blinds is to use a photo-film squeegee of the type that consists of a soft sponge on each end of a pair of tongs. These can be obtained in most photographic supply houses. Clean the blinds with a solution of soap and water

The Causes!

LEAKY EAVE TROUGHS, OR CLOGGED DOWNSPOUTS

FLOODED SEWERS

CLOGGED DOWNSPOUT DRAIN

WATER FROM HIGHER GROUND LEVEL

EAVE TROUGH

DOWNSPOUT

STANDING WATER

FLOOR-DRAIN TRAP

SURFACE SOIL

SURFACE SOIL

HARD SUBSOIL

HARD SUBSOIL

①

Where Water Enters

Ⓐ WALL CRACKS
Ⓑ POOR JOINT BETWEEN WALL AND FLOOR
Ⓒ FLOOR CRACKS
Ⓓ FLOOR DRAINS TO SEWER

②

TRENCH IS DUG NEXT TO WALL FOR TILING

③

CEMENT BLOCK WALL

COLD CHISEL

FOR BRICK, STONE OR CEMENT-BLOCK FOUNDATIONS ALL MORTAR JOINTS ARE CUT TO V-SHAPE, THEN BRUSHED WITH CEMENT

④

CRACKED AND POROUS CONCRETE WALLS GIVEN TWO COATS OF HOT TAR

Curing

IS YOUR basement damp, or likely to become flooded during rainy weather? Most leaky basements might have been made watertight if good construction practice had been followed when the foundation was built. A well constructed basement should be just as effective in keeping out water as a swimming pool is in keeping it in! However, much can be done to minimize water leaks and in many cases the trouble may be overcome completely. The first step is to locate, if possible, the source of the water.

Checking the Drainage System: Strangely enough, we must look first to the roof. Leaky eave troughs, as suggested in Fig. 1, are often the remote cause. Obstructions, such as roofing gravel or leaves, may block up the trough, causing it to rust and leak. Water then runs down the side of the building and accumulates next to the wall, where it gradually seeps through into the basement. Sometimes the soil next to the wall slopes toward it, forming a pocket, where water collects after a hard rain. Another offender is a clogged drain tile into which the downspout empties. The tile becomes clogged, causing the water to back up against the wall and seep through.

Outside Walls: If the drainage system is not at fault, or the building is so located that it cannot be adequately drained, provision must be made to waterproof the wall so that seepage will be prevented. Undoubtedly the best way

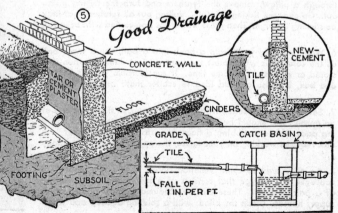

⑤ **Good Drainage**

CONCRETE WALL

TAR OR CEMENT PLASTER

FLOOR

FOOTING

SUBSOIL

NEW CEMENT

TILE

CINDERS

GRADE

CATCH BASIN

TILE

FALL OF 1 IN. PER FT

LEAKY BASEMENTS

to do this is to dig a trench wide enough for a man to work in, and as deep as the foundation, along as much of the wall as is usually damp. See Figs. 2 to 5. If your wall is built of brick, stone or cement block, the mortar joints must be raked out to a depth of ½ in. and all cracks cut back in a V-shape, as in Fig. 3. The wall should then be thoroughly sprayed with a hose, after which the cracks are filled with a mortar consisting of cement, 1 part, to sand, 1½ parts, and rammed in tight with a calking tool. The reason that the walls are kept wet is to prevent the absorption of water from the new cement in the patches. If this cement dries out too quickly, it will not stick. A grout of cement and water, having the consistency of thick cream, is brushed over the entire surface next. This is followed

⑥ WALL
UNDERCUT GROOVE
FLOOR

Where Floor Joins Wall

⑦ WET CONCRETE DRIED WITH BLOWTORCH

⑧ HOT TAR OR "EARLY CEMENT" MAKES WATERPROOF JOINT

⑨ FILLING THE WALL CRACKS

ing" and flaking, caused by the wall absorbing the moisture out of the new material before the chemical action is over. On a wall of solid concrete, which is in fairly good condition, two coats of hot tar, as in Fig. 4, may be used instead of the cement plaster, with good results and considerably less work and expense. However, the tar is not effective over a masonry wall.

If it is possible to secure drainage, a line of drain tile should be placed at the bottom of the trench, as indicated in Fig. 5. Be sure that sufficient fall can be obtained so that the water will drain into your catch basin, septic tank or other outlet, as indicated. The trench should be backfilled with coarse gravel or crushed stone, to a depth of 18 in. and then filled up with soil. The porous material around the tile permits the surface water to drain into the tile at the loose joints.

Inside Walls: If it is not possible to get at the outside walls, owing to sidewalks, shrubbery, etc., the next best thing is a treatment of the walls from the inside. The

immediately by a coat of cement and sand mortar (1 to 2 mix), about ⅜ in. thick. The mortar should be well worked with a wood float and when hardened sufficiently, roughed with a piece of wire lath to form a good bond for another coat, which also should be ⅜ in. thick. As soon as the cement has set, the new surface should be kept wet for several days until the cement has cured. This is done to prevent "craz-

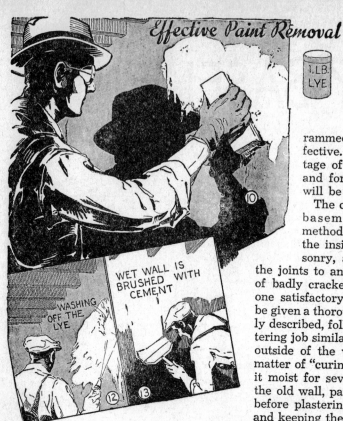

WET WALL IS BRUSHED WITH CEMENT

WASHING OFF THE LYE

rammed into the grooves to be effective. The tar has the advantage of being somewhat elastic and for this reason a tight seal will be assured.

The condition and type of your basement wall determines the method of waterproofing it from the inside. If the wall is of masonry, and the mortar is out of the joints to any extent, or if the wall is of badly cracked concrete, there is only one satisfactory remedy. The wall must be given a thorough patching, as previously described, followed by a two-coat plastering job similar to that suggested for the outside of the wall. Do not neglect the matter of "curing" the cement by keeping it moist for several days. Wetting down the old wall, painting with the grout just before plastering, roughing the first coat and keeping the surface moist after it has set, are the essential steps, all of which should be carefully followed in patching any old cement work successfully.

If your wall appears to be in fairly good condition, but does admit moisture, other than plain sweating, proceed as follows: Point up all mortar joints and patch up cracks with a mortar made with "quick drying" cement, 1 part, to sand, 2½ parts, as shown in Fig. 9. Allow the mortar in the patches to set for a period of 36 hrs. Then brush the walls thoroughly with a stiff brush, to remove all loose material and dirt. If the wall has been painted, the old paint must be removed by scrubbing with a wire brush or other means as in Fig. 10. Lye mixed with a thin paste of cornstarch, in the proportions shown in Fig. 11, is effective in removing oil paint. The lye paste should be allowed to remain on the surface for 45 min., then scrubbed with a wire brush and washed off with water as in Fig. 12. Water paint, calcimine and whitewash will respond to water and scrubbing. When working with lye, be sure to wear goggles and rubber gloves.

usual source of leaks is at the edge of the floor, where it joins the wall. This is caused by the fact that the walls are built first, and the floor is laid later when the concrete of the walls has thoroughly dried. The result is little or no bond between the two. The procedure in this case is to cut a groove next to the wall, to a depth of 1½ to 2 in., which is done by means of a cold chisel as in Fig. 6. The groove should be undercut as much as possible so that the seal will be anchored securely. Hot tar, or a mixture of tar and sand, is poured into this groove, as shown in Fig. 8. The tar will not adhere to wet material, and therefore it should be poured in when seepage is not occurring, if possible. Drying the groove with a blowtorch just before pouring the tar, as in Fig. 7, is also helpful to assure a good bond between the wall and floor. If the use of tar is objectionable, because of appearance, a mixture of any brand of "early strength" cement, one part to two of sand and four of gravel, may be used. It must be well

Laying a New Floor

Painting Walls: For painting concrete walls, the powder type of cement paints containing the same ingredients as cement, and mixed with water, actually bond with a masonry or concrete wall so that they become more than a surface coating. They produce a smooth, waterproof surface that is durable. The paint can be obtained in white and several colors, or can be tinted to suit. It is available in quantities as small as 5 lbs., which will cover about 50 sq. ft., two coats. Proceed with the painting as follows: Wet the wall thoroughly with a hose, and apply a coat of the paint, which has been mixed according to the manufacturer's directions. A large paint or calcimine brush is convenient for this work, as in Fig. 13. After 6 and not longer than 24 hrs., apply a second coat of the same paint, but mixed somewhat thicker than the first. The wall should not be moistened between coats. When the second coat is dry, you will have a beautiful and moistureproof wall.

Floor Repairs: Leaky floors are sometimes the cause of wet basements. If the leak is slight or of the seepage variety, patching the cracks in the floor with the cement mixture suggested for the joint between the wall and the floor, will often suffice. Another effective remedy for floors is by means of the "iron method." This is a powder with an iron compound as a base, which is used to fill cracks and also to serve as a coating over the entire floor, to waterproof it. If used in the latter manner, however, it should be covered with a coat of shellac or aluminum paint to prevent the color from bleeding through, and one or two coats of floor or deck paint,

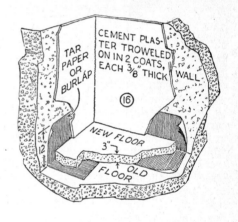

followed by a coat of varnish. If the pressure of ground water has cracked your basement floor, causing the basement to be flooded periodically, the remedies suggested above will not be effective and more drastic measures must be employed.

A new floor must be laid on top of the old one with a watertight membrane between, to prevent water coming up through the new floor. The surface of the old floor, or as much of it as is leaky, usually the area around the walls, should be covered with two or three layers of burlap, which is mopped and cemented into place with hot pitch or tar, as shown in Fig. 14. Tar paper and asphaltum are sometimes used instead of burlap where the surface of the

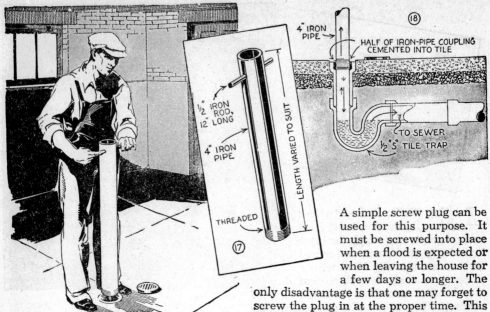

4" IRON PIPE

½" IRON ROD, 12" LONG

4" IRON PIPE

THREADED

LENGTH VARIED TO SUIT

⑰

HALF OF IRON-PIPE COUPLING CEMENTED INTO TILE

⑱

TO SEWER ½" S TILE TRAP

old floor is reasonably smooth, with equally good results. The tarred burlap or paper should extend a distance of a foot or so up the side wall, to insure a tight corner. A coating of cement plaster, applied as previously described, to the wall, is carried down over the tarred portion, as in Fig. 16. The thickness of the new floor, which is laid directly upon the tarred membrane, as shown in Fig. 15, depends largely on the amount of upward water pressure that must be overcome. A 3-in. thickness of concrete, including the cement topping, is usually considered safe unless an unusual amount of pressure has been experienced. In such a case it may be necessary to use metal reenforcing and additional thickness, to make sure that the floor will not heave up under pressure.

Excluding Sewer Water: In many neighborhoods the sewerage system is inadequate or antiquated so that unusually heavy rains cause the sewer to "back up" and flood the basements. While this water soon drains out again, it leaves a deposit of silt and sludge that is decidedly unsanitary. A tight wall and floor are no protection against this nuisance as the water enters through the floor drain. There are a number of devices on the market for closing this opening if the water backs up.

A simple screw plug can be used for this purpose. It must be screwed into place when a flood is expected or when leaving the house for a few days or longer. The only disadvantage is that one may forget to screw the plug in at the proper time. This difficulty is overcome by the ball-valve type of drain which permits water to run out of the basement, but closes when water backs up against it. The only possible objection to this type is that dirt will sometimes lodge in the valve and prevent it from functioning properly. Both the plug and the ball valve arrangements have one common fault—they may cause the floor to heave up if the pressure of the water backing up becomes too great.

Perhaps the simplest device which is not open to the above objection, and is useful where there is little likelihood of water rising more than 2 or 3 ft. temporarily, is the standpipe shown in Fig. 17. This consists of a length of 4-in. iron pipe from 2 to 4 ft. long. The pipe is threaded at one end and two holes are drilled in the other end to take a 12-in. piece of ½-in. iron rod which serves as a handle. With this arrangement, water may rise to the level of the water head without overflowing into the basement. All pressure against the floor is relieved. Fig. 18 shows how the standpipe is installed.

Where water in basements may rise over 2 ft., or over the height of a basement toilet bowl, an effective temporary measure to stop "back-up" water consists in plugging the toilet bowl with a sack containing sand, a cement sack being just the thing for this purpose.

Storm Sash Opens When Window Is Raised

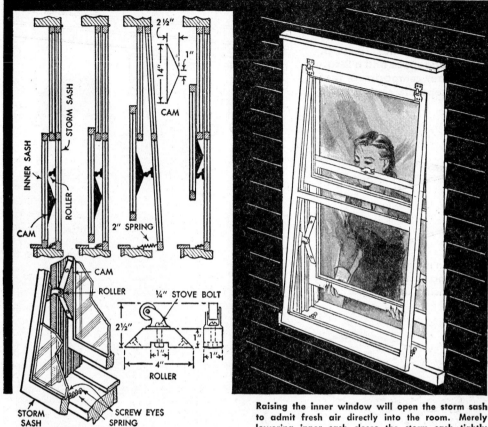

Raising the inner window will open the storm sash to admit fresh air directly into the room. Merely lowering inner sash closes the storm sash tightly

Designed particularly for use on bedroom windows, but an excellent idea for other windows where periodic ventilation along with adequate insulation is important, this novel device permits a hinged storm window to be opened and closed simply by raising and lowering the bottom sash of the inner window. It also prevents anyone from closing the inside window and forgetting to close the storm window. A caster-and-cam arrangement produces the automatic action while a tension-spring attachment for the bottom of the storm sash holds the sash tightly closed or firmly against the cam. As the inner window is raised, the storm sash opens, gradually reaching a maximum opening of approximately 3 in. when the roller is midway on the cam. Raising the window higher causes the storm sash to close entirely. In this closed position, air which normally enters around the storm sash gives a minimum amount of ventilation. The variety of positions of both sashes allowed by the device affords a wide range of ventilation. A wooden cam is fastened to each side of the lower sash and a caster assembly to each side of the storm sash with countersunk screws, as shown. Stove bolts anchor the casters to their mounting blocks. The 2½-in. dimension both for the cams and the roller assemblies should be varied, if required, to provide a clearance of ½ in. between cams and storm sash and rollers and inner sash. This clearance assures complete closing of the storm sash and avoids the possibility of rattling. When assembling the device, make sure that the casters and cams are in correct alignment so that the caster rolls true throughout the entire length of the cam. Two springs, 2 in. long and with a stretch of 4 in., are attached with screw eyes between the bottom rail of the storm sash and the window sill. The screw eyes should be fastened to the storm sash about 2 in. from each side and 1 in. from the bottom of the rail. Those on the sill should be attached opposite the ones on the storm sash and just outside the inner window sash.—Martin J. Gresho, Chicago.

30° Below HOME-FREEZER UNIT

Ordinary hand tools were used in building this home freezer, which has 18 cu. ft. of storage space and a 2-cu.-ft. freezer compartment that has a separate control valve

You can make the unit smaller by reducing dimensions and size of condensing unit proportionately

Trouble-free operation is the result of following the few simple service routines for freezer units.

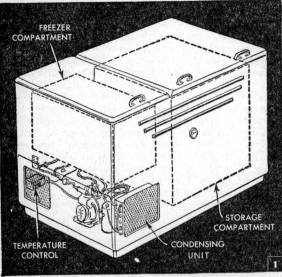

FREEZER COMPARTMENT

TEMPERATURE CONTROL

CONDENSING UNIT

STORAGE COMPARTMENT

By John F. Shrock

BUILDING your own home freezer is not a difficult job, especially this one; it's nothing more than a well-insulated plywood box or cabinet in which a purchased refrigerating unit is installed. The freezer has been tested in actual use and also in a laboratory, Fig. 8. The freezer and storage compartments can be separately controlled by shutoff valves and the freezer compartment can be brought down to about 30 deg. below zero for quick freezing of meats and vegetables before putting them in the storage compartment. The latter is held at a temperature of approximately zero. When not in use, the freezer

compartment may be shut off to ease the load on the compressor. It's best to use a new refrigeration or condensing unit, which comes charged with refrigerant and only has to be connected to the cooling or evaporator coils inside the compartments.

Construction begins with the cabinet, Fig. 1, which is divided into three parts: a freezer compartment, a storage compartment and the space for the condensing unit. Refer to Fig. 2 for the general dimensions. Since the over-all size of condensing units varies with different makes, this will affect the dimensions of the compartments because space allotted for the unit will vary. There should be several inches clearance on both sides and above the condensing unit. The dimensions given are for a hermetic ⅓-hp. unit.

After the base is cut, a 2 by 4-in. kick board is screwed to the underside 2 in. from the edges as shown in the lower right-hand detail of Fig. 2. The corners are mitered. The frame is of glued-and-screwed butt construction and all members are common 2 by 2 in. stock, actually 1⅝ by 1⅝ in. dressed. They are glued and screwed, using No. 14 screws 3 in. long. The screws, of course, are countersunk so the plywood panels will fit flush against the frame. The platform that forms the base of the freezer compartment is cut next and screwed to the supporting members. This is ¾-in. waterproof plywood, the width of which is determined by the space allotted for the condensing unit. To provide a partition and backing for the insulation for adjoining walls of the storage and freezer compartments, as well as to form one side of the condensing unit compartment, a ¼-in. waterproof plywood panel is used. This extends the full width and height of the box and is fastened to the frame members against which it rests.

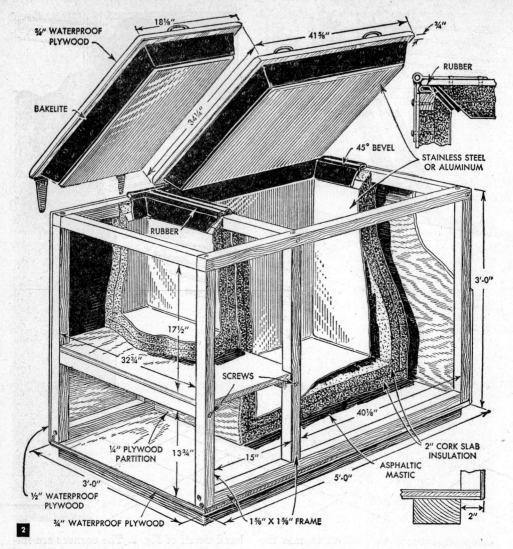

Next, the plywood sides, back and front are fitted to the frame. These are all ½-in. waterproof plywood, although hard-pressed board of a suitable thickness would do equally well. Before installing the front panel, cut an opening in it over the condensing unit compartment. Make the opening equal to the front area of the compartment and nail expanded metal over the inside of the opening. Any decorative grillwork can be used; but it must be remembered that air passing over the condenser enters through this opening and its area should not be restricted to retard movement of air as this would affect the efficiency of the refrigerating unit. That portion of the end panel covering the unit is hinged to provide a door for access to the unit. The door should be large enough to provide easy access to all parts of the com-

partment it covers. Toward the rear end of the door an opening is cut equal in area to the one in the front panel. This is the exhaust outlet for the condensing unit and remarks concerning the type of grille apply here as well as to the front panel.

After the panels have been fitted and assembled, they are screwed to the frame. Use flathead screws and countersink the holes so they can be filled. If the panels are cut so that one end comes flush with a corner frame member and the end of the adjoining panel extends slightly beyond the post, nicely rounded corners can be made. To do this, round the corners to the approximate curve desired with a plane or saw. Then use a sanding block that has the face cut to the desired contour to finish the curve. The lids for the deep-freeze and storage compartments should extend over the openings about ¾ in. on all sides, with very little clearance between the inner edges of the two lids. Approximate over-all dimensions are given in Fig. 2. After the lids have been cut to size, the corners and edges are rounded in the same manner as was done previously.

The next step is the application of the insulation and sheet-metal lining. A double layer of 2-in. compressed-cork slab, which is cut easily with a handsaw, is applied to the bottom and sides of both compartments and to the undersides of the lids. An asphaltic-mastic compound, which is a neat emulsified asphalt, is used as the bonding medium. Figs. 3 and 4 show how the mastic is troweled on. When applying the two layers of cork, spread mastic on all joining surfaces of the plywood and cork. After insulating the compartments and under-surfaces of the lids, roughly bevel the insulation at the upper edges of the compartments at a 45-deg. angle, using a saw to cut them. Then bring the bevels to a perfect 45-deg. angle by troweling on a mixture of ground cork and mastic, using a template as in Fig 5.

The metal lining is next. Either stainless steel or aluminum is used. A medium-gauge aluminum will prove very satisfactory. Before the metal is cut to shape, paper patterns should be fitted against the cork to determine the exact dimensions so the joints will be a perfect fit. This is necessary since the joints are not soldered, but depend on the mastic to hold the lining in place. The upper edges of the metal should overlap the bevels about 1 in. After the lining has been applied, using mastic to bond it to the cork, a Bakelite edging is cemented and screwed over the bevels. Again, paper patterns should be cut and tried to assure a perfect fit. After completing the compartments, bevel the insulation of the lids to fit the beveled surfaces of the compartments and apply metal and Bakelite as for the compartments. When preparing the lids it's a good idea to try them on the compartments frequently as the work progresses to compensate for any error that may have been made when beveling the compartments. A refrigerator cover-seal gasket of rubber, upper right-hand detail of Fig. 2, is screwed to the frame members before the Bakelite is attached. After the lids have been fitted, the hinges and handles are screwed in place. Chromium-plated hardware is used and the hinges should be attached firmly to the frame members and lids. A refrigerator dial thermometer, flush mounted, connects to the storage compartment. Any holes that are drilled are sealed with cork and mastic.

A ⅓-hp. condensing unit is used for a

Troweling the asphaltic mastic that forms a bonding medium between the cork and plywood

Here the final coating which forms a seal between the sheet metal and the cork is applied

A template must be used to gauge the correct bevel between the sides and lid of the unit

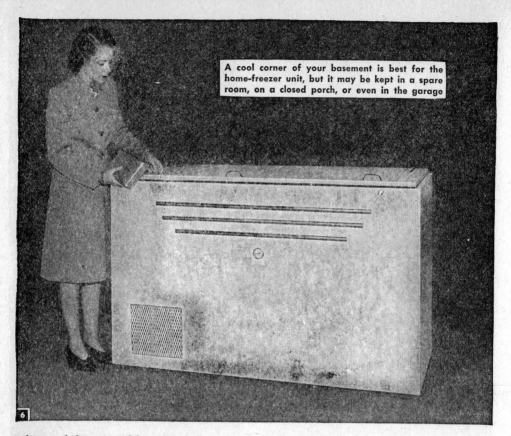

A cool corner of your basement is best for the home-freezer unit, but it may be kept in a spare room, on a closed porch, or even in the garage

cabinet of this size, although smaller units can be used if the size of the compartments is reduced proportionately. The so-called "open" type consists of a compressor, condenser, receiver, motor and fan, the compressor being driven by a V-belt. Hermetic units have the motor connected directly to the compressor and a separate motor is used to drive the fan. If a rebuilt unit is used, be sure that the compressor valves are not leaking, as this will affect the operating efficiency considerably. Freon 12 is the refrigerant gas commonly used. Other required parts for the refrigeration system are a dehydrator, sight glass, two shutoff valves, two tees, two thermostatic expansion valves and a check valve, or a two-temperature valve if available. Flare fittings are used throughout. About 100 ft. of ⅜-in. and 8 to 10 ft. of ¼-in. dehydrated copper tubing, as used for refrigeration work, are required. For this particular unit all parts are for ¼-in. connections except one tee, which is ⅜ in., as is the check valve. The expansion valves, which have ¼-in. inlets and ⅜-in. outlets, must be for a ⅓-hp. unit. A pneumatic temperature-control unit of suitable range is used to start and stop the motor. The connections to be made are shown in color.

Fig. 7 shows the complete refrigeration system installed. When making a flare joint, upper left-hand detail, the end of the tube is compressed against the seat of the fitting by screwing down the nut. The end of the tube must be perfectly round and cut off square. Carefully remove all burrs and chips of metal and keep all filings and chips out of the tube to prevent them from getting into the refrigeration system. Form the end of the tube with a flaring tool, making certain that the flare is the right length. If it is too short, it will not seat fully and the tube will pull out of the flare nut, while if the flare is too long it will not permit the nut to seat properly.

The manner in which the connections are made is indicated in Figs. 7, 9 and 10. The condensing unit, which is mounted on an integral base, is placed toward the front end of the compartment with the condenser against the grille in the front panel. The outlet connection from the receiver, which is for ¼-in. tubing, runs to the dehydrator, the sight glass and through a tee to the shutoff valves and the expansion valves. All these are ¼-in. fittings. All bends should have as large a radius as possible so the tubing is not compressed. The shutoff valves are made so they can be screwed to the top of the compartment. The evaporator coils, which are the coils inside the compartments, are ⅜-in. tubing. They connect to the outlets of the expansion valves and are secured with clips to the walls of the metal lining as shown in Fig. 9. About 50 ft. of tubing is required for each compartment. From the storage compartment, the line runs to a check valve and then to a ⅜-in. tee. The return from the freezer compartment goes directly to the same fitting from which a common return goes to the suction valve of the compressor, Fig. 7. Bending tools are used when making the evaporator coils, which should be formed before they are screwed to the metal lining. Two holes are drilled in each compartment, one for the ¼-in. inlet tubing and the other for the ⅜-in. outlet. In the case of the storage compartment, the outlet hole should be large enough to accommodate the capillary or temperature-control tubing which connects to the temperature control. The holes are hermetically sealed with the mastic-and-cork mixture. The bulb for the control is clamped to the evaporator coil, as indicated in Fig. 7. The control tubing for the expansion valves is clamped to the coils at a point about 2 ft. from where the coil leaves the compartment. The exact spot will have to be determined by experiment. After the system is in operation, there should be no frost on the suction-side

tubing outside the compartments. If there is, the control-tubing clamp should be moved farther back from the outlet. If a satisfactory adjustment does not result, the setting of the expansion valve will have to be changed. However, this is set at the factory and should be reset by a refrigeration serviceman. The manner of adjustment varies with the different makes of valves. The completed unit is then painted and finished with metal trim, Fig. 6.

If you are unfamiliar with refrigeration work, it's best to have a serviceman connect the condensing unit to the coils and put the system in operation. This includes purging the tubing of air, checking the suction and discharge pressures, and testing for refrigerant leakage. This work can be done for a nominal sum. It is necessary that there be no air in the system because air is much less compressible than Freon and, for that reason, may ruin the valves of the compressor. The simplest way to purge the coils of air is as follows: after the connections have been made and tightened, a standard refrigeration suction gauge is installed in the port provided on the suction valve, which is then opened slightly; open the receiver outlet valve and both shutoff valves to admit refrigerant to the evaporator coils. When the gauge pressure rises to about 20 lbs., close the suction valve on the compressor and the valve on the re-

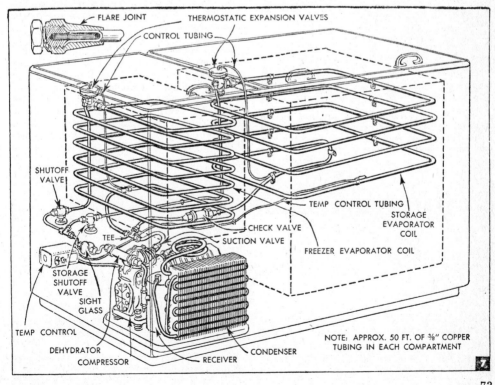

FLARE JOINT — THERMOSTATIC EXPANSION VALVES — CONTROL TUBING

SHUTOFF VALVE

TEMP CONTROL TUBING

STORAGE EVAPORATOR COIL

CHECK VALVE

SUCTION VALVE

TEE

FREEZER EVAPORATOR COIL

STORAGE SHUTOFF VALVE

SIGHT GLASS

TEMP CONTROL

DEHYDRATOR

COMPRESSOR

RECEIVER

CONDENSER

NOTE: APPROX. 50 FT. OF ⅜" COPPER TUBING IN EACH COMPARTMENT

Temperature readings are being taken with a thermocouple during the initial test of this home-freezer unit

ceiver outlet. The coils now contain a mixture of refrigerant and air; loosen the flare nut that connects the tubing to the suction valve to purge the tubing of this mixture, then tighten the nut again. It will be necessary to repeat the operation about three times. Care must be taken when purging the lines. Not following the proper sequence might result in excessive loss of refrigerant or cause damage to the condensing unit when it is put into operation.

After the system has been purged, all valves are opened and the motor is connected to a power source to put it into operation. All valves should be opened fully, otherwise damage may result. The temperature of the storage compartment is regulated by the temperature control. When it is not desired to use the freezer compartment, close the shutoff valve to put it out of service.

Since the home-freezer unit is not opened as frequently as a refrigerator, it will not require defrosting as often. However, when the coils are heavily frosted, the frost should be removed with a wire brush to keep the unit operating at its highest efficiency. For easy access, food should be kept in wire baskets, or dividers should be used.

A few of the common troubles experienced in the operation of refrigeration systems follow, together with the cause and correction. (When working around a condensing unit, always disconnect the motor as the operation is automatic and the unit may start at any time.) If the compressor runs in short cycles, it may be due to the fact that the suction and discharge valves are partially closed when they should be wide open and in the back-seated position. Obstructions over the grilles may cause insufficient ventilation. Periodically the grilles should be cleaned and the condenser gone over with a brush to be sure that there are no obstructions. A low charge of

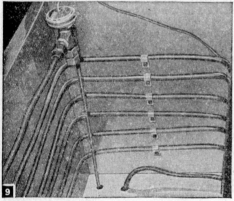

Above: The evaporator coil is attached to the sidewalls of the freezer compartment with small metal clips. Below: Arrangement of the condensing unit, valves, sight glass and dehydrator is shown here

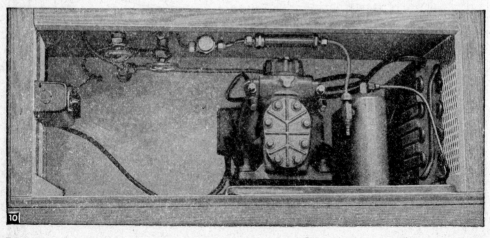

refrigerant will also cause the unit to run too frequently; if bubbles show in the sight glass or the liquid appears cloudy, this indicates the need of additional refrigerant. It should be noted that when food is put into the freezing compartment, there will be a heavy load placed on the refrigeration system and it will run more frequently than usual.

If the compressor knocks, it may be due to air in the system which should be purged, or in open models it may be due to a lack of oil in the crankcase. If the latter is true, a refrigeration serviceman should add the proper kind of oil. Frost on the compressor head is an indication that the suction pressure is too high and this is corrected by adjusting the control tubing on the expansion valves. As a general rule, there should be no frost on the lines after they leave the freezing and storage compartments. Compressors that are driven through a V-belt should have the drive tested for tension and alignment if belt slippage is suspected. When lubricating a unit, avoid dropping any oil on the belts.

Moisture is seldom found in a properly maintained refrigeration system, and no system will function correctly if there is moisture in it because the water will freeze at the expansion valve and then be blown free by accumulated refrigerant pressure, resulting in erratic suction pressure. If replacing the dehydrator fails to correct this condition, the expansion valve may have to be removed and dried out as well. In either case, it's best to have a serviceman do the work since the refrigerant must be exhausted from the evaporator coils and pumped into the receiver and condenser.

Should it become necessary to take the unit out of service, or should there be an extended power failure, dry ice can be put in the storage compartment to hold the temperature, or the food can be moved to a locker plant. However, care must be taken when using dry ice as its temperature is 110 deg. below zero and it may reduce the temperature in the box too far. The ice should not be handled with bare hands.

Repairing Refrigerator Gasket

When the rubber gasket surrounding the door of a refrigerator seemed to lose its life and to half collapse, permitting outside air to seep into the box, a slight incision was made at the right-hand corner into the collapsed air cell. Then a length of single-strand drop cord wire was worked around the whole face, thus filling out the insulation and preventing the entry of warm air.

Mousetrap That's Always Set

BAKING POWDER CAN
BOARD

With a pail, a baking-powder can, a board and a length of wire, you can make a mouse-trap that won't require resetting to catch any number of mice. Holes are punched in both ends of the can for the wire axle, which rotates in two holes punched in the side of the pail near the top. The board is used as an incline for the mice to walk on. To operate the trap, spread cooking fat over the can and cover with bread crumbs or grain; then fill the pail about one-third full of water. The mice will walk up the incline, and jumping for the food, roll off the baking-powder can into the water.

Improved Lock for Bathroom Door

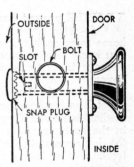
OUTSIDE / DOOR / SLOT / BOLT / SNAP PLUG / INSIDE

To keep a youngster from locking himself in the bathroom, one parent altered an ordinary bolt lock so that, in an emergency, it could be opened from outside the bathroom. The lock is installed in the usual manner, then the outside knob is removed and the end of the shaft is slotted to fit a screwdriver. Finally, the hole in the door for the knob is capped with a snap plug. To unlock the door from outside, remove the plug and turn the bolt back with a screwdriver.

Wood Strips Stiffen Stairs

1"x3" STRIP

If your basement stairs are weak and tend to spring up and down when you walk on them they can be stiffened by nailing 1 by 3 - in. strips along the lower edges of the supports. The strips will take part of the bending strain and add much rigidity to the stairs. Nails used in fastening these strips should be staggered about 10 in. apart to help avoid splitting.

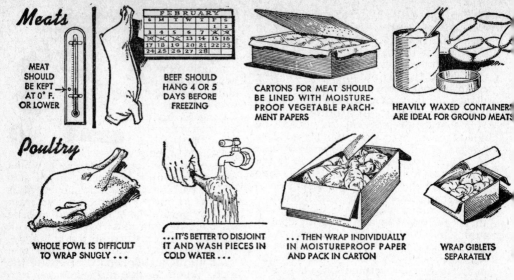

Meats

MEAT SHOULD BE KEPT AT 0° F. OR LOWER

BEEF SHOULD HANG 4 OR 5 DAYS BEFORE FREEZING

CARTONS FOR MEAT SHOULD BE LINED WITH MOISTURE-PROOF VEGETABLE PARCHMENT PAPERS

HEAVILY WAXED CONTAINERS ARE IDEAL FOR GROUND MEATS

Poultry

WHOLE FOWL IS DIFFICULT TO WRAP SNUGLY . . .

. . . IT'S BETTER TO DISJOINT IT AND WASH PIECES IN COLD WATER . . .

. . . THEN WRAP INDIVIDUALLY IN MOISTUREPROOF PAPER AND PACK IN CARTON

WRAP GIBLETS SEPARATELY

PREPARING FOOD for HOME-

WHILE prompt handling has much to do with success in storing foods in home freezers, it's equally important that you know how to process and, especially, package them to retain as much of the flavor and nutritive value as possible. Generally, the right time to prepare fruits and vegetables is when they are ready for immediate table use. They should be gathered in the early morning before they absorb the day's sun and should be processed and frozen with as little delay as possible. Loss of vitamin value occurs rapidly at room temperature, and holding products over to

the following day should be avoided, especially after shelling, scalding or cutting. It should be remembered that freezing does not necessarily sterilize the product. Consequently, it is important that all utensils as well as the hands be thoroughly clean before preparing the food.

In most cases, a storage temperature of 0 deg. F. will give satisfactory results when just a few packages of food are to be frozen at one time. Large amounts will require a lower temperature of —10 deg. F., although it's best not to try to freeze too many packages at once. As it is not as cold near the

Milk

FROZEN MILK WILL KEEP ONE OR TWO MONTHS

CREAM IS NOT GOOD AFTER FOUR MONTHS

Eggs

THE YOLKS OF WHOLE EGGS WILL JELL AT 22° F.

IT'S BETTER TO BREAK THEM AND STIR YOLKS AND WHITES TOGETHER ADDING 5% CORN SYRUP, SALT OR SUGAR

THESE ITEMS REQUIRE

SNAP BEANS

BANANAS

PEARS

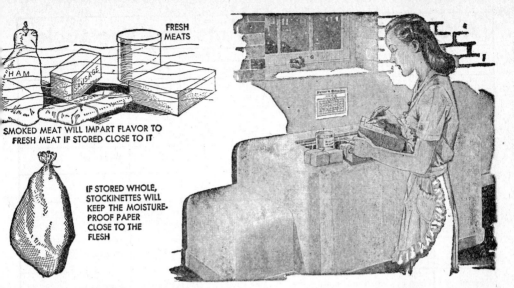

SMOKED MEAT WILL IMPART FLAVOR TO FRESH MEAT IF STORED CLOSE TO IT

FRESH MEATS

IF STORED WHOLE, STOCKINETTES WILL KEEP THE MOISTURE-PROOF PAPER CLOSE TO THE FLESH

FREEZER STORAGE

Label and date each package for future iden-tification. A waxed school crayon or grease pencil is just the thing for marking packages

top of the freezer, always check the temperature at this point. A periodic check should be made to detect possible power failure or mechanical breakdown. Should such an event occur, little thawing will take place during the first 15-20 hours. After this time it is best, if possible, to move the food to a locker plant or use dry ice to prevent excessive thawing until freezing is resumed. As a precaution against lowering the temperature too greatly, use dry ice sparingly. The length of time that products may be stored depends upon the temperature maintained. At 0 deg. F. fruits and vegetables may be stored 10-12 months,

while at 5 deg. F. the period is shortened to 8-10 months. In the case of meat, much is dependent upon the length of time it is held prior to freezing. Beef requires at least 4 or 5 days in a cool place for aging before it is cut up and packaged. Lamb, pork and veal should be frozen as soon as it is thoroughly chilled. Pork, especially, should be kept at a low temperature as it oxidizes easily and becomes rancid at higher temperatures. Dipping pork cuts quickly in hot lard will seal them and help prevent drying out during storage. Frozen meats should always be thawed thoroughly before cooking, especially large roasts, oth-

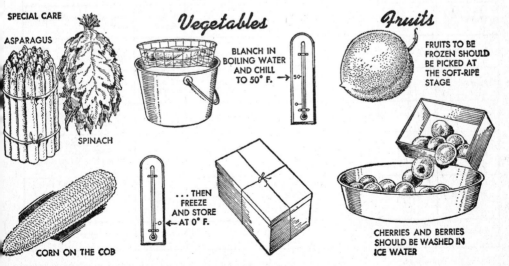

SPECIAL CARE

ASPARAGUS

SPINACH

Vegetables

BLANCH IN BOILING WATER AND CHILL TO 50° F. →

...THEN FREEZE AND STORE AT 0° F.

CORN ON THE COB

Fruits

FRUITS TO BE FROZEN SHOULD BE PICKED AT THE SOFT-RIPE STAGE

CHERRIES AND BERRIES SHOULD BE WASHED IN ICE WATER

A Guide for Freezing Fruits and Vegetables

Product	Maturity Desired	Preparation	Scalding		Type of Pack
			Boiling Water	Steam	
Asparagus	Tender tips best	Trim, wash, and discard all but upper 6 inches	Small stalks: 3 min. Large stalks: 4 min.	3½ min.* 4½ min.*	Without brine
Lima beans— bush or pole	Green beans best	Shell	Medium beans: 1½ min.* Large beans: 2 min.* Small beans: 1 min.*	2½ min. 3 min. 2 min.	Without brine
Soy beans	Green beans best	Scald pods, shell	2 min.*	3 min.	Without brine
Snap beans	Small beans best	Snip; cut into ¾-inch lengths	2 min.*	3 min.	Without brine
Beets	Young and tender	Cut off tops; mature beets should be cooked, then rub off peels; slice	1½ inches in diameter: 2½ min. Over 1½ inches: cook until tender	3½ min.* Cook until tender	Without brine
Peas	Sweet and not starchy	Shell, discard starchy peas	Small peas: 45 sec.* Large peas: 1 min.*	1½ min. 2 min.	Without brine
Spinach	Young	Cut and discard thick stems	2½ min.*	3½ min.	Without brine
Sweet corn, on cob	Before starch-iness develops	Husk; don't use immature and overmature ears	Small ears: 6 min. Medium ears: 8½ min. Large ears: 10½ min.	6½ min.* 8½ min.* 10½ min.*	Without brine
Sweet corn, cut	Before starchiness develops	Scald on cob as directed above, cool, then cut off whole kernels; or cut whole kernels from cob, then scald	Not recommended	2½ min.*	Without brine
Swiss chard	Small leaves best	Cut off and discard main stem	2 min.*	3 min.	Without brine
Apples	Fully mature	Peel, slice in 12ths	Not recommended	1½ min.; cool	Dry (no sugar or sirup)
Blueberries	Fully ripe	Stem, wash, crush slightly	Not recommended	Not recommended	4 or 5 pounds fruit to 1 pound sugar
Cherries, sour	Fully ripe	Wash, chill, pit	Not recommended	Not recommended	3 pounds fruit to 1 pound sugar
Gooseberries	Fully ripe	Stem, wash, crush slightly	Not recommended	Not recommended	3 pounds berries to 1 pound sugar
Peaches	Fully ripe	Peel, pit, slice	Not recommended	Not recommended	Cover with 60 or 70 percent sirup**
Pears	Fully ripe	Peel, core, quarter	Not recommended	Not recommended	Cover immediately with 60 or 70 percent sugar sirup**
Plums	Fully ripe	Wash, pit, quarter	Not recommended	Not recommended	Cover immediately with 60 or 70 percent sugar sirup**
Prunes	Fully ripe	Wash, pit, quarter	Not recommended	Not recommended	Cover immediately with 60 or 70 percent sugar sirup**
Raspberries	Fully ripe	Sort, wash in ice water, hull; crush or leave whole	Not recommended	Not recommended	4 or 5 pounds crushed berries to 1 pound sugar; cover whole ones with 50 or 65 percent sugar sirup**
Strawberries	Fully ripe	Sort, wash in ice water, hull and slice one quarter inch thick or leave whole	Not recommended	Not recommended	4 or 5 pounds sliced berries to 1 pound sugar; cover whole berries with 50 or 65 percent sugar sirup**
Rhubarb	Early spring best	Eliminate leaves; cut into 1-inch lengths	1½ min.	2 min.	Without sugar or sirup if desired

*Indicates preferred method.   ** For preparing sirup see table page 79.   New York State Agricultural Experiment Station.

Preparation of Sirup For Freezing Fruits

Dissolve the sugar in boiling water or mix the sirup with boiling water; cool to room temperature.

50-percent sirup: 2½ cups sugar per pint of water; 3 cups water to 4 cups crystal white corn sirup; 3½ cups water to 4 cups high-grade confectioners' corn sirup.

60-percent sirup: 3½ cups sugar per pint of water; 1½ cups water to 4 cups crystal white corn sirup; 2 cups water to 4 cups high-grade confectioners' corn sirup.

65-percent sirup: 4½ cups sugar per pint of water; ½ cup water to 4 cups crystal white corn sirup; 1½ cups water to 4 cups high-grade confectioners' corn sirup.

70-percent sirup: 5½ cups sugar per pint of water; ¼ cup water to 4 cups crystal white corn sirup; 1 cup water to 4 cups high-grade confectioners' corn sirup.

A moderately hot household iron, applied for a few seconds, will seal "bag-in-carton" containers. Cellophane bags may be sealed with a curling iron, taking care not to burn them

erwise the meat will not cook uniformly.

The importance of doing a thorough and careful job of packaging cannot be over-emphasized. The wrapping material used not only must protect the food from loss of moisture, but also must prevent transfer of odors. Ordinary waxed paper is not sufficiently moistureproof to package meat satisfactorily. In addition to special moistureproof paper for wrapping frozen foods, there are Cellophane, Pliofilm and rubber-latex bags which provide excellent protection. Present recommendations are that the size of the packages should not exceed 2 lbs. per package for fruits and vegetables and a package weight of 5 lbs. for chilled meats is about right. Roasts and other cuts of meat should be wrapped tightly to make them as airtight as possible and securely sealed with cellulose tape or tied with twine. Two separate wrappings, of course, are better than one. An outer covering of mesh cloth known as a stockinette will serve to protect the wrapping. Small cuts of meat are stored best in containers lined with moistureproof paper. To exclude as much air as possible, containers should be packed to the very top. Vegetable and fruit juices must have room for expansion. Containers most commonly recommended for storing fruits and vegetables are heavily waxed cylindrical and square cartons, "bag-in-box" types and special moisture and vapor-resistant bags of Cellophane. In filling Cellophane bags the tops must be kept clean for later heat-sealing. This can be done with a household iron, or a curling iron if not too hot. There is less moisture loss with a double bag than a single one.

In blanching, or scalding, the vegetables are placed in a wire basket and lowered into boiling water for the required time as given in the table on the opposite page. They are chilled immediately afterward in running water 50 deg. F. and packed for storing. Fruits require a covering of sirup prepared according to the table above. The sirup should cover the fruit completely.

It's best to prepare poultry during the colder months as it is difficult otherwise to cool it properly before freezing. Unlike meat, poultry is more tricky to prepare because chickens, ducks and turkeys have a soft layer of fat directly beneath the skin that oxidizes quickly. It also is difficult to package the whole fowl because of the awkward shape which hampers wrapping it snugly. A stockinette, if available, helps to solve this problem, but it is recommended that the bird be cut up into smaller sections and each of these wrapped individually. As is true with meat, poultry never should be thawed for cooking by placing in water. Allow it to thaw gradually while in the package at room temperature.

Ammonia Cleans Greasy Oven

Usually difficult to remove, grease which has spilled in stove ovens and baked on the enameled surface is removed with household ammonia. Saturate several cloths with the solution and spread them over the oven racks. Allow them to remain overnight and on the following day scrub the spots with soap and water. In stubborn cases, several applications may be necessary.

REMOVING ICE from a wire clothesline, above center, is done in a jiffy when the comb from a safety razor is fastened to the clothes pole and used as a scraper. Comb engages wire as pole is pulled

THAWING WATER PIPES, above, where it is not advisable to use a blowtorch can be done safely with the heat from an infrared bulb. Be careful in using it that the hand does not touch the unguarded bulb

IN-A-DOOR BOOKCASE, left, built in the recess of a shallow clothes closet found in some older homes, modernizes opening and puts it to practical use. Shelves rest on flat side of screw eyes turned into jambs

WATERPROOFING TREATMENT for boots and shoes consists of applying hot ski wax to the leather and rubbing it briskly with a stiff brush. Rub with a cloth after wax hardens

HOT POKER hung up after firing will not scorch wall if a wooden block is placed a little below the nail on which it hangs to hold the hot end of poker away from wall

TOASTING ONE SLICE at a time in a door-type toaster is done faster if the element on one side is covered with asbestos to direct the heat to the opposite side

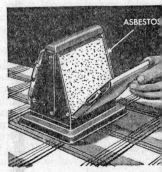

HOUSEHOLD HINTS

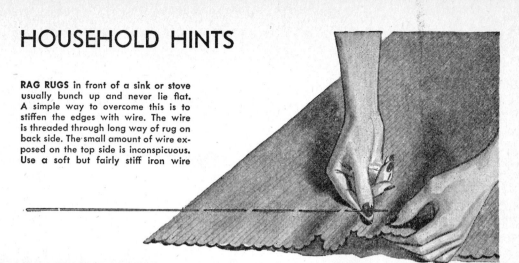

RAG RUGS in front of a sink or stove usually bunch up and never lie flat. A simple way to overcome this is to stiffen the edges with wire. The wire is threaded through long way of rug on back side. The small amount of wire exposed on the top side is inconspicuous. Use a soft but fairly stiff iron wire

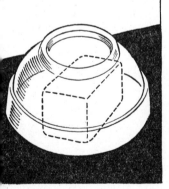

FLOWER FROG for narrow-neck vase, right, is improvised from the top of a scouring-powder can. Leave about ¼ in. of the cardboard container attached to the metal top to center and hold the frog in neck of vase

STERILIZING CORK of a vacuum bottle, left, requires that it be submerged. A good way to do this is to impale the cork on end of ice pick. Besides keeping the cork submerged, a handle is had to retrieve the cork

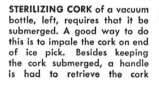

SOFTENING BUTTER taken from the refrigerator, above, can be done quickly and without waste due to melting if a bowl is heated and then placed over the butter for a short time

EGG CARTON in drawer of child's chest, right, provides individual storage compartments for socks. In addition to keeping them together in an orderly manner, idea promotes tidiness

ONE DOZEN EGGS

Paint-Locked Sash Loosened with Block and Hammer

WINDOW SASH — HARDWOOD BLOCK

If you can't loosen a newly painted window sash by cutting through the film of paint in the corner between the sash and frame, and it seems that some paint has run between the two, try this method. Set a small hardwood block endwise against the sash frame close to the top and strike it lightly with a hammer. Continue the procedure all the way across the top and down the sides of the sash frame. The hammer blows will break the paint film so that the sash can be opened without breakage.

Rack for Storing Storm Sash Safely Without Breakage

The problem of storing storm sash and window screens was solved by one man who hangs them on a rack like the one shown, where they are safe against breakage or other damage. Bolted to the ceiling joists or wall studs, the rack supports the sash and screens well above the floor in space not utilized in the average basement or garage. The rack consists of two end-pieces step-cut as indicated in the detail to receive 2 by 2-in. strips nailed to them. Hangers like those holding the sash and screens on the windows are screwed to these strips so that sash can be hung from them, each pair of hangers being numbered to correspond with the window to be hung on them. With this arrangement, each sash is hung on the rack as soon as it it removed from the window in the spring, at the same time taking down the screen from the rack and putting it up to the same window.

Faucet Washer Pivoted to Casing Stops Rattling of Window

The annoying rattle caused by a loose-fitting window can be prevented by screwing a faucet washer to the casing

FAUCET WASHER

WINDOW CASING

so that it presses against the sash as indicated. Use a screw of a size to permit the washer to rotate freely. In this way, the washer will not interfere with raising or lowering the sash, yet will apply sufficient pressure against the sash to prevent its vibrating in the wind. If the window is extremely loose, it may be necessary to install a washer at each side of the casing.

Hammering Pin on Shade Roller

SHADE ROLLER

SPOOL

If it's necessary to shorten a window-shade roller and then replace the pin, don't rest the other end on a floor or table when driving the pin. Instead, place it on an empty thread spool and insert the pin.

RACK

LAG SCREWS

JOIST

2"X2"

Part 2

PAINTING, DECORATING
AND FINISHING

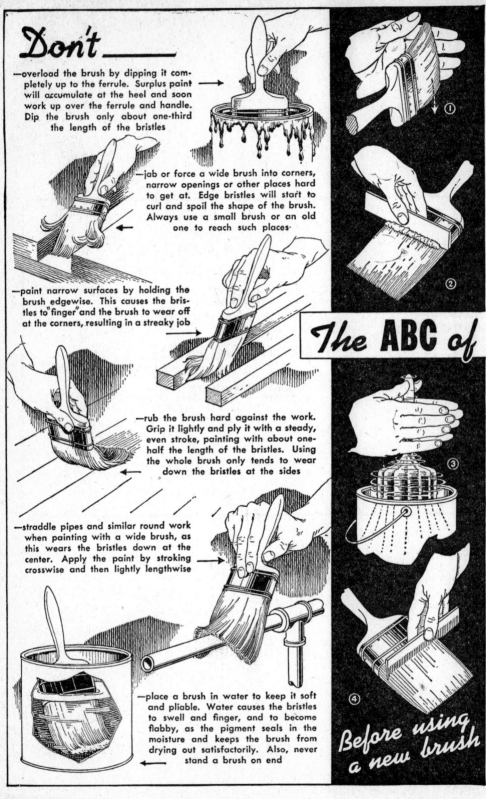

Don't____

—overload the brush by dipping it completely up to the ferrule. Surplus paint will accumulate at the heel and soon work up over the ferrule and handle. Dip the brush only about one-third the length of the bristles

—jab or force a wide brush into corners, narrow openings or other places hard to get at. Edge bristles will start to curl and spoil the shape of the brush. Always use a small brush or an old one to reach such places·

—paint narrow surfaces by holding the brush edgewise. This causes the bristles to "finger" and the brush to wear off at the corners, resulting in a streaky job

—rub the brush hard against the work. Grip it lightly and ply it with a steady, even stroke, painting with about one-half the length of the bristles. Using the whole brush only tends to wear down the bristles at the sides

—straddle pipes and similar round work when painting with a wide brush, as this wears the bristles down at the center. Apply the paint by stroking crosswise and then lightly lengthwise

—place a brush in water to keep it soft and pliable. Water causes the bristles to swell and finger, and to become flabby, as the pigment seals in the moisture and keeps the brush from drying out satisfactorily. Also, never stand a brush on end

The ABC of

Before using a new brush

TABLE FORK

Cleaning after using

⑤

⑥

⑦

WIRE

RIGHT

WRONG

⑧

PAINTBRUSH CARE

PAINTBRUSHES are used occasionally in most homes, and because of this wide distribution in inexperienced hands, brushes often are so misused and incorrectly cared for that they last for only one paint job. A good brush that is used and cared for properly will last for several years. A few of the most common abuses of brushes are illustrated on the opposite page.

When a new brush is purchased it should be broken in before using it. Figs. 1 to 4 inclusive show how this is done. First, hold the fingers of one hand extended as in Fig. 1 and flip the bristles sharply across them a few times. This causes any loose hairs to work forward and extend so they can be pulled out. As this operation is likely to tangle the bristles, they should be combed. Next, the brush is suspended in linseed oil for at least 12 hours. If this is not done, the paint pigment will adhere tightly to the dry bristles and make the brush hard to clean. Fig. 14 shows two handy containers in which brushes can be suspended in oil. One is a large glass jar having hooks in the lid to engage screw eyes in the ends of the brush handles. The other container is an open one in which the brushes are suspended from pieces of wire run through their handles. When ready to use the brush, remove all the oil from the bristles. One way of doing this is to use a wood strip as in Fig. 2. Start at the ferrule of the brush

and press the strip heavily across the bristles while moving it toward the tip of the brush. Centrifugal force will remove most of the remaining oil if you twirl the brush between the palms of your hands as in Fig. 3. It may now be necessary to again comb out the bristles as in Fig. 4.

Although often done, it is not good practice to press a brush across the edge of a paint can or pot to remove excess paint each time the brush is dipped. This bends the bristles at the corners of the brush and also results in an accumulation of congealed paint under the can rim that often drops back into the paint and has to be removed. A better way is to wipe the brush across a wire arranged as shown in Fig. 8.

Clean brushes are essential to good painting. A clean brush is more pliable,

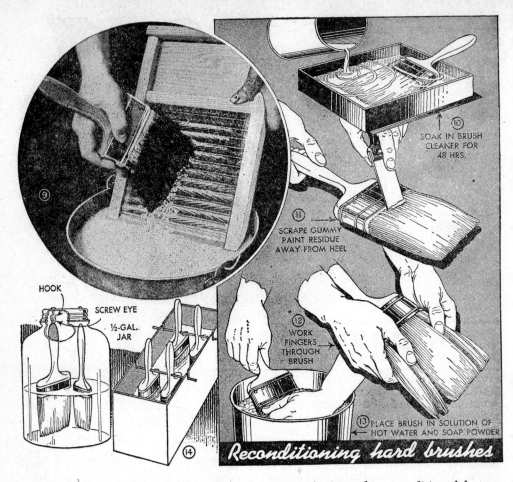

HOOK

SCREW EYE

½-GAL. JAR

⑨

⑩ SOAK IN BRUSH CLEANER FOR 48 HRS.

⑪ SCRAPE GUMMY PAINT RESIDUE AWAY FROM HEEL

⑫ WORK FINGERS THROUGH BRUSH

⑬ PLACE BRUSH IN SOLUTION OF HOT WATER AND SOAP POWDER

⑭

Reconditioning hard brushes

will work more easily and efficiently and will last much longer than one that is not kept clean. Therefore, always clean a brush in a suitable solvent before laying it away. The solvent recommended for the kind of paint in which the brush was used is the best for cleaning it. Use plenty of solvent and see that it is worked well up into the bristles, Fig. 7. A table fork or comb is handy for loosening gummy paint residue as in Fig. 5. If paint accumulates in the heel close to the binding, the bristles eventually will flare and ruin the shape of the brush. The back side of a knife can be used to good advantage for scraping away paint at the heel of a brush as in Fig. 6. When a brush is to be stored indefinitely, it should be cleaned thoroughly, first by washing it in liquid cleaner and then in soap and water. As soon as it is dry, the bristles are immersed in linseed oil and wrapped in paper. It's a good idea to remove the paper occasionally and apply a fresh coating of oil.

An old brush, which has been discarded because the bristles are full of hardened paint, often can be reconditioned by removing the dry paint. First, soak it in turpentine or liquid brush cleaner, Fig. 10, until the bristles have softened, working the bristles with the fingers from time to time as indicated in Fig. 12. A scraper like the one in Fig. 11 will be handy for removing the gummy paint residue that may accumulate at the heel. Next, place the brush in a pail containing hot water, 1 gal. and soap powder, ¼ lb., and work out the cleaner as in Fig. 13. Now comes the actual washing, which is done on a washboard. Sprinkle soap powder on the board, dip the brush in hot water and rub it over the board as you would when washing clothes. See Fig. 9. After the brush has been cleaned, rinse it in clear water to remove all traces of soap, comb out the bristles and wrap the brush in paper to dry, after which it is dipped in linseed oil, rewrapped and put away until needed. In replacing the brush each time in its paper wrapper, be sure that the bristles lie flat and straight; otherwise, the brush may assume a shape difficult to paint with.

OFF WITH THE OLD

Three methods of preparing painted and varnished surfaces for refinishing

SCRAPING — SANDING

is one of the most common methods used in removing either paint or varnish, but efficient use of a scraper depends on several factors, such as age of the varnish or paint and the wood underneath. If the finish has aged to the point of being dry and brittle, a sharp scraper may be used if the wood is hard. However, a scraper in the hands of an inexperienced person is likely to result in digs and gouges in the surface of softwoods. Grinding off the corners of the scraper will help some. The blade must be kept sharp by filing and turning the edge with a burnishing tool while the blade is held in a vise. It may be necessary to sharpen the scraper every few minutes while it is in use. If scrapers are used on rounded surfaces, even though the wood is hard, great care must be taken. The point of contact will be small and the pressure will be on a very small area. On some work the cutting edge should be slightly curved.

BLOWTORCH BURNING

is another method often used, especially where paint is to be removed from large areas, such as porch floors or sides of buildings on which several coats have been applied over a period of years. However, you must handle the torch carefully to avoid a fire. The torch should never be used on furniture and you should not attempt to remove varnish in this manner. When using a blowtorch most amateurs make the mistake of burning the paint too deeply. This scorches the wood underneath and does little to speed the work. Instead of trying to soften the entire paint film with one application of the torch, it's better to remove it momentarily as soon as the paint softens on top and then go over the surface with a scraper to cut off the softened paint. Repeat this operation until the wood surface appears, after which the use of the torch is discontinued.

CHEMICAL REMOVERS

are the best for use by inexperienced workmen. Although their use may raise the grain of the wood, which can be sanded down when dry, there is less chance of damaging the wood by nicking and gouging.

While not especially quick acting, trisodium phosphate, costing a few cents a pound, makes a safe remover for paint. It is not a corrosive agent, but rather a powerful alkaline solvent. Simply make up a saturated solution in a pail of hot water. This is brushed or "mopped" onto the surface to be treated, which should be flat and horizontal so that the solution will not drain off. Repeated applications usually must be made. The operation may be speeded up if a stiff scrubbing brush is used while the solvent is at work. At the end of a half hour or so, a scraper is employed. If all of the paint does not come off at this

Only small areas at a time should be treated and a brush should be used to keep the solvent active

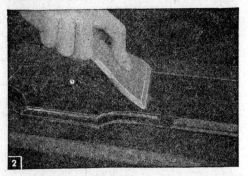

When removing varnish from veneers, use a scraper cut from hardwood and beveled on the scraping end

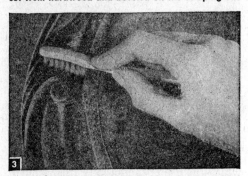

An old toothbrush is helpful in removing softened varnish from carved and other decorative surfaces

A hardwood dowel cut off at a sharp angle and then sharpened is ideal for cleaning varnished grooves

time, the applications are repeated until the paint film is softened through to the wood. A complete rinsing in warm, clean water follows and the bare wood is wiped dry to prevent warping.

Sodium metasilicate is another cheap chemical that performs much like trisodium phosphate. Although thorough and sure, both these materials are very slow acting. If you want speed, then prepared paint and varnish removers are best, although the precautions listed on the containers should be followed carefully in every detail. These removers usually contain dissolved wax or paraffin which slows down evaporation and protects the exposed wood. They should never be used in direct sunlight, which will cause them to evaporate with twice the normal speed. One should not make the mistake of trying to cover too much surface at once. A square foot, or even less, at a time is quite sufficient. For vertical or overhead surfaces where the material will run downward, a semipaste remover should be used. This type not only will stay put but also will stay wet a longer time. Paste removers are applied with a heavily loaded brush, using a flowing stroke. Lay on the paste with the flat of the brush rather than the tip, Fig. 1. Don't brush out as you would paint and don't brush back over material already applied. Allow 20 to 30 min. to penetrate, then scrape. If this doesn't expose bare wood another application is required. Allow time to penetrate and the finish then usually will come off. The job may be compared with taking off wallpaper. If there are several layers to be removed, it takes considerably more time and soaking.

When varnish is to come off, coarse rags may be employed after the solvent has had a chance to work for 8 or 10 min. Another application of remover is then made and followed by wiping. A final application of either turpentine or benzene stops action of the solvent. If rags are not sufficient on veneered surfaces, a scraper cut from hardwood may be used. This should be sharpened by beveling one end as in Fig. 2. If veneered drawer fronts have been covered with several applications of both paint and varnish, repeated applications of solvent usually are necessary for complete removal of the old finish. Removal from grooves will be aided greatly by several scrapers cut from dowels of various sizes. Any varnish-removal kit should have a set of all sizes along with several old toothbrushes to help in dealing with carved sections, Figs. 3 and 4. Such sections may require as many as ten applications of solvent before they are finally cleaned out. Be careful to prevent the staining of uncovered portions of furniture.

Rosin Removes Cold-Water Paint

Next time you have to remove cold-water paint from a wall or other surface, try using powdered rosin. Dust it lightly on a cloth which has been dipped in hot water and rub it over the paint. To apply the rosin to the cloth, use a large salt shaker

or similar dispenser. This will distribute it uniformly. The rosin has an abrasive action that is effective in removing this kind of paint.

Sawdust Absorbs Paint Remover

When refinishing woods, it's a good idea to have a supply of clean sawdust at hand to sprinkle on paint remover as the old finish is scraped off. A cleaner and neat-

er job will result than if rags were used and the sawdust can be disposed of when the work is done.

Bristles Attached to Paintbrush Make Dual-Purpose Tool

Fasten a section from a stiff wire brush to the handle of a paintbrush, as shown in the detail. This will be handy to use when scraping scale and rust from surfaces to be painted.

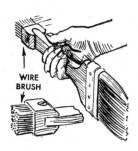

Solution to Clean Paintbrushes

Dirty paintbrushes that have been left in the following solution overnight and then washed in warm water will be perfectly clean. To make the solution, mix kerosene, 1 gal., and oleic acid, ½ gal. In a separate container, mix ammonia (28%), 1 pt., and denatured alcohol, 1 pt. Stir this mixture into the kerosene-oleic acid solution, continuing the stirring until the product is smooth.

Holder Suspends Paintbrushes in Cleaning Solution

When paintbrushes are set in a can of cleaner to keep them from hardening between jobs, the bristles may become bent out of shape. A simple holder to keep the bristles off the bottom of the can may be bent from a piece of heavy wire. The can sets on the lower end of the holder.

Nails in Legs Elevate Furniture to Simplify Painting

To do a better job of painting or varnishing chairs, occasional tables and other lightweight furniture, try driving a nail into the bottom of each leg to raise the piece above the bench top. This makes it easier to brush the finish down to the ends of the legs and keeps paper used to cover the bench top from sticking.

Water Soluble Paints Restored with Baking Soda

Some water soluble paints, if exposed to air and later stored, will become rancid in time. If this happens, the paint can be restored by straining it through a clean piece of cheesecloth and adding a small amount (about a teaspoonful to a gallon) of baking soda. Stir well and the paint will be ready for immediate use.

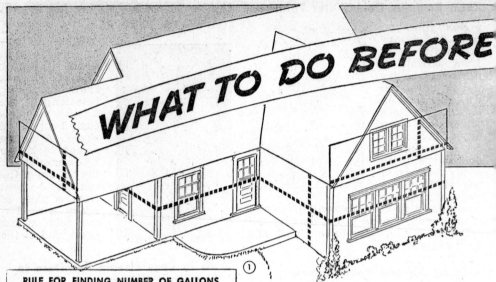

WHAT TO DO BEFORE

①

RULE FOR FINDING NUMBER OF GALLONS REQUIRED

Measure distance around house in lineal feet. Multiply by height to eaves. Divide by 600 where surface is in good condition—by 400 if surface is in poor condition. Measure width of gables and multiply by half the height

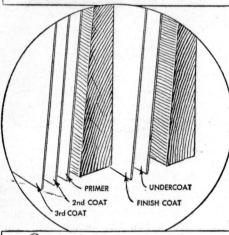

PRIMER UNDERCOAT
2nd COAT FINISH COAT
3rd COAT

② TWO ACCEPTED METHODS OF PAINTING THE AVERAGE FRAME HOME

By W. Clyde Lammey

GOOD paint will stick to almost any surface—for a while. How long it stays on is something else, for in the matter of durability it's what's under the paint film that counts. In general, the appearance of a house is not always a reliable guide to the condition of the surface over which paint is to be applied. Rather, adhesion of the paint film, original quality and formula of the paint and the condition of the building structurally are usually the factors determining the amount of work it will take to get the surfaces in proper condition for repainting.

Old paint worn thin by slow chalking and weathering—both normal processes—may appear to be in poor condition. But because of tight adherence to the wood and a solid bond between what remains of previous coatings, it still will provide a good painting surface, Fig. 3. However, if the surface presents one or more of the defects shown in Figs. 4, 5, 10 and 11, which have been somewhat exaggerated for purposes of illustration, then the job of preparation

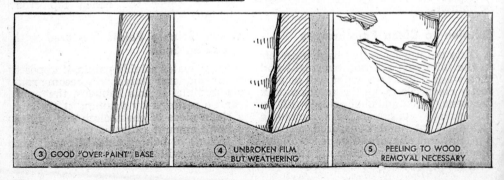

③ GOOD "OVER-PAINT" BASE

④ UNBROKEN FILM BUT WEATHERING

⑤ PEELING TO WOOD REMOVAL NECESSARY

YOU PAINT

CAREFUL ATTENTION TO SIMPLE PREPARATORY DETAILS WILL ASSURE A LASTING JOB

for repainting will be more extended. Scaling paint can be removed by scraping or wire-brushing, after which the surfaces are treated similar to new wood. But extensive blistering of the paint film and the peculiar "alligator," or "crackled-lacquer," surfaces less frequently seen are among the most difficult of all defects to remedy. In most cases complete removal is necessary, but if a blistered area is small a thorough scraping and sanding to level the paint film which still adheres sometimes will suffice. Paint remover in the paste form also is effective on small areas. Likewise, the prepared remover may be used in cleaning off small spaces presenting cracked, chipped or alligator surfaces. It also is especially effective in cleaning up turnings, newels and ornamental work which frequently adorns porches and cornices of very old houses. However, where the area is large, such as a side or gable end of the building, burning off the defective paint film to the wood with a blowtorch, Fig. 6, is considered the best practice. Unless you are accustomed to the work it's best to get experienced help for this job. In any case, it's essential that the siding be tight, that the flame be directed against the surface at an angle and slightly downward, and that the torch be moved continually to prevent charring the wood. Follow the flame with a scraper to remove the softened paint immediately. And always work with the torch on a quiet day—never when it's windy.

Fig. 2 illustrates two accepted methods

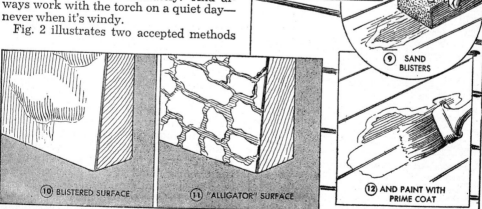

⑥

⑦ SURFACE BROKEN / HEAD FLUSH / DRIVE NAILS LIGHTLY

⑧ SHELLAC KNOTS

⑨ SAND BLISTERS

⑩ BLISTERED SURFACE

⑪ "ALLIGATOR" SURFACE

⑫ AND PAINT WITH PRIME COAT

(13) Siding should be thoroughly wire-brushed to remove all loose pigment. Follow wire-brushing with a light dusting immediately before applying fresh paint to the surface

FILL CRACKS WITH PRIMER

(15) End checks and cracks in trim boards, door stiles and rails, sash and window frames should be cleaned and coated with primer before filling with white-lead putty

BREAK OUT ALL LOOSE PUTTY

(16) Reconditioning old sash and frames preparatory to painting involves breaking out all loose putty, priming and filling cracks and checks, and in some cases tightening up the sash frames by nailing loose rails to stiles

of painting the average frame home—two coats over a primer, or one finish coat over a prepared undercoater. If you paint at intervals of less than four or five years the latter method is sufficient. But if the painting schedule calls for renewal only once in five years or longer, the three-coat job usually is recommended. Preparation begins with an estimate of the amount of paint required for the job. Unless the surfaces are in unusually poor condition this can be calculated with fair accuracy by means of the simple procedure and formula shown in Fig. 1. Of course, in using the formula other factors should be taken into account. For example, where there are more than the ordinary number of windows or glass-paneled doors, it is safe to deduct the area of the glass. "Cut-up" gable construction and varying heights to the eaves also will affect the accuracy of the calculation.

Next, where the house is of frame construction, the siding comes in for a thorough going over. Often it will be necessary to renail the siding, especially where it is exposed to weathering. Siding "cupped" outward between the studding calls for care in renailing. Use short, galvanized nails as these hold better when driven into the sheathing boards, and drill undersized pilot holes through the siding. Usually it's better to use two nails for each space between studs as in Fig. 7. Drive the heads flush, but do not sink them below the surface. After renailing go over all the siding, window frames, trim and cornices with a wire brush as in Fig. 13. This will remove any loose material that might flake off under the new coats of paint. It's a good idea to wear an approved respirator if you do much of this work. If any knots show through, sand off the paint and shellac as in Fig. 8. Some painters use spar varnish for this purpose. Any blistered spots where the paint chips off to the wood should be treated as in Figs. 9 and 12. Go over all sash and break out the loose putty as in the circular detail of Fig. 16. Conditions such as shown in Figs. 14, 15, 16, 17, 19 and 20 are quite common on the older houses. First clean the dirt out of all cracks and

openings of the kind shown, then apply the first coat of primer as it comes from the container, without thinning. Brush at right angles to the cracks as in Fig. 15 to work the paint well into them. At the same time coat all bared spots on the sash where old putty has been removed as in Fig. 18. After this paint coating is thoroughly dry fill the cracks with a paste white-lead putty, using a regular glazier's putty only on the sash. Paste white lead as it comes in the container usually will serve, but if it should be too soft it may be brought to proper consistency by adding a small quantity of whiting. It's important to fill the cracks completely, otherwise the putty soon will loosen and drop out. At this stage some master painters remove all outside doors and prime-coat the bottom edges, first making sure that the doors close easily without sticking. When applying paint in the manner described it's essential to brush out all excess to a thin film so that it does not show through succeeding coats. Siding boards which are lapped at the corners frequently warp and split and the end grain weathers badly in time. No amount of paint will hide this unsightly defect. Treat these corners as shown in Fig. 20, first renailing if necessary. Siding boards mitered at the corners sometimes warp slightly and pull apart, opening the joint. Master painters often gently pry these joints open far enough to fill the space with white-lead putty. Then renailing will tighten the joints once more to a neat fit. In any of these preparatory jobs where white-lead or glazier's putty is used it is of the greatest importance that the putty be allowed to dry thoroughly before paint is applied over it.

Fig. 16, details A to G inclusive, show the common defects one finds on old sash and window frames, particularly where intervals between paintings are longer than average. Frequently the lower rail will be loose, perhaps dropped partially at one or both ends due to opening of the joints and weight of the glass, as at D. In many cases this defect can be repaired by wedging the rail back into place and nailing through into the stile, using a single large finishing nail. Paint the cracks in the trim boards and fill with the lead putty as already described. Do the same with the sash frame where necessary, Fig. 17, A and B. Also, you may find small openings where the siding boards butt against the

All spaces bared by removal of loose putty from sash should be coated with primer

⑲ **Cracks in old porch columns must be filled with white-lead putty before painting**

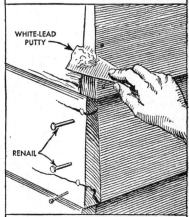

WHITE-LEAD PUTTY

RENAIL

⑳ **Coat the end grain of corner-lapped wide siding boards with white-lead putty and renail the corners if it is necessary to close wide cracks**

frames of brick buildings is a regular practice and usually the caulking should run all around the frame, including sills and thresholds, Fig. 24. Frequently, rather fine, irregular cracks following the mortar joints will be seen in brick walls. Those shown in Fig. 22 are quite common and are generally due to settling. Usually caulking compound gunned into such cracks makes a suitable repair as it will remain semiplastic after drying and will not break out even though there be slight movement between the edges. It also effectively keeps out water and frost. However, if the crack is wider than ¼ in. the repair generally should be made by pointing up with mortar. Likewise, brick walls in rather bad condition, Fig. 23, with brick faces eroded and mortar crumbled out of the joints, should be pointed before painting. Buildings and homes of ornamental brick seldom are painted, but homes of all other types of brick—common, soft, pressed and de-aired —often are made more attractive architecturally and more durable by painting. Either the so-called white-lead-and-oil paints or the water-soluble paints made especially for outside masonry can be used satisfactorily on brick. The oil paint dries with a slight gloss on brick in good condition while the water paints dry with a flat, nongloss surface. Either paint is especially effective in "dressing up" old homes of brick. Except for the hard-pressed and de-aired

window frames or the corner boards, B in Fig. 14. Here's where the caulking gun comes in handy. Run a line of caulking compound into corner board and siding cracks and all around the window frames, also into the crack under the sill, as at A in Fig. 17. If the stops, G in Fig. 16, are loose, gently pry out the strip, prime-coat it and tap it back into place. Finally, putty the sash in the manner described, Fig. 21. In most cases, it is better to remove the sash from the frame for puttying, as it is easier to do the job properly with the sash flat and on a solid support. Smooth the putty into place with considerable pressure of the knife so that it will bond properly to both the wood and glass without any open spaces beneath.

Caulking will effectively seal small cracks in both brick and stonework

Brick walls in badly eroded condition should be pointed with mortar before painting

Open cracks usually will be found underneath boxed cornices, Fig. 27, and, although the wood is not subjected to weathering, the open cracks allow passage of cold air in winter and insects in summer. Fill with a caulking gun as indicated. If you find it necessary to seal the joint between a porch roof and the siding with roofing compound, Fig. 28, this should be done before painting. Such roofs should be flashed to the siding, of course, but in some instances it is easier to maintain the seal with roofing compound where flashing was not originally used.

Figs. 22 and 23 show two common defects, due largely to natural causes, which must be remedied before painting brick walls. Caulking around window and door

Window frames in old brick homes must be recaulked before painting. Be sure that the cracks are filled flush with the surface

types, brick is porous and absorbs paint faster than most kinds of unpainted wood. For this reason the coverage per gallon on brick painted for the first time generally is considerably less than on any bare wood.

If the brick is in good condition and all common defects have been repaired as previously described, there need be little other preparatory work, except that on very old brick homes a light wire-brushing is helpful in removing dirt and loose sand. Sometimes there are discolorations beneath windows due to rusty screens, soot or dirt. Usually a thorough brushing with a handled wire brush will suffice. Discolorations due to other causes, such as mildew or "sweating" chimneys, should be treated with a zinc-sulphate solution or white asphaltum before painting. Follow the manufacturer's directions when applying any of these preparations.

"Before" and "after" views show how painting changes appearance

Before painting brick with a water-soluble paint it generally is recommended that the wall be kept moist just ahead of the paint application. This can be done with a wheelbarrow sprayer, wetting only a small area at a time. A damp wall retards drying, making it possible to apply these fast-setting paints without brush marks or laps showing. On the other hand, when applying a lead-and-oil paint it is essential that the brick be thoroughly dry.

Two more points to think of before you paint

Cracks around cornices usually are best filled with a caulking gun. Be sure to force sufficient compound into the opening so that the soft material will bond to the wood

are (1) the formula of the paint applied previously, and (2) how the paint you are to apply may change the appearance of the building. Using the lighter colors and white over a surface previously coated with a paint containing a tinting pigment of any of the so-called "earth" colors may under certain conditions cause "bleeding," that is, the darker color underneath may bleed through to the surface of the new paint, resulting in spotty discolorations. However, on old work in reasonably good condition where the previous paintings have been oxidized thoroughly, a good wire-brushing to remove all loose material down to the hard surface underneath and the use of a prepared undercoater is sufficient precaution against the possibility of bleeding.

Figs. 25 and 26 are an example of how painting sometimes changes the appearance of an old house, of either brick or frame construction. Note in this instance how certain constructional details have been almost completely hidden by the paint job, while other features, particularly the size of the house, have been emphasized. Generally the lighter colors, including white especially, will tend to make the house appear larger in its setting. It's always well to bear in mind that painting can be used to accentuate or minimize certain details of a structure as well as to preserve its surface.

Joints between siding and roofs should be resealed with paste roofing compound before painting, or better, flashed to the siding if this was not done on the original work

PAINT MAGIC

By Sam Brown

ALTHOUGH many types of paint are available for interior walls—including calcimine, powder-form water-mix paint, paste-form water-mix paint, and oil paints, characteristics of which are given in Table No. 1—the finishing methods described in this story are concerned chiefly with the paste type of water paint. There are two general types: casein base and synthetic-resin base.

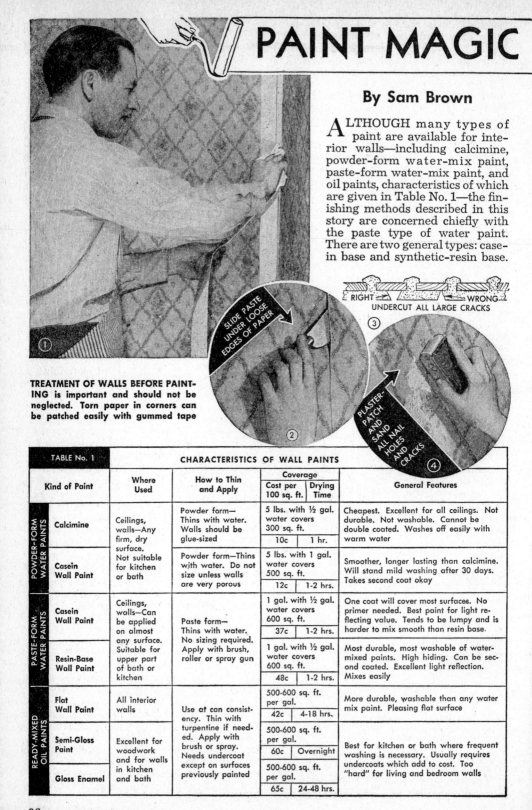

SLIDE PASTE UNDER LOOSE EDGES OF PAPER

RIGHT — WRONG
UNDERCUT ALL LARGE CRACKS

PLASTER-PATCH AND SAND ALL NAIL HOLES AND CRACKS

TREATMENT OF WALLS BEFORE PAINTING is important and should not be neglected. Torn paper in corners can be patched easily with gummed tape

TABLE No. 1			CHARACTERISTICS OF WALL PAINTS				
	Kind of Paint	**Where Used**	**How to Thin and Apply**	**Coverage**		**General Features**	
				Cost per 100 sq. ft.	**Drying Time**		
POWDER-FORM WATER PAINTS	Calcimine	Ceilings, walls—Any firm, dry surface. Not suitable for kitchen or bath	Powder form—Thins with water. Walls should be glue-sized	5 lbs. with ½ gal. water covers 300 sq. ft.		Cheapest. Excellent for all ceilings. Not durable. Not washable. Cannot be double coated. Washes off easily with warm water	
				10c	1 hr.		
	Casein Wall Paint		Powder form—Thins with water. Do not size unless walls are very porous	5 lbs. with 1 gal. water covers 500 sq. ft.		Smoother, longer lasting than calcimine. Will stand mild washing after 30 days. Takes second coat okay	
				12c	1-2 hrs.		
PASTE-FORM WATER PAINTS	Casein Wall Paint	Ceilings, walls—Can be applied on almost any surface. Suitable for upper part of bath or kitchen	Paste form—Thins with water. No sizing required. Apply with brush, roller or spray gun	1 gal. with ½ gal. water covers 600 sq. ft.		One coat will cover most surfaces. No primer needed. Best paint for light reflecting value. Tends to be lumpy and is harder to mix smooth than resin base.	
				37c	1-2 hrs.		
	Resin-Base Wall Paint			1 gal. with ½ gal. water covers 600 sq. ft.		Most durable, most washable of water-mixed paints. High hiding. Can be second coated. Excellent light reflection. Mixes easily	
				48c	1-2 hrs.		
READY-MIXED OIL PAINTS	Flat Wall Paint	All interior walls	Use at can consistency. Thin with turpentine if needed. Apply with brush or spray. Needs undercoat except on surfaces previously painted	500-600 sq. ft. per gal.		More durable, washable than any water mix paint. Pleasing flat surface	
				42c	4-18 hrs.		
	Semi-Gloss Paint	Excellent for woodwork and for walls in kitchen and bath		500-600 sq. ft. per gal.		Best for kitchen or bath where frequent washing is necessary. Usually requires undercoats which add to cost. Too "hard" for living and bedroom walls	
				60c	Overnight		
	Gloss Enamel			500-600 sq. ft. per gal.			
				65c	24-48 hrs.		

Treatment of walls before painting: Water-mix paints can be applied on almost any clean, dry surface. Finishing over wallpaper is popular, but don't depend too much on one coat to hide the pattern. A weak pattern can be covered nicely but strong designs usually show through, not so much because the paint is at fault but because certain wallpaper colors either bleed into or repel water-mix paint. An example is paper with gold or silver metallic printing. Often it is necessary to coat such a paper with a pigmented wall size before the water paint will take. On the average, 50 percent of all papers will cover with one coat; 45 percent will require two coats and 5 percent will require a primer coat. All loose edges of paper should be pasted down, Fig. 2. Don't tear them off, as a torn edge will be plainly visible. An exception is corners, where it usually is necessary to strip the paper

APPLICATION is simple with either brush or roller. Use masking tape to set off the borders

back about an inch. Patch the corner with two strips of 2-in. wide gummed-paper tape, turning the corner ¼ in. with the first strip and butting right into the corner with the second as in Fig. 1. Wet the plaster before applying tape and run the tape through water to get it really wet.

1-INCH WIDE MASKING TAPE IS EXCELLENT FOR OBTAINING BORDER EFFECTS

CEILING TAPE

MIX WATER PAINT WITH YOUR HANDS. IT WASHES OFF EASILY (SEE TABLE No. 2)

All cracks and nail holes should be patched and sanded smooth, Figs. 3 and 4. The finer spachtling compound is better than patching plaster for this work.

Painting procedure: Ceilings come first. Paint can be applied with brush or roller, Fig. 5. Determine the type of border you

PAINT CEILING SLIGHTLY BEYOND EDGE		PAINT CEILING COLOR 2" DOWN ON SIDEWALL		ROUGH PAINT COLOR BAND		TRIM CEILING TO TAPE		PAINT CEILING COLOR ON SIDEWALL		PAINT CEILING SLIGHTLY BEYOND EDGE	
TRIM SIDEWALL UP TO CEILING	AFTER PAINTING	APPLY 1" TAPE	AFTER PAINTING	TRIM SIDEWALL TO TAPE	AFTER PAINTING	USE STENCIL WHEN PAINTING SIDEWALL	AFTER PAINTING	APPLY PASTE OR GUM-PAPER BORDER	AFTER PAINTING		

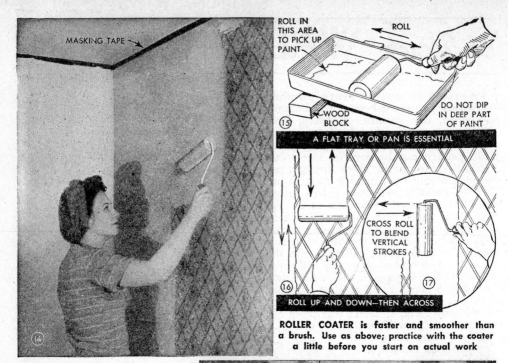

ROLL IN THIS AREA TO PICK UP PAINT

ROLL

WOOD BLOCK

DO NOT DIP IN DEEP PART OF PAINT

A FLAT TRAY OR PAN IS ESSENTIAL

CROSS ROLL TO BLEND VERTICAL STROKES

ROLL UP AND DOWN—THEN ACROSS

MASKING TAPE

ROLLER COATER is faster and smoother than a brush. Use as above; practice with the coater a little before you start on actual work

want before starting so that you will know whether or not to extend the ceiling color down the sidewall. Cheap masking tape is excellent for laying off borders as in Figs. 6 and 7. Two 8-ft. strips can be used several times and thus cover a whole room. Various ideas for borders are shown in Figs. 9 to 13. Mix the paint in a pan or pail as in Fig. 8, following the proportions given in Table No. 2. The roller coater, Fig. 14, is much faster and smoother than brushing. Break in your roller by washing in warm water and rolling dry on newspaper to remove loose fuzz. A flat tray (you can buy paper ones) is essential, Fig. 15. Apply paint with vertical strokes, leaving a slight space between the paint strips as in Fig. 16, then roll crosswise as in Fig. 17 to blend. Don't load the roller with too much paint until you have had a little practice, and don't press heavily on a roller freshly filled with paint. To reach low spots in the surface, increase pressure as the roller becomes dry. Don't worry about sags in the paper, as they will flatten out when the paint dries.

Special colors: You can buy water-mix colors in solid deep tones. Use these to tint white or any of the light pastel shades the color you desire. Mix the tinting color in a separate container with a little water, Fig.

MIX COLOR WITH WATER IN SEPARATE CONTAINER

ORIGINAL PASTE WITH ABOUT ½ OF WATER ADDED

GLYCERIN (SEE TABLE No. 2)

18, then add gradually to the slightly thinned paint. A casein base product will mix with a resin base product. Add water gradually, stirring as you go, especially if you are using a casein paint, which will be lumpy and hard to mix if all the water is poured in at once. If you are going to brush on the paint, it is a good idea to add a small quantity of glycerin. This holds the coat open (wet) longer so that you have plenty of time to paint a strip and still have a wet edge for a smooth blend when you paint the adjoining strip. If you can't get glycerin, use boiled linseed oil, and work it in while the paint is in paste form. It emulsifies nicely with the paste but is hard to work in after the paint has been thinned.

Spray application: Water paints spray nicely but are dusty. Be sure everything is out of the room before you start. Cover the floor with newspapers. Mask all trim with masking tape as in Fig. 19, and then use a shield while spraying, Fig. 20. Go over all woodwork and glass with a damp rag as soon as dust has settled. Dusting is held to a minimum by using the paint as thick as the gun will take. It can be sprayed with exceptionally heavy body by using a pressure feed gun coupled to a small compressor. Don't try to spray the ceiling unless you have suitable equipment, Fig. 21.

Mottle finishes: These are attractive, especially if the surface is a little too rough to look nice in a single flat color. First, apply a

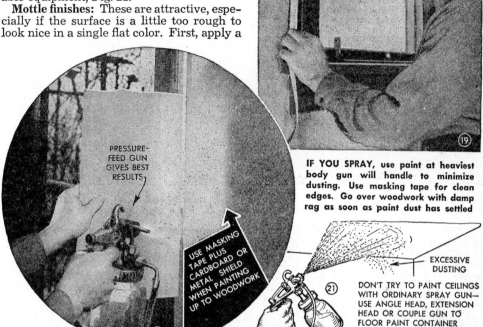

MASKING TAPE

PRESSURE-FEED GUN GIVES BEST RESULTS

USE MASKING TAPE PLUS CARDBOARD OR METAL SHIELD WHEN PAINTING UP TO WOODWORK

IF YOU SPRAY, use paint at heaviest body gun will handle to minimize dusting. Use masking tape for clean edges. Go over woodwork with damp rag as soon as paint dust has settled

EXCESSIVE DUSTING

DON'T TRY TO PAINT CEILINGS WITH ORDINARY SPRAY GUN— USE ANGLE HEAD, EXTENSION HEAD OR COUPLE GUN TO FLOOR PAINT CONTAINER

ground coat of water-mix paint, Fig. 22, let dry overnight, then mottle with roller or sponge as shown in Figs. 23 to 28. A two-color mottle usually is the most attractive. Rules for using color are given in Table No. 3. Do a couple of practice panels on paper or wallboard before you start.

News roll: The ground coat for this is preferably a pigmented wall paint or other hard-finish undercoat. Applied over a water-mix paint base, the effect tends to be soft and fuzzy. This makes a nice finish and is easy to do as shown in Figs. 29 to 31. The news roll makes a good base for a mottle finish when redecorating.

Spatter finish: This is obtained by tapping the surface with a fiber brush loaded with paint as in Figs.

Surface or Finish	Method of Application	Water		Other Ingredients
		Per qt.	Per gal.	
Paper, Wallboard, Plaster, Flat Paint	Brush	16 oz. (1 pt.)	4 pts.	Recommended but not essential: 2 oz. glycerin per gal. of paste for smoother brushing and slower drying. Boiled linseed oil can also be used.
Oil Paint— All Non-porous Surfaces	Brush	12 oz. (¾ pt.)	3 pts.	
All Surfaces	Roller	12 oz.	3 pts.	
All Surfaces	Spray (suction feed)	12 oz.	3 pts.	None
All Surfaces	Spray (pressure feed)	8 oz.	2 pts.	None
Sponge or Roller Mottle	Sponge or roller	10 oz.	1 qt. 8 oz.	4 oz. glycerin per gal. of paste
Streak Glaze	Brush on— wipe with cloth	24 oz.	3 qts.	None
Flat Stipple	Brush	8 oz.	2 pts.	1 pt. spar varnish per gal. of paste. Add water last
News Roll *	Brush on— wipe with newspaper	18 oz.	2 qts. 8 oz.	6 oz. glycerin per gal. of paste

MIXING PROPORTIONS FOR PASTE WATER PAINT TABLE No. 2

* Works best over ground coat of pigmented wall size

GROUND COAT is required for all two-tone finishes. Let water paint dry overnight before applying color coat

32 and 33, or by snapping the color onto the wall as shown in Fig. 35. A widely spaced spatter in two colors is effective if the paint dots are brushed out with a dry brush before they dry hard. Fig. 34 shows the result.

Streak glaze: It is a simple matter for anyone to imitate the appearance of wood grain with this finish, which is easy to apply. First, apply a coat of white or cream water paint and allow it to dry overnight. Then, brush on a thin coat of colored water paint and immediately wipe the color with a crumpled soft cloth. You will get the streaked, wood grain effect shown in Fig. 36. Although any colored paint can be used over a white or cream ground coat, good color combinations for this finish are brown over a cream ground coat, or green over a white ground coat. It may take a little practice

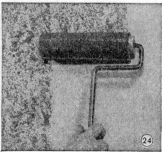
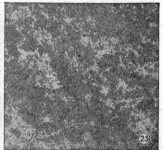

ROLLER MOTTLE—Pick up color on roller, Fig. 23, then apply roller to wall, being careful not to overlap. Two times over makes a heavier mottle, as shown in Fig. 25. Use a stippling roller, not a roller coater

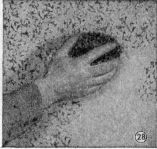

SPONGE MOTTLE—Trim sponge so that it has a flat side. Dip in water to soften, then wring dry. Press onto the color slab, Fig. 27, then transfer the paint to the wall. Two color mottles are very effective

NEWS ROLL—Use a pigmented ground coat for this, not water paint. When dry, apply color coat of water paint. Crumple a sheet of newspaper, Fig. 29, and roll this over the fresh paint, Fig. 30. Change the paper as often as may be necessary. Fig. 31 shows a heavier pattern obtained by double rolling

SPATTER FINISH—This novel effect can be obtained in three or four different ways, as shown above and described in the text. Two or more complementary colors may be spattered on one ground coat if desired

to produce the desired effect, but if any particular area does not please you, just apply a new coat of colored paint and try wiping again. You will find that it is not necessary to wipe in continuous strokes from the ceiling to the floor as the strokes can be blended together easily.

Flat stipple: Mix the paint for this according to Table No. 2. This is a single-coat finish and does not require the ground coat common to other novelty finishes described. Just brush it on, let it stand about 5 min., and then stipple. This can be done with a brush, preferably a stippling brush if available, by merely tapping the surface with the face or bristle end of the brush.

STREAK GLAZE

Or, it can be done with a wood float as shown in Fig. 37. The float is merely applied to the surface and then pulled straight out as indicated. The mild texture is effective in a single color, or it can be highlighted by applying a thin coat of contrasting color and immediately wiping with a cloth.

FLAT STIPPLE

COLORS FOR TWO-TONE FINISHES		TABLE No. 3
Finish	General Rules	Examples
Mottle or Spatter	Tints of same color	Light blue over dark blue
	Any color on cream or white	Blue over cream
	Contrasting colors (Not too strong)	Rose over blue-green
	Two mottle coats are usually more pleasing	White and light blue over orange
News Roll	Any color on cream or white	Green over white
	Complementary colors	Orange over blue
Streak Glaze	Any color on white or cream	Brown over cream Green over white

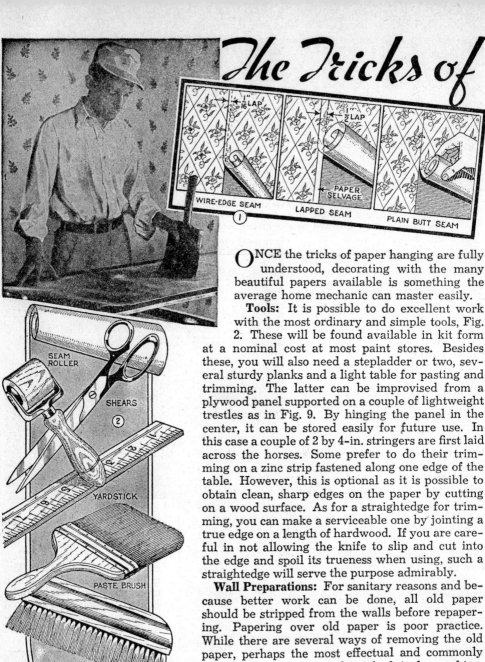

WIRE-EDGE SEAM

LAPPED SEAM

PAPER SELVAGE

PLAIN BUTT SEAM

The Tricks of

ONCE the tricks of paper hanging are fully understood, decorating with the many beautiful papers available is something the average home mechanic can master easily.

Tools: It is possible to do excellent work with the most ordinary and simple tools, Fig. 2. These will be found available in kit form at a nominal cost at most paint stores. Besides these, you will also need a stepladder or two, several sturdy planks and a light table for pasting and trimming. The latter can be improvised from a plywood panel supported on a couple of lightweight trestles as in Fig. 9. By hinging the panel in the center, it can be stored easily for future use. In this case a couple of 2 by 4-in. stringers are first laid across the horses. Some prefer to do their trimming on a zinc strip fastened along one edge of the table. However, this is optional as it is possible to obtain clean, sharp edges on the paper by cutting on a wood surface. As for a straightedge for trimming, you can make a serviceable one by jointing a true edge on a length of hardwood. If you are careful in not allowing the knife to slip and cut into the edge and spoil its trueness when using, such a straightedge will serve the purpose admirably.

Wall Preparations: For sanitary reasons and because better work can be done, all old paper should be stripped from the walls before repapering. Papering over old paper is poor practice. While there are several ways of removing the old paper, perhaps the most effectual and commonly used method is by soaking. Take a pail of hot water and a whitewash brush and go around the entire room, Fig. 3, wetting the paper until it will absorb no more water. The work will go much faster than if small patches are done here and there. Oftentimes a little

SEAM ROLLER

SHEARS

YARDSTICK

PASTE BRUSH

SMOOTHER

SCRAPER

TRIMMING KNIFE

7 FT. STRAIGHTEDGE

Hanging WALLPAPER

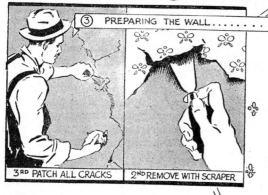

③ PREPARING THE WALL.......

3RD PATCH ALL CRACKS | 2ND REMOVE WITH SCRAPER

1ST SOAK WITH HOT WATER

⑤ APPLYING GLUE SIZE

④ WASHING THE WALL

⑥

PASTE FORMULA
BEST FLOUR, 4 LBS.
ALUM, 1 OZ
MIXED WITH COLD WATER

baking soda, sal soda, borax or ammonia added to the water will aid in softening up the old paste. By the time you have finished soaking, the paper where you first started should be loose enough so that it can be taken off in sheets with a scraper blade. When all the old paper has been removed, wash down the walls with a sponge and let dry. A little carbolic acid added to the clear water will make a sanitary job of it. Any defects or cracks in the walls, of course, should be filled smoothly with a prepared patching compound. Porous plaster as well as new plaster should be glue-sized preparatory to papering. The size should be rather thin and applied hot in a warm room, using a large brush to apply it quickly before it jells, Fig. 5. As a rule, one coat will suffice.

If the walls you intend to paper have been painted previously, it will be necessary, in order to make the paste stick, to kill the gloss and oil in the paint by first sanding with rough paper and then washing with a weak solution of sal soda and water, Fig. 4. Follow this with a size of plain vinegar. In the case of particularly rough walls such as a sand finish, you must first cover with a lining paper available especially for the purpose or, if you should have a number of odd rolls of paper you wish to use up, you can use this instead, placing the figure of the paper next to the wall. For lining papers the paste should be fairly stiff. Use a wide, stiff, smoother

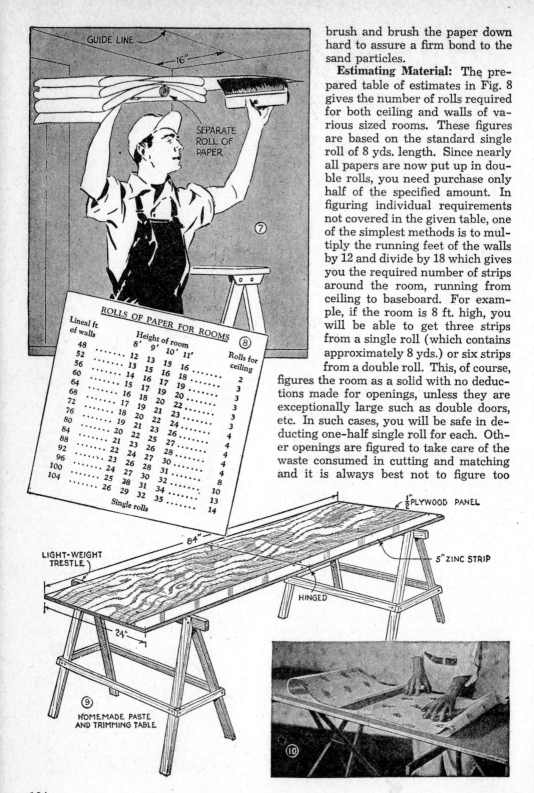

ROLLS OF PAPER FOR ROOMS

Lineal ft of walls	Height of room				Rolls for ceiling
	8'	9'	10'	11'	
48					
52	12	13	15	16	
56	13	15	16	18	
60	14	16	17	19	2
64	15	17	19	20	3
68	16	18	20	22	3
72	17	19	21	23	3
76	18	20	22	24	3
80	19	21	23	26	4
84	20	22	25	27	4
88	21	23	26	28	4
92	22	24	27	30	4
96	23	26	28	31	4
100	24	27	31	32	8
104	25	28	31	34	10
	26	29	32	35	13
					14

Single rolls

GUIDE LINE

16"

SEPARATE ROLL OF PAPER

⑦

⑧

½" PLYWOOD PANEL

84"

LIGHT-WEIGHT TRESTLE

5" ZINC STRIP

HINGED

24"

⑨

HOMEMADE PASTE AND TRIMMING TABLE

⑩

brush and brush the paper down hard to assure a firm bond to the sand particles.

Estimating Material: The prepared table of estimates in Fig. 8 gives the number of rolls required for both ceiling and walls of various sized rooms. These figures are based on the standard single roll of 8 yds. length. Since nearly all papers are now put up in double rolls, you need purchase only half of the specified amount. In figuring individual requirements not covered in the given table, one of the simplest methods is to multiply the running feet of the walls by 12 and divide by 18 which gives you the required number of strips around the room, running from ceiling to baseboard. For example, if the room is 8 ft. high, you will be able to get three strips from a single roll (which contains approximately 8 yds.) or six strips from a double roll. This, of course, figures the room as a solid with no deductions made for openings, unless they are exceptionally large such as double doors, etc. In such cases, you will be safe in deducting one-half single roll for each. Other openings are figured to take care of the waste consumed in cutting and matching and it is always best not to figure too

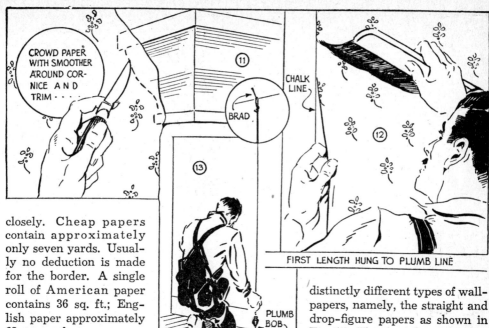

FIRST LENGTH HUNG TO PLUMB LINE

closely. Cheap papers contain approximately only seven yards. Usually no deduction is made for the border. A single roll of American paper contains 36 sq. ft.; English paper approximately 63 square feet.

Making Paste: Good paste is not difficult to make, yet it requires some pains. The worker can use either a commercial ready-made paste sold in 5-lb. packages or he can make his own, following the formula given in Fig. 6. Mix your flour with cold water until it has the consistency of thick cream. Be thorough in beating the batter smooth. Any lumps present in the mixture can be removed by straining through a fine sieve. The addition of alum makes the paste firmer, preserves it from spoiling and makes it easier to spread. Place the mass over a flame and boil, stirring continuously; then remove and add cold water until about like cream. Let the paste stand until perfectly cold before using. A tablespoonful of Venice turpentine to a pail of paste, added while the mixture is hot, will increase its adhesiveness considerably. The proper consistency of the paste, of course, depends upon the quality of the paper to be hung. If delicate, lightweight paper is to be used, make the paste fairly thin, while with heavier material use the paste quite stiff.

Cutting the Paper: Prior to cutting the paper to length, you must first examine and study the pattern to be able to cut it with the least waste. You will find two distinctly different types of wall-papers, namely, the straight and drop-figure papers as shown in Fig. 17. The drop figure is usually a floral design which will not match immediately opposite and consequently must be dropped or moved downward to match the adjacent strip. This drop measures one-half of the full figure and must be cut accordingly. For example, if your pattern is 18 in. long, the opposite length of paper must be lowered 9 in. Along the margin of commercial papers you will find equally spaced markings which indicate where the pattern should be cut. This makes it simple for the worker as he will cut one strip the required length by cutting on the "join here" mark of the paper and the next strip he will cut half-way between the "join

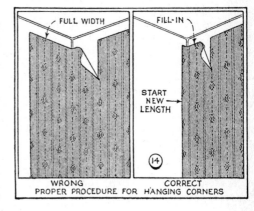

WRONG   CORRECT
PROPER PROCEDURE FOR HANGING CORNERS

START THE BORDER IN AN OBSCURE CORNER

Pasting and Trimming: Fig. 2 shows three types of joints or seams which can be used; namely, the butt, lap and wire edge. Of the three, the lapped seam is the simplest, requiring only the trimming of one edge. On some papers the edge is trimmed, that is, the edge is perforated so that it can be folded over and torn off. A ready-trimmed edge is only suitable for a lapped seam. For a butt seam both edges of the paper must be trimmed by hand regardless of whether it may be ready-trimmed. This type of joint is preferable as the seam is visible only upon close inspection and therefore makes a neater job. The wire-edge seam is more or less a lapped joint, which resembles a butt joint with less skill required in keeping the joint closed. Trimming is done after the length has been pasted. Here the pasted ends of the paper are temporarily folded over midway as shown in Fig. 10, keeping the edges perfectly even, after which the straight edge is laid parallel to the edge of

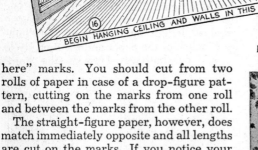

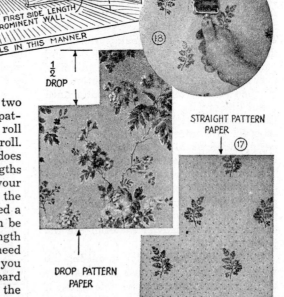

STRAIGHT PATTERN PAPER

DROP PATTERN PAPER

here" marks. You should cut from two rolls of paper in case of a drop-figure pattern, cutting on the marks from one roll and between the marks from the other roll.

The straight-figure paper, however, does match immediately opposite and all lengths are cut on the marks. If you notice your particular pattern has half figures on the margin of the paper, this is also termed a straight-figure pattern, and it, too, can be cut on the marks. In measuring the length of strips for a 9-ft. ceiling, there is no need of cutting the paper full 9 ft. long as you have a border at the top and a baseboard at the bottom. For a 9-ft. room, cut the paper in 8½-ft. lengths.

the paper to guide the knife in trimming the selvage (Fig. 19). When only one edge of the paper is to be trimmed, first make sure you are trimming the correct edge. In pasting thin and delicate papers you will have to work a little faster as the paper will become overly wet and if left too long it is apt to tear while hanging. Also, above all, get the habit of wiping your paste board off each time. Otherwise you will have some objectionable stains on your finished paper.

Hanging the Paper: Papering the ceiling is looked upon by many as the most difficult part of the whole job but, through actual experience, you will find this to be easier than fitting paper around window and door cornices, fixtures, etc. The whole secret of the job is the manner in which the paper is prepared prior to hanging. With a butt-type seam it makes little difference whether the paper is run the length or width of the room. But with a lap seam, it is important to work from the lighted side of the room, as shown in Fig. 16, for the reason that if not done, shadows will be cast from each seam, making the ceiling very noticeable upon entering the room. As the length of paper is gradually pasted, it is folded back and forth in loose folds as shown in Fig. 7 and is carried up on the scaffold with a roll stick or an odd roll of wallpaper. If the angle of the ceiling is not true, you first strike a guide line about 16 in. from the wall and hang to this. "Tack" the end of the strip in place with the smoother brush, allowing it to extend down the side wall about ½ in. As you continue across the room, the paper will unfold. Brush it out smoothly and avoid blisters. Follow this strip with succeeding ones. The seams are rolled down firmly as shown in Fig. 18. After the ceiling has been completed, the

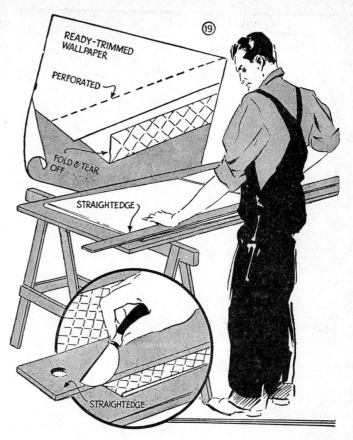

first consideration in hanging the first side wall strip is having it plumb. Select a prominent wall on which to center the strip, Fig. 16. A plumb line from the ceiling to the baseboard is snapped as shown in Fig. 13. The starting length of paper is hung to this line as in Fig. 12, working each way from this center strip. If a lap seam is employed, it is not necessary to trim either edge of this first strip. In entering a corner, do not continue a full width strip around the angle as shown in the left detail of Fig. 14. Instead, cut a "fill-in" strip of the proper width as shown on the right. Use your trimming knife in cutting the paper to length at the baseboard. At window and door cornices, crowd the paper around the molding with the smoother and trim carefully with a knife as in Fig. 11. Finally the border is hung, starting in an obscure corner of the room, Fig. 15. Keep the pasted side off of the lower side wall while hanging to avoid staining.

CHECK VISCOSITY

STRAIN MATERIAL

"Manual of arms" for SPRAY

TOO CLOSE LESS THAN 6 INCHES

RIPPLES AND RUNS

TOO FAR MORE THAN 10 INCHES

DUSTING AND SANDY SURFACE

GET THE RANGE!

Holding the gun too close causes an uneven coat, air ripples and possible runs. If the gun is held too far from the work results are dry, sandy spray and excessive dusting. With average home shop equipment, a distance of 7 or 8 in. from the gun to work gives good results

HEAVY COAT DEPOSITED HERE

HEAVY COAT DEPOSITED HERE

AVOID ARCING

ANGLE OF FIRE

Gun should be held "square-on" when spraying vertical panels. Pointing down, as shown at extreme left, deposits heavy coat along upper edge of spray pattern. At left, keep same distance from work throughout stroke—arcing deposits a heavy coat at the center of the stroke

PULL TRIGGER HERE

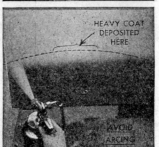

BANDING PANELS IS GOOD PRACTICE

CORRECT TRIGGERING

Pull the trigger before your gun stroke hits the work; do not release trigger until gun stroke has passed work. Practice triggering to hold overspray at ends to a minimum. Banding panel ends previous to horizontal stroking is good practice and reduces overspray

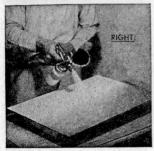

RIGHT!

WRONG!

HIT THE FRONT LINE!

When spraying horizontal surfaces, start at the near edge. Spray dust then is projected forward to land on uncoated work where it is dissolved by full spray stroke. Starting at far edge is wrong as it shoots spray dust onto the finished surface coat causing a rough finish

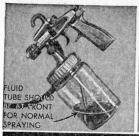

FLUID TUBE SHOULD BE AT FRONT FOR NORMAL SPRAYING

CHECK POSITION OF FLUID TUBE AND MAKE GUN ADJUSTMENTS

GUNNERS

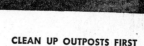

RIGHT

CAP SET FOR HORIZONTAL FAN

SHOOT SQUARE AT OUTSIDE CORNERS

CLEAN UP OUTPOSTS FIRST

If you shoot the edges and other out-of-the-way places last, you will have a lot of spray dust falling on surfaces already coated. The right way is to shoot edges and similar surfaces first, as spray dust falling on uncoated main areas is dissolved by later full spray coat. Turnings should be sprayed with an up-and-down stroke, with air cap of gun set for vertical fan (horn holes horizontal). Make use of a simple turntable—walking around the work or shifting it by hand is poor practice. Always spray full wet coats just short of running and work under a good light so that you can actually see the finish as it goes on

GUNNING CORNERS

Shoot square-on at outside corners. This deposits a heavy coat at the corner edge where it is needed. The air cap of gun should be set for horizontal fan. Finish the job with horizontal strokes. Don't shoot square-on at inside corners. This deposits a heavy coat at either side of corner. The right way is to shoot each corner in turn, as shown at extreme right, with air cap set for vertical fan. Finish the surface with horizontal strokes, triggering each stroke to minimize overspray on coated surface. Avoid closed or box openings. It is almost impossible to prevent dusting when you shoot right into them. On many jobs you can remove back panel and spray from both ends of opening

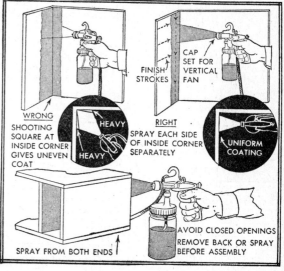

WRONG
SHOOTING SQUARE AT INSIDE CORNER GIVES UNEVEN COAT

HEAVY
HEAVY

FINISH STROKES

CAP SET FOR VERTICAL FAN

RIGHT
SPRAY EACH SIDE OF INSIDE CORNER SEPARATELY

UNIFORM COATING

SPRAY FROM BOTH ENDS

AVOID CLOSED OPENINGS
REMOVE BACK OR SPRAY BEFORE ASSEMBLY

| A SAME-COLOR FILLER | B DARK-COLOR FILLER | C LIGHT-COLOR FILLER |

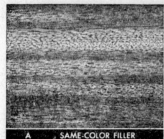

Mixing the filler—

1 Paste wood filler is thinned with naphtha or gum turpentine to resemble thick paint

Brushing the filler—

2 Apply a liberal quantity of filler; brush thoroughly in the direction of wood grain

Application of

By Sam Brown

WOOD having open pores, such as oak, walnut and mahogany, requires a coat of paste wood filler to build a level surface for the application of top finish coats. Besides this prime purpose, the filler plays an important role in coloration and in emphasizing the grain. The color of the filler usually is a shade darker than the stained color of the wood, producing the effect shown in photo A above. A very dark, nearly black filler often is used to bring out the grain, photo B, while white and brightly colored fillers are used for novelty effects as in photo C.

Mixing the filler: Filler is purchased in 1, 5 and 25-lb. cans, and also in pint and quart containers. The material is in heavy paste form, the mix consisting mainly of silex (powdered rock quartz), together with a small amount of linseed oil and japan drier. Before use, the paste is thinned to the desired consistency as needed with naphtha or gum turpentine, Fig. 1, the amount of dilution depending on the size of the pores to be filled. Obviously, large pores require a thicker mix than small ones. Table No. 2 is a partial guide to the mix required for various domestic and im-

PROPORTIONS FOR MIXING VARIOUS QUANTITIES OF FILLER								TABLE NO. 1
HEAVY MIX (16-LB. BASE)			MEDIUM MIX (12-LB. BASE)			THIN MIX (8-LB. BASE)		
APPROX. AMT. NEEDED *	PASTE	THINNER	APPROX. AMT. NEEDED *	PASTE	THINNER	APPROX. AMT. NEEDED *	PASTE	THINNER
2 GALS.	16 LBS.	1 GAL.	1 GAL., 3 QTS.	12 LBS.	1 GAL.	1½ GALS.	8 LBS.	1 GAL.
5 PTS.	5 LBS.	2½ PTS.	3 QTS.	5 LBS.	3 PTS., 5 OZ.	1 GAL.	5 LBS.	5 PTS.
2 QTS.	1 QT.	1 QT.	2 QTS., 10 OZ.	1 QT	2 PTS., 10 OZ.	3 QTS.	1 QT.	2 QTS.
2 PTS.	1 PT.	1 PT.	1 QT., 5 OZ.	1 PT.	1 PT., 5 OZ.	3 PTS.	1 PT.	2 PTS.
1 PT.	1 LB.	½ PT	1 PT., 2 OZ.	1 LB.	10½ OZ.	1½ PTS.	1 LB.	1 PT.
½ PT.	½ LB.	4 OZ.	9 OZ.	½ LB.	5¼ OZ.	12 OZ.	½ LB.	½ PT.
* 1 PINT THINNED FILLER COVERS APPROX. 35 SQ FT								

FILLER MIX REQUIRED FOR VARIOUS WOODS			TABLE NO. 2
NO FILLER NEEDED	THIN FILLER	MEDIUM FILLER	HEAVY FILLER
BASSWOOD	ALDER	AMARANTH	ASH
CEDAR	BEECH	AVODIRE	BUBINGA
CYPRESS	BIRCH	BENIN	CHESTNUT
FIR	BOXWOOD	BUTTERNUT	KELOBRA
HEMLOCK	CHERRY	MAHOGANY	LOCUST
MAGNOLIA	GUM	ORIENTALWOOD	MAHOGANY (Phil.)
PINE	IRONWOOD	PRIMA VERA	OAK
POPLAR	MAPLE	PURPLEHEART	PADAUK
SPRUCE	SYCAMORE	ROSEWOOD	TEAK
WILLOW	TUPELO	WALNUT	TAMO
		ZEBRAWOOD	

FILLER in Finishing

ported woods. Table No. 1 gives proportions for heavy, medium and thin mixtures in various quantities. Only enough filler needed for the job at hand should be mixed, as the thinned filler thickens after a few hours and becomes useless. Mixing by exact weights (Table No. 1) is always good practice. The heavy mix (16 lbs. of paste per gallon of thinner) can be approximated in any quantity by adding thinner in the same volume as the paste. The heavy mix should not be confused as meaning a heavy-bodied material. Actually, the consistency is no heavier than varnish. The first step in mixing is to spade thoroughly the original paste in the container with a putty knife, then add a very small amount of thinner and stir again until thoroughly mixed. After the initial mixing, increasingly larger amounts of thinner can be added and stirred in until the mix is the proper consistency. Do not make the mistake of adding a lot of thinner at the start, as this makes mixing doubly difficult. Use naphtha for thinning if you want the filler to set up quickly for wiping, and use turpentine to hold the coat open longer. Or, you can mix the two liquids together if desired, making the proportions suitable to obtain the desired results. A small amount of boiled linseed oil can be added to hold the coat open for 30 or 40 minutes. The reverse of this—a very quick-setting filler—can be obtained by adding a small amount of japan drier.

Brushing the filler: Use a short-bristle brush of convenient size. Apply filler liberally, brushing thoroughly with the grain of the wood as shown in Fig. 2. Do not cover more than 8 to 10 sq. ft. of surface at one time, otherwise you will get ahead of the wiping and cleaning-up operations that follow.

Padding-in: As soon as spots on the

Padding-in-
3 This is done easily with a felt pad, which is used with a circular motion to pack the filler tightly into the pores of the wood

Towing-off-
4 Cuts surplus filler from wood surface and is done as soon as the filler starts to dry

Wiping-
5 This is done with the grain to remove all remaining traces of filler on the surface

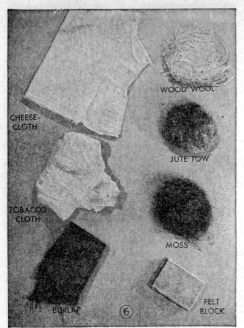

CHEESECLOTH is an excellent wiper but is a little **too** expensive for regular work. Open-mesh grade is best

TOBACCO CLOTH is unbleached cheesecloth. This provides an excellent wiper and is clean to use. Cheapest grade gives best results because of its open mesh

BURLAP is an old favorite for wiping. It is clean to use and cuts the filler level with wood surface. The cheaper grades are best because of more open mesh

WOOD WOOL or excelsior in the finer grades is very inexpensive and makes an excellent wiping material. The coarse grades will scratch fine cabinet woods

TOW from jute fibers is good, inexpensive wiper. Breaking up of material can be avoided by dampening

MOSS costs more than tow but it hangs together much better; is a cleaner as well as a faster wiper

FELT BLOCK is for padding-in before towing-off filler. It should be ½ in. thick, or thinner piece wood-backed

Wipers-

These are for removing surplus filler from the work and can be any cheap, coarse material. Open-weave cloth wipers are cleanest to use but most expensive

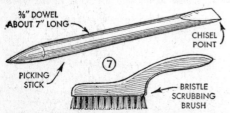

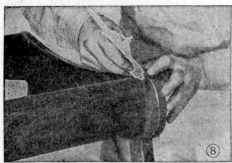

STANDARD FILLER COLORS	TABLE NO. 3

BLACK: Add drop black to natural filler. Suitable for blackwood or dark mahogany.

WHITE: Color natural base with zinc oxide. Used for limed oak and similar effects on chestnut and ash.

LIGHT BROWN: Tint with Van Dyke brown to required shade. Can be used on any light brown-color wood.

DARK BROWN: Van Dyke brown with a touch of drop black. For walnut, mahogany, etc. Suitable for any medium to dark-color wood.

WALNUT: Half and half Van Dyke brown and burnt umber.

LIGHT RED: Use any red color (Indian red) in oil or japan, toning darker or lighter with drop black or zinc white.

DARK RED: Equal parts of burnt umber and rose pink. Add drop black for darker shade. Used for Sheraton mahogany or any other red finish where dark pores are desirable.

AMBER: Tint natural base with yellow or orange oil colors. Suitable for ambered walnut, harvest wheat mahogany and other bleached finishes.

Coloring the filler-

Pigment colors ground in oil of japan are used for this purpose, usually only a very small quantity of color being required to produce the desired shade

filled surface being worked become dull, the filler coat is ready for wiping. Do not wait until the whole surface becomes dull as this will make the job more difficult. The first stage in cleaning off the surplus filler is padding-in. This is done with a felt block or a smooth pad of cloth, the motion of the pad being circular but mostly across the grain, Fig. 3. This operation does not

clean off the filler. Instead, it is intended only to force or pack the filler into the wood pores. You can do a very good job of padding-in with the heel of your hand. Many finishers omit padding-in altogether, proceeding directly after application to towing-off, Fig. 4, in which the surplus filler is packed into the wood and cut off level with the surface in one operation.

Towing-off: The work is towed-off with tow, moss, burlap or any other coarse, cheap material (see Fig. 6). Wiping is done across the grain, as shown in Fig. 4. The pad of wiping material should be turned around or refolded frequently to bring a clean surface in contact with the filler. The work should be cleaned thoroughly and progressively from one end to the other, not just half-wiped all over and then gone over again. If the filler has set up too hard for easy wiping, the surface of the work or wiping pad can be moistened with naphtha or the whole surface can be recoated with filler, which will tend to soften the filler coat underneath.

Wiping: Final wiping is done with the grain of the wood, using any soft lintless cloth, Fig. 5. This serves to remove any slight traces of filler missed in towing-off. The cloth can be moistened with benzine for a final wipe. Inside corners and other hard-to-reach places can be wiped clean with a picking stick as shown in Figs. 7 and 8. The stick consists of a short dowel having a round point at the end and a chisel edge at the other. A bristle scrubbing brush is useful for cleaning filler from intricate carvings, but in no case should it be used when the work can be wiped. If one coat of filler fails to fill the pores flush with the surface, apply another, tow-off as before and wipe lightly to avoid pulling out the filler.

'Turned work-

Turnings can be towed-off while the work is rotating at slow speed in the lathe. The work should be sanded very smooth as any sandpaper rings will pick up and hold filler. Turnings on furniture are towed-off by hand

The finishing schedule: The place of filler in the finishing schedule is best told by following a typical complete schedule. Staining usually is the first operation. The stain coat should be sealed with a wash coat of shellac or lacquer (1 part shellac or lacquer to 6 parts thinner). The work is sanded lightly with 5/0 paper when dry and, after a thorough cleaning with a duster or compressed air, it is ready for the filler coat. The filler coat should dry 6 hours if the filler is the quick-drying type. If a slow-drying type is used, 24 to 36 hours drying time should be allowed. The dry filler coat then is sealed with a light coat of shellac or lacquer sealer. When dry, this is sanded lightly, after which the work is given a full-bodied coat of varnish (varnish finish) or lacquer sealer (lacquer finish). This coat fills any tiny open pores, and should be sanded thoroughly to a flat, smooth surface. Top coats of varnish or lacquer complete the finish.

Filler colors: Paste filler can be obtained in all standard wood colors, also white and natural (the color of pale linseed oil). Common colors such as walnut, oak and mahogany are best purchased ready-mixed. These can be shaded lighter or darker to suit by adding a small amount of pigment color ground in oil or japan, and the natural filler can be shaded any color desired by adding oil or japan colors. The color should be mixed separately, using a very small amount of turpentine, Fig. 9, after which it can be added to the filler, preferably through a strainer. Table No. 3 gives formulas to mix colored fillers for various finishes.

Staining filler: Filler that stains and fills in one operation can be made by adding a small amount of oil stain to the paste filler. This is sometimes useful when exact mono-tone effects are desired, but generally is considered a short-cut practice suitable only for cheap work.

Turnings: Any turning that is a complete project in itself, such as a candlestick, can be filled and then towed-off with the work rotating at slow speed in a lathe as shown in Fig. 10.

Two-toning: One of the many methods of producing two-tone work can be done with filler. Areas to remain light are masked with tape after the whole panel has been stained, Fig. 11. The filler then is applied, Fig. 12, and when the tape is removed it produces the effect shown in Fig. 13, the

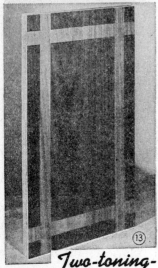

Two-toning—

This is done by masking areas to remain light and then applying filler in the usual manner

FILLER DEFECTS		TABLE NO. 4
Defect	Cause	Remedy
PIN-HOLES	Usually too thick filler which bridges pores. Trapped gas in pores then explodes forming miniature volcano.	Use a thinner filler. Avoid use of japan in mixing. Dust work thoroughly before filling.
RAISED GRAIN	Filler not given enough drying time. Also, in lacquer finish, the use of a filler not suitable under lacquer.	Allow plenty of drying time. Use 5/0 paper to sand off surface fuzz before and after staining.
GRAY PORES	Moisture in wood. Not enough drying time. Filler too light in color.	Check moisture content of wood. Always use filler as dark or darker than stain.
STREAKED CLOUDY FINISH	Filler not cleaned off completely. Use of wood turpentine instead of gum turpentine in mixing filler.	Moisten wiping rag with naphtha for final wipe of filler coat. Use gum turps or naphtha for mixing filler.

protected areas standing out both because they are lighter and also because they were not filled. For sharper contrast, a small amount of oil stain can be added to the filler.

Filler defects: The four most common finishing defects traceable to improper application of filler are described in Table No. 4. Augmenting this table and summarizing good filler practice, the finisher should observe the following general rules: Don't make the filler too heavy; it should have enough fluidity to sink to the bottom of the pores. Stick to one brand of filler and mix it the same way every time for any certain wood. Allow plenty of drying time; the two types of paste filler are commonly described as 4-hour and overnight-dry, but it is advisable to increase these minimum schedules by about half. Don't worry about a special type of filler for use under lacquer. If the filler has been made within the last two years, it will be compatible with lacquer, synthetic or varnish.

Oil Colors Applied to Scratches Touch Up Furniture

To touch up scratched spots on furniture, obtain a tube of oil color to match the finish, and mix this putty-like pigment with a small amount of turpentine. Apply with a brush and wipe off with a soft, dry cloth. This will cover all scratches or spots except those that are very deep. These spots should be filled with stick shellac, after which color as it comes from the tube is applied with the tip of your finger. After the color and shellac have hardened, the entire piece is either varnished or shellacked to complete the job.

Painting a Straight Line on Wood Without the Paint Creeping

Painting a straight line on wood, composition material or metal is made easier if the line is first scribed with a sharp knife blade. The cut forms a barrier beyond which the paint does not spread easily. The scribed line should be very light, just enough to break the surface.

Easy Way to Pour Half of Contents from Open-Top Container

When you wish to pour half the contents of a full can of paint, gasoline or other liquid into another container, here's a way to get a

close approximation of this amount. Pour the liquid in the usual manner until the level of the liquid remaining in the can forms a line between the lower edge of the rim, A, and the upper edge of the bottom, B. At this point you have poured about one half of the contents from the can. This rule will hold true for both round and square cans, but, of course, it can be done only with open-top containers. If you want to divide the contents of a partially empty can equally, make a mark or place your finger on the outside of the can at the level of the liquid when the can is vertical. Then, use this mark as you would the lower edge of the rim when pouring from a full can.

HOT WAX FINISH

Ideal for Small Projects

THIS finish differs from conventional wax treatment in that it is applied directly to the bare wood. Best woods to use for this treatment are beech, birch, cherry or maple. Both the work and wax must be kept hot throughout the entire application. Buffing the work after the wax coating has cooled should be done across the grain of the wood to give a filling action, following this treatment by a light buffing with the grain. Colored finishes can be obtained by first staining the work before the wax is applied. Also, excellent effects can be had by using tinted wax, which is obtained by coloring the wax with a small amount of oil color while mixing it.

Buffing is final step in finishing, after wax coating has cooled for an hour. Use a 6-in. loose muslin wheel at about 2,500 r.p.m.

① Shred the lump of wax. Carnauba wax is by far the best natural wax to use by virtue of its extreme hardness, but beeswax, ceresin, candelilla or even paraffin can be used

② Add to 2 oz. of shredded wax, 1 pt. of naphtha or turpentine, naphtha preferred. Colored wax can be made by adding a small amount of oil color

WATER · 1 PINT NAPHTHA · 2 OZ. CARNAUBA WAX. · HEAT TO 165°

③ (Above) Place the mixture in a pan of water and heat. The wax will dissolve at about 165° F. Use electric fan to blow naphtha fumes out of open window

④ Work must be sanded very fine and must be heated to at least 110° before wax is applied. An electric light bulb in cardboard box can be used for heating

⑤ (Left) Wax must be applied hot, either a freshly made solution or old solution reheated. Temperature should be 150° F. or higher. Wax should be applied quickly and evenly while work is still warm

TEST FOR SOLUBILITY

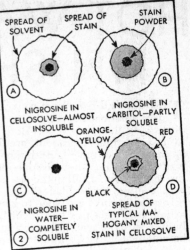

SPREAD OF SOLVENT — SPREAD OF STAIN — STAIN POWDER

A · NIGROSINE IN CELLOSOLVE—ALMOST INSOLUBLE

B · NIGROSINE IN CARBITOL—PARTLY SOLUBLE

ORANGE-YELLOW — RED

C · NIGROSINE IN WATER—COMPLETELY SOLUBLE — BLACK

D · SPREAD OF TYPICAL MAHOGANY MIXED STAIN IN CELLOSOLVE

2

STAINS

By Sam Brown

STAINING is the first and most important step in applying a clear finish on wood. It gives the wood color and enhances the beauty of the grain. No other step in finishing brings about so radical a change in the appearance of the wood.

Types of stains: Essential ingredients of any stain are a liquid or solvent, and coloring matter. The solvent usually is water, oil or alcohol, and the general description of the stain is the same as the solvent used, that is, water stain, oil stain, spirit stain. There are several branches of these main groups, including non-grain-raising stain, wiping stain, shading stain, etc. The coloring matter usually is an aniline dye, which is available as a dry powder in numerous colors, and comes in cans as small as 1 oz. All types of stains can be made by mixing the dry powder with the required solvent. Also, all types, except water stain, can be obtained in liquid form if a ready-to-use product is desired.

Mixing powder stain: Directions for mixing powder stains are shown in Figs. 3 and 4. As a general rule, 1 oz. of powder will make 1 qt. of stain. The powder dissolves better if the solvent is warmed to about 160 degrees F. Where inflammable oils or alcohol are being used, the bottle containing the solvent can be placed in a

PENETRATING OIL STAIN
Add to 1 oz. oil soluble stain powder, 1 qt. warmed, light oil (benzol, turpentine, naphtha, gasoline) or a blend. Half and half benzol and VMP naphtha is recommended. A small amount of asphaltum or 4-hour varnish (⅛ to ½ pt.) can be added for body if desired.

POWDER STAIN (OIL SOLUBLE)

WATER STAIN
Add to 1 oz. water soluble stain powder, 1 qt. of hot but not boiling water Allow to cool and then strain. Keep in glass jar

NON-GRAIN-RAISING STAIN
Add to 1 oz. water soluble stain powder, 1 qt. Carbitol or Cellosolve (see text). Keep in glass. Dilute as used with denatured alcohol but not over 3 parts alcohol to 1 part stain.

SPIRIT STAIN
Add to 1 oz. alcohol soluble stain powder 1 qt. of warmed denatured alcohol. A small amount of white shellac (⅛ to ½ pt.) can be added for body if desired. A small amount of VMP naphtha can be added to retard drying if stain is to be applied by brushing.

HOW TO MIX POWDER STAINS

3

4 · OTHER TYPES OF STAIN
Pigment Oil Stain: 4 oz. any color pigment ground in oil with 1 pt. of benzol, turpentine and boiled linseed oil in equal parts. Under lacquer, use colors ground in japan and mix with turpentine.

Wiping Stain: Same as above.

Shading Stain: 1 oz. oil soluble stain powder to 1 qt. lacquer thinner Add to clear lacquer in any proportion.

Staining Filler: Color regular paste wood filler with penetrating oil stain.

WARM THE SOLVENT

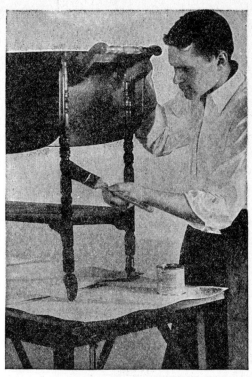

in wood finishing

pan of hot water as shown in Fig. 5. It is good practice to strain all stains through muslin or cheesecloth after they have cooled to room temperature. This removes impurities and filters undissolved pigment.

Non-grain-raising stains (NGR): These are made from water-stain powders dissolved in a synthetic chemical. The result is a stain with all the good features of water stain, but minus the grain-raising fault. The solvents Carbitol and Cellosolve mentioned in the lower right-hand corner of Fig. 3, are the commercial names for diethylene glycol and ethylene glycol respectively. Both are obtainable from finishing supply houses, and are of the alcohol family, miscible in all proportions with water and each other. They are solvents for practically all of the water-soluble powders. However, two important exceptions in solubilities should be remembered. Cellosolve is not a solvent for walnut crystals or nigrosine and Carbitol is not a solvent for walnut crystals, and only a partial solvent for nigrosine. If these solvents are used in mixing a powder containing any part of nigrosine, the resulting color will be lighter than the same powder mixed with water, as the black (nigrosine) will not dissolve. As manufacturers of stain powders generally favor the purer form of mixing colors from the primary colors (red, yellow,

⑥ TREATMENT OF VARIOUS WOODS	
WALNUT and MAHOGANY	Often finished natural, without stain. Stain used for wide variety of brown and red tones. Preferable stain, water or NGR; seldom oil or spirit. Excellent for bleaching, after which wood may be stained light amber, straw, etc., or sufficient color can often be obtained by filler alone.
OAK	Seldom finished natural or red. Attractive in any brown tone. Grain raising very bad with water stain, hence NGR preferable. Excellent for bleaching. Good for novelty effects.
PHILIPPINE MAHOGANY	Same as mahogany, NGR stain preferable. Sometimes filled direct on bare wood with an orange-brown filler (pigment coloring, not dye) and further toned by adding shading stain to first finishing (sealer) coat.
FIR SPRUCE CYPRESS BASSWOOD POPLAR REDWOOD PINE	Usually stained mahogany or walnut color, using penetrating oil stain, which brings out grain. To kill grain, use wiping stain. Water stain not commonly used but if used will penetrate better on resinous wood if work is first washed with an alkali solution (4 oz. of sal soda, 1 oz. washing soda per gal. of water).
MAPLE	Use water or NGR stain. Add further color with shading or wiping stain between finishing coats. Often stained with wiping stain on bare wood.
POPLAR BIRCH GUM BEECH	Commonly used in combination with walnut or mahogany. A uniform color is obtained by spraying NGR stain overall; heavy on birch or gum; light on walnut or mahogany. After filling, birch or gum can be darkened to match by using shading or wiping stain.
CEDAR	Always finished natural. A red wiping stain can be used to blend or smooth any excessive contrast between the white and red wood.

PROTECT INLAYS WITH SHELLAC

blue), it is not likely that much trouble will be encountered in this respect. When mixing stains, a deep blue-violet will answer all color requirements for a black. Walnut crystals are mixed usually as a single color to produce a walnut brown for which there are many good browns as substitutes.

Solubility rings: A good check for solubility when making NGR stains is as follows: Take a blotter or a folded facial tissue and place a small pinch of the powder on the paper. If you are checking more than one solvent, put down a separate pinch of powder for each. Now, wet each mound of powder with several drops of warm solvent, so that the wet ring of solvent makes a circle about 2 in. in diameter, as shown in Fig. 1. Observe the stain color obtained. If it spreads instantly in a uniform color to the fullest extent of the wet solvent ring, the powder is very soluble in the solvent being tested. A color spread of about two-thirds the diameter of the wet solvent ring can be considered satisfactory. Note the examples in Fig. 2. Data contained in the tables of Figs. 6 and 8 should enable the finisher to make a satisfactory selection as to the type of stain he should use for any particular job.

Application of stain: One rule that applies to all types of stains is to start on less important parts. When using water stain, sponge the wood with warm water just enough to dampen it, Fig. 13, and sand smooth when dry as in Fig. 14. Apply the stain with brush or spray. Use a fairly large brush and apply the stain freely and rapidly, shaking out the brush after finishing each surface. Brush lightly with the grain to obtain a smooth color. End grain should be brushed with water immediately before staining to prevent darkening. Touch up sap streaks to same color as

(8)		TYPE OF STAIN				
		WATER STAIN	NON-GRAIN-RAISING STAIN	PENETRATING OIL STAIN	PIGMENT OIL STAIN	SPIRIT STAIN
	COLORING MATTER	Water-soluble aniline powder	Water-soluble aniline powder	Oil-soluble aniline powder	Pigment colors in oil	Alcohol-soluble aniline powder
	SOLVENT	Water	Carbitol or Cellosolve plus alcohol	Benzol, turpentine, etc.	Benzol, turpentine, naphtha	Denatured alcohol
	COST	Low	High	Medium	Medium	High
	APPLICATION	Brush or spray	① Best sprayed but can be brushed	Brush and wipe with cloth	Brush and wipe	Spray only
	GRAIN RAISING	② Bad	③ Very little	None	None	③ Very little
	CLARITY	Excellent	Excellent	Good	Fair	Good
	BLEEDING	None	None or very little	⑤ Bad	None	④ Bad
	PERMANENCE OF COLOR	Excellent	Excellent	Fair	Excellent	Poor
	EFFECT ON TOP COATS	None	Possible slight bleeding	⑤ Bleeds. Must be sealed with shellac	⑥ None	④ Bleeds
	MIXES WITH LACQUER	No	Yes	Yes	No	Yes
	MIXES WITH VARNISH	No	Yes	Yes	Yes	Yes
	DRYING TIME	12-18 hrs.	1-4 hrs.	⑦ 2-18 hrs.	⑦ 6-18 hrs.	1 hr.
	PRINCIPAL USE	Staining quality hardwoods	Same as water stain. Also for refinishing	Staining softwoods	Softwoods. Also as a glaze coat or wiping stain	⑧ Patching and quick work

(Left margin, vertical: CHARACTERISTICS OF STAIN)

Notes Applying to Table Above:

1. Some types, factory mixed in liquid form, dry very quickly and are difficult to brush smoothly.

2. The only fault of water stain — water solvent causes wood fibers to lift. Work must be resanded smooth when dry. The addition of up to 25% Carbitol or Cellosolve will help correct this fault.

3. Alcohol solvent absorbs moisture from air causing slight grain raising in muggy weather.

4. Refers to own-mix stain. Some factory-mixed stains of the alcohol series are strictly non-bleeding.

5. Seal with shellac when used under varnish. Do not use under lacquer.

6. Refers to factory-mixed product, made with specially treated oils to work under lacquer.

7. Use benzol as solvent for fast-drying. Retard drying with turpentine or turpentine substitute.

8. Non-grain-raising stains answer all requirements for a spirit stain and the colors are more permanent.

GLASS GRADUATE
MARKED OFF
IN OUNCES

BATTERY
FILLER

½" GLASS
TUBE

⑩ **COLOR MIXING**

heartwood before staining the entire surface. Stain should dry 12 hours. Then a wash coat consisting of shellac, 1 part and alcohol, 6 parts is applied and sanded smooth, after which the work is ready for filling if the wood is open grain, or for finishing if it is close grain. Non-grain-raising stain is handled the same as water stain except that preliminary sponging with warm water is unnecessary. This stain usually is sprayed. Penetrating oil stain is sprayed or brushed on. No particular care is needed in application. The color is spread uniformly by wiping with a cloth 10 to 15 min. after application.

⑪ **STAIN COLORS BY LIQUID PARTS**

Color **	Yellow	Orange	Red	Dark * Blue	Black *
Sheraton Mahogany (Lt. Red)	—	12	5	3	—
Medium Red Mahogany	2	6	6	—	3
Red Mahogany	—	9	7	4	—
Dark Red Mahogany	2	6	7	—	4
Brown Mahogany	1	18	—	4	—
Light Walnut	—	12	1	—	4
Medium Walnut	—	14	1	—	6
Oriental Walnut	—	3	—	—	2
Light Oak	1	10	—	2	—
Dark Oak	2	10	—	5	—
Golden Oak	—	22	1	3	—
Honey Maple	4	11	—	2	—

** Lighter tints of same color can be obtained by diluting with solvent.
* Add dark colors last.

WIPING STAINS
For Mahogany or Walnut—Van Dyke Brown
For Red-Orange Maple—Half and half raw Sienna and Burnt Umber
For Brown Maple—Burnt Umber

Color palettes for mixing stains ⑫

	Color	Water Stain and NGR Stain	Penetrating Oil Stain	Spirit Stain	Pigment ** Oil Stain
Primary colors and black make all other colors	Red	Brilliant Scarlet ZR Azo Rubine	Oil Red Oil Scarlet	Fuchine Safranine Y	Alizarin Scarlet Crimson Lake
	Yellow	Tartrazine Metanil Yellow	Oil Yellow	Auramine O	Alizarin Yellow Cadmium Yellow Golden Ochre
	Blue	Acid Green B Pontacyl Brilliant Blue	Oil Blue Victoria Blue	Methylene Blue	Prussian Blue Cobalt Blue
Additional colors often simplify mixing	Black	Nigrosine * (Use any deep blue, buffalo black) for NGR stains	Oil Black	Nigrosine	Mixture of Raw Umber and Ultramarine Blue
	Brown	Walnut Crystals * Loutre Brown Sap Brown	Oil Brown	Bismarck Brown	Brown Ochre Raw and Burnt Umber Raw and Burnt Sienna
	Orange	Orange A Grocein Orange	Oil Orange	Chrysoidine	Alizarin Orange
	Green	Naphthol Green	Oil Green	Malachite	Alizarin Green Transparent Green

* For water stain only   ** Colors in oil—All others are powder stains

119

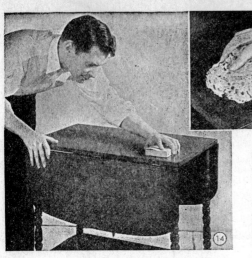

Immediate wiping of end grain will prevent darkening. Allow the stain to dry overnight, and then seal with shellac but do not use this stain under lacquer. Spirit stain dries almost instantly and must be sprayed. If necessary to brush it, add Cellosolve and shellac. It is best to spray the wash coat of shellac over stain as it must be applied deftly to prevent lifting the stain. Pigment oil stain is handled the same as penetrating oil stain. Also, it is used as a glazing or shading stain over the filler or between finishing coats. In either case, it is applied and wiped with cloth.

Mixing stain colors: While all standard colors are obtainable ready-mixed in powder form, the finisher may wish to mix his own color or modify the color of a commercial mixture. The table in Fig. 9 gives a few rules on color mixing that generally are useful, while Fig. 12 gives complete color palettes for all types of stain. The apparatus shown in Fig. 10 simplifies the job. Where two or more colors are given, any one will be satisfactory. Fig. 11 shows how various standard wood colors are mixed, using liquid parts. As the exact color will depend on the original selection of basic colors, these formulas will not be exactly correct but will serve as a rough guide. Mixing is done easily if a stock solution of each of the required colors is on hand. The unit or part for mixing can be any convenient measure, a drop for very small test runs, the cubic centimeter (c.c.) for accurate tests, and the liquid ounce for final measuring. Liquid stain is drawn by using a small syringe or rubber bulb battery filler. Wet pour-tests can be used as a preliminary in judging color, but the final selection should be made on the basis of a completely finished panel.

Special applications: Where it is necessary to stain over inlays, the wood, if light colored, should be protected with a coat of white shellac as in Fig. 7. The stain is brushed or sprayed right over the shellac, but will not "take" and is wiped off easily. An equally good method is to mask off the inlay with masking tape previous to staining. Tape or stencils can be used also for a two-tone effect, spraying stain lightly or not at all on the protected areas. Various highlighted and antique effects are obtained easily with wiping stain. The initial staining is done as usual with any type of stain. The wiping stain is applied over the sealer coat and is wiped to produce highlights as required. Similar work is done with shading stain. This is sprayed and is a somewhat different technique in that the wood is darkened in certain areas as desired by the finisher.

Mixture for Finishing Cabinets Made from Plaster and Paint

A paint that is especially effective for radio and other cabinets can be made by mixing patching plaster with ordinary flat paint to produce a fairly thick mixture, which is applied with a brush. A variety of rough-textured effects can be worked out with a stippling brush or knife. The mixture covers well and is not apt to flake off.

Blotter Removes Decals

A wet blotter placed over a decal on a painted surface will loosen it sufficiently to permit removal with a dull knife without marring the finish. The blotter should remain over the decal for 2 hours.

Giving Wood a Rough Finish

Rough finishes on wood can be made with a rotary wire brush, which tends to cut away the softer portions and leave the harder ones standing out in relief. The brush can be attached to any machine which will rotate it, such as a grinder or, it can be fitted to a flexible shaft.

Hint for Applying Oak Stain

To obtain an even color over the entire surface when applying a medium oak stain to softwood floors, first seal the surface with a filler of thinned, hot glue. Allow the glue to dry and rub it down with sandpaper before applying the stain to the floor.

Modern FINISHES for your Furniture Projects

Bleaching

WITH the increased use of small spray-painting outfits, and the many new types of paints and lacquers recently developed, the craftsman can duplicate the finest finishes seen on manufactured furniture. Beautiful blond tones in ambered walnut, honeytone maple and harvest-wheat mahogany, interesting novelty effects such as limed oak, bone white and pickled pine, as well

Photo courtesy
American Furniture Mart

MAHOGANY   WALNUT

MAKE TEST STRIPS TO SHOW ACTION OF BLEACH ON WOOD

WHITE OR TAN LACQUER, 1 PART

CLEAR LACQUER, 4 PARTS

WHITE LACQUER

Honey-tone Maple

MAPLE

Toning

as smart contemporary finishes such as antique maple and natural birch are all within his scope. The man with the brush is not altogether out of the picture either, as most of these finishes can be applied nearly as well by hand brushing.

Bleaching: One of the basic processes for many of the newer finishes is bleaching, which entails the removal of the natural wood color with various chemical solutions that you can buy. Most of the solutions consist of two liquid chemicals, which are mixed together in the proportions of about four-to-one immediately before using. Apply the bleach to the wood with a rubber sponge as in Fig. 1. Wear rubber gloves as all bleaching solutions are corrosive. Get the work wet evenly all over, and let the bleach dry on the wood. Most commercial bleaches having a hydrogen-peroxide or similar base, when thoroughly dry, leave

Limed Oak

BLOND FINISHES

FINISH	APPLICATION
AMBERED WALNUT	Bleach. Stain with amber stain. Apply sealer coat of thin lacquer. Fill with natural filler. Finish with clear lacquer.
HONEYTONE MAPLE OR BIRCH	Tone with bond toner, using 1 part white lacquer to 4 parts clear flat lacquer. Finish with water-white lacquer.
HARVEST-WHEAT MAHOGANY	Bleaching will give required wheat color. Fill with natural filler lightly tinted with raw sienna color in oil. Lacquer.
PICKLED PINE	Bleach. Stain with gray stain for pine. Finish with water-white lacquer.
PICKLED PINE	Spray toner coat (gray or cream). Apply white wiping stain and wipe for highlights.
LIMED OAK	Bleach. Seal. Fill pores with white paste wood filler. Finish with water-white lacquer.
TWEED MAHOGANY	Bleach. Seal. Fill pores with red paste wood filler. Water-white lacquer.
HEATHER MAHOGANY	Bleach. Seal. Fill pores with white paste wood filler. Finish with water-white lacquer.
OLD-WORLD WALNUT	Bleach. Seal. Fill with natural filler lightly tinted with burnt umber. Seal. Shade with brown wiping stain. Finish with clear lacquer.

Silver Oak

nothing in the wood to harm the finishing coats. One application of the bleach is generally sufficient. Check the effect before you start, on a test strip as in Fig. 2.

Toning: Toning, Fig. 4, is the second basic process. This calls for the spraying of a semi-transparent undercoat to lighten the wood rather than the more expensive and longer bleaching schedule. It is not successful on dark wood like walnut, but very successful on naturally light-colored woods such as birch and maple. The toner is made by adding white lacquer, 1 part, to clear flat lacquer, 4 or 5 parts, as in Fig. 3. This mixture is sprayed directly on the bare wood. Its semi-transparent nature does not obscure the grain, but at the same time it makes the wood much lighter. On oak and mahogany, the toner should be made with tan lacquer instead of white.

Honeytone maple: This attractive effect of blond wood, shown in Fig. 5, can be worked on white maple or birch by toning. Spray a thin coat of white toner directly on the bare wood after sanding. Finish with two coats of water-white lacquer. This is almost as clear as water and does not have the amber color of ordinary clear lacquer. It should be used on all extremely light finishes. If a bleaching instead of toning process is used, bleaching is the first operation, followed by three or four coats of water-white lacquer.

Ambered walnut: The light amber finish so popular on walnut can only be obtained by using a commercial bleaching solution. Toning, if carried to a stage of light coloring, will completely kill the grain of the wood, giving the piece a painted appearance. Start by applying the bleach. Let it dry on the wood overnight and then sand lightly with No. 6-0 paper. Dust the work, and stain it with a non-grain-raising, quick-drying stain. This should be light amber color and should be thinned as much as needed with the required thinner until the tone is just a shade darker than the bleached color of the wood. Seal the stain with a wash coat of shellac to prevent further darkening of the wood by the oil in the filler. Apply natural (transparent) filler. Let dry thoroughly. Finish the schedule by applying two or

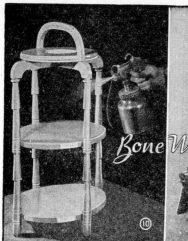

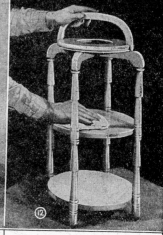

Bone White

| SPRAYING BONE-WHITE LACQUER COAT | APPLYING WARM-BROWN WIPING STAIN | WIPING STAIN WITH SOFT RAG |

three coats of clear gloss lacquer, rubbing the last coat to a satin finish.

Limed oak: To produce limed oak, Fig. 6, bleach the work with a commercial bleach. Stain or leave the wood in its natural bleached color as you desire. Apply a wash coat of water-white lacquer. Fill the pores of the wood with white filler. This can be obtained ready-mixed or made by adding zinc-white oil color to natural filler. Use only water-white lacquer as a top coat over this finish—ordinary clear lacquer will spoil the color.

Silver oak: This is similar to limed oak but is obtained by the toning method. Mix light gray lacquer, 1 part, with clear lacquer, 3 parts, and spray directly on the bare wood until an even color is obtained. Fill the pores of the wood with white filler, Fig. 8, and finish with water-white lacquer. Many novel effects can be obtained in this manner, Fig. 9, using different colors for the toner.

Other blond finishes: All other blond finishes, Fig. 7, feature the same application of the basic processes already described. Mahogany, bleached and filled with white filler, is known as "heather mahogany." When filled with red filler (made by adding red oil color to natural filler) the delightful pink tone is called "tweed." Bleached mahogany with a natural filler is one of the most attractive in the blond mahogany group and is variously known as "harvest-wheat mahogany," "bronze mahogany," etc. After obtaining an almost white wood color by bleaching, the worker can give the wood a coat of

Antique Maple

diluted stain to produce almost any color desired.

Bone white: Bone white, Figs. 10, 11 and 12, is a popular enamel finish. Start by giving the work a coat of bone-white enamel. This is purchased ready-mixed and is simply an off-tone shade of white which the finisher can mix himself, if desired, by adding a little black or brown lacquer to white lacquer. Next, spray or brush a coat of warm brown wiping stain. Wiping stain is ordinary oil pigment stain, but somewhat more concentrated. Before the stain dries, start to wipe it off with a soft rag. This operation is called high-

123

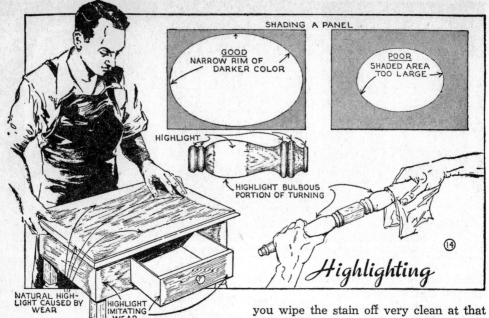

SHADING A PANEL

GOOD
NARROW RIM OF
DARKER COLOR

POOR
SHADED AREA
TOO LARGE

HIGHLIGHT

HIGHLIGHT BULBOUS
PORTION OF TURNING

NATURAL HIGH-
LIGHT CAUSED BY
WEAR

HIGHLIGHT
IMITATING
WEAR

Highlighting

lighting. A few pointers on proper high-lighting will be given later. After wiping and after the stain is dry, the finish is completed with two coats of clear lacquer.

Antique maple: The popular color for maple pieces in Early American styling is a red-orange, usually sold under the label, "antique maple," Fig. 13. After staining, the work should be coated with orange shellac or clear lacquer. Staining alone seldom gives the mellow aged appearance so essentially a part of this finish, making it necessary to apply a second coat of stain to obtain highlights. This second stain coat is a warm brown wiping stain, the same as used in the bone-white finish. It is sprayed or brushed on the work and then wiped off rather cleanly. Even on areas wiped perfectly clean with a dry cloth, a portion of the stain will remain on the wood to give a shaded effect to the finish. Extra clean highlights are obtained by wiping the stain with a rag moistened with benzine. After the wiping stain has dried, the work can be finished with clear lacquer or varnish.

Highlighting: This technique plays an important part in the bone-white and antique-maple finishes already described. Highlights can be obtained in many different ways, but these few remarks are confined to highlighting with the use of wiping stain. The basic principle is easily understood—if you want a light-colored area,

you wipe the stain off very clean at that point. The proper application of the idea is best learned by observing store furniture and doing a little experimenting. In most cases a very clean wiping should be practiced. Turnings are easy—just wipe them from end to end. In this way you will hit only the high spots or bulbous portions of the turning, and this is the correct technique. On panels, leave a narrow dark rim around the edges, spreading a little at the corners, and wipe the center portion clean. The highlighted area should predominate, as shown in Fig. 14. The rule of natural wear often serves as a guide. Notice how a table top is highlighted at the natural wearing points. Highlight small drawers along the outer edges—the area which the hand would naturally polish through wear. If you fail to get a good-looking job the first time, sponge the work clean with benzine and try again.

Applying Shellac Without Smear

When brushing shellac or varnish over a stained finish, the stain is sometimes softened and smeared by the brush, especially if more than one stroke is made over the same surface. If the shellac is sprayed on with an inexpensive atomizer, this trouble will be eliminated. After the shellac has dried for a few hours, it should be rubbed lightly with curled hair or very fine sandpaper to remove the grain before applying the finishing coats.

A Lustrous OIL FINISH

ROTTENSTONE

LINSEED OIL

BOILED LINSEED OIL

SPAR VARNISH

TURPENTINE

PASTE FILLER

ALKANET ROOT

MULE-HIDE LEATHER FACING

BUFFING BLOCK

BUFFING STICK

① MATERIALS AND TOOLS NEEDED

② After sanding, the wood is moistened with water, using either a sponge or cloth pad

③

Then the surface is steamed by playing the flame of a blowtorch over the dampened wood

④

This raises the grain which is removed by sanding lightly with very fine sandpaper

⑤

MANY articles made of wood, particularly of walnut, mahogany, and other hardwoods, can be beautified and the life of their finishes increased if the worker follows to some extent the methods of gunsmiths, to produce a soft, beautiful oil finish. The finish is in the wood, not on it—the surface is quite bare—but it is highly resistant to moisture and ordinary use will not scratch it.

Few materials are needed, and only two tools—a buffing stick and a buffing block, Fig. 1. The stick is used somewhat like a file, to buff off legs, spindles, arms and other rounded surfaces while the block is used on table tops and other flat surfaces. The working surfaces of both tools are covered with a leather known to saddlers as mule hide. For materials you need a lump of rottenstone about the size of your fist, 1 pt. each of pure raw linseed oil and boiled linseed oil (no fishoil substitutes), ½ pt. good spar varnish, ½ pt. pure turpentine, and a small can of any dark col-

Apply a coat of raw linseed oil and turpentine to the sanded work, wipe off after 30 min., and then let the work stand overnight

ored paste filler. Keep the can of raw linseed oil closed tightly, but the can of boiled oil open—but protected from dust—and let it oxidize and get as thick and syrupy as possible. A small amount of aniline red, or a handful of alkanet root may be added to the oils to produce a reddish tinge, which greatly enhances the appearance of most brownish woods.

First, the work should be sanded thoroughly, beginning with coarse abrasive and ending with the finest, Fig. 2. Aluminous oxide cloth, or garnet paper will do the job much better than sandpaper. Next, moisten the entire surface with a wet sponge or pad of cloth, and dry quickly by playing a blowtorch flame over it, Figs. 3 and 4. This will raise the grain, after which it should be sanded down very lightly, with the finest grade of abrasive, Fig. 5. Repeat the process of wetting, flaming, and sand-

Next, seal the sanded surface, including the end grain, against further absorption of oil with a coat or two of paste filler

After 12 hrs., apply from three to six coats of boiled oil 24 hrs. apart, rubbing each coat into the wood with the bare hands

Follow the oil treatment with a coat of boiled oil and drier and let dry until tacky; then rub it off across the wood grain

ing until the grain does not rise. If you have no blowtorch and the work is too large to hold over a gas flame, place a layer or two of cloth over the work and press with a hot flat iron.

The first treatment of the sanded wood consists of spreading on a coat of raw linseed oil, 3 parts, mixed with turpentine, 1 part, Fig. 6. Let this stand 30 min., then wipe off the surplus oil, and let stand overnight. Next, seal all end grain against further absorption of oil, with a coating or two consisting of paste filler, spar varnish and japan drier, in equal parts, rubbed in, Fig. 7. When nearly dry, rub off the surplus paste and let dry hard for at least 12 hours. Now apply from three to six coats of the boiled oil, well rubbed in with the bare hands, 24 hrs. apart, Fig. 8. Allow the last coat to dry 24 hrs. or longer, after which you apply a coat consisting of equal parts of boiled oil and drier. Let stand until quite "tacky," rub off surplus across the grain with burlap or other coarse material, Fig. 9, and let dry 24 hrs. By this time the pores in the grain should be almost filled up. If not, hasten the work with a coat of filler, well thinned with turpentine and a little boiled oil. Rub off the surplus when dry, apply another coat of boiled oil and drier, and rub off all surplus when it gets tacky.

Now comes the rubbing. Take your buff stick and rub the leather surfaces several times over a lump of rottenstone, Fig. 12, and use it with a light, brisk filing motion, diagonally across the grain on legs and other rounded surfaces. Use the buffing block in the same way on all flat surfaces, Fig. 11, always working at a slight angle with the direction of the grain. Rub the leather over the rottenstone frequently—and be sure you do not pick up any small

Rottenstone is applied to flat surfaces with buffing block, rubbing slightly across grain with long, even strokes

particle of grit that would make a scratch. As the leather becomes slick and shiny from the oil it picks up, scrape it clean with a knife, Fig. 13, and apply more rottenstone. The more you rub the better will be the finish. This finish is never completed, but is renewed at intervals as needed. A drop or two of the syrupy boiled oil on the heel of the hand may be rubbed in over a square foot or two of surface, whenever you feel ambitious but not too often—say once a month or so for six months. Age— and rubbing—bring out the beauty even in plain grained woods.

When satisfied that you have done your best, fill the formula in Fig. 10 and use it, and nothing else, as a polish in the future. Melt carnauba wax and Venice turpentine over a water bath, add the oil and drier, and simmer slowly for 10 min. Then add the spirits of turpentine, and stir until the mixture is cool. It can be stored in a screw-topped glass jar. A small amount of this polish applied with a rag and rubbed vigorously gives a superior and lasting finish to any wood and is harmless to varnished surfaces. It will not cause the finish to check, no matter how long it is used.

Maple and some other light colored woods possess many hidden beauties brought out by judicious darkening with stains. One of the best stains for maple is a strong solution of potassium permanganate. After applying, allow the solution to dry for an hour or so and then play a torch flame over the sur-

When the leather face of the buffing stick becomes slick from the oil, scrape it clean with a knife and apply more rottenstone, repeating this as may be necessary

ROTTEN-STONE

BUFFING STICK

CHAIR LEG

BUFFING STICK

face, which changes the color to a deep, rosy brown. After staining, sand the surface lightly with very fine abrasive to bring out the highlights, and proceed with the oil finish as already described.

Fine Finish on Interior Woodwork

To get a smooth finish on interior wood work that has been painted previously, first clean off the old paint with remover and brush over the entire surface with turpentine. After this is dry, sand and apply a coat of the selected color, thinned with turpentine to act as a filler. When this in turn has dried, putty all holes and broken or splintered parts. Then apply as many coats of paint as needed, allowing each coat to dry before adding the next.

❡ A little starch added to calcimine before brushing it on a wall will make it adhere firmly and help prevent streaking.

Chart Gives Paint Mixes for Many Purposes

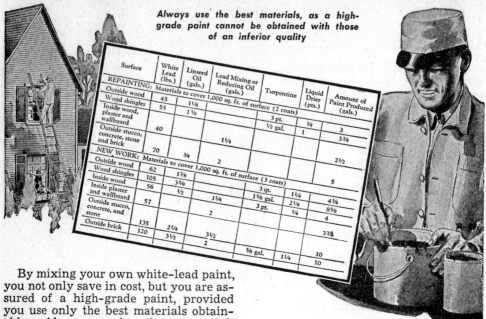

Always use the best materials, as a high-grade paint cannot be obtained with those of an inferior quality

Surface	White Lead (lbs.)	Linseed Oil (gals.)	Lead Mixing or Reducing Oil (gals.)	Turpentine	Liquid Drier (pts.)	Amount of Paint Produced (gals.)
REPAINTING: Materials to cover 1,000 sq. ft. of surface (2 coats)						
Outside wood	45	1⅛		3 pt.	¾	3
Wood shingles	55	1⅜		½ gal.	1	3¾
Inside wood, plaster and wallboard	40		1¼			2½
Outside stucco, concrete, stone and brick	70	¾	2			5
NEW WORK: Materials to cover 1,000 sq. ft. of surface (3 coats)						
Outside wood	62	1⅞		3 qt.	1¼	4¾
Wood shingles	105	3⅝		1⅝ gal.	2¼	8⅝
Inside wood	56	½	1¼	3 pt.	¼	4
Inside plaster and wallboard	57		2			3¾
Outside stucco, concrete, and stone	135	2¼	3½			10
Outside brick	120	3½	2	⅝ gal.	1¼	10

By mixing your own white-lead paint, you not only save in cost, but you are assured of a high-grade paint, provided you use only the best materials obtainable. Also, remember that a careful, thorough mixing of the paint is just as important as good materials. The table above gives the recommended proportions of ingredients in mixing enough paint to cover 1,000 sq.ft. of surface two coats in refinishing old work, and for covering the same area three coats on new work. Do not guess at the proportions. Always accurately measure or weigh the materials as stated in the table. And don't forget the surface to be painted. It is not only a waste of money to paint a surface that is not clean and dry, but it is discouraging to see the paint come off after a few months.

Rim of Paint Can Kept Clean to Effect Tight Seal

To keep the rim of a can of paint free of hardened paint accumulations so that the cover will make a good seal, fill the groove with a length of plastic weather strip each time before you paint from the can. Rope-type calking compound which is sold in roll form is ideal for this purpose. Although not as satisfactory as a plastic compound, a length of cord also may be used.

When each coat of house paint is allowed to dry thoroughly for at least ten days before the next coat is applied, the resulting finish will last longer and stay brighter.

A Non-Reflecting Paint

You camera fans will cheer this formula for a non-reflecting paint. Suitable for covering the inside surfaces of cameras, telescopes, binoculars, and other optical instruments, a paint that will not reflect light is made by mixing lamp-black with shellac, varnish or lacquer which has been thinned with a solvent. The paint must be stirred frequently while using to prevent settling of the pigment.

When applying only one finish coat to interior walls, better coverage will be insured if the white undercoat is tinted with a little of the finish color. This will be especially helpful if the walls are to be finished in a delicate shade.

Prevent paint from hardening in the can after exposure to the air by pouring a thin layer of turpentine over the surface. Put a bit of the paint in the groove in the friction top of the can also, and then drive the cover down tightly.

Tips on a BETTER FINISH

LITTLE TRICKS THAT HELP IN APPLYING A PERFECT VARNISH FINISH

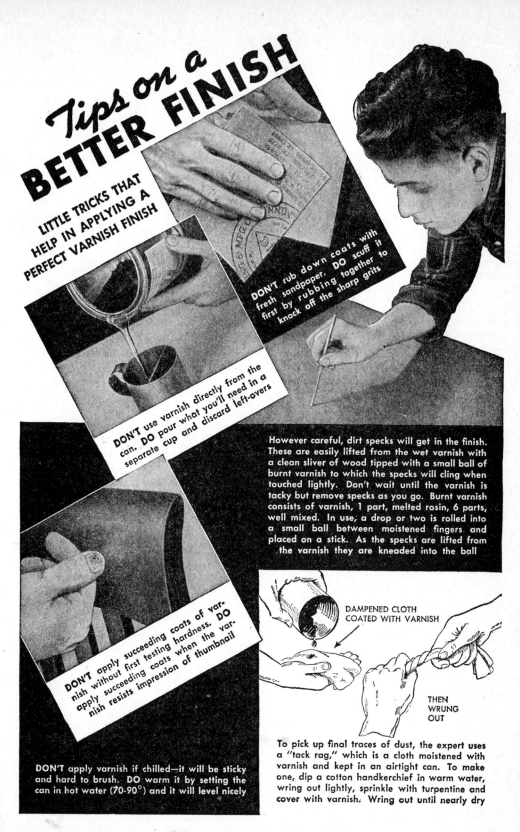

DON'T rub down coats with fresh sandpaper. **DO** scuff it first by rubbing together to knock off the sharp grits

DON'T use varnish directly from the can. **DO** pour what you'll need in a separate cup and discard left-overs

DON'T apply succeeding coats of varnish without first testing hardness. **DO** apply succeeding coats when the varnish resists impression of thumbnail

DON'T apply varnish if chilled—it will be sticky and hard to brush. **DO** warm it by setting the can in hot water (70-90°) and it will level nicely

DAMPENED CLOTH
COATED WITH VARNISH

THEN WRUNG OUT

However careful, dirt specks will get in the finish. These are easily lifted from the wet varnish with a clean sliver of wood tipped with a small ball of burnt varnish to which the specks will cling when touched lightly. Don't wait until the varnish is tacky but remove specks as you go. Burnt varnish consists of varnish, 1 part, melted rosin, 6 parts, well mixed. In use, a drop or two is rolled into a small ball between moistened fingers and placed on a stick. As the specks are lifted from the varnish they are kneaded into the ball

To pick up final traces of dust, the expert uses a "tack rag," which is a cloth moistened with varnish and kept in an airtight can. To make one, dip a cotton handkerchief in warm water, wring out lightly, sprinkle with turpentine and cover with varnish. Wring out until nearly dry

WHAT PRIMER to Select

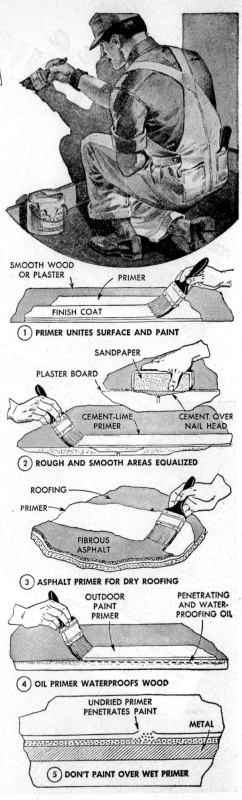

SMOOTH WOOD OR PLASTER — **PRIMER** — **FINISH COAT**

① PRIMER UNITES SURFACE AND PAINT

SANDPAPER — **PLASTER BOARD** — **CEMENT-LIME PRIMER** — **CEMENT OVER NAIL HEAD**

② ROUGH AND SMOOTH AREAS EQUALIZED

ROOFING — **PRIMER** — **FIBROUS ASPHALT**

③ ASPHALT PRIMER FOR DRY ROOFING

OUTDOOR PAINT PRIMER — **PENETRATING AND WATER-PROOFING OIL**

④ OIL PRIMER WATERPROOFS WOOD

UNDRIED PRIMER PENETRATES PAINT — **METAL**

⑤ DON'T PAINT OVER WET PRIMER

SELECTING the right primer for any paint job depends upon the kind of paint you intend to use and the surface to be covered. As shown in Fig. 1, on a smooth, indoor wood or plaster surface, the primer acts as a seal over the work surface, and combines readily with the paint to form a uniform, even finish coat. If, however, the surface is made up of both hard, compact areas and rough, soft spots, such as are produced on plaster board when cemented areas over joints or countersunk nail heads are sanded smooth, Fig. 2, the primer must equalize the surface texture so that when painted the hard areas will not show as slick spots and the rough areas will not absorb the paint and appear as dull blotches. Where oil paint having a lustrous finish is used on such a surface, it is best to apply two primers, one consisting of a cement-lime ingredient to produce a toothy layer that will equalize the surface, and another made up of the proper base ingredients to unite with the paint. Since primers are cheaper than finish paint, it is more economical to use two primer coats than to try to cover an imperfectly-prepared surface with several coats of finish paint.

A primer used on dried-out composition roofs should be some nonfibrous asphalt liquid capable of resaturating the felt, after which a coat of heavy fibrous asphalt is applied, Fig. 3. Under heavy-bodied outdoor paints, primers having greater bonding strength than those applied on indoor work should be used. To gain this additional bonding strength, a primer must be able to penetrate the surface of wood or other porous material, Fig. 4. Therefore, it should contain penetrating and waterproofing oil. A satisfactory primer for metal surfaces must adhere firmly, be waterproof, and provide a suitable base for the finish paint. Also, it must have full drying time. Red lead and outdoor aluminum paint are commonly used over metals. If paint is applied before the primer has dried, the unevaporated, volatile content, sealed underneath by the nonporous metal, will be forced to penetrate the paint layer over it, Fig. 5. The result is a breakdown of the entire paint surface and a spoiled job.

Part 3

ELECTRICITY AND PLUMBING

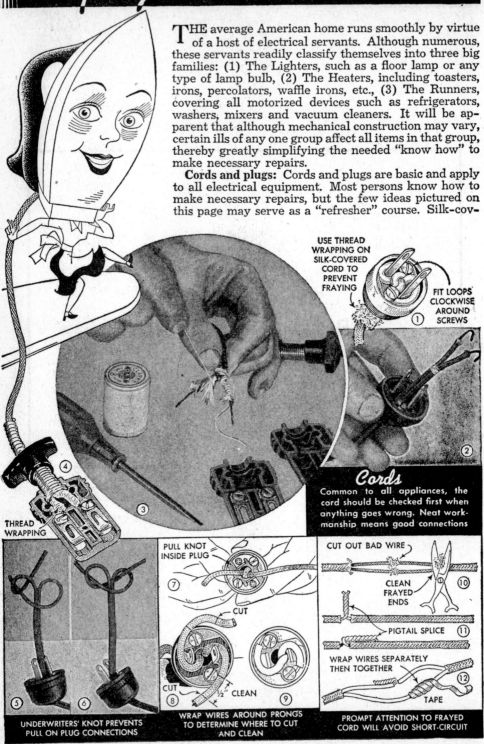

THE average American home runs smoothly by virtue of a host of electrical servants. Although numerous, these servants readily classify themselves into three big families: (1) The Lighters, such as a floor lamp or any type of lamp bulb, (2) The Heaters, including toasters, irons, percolators, waffle irons, etc., (3) The Runners, covering all motorized devices such as refrigerators, washers, mixers and vacuum cleaners. It will be apparent that although mechanical construction may vary, certain ills of any one group affect all items in that group, thereby greatly simplifying the needed "know how" to make necessary repairs.

Cords and plugs: Cords and plugs are basic and apply to all electrical equipment. Most persons know how to make necessary repairs, but the few ideas pictured on this page may serve as a "refresher" course. Silk-cov-

USE THREAD WRAPPING ON SILK-COVERED CORD TO PREVENT FRAYING

FIT LOOPS CLOCKWISE AROUND SCREWS

①

②

THREAD WRAPPING

Cords

Common to all appliances, the cord should be checked first when anything goes wrong. Neat workmanship means good connections

③

④

PULL KNOT INSIDE PLUG

⑦

CUT

CUT OUT BAD WIRE

CLEAN FRAYED ENDS

⑩

PIGTAIL SPLICE

⑪

WRAP WIRES SEPARATELY THEN TOGETHER

⑫

TAPE

CUT

⑧ ½" CLEAN

⑨

⑤ ⑥

UNDERWRITERS' KNOT PREVENTS PULL ON PLUG CONNECTIONS

WRAP WIRES AROUND PRONGS TO DETERMINE WHERE TO CUT AND CLEAN

PROMPT ATTENTION TO FRAYED CORD WILL AVOID SHORT-CIRCUIT

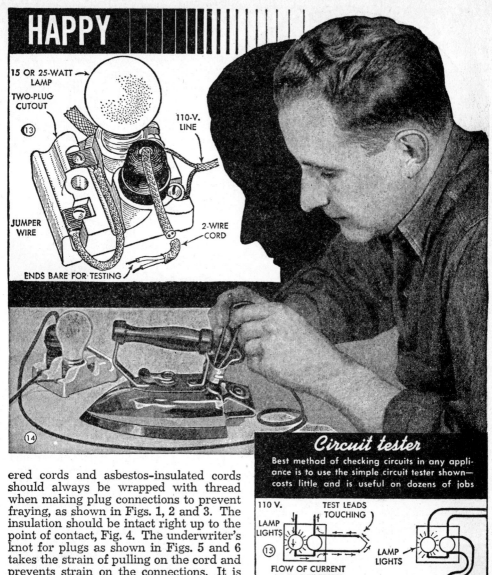

15 OR 25-WATT LAMP

TWO-PLUG CUTOUT

13

110-V. LINE

JUMPER WIRE

2-WIRE CORD

ENDS BARE FOR TESTING

14

Circuit tester

Best method of checking circuits in any appliance is to use the simple circuit tester shown—costs little and is useful on dozens of jobs

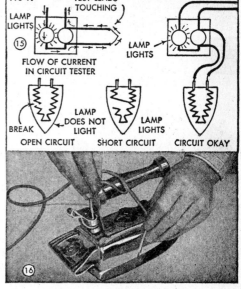

110 V.

TEST LEADS TOUCHING

LAMP LIGHTS

15

FLOW OF CURRENT IN CIRCUIT TESTER

LAMP LIGHTS

BREAK

LAMP DOES NOT LIGHT

OPEN CIRCUIT

LAMP LIGHTS

SHORT CIRCUIT

CIRCUIT OKAY

16

ered cords and asbestos-insulated cords should always be wrapped with thread when making plug connections to prevent fraying, as shown in Figs. 1, 2 and 3. The insulation should be intact right up to the point of contact, Fig. 4. The underwriter's knot for plugs as shown in Figs. 5 and 6 takes the strain of pulling on the cord and prevents strain on the connections. It is especially good with the popular parallel-wire rubber cord. Steps in making plug connections after tying the knot are shown in Figs. 7 and 8. The best practice is to leave the wire long and the insulation intact until actual fitting. Fig. 8 shows where to cut and clean. Fig. 9 shows a plug properly connected—the wire is pulled around the prongs and fitted clockwise under the screw heads. A frayed weak spot in a cord should be spliced promptly instead of waiting until the wire or fuse burns out due to a short circuit. The common splice joint is best made with pigtail splices, as shown in Figs. 10, 11 and 12. Each joint is wrapped separately with friction tape; then the two wires are wrapped together.

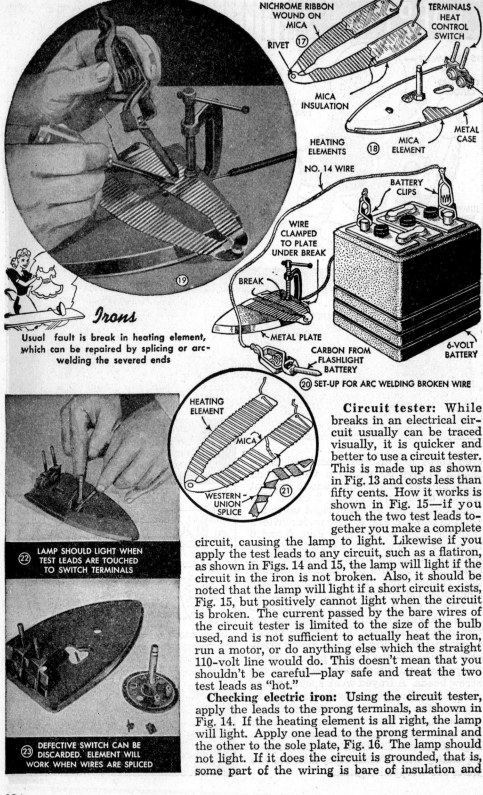

NICHROME RIBBON WOUND ON MICA

RIVET (17)

TERMINALS HEAT CONTROL SWITCH

MICA INSULATION

HEATING ELEMENTS (18) MICA ELEMENT

METAL CASE

NO. 14 WIRE

BATTERY CLIPS

WIRE CLAMPED TO PLATE UNDER BREAK

BREAK

(19)

Irons

Usual fault is break in heating element, which can be repaired by splicing or arc-welding the severed ends

METAL PLATE

CARBON FROM FLASHLIGHT BATTERY

6-VOLT BATTERY

(20) SET-UP FOR ARC WELDING BROKEN WIRE

HEATING ELEMENT

MICA

WESTERN-UNION SPLICE

(21)

(22) LAMP SHOULD LIGHT WHEN TEST LEADS ARE TOUCHED TO SWITCH TERMINALS

(23) DEFECTIVE SWITCH CAN BE DISCARDED. ELEMENT WILL WORK WHEN WIRES ARE SPLICED

Circuit tester: While breaks in an electrical circuit usually can be traced visually, it is quicker and better to use a circuit tester. This is made up as shown in Fig. 13 and costs less than fifty cents. How it works is shown in Fig. 15—if you touch the two test leads together you make a complete circuit, causing the lamp to light. Likewise if you apply the test leads to any circuit, such as a flatiron, as shown in Figs. 14 and 15, the lamp will light if the circuit in the iron is not broken. Also, it should be noted that the lamp will light if a short circuit exists, Fig. 15, but positively cannot light when the circuit is broken. The current passed by the bare wires of the circuit tester is limited to the size of the bulb used, and is not sufficient to actually heat the iron, run a motor, or do anything else which the straight 110-volt line would do. This doesn't mean that you shouldn't be careful—play safe and treat the two test leads as "hot."

Checking electric iron: Using the circuit tester, apply the leads to the prong terminals, as shown in Fig. 14. If the heating element is all right, the lamp will light. Apply one lead to the prong terminal and the other to the sole plate, Fig. 16. The lamp should not light. If it does the circuit is grounded, that is, some part of the wiring is bare of insulation and

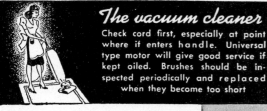

The vacuum cleaner

Check cord first, especially at point where it enters handle. Universal type motor will give good service if kept oiled. Brushes should be inspected periodically and replaced when they become too short

touching the sole plate or cover. No light across the terminals shows that the circuit is broken. In this case, remove the handle, cover, and any other parts necessary to expose the heating element. The most common type of heating element is ribbon Nichrome wire wrapped on mica and insulated on either side with mica, as shown in Fig. 17. Better grade elements are covered with a metal case, Fig. 18, and it is necessary to pry off the case. Still other elements are built right into the sole plate in a solid mold; this type is not repairable except by obtaining a new replacement part.

Patching Nichrome wire: A break in the Nichrome ribbon or wire can be patched by twisting the two ends together, as shown in Fig. 21. A better method is to fuse the broken ends together with a small makeshift arc-welding outfit, as in Figs. 19 and 20. In use, the pointed carbon should be touched to the break delicately and only for an instant. You will get a flash of white hot wire and the two ends will fuse together. Prolonged contact generates too much heat and burns the wire completely. No flux is needed although borax can be used if desired. Sometimes the break is within a few turns of the post terminals, and in this case it is practical simply to unwind the broken section and make a new connection.

Electric-iron switch: If the iron has a heat-control switch, test it across the terminals, as shown in Fig. 22, to determine if the fault is in the heating element or the switch. If the switch is defective and a replacement not available, the iron can be made usable by twisting or welding the two ends together, as indicated in Fig. 23. There is little that can be done with a defective switch; make certain, however, that the thermostatic disk is not jammed open (saucer shape). Try mild pressure with your fingers in manipulating the disk—it should have a curved bell shape when the iron is cold.

Other heater-type appliances: Apply the same general tests as described. Always

㉔ CLEAN COMMUTATOR WITH FINE (8-0) SANDPAPER

㉕ INSPECT BRUSHES AND FIT NEW ONES IF NEEDED

check the cord first (use test lamp and run current through both wires separately), and then proceed systematically until the fault is discovered. Some appliances, such as inexpensive toasters, can be checked visually since the heating element is in full view. Breaks in round Nichrome wire can be spliced much the same as described for ribbon wire. In all cases, press the splice flat and make it as tight as possible—any slight amount of arcing from a loose joint will immediately burn the wire.

Vacuum cleaners: With so many different makes and styles, about the only thing vacuum cleaners have in common is the motor. This is usually a series-wound universal type, a high-speed motor suitable for sweepers, mixers, fans and other light duty applications. If the motor goes bad, the first check point should be the brushes. These can be removed by unscrewing the caps which hold them in place, as shown in Fig. 25. Replace the brushes if they are worn too short. Test the spring tension to make sure that the springs keep the

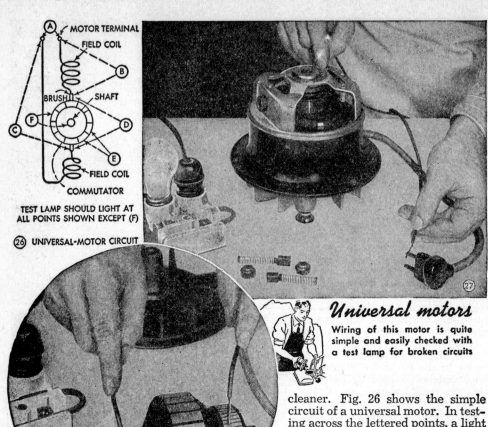

MOTOR TERMINAL
FIELD COIL
BRUSH
SHAFT
COMMUTATOR
FIELD COIL

TEST LAMP SHOULD LIGHT AT
ALL POINTS SHOWN EXCEPT (F)

(26) UNIVERSAL-MOTOR CIRCUIT

Universal motors

Wiring of this motor is quite simple and easily checked with a test lamp for broken circuits

cleaner. Fig. 26 shows the simple circuit of a universal motor. In testing across the lettered points, a light shows that the circuit is continuous. Fig. 27 illustrates test B. A light shows that this field coil is continuous, but although the wiring is intact, the insulation may be burned off. Test D checks the coils of the rotor or armature. If no light is obtained, test each adjacent pair of commutator segments all around, as at E. Each pair should light; no light indicates that the coil is burned out between these two segments. This condition will cause considerable sparking at the commutator, also the motor will be dead if it stops with the dead coil in contact with the brush. A repair job can be done by "jumping" the segments together by soldering a copper wire across the ends. If the test lamp lights when making test F also shown in Fig. 28, insulation has been scraped or burned from armature coil or coils, and the wire is touching the shaft causing a "ground."

When the test lamp does not light when it should, careful inspection should be made of the circuit being tested. Unless the motor is burned out, breaks usually will be found at the ends of the wires and can be repaired. When it is definitely determined that the motor is burned out, it should be junked or turned over to a service shop for rewinding.

brushes in contact with the commutator, (part against which the brushes bear). When replacing old brushes, be sure to fit them properly to the curve of the commutator. If new brushes are fitted, break them in by slipping a piece of fine sandpaper under a brush with the sand facing the end of the brush, then swing the rotor back·and forth until the brush is ground to fit. Clean the commutator with gasoline, or sand it bright with fine (8/0) sandpaper, as shown in Fig. 24. If the commutator is grooved, the rotor should be removed to permit turning the commutator down smooth on the lathe. Other than motor failure, the most common causes of trouble are dirt and lint tightly wound around the motor shaft or the belt-driven brush, lack of oil, and poor bearings.

Universal motors: When checking a vacuum cleaner's universal motor with the test lamp, remove the motor from the

Proper care will make them last longer

Electric iron

Polish bottom with very fine steel wool. Rub frequently with waxed paper. Always plug in at outlet; keep the iron plug in place. If arcing occurs at plug, take plug apart and squeeze contacts lightly with pliers. Keep cord in good condition

Toaster

Have a long bristle brush handy for wiping out crumbs. Never immerse toaster in water—clean only with damp cloth. Breaks in heating element can be repaired the same as described for irons (see text). Never use a fork to remove toast

Refrigerator

Replace door seal if it does not hold sheet of paper with door closed. Keep condenser clean by brushing or vacuum cleaner attachment—dirt and dust make motor run overtime. Allow room at back and over top so that refrigerator can breathe

Coffee maker

Never dip electric parts in water. Percolator has fuse in bottom to prevent overheating if it boils dry—remove with screwdriver and replace if needed. Glass vacuum coffee maker should be cleaned once a week with baking soda in water just as if you were making coffee

Motors

Oil regularly and keep clean so that motor can breathe. See that pulleys are properly aligned and tight on shaft. Be very careful not to stall split phase motors. If motor is universal type, check brushes regularly and clean commutator. Use proper size fuse to protect motor

Washing machine

Don't overload. Always clean after using and release pressure on wringer rolls. If stored in cold place, give it time to warm up in warm location to soften grease in gear case. Be sure that all moving parts are well lubricated. Check periodically for loose bolts and screws

Fuses

Under average conditions, circuits with lights should not have fuses larger than 15 amperes. Convenience outlets take 20 ampere fuses. Large fuses are no protection—the house wiring itself will burn up before the fuse blows. When installing new fuses, play safe—pull the switch

Cords and plugs

If plug does not make contact at outlet, bend prongs slightly outward. Avoid overloading outlets—the maximum load on any one circuit should not exceed 1400 watts. Keep all cords free of kinks. Hang cords on round peg when not in use—don't throw them in a drawer

Lamps

Keep lamp bulbs clean for maximum illumination. Use one large bulb instead of several small ones—a 100-watt lamp gives 50% more light than four 25-watt lamps. Do not use fuses larger than 15 amperes when there are lamps on the circuit. Use proper type of shade

VACUUM CLEANER
Check-up and Repair

PATH OF AIR AND DUST

HANDLE SOCKET

COMMUTATOR

VENTILATING FAN

BRUSHES

MOTOR HOOD — ARMATURE

LAMP

FIELD COIL

BODY

AGITATOR OR BRUSH

BAG

RUBBER BELLOWS

SUCTION FAN

BELT

WHEELS

Courtesy The Hoover Company

① CROSS SECTION OF VACUUM CLEANER

By Vito W. Mazzara

ALTHOUGH a vacuum cleaner is one of the most reliable mechanical devices in the home, there comes a time when it needs servicing and minor repairs—if for no other reason than to keep it in top-notch working condition. In doing its job of collecting dirt in the dust container, certain parts of the cleaner take plenty of punishment. Cut a cleaner in half, as in Fig. 1, so you can view it "in section," as the draftsman calls it, and it looks like a complicated piece of machinery. But in reality its operation and its parts are quite simple. Essentially it consists of a centrifugal suction fan, a dust bag or container, a suction nozzle and a small electric motor which drives the fan. And that's all, except a handle perhaps, a light to illuminate dark corners and, on certain types such as that in Fig. 1, small wheels and casters for easy maneuverability. Most cleaners of this particular type also are fitted with an agitator brush, its purpose being to loosen embedded dirt so that it can be picked up by the air stream. This brush and the dust bag or container are the two parts requiring the most frequent attention. When emptying the bag, the directions furnished by the manufacturer of the cleaner should be carefully followed, of course, but a common procedure is to hold the bag over a sheet of paper with the open end down, place your feet on the corners of the frame and shake the bag vigorously, as in Fig. 2. Turn the bag inside out occasionally and carefully brush off the accumulated film of fine dust. Never wash the bag as this will likely destroy its properties of dust retention.

The agitator brush should be removed occasionally and thoroughly cleaned. Lint, thread and string often wind so tightly on this brush that it's impossible to untangle the mass. But you can cut through the strands with shears and remove them with a comb as in Fig. 4. Be careful not to break the bristles of the brush. Check the length of

② EMPTY THE BAG AFTER EVERY CLEANING

③ IF PLUG DOES NOT MAKE CONTACT, BEND PRONGS OUTWARD SLIGHTLY

④ CUT TANGLED THREAD WITH SHEARS AND REMOVE WITH COMB

⑤ CHECK LENGTH OF BRISTLES BY LAYING CARD ACROSS NOZZLE

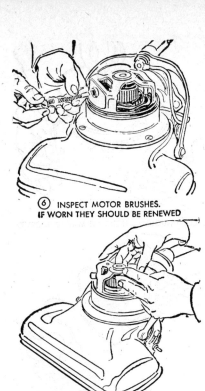

(6) INSPECT MOTOR BRUSHES.
IF WORN THEY SHOULD BE RENEWED

(7) EXAMINE THE COMMUTATOR AND
CLEAN WITH FINE (8-0) SANDPAPER

(8)
A TEST LAMP IS USED TO CHECK FOR "OPEN"
CIRCUIT IN FIELD OR ARMATURE COILS

the bristles occasionally as in Fig. 5. Also check the agitator belt tension to see that there is no slippage.

Sometimes a cleaner will start and stop at intervals when the switch is turned on, or it may simply refuse to run. When this happens the first part to examine is the plug, Fig. 3. Usually you'll find that the plug is loose in the receptacle and this means that the prongs are making only intermittent contact. The remedy is to bend the prongs outward slightly, or if the prongs are unusually loose when inserted in the receptacle it often helps to bend the ends of the prongs with pliers.

At long intervals it will be necessary to replace worn motor brushes, Fig. 6. Unscrew the brush caps and examine the brushes occasionally. Handle brushes carefully and be sure to return them to the sockets exactly as they were taken out. Don't turn the brush over. A commutator in good condition should be reasonably clean with the brush track somewhat darker in color. If the track is pitted, burned or coated, the brushes are not making proper contact. This causes arcing and results in a rough commutator surface, which of course grows worse with continued use. The remedy depends on the condition of the parts. Sometimes merely cleaning the commutator surface with fine sandpaper as in Fig. 7 will be sufficient. However, if it is rough and pitted or grooved, then, if tests show the motor otherwise in good condition, it will pay to have the commutator trued up and the mica undercut by a competent service shop. Whenever you have the cleaner apart for any reason, give the fan a thorough going over. There might be a cracked or bent blade or maybe a piece broken out as in Fig. 9. This will cause vibration which in turn greatly accelerates wear. If any of the blades are cracked or broken, a new fan is the surest remedy.

If you suspect there's need to check over the cleaner electrically, then make up the simple circuit tester detailed in Fig. 10. Begin by plugging the cleaner cord into the tester and turning the switch to the "off" position. If the lamp lights there's a short somewhere in the cleaner. Check switch cords and leads to the motor to locate it. If, on the other hand, the lamp does not light with the switch in the "off" position, snap it to the "on" position. If the lamp still does not light, there's a short somewhere along the line of the electrical circuit. Check the plug for breakage or loose wire connections, also

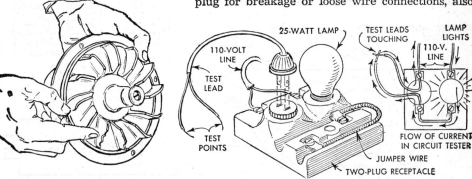

25-WATT LAMP
TEST LEADS TOUCHING
LAMP LIGHTS
110-VOLT LINE
110-V. LINE
TEST LEAD
TEST POINTS
FLOW OF CURRENT IN CIRCUIT TESTER
JUMPER WIRE
TWO-PLUG RECEPTACLE

(9) BROKEN FAN BLADES WILL CAUSE
VIBRATION AND WEAR ON MOTOR BEARINGS

(10) A SIMPLE CIRCUIT TESTER FOR CHECKING
CIRCUITS IN ANY ELECTRICAL APPLIANCE

the wires to the cleaner switch plate. Shake the cord all along its length and note if the lamp flickers at any point. If nothing happens, disconnect the cord from the motor, twist the wires together and plug the cord into the circuit tester. The lamp will light if the cord and switch are intact.

To test for open circuit in field or armature coils proceed as in Figs. 8 and 12. The lamp will light unless there is a burned or open field coil. If turning the fan slowly, Fig. 12, produces a uniform flicker of the light, everything is okay. But if the flicker is unsteady, turn slowly to find a point where the lamp goes out. Ordinarily this will indicate an opened commutator segment.

To test field coils proceed as in Fig. 14, connecting the complete set in series across the line voltage and measuring the voltage drop across each coil. A low reading indicates a short in the coil being tested. Fig. 15 shows the circuit of a universal motor, a common type in vacuum cleaners. Fig. 11 illustrates tests B and C, shown diagrammatically in Fig. 15. Although a light shows that the coil being tested is continuous, the insulation may be burned off. Test D, Figs. 12 and 15, checks coils of the rotor or armature. If the lamp does not light then test each adjacent pair of commutator segments as at E, Fig. 15. No light indicates that the coil is burned out between those two segments. The motor will not start if it should stop when a brush is in contact with the dead coil. If the test lamp lights when making the test F in Fig. 15, illustrated in Fig. 13, insulation has been scraped or burned from the armature coil, or coils, and the armature is grounded to the shaft.

If the test lamp fails to respond when it should light, make a careful inspection of the particular circuit you are testing. Unless the motor is burned out or otherwise damaged, making replacement of the whole unit necessary, breaks usually will be found near the ends of the wires where it is easy to make a lasting repair. Generally the cord is the first offender. When you coil or uncoil it from the cord brackets on the cleaner be careful not to kink it. If you should happen to pull out a sharp kink you may break the strands of one or both the wires as well as the insulation. Other than the cord, most repairs are necessary only after a long period of hard service, unless of course the cleaner is damaged. Often it's a question of deciding which to do, repair the damaged part or renew it entirely.

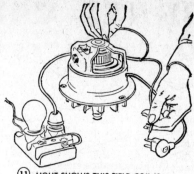

(11) LIGHT SHOWS THIS FIELD COIL IS CONTINUOUS ALTHOUGH IT MAY BE SHORTED

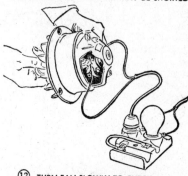

(12) TURN FAN SLOWLY TO CHECK ARMATURE COILS FOR "OPEN" CIRCUIT

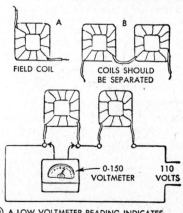

(13) LIGHT HERE INDICATES THE ARMATURE COIL IS GROUNDED TO THE SHAFT

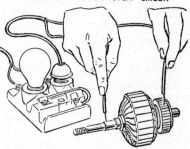

FIELD COIL   COILS SHOULD BE SEPARATED

0-150 VOLTMETER   110 VOLTS

(14) A LOW VOLTMETER READING INDICATES A SHORT CIRCUIT IN THE FIELD COIL

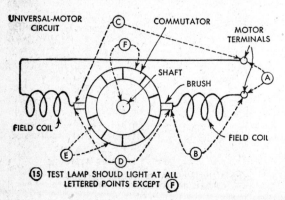

UNIVERSAL-MOTOR CIRCUIT — COMMUTATOR — MOTOR TERMINALS — SHAFT — BRUSH — FIELD COIL — FIELD COIL

(15) TEST LAMP SHOULD LIGHT AT ALL LETTERED POINTS EXCEPT (F)

BRASS CANDLE SCONCE
gives emergency light

WHEN STORMS damage the power lines and leave you in the dark, you'll appreciate this attractive candle sconce to furnish an emergency light while service is being restored. It consists of a chimney of eight strips of glass held vertically by two bands of hammered brass, part A, the bands being attached to an oval plaque of fancy wood. Four of the glass strips measure 1 x 8 in. and the others are cut about 1 in. shorter. Each one is drilled for attaching to the bands with short machine screws. One of the best ways to drill glass is with a piece of rod chucked in a drill press. Putty is used around the hole to retain an abrasive mixture of turpentine and emery which is used to grind through the glass. Parts B, C and D are cut according to the patterns and assembled in the order given. Drip cup, C, is formed over the edge of a wooden disk as shown in the photo.

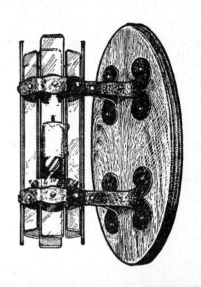

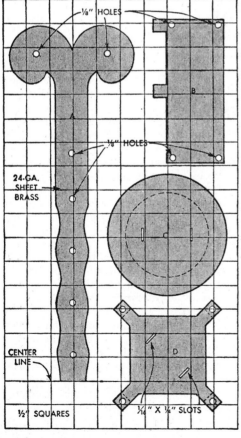

⅛" HOLES

⅛" HOLES

24-GA. SHEET BRASS

CENTER LINE

½" SQUARES

¹⁄₁₆" X ¼" SLOTS

A

B

C

D

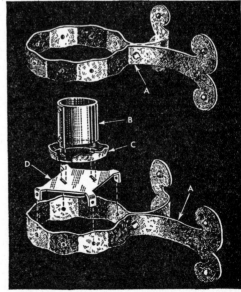

A

B

C

D

A

ELECTRIC WIRING

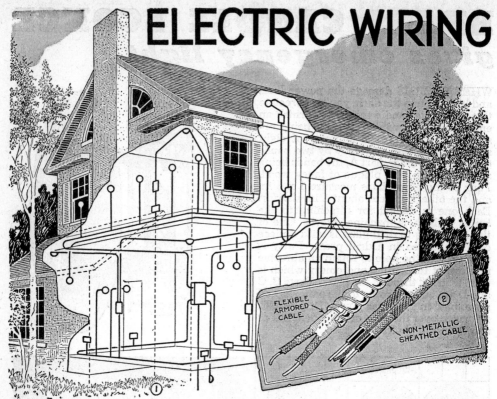

FLEXIBLE ARMORED CABLE

NON-METALLIC SHEATHED CABLE

PART I

Planning the Installation and Arranging for Service Connections

By C. A. CROWLEY

WHEN wiring old houses or adding new convenience outlets in houses already wired, it is first of all a job of careful planning to determine all the requirements including the location of the outlets, materials to use, wire size, load distribution and other factors. Then, it is just as important to do the work entirely in accordance with approved wiring practice to meet electrical and safety requirements.

Materials: For wiring an old house, the most convenient materials to use are armored cable, commonly known as B-X, and non-metallic sheathed cable, Fig. 2. General installation methods are the same for both. Knob-and-tube and conduit installations are more difficult in finished buildings and will not be considered as they occasion considerable damage to walls and floors. Also, knob-and-tube work is not permitted in many localities.

Code Requirements: The National Electrical Code, published by the National Board of Fire Underwriters, gives minimum requirements for safe electrical installations. All recommendations contained in these articles are in accord with the national code. However, some localities have additional restrictions and one should find out about these before undertaking a wiring job.

Types of Service: Service supplied by the power company may be alternating or direct current, usually the former at between 110 and 120 volts. Before making any plans, find out what type of service is to be used. In the case of both a.c. and d.c. there are two types of service commonly furnished; two-wire and three-wire. Fig. 3 shows the difference. Most power companies supply three-wire service, except for very small installations. The power company will install lines up to the house. From that point on the service connections (lines to the fuse boxes, including switches, meter, etc.,) are usually installed at the expense of the owner. The power company

in the HOME

lays down specifications as to type and size of equipment and its location.

Service Connections: The easiest, and in most cases the required, method will be to inclose the wires from the power line inside rigid conduit, which is a special smooth pipe designed for holding electric wires. It must be galvanized. Conduit of the 1-in. size should be used for three No. 8 wires; ¾-in. conduit will take two No. 8 wires. The conduit is run outside the building, where it is secured with pipe straps. A service cap of the type shown is installed at the top to keep out water. The conduit is bent into a curve of large radius where it enters the building as shown in Fig. 4.

All convenience outlets should be spaced the same distance from the floor for uniformity of appearance

The meter and main switch and fuses are often located in the basement, as close as possible to the service entrance. In some localities it is customary to install the meter outside the house to facilitate inspection, in which case special exterior equipment is required, which

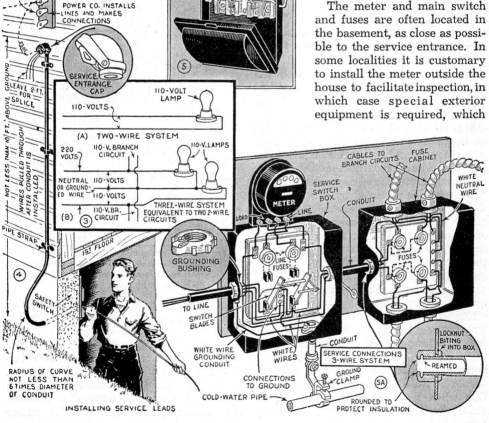

143

Table I. As pointed out before, the power company will generally specify this part of the equipment.

Two-Wire and Three-Wire Connections: Typical service connections for two and three-wire 110-volt a.c. or d.c. are shown in Figs. 5A and 7. The connections to ground, and the use of white and black wires should be noted in particular. The white wire always should be grounded for convenience in tracing. Grounding of all electric conduits and boxes is a matter of safety as it automatically causes a fuse to blow if a live wire accidentally touches exposed metal parts, thus preventing dangerous shock and possible fires. For

Effective grounding is accomplished by connecting a conduit from the switch box to a cold-water pipe by means of a special clamp

can be determined by consulting with the power company. For a basement installation, a board is nailed to the wall for mounting these units. The end of the conduit is cut off and threaded, leaving about ⅜ in. to extend inside the switch box. After the conduit has been cut, it should be carefully reamed to remove all burrs. One of the numerous round depressions called "knockouts" is removed by a sharp blow with a screwdriver or hammer, and the hole is reamed. An approved safety-switch of the general type shown in Fig. 5 must be used. A locknut is put on the end of the conduit, the box is put in place, and a bushing is screwed onto the end of the conduit, as shown in a detail of Fig. 5A. The locknut is then tightened.

The wires are fished through the conduit by passing a light wire through the conduit, attaching the wires to it, and pulling them through. Usually, for average-size homes, the wires for service connections should be No. 8 rubber-and-cloth covered. One white and one or two black wires should be used. This size wire will carry a maximum load of 30 amperes. For larger loads, larger feeders are required. See

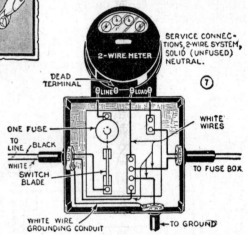

TABLE I—SERVICE CONNECTIONS

Wire Size	Fuse Size, Amperes	Max. Load (Watts at 115 V.)	Minimum Conduit Size (in inches) 3-wire	2-wire	1-wire*
8 Type R	40	4600	¾	¾	½
8 Type RH	45	5175	¾	¾	½
6 Type R	55	6325	1	1	½
6 Type RH	65	7475	1	1	½
4 Type R	70	8050	1**	1**	½
4 Type RH	85	9775	1**	1**	½

* For grounding wire only, when required.

** If a service run exceeds 50 feet and includes more than the equivalent of two quarter bends, 1¼-inch conduit must be used.

grounding, a conduit is run from the switch box to a water pipe and clamped to the pipe with a ground clamp of the type shown in Fig. 6. A single No. 8 white wire is run inside this pipe and securely fastened to the terminal provided at the pipe. A No. 8 copper wire should be fastened to this conduit and the power-line conduit. The grounding bushing, detail of 5A, makes this easy. The wire inside the ground conduit is attached to the proper terminal.

Fuses and Meter Connections: The main-line fuses should be installed in the box with the service switch. For most homes 30-amp. fuses are required. The connections to the meter are usually made by the power company. A short length of conduit can be run from the line-switch box to the fuse cabinet, and the wires can be pulled through readily. Bushings and locknuts must be used. The fuse box or cabinet contains one fuse for each branch circuit. The neutral or grounded wire is continuous or unfused at all points. However, some localities require fusing the neutral wire also. The "hot" wires (black wires) are fused in all cases as shown. When a fuse blows, the reason should be located and eliminated. A fuse block for a four-branch-circuit installation is shown in the circular insert above Fig. 10, while methods of wiring are shown in details A, B and C of Fig. 10. It is wise to get a fuse box larger than needed, to provide for future expansion.

Survey of Needs: Next determine the number and location of electrical outlets. By an outlet is meant any point at which

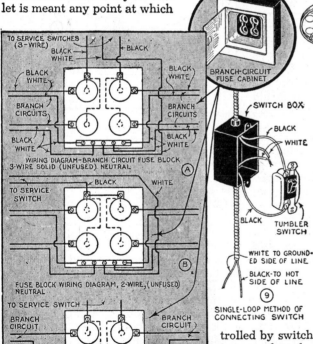

ARMORED CABLE TO SWITCH — ARMORED CABLE TO LINE

CEILING OUTLET BOX
BLACK FROM SWITCH TO FIXTURE
WHITE FROM LINE TO FIXTURE

SPLICED { WHITE FROM SWITCH
BLACK FROM LINE

SWITCH BOX

SWITCH

⑧

DOUBLE-LOOP METHOD OF CONNECTING SWITCH

ARMORED CABLE

WIRES FOR CONNECTING FIXTURE

CEILING OUTLET BOX

The double-loop and single-loop methods of connecting wall switches to outlets are shown in Figs. 8 and 9

BRANCH-CIRCUIT FUSE CABINET

SWITCH BOX
BLACK
WHITE

BLACK   TUMBLER SWITCH

WHITE TO GROUNDED SIDE OF LINE
BLACK TO HOT SIDE OF LINE

⑨

SINGLE-LOOP METHOD OF CONNECTING SWITCH

TO SERVICE SWITCHES (3-WIRE)
BLACK
WHITE
BLACK
BLACK WHITE
BLACK WHITE
BRANCH CIRCUITS
BRANCH CIRCUITS
BLACK WHITE
BLACK WHITE
WIRING DIAGRAM—BRANCH CIRCUIT FUSE BLOCK 3-WIRE SOLID (UNFUSED) NEUTRAL   Ⓐ

TO SERVICE SWITCH
BLACK   WHITE
FUSE BLOCK WIRING DIAGRAM, 2-WIRE, (UNFUSED) NEUTRAL   Ⓑ

TO SERVICE SWITCH
BRANCH CIRCUIT
BRANCH CIRCUIT
Ⓒ
⑩
FUSE BLOCK WIRING DIAGRAM 2-WIRE, BOTH SIDES FUSED

electricity can be drawn from the line. This includes lighting fixtures, heating devices and machines that are permanently attached to the line, and convenience outlets for attaching portable lamps and apparatus. Switches are not counted as outlets. It is best to be rather liberal in planning outlets. There is no reason for omitting lights in any room, even closets. All ceiling lamps should be controlled by wall switches. Lights on stairways should be controlled by switches at top and bottom. Convenience outlets should be spaced about one every 10 ft. of wall space (counting doors and windows), in living rooms, and usually 15 to 20 ft. in bedrooms and dining room. It is best to locate them where particularly needed. Generally they are placed just above the baseboard. At least

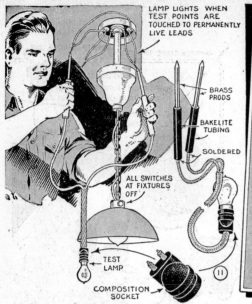

LAMP LIGHTS WHEN TEST POINTS ARE TOUCHED TO PERMANENTLY LIVE LEADS

BRASS PRODS

BAKELITE TUBING

SOLDERED

ALL SWITCHES AT FIXTURES OFF

TEST LAMP

COMPOSITION SOCKET

⑪

Locating live wires with test-prod-and-lamp assembly when adding new outlets to a branch circuit

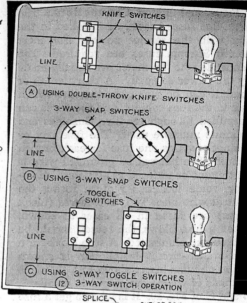

KNIFE SWITCHES

LINE

(A) USING DOUBLE-THROW KNIFE SWITCHES

3-WAY SNAP SWITCHES

LINE

(B) USING 3-WAY SNAP SWITCHES

TOGGLE SWITCHES

LINE

(C) USING 3-WAY TOGGLE SWITCHES
⑫ 3-WAY SWITCH OPERATION

TABLE II—WIRE SIZE FOR BRANCH CIRCUITS

Wire Size	Max. Safe Load Watts—115 V.	Use Fuse Size Amps.
14	1725	15
12	2300	20
10	3450	30
6	5750	50

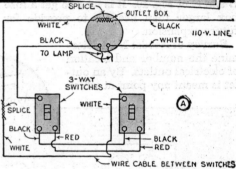

SPLICE
OUTLET BOX
WHITE
BLACK
110-V. LINE
BLACK
WHITE
TO LAMP

3-WAY SWITCHES
WHITE
SPLICE
BLACK
WHITE
RED
BLACK
WHITE
BLACK
RED

(A)

WIRE CABLE BETWEEN SWITCHES

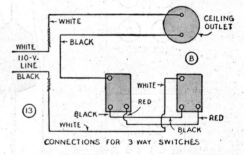

WHITE
BLACK
CEILING OUTLET

WHITE
110-V. LINE
BLACK

(B)

WHITE
RED
BLACK
WHITE
BLACK
RED
BLACK

⑬

CONNECTIONS FOR 3 WAY SWITCHES

two outlets should be provided in the kitchen and outlets in the basement should be located to care for washing machine, iron, mangle and workshop.

Branch Circuits: Each branch circuit usually feeds a number of outlets. In most homes all branch circuits are wired with No. 14 wire. The load on each branch circuit is therefore limited by the carrying capacity of this size wire, or to 15 amperes. In planning branch circuits, therefore, it is wise to limit the possible demand to a value below 15 amps. As most electrical appliances are rated according to power consumption in watts, and volts times amperes equal watts, the maximum safe load for No. 14 wires is 115 times 15, or 1725 watts. Generally circuits are designed for an estimated load of 1200 watts at most, as required in many cities. Frequently it is also required that no branch circuit include more than twelve outlets.

Generally it has been found that independent circuits should be used for the following devices or groups of devices: Oil burners; laundry lights and outlet for washing machine or mangle; workshop lights and outlets for power-driven tools; refrigerator; any heating appliance drawing more than 1000 watts; any apparatus with larger than ¼-hp. motor. Should any appliance draw more than 1500 watts, larger wire as specified in Table II will be required for its circuit.

In three-wire systems it is quite important that the load be balanced or evenly distributed between the two legs of the circuit. There is a complete 110-volt circuit between each hot wire (black wire) and the grounded wire (white wire) of a three-wire system. The loads on these two legs should be approximately equal.

Connecting Wall Switches: There are two methods of connecting wall switches. In the double-loop method, Fig. 8, the hot and grounded wires are led into the outlet box. A cable is run from the outlet box to the wall switch and is connected as shown. Note particularly the use of the different colors of wire. The hot wire to the outlet box is black as usual. This is connected to the white wire leading to the switch. The black wire from the switch, which is hot when the switch is closed, and the white or grounded wire are then connected to the fixture.

The single loop is an alternative method which can be used where the double loop would be inconvenient. For example, if the lead to a fixture passes right past the site for the switch; or if the lead to a fixture must be brought up from below. Connections are made as shown in Fig. 9. The hot wire is broken before it comes into the outlet box.

Use of Three-Way Switches: Three-way switches are installed to act as illustrated in Fig. 12. They are always used in pairs so that lights may be turned on or off independently at two locations. The color scheme for single and double loop methods of connecting this type of switching circuit is shown in Fig. 13.

Locating Live Leads: When adding new outlets to a branch circuit, it is necessary to locate live wires into which the new lines can be tapped. To accomplish this, first open the switch at the meter, and then open an outlet box that you think will offer the desired leads. The tape is removed and the wires are separated carefully so that there is space of at least an inch between them and no chance of their touching each other. Then the main switch is closed and all other switches turned off. Each pair of wires is now touched with the prods of a test lamp, as in Fig. 11. If the lamp lights, the two wires it is touching are permanently hot and will serve as a starting point for the new connections.

❡ If you have trouble with your windows sticking during the winter months, apply a small amount of liquid wax where the sash slides in the frame.

❡ A handful of salt thrown at the base of a flame caused by burning grease will extinguish it quickly.

Toggle Bolts Anchor Outlet Box in Soft Wallboard

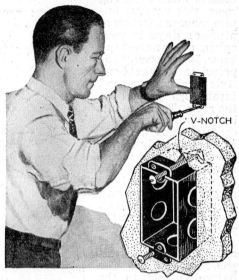

V-NOTCH

One man solved the problem of installing electrical outlet boxes in walls paneled with soft wallboard by anchoring the boxes with small toggle bolts instead of wood screws, which, of course, couldn't be made to hold firmly in wallboard. The openings for the boxes were cut slightly oversize and then V-notched at the top and bottom to take the toggle part of the bolt. The notches were aligned with holes in the mounting brackets and then both box and bolts were slipped into the opening at the same time, thus getting the toggle in position to grip the wallboard at the rear when the bolts were tightened. The outlet surface plate covers the notches.

Polarity Tester for Electric Current

A simple polarity tester can be made from two small copper rods and a glass jar that measures 2 to 3 in. across the top. Select a cork that will fit the jar and slot opposite sides of the cork to take the copper rods. Dissolve 1½ teaspoonfuls of table salt in a cup of water and pour into the jar. Adjust the rods so they just touch the liquid, and hold the bared ends of the wires in the circuit against the ends of the rods. The rod that sparks is positive side of circuit.

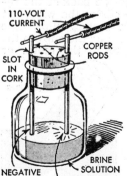

110-VOLT CURRENT
COPPER RODS
SLOT IN CORK
BRINE SOLUTION
NEGATIVE
POSITIVE ELECTRODE SPARKS

Suspended from the ceiling of a studio living room or informal dining room, this unusual fixture conveys a feeling of pioneer days to your cabin or ranch-type home. It's especially appropriate if western-style architecture and furnishings prevail in the room. The yoke can be bandsawed from a 2 or 3-in.-thick piece of wood, preferably oak, to the size indicated in the squared pattern. The bows may be bent by steaming them and clamping in shape, and they are fastened to the yoke by means of wedges, as shown. Hickory, if available, is excellent wood for the bows. The fixture is held to the ceiling with two lengths of chain which are attached to eyes in the yoke. Although these parts on the original were taken from an old lighting fixture, threaded brass tubing and eyes can be purchased for this purpose. The yoke is drilled to take the tubing and the eyes for the chain and light are turned on each end of this. Then, a lantern-type light, which is attached to the lower eye, is wired through the tubing and along the

Oxen-Yoke Ceiling Fixture for Dining Room Imparts Pioneer Atmosphere to Ranch Home

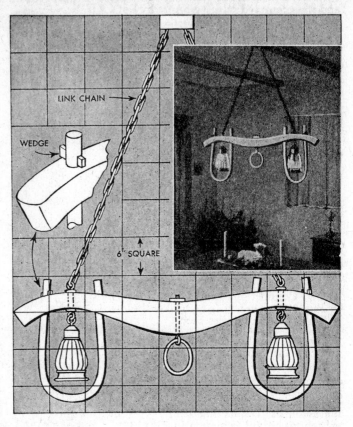

LINK CHAIN

WEDGE

6" SQUARE

chain to the ceiling outlet. Finally, a large iron ring is bolted through the center of the yoke.

Flashlight Used as Trouble Lamp

You can make good use of an old flashlight by converting it into an auto trouble light. After the cells have been removed, solder a wire to the end of the bulb and another to the back of the reflector. The other ends of the wires are fitted with radio or battery clips. The light is used by attaching the clips to the battery terminals, or to the motor or frame and any "hot-wire" terminals. The wires should be long enough so that the light, a 6-volt bulb, will reach any part of car. When not using, store wires and clips in flashlight case.

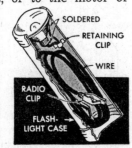

SOLDERED

RETAINING CLIP

WIRE

RADIO CLIP

FLASH-LIGHT CASE

Pipe Cleaner Used as Lighter Wick

As a substitute for a standard wick, a pipe cleaner can be used in some cigarette lighters. Coil the cleaner inside the windshield and insert the end in the wick hole. It will be necessary to shorten the cleaner. Be sure not to obstruct the small holes in the shield when coiling the wick.

CIGARETTE LIGHTER

PIPE CLEANER

❡ If the V-belt on a refrigerator unit is slipping or making noise, the trouble can be corrected in some cases by rubbing a little naphtha laundry soap on the sides of the belt while the unit is running. When working around a unit in operation, watch your tie or loose clothing.

ELECTRIC WIRING *in the* HOME

PART II

Installing the Equipment

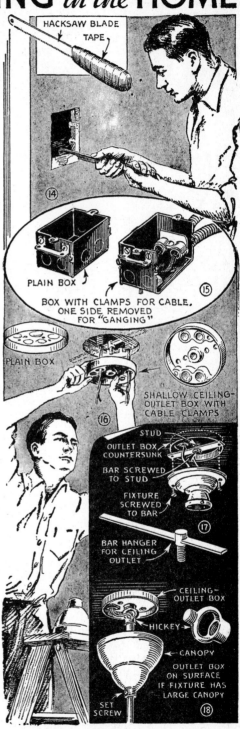

HACKSAW BLADE
TAPE

⑭

PLAIN BOX

BOX WITH CLAMPS FOR CABLE.
ONE SIDE REMOVED FOR "GANGING"

⑮

PLAIN BOX

SHALLOW CEILING-
OUTLET BOX WITH
CABLE CLAMPS

⑯

STUD
OUTLET BOX
COUNTERSUNK
BAR SCREWED
TO STUD
FIXTURE
SCREWED
TO BAR

⑰

BAR HANGER
FOR CEILING
OUTLET

CEILING-
OUTLET BOX

HICKEY

CANOPY

OUTLET BOX
ON SURFACE
IF FIXTURE HAS
LARGE CANOPY

SET
SCREW

⑱

ALTHOUGH the switch and outlet boxes are not installed until after the cables have been pulled through partitions and floors, it will be necessary to locate the exact position of the switch and outlet boxes first, and then to make the wall and ceiling openings. In this way the cables can be pulled from one opening to the next, and the ends of the cable left extending from the openings for later testing and subsequent attachment of the boxes.

Openings for Outlet Boxes: Switch boxes may be used singly or a number of them can be combined side by side which is called "ganging." In the latter case the sides of the boxes are removed and the remaining portions attached together to form a single large box. Whether the wall opening is to accommodate one switch box or a number of them, the procedure of cutting an opening just large enough, and no larger, is the same. First locate the approximate position between two studs, carefully drill a hole in the wall and remove just enough plaster to find the opening between laths. Then, mark the outline of the box on the wall with a pencil so that one lath will cross the center. Then, with a hacksaw blade, carefully cut out a section of this lath along the pencil marks and saw into the adjacent ones just enough to form a hole to take the box, Fig. 14, so that the small tabs at the top and bottom of the box can be screwed to the uncut portions of lath. The hacksaw blade should be used so that it cuts on the pull stroke.

To install a ceiling outlet box, the most common types of which are shown in Fig. 16, use a bar hanger of the type shown in Fig. 17. A wire is fastened to the movable stud and the bar is pushed through a hole in the ceiling, after which the wire is used to pull the stud back to project through the opening. The hanger is turned so that the bar lies across the lath, which will distribute the load. The outlet box is to be attached to this stud as in Fig. 16. The box may or may not be countersunk in the

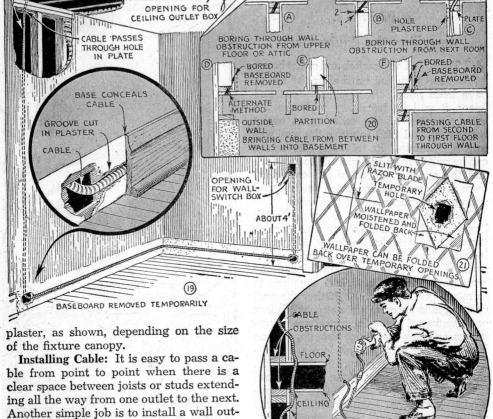

CABLE PARALLEL TO JOIST AND STUDS

OPENING FOR CEILING OUTLET BOX

CABLE PASSES THROUGH HOLE IN PLATE

BORED FOR CABLE HOLE IN FLOOR PLUGGED

FLOOR

CABLE

A

2 1

B

HOLE PLASTERED

PLATE

C

BORING THROUGH WALL OBSTRUCTION FROM UPPER FLOOR OR ATTIC

BORING THROUGH WALL OBSTRUCTION FROM NEXT ROOM

D

BORED BASEBOARD REMOVED

E

F

BORED BASEBOARD REMOVED

ALTERNATE METHOD

BORED PARTITION

20

PASSING CABLE FROM SECOND TO FIRST FLOOR THROUGH WALL

OUTSIDE WALL

BRINGING CABLE FROM BETWEEN WALLS INTO BASEMENT

BASE CONCEALS CABLE

GROOVE CUT IN PLASTER

CABLE

OPENING FOR WALL-SWITCH BOX

ABOUT 4'

SLIT WITH RAZOR BLADE

TEMPORARY HOLE

WALLPAPER MOISTENED AND FOLDED BACK

WALLPAPER CAN BE FOLDED BACK OVER TEMPORARY OPENINGS

21

19

BASEBOARD REMOVED TEMPORARILY

CABLE OBSTRUCTIONS

FLOOR

CEILING

HOLES PLASTERED

WALL

CABLE AROUND OBSTRUCTIONS WHEN TOO DIFFICULT TO GO THROUGH

22

plaster, as shown, depending on the size of the fixture canopy.

Installing Cable: It is easy to pass a cable from point to point when there is a clear space between joists or studs extending all the way from one outlet to the next. Another simple job is to install a wall outlet on the first floor, as you can usually drop the cable down into the basement where it is connected to the nearest outlet box. But where the cable must cross studs as in Fig. 19, you can either drop into the basement or you can run the cable behind the baseboard, removing plaster to form a groove for the cable. To drop the cable into the basement you will have to pass it through the partition plate. Two methods of doing this are shown in details D and E of Fig. 20. To pass the cable through partition plates at the ceiling as in Fig. 19, it may be possible to drill this hole from above, as in detail A of Fig. 20. The hole can be plugged later. Otherwise the method shown in details B and C, Fig. 20, can be followed. To do this, first slit the wallpaper as in Fig. 21, fold the paper back and make a hole large enough so that you can insert the bore at an angle to go through the plate. Then drill a second hole straight

across at the bottom but only partly through the sill, after which the cable can be passed through the plate easily as in detail C of Fig. 20.

When passing a wire from one floor to another, it may be necessary to go through a sill and plate as in detail F of Fig. 20. When encountering other forms of obstructions, it is sometimes possible to run the cable exposed through attics, and in closets where exposed cable is not objectionable. For example, Fig. 22 shows a cable run around the obstruction that was drilled through in detail F of Fig. 20. In some cases the baseboard can be removed and the cable can be hidden behind it where it comes up through the floor, making it even less noticeable.

In pulling cables from point to point, you will find a "fish wire" handy. This is first passed through the channel and then the attached cable is pulled through. Any fairly stiff wire will be suitable. In some cases it is necessary to use two lengths of fish wire as in Fig. 26. In this case one length is pushed into the opening at the ceiling and pulled out at the baseboard opening. A hook is formed on the end of this wire and pushed up through the hole in the sill. A hook is also formed on the end of the second wire, which is pushed down from the top. The two wires must be hooked together, which may require some effort and patience. Then by pulling at the upper outlet and guiding the wire at the other openings, it is possible to pull the hooked joint out at the top, which leaves a continuous length of wire between outlets. Besides

END OF WIRE BENT BACK
WIRES TIGHTLY TWISTED, THEN SOLDERED
END OF INSULATION TAPERED,
RUBBER TAPE
JOINT SOLDERED
COVER WITH RUBBER TAPE
FINISH WITH TWO LAYERS OF FRICTION TAPE
(24) TAPING A PIGTAIL SPLICE

HACK SAW AT RIGHT ANGLES TO METAL STRIP
CUTTING ARMORED CABLE
(25)

the use of fish wires, ordinary furnace chain is useful for pulling up wires through partitions. It is dropped down from an upper opening and the lower end is pulled through sill holes by means of short wire hooks, after which the wires of the cable are attached and the cable is pulled up.

A length of cable long enough to reach from one outlet to the other, with a couple of feet surplus, is cut next. The manner of cutting B-X is shown in Fig. 25. Nonmetallic cable is cut with a sharp knife. The wires are cut with a pair of side-cutting pliers. The end of the cable is fastened securely to the end of the fish wire and it is then fed in at one opening while the wire is pulled at the other opening and guided at temporary openings between the two. The entire cable is pulled in leaving only about 8 or 10 in. for connections at the outlets.

Connecting Cable to Boxes: After all cables have been located and their ends project from the holes, the switch and outlet boxes are installed. Each box has a number of "knock-outs" and the required number of these must be removed by striking them with a ball-peen hammer.

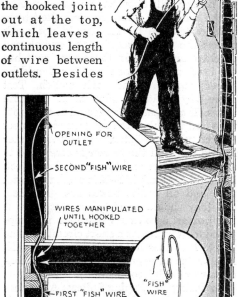

OPENING FOR OUTLET
SECOND "FISH" WIRE
WIRES MANIPULATED UNTIL HOOKED TOGETHER
FIRST "FISH" WIRE INSERTED HERE
"FISH" WIRE
(26)
BASEBOARD OPENING AT WHICH CABLE IS FED IN

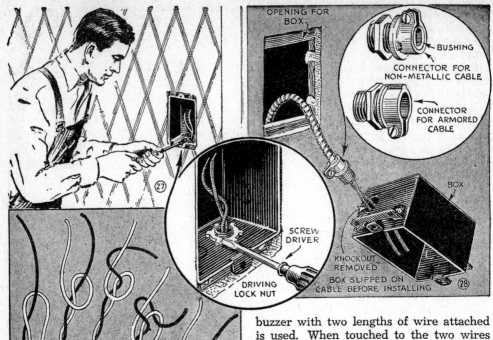

OPENING FOR BOX

BUSHING

CONNECTOR FOR NON-METALLIC CABLE

CONNECTOR FOR ARMORED CABLE

BOX

SCREW DRIVER

KNOCKOUT REMOVED

BOX SLIPPED ON CABLE BEFORE INSTALLING

DRIVING LOCK NUT

TYING UNDERWRITERS' KNOT

Then the cable covering is removed about 8 in. from the end. Do this carefully to avoid damage to the wires which are left extending. Now fit a connector to the cable and attach to the box as in Fig. 28, driving the locking nut home with a screwdriver as in Fig. 27. Before a switch box is screwed to the lath, the tabs on the top and bottom are adjusted so that when fastened in place, the front edges of the box will be flush with the surface of the wall.

Splices: As all connections are made within outlet boxes, there will be no great strain on splices, except in the case of drop lights. For all connections but drop lights, use the pigtail splice shown in Fig. 24, although this can be used also for drop lights if strain on the splice is relieved by tying an underwriters' knot in the drop cord, Fig. 29. The knot rests on the bushing of the outlet-box cover and takes the strain.

Testing: Before soldering splices, and before attaching fixtures, switches, or wall outlets, the circuits must be tested. With the main switch off, connect two or three dry cells in series to the new circuit. A buzzer with two lengths of wire attached is used. When touched to the two wires which are to be attached to a wall outlet or to any outlet not controlled by a switch, the buzzer will operate. When connected to the wires for a fixture controlled by a wall switch the buzzer should not work unless the two wires for the switch are touched together. If three-way switches are used, all three of the wires should be joined together at each switch. Test three-way switches also with separate wires. If one lead is connected to the "hot" wire and the other to any grounded object (water pipe, radiator, etc.), the buzzer should work. If the buzzer is connected to a grounded wire and to a grounded object, it should not buzz. If B-X is used, the metal tube and all outlet boxes are grounded, and they should be tested in this way. If the buzzer operates when it is not supposed to, it indicates a short circuit at some point. If it does not work when it should, it indicates an open circuit (a broken conductor or faulty connection).

Soldering and Taping Splices: All splices must be made mechanically and electrically sound, and they must be soldered and insulated in a manner equal to the original insulation. The copper wires must be scraped or sanded clean before joining. After testing, rosin or non-corrosive paste soldering flux—not acid flux—is applied and the wire is heated with a blowtorch or a hot soldering copper. Then wire solder, either plain or rosin-cored, is applied to the hot joint. If properly performed, this operation will give a perfectly tight and secure joint that will not loosen. The soldered joint is next wrapped with rubber tape as shown in Fig. 24. First fold a short length over the tail of the splices. Then wrap the splice spirally with rubber tape, starting from the insulation on one wire and overlapping the turns, completely covering the bare wire with rubber as thick as the original insulation. Finally wrap the whole splice with friction tape in the same manner, applying two layers to complete the splice.

Attaching Fixtures: Switches, wall outlets and fixtures are attached next. If the screws for attaching the wires to the device are of different colors, the silver colored one is to be attached to the white wire and the brass colored one to the black wire. In the case of lighting fixtures which come wired with lampcord, one of the wires will probably have a tracer thread of a distinct color woven into the insulation. This is to be connected to the white or grounded wire in the outlet box. Large ceiling fixtures generally employ a "hickey" which attaches to the stud in the outlet box and also to the stem of the fixture. See Figs. 18 and 23. A canopy sliding up and over the stem conceals all connections. Small fixtures may be fastened as shown in Fig. 17, by means of a strap screwed to the box or to the stud, and to which the fixture itself is screwed.

Finishing: To finish the job, flush plates are installed over all wall outlets and switches. Bakelite plates in a variety of colors are generally used, although mirror or metal plates are also available. All temporary openings should be plastered over with patching plaster, which is available at any hardware store.

Baseboards and molding that were removed should be nailed to the studs, not to the lath. Holes in the floor should be plugged. A plug of the same kind of wood should be used as a rule, but in an inaccessible place, a cork held in place with shellac is often satisfactory. Finally, wallpaper that has been removed should be pasted back and any place where paint has been damaged should be touched up.

Joining Glass and Metal

Alum melted in an iron container forms a strong cement for joining glass and metal.

Gauge Marks Electrical Outlets

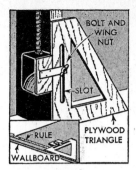

When installing wallboard, locating the areas to be cut for electrical outlets is always a problem. However, with this gauge, the task is simplified. Cut from plywood a template the same shape and size as the front of the outlet and fasten it to a wooden triangle so that it can be adjusted vertically by means of a bolt and wing nut riding in a slot. Then, using a rule and the triangle, locate the outlet in relation to the studding and transfer these measurements to the wallboard and cut the hole for the outlet.

Batteries Operate Electric Shaver

A vacation away from any source of electricity need no longer be marred by shaving irritations for the man who uses an electric shaver. All you need are two 45-volt radio batteries connected in series to operate the shaver. While this method is somewhat expensive, it is convenient when one has no 110-volt supply at hand.

Guard Catches Drill Shavings

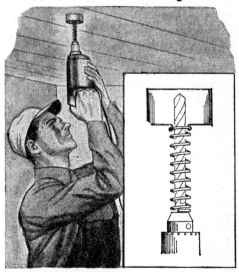

To protect his eyes from falling particles when drilling through ceilings, one electrician placed a small tin can over the end of the drill bit. A coil spring holds the can flush with the ceiling, as shown. Both the spring and the hole in the can must be larger than the bit.

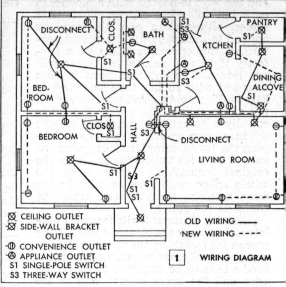

REWIRE YOUR HOME FOR

If your home is more than 10 years old, it probably is not wired adequately to enable you to enjoy fully the convenience of modern electrical appliances

By Thomas Trail

OLDER homes usually are not wired to make full use of all electrical conveniences now available or being developed. In many houses, the wiring is not of approved sizes to carry modern appliance loads; there are too few switches for control of the lights and an insufficient number of convenience outlets. Rewiring a home to take care of present and possible future requirements is quite simple to do. While most localities have no regulations prohibiting a homeowner from doing his own wiring, it generally is required that the completed job be inspected by a competent electrician for compliance with both the national and local electrical codes. Therefore, before going ahead with a wiring job, the homeowner should study all the local ordinances and codes and should be familiar with the requirements of the national electrical code.

A rewiring job requires careful planning, so the first thing to do is make rough pencil sketches of the present wiring, as shown in black lines on the wiring diagram, Fig. 1. Make a separate diagram for each floor of

the house. If there is a garage or other building wired for electricity, include this on the ground-floor sketch. On each sketch, simply mark the approximate location of each lighting fixture, wall switch, convenience outlet, etc. Next, make pencil notes of the various conveniences and appliances desired. Among those that may be needed are fluorescent lighting, combination receptacles for radio power, aerial and ground, Fig. 4, and switches that permit lights to be turned on and off from any entrance to a room or from the top or bottom of a stairway. Other modern conveniences include door switches in all clothes closets, Fig. 5, that turn on the lights when the doors are opened, and outlets that provide plug-in receptacles easily reached from any part of the room. Locate separate outlets for the kitchen clock, mantel clock, electric iron, washing machine, dishwasher, garbage-disposal unit and a ventilating fan. Any other special lighting problems should be considered and provided for in the rough plan.

If wires are not large enough to handle maximum current requirements, lights and appliances will not deliver their rated output. The national code recommends No. 12 wire as the smallest size to be used on branch circuits. Furthermore, the code specifies that wiring capacity be sufficient to provide at least 2 watts of lighting for every square foot of floor area in the house,

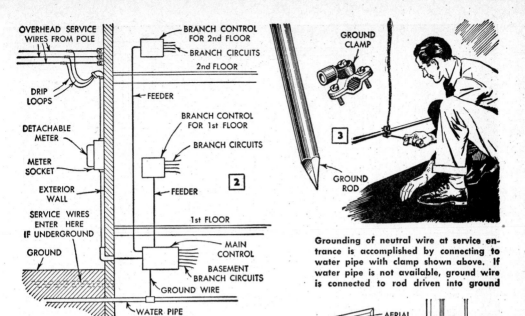

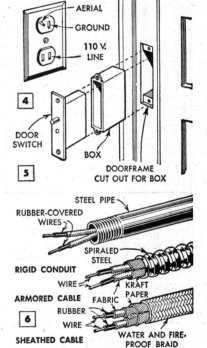

Grounding of neutral wire at service entrance is accomplished by connecting to water pipe with clamp shown above. If water pipe is not available, ground wire is connected to rod driven into ground

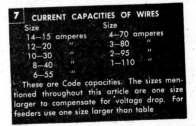

MODERN LIVING

excluding unfinished areas such as the basement and attic unless these require special lighting.

In addition to lighting requirements, capacity for 1500 watts of appliance load must be provided on circuits separate from the lighting and convenience-receptacle circuits. Appliance circuits usually are provided for the kitchen, dining room, utility room and laundry, or whichever of these are on the floor plan. If a total of more than six receptacles is required in these locations, two or more circuits are provided. When planning appliance circuits, remember that other heavy-load appliances such as a home freezer, clothes drier and perhaps a room-type air conditioner may be added in the future. If you are considering these extra units, plan one or more extra circuits or provide sufficient capacity in the branch control center and feeders to take care of the requirements.

In deciding on the location of convenience outlets and circuits, the following suggestions may be helpful as they follow approved procedure: Place a receptacle in each usable wall space 3 ft. or more in width. Have a receptacle located within 6 ft. (at the floor line) of any location in any usable wall space. Provide receptacles on enclosed porches. All outdoor receptacles must be of the weatherproof type. Receptacles for television sets should be located so that the set can be placed where light from windows will not strike the screen directly. Place at least one receptacle at each work space in the kitchen, workshop, garage and utility room. Locate separate receptacles for fixed appliances such as the garbage eliminator, dishwasher, ventilating fan and bathroom heater. Workshop motors should be on the

7 CURRENT CAPACITIES OF WIRES	
Size	Size
14—15 amperes	4—70 amperes
12—20 "	3—80 "
10—30 "	2—95 "
8—40 "	1—110 "
6—55 "	

These are Code capacities. The sizes mentioned throughout this article are one size larger to compensate for voltage drop. For feeders use one size larger than table

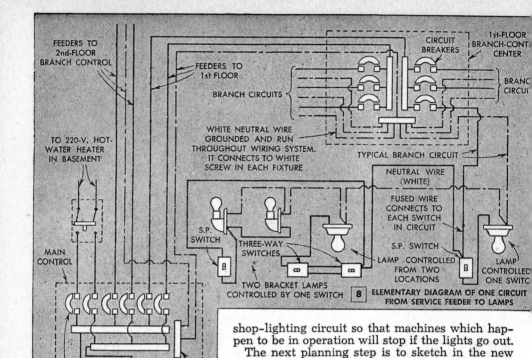

FEEDERS TO 2nd-FLOOR BRANCH CONTROL

FEEDERS TO 1st FLOOR

BRANCH CIRCUITS

CIRCUIT BREAKERS

1st-FLOOR BRANCH-CONT CENTER

BRANC CIRCUI

TO 220-V. HOT-WATER HEATER IN BASEMENT

WHITE NEUTRAL WIRE GROUNDED AND RUN THROUGHOUT WIRING SYSTEM. IT CONNECTS TO WHITE SCREW IN EACH FIXTURE

TYPICAL BRANCH CIRCUIT

NEUTRAL WIRE (WHITE)

FUSED WIRE CONNECTS TO EACH SWITCH IN CIRCUIT

MAIN CONTROL

S.P. SWITCH

THREE-WAY SWITCHES

S.P. SWITCH

LAMP CONTROLLED FROM TWO LOCATIONS

LAMP CONTROLLED ONE SWITC

PULL-OUT FUSED SWITCHES

NEUTRAL BUS

UNGROUND-ED FEEDERS

MAIN-ENTRANCE SWITCH

GROUNDED NEUTRAL WIRE

WATER PIPE

TWO BRACKET LAMPS CONTROLLED BY ONE SWITCH

8 ELEMENTARY DIAGRAM OF ONE CIRCUIT FROM SERVICE FEEDER TO LAMPS

WEATHERPROOF CONNECTOR

METER SOCKET

GROUNDING ELECTRODE

WEATHER-PROOF CONNECTOR

SILL PLATE

INDOOR CONNECTOR

GROUND CLAMP

BLACK

BARE

RED GROUND

WHITE RED BLACK

MAIN FUSES

RANGE CIRCUIT

RANGE FUSES

BRANCH-CIRCUIT FUSES

BRANCH CIRCUITS

9

shop-lighting circuit so that machines which happen to be in operation will stop if the lights go out.

The next planning step is to sketch in the new wiring system with a colored pencil on the wiring diagram as shown in red, Fig. 1. Make use, if possible, of all existing outlets to eliminate unnecessary work. Opposite each permanently connected lamp mark the wattage required. Total up the wattage of the lighting fixtures. As 1725 watts are allowed on each circuit, divide the total wattage by 1725 to find the number of circuits required. In wiring lights on two or more circuits, it is best, where possible, to arrange them so that all lights on each floor are not on one circuit. Otherwise, the blowing of a fuse will cause all the lights on that floor to go out. To figure the number of receptacle circuits required (other than the special ones feeding kitchen, laundry, etc.) allow one circuit for each six or seven receptacles. As in Fig. 2, it is best to provide a branch control center for each floor in the house. These branch control centers are fed from a main control center located near the point where the service feeder from the power lines enters the house.

When the number of lighting and convenience-receptacle circuits have been calculated for each floor, mark this information on the sketch. Branch circuits should be of No. 12 wire, each circuit being rated at 15 amp. The rated amperage of all the circuits in a branch control center added together will give the total amperage required for that control center. This will apply where two-wire feeders are used between the branch control centers and the main control center. However, three-wire service lately has come into common use in new installations. With three-wire feeders, the amperage will be halved. The correct size of wire required for each branch feeder can be determined easily from the table in Fig. 7. The feeder circuits remaining to be calculated are the individual branch circuits

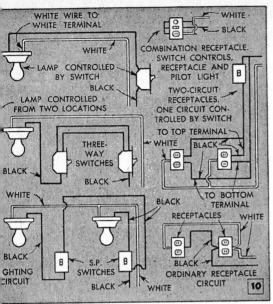

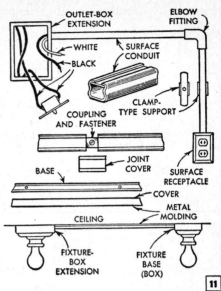

which feed directly to heavy-load appliances such as a water heater or range. If the power company does not require a separate meter on the water-heater circuit, both the heater and the range may be connected to the same branch circuit. To calculate the size of the feeders required, simply divide the wattage of each appliance by the voltage. This will give the amperage required. For example, a water heater consuming 3000 watts at 230 volts will require 13 amp. (3000 divided by 230). Use No. 10 wire for this load. The range load is calculated in the same manner. While ranges usually operate on both 115 and 230 volts, depending upon how many burners are in use at a time, only the 230 voltage is used to calculate the amperage. For a range rated at 7000 watts, the load would be 30.4 amp. Use a three-wire feeder of No. 8 wire.

Branch control centers may be arranged in three ways. They may consist of only 15-amp. circuits for lamps and convenience receptacles. Secondly, they may contain one or more 15-amp. circuits and one or more 20-amp. appliance circuits. Or, they may contain only 20-amp. circuits. A fuse or circuit breaker protects each circuit, but the fuse or breaker must be of no greater capacity than the circuit. The main control center will contain two fuses or a double-pole circuit breaker for each feeder from the branch control center and for each feeder from the appliance branch-circuit feeder where three-wire feeders are used. These overload devices must have a rating no higher than the carrying capacity of the wires they feed. If two-wire feeders are used, only one fuse is required. The grounded wire, Fig. 3, is not fused.

After the calculations have been made, mark this information on the rough sketch of the circuits and control centers of the new system. The installation of new conduit runs is not difficult. Some local codes permit only thin-wall conduit to be used in certain locations. Check before making the installation. In all conduit work, whether using rigid or flexible metal conduit, Fig. 6, the structure of the house determines to some extent the procedure to be followed. Usually, there is a way to feed flexible conduit either through or around ordinary obstructions, but sometimes it will be found impossible to run conduit to certain locations. Such outlets may have to be relocated or surface conduit, called metal molding, may have to be used as in Fig. 11. A suitable box should be installed in the basement or utility room to contain the doorbell transformer, which should be connected to a branch lighting circuit and protected with fuses.

Of course, rewiring an old house is more involved than wiring a new one. Service will have to be maintained to some lights while other circuits are being installed. Start by installing the service-entrance wires and equipment, as shown in Figs. 8 and 9. The service switch shown in Fig. 9 is ideal for a house utility room where all the rooms are on one floor. Next, run the branch-circuit feeders and the individual appliance circuits. The latter should terminate in suitable receptacles or switch boxes to which the appliances are to be connected. Follow this by removing all the

TEST LEADS

TAPE

12

DRY CELLS   DOOR-BELL

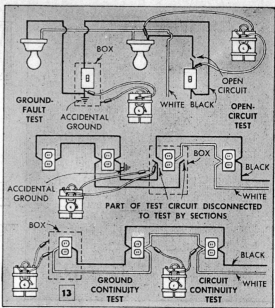

GROUND-FAULT TEST

ACCIDENTAL GROUND

BOX

WHITE BLACK

OPEN CIRCUIT

OPEN-CIRCUIT TEST

ACCIDENTAL GROUND

BOX

BLACK

WHITE

PART OF TEST CIRCUIT DISCONNECTED TO TEST BY SECTIONS

BOX

BLACK

13   GROUND CONTINUITY TEST   CIRCUIT CONTINUITY TEST   WHITE

existing wires from one circuit at a time and installing new, larger-capacity wires. Where armored cable, nonmetallic cable or knob-and-tube wiring is to be replaced, remove all the old wiring. Next, fish in the new armored cable or flexible metal conduit and attach to the boxes. Larger-capacity armored cable may be installed, or three-wire armored cable substituted and the outlets divided evenly between the two circuits.

If rigid conduit is merely to be rewired, pull out the old wires and replace them with larger-capacity wiring of the new S.N. type having a smaller diameter. This can only be used for rewiring of existing conduits or metal molding. Either the same number of wires of larger capacity can be used, or the circuit can be split into two parts and two circuits installed, using three or four wires of the same capacity. Where three-wire branch circuits are used, they must be considered as two separate circuits. Each ungrounded wire is protected at the branch control center by a single-pole breaker or by a fuse, Fig. 8.

As each circuit is completed and the connections made, it is tested and connected temporarily to the old distribution fuses. Figs. 8 and 10 show how various devices and fixtures are connected to circuits. In splicing wires in outlet boxes, solder the joints and cover with rubber tape and friction tape, or use approved solderless connectors. When all the new circuits are finished they may be disconnected from the old fuses and connected to the new branch control centers, or

main control center, as the case may be. The feeders are then connected and the branch control centers are mounted in proper location. Then the feeders are connected to the main control center, but all circuit breakers are left in open-circuit position until the feeders and circuits have been tested. To feed individual branch circuits, appliance circuits, feeders and service feeders, a simple test set is assembled from a doorbell, two dry cells and test prods as in Fig. 12. Fig. 13 shows how to test the various circuits.

If a ground shows up, check all boxes through which the circuit feeds for the cause of the trouble. It may be caused by the end of a bare wire touching some metal part of an outlet box, or the insulation may have been cut on a wire where it enters a box. If the defective circuit can be tested in sections, this may save considerable time in locating the trouble. The same general procedure is followed in searching for an open circuit, except that in the case of an open circuit a defective splice or broken wire usually is the cause of the fault. If all circuits test free of grounds and show complete circuit continuity, then test for ground continuity at each outlet. Sometimes paint will prevent a good ground connection between a box and the conduit or cable attached to it. To insure against defects in the wiring, be sure to tighten all wire-terminal screws, cable clamps, locknuts and bushings in boxes. Insulate splices carefully and use fiber bushings in the ends of flexible metal cable. Fasten all switches, outlets and fixtures securely.

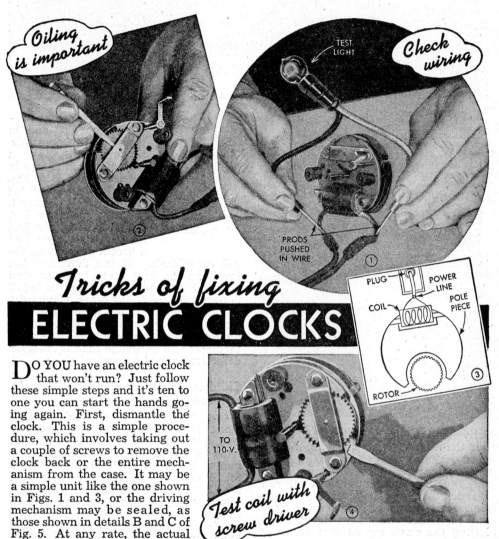

Oiling is important

TEST LIGHT

Check wiring

PRODS PUSHED IN WIRE

PLUG
POWER LINE
COIL
POLE PIECE
ROTOR

Tricks of fixing
ELECTRIC CLOCKS

TO 110-V.

Test coil with screw driver

DO YOU have an electric clock that won't run? Just follow these simple steps and it's ten to one you can start the hands going again. First, dismantle the clock. This is a simple procedure, which involves taking out a couple of screws to remove the clock back or the entire mechanism from the case. It may be a simple unit like the one shown in Figs. 1 and 3, or the driving mechanism may be sealed, as those shown in details B and C of Fig. 5. At any rate, the actual operation is the same as diagramed in Fig. 3—the current flows through the coil, setting up a magnetic field in the pole piece that causes the rotor to revolve.

Obviously, the first thing to check is the coil. Plug in at power source, then hold the clock to your ear. A faint hum indicates that the coil passes current. The coil hum is sometimes very faint and a more positive check is to touch a screwdriver to the pole piece near the rim of the rotor, as shown in Fig. 4. A gentle vibration indicates that the coil is in good condition. If the coil does not seem to pass current go over the wiring. Use any kind of electrical

tester and test the current flow right up to the coil, which is easily done by using sharp test prods and sticking them into the wires near the coil, as shown in Fig. 1. If the line tests okay and if the coil is not dead, the trouble, then, must be at the rotor or other point of the mechanism. Perhaps something is jammed.

In many cases, a dry, gummy bearing at the rotor is the source of the trouble. Clean the clock as well as you can with a small piece of cloth wrapped around a matchstick and dampened with any kind of cleaning fluid. Then, with a pointed match, care-

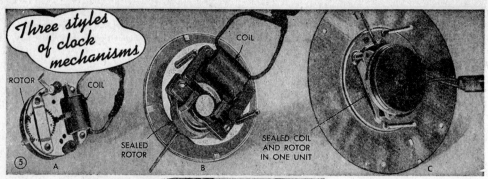

Three styles of clock mechanisms

ROTOR — COIL

SEALED ROTOR

COIL

SEALED COIL AND ROTOR IN ONE UNIT

⑤   A   B   C

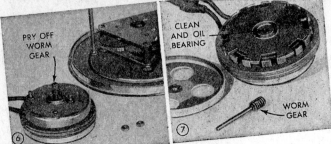

PRY OFF WORM GEAR

CLEAN AND OIL BEARING

WORM GEAR

⑥   ⑦

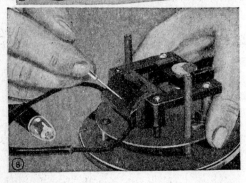

⑧

Coil repairs are usually impractical and, in sealed units, impossible. However, with the open type of coil as shown in details A and B of Fig. 5, it is worth looking into as a last resort. Split the insulation, Fig. 8, and unwind the first layer of wire. If you find a break, you can fix the coil by soldering. If you don't find the break in the first layer you can stop right there because invariably the break is near one end or the other. Obviously, you can't get at the inside end. The final remedy is to write the manufacturer for a quotation on a new coil. Many manufacturers will exchange rebuilt units for defective ones at a nominal charge.

Children Learn How to Tell Time by Hand-Operated Clock

One teacher uses a hand-operated clock in her classroom for teaching pupils to tell time. The clock face is cut from plywood and shellacked, then numerals are painted on it with India ink. The hands are operated from the rear by a knob connected to the works of a discarded alarm clock, as shown in the detail. Only the gear mechanism is needed, so that the hour and minute hands will travel in correct ratio when the knob is rotated.

fully oil all the bearings that you can see, and the rotor shaft, as in Fig. 2. Use any good grade of nondrying, nongumming oil, such as watch oil, gun oil, etc. After this, it's probable that the clock will run. If it doesn't, check the mounting—sometimes this is rubber tubing over studs and the rubber may have deteriorated, letting the clock sag so that hands or other parts rub. Rubber mounting can be replaced with "spaghetti" tubing used in radio work. Spin the rotor of the clock with your finger—it should revolve freely. Don't worry about end play at rotor shaft; it centers automatically in the magnetic field when clock runs.

If your clock has combined coil and motor like the one shown in detail C of Fig. 5, remove the whole unit by unscrewing two nuts that hold it in place. It will then look like Fig. 6. With slim pliers or other suitable tool, pry off the worm gear. Parts shown at Fig. 7. Clean and reoil long bearing surface.

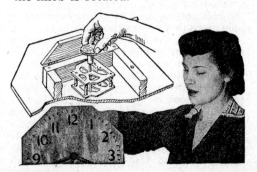

160

Converting Electric Clocks
to TIME SWITCHES

By C. A. CROWLEY

DO YOU need a time switch to turn off lights or electrical appliances at a predetermined time when no one will be there to turn the switch by hand? Perhaps your problem is to turn one circuit off and another on at the same time, or after an elapse of time. By simply making a few alterations in one or two electric alarm clocks and making relays from some scrap iron and some copper wire, you can have these automatic servants to save your time and labor. In effect you are altering them to form time switches, which turn electric circuits on and off at any time for which the clocks are set.

Three models: Three models of time switches will cover many needs. The relays used are the same but the circuit connections vary, as shown in the diagrams Figs. 7, 8 and 9. The arrangement in Fig. 7 is a straight cut-off switch. Merchants will

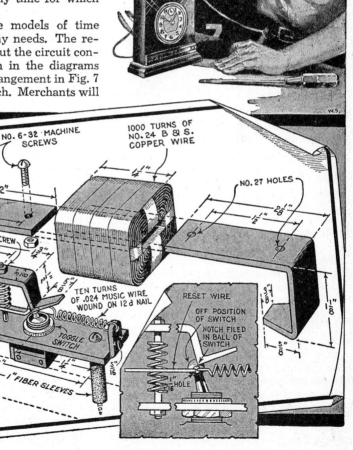

NO. 6-32 MACHINE SCREWS

1000 TURNS OF NO. 24 B & S. COPPER WIRE

NO. 27 HOLES

MACH. SCREW

RESET WIRE

NO. 4 d FINISHING NAIL

TEN TURNS OF .024 MUSIC WIRE WOUND ON 12 d NAIL

TOGGLE SWITCH

SIX TURNS OF WIRE WOUND ON 12 d NAIL

1" FIBER SLEEVES

RESET WIRE

OFF POSITION OF SWITCH

NOTCH FILED IN BALL OF SWITCH

HOLE

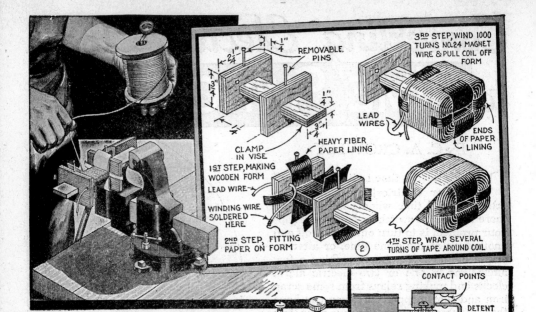

3RD STEP, WIND 1000 TURNS NO. 24 MAGNET WIRE & PULL COIL OFF FORM

REMOVABLE PINS

LEAD WIRES

ENDS OF PAPER LINING

CLAMP IN VISE

HEAVY FIBER PAPER LINING

1ST STEP, MAKING WOODEN FORM

LEAD WIRE

WINDING WIRE SOLDERED HERE

2ND STEP, FITTING PAPER ON FORM

4TH STEP, WRAP SEVERAL TURNS OF TAPE AROUND COIL

CONTACT POINTS

COIL

CORE

DETENT OF CLOCK

INSULATED SIDE VIEW

VIBRATING ARM CUT OFF HERE

CLOCK MOTOR COIL

WIRE SOLDERED TO DETENT

BRASS

TO SUIT CLOCK

CONTACT POINT FORMED FROM SILVER WIRE

FIBER WASHERS AND SLEEVE INSULATE BOLT

find it useful for shutting off display lights. Or, this arrangement is useful for turning off a radio, ventilating fan, outdoor lights and other appliances. A slight elaboration of the circuit, as shown in Fig. 8, enables one to turn one circuit off and another on at the same time, or either one of these functions separately. With this switch a radio can be turned on in the morning, or a solenoid-type water valve can be opened to start a sprinkler system, etc. The third model has two electric alarm clocks and two relays, Fig. 9. This one will turn a circuit on and then off after a lapse of time, such as turning hall and porch lights on early in an evening and off at a later time. As all of these time switches are designed to be portable and compact, they can be moved around wherever needed.

Making the relay: Fig. 1 shows the general assembly of the relay, and the parts comprising it. Flat iron ⅛ in. thick is used for the frame, pole piece and armature. It is advisable to anneal the bends from a cherry-red heat to relieve the strains set up in them. This can be done over a gas stove or even in the furnace of your heating plant. Dress up the pieces with a file

and drill the holes as indicated. When drilling the holes to fasten the pole piece to the frame, it is advisable to clamp them together and drill through both pieces at once to insure a perfect matching of these holes when the relay is assembled. Drill the hinge-pin holes in the frame and armature before notching them out to fit each other. Care must be used not to allow the holes to wander off center.

To wind the armature and switch springs, a small flat is filed on the side of the nail so that the end of the music wire can be clamped to it in the vise. Wind the turns as closely together as possible. No. 24-ga. music wire is used for making both springs. See Fig. 1. In notching up the ball tip of the toggle switch do not attempt to form it by hammering. Use a file, as the toggle is usually made of hard brass and is brittle.

The notch for the switch catch is filed on the side of the toggle that is held by the relay armature when the switch is in the on position. Details of winding the coil on a form are shown step by step in Fig. 2. It is not necessary to wind the coil in layers. Single cotton-covered magnet wire, No. 24, is satisfactory, but enameled or other insulated wire may be used.

In assembling the relay, first place the mounting screws in their holes, then hinge the armature and mount the toggle switch. The armature or switch catch and the toggle switch usually have to be adjusted to each other. This can be accomplished by carefully bending the catch with a pair of pliers if necessary, and also by moving the switch up and down by means of the mounting nuts. A piece of stiff wire will serve as the reset catch when bent to shape. Slip the coil on the frame, insert the pole piece, and fasten the two together. Tighten the fastening screws securely to prevent the pole piece from chattering.

Modifying the clock: Alterations on the clock are the same for all the models and consist of installing a pair of electrical contacts in the alarm system. Where two clocks are used, the procedure is exactly the same for both clocks. The clocks do not need to be alike so long as they both have an alarm system. The alarm system of an electric clock is very simple. As shown in Fig. 4, a vibrator arm, which lies next to the motor coil, is riveted at one end to the laminated core of the clock and is held in place at the other end by a movable detent or catch, which releases the arm, allowing it to vibrate. The vibrating arm is cut off as indicated. A contact point on the detent is made by removing the detent, drilling a hole in it at the point shown, inserting a short piece of silver wire, (obtainable at jewelers) and riveting over the ends with a hammer. Use a hardwood block to back up the work while riveting the wire, to prevent excessive flattening of the contact on the other side. A second silver contact is mounted

in the same way on a piece of sheet brass cut to fit your particular clock. This contact must be electrically insulated from the rest of the works when mounting it on the laminated core as shown in Figs. 3 and 5. Then the lead wires are soldered in place. Bring these lead wires through the cord hole in the back cover plate and close up the clock. Cut off the clock cord about 3 in. outside of the cord hole. If, by chance, you have clocks already equipped with contacts, these may be used and this part of the work omitted by simply bringing out leads from them after disconnecting them from the rest of the clock works.

Mounting the parts, wiring and testing: If the clock has a wooden frame, the relay, the lamp receptacle and the load plug-in socket can be screwed to the top and sides.

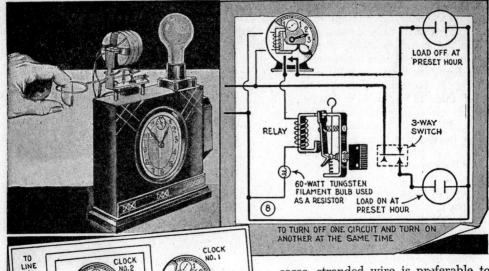

LOAD OFF AT PRESET HOUR

RELAY

3-WAY SWITCH

60-WATT TUNGSTEN FILAMENT BULB USED AS A RESISTOR

LOAD ON AT PRESET HOUR

8

TO TURN OFF ONE CIRCUIT AND TURN ON ANOTHER AT THE SAME TIME

TO LINE

CLOCK NO.2

CLOCK NO. 1

9

CONTACT MOUNTED IN CLOCKS

RELAY

RELAY

60-WATT TUNGSTEN FILAMENT BULBS USED AS RESISTORS

LOAD

USING TWO CLOCKS TO TURN ON CIRCUIT AND TURN IT OFF AFTER LAPSE OF TIME

Otherwise these parts and the clock are all mounted on a wooden base of suitable size. In wiring, do not use a wire size of less than No. 14 gauge where the lines on the diagram are heavy, but No. 20 gauge wire is sufficient for the lighter wiring. In all cases, stranded wire is preferable to solid conductors.

Use a 60-watt lamp in the resistance receptacle, pull the reset back until the catch holds the switch, and plug the switch clock into the line. Do not touch anything until you have made a test to find the grounded side as in Fig. 6. This is done by touching one lead from a lamp to the metal back of the clock and the other lead to a water pipe or radiator valve to obtain a good electrical ground connection. If the lamp lights, reverse the cord plug used to connect the clock to an outlet. After this has been done, plug some convenient test load such as a desk lamp into the load receptacle. The lamp should now go off at any time to which the alarm is set. In Figs. 8 and 9, three-way switches are used. In the diagrams, connections are made to the switch as indicated in the dotted portion although the switch itself is shown attached to the relay without any connections.

Prongs of Electric Plug Shielded with a Large Cork

Many a homeowner has experienced the annoyance of loose or bent electric plugs. If the prongs of the plugs on electric appliances in your home are sometimes dropped on the floor and damaged or stepped on and bent, get a few corks and use them as shields on the prongs when the plugs are pulled from the receptacles. Slits for the prongs are made with a knife.

Midget D.C. Current Converter Fits Phonograph or Clock

Phonographs, clocks, electric razors and other electrical equipment designed to operate on alternating current can now be used with direct current by means of a vibrator inverter which converts the d.c. to a.c. Weighing only 14 ounces and measuring 2¼ by 4 by 4½ inches, the compact unit can be installed in the corner of a phonograph cabinet or some other convenient location. With an input of 115 volts d.c., the inverter's output is 110 volts, 60 cycle a.c., providing a maximum load of 25 watts.

Frozen Water Pipe in Wall Thawed by Hot Air

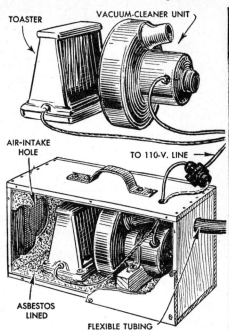

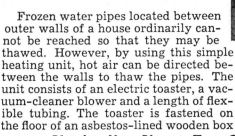

Frozen water pipes located between outer walls of a house ordinarily cannot be reached so that they may be thawed. However, by using this simple heating unit, hot air can be directed between the walls to thaw the pipes. The unit consists of an electric toaster, a vacuum-cleaner blower and a length of flexible tubing. The toaster is fastened on the floor of an asbestos-lined wooden box and just behind an air-intake hole cut in the end of the box. Behind the toaster the blower is set in position to force air heated by the toaster out through the tubing. The method of attaching the tubing to the blower will be determined by the type of blower used.

Plumber Uses Plunger-Type Gun to Apply Thread Compound

Working on the principle of an ordinary grease gun, this handy dispenser for pipe-joint compound is assembled from scrap materials. It consists of a metal tube which is fitted with a plunger and an improvised nozzle, as shown. To simplify spreading the compound, a brush is added by anchoring bristles around a hollow tube driven into the nozzle. As pressure is applied to the plunger, compound is forced through the hollow brush and spread in a smooth layer on the desired fitting.

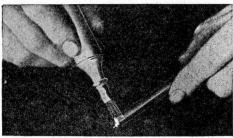

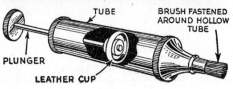

Plumber's Tape Secured by Hose for Measuring Pipe

The problem of holding the end of a tape measure while measuring lengths of pipe was solved by one plumber who used a short piece of split garden hose.

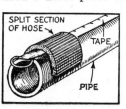

The tape was placed at one end of the pipe and the hose slipped over it to act as a clamp. This method will work on pipe of various diameters.

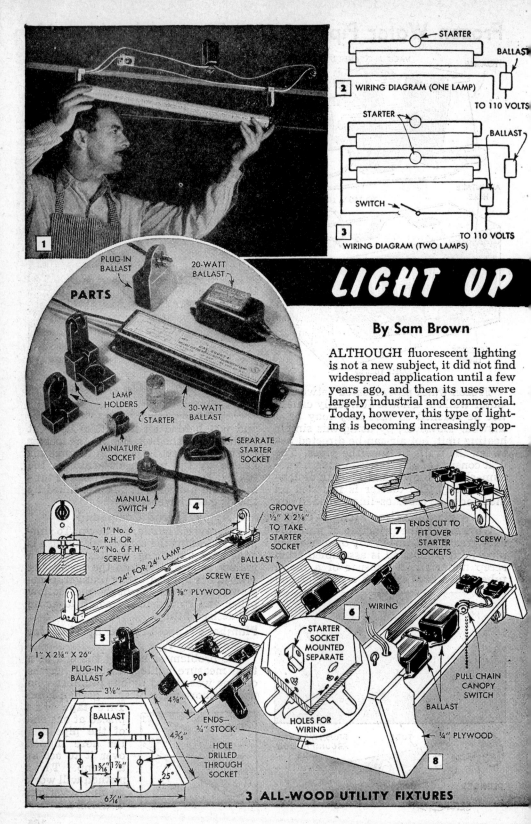

LIGHT UP

By Sam Brown

ALTHOUGH fluorescent lighting is not a new subject, it did not find widespread application until a few years ago, and then its uses were largely industrial and commercial. Today, however, this type of lighting is becoming increasingly pop-

2 WIRING DIAGRAM (ONE LAMP)

STARTER · BALLAST · TO 110 VOLTS

3 WIRING DIAGRAM (TWO LAMPS)

STARTER · BALLAST · SWITCH · TO 110 VOLTS

PARTS

PLUG-IN BALLAST · 20-WATT BALLAST · LAMP HOLDERS · STARTER · 30-WATT BALLAST · MINIATURE SOCKET · SEPARATE STARTER SOCKET · MANUAL SWITCH · **4**

1" No. 6 R.H. OR ¾" No. 6 F.H. SCREW

24" FOR 24" LAMP

GROOVE ½" X 2⅛" TO TAKE STARTER SOCKET

BALLAST · SCREW EYE · ⅜" PLYWOOD

1" X 2⅛" X 26"

PLUG-IN BALLAST · **3**

7 ENDS CUT TO FIT OVER STARTER SOCKETS · SCREW

6 WIRING

STARTER SOCKET MOUNTED SEPARATE

90°

4⅝"

ENDS—¾" STOCK

HOLE DRILLED THROUGH SOCKET

HOLES FOR WIRING

4³⁄₁₆"

PULL CHAIN CANOPY SWITCH · BALLAST · ¼" PLYWOOD · **8**

9 BALLAST

3⅛" · 1³⁄₁₆" 1⅞" · 25° · 6⁷⁄₁₆"

3 ALL-WOOD UTILITY FIXTURES

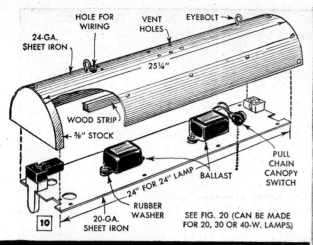

HOLE FOR WIRING — VENT HOLES — EYEBOLT →

24-GA. SHEET IRON

25¼"

WOOD STRIP

⅝" STOCK

24" FOR 24" LAMP — BALLAST — PULL CHAIN CANOPY SWITCH

RUBBER WASHER

20-GA. SHEET IRON

SEE FIG. 20 (CAN BE MADE FOR 20, 30 OR 40-W. LAMPS.)

10

FLUORESCENT

with Homemade FIXTURES

ular in the home and workshop as a source of superior, low-cost illumination. Assembled from standard parts, fluorescent fixtures are not difficult to build for almost any lighting condition. Like ordinary filament lamps, the simplest installation of the fluorescent tube is a surface mounting, such as shown in Fig. 1. Bare as this is, it does the trick in certain locations. The basic wiring diagram is shown in Fig. 2, consisting of two circuits, one of which supplies current to start the lamp or tube and then plays no further part in operation, while the second circuit supplies the operating current. This line must carry a suitable ballast to limit the current to the amount needed for any particular lamp. A two-or-more lamp circuit is shown in Fig. 3, and requires either a separate ballast for each lamp, or two ballasts mounted in one case.

Parts: Parts are shown in Fig. 4. Included are ballasts having the proper capacity, and lamp holders, the latter consisting of one lamp holder and one combination lamp holder and starter socket. Also needed are either automatic starting switches, or one of the manual types which are for push, turn and pull operation and control one or two lamps. Always be sure the ballast is for the proper wattage, frequency and voltage range.

All-wood fixtures: Fluorescent lamps generally are considered to radiate less than one half the heat of filament lamps and can be mounted satisfactorily in all-wood fixtures, such as shown in Figs. 5 to 9. Fig. 5 is a simple light strip using a plug-in type of ballast, while the other two use standard ballasts mounted inside the fixture. These units can be made up to 40-watt size, the lamp length determining the length of fixture (see Fig. 20 for lamp sizes). The lamp-holder mounting for the fixture shown in Fig. 8 is not

11

A TWO-LAMP SHOP LIGHT

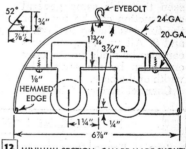

52° — ¾" — ⅞" — EYEBOLT — 24-GA. — 20-GA.

1³⁄₁₆" — 3⁷⁄₁₆" R. — ⅛" HEMMED EDGE — 1¼" — ¼" — 6⅞"

12 MINIMUM SECTION—CAN BE MADE SLIGHTLY LARGER AS DESIRED. FOR TWO 40-WATT LAMPS USE TULAMP THIN SECTION BALLAST (1⅜" X 2¼" X 18¼").

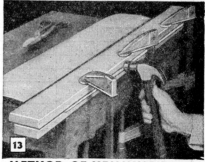

13

METHOD OF HEMMING EDGE

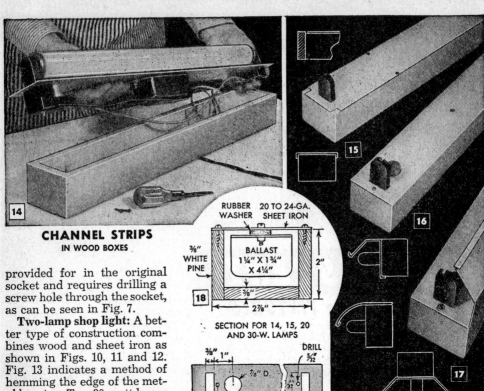

CHANNEL STRIPS
IN WOOD BOXES

RUBBER WASHER 20 TO 24-GA. SHEET IRON

⅜" WHITE PINE

BALLAST 1¼" X 1¾" X 4¼"

2"

⅜"

2⅞"

SECTION FOR 14, 15, 20 AND 30-W. LAMPS

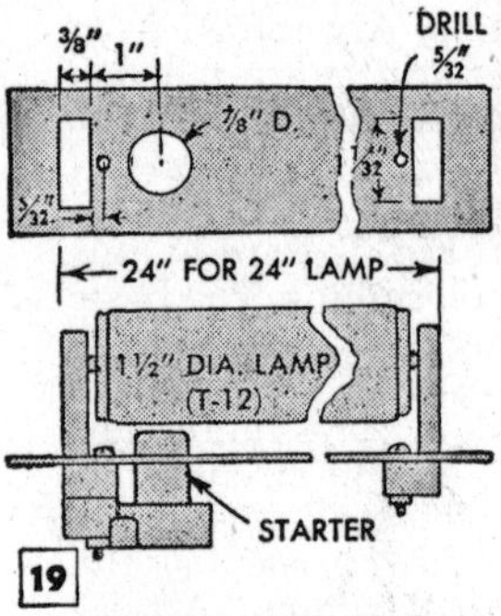

⅜" 1" DRILL 5/32

⅞" D.

1 1/32 D.

5/32

24" FOR 24" LAMP

1½" DIA. LAMP (T-12)

STARTER

MOUNTING DIMENSIONS

provided for in the original socket and requires drilling a screw hole through the socket, as can be seen in Fig. 7.

Two-lamp shop light: A better type of construction combines wood and sheet iron as shown in Figs. 10, 11 and 12. Fig. 13 indicates a method of hemming the edge of the metal housing. Two 20-watt lamps make an excellent bench light, while two 40s serve nicely for general illumination. It can be seen that this same general construction can be used for the fixtures shown in Figs. 6 and 8. All two-lamp fixtures can also be made up for only one lamp by narrowing the width of the base.

Channel strips: Channel strips, Figs. 14 through 17, are basic fluorescent-light units used extensively as fixture bases or for special built-in installations. The strips can be made up of wood boxes with sheet iron or metal mounting bases, as shown. Sectional

20	**FLUORESCENT LAMP SIZES**① **AND ELECTRICAL DATA**						
Lamp	Diameter	Length②	Lamp Holder	Total③ Watts	Filament④ Lamp Equal	Lamp Life (Hrs.)	Ballast Size ⑤
6-Watt	⅝"	9"	Miniature Bipin	8	20-Watt	2500	1¼" X 1¾" X 4¼" (1 Lamp)
8-Watt	⅝"	12"	Miniature Bipin	11	25-Watt	2500	
13-Watt	⅝"	21"	Miniature Bipin	20	40-Watt	2500	
14-Watt	1½"	15"	Medium Bipin	18	30-Watt	2000	1¼" X 1¾" X 4¼" (1 Lamp)
15-Watt	1"	18"	Medium Bipin	20	40-Watt	2500	
15-Watt	1½"	18"	Medium Bipin	20	40-Watt	2500	1¼" X 1¾" X 6½" (2 Lamps)
20-Watt	1½"	24"	Medium Bipin	25	50-Watt	2500	
30-Watt	1"	36"	Medium Bipin	40	75-Watt	2500	1¼" X 1¾" X 6½" (1 Lamp)
40-Watt	1½"	48"	Medium Bipin	50	100-Watt	2500	1⅜" X 2¼" X 8¾" (1 Lamp) 2⅜" X 3⅛" X 9½" (2 Lamps)
100-Watt	2⅛"	60"	Mogul Bipin	125	200-Watt	3000	2⅜" X 3⅛" X 14⅜" (1 lamp)

① Lists all common sizes — some other sizes and styles also available.

② Over-all mounted length of one-lamp and **two-lamp** holders.

③ Lamp watts plus watts lost at ballast.

④ Filament lamp which gives same approximate light as fluorescent lamp listed.

⑤ Smallest size — some other sizes available.

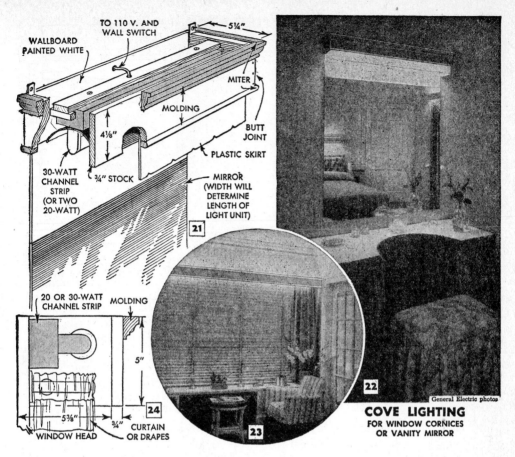

WALLBOARD PAINTED WHITE

TO 110 V. AND WALL SWITCH

5¼"

MITER

MOLDING

BUTT JOINT

PLASTIC SKIRT

4⅛"

30-WATT CHANNEL STRIP (OR TWO 20-WATT)

¾" STOCK

MIRROR (WIDTH WILL DETERMINE LENGTH OF LIGHT UNIT)

21

20 OR 30-WATT CHANNEL STRIP

MOLDING

5"

24

5⅜"

¾"

CURTAIN OR DRAPES

WINDOW HEAD

23

22

General Electric photos

COVE LIGHTING
FOR WINDOW CORNICES
OR VANITY MIRROR

dimensions, Fig. 18, will accommodate lamps up to 30 watts. The 40-watt size will require a slightly larger box to suit the larger size ballast. Fig. 19 gives dimensions for socket mountings, and these dimensions apply to any style of fixture using 14, 15, 20, 30 or 40-watt lamps.

Cove lighting: The two examples of cove lighting, Figs. 21 through 24, are typical channel strip installations. General construction details, which can be altered to fit individual requirements, are given in Figs. 21 and 24. If possible, the power line should be concealed in the wall, with control from a wall switch. However, the simpler method of tacking the wiring along woodwork and then to a receptacle can be used.

Bed lamps: Bed lamps, Fig. 25, introduce the problem of magnetic ballast hum. All fluorescent-lamp ballasts make a low humming sound, which is inaudible in most locations but like a bee in flight in the quiet of a bedroom. Fortunately, it is practical to cut the ballast in at some remote point in the power line, and the noisemaker thus can be shifted to a far corner of the room, or, even better, to some distant location like the basement or attic. However, for successful operation, the voltage drop must not be too great, and this may occur when the ballast is located too far from the lamp. As a general rule, do not locate the ballast more than 50 ft. from the lamp and avoid locations where there is extreme moisture or where the surrounding air temperature is higher then 120 deg. F. Without the ballast, the basic light unit takes the form of a flat box housing the lamp holders and starting switch. All-wood construction can be used for the 1-in.-dia. tubes (15 and 30 watts) and the housing can be held to 1 in. thickness, as shown in Figs. 28 and 29. This tiltboard style makes a very practical bed lamp, allowing rotation of the light to any desired position. The fixed headboard style, as shown in Fig. 30, uses the lamp-housing box flat against the wall, with a combination wood and metal shade extending outward, as can be seen in Fig. 31.

Series hookup: Two 14-watt lamps (this one size only) can be connected in series and operated with a small 60-volt lamp as a resistance ballast, as shown in Fig. 27. Total wattage of lamps and ballast is about 45 watts. This circuit can be used on alternating or direct current. It has no ballast

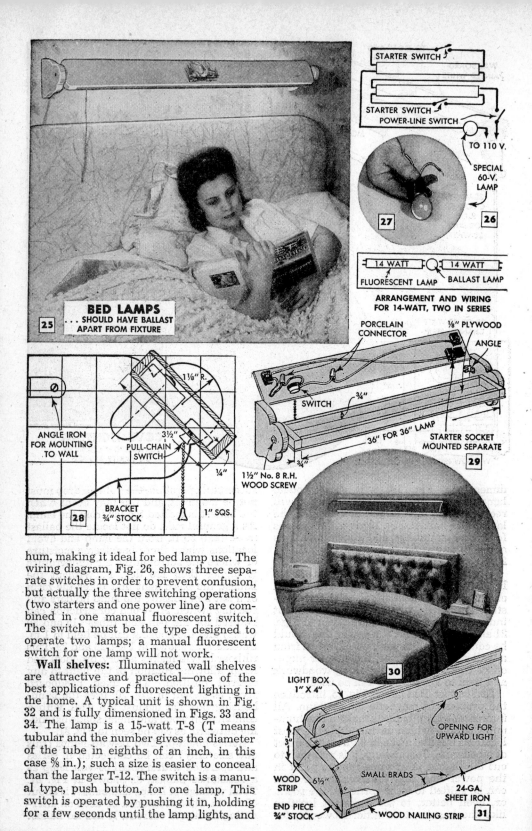

BED LAMPS
... SHOULD HAVE BALLAST
APART FROM FIXTURE

25

27

26

STARTER SWITCH

STARTER SWITCH
POWER-LINE SWITCH

TO 110 V.

SPECIAL
60-V.
LAMP

14 WATT   14 WATT
FLUORESCENT LAMP   BALLAST LAMP

ARRANGEMENT AND WIRING
FOR 14-WATT, TWO IN SERIES

PORCELAIN
CONNECTOR

⅛" PLYWOOD

ANGLE

SWITCH

¾"

36" FOR 36" LAMP

STARTER SOCKET
MOUNTED SEPARATE

29

¾"

1½" No. 8 R.H.
WOOD SCREW

ANGLE IRON
FOR MOUNTING
TO WALL

1⅛" R.

3½"

PULL-CHAIN
SWITCH

¼"

BRACKET
¾" STOCK

1" SQS.

28

30

LIGHT BOX
1" X 4"

3"

WOOD
STRIP

6½"

END PIECE
¾" STOCK

SMALL BRADS

OPENING FOR
UPWARD LIGHT

24-GA.
SHEET IRON

WOOD NAILING STRIP

31

hum, making it ideal for bed lamp use. The wiring diagram, Fig. 26, shows three separate switches in order to prevent confusion, but actually the three switching operations (two starters and one power line) are combined in one manual fluorescent switch. The switch must be the type designed to operate two lamps; a manual fluorescent switch for one lamp will not work.

Wall shelves: Illuminated wall shelves are attractive and practical—one of the best applications of fluorescent lighting in the home. A typical unit is shown in Fig. 32 and is fully dimensioned in Figs. 33 and 34. The lamp is a 15-watt T-8 (T means tubular and the number gives the diameter of the tube in eighths of an inch, in this case ⅝ in.); such a size is easier to conceal than the larger T-12. The switch is a manual type, push button, for one lamp. This switch is operated by pushing it in, holding for a few seconds until the lamp lights, and then releasing. It combines a starting switch and power-line switch in one unit, and has four lead wires. Power leads usually are black and are wired into the power circuit (see Fig. 2), while the second pair of wires is cut in on the starting circuit. The ballast is mounted apart from the shelf, using a plug-in type or running wiring to the regular ballast which can be mounted in the basement or on a wall. A modification of the shelf-type holder, a living-room installation, is illustrated in Fig. 35, and a method of

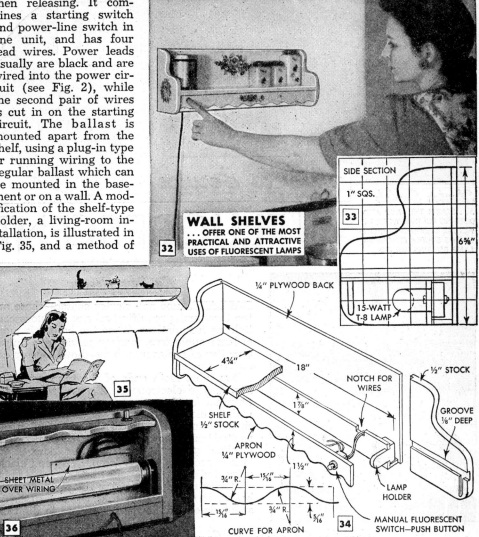

WALL SHELVES
... OFFER ONE OF THE MOST PRACTICAL AND ATTRACTIVE USES OF FLUORESCENT LAMPS

SIDE SECTION
1" SQS.

33

6⅝"

¼" PLYWOOD BACK

15-WATT T-8 LAMP

4¾"

18"

NOTCH FOR WIRES

½" STOCK

GROOVE ⅛" DEEP

1⅞"

SHELF ½" STOCK

APRON ¼" PLYWOOD

1½"

¾" R. 15⁄16"

15⁄16" ¾" R.

5⁄16"

LAMP HOLDER

CURVE FOR APRON

34

MANUAL FLUORESCENT SWITCH—PUSH BUTTON

SHEET METAL OVER WIRING

35

36

keeping wiring from coming in contact with the lamp for this and similar fixtures is shown in Fig. 36.

T-5 lamps: T-5 lamps are available in 6, 8 and 13 watts, as tabulated in Fig. 20. Although not shown in any of the plans, these lamps are excellent for shelves, picture lighting, portable trouble lamps, etc., where their small dimensions and low wattage are important considerations. Wiring is standard, and switching can be done with automatic starters or manually, the same as with the larger-diameter lamps. Whenever connecting starters, ballasts, etc., if wiring diagrams are included with the equipment, refer to these as a double check.

Installation applications: Don't use a one-lamp fixture as a lathe light or for illuminating any revolving machinery; the best unit for such installations is a two-lamp unit and, further, ballasted with a two-lamp high power-factor ballast. Don't overrate the light value of fluorescent lamps; a sound conservative rating is twice the illumination of a similar wattage filament lamp. "Light Up Fluorescent" with one or two simple units, and then, as your appreciation of this new and better lighting grows, make other installations as dictated by your own experience.

❡Carriage lamps on an old surrey make excellent door lamps. After rubbing down, paint them black, wire for electricity and install on each side of the entrance door.

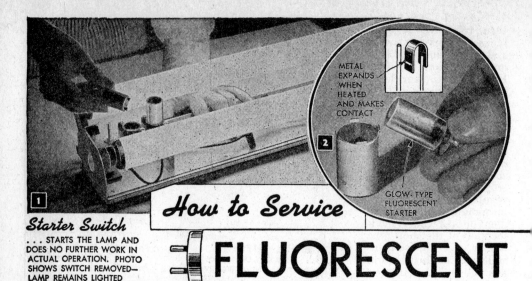

Starter Switch

... STARTS THE LAMP AND DOES NO FURTHER WORK IN ACTUAL OPERATION. PHOTO SHOWS SWITCH REMOVED—LAMP REMAINS LIGHTED

METAL EXPANDS WHEN HEATED AND MAKES CONTACT

GLOW-TYPE FLUORESCENT STARTER

How to Service

FLUORESCENT

End Blackening ... IS A NORMAL DEVELOPMENT OCCURRING LATE IN LIFE OF TUBE

FLUORESCENT COATING

FILAMENT (Cathode)

By Sam Brown

BALLAST, tube and starter switch—these are the three units requiring service in fluorescent lighting installations. Since the ballast is more or less trouble-free, common servicing is simply a matter of replacing a burned-out tube or defective starter.

The tube: Both ends of the tube are alike, Fig. 4. The electrode or filament furnishes a terminal for the arc and originally is covered with an electron-emissive material. This is dissipated during the life of the lamp and is deposited inside the tube, causing the familiar end blackening, Fig. 3, which is a fair index of the "life expectancy" of the lamp. Early end blackening indicates faulty starting.

Starter switch: Following the lamp diagram below, it can be seen that when the starter switch is closed, power is supplied to the tube

How the Fluorescent Lamp Works

MAIN SWITCH 1, IS TURNED ON. BALLAST 2, LIMITS CURRENT TO AMOUNT REQUIRED BY LAMP. STARTER SWITCH 3, IS CLOSED (USUALLY AUTOMATIC) TO COMPLETE CIRCUIT. LAMP FILAMENTS BECOME HEATED AND SEND OUT ELECTRONS 4, AND IN A FEW SECONDS THE ARC 5, STRIKES. STARTER SWITCH THEN IS OPENED AUTOMATICALLY OR MANUALLY AND PLAYS NO FURTHER PART IN OPERATION. ARC 5, SENDS OUT SHORT-WAVE, INVISIBLE LIGHT, WHICH ACTIVATES FLUORESCENT COATING ON INSIDE OF TUBE CAUSING IT TO GLOW AND PRODUCE VISIBLE LIGHT.

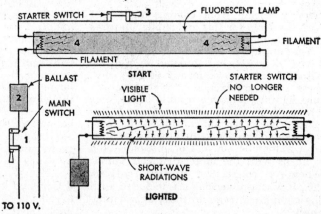

STARTER SWITCH → 3

FLUORESCENT LAMP

FILAMENT

FILAMENT

BALLAST

MAIN SWITCH

START

VISIBLE LIGHT

STARTER SWITCH NO LONGER NEEDED

SHORT-WAVE RADIATIONS

LIGHTED

TO 110 V.

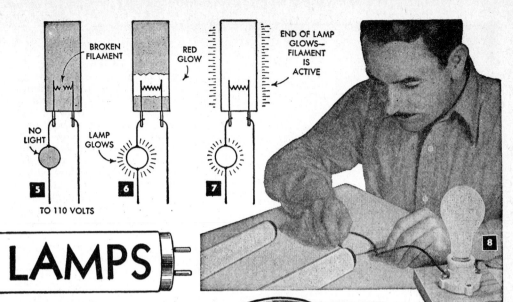

BROKEN FILAMENT

RED GLOW

END OF LAMP GLOWS— FILAMENT IS ACTIVE

NO LIGHT

LAMP GLOWS

TO 110 VOLTS

5　**6**　**7**

8

LAMPS

filaments, and they heat and become a dull red. Modern fixtures are fitted with an automatic starter, commonest of which is the glow lamp, Fig. 2. When the fluorescent fixture is turned on, the glow switch receives a full supply of current, causing the movable metal strip to heat and make contact. When the arc strikes, voltage to the glow switch is lowered and the metal strip cools and opens the circuit. Because the glow switch must heat on a certain voltage and not heat on a slightly lower voltage, it is impractical to test the

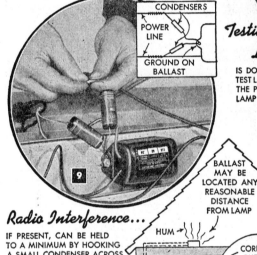

CONDENSERS

POWER LINE

GROUND ON BALLAST

9

Testing Lamps.... IS DONE BY USING A TEST LAMP AS SHOWN. THE PROPER SIZE TEST LAMP MUST BE USED.

Radio Interference... IF PRESENT, CAN BE HELD TO A MINIMUM BY HOOKING A SMALL CONDENSER ACROSS THE POWER LINE

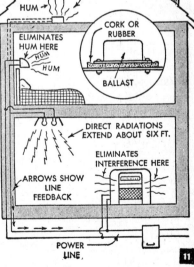

BALLAST MAY BE LOCATED ANY REASONABLE DISTANCE FROM LAMP

HUM

CORK OR RUBBER

ELIMINATES HUM HERE

HUM

HUM

BALLAST

DIRECT RADIATIONS EXTEND ABOUT SIX FT.

ELIMINATES INTERFERENCE HERE

ARROWS SHOW LINE FEEDBACK

POWER LINE

11

10

Ballast Hum . . . . USUALLY IS LOW AND INAUDIBLE UNDER AVERAGE CONDITIONS. BALLAST CAN BE INSULATED TO MIN-IMIZE HUM, OR IT CAN BE LOCATED SOME DISTANCE FROM LAMP

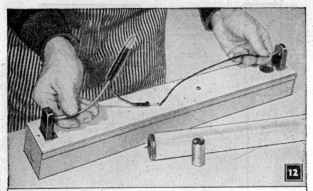

Circuit Testing . . . CAN BE DONE WITH A TEST LAMP. ONE SIDE OF EACH SOCKET SHOULD BE ALIVE AND LIGHT SHOULD SHOW BETWEEN THEM.

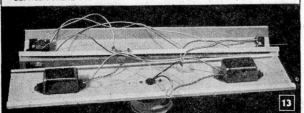

switch electrically by any method other than placing it in the fixture.

Lamp blinking: Near the end of life, the electron-emissive deposit on tube filaments is exhausted, the filaments are no longer self-sustaining and a cycle of blinking continues until either lamp or starter ceases to function. To prevent blinking, auxiliary equipment was added to the glow switch, making a double switch, the second switch turning off the first when the fixture is not functioning correctly.

Testing lamps: Use an extension cord with the ends scraped clean. Connect a socket in one of the power lines, as in Figs. 5 to 8 inclusive. When the test wires are touched to the prongs of the tube, the test lamp should light. If it does not, a broken filament is usually indicated.

FAULT	POSSIBLE CAUSE	REMEDY
LAMP BLINKS (This fault should be corrected at once to avoid undue wear on lamp and starter)	END OF LIFE (Normal life is 2500 hours)	INSTALL NEW LAMP
	DEFECTIVE STARTER	TEST WITH NEW STARTER
	LOOSE CONTACTS	CHECK CONTACTS AT LAMP ENDS
	WITH NEW LAMP: MAY BE CAUSED BY DEFECTIVE LAMP	CHECK WITH A LAMP KNOWN TO BE SATISFACTORY
	WITH PLUG-IN FIXTURES: LOOSE CONNECTION AT PLUG	CHECK PLUG. TRY NEW PLUG-IN. TEST FROM DIFFERENT OUTLET
POOR OR SLOW START	USUALLY DEFECTIVE STARTER	REPLACE STARTER
	COLD WEATHER (Fluorescent lamps are unsatisfactory below 50° F.)	SHIELD LAMP (A special lamp for low-temperature operation is available)
NO START	LAMP OR STARTER OR CIRCUIT DEFECTIVE	CHECK LAMP, STARTER AND CIRCUIT IN ORDER NAMED
ENDS OF LAMP REMAIN LIGHTED	DEFECTIVE STARTER	REPLACE STARTER
BALLAST HUM	NORMAL. MOST PRONOUNCED IN CHEAP SINGLE-LAMP BALLAST	INSULATE WITH RUBBER BASE. TIGHTEN SCREWS. BE SURE BALLAST HAS SOME MEANS OF VENTILATION. (See also Fig. 11)
RADIO INTERFERENCE	DIRECT RADIATION FROM LAMP OR LINE FEEDBACK	MOVE RADIO AWAY FROM LAMP. CONNECT CONDENSER ACROSS POWER LINE
STROBOSCOPIC EFFECT	NORMAL TO SOME EXTENT WITH ALL SINGLE-LAMP BALLASTS	REPLACE FIXTURE WITH TWO-LAMP UNIT USING TWO-LAMP BALLAST
	MOST PRONOUNCED WITH BLUE AND DAYLIGHT LAMPS	CHANGE TO WHITE LAMPS
FLICKER OR SWIRL	NORMAL, ESPECIALLY WHEN LAMP IS FIRST USED, BUT MAY OCCUR AT ANY TIME	SWITCH LAMP ON OR OFF A FEW TIMES OR LET IT ALONE AND IT WILL CLEAR UP ITSELF
DECREASE IN LIGHT OUTPUT	LIGHT OUTPUT DURING FIRST 100 HRS. IS ABOVE NORMAL	LAMPS ARE RATED AT 100 HR. VALUE (About 10% above normal)
	COLD WEATHER. A LIGHT LOSS OF ABOUT 1% PER DEGREE BELOW 65° F.	ENCLOSE OR PROTECT LAMP. USE SPECIAL COLD-WEATHER LAMP
END BLACKENING	NORMAL NEAR END OF LIFE. CAUSED BY BURNING OF COATING ON FILAMENT	IF OCCURRING EARLY IN LIFE, CAREFUL CHECK OF ENTIRE FIXTURE SHOULD BE MADE

FLUORESCENT-LAMP, TROUBLE-SHOOTING CHART

If the tube glows red, Fig. 6, the filament is operating correctly but the activating material has been burned off. When the lamp lights and the end of the tube glows, Fig. 7, that end of the tube is good. If both ends test, the tube is satisfactory. For accurate results, and also to avoid overloading the tube filament, the test lamp should be 60 watts for 14, 15, 20 and 30-w. tubes. Use a 100-w. test lamp for 40-w. tube; 20-w. test lamp for 65 and 100-w. tubes; 25-w. test lamp for the small miniature tubes.

Radio interference: Direct radiation from the tube is eliminated easily by simply moving the lamp or radio. Line feedback can be cut to a very low level by connecting a small condenser across the line, Fig. 9. Special condensers are made for this purpose. Ground the free end of each condenser to the fixture.

Ballast hum: Correction for ballast hum often is made by simply tightening loose screws holding the ballast, as shown in Fig. 10. A rubber shim under the ballast, Fig. 11, will give a more positive reduction of noise. For complete elimination of noise, the ballast can be moved any reasonable distance from the lamp without affecting its performance, Fig. 11. As a general rule, keep ballast within 50 ft. of lamp, avoid damp locations, air temperatures 120 deg. F. and above.

Circuit testing: If both lamp and starter check correctly, the fault is in the circuit. Test with an electrical tester or a 220-v., 100-w. lamp, as shown in Fig. 12. If the test lamp does not light, the fault is farther along the line and the whole wiring system must be checked.

Power factor: This means that the line must carry an over-supply of current in order to transmit a smaller amount of current which is actually used. Thus, if a ballast requires twice as much current in the line as it actually uses, it has a low power factor of 50 percent. Power factor does not affect lamp performance. Its only effect: need for heavier wiring.

Stroboscopic effect: This should not be confused with an actual flicker or blink. Stroboscopic effect shows itself on moving machinery, where, when the moving part and the lamp cycle happen to be timed just right, rotating parts may appear to stand still or to rotate backwards. The highest correction is obtained by using two lamps arranged so that one is "off" while the other is "on." However, a two-lamp fixture is not insurance against stroboscopic effect as many are two single lamps, each with separate ballast, Fig. 13. Current surge of each is the same. Correction is made only with a two-lamp high power-factor ballast.

Inexpensive Ceiling Fixture

If you are fixing up a basement recreation room and are looking for an inexpensive indirect-lighting fixture, here's one that is modern in appearance and extremely easy to make. It's nothing more than a 24-in. disk of sheet aluminum, with a hole in the center, supported by a standard bowl-type bulb which has a silver coating over the lower half to reflect the light upward. The hole in the disk should be of a size to permit the reflector to rest horizontally on the bulb at the point where it is coated. Galvanized sheet metal also can be used for the reflector, although a highly polished metal, such as aluminum or tinplate, is preferred as it will provide better reflection. The underside of the reflector can be painted to match or harmonize with the color treatment of the room. Silver-coated bulbs can be purchased at any electrical store.

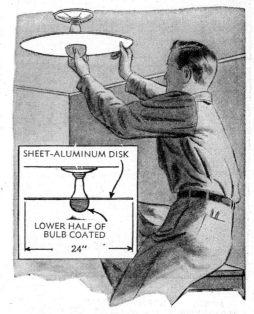

SHEET-ALUMINUM DISK

LOWER HALF OF BULB COATED

24"

Increasing Life of Lamp Cord

When the rubber covering of a floor-lamp cord shows signs of deterioration, change it end for end in the lamp. As the length of wire protected within the lamp standard is approximately equal to the length of the exposed wire outside the lamp, reversing the wire brings an entirely new portion into use. Before making the change, however, all broken parts of the rubber insulation should be taped carefully, and care should be taken to see that the same worn and chafed portions are not exposed where the wire enters the lamp base.

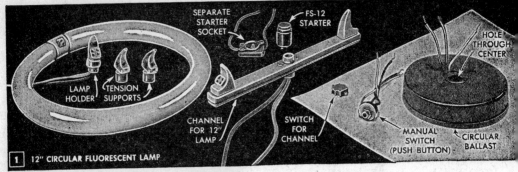

1 12" CIRCULAR FLUORESCENT LAMP

Labels: SEPARATE STARTER SOCKET · FS-12 STARTER · HOLE THROUGH CENTER · LAMP HOLDER · TENSION SUPPORTS · CHANNEL FOR 12" LAMP · SWITCH FOR CHANNEL · MANUAL SWITCH (PUSH BUTTON) · CIRCULAR BALLAST

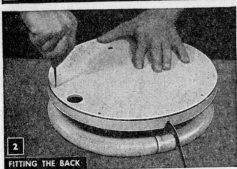

2 FITTING THE BACK

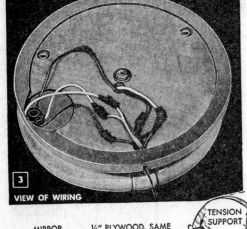

3 VIEW OF WIRING

RINGS OF

By Sam Brown

CIRCULAR fluorescent lamps offer new possibilities for making special fixtures in more compact and attractive designs than was possible with the long, tubular lamps. Although a complete range of sizes of the new circular lamps is not yet available, simple ceiling and wall fixtures for the small and medium-size lamps can be made by any craftsman.

Circular lamps can be used for large, illuminated magnifiers or opaque projectors, and are excellent, too, for house-number lights, merchandise-display fixtures and illumination for certain power tools. The square ballast can be housed in most ceiling fixtures and is considerably cheaper than the circular type. The mirror style of fixture is excellent for close work like

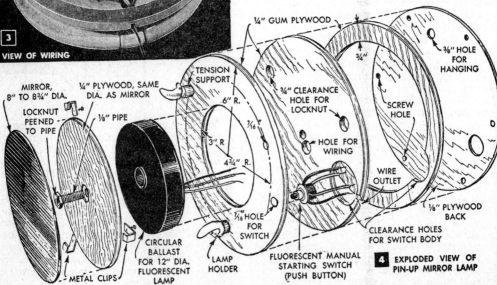

4 EXPLODED VIEW OF PIN-UP MIRROR LAMP

Labels: ¼" GUM PLYWOOD · ⅜" HOLE FOR HANGING · MIRROR, 8" TO 8¾" DIA. · ¼" PLYWOOD, SAME DIA. AS MIRROR · TENSION SUPPORT · ¾" CLEARANCE HOLE FOR LOCKNUT · SCREW HOLE · ¾" · LOCKNUT PEENED TO PIPE · ⅛" PIPE · 6" R. · 7/16 · 3" R. · HOLE FOR WIRING · 4¾" R. · WIRE OUTLET · ⅛" PLYWOOD BACK · CIRCULAR BALLAST FOR 12" DIA. FLUORESCENT LAMP · 7/16 HOLE FOR SWITCH · LAMP HOLDER · FLUORESCENT MANUAL STARTING SWITCH (PUSH BUTTON) · CLEARANCE HOLES FOR SWITCH BODY · METAL CLIPS

176

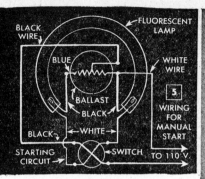

LIGHT

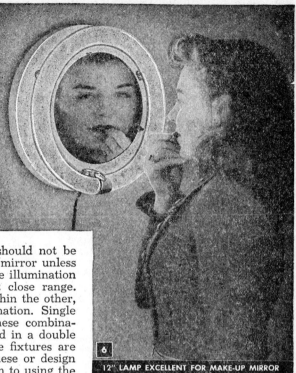

12" LAMP EXCELLENT FOR MAKE-UP MIRROR

applying make-up. However, it should not be employed as a general long-view mirror unless a special reflector is used, because illumination blacks out the mirror except at close range. Lamps of three sizes nest one within the other, offering scope for added illumination. Single ballasts are available to work these combinations. Lamps also can be arranged in a double deck. Although only three simple fixtures are shown here, anyone can adapt these or design others to fit individual needs, even to using the circular lamps in floor and table units. Study the details carefully and notice how the various parts fit together to form a neat, compact unit.

Parts: Other than lamps, the special parts needed are shown in Fig. 1. The supporting or mounting members for the lamp consist of a fixed lamp holder with four wire leads, and two spring-actuated tension supports. A second type of mounting is the channel, which has one fixed lamp holder and one tension support. A special starter, FS-12, is needed for all fixtures using automatic starting. All units require a special size of ballast, which can be obtained in either the rectangular or circular type. Other parts, such as manual switches and starter sockets, are standard fluorescent-lamp equipment.

Pin-Up Mirror Lamp: Construction of this unit, which is pictured in Fig. 6, is shown in Fig. 4. The unit uses a 12-in. circular lamp. The body or base consists of three rings of ¼-in. plywood, which are glued together after the various openings required have been cut or drilled. Fig. 7 shows how the lamp looks in section, the circular ballast projecting forward and serving as a base for the plywood-backed mirror. Note that the mirror is attached to the plywood backing by means of small metal clips, Fig. 4. These are exposed in the finished fixture so care should be taken to space them equally. The backing piece is counterbored to take a standard ⅛-in. locknut which is peened to a ⅛-in. pipe nipple. This nipple passes through the plywood backing plate, the circular ballast unit and also the third spacing disk, Fig. 7. In assembling, a locknut turned

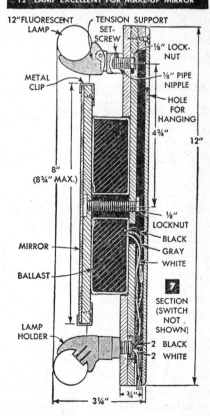

12" FLUORESCENT LAMP

TENSION SUPPORT
SET-SCREW

⅛" LOCK-NUT

METAL CLIP

⅛" PIPE NIPPLE

HOLE FOR HANGING

4¾"

12"

8"
(8¾" MAX.)

⅛" LOCKNUT

MIRROR

BLACK
GRAY
WHITE

BALLAST

7

SECTION (SWITCH NOT SHOWN)

LAMP HOLDER

2 BLACK
2 WHITE

3¼"

¾"

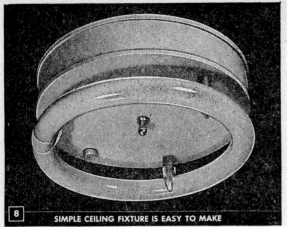

SIMPLE CEILING FIXTURE IS EASY TO MAKE

onto the projecting end of the nipple draws the parts tightly together ready for gluing and screwing to the mounting disk and spacer. Finish the edges of the plywood smooth to provide a good base for enamel. The lamp holder and tension supports are spaced equally around a circle having a radius of 4¾ in., mounting being made by means of a pipe nipple and locknut. Fig. 2 shows how the back is fitted. The whole unit is easy to make despite its complex appearance in the drawings. The finish should be white or a pastel shade of enamel. Lamp temperature is about 110 deg. so there is no danger of heat discoloring the finish or causing the wooden parts to catch fire.

Wiring: The wiring diagram for the pin-up lamp is shown in Fig. 5. The view of the wiring shown in Fig. 3 looks involved, but it really is simple as the various units have colored lead wires. If the small, 8¼-in. circular lamp is used, its low-voltage rating permits it to be used with a simple, series type of ballast. This has two leads, and wiring is just a matter of cutting the ballast into one wire of the power line. Medium and large circular lamps require an auto-transformer type of ballast which has three lead wires.

Ceiling Fixture: A basic type of ceiling fixture consists of a circular mounting frame or body with a 12-in. circular lamp supported by a three-point mounting. Fig. 8 shows a typical unit, excellent for kitchen or game room. This unit employs the automatic starter, and is constructed as indicated in Figs. 9, 10 and 11. Instead of using a sheet-metal rim to enclose the unit, as specified in Fig. 9, the rim of the fixture can be made a solid-wood turning as suggested by the two left-hand details of Fig. 15. Ornamentation of the rim can be done by fluting, turning or carving. If fluting or turning is used, a hardwood that will harmonize with other wood finishes in the room is best but, if the rim is to be carved, it should be made of softwood to simplify the carving job. If desired, you could use aluminum or stainless steel and corrugate or otherwise ornament it. However, the simple base unit shown, with a gleaming

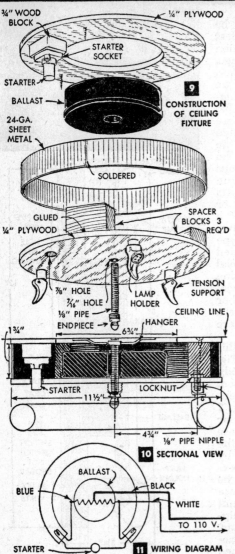

¾" WOOD BLOCK

¼" PLYWOOD

STARTER SOCKET

STARTER

BALLAST

24-GA. SHEET METAL

9 CONSTRUCTION OF CEILING FIXTURE

SOLDERED

GLUED

¼" PLYWOOD

SPACER BLOCKS 3 REQ'D

⅞" HOLE
7/16" HOLE
⅛" PIPE
ENDPIECE

LAMP HOLDER

TENSION SUPPORT

CEILING LINE

HANGER

1¾"

6¾"

STARTER

LOCKNUT

11½"

4¾" ⅛" PIPE NIPPLE

10 SECTIONAL VIEW

BALLAST

BLUE

BLACK

WHITE

TO 110 V.

STARTER

11 WIRING DIAGRAM

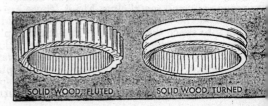

SOLID WOOD, FLUTED   SOLID WOOD, TURNED

white finish, is nice enough for almost any location. This fixture can be flush-mounted, as shown in Fig. 10, or it can be dropped down from the ceiling by using a standard ceiling outlet box as a spacer.

Shelf Fixture: This fixture, shown in Figs. 12, 13 and 14, illustrates a neat idea in a whatnot shelf, and also serves to show the wiring for the medium and large circular lamps when the ballast is mounted some distance from the fixture. As indicated in Fig. 14, three wires run from the fixture to the ballast. With average lamp cord, the ballast can be installed a distance up to 50 ft. from the fixture without any danger. Advantages of this mounting are a more compact fixture, freedom to use the less expensive square or rectangular ballast instead of the circular form, and no ballast hum. With a good ballast, hum is reduced to the minimum. Note in this unit that only two lamp supports are used, this mounting being practical in all cases except where the lamp hangs straight down from the supports. Also note how the over-all extension from the wall is decreased a little by recessing the supports into the base. The plastic shelf is in the form of a full, half circle, cut either from clear plastic or from colored plastic in blue or yellow. The curved edge is highly polished. The shelf is edge-screwed to the wooden backing disk. Take care in drilling and tapping the plastic for the screws, making the diameter of the holes very slightly smaller than the screws. If the screws fit too tightly, they may crack the plastic when driven into it. If they are too small, any weight on the shelf may strip the threads. Do not pull the screws up too tightly as this also may strip them.

Channel Mounting: The channel mounting shown in Fig. 1 is not illustrated with a specific fixture application. This mounting has central connections on both sides for ⅛-in. pipe. In combination with the small 8¼-in. lamp, fixture-making with the channel mounting is almost as simple as making one for a filament-bulb lamp. The ballast is cut into the power line, or a plug-in type of ballast is used.

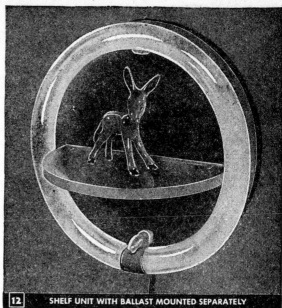

12 SHELF UNIT WITH BALLAST MOUNTED SEPARATELY

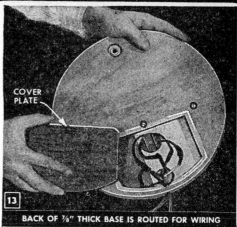

13 BACK OF ⅞" THICK BASE IS ROUTED FOR WIRING

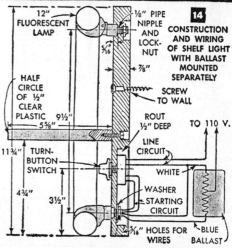

14 CONSTRUCTION AND WIRING OF SHELF LIGHT WITH BALLAST MOUNTED SEPARATELY

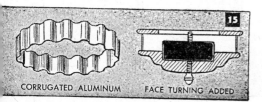

15 CORRUGATED ALUMINUM   FACE TURNING ADDED

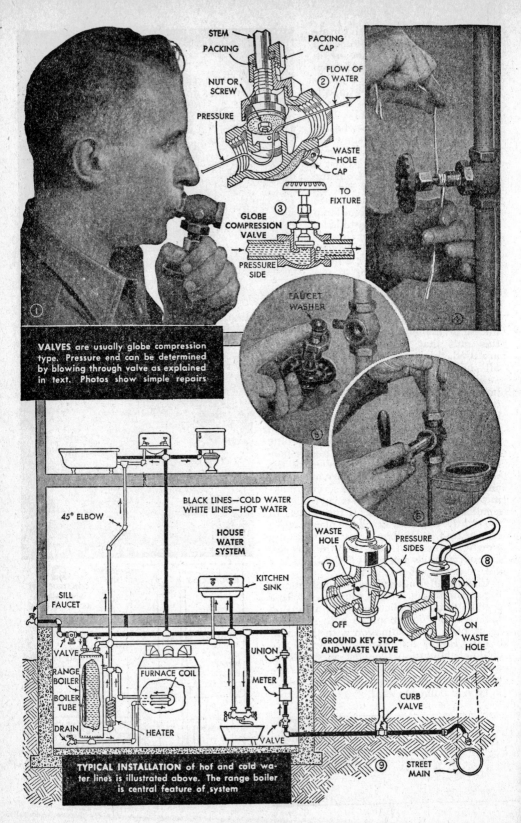

STEM

PACKING

PACKING CAP

NUT OR SCREW

② FLOW OF WATER

PRESSURE

WASTE HOLE

CAP

③ GLOBE COMPRESSION VALVE

TO FIXTURE

PRESSURE SIDE

FAUCET WASHER

⑤

⑥

VALVES are usually globe compression type. Pressure end can be determined by blowing through valve as explained in text. Photos show simple repairs

BLACK LINES—COLD WATER
WHITE LINES—HOT WATER

HOUSE WATER SYSTEM

45° ELBOW

KITCHEN SINK

SILL FAUCET

VALVE

RANGE BOILER

BOILER TUBE

DRAIN

FURNACE COIL

HEATER

UNION

METER

VALVE

WASTE HOLE

PRESSURE SIDES

⑦

⑧

OFF

ON WASTE HOLE

GROUND KEY STOP-AND-WASTE VALVE

CURB VALVE

⑨

STREET MAIN

TYPICAL INSTALLATION of hot and cold water lines is illustrated above. The range boiler is central feature of system

180

IS THERE A *Plumber* IN THE HOUSE?

PIPE LEAKS can be repaired permanently with rubber hose, as shown above. Other temporary methods are shown below together with table for determining length of pipe replacements

THERE are several small plumbing repair jobs that need only a little "know how" plus a few minutes work, and still another half dozen heavier repairs that are well within the capabilities of the average person.

Valves: No. 1 rule in plumbing is "Know your valves." If a leak should develop anywhere in the system, muss is held to a minimum if you know exactly where the main shut-off valve is located. Take the family downstairs some evening and show every member just where and how water, gas and electricity can be shut off in case anything goes wrong. The main shut-off valve usually is a stop-and-waste valve, which stops the water when turned off, and also has a small opening in one side or the bottom to drain off waste water standing in the pipes on the house side. The most common style of stop-and-waste valve is made in the familiar globe pattern, as shown in the cutaway view Figs. 2 and 3. This valve is of the compression type—being worked by turning the handle, which compresses a composition or rubber washer against the seat of the valve. The most common repair to globe valves is replacement of the washer, Fig. 5. Ordinary faucet washers are used, and the size is determined by the size of recess into which the washer fits. Leakage around the stem can be cured by unscrewing the packing nut and wrapping four or five turns of candle wicking moistened with soap or oil around the stem, as in Fig. 4. Ordinary string will do in an emergency.

The ground-key stop-and-waste valve, Figs. 7 and 8, is used in the same capacity as the globe valve, but works in an entirely different manner. This valve is a metal-to-metal contact, the tapered stem having a hole at its center which blocks or

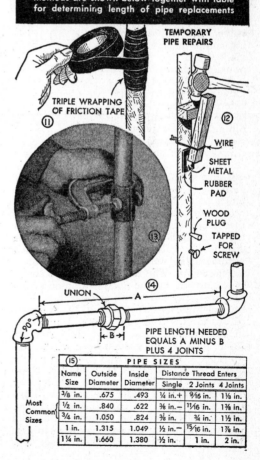

TEMPORARY PIPE REPAIRS

TRIPLE WRAPPING OF FRICTION TAPE

WIRE
SHEET METAL
RUBBER PAD
WOOD PLUG
TAPPED FOR SCREW

UNION — A

PIPE LENGTH NEEDED EQUALS A MINUS B PLUS 4 JOINTS

Most Common Sizes

Name Size	Outside Diameter	Inside Diameter	Distance Thread Enters		
			Single	2 Joints	4 Joints
3/8 in.	.675	.493	1/4 in.+	9/16 in.	1 1/8 in.
1/2 in.	.840	.622	3/8 in.−	11/16 in.	1 3/8 in.
3/4 in.	1.050	.824	3/8 in.	3/4 in.	1 1/2 in.
1 in.	1.315	1.049	1/2 in.−	15/16 in.	1 7/8 in.
1 1/4 in.	1.660	1.380	1/2 in.	1 in.	2 in.

PIPE SIZES

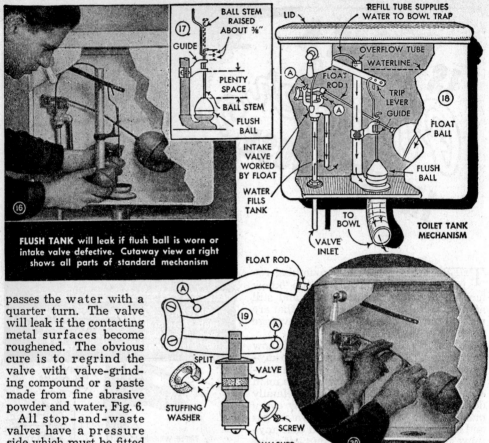

FLUSH TANK will leak if flush ball is worn or intake valve defective. Cutaway view at right shows all parts of standard mechanism

VALVE LIFTED AFTER REMOVING SCREWS AT POINTS A

passes the water with a quarter turn. The valve will leak if the contacting metal surfaces become roughened. The obvious cure is to regrind the valve with valve-grinding compound or a paste made from fine abrasive powder and water, Fig. 6.

All stop-and-waste valves have a pressure side which must be fitted to the pressure side of the piping. If the valve is installed backward, it will leak water continually through the waste hole. Fig. 1 shows how a check can be made by blowing through the valve. If the valve is the globe type, open the cap that closes the waste hole. Now, with valve turned off and the waste hole open, you can blow through the house or fixture end, but you can't blow through the pressure end. On the ground-key valve, the waste hole is opened automatically when the valve is closed.

Pipe leaks: The best "fix-it" for a leaky pipe is to cut out the poor section and couple the pipe ends with rubber hose and hose clamps, as shown in Fig. 10. A repair of this kind will last for years. 1-in. automobile radiator hose is the right size for ¾-in. pipe; ¾-in. garden hose will fit ½-in. pipe. Other emergency ways to stop a leak are shown in Figs. 11, 12 and 13. Doping with white lead, varnish or anything of similar nature under the patch will assure a good job. Of course, the best way is to install a new pipe. When you do this you will need a union connection as in Fig. 14, since you can't screw both ends of a

pipe in place at the same time. The last column of the table in Fig. 15 will help when calculating pipe lengths required.

Toilet flush tank: Likely about every 2 or 3 years the toilet flush-tank mechanism will need attention. Worst offender is the flush ball, Fig. 18, which becomes worn and permits water to escape continually into the bowl trap. Fix it by installing a new ball, observing the clearances required, as shown in Fig. 17. Fig. 16 shows the operation, but in actual practice you lift the ball stem and then turn the stem with one hand while you hold the ball in the other. Be sure that the guide is high enough. If it is too low, the ball will immediately drop back into the opening unless held up by holding the trip handle. If the new ball doesn't stop the flow of escaping water in the bowl trap, check the intake valve. First, pull up the float rod. If this stops the leak, all you have to do is bend the float rod as in Fig. 20, to put more pressure on the valve. If this does not stop the leak, the trouble is probably in the valve itself. Remove the valve core, float

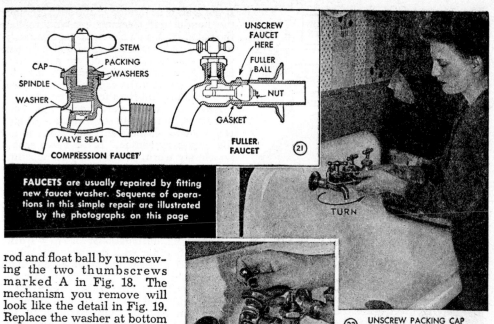

STEM
PACKING
CAP
WASHERS
SPINDLE
WASHER
VALVE SEAT

COMPRESSION FAUCET

UNSCREW FAUCET HERE
FULLER BALL
NUT
GASKET

FULLER FAUCET

(21)

FAUCETS are usually repaired by fitting new faucet washer. Sequence of operations in this simple repair are illustrated by the photographs on this page

TURN

rod and float ball by unscrewing the two thumbscrews marked A in Fig. 18. The mechanism you remove will look like the detail in Fig. 19. Replace the washer at bottom (use a faucet washer of the right size), also inspect and replace, if necessary, the leather stuffing washer at the center of the core. When repairing a flush-tank valve, the water supply must be shut off. If the job is merely a new flush ball you can shut the water off at the tank itself by holding up the float rod.

After the flush-tank mechanism has been put in good condition, oil the trip-lever mechanism occasionally. Check the float ball for leaks by shaking it gently with the tank empty. If desired, the end of the refill tube can be pinched together slightly to conserve water since it supplies more than enough water to fill the bowl trap; the end must not be below water level.

Faucets: These need attention more frequently than any other part of the plumbing system. They differ in external appearance, but the working mechanism is always the same. Chances are your faucets are compression type. If the water comes on full blast with half a turn of the handle, they are quick-compression type. If it takes four or five turns, they are ordinary or slow-compression

(22) **UNSCREW PACKING CAP WITH MONKEY WRENCH**

type. Both work the same way. The fuller-ball type of faucet has been off the market for a number of years, but is still found in actual use. Typical compression and fuller faucets are shown in Fig. 21. The compression type is repaired by replacing the washer at the end of the spindle, the whole operation being as shown in Figs. 22

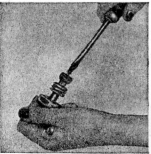

(23) **TURN COUNTER-CLOCKWISE AND PULL OUT SPINDLE**

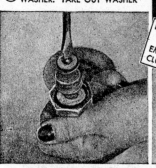

(24) **REMOVE SCREW HOLDING WASHER. TAKE OUT WASHER**

(25) **FIT NEW WASHER OF PROPER SIZE. REASSEMBLE**

DOWEL
EMERY CLOTH GLUED

(26) **IF VALVE SEAT IS ROUGH, SANDPAPER SMOOTH**

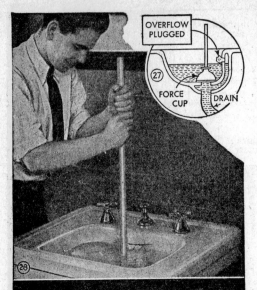

REMOVING OBSTRUCTIONS is less trouble when proper tools such as force cup and coil-spring augers are used. Obstructions treated promptly seldom become serious

If the leak is at the top of the stem, remove the handle and packing cap and replace the packing. If you haven't a regular packing ring, you can use candle wicking or string moistened with oil or soap. If a faucet leaks at the threaded part of packing cap, unscrew the cap and wrap a piece of thread around the threaded portion.

After a faucet valve seat has been smoothed by reaming several times, it may require two washers instead of one to get the necessary contact. If the valve seat is hopelessly worn, you can buy composition insert seats and make the valve as good as new. For a few cents extra you can buy a faucet washer fitted with a ball bearing ring, which reduces abrasion wear to zero and gives good results even on roughened valve seats.

Removing obstructions: Every home owner is familiar with the force cup shown in Figs. 27 and 28. On lavatory and bath connections, you can get more positive results if the waste opening is plugged with a wet cloth as shown in Fig. 27. Obstructions in the toilet bowl usually are easily removed with an inexpensive closet

to 25 inclusive. Equally simple, the fuller faucet is repaired by unscrewing the portion shown in Fig. 21 and fitting a new rubber fuller ball.

Be sure the main valve is turned off before you fix faucets. Open the faucet to release standing water and back pressure, then go ahead with the repair. While you're at it, inspect the valve seat (compression faucets) since a new washer is of little use if the seat is rough or scratched. If mildly rough, smooth it with a disk of sandpaper on a stick as shown in Fig. 26; if very rough, invest fifty cents in a faucet reamer. Of course, the faucet can leak at other points independent of the washer.

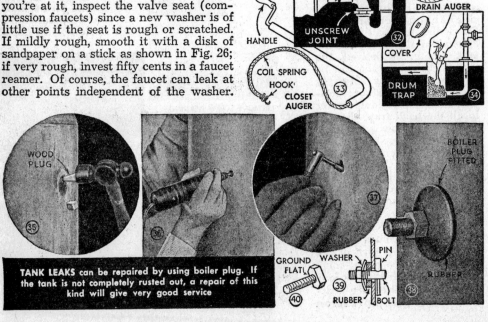

TANK LEAKS can be repaired by using boiler plug. If the tank is not completely rusted out, a repair of this kind will give very good service

auger as in Figs. 29 and 33. A somewhat similar gadget called a drain auger, Figs. 30 and 31, is useful for a wide variety of "stopped-up" conditions. If force cup and auger fail to remove an obstruction in a lavatory or sink, remove the trap by slightly loosening the slip joint and unscrewing the ring at gasket joint, Fig. 32. When replacing trap, inspect gaskets and use new ones if needed. If the trap is the drum type, unscrew the cover and scoop out the dirt and grease with spoon as Fig. 34 shows.

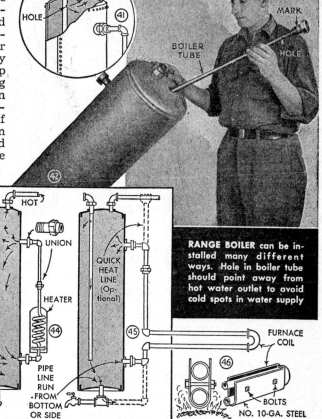

RANGE BOILER can be installed many different ways. Hole in boiler tube should point away from hot water outlet to avoid cold spots in water supply

Tank leaks: The average galvanized water tank has a life of about seven years. When it starts to leak, you might as well get a new one. Leaks can be stopped temporarily by driving in soft wooden plugs, as shown in Fig. 35. More permanent is the regular boiler plug sold for this purpose. To fit the plug, enlarge the hole, Fig. 36, so that the plug can be inserted as in Fig. 37, then fit the rubber washer and draw up tight to complete the job as in Figs. 38 and 39. A similar repair can be done by grinding the head of a bolt, Fig. 40, enlarging the opening to admit it and turning it crosswise, using a rubber disk in the same manner as with the boiler plug.

Installing new range boiler: Any of the installations shown in Figs. 43 to 46 inclusive will give good results at minimum expense for new parts. Simplest of all is the gas ring below the tank, shown in Fig. 43, its only fault being that heat absorption is not efficient due to the small tank area exposed to the gas flame. The side-arm gas heater, Fig. 44, makes a good set-up. A furnace coil is seldom used alone since it works only when the furnace is going. Fig. 9 shows how a furnace coil is combined with a side-arm gas heater or gas ring. The "quick heat" line, Fig. 45, can be installed in any set-up, and has the feature of supplying a small but very hot supply of water almost instantly. In making any installation, remember that hot water always rises to the highest point. Follow the natural flow of hot water in your system and be sure that all lines pitch slightly upward. This insures good circulation, and eliminates air pockets and cracking noise when water is turned on.

The boiler tube must be inserted before the tank is set upright, Fig. 42, since it is too long to be fitted in the average height of a basement. The hole at top of tube prevents water from being siphoned out of the tank when the water is turned off. Mark its position so that it can be located facing away from the hot water outlet, otherwise cold water from the hole mixes with the hot water, Fig. 41.

Testing Christmas-Tree Bulbs

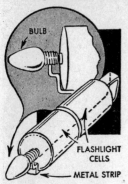

Locating a burned-out lamp bulb in a string of series - wired Christmas - tree lights is done quickly with this little tester. It consists of two flashlight cells and a metal strip bent as shown to hold the cells. To test a bulb, hold the bottom contact against the front-cell contact and let the threaded part of the base touch the metal strip. The flashlight cells are strong enough to make the bulb glow dimly if it is not burned out.

Flashlight Bulbs Illuminate Tree if Electricity Is Not Available

One man, whose home is not wired for electricity, illuminates his Christmas tree with a battery-operated string of flashlight bulbs, thus eliminating the fire hazard of candles. He removed the male plug from an ordinary light string and connected the ends of the string to the terminals of a car battery. For convenience, he wired a feed-through switch into the circuit. The length of the base of the flashlight bulbs was increased to fit the sockets by adding a drop of solder to the contact point of each bulb. To give the tree a more pleasing appearance, he tinted each one of the bulbs with water colors.

Wall Lamp Easily Assembled from Socket and Metal Angle

When regular fixtures are not available, a small metal bracket and a brass socket can be used as a wall lamp. The socket is fastened to the bracket which, in turn, is screwed to a door or window casing. Small shades that clamp on the bulb complete the lamp. If additional outlets are desired, an extension outlet is screwed into the socket, but care should be taken not to overload the circuit.

Cement to Extend Life of Broken Element in Electric Heater or Stove

The life of a broken element in an electric heater or stove can be extended if the broken ends of the wire, after first being cleaned with fine sandpaper or emery cloth to remove corrosion, are twisted together and then coated liberally with a paste consisting of common borax, 1 part, and commercial iron cement, 3 parts by volume. The ingredients are mixed with just enough water to make a workable paste and then forced in and around the junction point of the wires. After cementing, the current should be turned on to heat and set the cement. Of course, rough treatment should be avoided after making the repair.

◖ An attractive globe for an outside entrance light can be made from a wide-mouthed coffee jar having a frosted top and bottom and a clear band around the center. The jar will fit into globe holders of many types. For decoration, and also for protection from broken glass, add a guard of sheet metal strips riveted together.

Part 4

HEATING AND INSULATION

TOP PERFORMANCE

ROTARY BURNER CAN BE INSTALLED IN ROUND, SQUARE OR RECTANGULAR FIREBOX

1   VERTICAL ROTARY BURNER

OWNERS of household oil burners have come to expect uninterrupted performance as a matter of course. This is due largely to the cooperative research and ingenuity of manufacturers, dealers and servicemen in an effort to produce ever-better burners and more efficient installations.

Because of its ease of handling and its own peculiar burning characteristics, oil is one of the comparatively few fuels which lend themselves readily to fully automatic control. To the average user, efficiency of the burner is measured by the amount of useful heat delivered per dollar expended for fuel and maintenance. Owners can do much toward maintaining a high efficiency by proper selection and care of a burner.

Figs. 1 and 2 show two types of oil burners commonly installed in home-heating plants. There are variations of these types. All are good, and the problem in selection of a burner is not so dependent on any spe-

By W. Clyde Lammey

cial merit of the burner unit as on its suitability for the heating system, the average seasonal heating load in your locality, and the peculiarities of the individual centrally fired plant, the building and its immediate surroundings. In addition to the two burners shown in Figs. 1 and 2, one of which operates by mechanical draft, the other by a combination of natural and mechanical draft, there is the natural-draft pot burner, sometimes called the vaporizing bowl burner. This burner usually is supplied in oil-burning space heaters, but also is furnished in oil-fired furnaces as in Fig. 10. This latter type of burner operates with a forced or mechanical draft. When installed in correctly designed furnaces and supplied with uniformly high-grade fuel it is very efficient. With mechanical draft, the burner is somewhat less sensitive to fuel characteristics than the natural-draft pot burner. It is especially suitable in small homes where

FROM YOUR OIL BURNER

WHEN GUN BURNER IS ADJUSTED CORRECTLY FLAME LOOKS LIKE THIS

2   GUN-TYPE BURNER

the fuel required runs less than 1½ gallons per hour. The vertical rotary burner, Fig. 1, also made in the horizontal type, is simple in design and construction and is noted for its quiet operation. Oil is fed either by pump or by gravity to a rapidly rotating distributor which combines a fan and oil "slinger." The distributor projects the oil against a hot flame ring, which may be made of metal or refractory material. Heat from the ring vaporizes the fuel and the air-oil mixture burns with a yellow-tipped blue flame that sweeps or "wipes" the walls of the firebox. Because of this characteristic it is often called the wall-flame burner. The flame ring can be installed in a round, square or rectangular firebox. Fig. 3 shows the principle of operation more clearly. Burners of this type often are recommended for installation in older-type heating plants and in small homes where fuel requirement in gallons per hour is quite low.

The so-called gun burner, Fig. 2, is per-haps the most common type installed in centrally fired home-heating plants. These burners operate on two principles, atomization by oil pressure and atomization or emulsification of the fuel by low-pressure air. Low-pressure burners of this type, Fig. 8, can provide the low flame necessary in heating small homes, and because of the large openings through which oil and air flow together, the nozzle does not clog so readily when lower-grade fuel oils are used. Fig. 9 details the nozzle of a burner of the high-pressure type. Here oil is fed from a pump through an oil line to an atomizing nozzle under high pressure, as much as 100 lbs. per sq. in. in some burners. This burner is more sensitive to the quality of the oil but is a highly efficient unit when supplied with high-grade fuel. Although both high and low-pressure burners are similar in design and installation requirements, the low-pressure type differs from the former in that a portion of the combus-

CORRECT OIL-AIR MIXTURE GETS ALL THE HEAT FROM THE FUEL OIL

Courtesy Timken Silent Automatic Div.,Timken-Detroit Axle Co.

Because fuel oil is so easy to handle and requires comparatively small space for storage of a season's supply, oil-fired heating plants are among the first requirements of present-day home-owners. Clean-burning characteristics of oil make it easy to have fully automatic heat in any home

4 HEAT LOSSES:

Walls and Roof	44.4
Glass and Doors	26.0
Cracks	20.8
Floors	8.8
Total	**100.0**

5 FIT STORM SASH

6 WEATHER-STRIP OUTSIDE DOORS

7 INSULATE WALLS AND CEILING

tion air is drawn in with the oil by an atomizing pump. Expansion of the air causes the oil to froth or emulsify and thus enables the burner to deliver an oil-air mixture to the combustion chamber under low pressure through a comparatively large orifice. For this reason the low-pressure burner will operate satisfactorily on a wide range of fuels.

With the exception of the pot burners, in which the fuel is ignited manually and thereafter burns continuously, all late-type burners have some means of automatic ignition. There are several methods, the most common employing a pair of electrodes with high-voltage current supplied by a transformer built into the burner unit. Some burners are fitted with a resistance coil which is heated to incandescence to ignite the air-oil mixture. A few burners use a gas-pilot ignition which burns continuously; others a gas-electric system.

A control unit for an oil burner is designed to maintain automatically the desired room temperature with very little variation from the manual setting. It consists of a room thermostat, a primary control and a limit control. The ordinary room thermostat is the most used. Several types are available for special conditions. Some are clock controlled to give variable

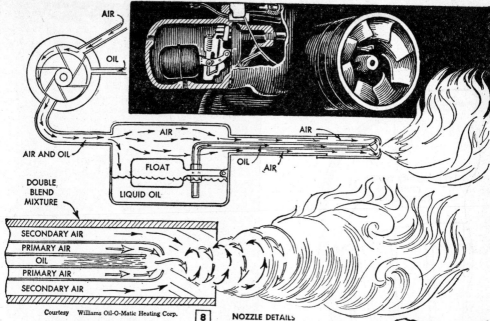

DOUBLE
BLEND
MIXTURE

SECONDARY AIR
PRIMARY AIR
OIL
PRIMARY AIR
SECONDARY AIR

Courtesy Williams Oil-O-Matic Heating Corp.

8 NOZZLE DETAILS
LOW-PRESSURE GUN TYPE

day and night temperatures, and automatically change the settings according to a predetermined schedule. Others are special double-contact types for controlling mechanical-draft pot burners that operate continuously with several stages of fire. When the room temperature is in the range between the two sets of contacts the flame is at "medium fire"; when below, "high fire," and when above, at "pilot fire." In the event of power failure this type of thermostat automatically places the burner at pilot fire with natural draft. Some thermostats are more sensitive than others but usually adjustments are provided for varying the range, or differential, between the "cut-in" and "cut-out" points. This makes it possible to adjust performance to the needs of the individual installation.

Most primary controls are merely safety devices. This control usually is installed between the thermostat and burner and, in addition to closing motor and ignition circuits when the thermostat calls for heat, it will cut out the motor if the fuel oil fails to ignite on starting and also will stop the burner in case of flame failure at any time during the running

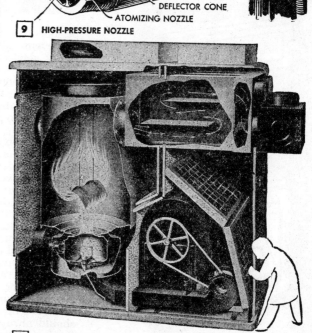

IGNITERS AIR TUBE
DEFLECTOR
BLADES

OIL LINE
DEFLECTOR CONE
ATOMIZING NOZZLE

9 HIGH-PRESSURE NOZZLE

10 POT-TYPE BURNER, FORCED DRAFT *Courtesy* Perfection Stove Co

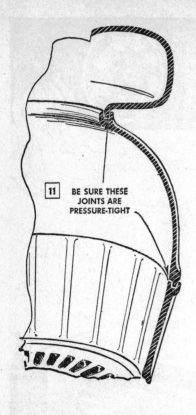

11 BE SURE THESE JOINTS ARE PRESSURE-TIGHT

13 POSSIBLE AIR LEAKS

12 SEAL DOORS WITH FURNACE CEMENT

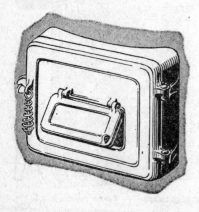

period. At a time of current interruption it prevents starting of the burner until all safety devices are in starting position. Primary controls are designed to meet various conditions and should always be installed in accordance with the directions of the manufacturer. Purpose of the limit controls is to prevent the generation of excessive temperatures or pressures in the furnace or boiler. When, for any reason, the room thermostat is still calling for heat after the safety limits of pressure or temperature have been reached, the limit control "takes over" and shuts off the burner. When pressure or temperature returns to the predetermined "cut-in" point, the control again closes the burner circuit and the burner resumes operation. A pressure limit control is installed on a steam boiler, while a temperature limit control is required for a warm-air furnace or hot-water boiler. In addition, other controls are often furnished. The burner manufacturer's directions and recommendations should always be followed when making the installation.

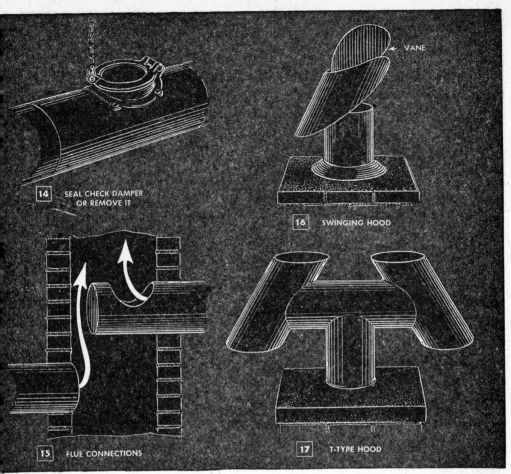

14 SEAL CHECK DAMPER OR REMOVE IT

16 SWINGING HOOD

VANE

15 FLUE CONNECTIONS

17 T-TYPE HOOD

Courtesy Standard Oil Co. (Indiana)

When installing the fuel-storage tank either inside or outside the building, the requirements of the local codes should be carefully followed. General requirements are that unenclosed tanks inside the building should be not less than 7 ft. from any fire or flame and should not exceed 275 gallons capacity. Certain universal requirements that govern the installation of underground tanks outside buildings also are subject to the installation codes in your locality. Specifications usually cover size and spacing of the tank or tanks, depth, footings, fill and suction lines, venting, location with respect to property boundaries, swing joints in the fill and vent pipes if these are of iron, distance of tank from foundation wall, etc.

Although many experienced **servicemen** can set a burner

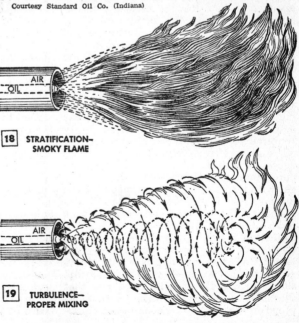

18 STRATIFICATION— SMOKY FLAME

AIR
OIL

19 TURBULENCE— PROPER MIXING

AIR
OIL

193

WHAT'S WRONG??

A. High oil consumption.
1. Excessive air infiltration.
2. Boiler too small—insufficient radiation.
3. Boiler controls improperly set.
4. Dirty heat-absorbing surfaces.
5. Incorrect firing rate.
6. Excessive temperatures carried.

B. Burner starts and burns satisfactorily but fails after one minute of operation.
1. Air in suction lines.
2. Excess draft.
3. Strainers clogged.
4. Oil-tank vent obstructed.
5. Dirt or water in oil.
6. Controls out of order.
7. Insufficient fire.

C. Burner puffs when first started.
1. Poor or delayed ignition.
2. Insufficient draft.

D. Carbon forms in combustion chamber.
1. Improper or defective nozzle.
2. Nozzle clogged or dirty.
3. Insufficient air.
4. Oil spray impinges on walls. May be caused by misalignment of burner.
5. Drip from nozzle.
6. Excessive oil-burning rate.

E. Burner starts, runs properly and has proper oil pressure, but fails to ignite.
1. Nozzle may be clogged.
2. Electrodes out of adjustment.
3. No spark.

F. Objectionable odors or smoke.
1. Insufficient air admitted.
2. Excessive baffling of flue passages.
3. Combustion chamber too small.
4. Leaks in fuel-oil lines.
5. Insufficient draft.

Certain of the above suggestions are applicable only to gun-type burners.

Courtesy Standard Oil Co. (Indiana)

very accurately "by eye," most careful workmen will check performance with special instruments just to make sure before they okay the job, whether it be a routine seasonal servicing or a checkup on a new installation. One of the visible evidences of good or poor performance is indicated in Figs. 18 and 19. Poor or defective atomization forms large particles of oil which take a longer time to burn. Many particles do not burn at all and form coke deposits and soot. If the air supply is insufficient and mixing inadequate, unburned gases leave the furnace, resulting in a material loss of heat. Partly clogged nozzles or deflector vanes coated with soot deposit, often cause stratification of the oil-air stream, Fig. 18, which results in only a part of the atomized oil mixing properly with the air. This slows the burning rate, thereby producing smoky flames and undue quantities of excess air. Some excess of air over the theoretical quantity required to burn a given amount of fuel oil is always necessary. The quantity of excess air can be gauged by checking the percentage of carbon dioxide in the flue gas with a special instrument made for the purpose. This is an important test in determining the efficiency and performance of an oil burner. The carbon-dioxide, CO_2, content of the flue gases should be at least 10 percent with the burner properly adjusted. When everything is working correctly you get a flame something like that shown in Fig. 19. It's also important that the flames from a gun burner do not impinge on the sides of the combustion chamber at any point. Manufacturers specify the size and shape of the combustion chamber in their installation instructions and these directions should be followed in detail.

Insufficient draft is a common cause of minor oil-burner troubles. In some basements there is so little air infiltration due to a lack of ventilation, that the furnace room may be "air locked." Such a condition can result in insufficient air for complete combustion. The chimney may be inadequate, partially clogged with soot, a piece of tile lining or other material, and the top may be lower than the roof ridge or a nearby tree or building. Any of these conditions can affect the efficient operation of the burner. In older heating plants, air leaks in the furnace firebox, especially in a cast-iron warm-air furnace, Fig. 11, and in the cleanout and fire doors, Fig. 12, may affect the operation of the burner and also can be the cause of objectionable odors in the house. Any openings in the smoke pipe, chimney or furnace cleanout doors, Fig. 13, details A, B and C, act as tiny check dampers. Figs. 14 to 17 inclusive suggest methods of remedying other chimney and smoke-pipe defects. Inspect the draft regulator supplied with the burner periodically to be sure it is working properly. Fig. 20 lists a number of ordinary troubles that sometimes occur. Although the remedies vary with different types of burners, in most cases correction of the trouble is quite simple.

In addition to the hints mentioned on care of your burner, remember that what is true of almost all home-heating plants fired by other fuels is equally true of the oil-burning installation, that is, in rating efficiency the whole plant should be considered, and not merely the burner alone. Some of these points to be taken into account in both new and old installations do not relate directly to the operation of the burner, but do affect its efficiency indirectly. Take, for example, the heat loss from a building of average construction. Where the temperature inside the house must be maintained at a level higher than that outside—even though the variation is only a few degrees—there will be a constant loss of heat to the atmosphere. The variables which affect the rate of heat loss during a season are outside temperature, rain or snow, sunshine or cloudiness and wind velocity or exposure. Fig. 4 gives the average percentages of loss through various parts of the structure. Since the greatest loss is through the walls and roof, it is easy to see the value of insulation, Fig. 7, in slowing the rate at which heat is lost. Tight-fitting storm windows and storm doors, Fig. 5, will materially reduce the second percentage value given in Fig. 4 and weather stripping, Fig. 6, and caulking will stop infiltration of air through cracks. In many cases these inexpensive installations will reduce heat losses as much as 50 percent or more in old buildings as well as in new construction. Repeated opening and closing of doors in cold weather, windows open at night in sleeping rooms, hot water for baths, laundry, and dishwashing all add to the load on the heating plant and require extra fuel. Roughly, depending on locality, fuel consumption increases 2½ percent or more for each degree that the inside temperature is maintained above 70 deg. F. This can be offset by lowering the inside temperature 10 deg. during the 8-hour sleeping period. However, as heat loss is directly related to outside temperature, it is likely that, as an average, the greatest saving will be effected by insulation on walls and ceilings and by installation of storm sash or double-glazed windows, and weather stripping.

Patching Small Holes in Walls

The small hole that remains in a wall after a gas or water pipe has been removed is easily patched if a cork is used to back up the plaster. The cork is trimmed to size and pressed in the hole flush with the lath.

❡ To reduce the tendency of furnace pipes to rust in a damp basement in summer, burn papers in the firebox 10 or 12 times throughout the season.

Ventilator Formed from Plastic Admits Light and Air

Novel because it is made of transparent plastic that will admit light, this ventilator can be made to fit almost any window. One half is formed to slide inside the other with the tops and bottoms curved as shown in the detail. The louvers are bent in to provide protection from rain and snow, and this also serves to direct drafts upward.

Groove in Door Edge Stops Leaks

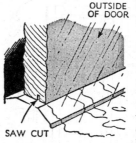

If water from a driving rain seeps under an outside door, this trouble can be corrected in most cases by merely making a ¼ in. saw cut in the lower edge of the door. Drops of water passing under the door will, when they reach the groove, fall to the threshold and drain back outside. To cut the groove, remove the door from its hinges and nail two guide strips to the lower edge, spacing them just far enough apart to take the saw blade.

❡ Window screens are converted to temporary storm windows by coating them with thinned cellulose cement or clear lacquer. In spring, the screens are restored to original condition with thinner.

COME OUT OF YOUR IGLOO

DOES IT TAKE more fuel than it should to keep your home comfortably warm? Then, now is the time to come out of your igloo and plug the cracks that are letting the heat escape. Heat loss from the average house can be figured in approximately equal proportions: 25 percent through the glass of windows and doors and 25 percent through openings around them. Another 25 percent is lost through uninsulated side walls and 25 percent more through the roof. These figures will vary, of course, with each type of house, but they offer a basis for weighing the value of storm sash, weather stripping, caulking and insulation. Insulation, besides reducing fuel costs, adds healthful comfort both winter and summer; for just as it keeps the heat in, it also keeps the heat out. Rooms will be 8 to 15 percent cooler in summer. Below are things you can do to help keep the heat at home and money in your pocket.

Storm sash can save you 15 percent or more on winter fuel bills by reducing heat loss through windows. It pays to put them on every window of the house, including basement windows, and especially on those with a north and west exposure

Like windows, exterior doors let heat escape, too, if they are left unprotected. The best storm door to use here is the popular combination type which has an interchangeable sash-and-screen unit. For best results the storm door should fit snugly

Closing off unused rooms during the winter months is another way of saving the heat and promoting greater comfort. If the opening is large, French doors are both practical and smart looking. A heavy drape can be used to close off a doorway

Cracks around doors and window sash provide another exit for heat and an entrance for drafts, but you can seal them effectively with a metal weather stripping which is simply tacked to the casing. Being flexible, it bears against the door

By Wayne C. Leckey

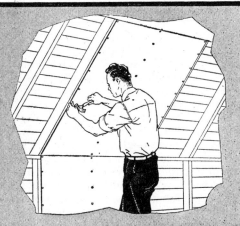

Lining an unfinished attic with wallboard will help keep the heat in and provide useful rooms at the same time. Standard-width sheets permit direct application to studs and rafters. Joints can be covered neatly with plain wooden battens

Up to 25-percent saving in fuel can be had by insulating your home. Not only will you have a warmer home in winter, but a cooler one in summer. Blanket and batt-type insulation are ideal for new construction and fill insulation for old

Sealing cracks due to shrinkage that develop around window frames of brick homes can be done with caulking compound. You can use either a mastic-type compound, or one marketed in rope form which is pressed into the joint with a knife

Cold and drafty floors of homes constructed without foundations can be eliminated by banking straw and leaves around the outside. Asphalt roofing felt is first tacked to building as shown, and boards weighted with stones anchor the straw

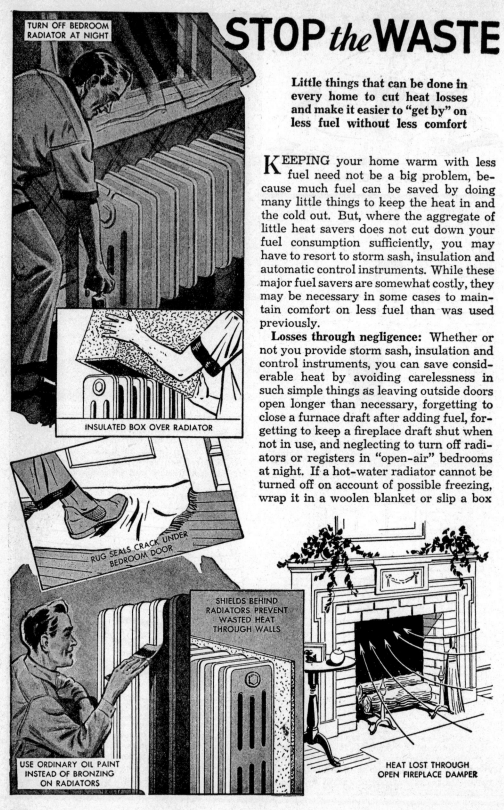

STOP *the* WASTE

Little things that can be done in every home to cut heat losses and make it easier to "get by" on less fuel without less comfort

KEEPING your home warm with less fuel need not be a big problem, because much fuel can be saved by doing many little things to keep the heat in and the cold out. But, where the aggregate of little heat savers does not cut down your fuel consumption sufficiently, you may have to resort to storm sash, insulation and automatic control instruments. While these major fuel savers are somewhat costly, they may be necessary in some cases to maintain comfort on less fuel than was used previously.

Losses through negligence: Whether or not you provide storm sash, insulation and control instruments, you can save considerable heat by avoiding carelessness in such simple things as leaving outside doors open longer than necessary, forgetting to close a furnace draft after adding fuel, forgetting to keep a fireplace draft shut when not in use, and neglecting to turn off radiators or registers in "open-air" bedrooms at night. If a hot-water radiator cannot be turned off on account of possible freezing, wrap it in a woolen blanket or slip a box

TURN OFF BEDROOM RADIATOR AT NIGHT

INSULATED BOX OVER RADIATOR

RUG SEALS CRACK UNDER BEDROOM DOOR

SHIELDS BEHIND RADIATORS PREVENT WASTED HEAT THROUGH WALLS

USE ORDINARY OIL PAINT INSTEAD OF BRONZING ON RADIATORS

HEAT LOST THROUGH OPEN FIREPLACE DAMPER

and SAVE the HEAT

POOR CIRCULATION

GOOD CIRCULATION

A COVER THAT DEFLECTS HEAT INTO ROOM

DISCARD RADIATOR COVERS THAT IMPEDE FREE CIRCULATION

ALL CRACKS AT DOOR AND WINDOW FRAMES, AND THOSE BETWEEN WARPED SIDING, SHOULD BE FILLED WITH CALKING COMPOUND

made of insulating board over it, and leave it turned on. The object is to avoid the lowering of water temperature in the entire system, which causes more fuel to be burned to restore the temperature to normal. Likewise, cold-air returns in an open bedroom should be shut off to prevent extremely cold air from entering. It is best to turn off the heat in a bedroom a few hours before retiring so that the temperature will decrease gradually, instead of attempting to chill the room suddenly and wasting heat through an open window. Space under a bedroom door should be closed with a throw rug or folded blanket to prevent cold air from circulating into the rest of the house.

More heat from radiators: Some heat can be saved by providing shields behind radiators that are set against uninsulated outside walls. Such shields, which prevent absorption of heat by the walls and consequent waste, may be of insulating or reflective material, or simply hard-pressed board mounted so that there will be an air space of at least 1 in. between it and the wall. If your radiators are covered with boxes or grills that allow little circulation of air, you'll get more heat from the system by removing these impediments. Only those that do not impede the free circulation of air are satisfactory. Also keep dust and lint from accumulating in the open spaces by frequent cleaning, to assure good air circulation. Paint on radiators has much more to do with the amount of heat that they radiate than most people suppose. If painted with bronzing, especially aluminum, they produce from 12 to 15 percent

less heat than if painted with ordinary oil paint. Bronzing tends to reflect heat back into the radiator. Liberal use of calking compound on all cracks in the walls and at door and window frames will help to save some heat, whether or not the house is provided with storm sash and is insulated. Cracks in brick and stucco walls should be filled with mortar.

Directing heat to living quarters: In case the simple measures already mentioned are not enough to effect a substantial saving of fuel, and the living quarters are not fully comfortable, you may have to shut off heat to quarters where it is not required, such as an attached garage or a storeroom, precautions being taken to prevent freezing of water in pipes and radiators. Even bedrooms may have to be closed during the

INSULATION ON STEAM AND HOT-WATER PIPES IN BASEMENT BRINGS MORE HEAT TO LIVING QUARTERS

CUT OFF HEAT TO GARAGE

A 2-IN. LAYER OF SHREDDED ASBESTOS PUT ON BOILER AND COVERED WITH MUSLIN

REGISTER IN FIRST FLOOR ADMITS EXCESS HEAT FROM BASEMENT

day and heat turned on only a few hours in the evening to eliminate the chill, to direct most of the heat to the living quarters during the day. Many basements are much warmer than is necessary and much of the heat can be directed to the living quarters by insulating the steam or hot-water pipes and covering a boiler with a 2-in. layer of shredded asbestos confined with muslin. Excess heat in a basement where a hot-air furnace is located can be directed into the rooms above by installing registers. Although much basement heat is transmitted to the rooms above through the floor, absorption of heat by basement walls and floor represents a loss.

Hot-water heater and smoke pipe losses: An unsuspected heat loss occurs when a hot-water heater connected to the furnace or boiler is not insulated, as considerable heat is radiated from the tank into the air around it. Similarly, the top of a furnace bonnet can be covered with a 6-in. layer of non-burning insulation to keep the heat

in. Then excessive loss of heat through chimneys should be stopped if possible. One home owner fitted heat-radiating fins on a long smoke pipe to "rob" it of excess heat, while another slipped a sheet-metal duct over the smoke pipe, allowing cool air to enter at the lowest point and the heated air to come out at the other end. Another method used was the provision of a steel drum through which the gases are passed. This method is applicable also to a stove. While on the subject of heat losses through the chimney, one should remember that the draft opening below the firepot of a boiler or furnace should be tight when closed so that no more air is supplied to the fire than just enough to keep it barely going, except of course, when the draft is opened intentionally. On the other hand, a leaky chimney allows air to enter, which acts as a check damper, preventing necessary draft for proper combustion of the fire. Such chimneys should be pointed up with mortar.

Economical firing: Firing a boiler or furnace by hand economically is not just a matter of following a set of rules, but adapting the technique of firing to a number of variable factors such as the type of fuel used, the atmospheric conditions and the peculiarities of the heating system. Generally it is most economical to keep the fire burning slowly to provide constant heat, instead of burning the coal with considerable draft at intermittent periods, and allowing the fire to die down slowly before adding more fuel. Such forcing results in smoky fires and the loss of combustible gases that would produce heat if ignited. For efficient burning of coal, be sure to remove the ashes each time that the grates are shaken, as accumulated ashes limit the air supply besides being largely responsible for warped grates. Grates should be shaken gently to avoid dumping the fire; one should stop when a few live coals drop into the ashpit. The opening in the fire door or directly below it admits air into the combustion chamber. This should always be kept open when burning soft fuels as it helps to burn combustible gases. Soft coal requires more frequent furnace regulation to keep it burning slowly than hard coal or coke. During cold, clear weather, the fire must be kept checked for longer periods than on foggy days and nights when the air is heavy and the fire tends to burn sluggishly. When adding fresh fuel, open the draft for a few minutes to brighten up the fire, and then scatter the coal on uniformly, leaving the draft open until the fuel is ignited. When banking the fire for the night, add fresh fuel in two batches at intervals. Allow the first batch to ignite, then add a second and leave the draft open until the flames appear. This method produces less smoke and a minimum loss of combustible gases. If you have trouble holding a fire overnight, a light sprinkling of fine ashes over the second batch of fresh fuel will help. However, if you are using fine coal of the grade known as "mine run," this is not advisable as it tends to form clinkers. As a general rule, it is best to avoid disturbing a fire, although mine-run coal tends to crust over and should be broken up occasionally with a poker. Also be sure to pick the clinkers out of the firepot or the fire will go out unexpectedly.

Limed pipes and "stale" water: In steam and hot-water systems, the inside of the pipes and radiators tend to accumulate a coating of lime, especially where the water is hard. Thick accumulations act as insulation, preventing the transfer of heat from the water to the pipes and radiators. Also, deposits will restrict the flow of water in the pipes, especially at elbows. Rain water is best because it is free from lime. However, if you use hard water, do not drain the system but retain the "stale" water un-

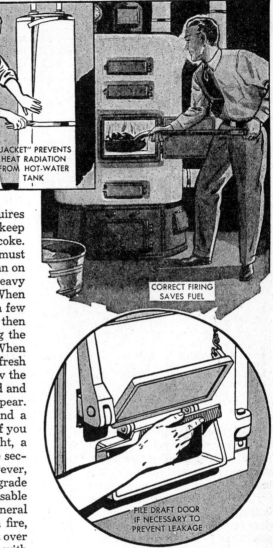

"JACKET" PREVENTS HEAT RADIATION FROM HOT-WATER TANK

CORRECT FIRING SAVES FUEL

FILE DRAFT DOOR IF NECESSARY TO PREVENT LEAKAGE

less repairs on the system are necessary, or the house is closed and the water in the pipes may freeze. Stale water is soft because the lime has already been "boiled out." Also, it contains less oxygen than fresh water, and the tendency of rusting is decreased greatly. To prevent the need of frequent additions of water to the system, be sure that none of the valves on the radiators leak.

Automatic controls: Control of a boiler or furnace draft and damper by means of a thermostat eliminates the waste of fuel and unnecessary high temperatures that result when several members of a family

eral methods of humidifying the air automatically. Apparatus for this purpose can be installed to work in conjunction with the heating system, the exact type of unit depending on the kind of heating system you have. A coil can be installed in the firing chamber, to which water is fed in small, controlled amounts, and the resulting steam is conducted through a short pipe to a radiator in a room above, where the steam is carried off by the warm air.

Storm sash and weather stripping: Tests have shown that as much as 20 percent of fuel can be saved in many cases by having tight-fitting storm sash on all windows and doors. The initial cost will be repaid in savings on fuel bills over a period of years. If you can afford a few sash only, put them on the sides exposed to prevailing cold winds. The

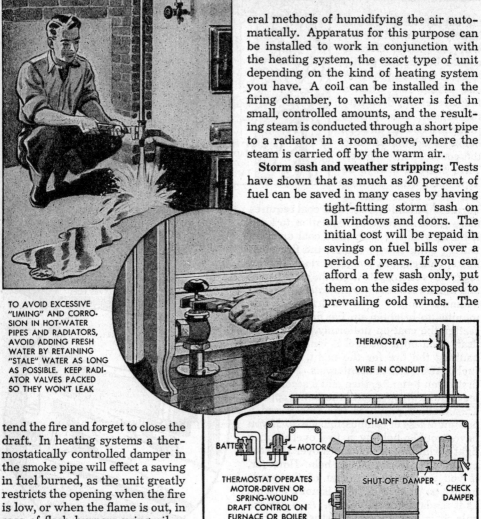

TO AVOID EXCESSIVE "LIMING" AND CORROSION IN HOT-WATER PIPES AND RADIATORS, AVOID ADDING FRESH WATER BY RETAINING "STALE" WATER AS LONG AS POSSIBLE. KEEP RADIATOR VALVES PACKED SO THEY WON'T LEAK

THERMOSTAT →

WIRE IN CONDUIT →

CHAIN

BATTERY ← MOTOR

SHUT-OFF DAMPER

CHECK DAMPER

THERMOSTAT OPERATES MOTOR-DRIVEN OR SPRING-WOUND DRAFT CONTROL ON FURNACE OR BOILER

DRAFT →

tend the fire and forget to close the draft. In heating systems a thermostatically controlled damper in the smoke pipe will effect a saving in fuel burned, as the unit greatly restricts the opening when the fire is low, or when the flame is out, in case of flash burners using oil or gas. Due to the restricted draft, the coils of a boiler or the bonnet of a warm-air furnace will not be cooled off as quickly as otherwise by incoming cold air which, after absorbing heat, passes up the chimney.

Humidity: By keeping the moisture content or humidity of the air in your home between 30 and 40 as determined by a reliable humidity indicator, you will be able to reduce the temperature a few degrees lower than necessary when the air is dry, the reason being that moist air feels warmer than dry air of the same temperature. For the average home, several gallons of water must be evaporated daily to maintain the desired humidity. There are sev-

space between the regular sash and the storm sash should be as much of a dead-air space as possible. Therefore, the regular sash should be fitted with weather stripping—strips of wood and felt set snugly against the sash if regular metal weather stripping is not available. Also, the storm sash should be fitted into the window frames tightly, which can be done by gluing strips of felt to the sash where they contact the frames. In some cases it may be advisable to seal cracks between sash and frames by means of adhesive tape.

"Weep holes" in storm sash are handy to admit a slight amount of fresh air when the temperatures are extremely low. However, when not used for this purpose, these holes should be closed tightly by corks or snug-fitting covers, as leakage at these points defeats the purpose of sealing the sash.

Insulating: A major saving of fuel can be accomplished by insulating. If your expenditure for this must be limited, start by covering the ceiling below the attic if the latter is not in regular use, as more heat is lost through the ceiling than through walls of the same area, other conditions being equal. If you make use of the attic regularly, insulating bats should be placed between the rafters. However, before installing insulation, check up for leaks in the roof and at the flashing along the chimney and valleys, and make repairs,

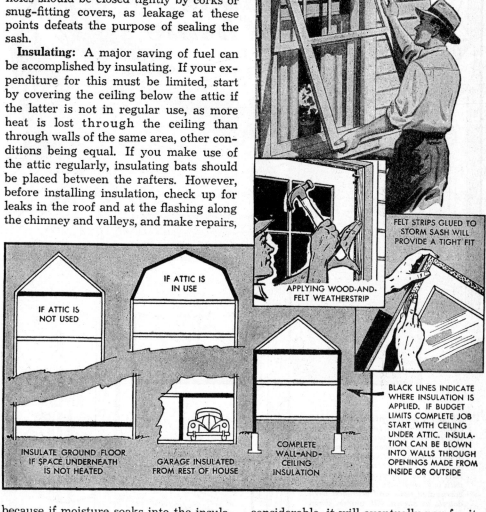

TIGHT-FITTING STORM SASH ON ALL WINDOWS AND DOORS WILL REDUCE FUEL CONSUMPTION AS MUCH AS 20 PERCENT

FELT STRIPS GLUED TO STORM SASH WILL PROVIDE A TIGHT FIT

APPLYING WOOD-AND-FELT WEATHERSTRIP

IF ATTIC IS IN USE

IF ATTIC IS NOT USED

INSULATE GROUND FLOOR IF SPACE UNDERNEATH IS NOT HEATED

GARAGE INSULATED FROM REST OF HOUSE

COMPLETE WALL-AND-CEILING INSULATION

BLACK LINES INDICATE WHERE INSULATION IS APPLIED. IF BUDGET LIMITS COMPLETE JOB START WITH CEILING UNDER ATTIC. INSULATION CAN BE BLOWN INTO WALLS THROUGH OPENINGS MADE FROM INSIDE OR OUTSIDE

because if moisture soaks into the insulation it will reduce its effectiveness greatly. On ground floors that have no basement under them, and are subject to outside temperatures, insulation is applied between the joists below the floor. Similarly, any room over a built-in garage should be insulated from the garage. If you wish to continue insulating, have the insulating material blown between the studs through openings cut through from either the outside or the inside of the house. While the expense of providing insulation may be considerable, it will eventually pay for itself in the course of years by the savings in fuel that will result.

Keeping Outboard Motor Clean

An ideal way of keeping the cooling system of an outboard motor clean is to operate it in a barrel of clear water after using it. This is especially desirable after use in dirty or salty water, but it's also desirable when using the motor on lakes and rivers to remove sand and silt.

Storm Sash and Doors

can be made at home

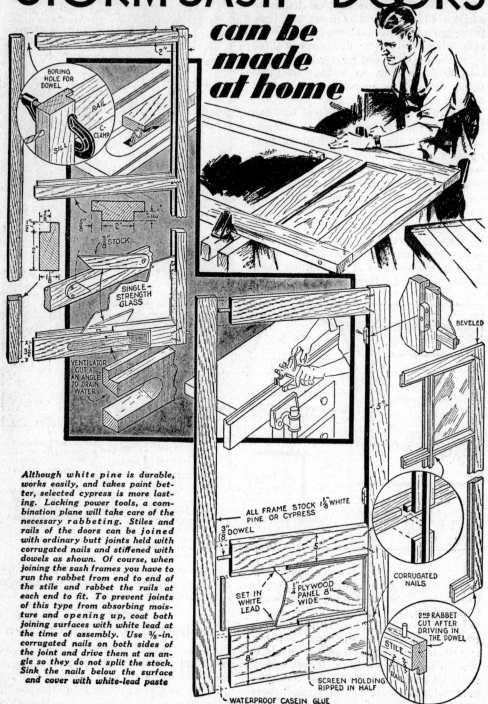

BORING HOLE FOR DOWEL

RAIL

SILL

C-CLAMP

2"

⅜" STOCK

SINGLE-STRENGTH GLASS

VENTILATOR CUT AT AN ANGLE TO DRAIN WATER

BEVELED

ALL FRAME STOCK 1⅛" WHITE PINE OR CYPRESS

⅜" DOWEL

SET IN WHITE LEAD

¼" PLYWOOD PANEL 8" WIDE

5"

8"

CORRUGATED NAILS

2ND RABBET CUT AFTER DRIVING IN THE DOWEL

STILE

RAIL

SCREEN MOLDING RIPPED IN HALF

WATERPROOF CASEIN GLUE

Although white pine is durable, works easily, and takes paint better, selected cypress is more lasting. Lacking power tools, a combination plane will take care of the necessary rabbeting. Stiles and rails of the doors can be joined with ordinary butt joints held with corrugated nails and stiffened with dowels as shown. Of course, when joining the sash frames you have to run the rabbet from end to end of the stile and rabbet the rails at each end to fit. To prevent joints of this type from absorbing moisture and opening up, coat both joining surfaces with white lead at the time of assembly. Use ⅜-in. corrugated nails on both sides of the joint and drive them at an angle so they do not split the stock. Sink the nails below the surface and cover with white-lead paste

SAVE FUEL
by Calking

In most houses, slight settling of foundations and shrinkage of materials cause cracks around doors and windows. Sometimes there will be cracks in mortar joints of masonry or stucco walls. As such cracks are heat wasters, and wall cracks in masonry may weaken the structure, all of them should be made wind and weatherproof as soon as they are noticed.

Cracks around doors and windows can be sealed best with calking compound, a material elastic enough to compensate for the movements of settling. It sticks tightly to all materials, becomes dry on the surface but remains semi-plastic underneath, and is water and weatherproof. It can be bought in several colors and in two consistencies; a soft grade that can be pressed through a calking gun, and a heavier grade that can be applied with a knife.

Application of calking compound is done most easily with a gun which pushes a ribbon of material into the cracks. Used in this way, the compound must be free from skins and lumps which might clog the nozzle. Around hinges and in some corners, it may be necessary to force down the compound and smooth it with a wooden paddle about ½ in. wide, which has been soaked in oil to prevent the compound from adhering.

Before filling cracks, see that they are dry, and clean out all loose dirt, mortar and paint scales. Metal framework should be scraped or wire-brushed to remove rust, and given a coat of paint before calking. Wide cracks should be painted before applying the compound, but if they are more than ¼ in. wide they should be filled with oakum forced in with a blunt chisel, putty knife or calking iron and packed down by tapping the iron with a hammer until the filling comes up to ¼ in. of the surface. Cracks in masonry or stucco should be filled with cement mortar consisting of portland cement, 1 part, hydrated lime, 1 part, and clean sand, 2 or 3 parts. Wet the cracks before filling with cement, using a small putty knife or tuckpointer's trowel. When the cement is dry, cover it with a ribbon of calking compound to keep out the water.

❑ To clean a broom and extend its life, dip it in warm water once a week.

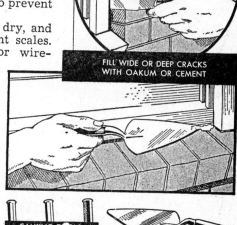

FIRST BRUSH OUT LOOSE DIRT

FILL WIDE OR DEEP CRACKS WITH OAKUM OR CEMENT

CALKING TOOLS

TROWEL

PUTTY KNIFE

HAND FIRING

Getting at the causes of common
Helpful tips that make hand firing
your plant at peak efficiency

①

DENSE
SMOKE

FRESH FUEL

LIVE COALS

②

"SPREADING" METHOD OF FIRING
NOT RECOMMENDED

NORMAL HEATING REQUIREMENTS BY MONTH

CUMULATIVE TO LAST
DAY OF MONTH

MONTHLY FUEL
REQUIREMENTS

OCT.	5%	5%
NOV.	12%	17%
DEC..	18%	35%
JAN.	20%	55%
FEB.	18%	73%
MARCH	16%	89%
APRIL	9%	98%
MAY	2%	100%

NO ONE would deliberately throw a shovel or two of coal outside every day, yet the equivalent of this waste is discharged into the air in the form of combustible gases by many home heating plants. A smoky fire consumes fuel but produces insufficient heat, which is one of the most common complaints of home owners. The causes of this trouble are many and varied, and are best found by the process of elimination—starting with the most likely cause, which is incorrect firing, and then proceeding with other causes until the trouble is found and corrected.

Keep the ash pit clean: It should always be nearly empty. Ashes banked up in the pit as indicated by A in Fig. 1, reduce air supply, increase the velocity of what air does reach the fire when the lower draft is open, and result in "live" and "dead" spots here and there over the fire bed. Ashes touching the grates at any point tend to concentrate the heat and warp or break the grates. It's best to clean the ash pit before shaking the grates. A thin, skimpy fire, B in. Fig. 1, also Fig. 22, is wasteful of both heat and time as it requires more frequent attention. Fuel bed should be level with or slightly above the bottom of firing door.

Spreading method of firing causes slow "pickup": Spreading fresh fuel over the whole fire bed as in Fig. 2, "blankets" the fire, shuts off the heat, and results in the release of great quantities of valuable gases, which escape unburned up the chimney. In firing soft coal, a dense smoke is produced when a bed of live coals is covered with fresh fuel. Before ignition can take place over the whole fire bed the furnace and the house cool down. As a result, there is a tendency to force the fire with full draft, which speeds

with COAL

troubles in home heating plants.
easier and enable you to operate
and greatest economy

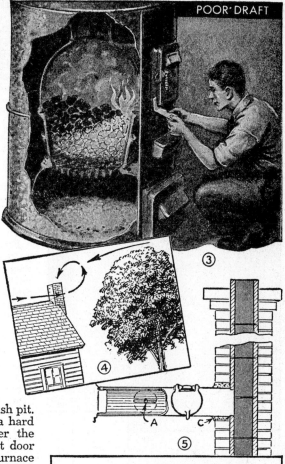

POOR·DRAFT

③

④

⑤

up the rate of ignition and makes the fire wasteful and difficult to control.

House cold in the morning: This condition can be due to many causes and to defects in the heating plant. The chart in Fig. 9 is the result of a study of reasons for the unsatisfactory operation of home heating plants. Banking the fire with ashes is one of the causes. Ash placed on live coal gradually stops the burning. The heat is absorbed by the ash which reaches the fusion point and forms a clinker. The latter slows down flow of air through the fuel bed. By morning the fire will be practically out. The remedy is to be sure the equipment is in good condition and then fire by approved methods, leaving a trifle more draft on the fire over night.

Fire picks up slowly or is sluggish: This condition usually is caused by a poor draft. Check the ash pit. Probe the fire bed for clinkers or a hard crust, which sometimes forms over the burned-out ash. Open the cleanout door and examine the interior of the furnace with a flashlight for heavy deposits of soot and fly ash which sometimes collect in sufficient amounts to hamper the draft. Be sure the turn-damper, A in Fig. 5, is open. If correcting these conditions fails to remedy the trouble, then use a strip of tin as a feeler gauge and "feel" along the edges of all doors, as in Fig. 3. Check fire doors, clean-outs on furnace and at the bottom of chimney as at B in Fig. 5. If you can insert the "feeler" and move it a distance of more than 3 or 4 in. along any of these openings, you have an air leak that may interfere with the draft. This can be corrected by filing the edge of the door until it fits.

Chimney or surrounding structures reduce draft: A large tree near the house, Fig. 4, with its top higher than the chimney, can be the cause of impaired draft, as it creates an eddy air current, and sometimes a strong down-draft when the wind is blowing. Likewise, adjacent buildings higher than the chimney will cause the same condition as indicated in Fig. 6. If the top of the chimney is lower than the roof ridge you are almost sure to have trouble.

HOW TO FIND YOUR TROUBLE

When your heating plant operates unsatisfactorily there are usually many possible causes for one effect. Generally the causes of insufficient heat, poor draft, excessive consumption of fuel, clinker formation, etc., are easy to discover and remedy if one takes the time to apply a simple process of elimination. As an example, the cause of poor draft may not lie in the heating plant at all. In certain cases it has been found that simply opening the basement door or a window has completely cured the trouble. In these instances the remedy was simply more air circulation in the basement. Often cures for other troubles are just as simple

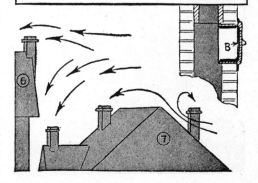

⑥

⑦

207

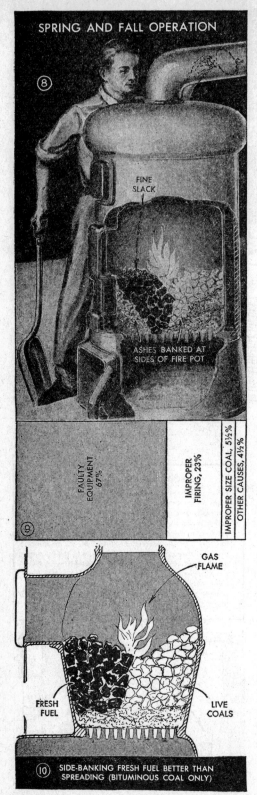

⑧

FINE SLACK

ASHES BANKED AT SIDES OF FIRE POT

FAULTY EQUIPMENT 67%

IMPROPER FIRING, 23%

IMPROPER SIZE COAL, 5½%

OTHER CAUSES, 4½%

⑨

GAS FLAME

FRESH FUEL

LIVE COALS

⑩ SIDE-BANKING FRESH FUEL BETTER THAN SPREADING (BITUMINOUS COAL ONLY)

Air striking the roof is deflected as in Fig. 7 and the resulting eddy currents create down-drafts in the chimney. In severe winter weather, the cold air in the upper part of the flue of the outside chimney may act as a baffle, checking the free movement of gases from the chimney. The procedure in correcting any of these faults depends, of course, on the conditions. If there is no outside defect, then it's well to examine the chimney itself. Any large cracks in the mortar or at the smokepipe opening, C of Fig. 5, will act as check dampers. Finally, remember that nests of chimney swallows, or swifts, sometimes block the flue. Also, a basement or cellar that is shut up tightly is nearly always "air-locked." Records show that sometimes opening the basement door or a window slightly will cure a stubborn case of poor draft.

Fuel bed for mild weather: The entire grate area is not needed during mild weather so only the center is kept clear with the poker. The grates are not shaken and ash is allowed to bank up on the sides of the fire pot as in Fig. 8. This cuts down the heat output of the fire bed and, at the same time makes it easy to control. Due to adding smaller amounts of fresh fuel, such a fire will burn low in a shorter time, making it advisable to put on full draft a few minutes before firing so there will be a bright coke bed to receive the fresh fuel. Note in Fig. 8 that the live coals are pushed to one side before firing the fresh charge of coal. To hold the fire longer, cover the nut coal with a shovelful of fine slack as shown. This can be made by breaking up larger pieces of coal to the pea size. Be sure, before leaving the fire, that a gas flame has started, otherwise it will smolder. Also, there is the likelihood that the column of gases from a long-smoldering coal fire will ignite suddenly and cause a serious explosion. See that there is a fairly strong draft just after firing, especially on windless days. Once the gas is ignited, the drafts usually can be closed and the fire checked to conserve the heat.

"Side-banking" when firing soft coal: In any weather, side-banking the fresh fuel as in Fig. 10, is a great improvement over the spreading method in that it prevents rapid escape of gases which takes place when fresh fuel is spread over a hot bed of coals. Grates are shaken lightly to remove surplus ash, live coals are worked to the back or side of the fire pot, and fresh coal is placed in the pit or depression thus formed. The charge is not heaped but live coals and fresh fuel are sloped to the center as indicated. By this method ignition of the fresh fuel takes place slowly and the gases are burned as they are driven off. It is essential to remove all live coals from the bottom of the depression where the fresh fuel is placed, as otherwise ignition will take place from the bottom as well as the side and the value of the practice will be lost.

Don't burn garbage in furnace: Garbage thrown on a hot fire, Fig. 11, will immediately cut the heat output by as much as 50 percent, and it will take the fire some time to recover even a part of the loss. Even a small quantity of garbage or other foreign material is almost sure to form a hard clinker when thrown on a hot fire. In addition to the heat loss and consequent waste of fuel, a large clinker is often very difficult to remove. Sometimes the furnace and grates are damaged in the process. A clinker forming in the hot fire also tends to blanket the heat and, in effect, force it downward, sometimes heating grates to the danger point.

Avoid closing drafts on a high fire: Closing the drafts suddenly on a very hot fire often causes a hard clinker to form as the furnace surfaces cannot absorb the excessive heat that is suddenly bottled up and reflected back into the fire bed which quickly fuses or makes clinkers under the excessively high temperature. It's better to close the drafts on a hot fire by stages, leaving the lower draft open just the width of a match stick, and opening the check damper only part way until the burning rate slows down to more nearly normal.

Water in ash pit aids combustion: With certain grades of fuel, clinkering can be prevented and combustion aided considerably by leaving a small quantity of ash in the ash pit and keeping this moist by adding water occasionally, as in Fig. 13. In this connection it's also a good idea to wet or "temper" the fuel. This should not be done immediately before firing but the fuel should be sprayed at regular intervals with water so that the coal particles have a chance to absorb moisture.

Tools needed in hand firing: In firing a furnace by any of the recommended methods you will need two pokers and the wire cleanout brush shown in Fig. 14. Of the two pokers the oblique-angled type is the more important as it is efficient in probing the fire bed and in working live coals to the side of the fire pot. The wire flue brush is essential for loosening soot and fly ash.

Use the right size coal: Usually this is more important when burning the smokeless fuels, such as hard coal and coke, but it also applies in the extremes to soft fuels.

PREVENTING FORMATION OF CLINKERS

(11)

GARBAGE — CLINKER FORMS HERE

(12) SMOKE RECORDS OF BITUMINOUS COAL FIRED BY FOUR METHODS

SPREADING METHOD	SIDE-BANK METHOD	IMPROVED SIDE-BANK METHOD	NUT-AND-SLACK METHOD

100 80 60 40 20 0

0 20 40 60 20 40 60 80 20 40 60 80 20 40 60 80

SMOKE DENSITY IN PERCENT

MINUTES AFTER FIRING

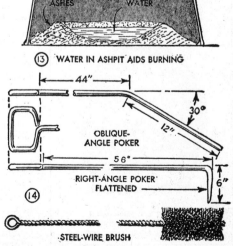

ASHES WATER

(13) WATER IN ASHPIT AIDS BURNING

44"

30°

12"

OBLIQUE-ANGLE POKER

56"

RIGHT-ANGLE POKER FLATTENED

6"

(14)

STEEL-WIRE BRUSH

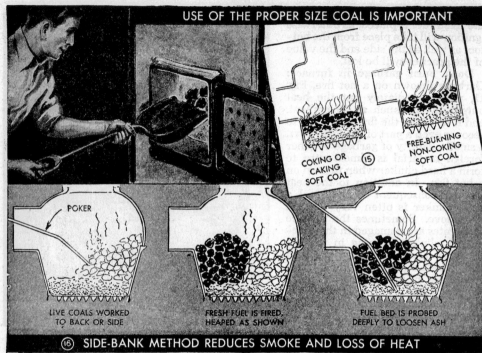

COKING OR CAKING SOFT COAL ⑮ FREE-BURNING NON-COKING SOFT COAL

POKER

LIVE COALS WORKED TO BACK OR SIDE

FRESH FUEL IS FIRED, HEAPED AS SHOWN

FUEL BED IS PROBED DEEPLY TO LOOSEN ASH

⑯ SIDE-BANK METHOD REDUCES SMOKE AND LOSS OF HEAT

⑰ LARGE LUMP FUEL RESULTS IN EXCESSIVE HEAT LOSS

⑱ SMALLER LUMP SIZES ADMIT LESS AIR, BURN MORE EFFICIENTLY; APPLIES TO ANTHRACITE COAL AND COKE

As an example, fine soft-coal slack and forkings cannot usually be burned successfully in the average home furnace without a forced draft. When firing soft coals by any of the three approved methods the sizes generally referred to as nut, stove and range, usually will be found satisfactory. Most soft fuels are divided into two types known as coking or caking coals and the free-burning non-coking type, Fig. 15. These terms refer to the burning characteristics rather than to the lump size. Also, the two are sometimes referred to as short and long-blaze coals. In the hard fuels, particularly coke, the large lumps bulk up loosely admitting the passage of excess air through the fire bed. This condition moves the heat so rapidly that only a part of it is absorbed and transferred by the exposed surfaces of the furnace, Fig. 17. Loss of heat up the chimney is sometimes excessive. The smaller lump sizes, Fig. 18, admit less air, burn more efficiently in a deep fire, Fig. 23, and produce more useable heat. Where the natural draft is very strong the burning rate can be controlled better if a small amount of fine lump fuel is placed on top of the regular charge.

Improved side-bank method: With two exceptions in procedure, this is the same as the ordinary side-bank method. The sequence of the firing operations is detailed in Fig. 16. By this method the grates are rarely, if ever, shaken. The fresh fuel is heaped slightly as indicated and as the final step the fuel bed is deeply probed over the whole grate area to loosen and sift out the fine ash.

Nut-and-slack method: This method of firing is essentially the same as the side-banking procedure except that two sizes of coal are used. Fig. 21 de-

HEAT LOSS FROM
FLY ASH AND SOOT
IN TERMS OF COAL

1/32" DEPOSIT
9.5% LOSS
190 LBS.
OF COAL

1/16" DEPOSIT
26% LOSS
250 LBS.
OF COAL

1/8" DEPOSIT
45% LOSS
906 LBS. IN EACH
TON OF COAL

⑳

GASES RISING
FROM FRESH
FUEL

GASES
IGNITE
HERE

SLACK

GRATES ARE SHAKEN,
LIVE COALS WORKED TO SIDE

FRESH COAL IS FIRED
AND FUEL BED LEVELED

SLACK IS PLACED
OVER FRESH FUEL

㉑ NUT-AND-SLACK METHOD IS THE MOST ECONOMICAL OF ALL

tails the steps. Grates are shaken gently, with only a few long strokes as in Fig. 25. Coals and coke remaining from the previous charge are worked to the side of the fire pot. After firing the fresh charge, the fuel bed is leveled and slack is placed over the fresh fuel. Slack from the same kind of coal should be used if possible. Following the sequence of this method requires somewhat more coal for each fresh charge but actually the overall consumption of fuel is less than that when using other methods because of the greater heat output from a given amount of coal, assuming that the heating plant is in good condition. In addition, the latter method as described produces less smoke than any other as you can see from the smoke chart, Fig. 12. It's important to note that success with any of the three approved methods depends on careful attention to details.

Heat loss from fly ash and soot: Fig. 19 illustrates this loss graphically. One of the essentials to satisfactory operation is that the furnace and flue be kept clean, Fig. 20. On some of the later type hot-water and steam plants, passageways in the furnace can often be cleaned more efficiently by compressed air. Periodically scrubbing the radiator dome and the upper part of the fire pot with a wire flue brush usually will suffice for the average warm-air plant. Three other methods of ridding the furnace of soot as approved by the U. S. Bureau of Mines and the Engineering College, University of Illinois, are shown in Figs. 26, 27 and 28. Common granulated rock salt placed on a bright fire at regular intervals is quite effective. The methods shown in Figs. 27 and 28 also are effective in cleaning the flue but it should be remembered that on wood-shingled buildings there is some danger of a roof fire so it's

㉒ SHALLOW FIRE WASTES
FUEL AND HEAT

㉓ DEEP FIRE BURNS SLOWLY,
CONSERVES HEAT AND COAL.
APPLIES TO HARD AND SOFT FUELS

MOVE GRATE LEVER IN UNIFORMLY LONG STROKES

DRAFT DOOR CLOSED

METHODS OF CLEANING OUT SOOT

1½ TO 2 LBS. OF COMMON SALT

CHECK DAMPER OPEN →

WASTE PAPER

MATCH

IGNITE WASTE PAPER IN CHIMNEY CLEAN-OUT DOOR

a good idea to burn out the flue only on damp or rainy days when the roof is wet. It should never be done in a chimney in poor condition or where the soot accumulation is unusually heavy. Clean out the bulk of the soot by other methods, such as dragging a chain up and down in the flue.

Over-draft damper: When burning soft coal the use of the over-draft damper, Fig. 24, in the fire door is important as gases evolved from the fresh fuel will not ignite in the furnace unless mixed with air. Just how much the over-draft should be opened depends somewhat on the fuel and the peculiarities of the individual furnace.

Kindling the fire: Ordinarily, paper is first placed in the furnace, the kindling next, and finally a small quantity of coal. A better method reverses this procedure as in Fig. 29. First, ash is worked through the grates until only about a 2-in. layer remains. Then the coal is placed as shown, with slack on top, leaving a depression at the front near the fire door. Into this is placed the kindling with rolled and twisted waste paper on top, which is lighted.

THE RIGHT WAY TO KINDLE A FIRE

PAPER, ROLLED AND TWISTED

SLACK

KINDLING

FRESH COAL

2" OF ASHES

CLEAN ASHPIT

WEATHER-STRIP

FOR COMFORT

AND ECONOMY

By E. J. Lucas

WHEN sharp wintry winds reach full velocity and temperatures drop below freezing, the unsealed doors and windows of your home may account for as much as 40 percent of the total heat loss during an average day. Weather stripping alone can reduce this loss as much as 20 percent, even without the addition of storm sash and storm doors. There are many kinds of weather stripping, some designed only for temporary use, such as plain felt strips, felt strips with a wood or metal backing, and rubber-coated fabrics. The interlocking types made from bronze, brass or other rustproof metals are designed for permanent installations. The interlocking types are, of course, the best in the long run as they do not require a friction contact to form an effective seal. Doors and windows fitted with these types open and close as easily as before stripping, while the friction-seal stripping makes window sash somewhat harder to raise and lower and doors a bit more difficult to close. Both types, however, make a very effective seal against heat loss.

Except along the bottom edge, a door can be weather-stripped with the interlocking type, cut and bent to the shape shown in detail A of the series of detail illustrations A to K inclusive. If this material is not available from local hardware, lumber, or building-materials dealers, a sheet-metal shop can prepare it at small cost. Zinc is quite commonly used as it is easy to work, but any other corrosion-resistant metal, soft enough to be formed to the desired shape, may be used. A splice is made by snipping a tongue out of the sheet metal

One way to test a weather-stripped door for air leaks is by moving a lighted match along opening between door and jamb. Flame flickers if air is entering

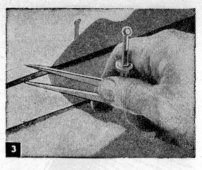

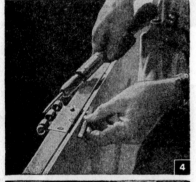

Before weather-stripping a door, true it up to assure uniform clearance between door and jamb. Be sure to plane edges square

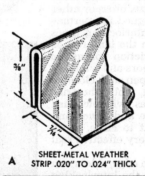

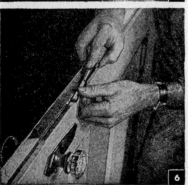

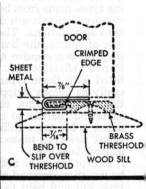

as in detail B and inserting it in the folded flange of the other piece. Rustproof nails should be used.

The first step before removing the door is to see that it is hung properly. It may be necessary to plane off some high spots, as in Fig. 2, or to shim up one of the hinges. If the wooden threshold is worn down in places, plane it level. Then, with dividers, scribe a line along the bottom of the door as in Fig. 3, using the threshold as a guide for the lower point of the dividers. These should be set so that the bottom of the door, when sawed along the scribed line, will clear by $\frac{1}{16}$ in. the top of the brass threshold to be installed, Fig. 10. After marking the bottom of the door, remove the door from the frame, block it on the floor with the hinged edge up, and remove the hinge butts. Using a rabbet plane or an electric hand plane such as shown in Fig. 7, cut a $\frac{1}{8}$ by $\frac{3}{8}$ in. rabbet the entire length of the door. With a hacksaw, cut a piece from the outside edge of each hinge

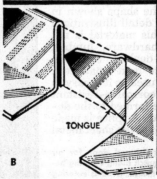

$\frac{3}{8}''$

$\frac{3}{16}''$

SHEET-METAL WEATHER
STRIP .020" TO .024" THICK

A

TONGUE

B

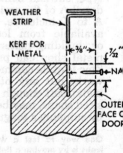

DOOR

CRIMPED
EDGE

SHEET
METAL

$\frac{7}{8}''$

$\frac{3}{16}''$

BEND TO
SLIP OVER
THRESHOLD

BRASS
THRESHOLD

WOOD SILL

C

WEATHER
STRIP

KERF FOR
L-METAL

$\frac{3}{8}''$

$\frac{7}{32}''$

NA

OUTE
FACE C
DOOR

D

butt just wide enough so that, when the butt is replaced on the door, it will clear the rabbet, Fig. 4.

Now, following the line scribed near the bottom of the door, saw off just enough to clear the brass threshold. If a felt door bottom is to be used, this can be nailed or screwed to the door after rehanging; but if the metal threshold is of the interlocking type with overhanging lip, then be sure that allowance is made for the interlocking bottom strip which is nailed to the bottom of the door, as in detail C, to interlock with the threshold lip. This can be bent to the dimensions given from the same material as the weather strip used on the rest of the door, unless, of course, a similar strip is purchased ready-made. Attach the strip, as shown, with the back of the hook flush with the inside face of the door.

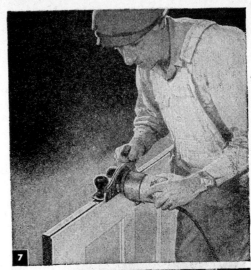

As the lock side and the top of the door are weather-stripped in the same manner, rabbet the outside edge of each as in detail D. Dimensions should be maintained closely so that the edge of the weather strip will not extend beyond the outside face of the door, Fig. 8, as the strip which later is installed on the jamb must be fitted to interlock closely without binding. A suitable kerfing tool to cut the groove for the metal edge can be made from a piece of steel, with a cutting point filed or ground as in detail E. A short length of saw blade not less than ½ in. wide and bolted to a handle, also will serve this purpose. If there is sufficient clearance between the striker plate and the edge of the door, the weather

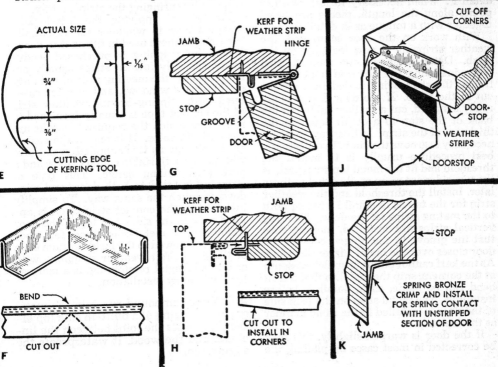

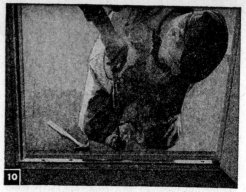

strip can be installed for the entire length of this side. Otherwise, cut the rabbet up to the striker plate and then taper the cut with a chisel as in Fig. 6.

The metal strip now can be nailed in place as in Fig. 5, with the outside edge flush with the edge of the door. Fit the strip at the corner by snipping out a vee and bending around the corner as shown in detail F. When necessary to join at other points along the length, pieces are fitted together with a tongue as in detail B.

With work on the door completed, the weather stripping is now installed on the jamb. Detail G shows one method used when installing the strip on a new door frame, the strip being nailed in a groove cut in the jamb. If the door frame is already installed, cut a shallow rabbet in the back of the stop to a depth equal to the thickness of the strip. In this way, it is unnecessary to groove the jamb. In either case, best procedure usually is to install the threshold and fit the metal top strip first, as the two sides are more easily fitted to these later. Install the threshold and the weather strip for the top as in detail H, fitting both to the mating strips on the door. Then the vertical strips are installed, making sure that the groove in the hinged edge of the door closes over the metal without binding. As the kerf cannot be cut to sufficient depth at the corners, snip the metal so that a neat bend can be made, as in detail J, before installing. The metal strip on the lock side of the door is installed in the same manner as the top strip.

If the door is warped slightly, this may be corrected in most cases by planing the stop to make uniform contact with the outer edge of the door before installing the metal strip. Where the stop on the lock side of the door is planed to fit the warped door, it will be necessary to relocate the striker plate so that the door can be closed securely without rattling. Finally, crimp a strip of spring bronze and nail to the stop, as in detail K and Fig. 9, to close the gap at the striker plate. One way of testing a weather-stripped door for leaks is to move a lighted match slowly along the opening between the door and the jamb as in Fig. 1. If air is leaking in at any point the flame will flicker. Generally, the leak can be stopped by springing the strip slightly.

Methods of applying the interlocking weather strip to windows are essentially the same as those used in fitting it to doors. When the stripping is purchased ready-made, specially formed strips usually are furnished for the meeting rails of ordinary double-hung windows, and also for casement sash. Spring-bronze weather strip of the contact type is usually furnished in rolls from which the required lengths are cut with tin snips. It is one of the easiest of all to apply as it is supplied in uniform widths with adjustable contact edges and a perforated nailing flange. This type of stripping is fitted to both doors and windows in much the same way. To simplify installation, the contact strip often is applied only to the sides and top of the door frame and a metal-reinforced felt door bottom is screwed to the inside bottom edge of the door. Felt weather stripping, with or without metal reinforcing, is a more or less temporary installation.

❡ Calking compound run into the metal or plastic edging of a built-in sink top effectively seals the joint between the linoleum and the wood. It waterproofs the edging, too.

HAS STORAGE SPACE AND FOUR SCOOP CHUTES

Capacity		
Size	Tons	
6 X 7 X 7 Ft.	6½	
6 X 8 X 8 Ft.	8	
6 X 9 X 9 Ft:	9¾	

3 *Step-saving* COAL BINS

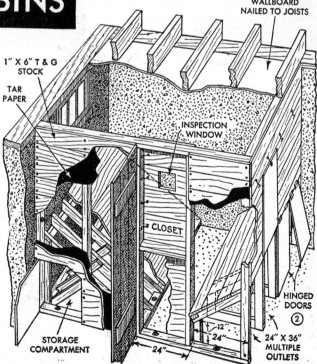

WALLBOARD NAILED TO JOISTS

1" X 6" T & G STOCK

TAR PAPER

INSPECTION WINDOW

CLOSET

STORAGE COMPARTMENT

HINGED DOORS

24" X 36" MULTIPLE OUTLETS

12"

24"

24"

IT TAKES no more skill to build a neat, long-lasting coal bin that is planned for convenience than it does to nail up two or three walls merely to retain fuel in one corner of your basement. A well planned bin should be as close as possible to the heating plant and yet be easily accessible for fuel delivery. It should be as nearly dust-tight as possible to help keep the basement clean. Also, if possible, it should be large enough to hold a season's fuel supply, thus making frequent deliveries unnecessary. Size of the bin will depend on the amount of fuel required. The bins shown here were designed by Anthracite Industries Incorporated, and the capacity tables are for anthracite coal. Similar types of bins,

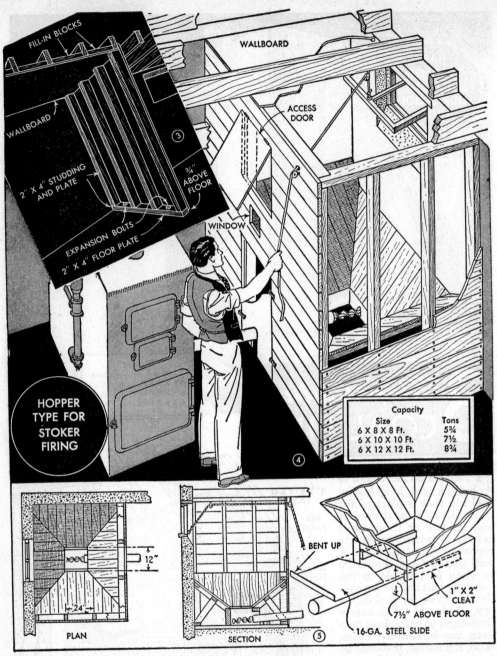

FILL-IN BLOCKS

WALLBOARD

WALLBOARD

2" X 4" STUDDING AND PLATE

3/4" ABOVE FLOOR

EXPANSION BOLTS

2" X 4" FLOOR PLATE

③

WALLBOARD

ACCESS DOOR

WINDOW

HOPPER TYPE FOR STOKER FIRING

④

Capacity	
Size	**Tons**
6 X 8 X 8 Ft.	5¾
6 X 10 X 10 Ft.	7½
6 X 12 X 12 Ft.	8¾

12"

24"

PLAN

SECTION

⑤

BENT UP

1" X 2" CLEAT

7½" ABOVE FLOOR

16-GA. STEEL SLIDE

larger in size, can be used for soft coal. For estimating the size required, it is best to ask your dealer how many cubic feet there are in a ton of the coal you are using, and then build your bin accordingly. When planning it, allow for a clearance of 1½ to 2 ft. between the fuel and the ceiling. It is hard work to shovel the coal up against the ceiling, and some dealers won't do it.

Well seasoned tongue-and-groove lumber, waterproof plywood (the plies of regular plywood may separate in a damp basement), and masonry (concrete or cinder blocks) are the materials most used for coal bins. The type of bin bottom, flat or sloped, is a matter of choice. A sloped bottom is practically a necessity for a bin-type stoker, and has the advantage of feeding the coal to the scoop chute when hand firing.

The bin pictured in Fig. 1 and detailed in Fig. 2 has the bottom sloped on two sides, and has four scoop chutes along the front, each being covered with a hinged door. Also, space under the other slope is utilized for storage, and a door to enter the bin is provided. Boards hinged to the inner edge of the door frame retain the fuel and the space between the boards and door provides a closet to hold firing tools. The ceiling is made dust-tight with wallboard nailed to the joists as in Fig. 3, and all framing is of 2 by 4-in. stock. Floor plates are fastened with expansion bolts as are the studs that join the basement walls.

The hopper-type bin for stoker firing in Fig. 4 is of similar construction except that scoop chutes are eliminated. The bottom is sloped from all four sides to a small box containing the stoker conveyor. The box is detailed in Fig. 5 and is about 7½ by 12 by 16 in. in size. A steel slide is used to close the hopper when the stoker conveyor needs attention. A small access door is provided and the fuel delivery window can be operated from outside the bin.

Although more expensive, the neat masonry bin shown in Fig. 7 has the advantage of being the most nearly dust-tight, and it will not deteriorate in a damp basement. The bottom slopes four ways toward the scoop chute, which is at the forward corner. The sloped portions are covered with

a 2-in. layer of concrete poured over a fill of earth or ashes well compacted.

Notice in Fig. 7 that the sides of the scoop chute are of the same material as the walls and are sloped at the same angle as the bottom. A wooden panel made up from short boards covers the sloped top of the chute as indicated.

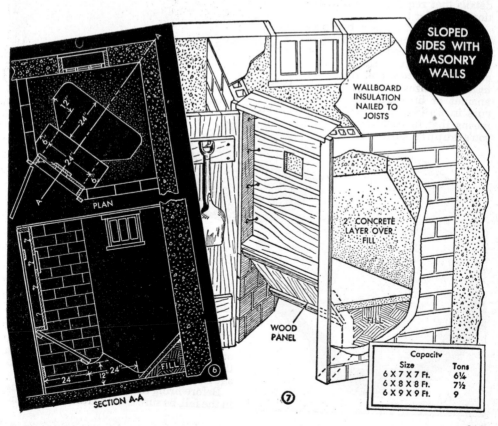

SLOPED SIDES WITH MASONRY WALLS

WALLBOARD INSULATION NAILED TO JOISTS

2" CONCRETE LAYER OVER FILL

WOOD PANEL

FILL

PLAN

SECTION A-A

⑥

⑦

Capacity	
Size	Tons
6 X 7 X 7 Ft.	6¼
6 X 8 X 8 Ft.	7½
6 X 9 X 9 Ft.	9

"READING" YOUR STOKER FIRE

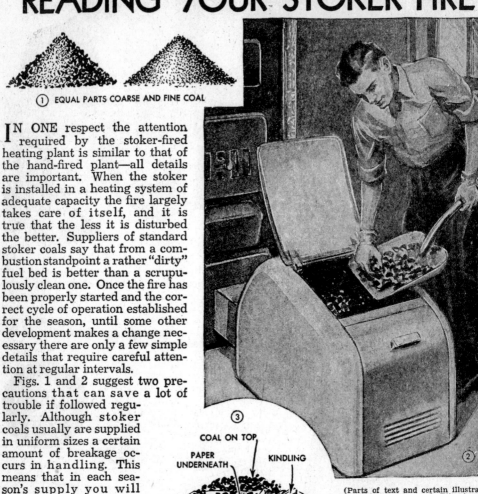

① EQUAL PARTS COARSE AND FINE COAL

③

COAL ON TOP

PAPER UNDERNEATH   KINDLING

②

(Parts of text and certain illustrations by courtesy of Bituminous Coal Institute and Appalachian Coals, Inc.)

④

IN ONE respect the attention required by the stoker-fired heating plant is similar to that of the hand-fired plant—all details are important. When the stoker is installed in a heating system of adequate capacity the fire largely takes care of itself, and it is true that the less it is disturbed the better. Suppliers of standard stoker coals say that from a combustion standpoint a rather "dirty" fuel bed is better than a scrupulously clean one. Once the fire has been properly started and the correct cycle of operation established for the season, until some other development makes a change necessary there are only a few simple details that require careful attention at regular intervals.

Figs. 1 and 2 suggest two precautions that can save a lot of trouble if followed regularly. Although stoker coals usually are supplied in uniform sizes a certain amount of breakage occurs in handling. This means that in each season's supply you will have at least a small quantity of fine particles of coal. The important thing when filling the stoker with varying sizes of coal is to mix equal parts of fine and coarse fuel in the hopper. This will assure uniform feeding of the fine and coarse particles into the retort. Where the coal varies in size this precaution should always be observed. When filling the hopper, wear gloves and inspect each shovelful. It takes more time, of course, but by this process you are almost certain to discover a chance spike, bolt, or other foreign object before it can get into the mechanism and cause delay or breakage at a critical time.

Before firing the stoker for the first time in the fall, be sure that the furnace is clean.

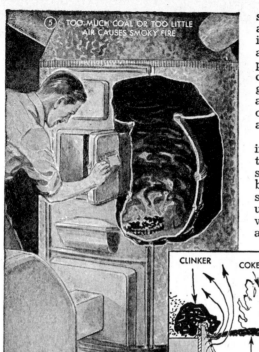

⑤ TOO MUCH COAL OR TOO LITTLE AIR CAUSES SMOKY FIRE

CLINKER COKE ASH

AIR

⑥ AIR PLASTIC COAL

speed control for coal feeds. A correct air adjustment is one that will maintain a maximum depth of fuel bed without objectionable soot formation in the firebox and gas passages, or smoke discharge from the chimney. Avoid mixing different kinds or grades of coals. Once the stoker has been adjusted for a satisfactory grade and size of fuel it's best to continue with that size and grade.

Although one of the most common errors in household stoker operation is the use of too much air, too little air will cause a smoky fire. Also, if too much coal is being fed, the fire will be sluggish and smoky, Fig. 5, and soot deposits will build up on the heating surfaces. The fuel bed will form a heavy coke tree as in Fig. 12, and the clinker "ring" will be thin and irregular, and may not form in the normal length of time. Large pieces of the coke tree will break away from the central mass and die out, resulting in an accumulation of unburned fuel around the sides of the firebox. On the other hand, if the fuel bed is supplied with too much air the fire will become steadily thinner and

Fuel and air ratio

If you have a steam or hot-water system, always check the water level. See that the stoker is properly serviced and lubricated, and be sure that the feed screw, windbox and tuyere openings are free of ashes, clinker or other obstructions. If the hopper is fitted with smokepipe, check to see that it is clear. Fill the hopper to about one fourth its depth, start the stoker and allow it to run until the retort fills level with the top. Then stop it and check all the controls, both manually operated and automatic, to see that they are in working order. Place several small pieces of dry kindling and twisted newspapers on top of the coal in the retort, sprinkle a scoopful of coal over this as in Fig. 3, ignite the kindling, Fig. 4, and immediately start the stoker again. Don't forget to fill the hopper after making the necessary adjustments.

Proper depth of fuel bed to maintain will vary according to the coking properties of the coal used. Coals that form hard, strong coke usually require a deep fuel bed, while those that form soft coke generally burn best in a shallow fuel bed. In the average household stoker a fuel-bed depth ranging from 6 to 10 in. gives best results. Most late model stokers are equipped with automatic air-control devices and variable-

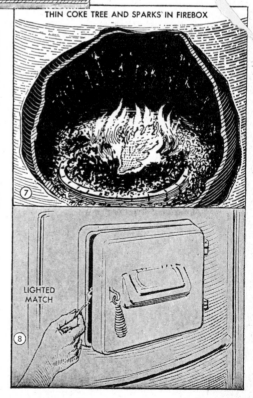

THIN COKE TREE AND SPARKS IN FIREBOX

⑦

LIGHTED MATCH

⑧

ash will be blown clear of the fuel bed to settle on the heating surfaces. A thin coke tree, Fig. 6, will appear at the center of the fuel bed, the tree sometimes being surrounded by dead, burned-out areas adjacent to the edges which act as passages for the excess air. If the fire door is opened while the stoker is running likely you will see streamers of sparks in the firebox, Fig. 7, and perhaps even in the smokepipe or chimney.

Another reliable and perhaps more sensitive indicator with most stoker coals is the nature and shape of the clinker formed by fusion of the ash and residues. With even a comparatively small amount of air in excess of requirements, the clinker tends to form deep in the fire bed and sometimes so low that it will partially obstruct the tuyere openings. The remedy for any of these troubles is to cut down the excess air or coal, as the case may be. Generally, it is best to adjust one or the other, then observe results before making other changes. If too much air is indicated, cut down the air and note results before increasing the coal feed. Proceed in the same way where too much coal is indicated.

The amount of "free" or natural draft in the firebox is very important when burning high-volatile coals. As a general rule it should be kept at the minimum. In most heating plants this will be indicated by the simple check pictured in Fig. 8. With the stoker running and the smokepipe and chimney heated to normal operating temperatures open the fire door about 1 in., then strike a match and hold it in the position shown. The natural draft should be just strong enough to draw in the flame gently toward the firebox. If the draft is excessively strong, set the smokepipe dampers to produce the correct draft as indicated by the match flame. However, if the installation is equipped with an automatic damper, the check damper should not be used. Instead adjust the automatic damper. It should be kept in mind, too, that there are many other conditions, both inside and outside the building, that will affect the natural draft.

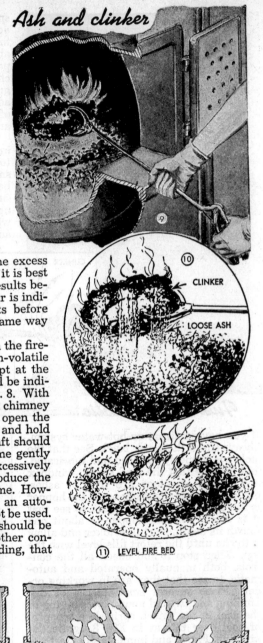

Ash and clinker

CLINKER

LOOSE ASH

⑪ LEVEL FIRE BED

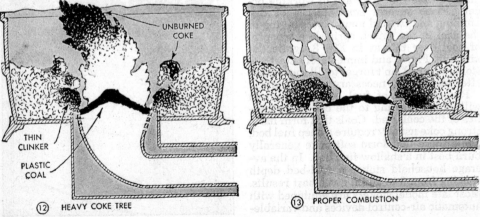

UNBURNED COKE

THIN CLINKER

PLASTIC COAL

⑫ HEAVY COKE TREE

⑬ PROPER COMBUSTION

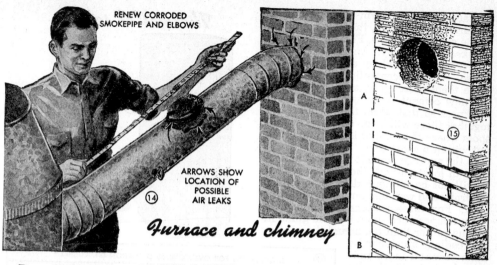

RENEW CORRODED SMOKEPIPE AND ELBOWS

ARROWS SHOW LOCATION OF POSSIBLE AIR LEAKS

(14)

A

(15)

B

Furnace and chimney

Remove the clinker at regular intervals as in Fig. 9, using special clinker tongs. Be careful to disturb the fire bed as little as possible. Before withdrawing the clinker from the firebox turn it over as in Fig. 10 and shake off the loose ash and live coals. Then with a curved poker rake the surrounding loose ash into the cavity and level the fuel bed as in Fig. 11. In mild weather it's a good idea to run the stoker for a short interval to recondition the fire after removal of the clinker. The frequency of cleaning the fire depends on the ash content of the coal and the amount of fuel consumed.

Most late model stokers are equipped with an electric clock type of hold-fire control, the purpose of the device obviously being to keep the fire from going out during long intervals in mild weather when there is no demand for heat. It serves the dual purpose of promoting good combustion, Fig. 13, and of converting ash into clinker. For this reason its proper adjustment is important. In adjusting for a given kind and size of coal, carefully follow the directions of the stoker manufacturer. Some older model stokers are fitted with a stack thermostat to control hold-fire. This device is, of course, set to operate the stoker for short intervals during the "off" period when stack temperature drops below a certain point. Due to variations in heating plant installations proper adjustment of any hold-fire control device is often a matter of "cut and try" until you attain the cycle or time interval of operation which gives best results. General practice favors the longer cycle; that is, it will be found that 4 min. operation once every hour is better than 2 min. twice every hour.

In any home installation it's well to check the chimney and smokepipe at the start of each season. Unused stovepipe openings into the chimney, detail A, Fig. 15, should be closed permanently, and the brick should be examined for cracks, detail B. A corroded smokepipe should be replaced, and care must be taken that there are no air leaks at the check damper or where the pipe enters the chimney, Fig. 14. Any of these openings, even though quite small, will act as miniature check dampers. If the

CEMENT

RADIATOR

COMBUSTION CHAMBER

(16)

FIREBOX

ASHPIT

furnace is of the warm-air type and of cast-iron construction, then the condition of the cemented joints, Fig. 16, should be checked periodically. Any leaks in these will permit gas and fly ash to enter the house. When recementing these joints, clean them thoroughly, and be sure that the new cement is spread to a uniform thickness so that when the parts are set together there will be no openings or thin spots where the cement is likely to crack out within a short time.

In the average home it is almost impossible to locate a wall thermostat so that it will not be influenced to some extent by drafts and wall temperatures that may vary. For these reasons a comfortable room temperature should be the guide in setting rather than the actual thermometer reading. Much can be done toward more uniform heat distribution by adjusting register shutters. In addition, the best practice has shown that there is little, if any, economy in a variation of more than 5 to 7 degrees between the day and night setting of the thermostat, Fig. 17. Wider variations throw a heavy load on the heating plant during the early morning warm-up period, and after a night at the low thermostat setting, the fire will not be in the best condition to deliver peak efficiency just when needed most. It is better to remove the clinker and condition the fire in the morning before setting up the thermostat, as the clinker then has had time to cool and harden and will be easy to handle.

The table in Fig. 18 explains common stoker troubles, their causes and remedies. This does not in any way supplant the specific instructions furnished by the manufacturer of your stoker. If there is any variation, follow the maker's instructions. However, close study of the causes and remedies given will enable you to cope with most of the ordinary difficulties which usually are quite simple to remedy.

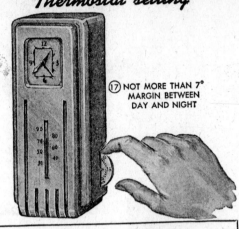

Thermostat setting

⑰ NOT MORE THAN 7° MARGIN BETWEEN DAY AND NIGHT

⑱ SUGGESTIONS FOR OVERCOMING OPERATION DIFFICULTIES *		
TROUBLE	CAUSE	REMEDY
Hopper gas	Excessively dirty fuel bed Clinker in retort Fuel bed too thick Hopper lid not sealed Hopper smokepipe plugged	Clean the bed thoroughly Remove the clinker Reduce thickness of bed Refit lid and gasket Remove cap and clean pipe
Smoke (chimney) (Either during "on" or "off" period, or both)	Fuel bed too thick Not enough air Poor draft Coarse coal Faulty chimney or smokepipe	**Reduce coal feed **Increase air Adjust smokepipe damper Mix fine and coarse coal Repair chimney and pipe
Smoke (basement) "on" period	Firebox draft too weak Too much air	Adjust smokepipe damper Decrease air by fan adjustment
Coke trees	Heavy trees—feed too fast Thin trees—too much air Coal too fine	**Increase air, or reduce feed **Increase feed, or decrease air, or maintain thicker fuel bed Mix coarse and fine coal
Not enough heat	Coal feed rate too low Air supply rate too low Poor draft Dirty fuel bed Heating surfaces dirty Coal too fine Limit switch set too low	Increase feed Increase air Adjust smokepipe damper Clean fuel bed Clean castings thoroughly Mix coarse and fine coal See stoker instructions
Too much heat	Wrong setting of hold-fire control (in mild weather) Coal feed rate too high	Reduce operating time Reduce rate of coal feed
Fly ash	Fuel bed too thin Too much air Dirty fuel bed	Increase rate of coal feed Decrease air Clean fuel bed
Soot	Fuel bed too thick Air supply rate too low Hold-fire control set incorrectly	**Decrease coal feed Increase air supply Increase operating periods of hold-fire control
Not enough air	Fan adjustment too low Siftings in windbox Water in air duct Retort openings blocked Basement too air-tight	Increase fan opening Clean windbox Remove the water Remove foreign material Admit more air
Fire goes out	Switch off, or fuses blown Hold-fire set improperly Clutch out, or pin sheared Coal arched in hopper Fuel-air ratio wrong Excessive draft Drive belt slipping	Rebuild fire Close switch or renew fuses Change setting Throw in clutch, or renew shear pin, or remove obstruction Break arch and push coal down to worm Adjust one or the other Reduce firebox draft Tighten, or renew belt

* It is assumed that the stoker has been properly installed and that heating plant is of adequate capacity
** Always do one then observe results before proceeding.

Automatic Check Damper for Use with Stoker

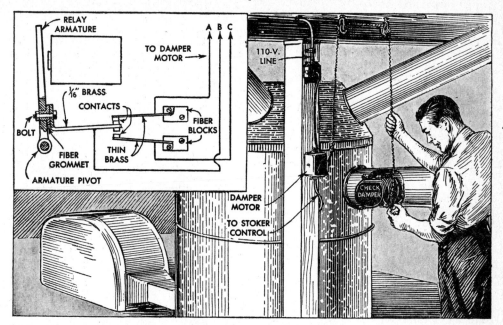

On older types of stokers that are not equipped with an air control for limiting the amount of natural draft through the firebox, a reasonably close control can be provided by automatically operating a check damper in the smokepipe as indicated. The damper closes when the stoker starts to operate and opens when it stops, thus checking the draft.

The check damper is operated by a motor unit of the type used with a wall thermostat for automatic damper control in hand firing. For use with a stoker, the unit is wired to a double-contact switch instead of a thermostat, the switch having connections for three wires the same as the thermostat and being actuated by the armature relay of the stoker control.

The particular type of relay in the stoker control will determine the method of making and mounting the switch. In the switch shown, an arm with double contacts at one end was mounted on the relay armature so that when the armature moved in starting or stopping the stoker it also moved the arm slightly to make or break the circuit between two spring contacts. The arm was insulated from the armature by a fiber grommet and the two brass contacts were insulated by being mounted in fiber blocks.

Most damper motor units have two electrical circuits, one of 110 volts to operate the motor and one of low voltage which flows through the thermostat to control the motor. The low-voltage circuit consists of the three wires that were formerly connected to the room thermostat. These wires are now connected to the switch you installed in the stoker control in the same way as they were connected to the thermostat. The common wire, or wire B in the detail, which was connected to the blade or movable arm of the thermostat, is soldered to the arm of the switch, and the two remaining wires A and C are soldered to the two spring-brass contacts in the switch.

Mount the motor unit on a post, wall or other convenient place and connect one of its arms to the check damper by means of a small chain passed over pulleys as indicated. Plug the motor into the 110-volt circuit and check its operation by starting and stopping the stoker. If the damper closes when it should open, reverse the connections of wires A and C, or change the position of the arm on the motor unit.

❢ A small clean-out door in the cold-air return of your furnace will provide easy access when removing accumulated dirt. The opening in the duct should be ½-in. smaller all around than the dimensions given for the door so that the door will overlap the edges to provide a seal and prevent basement air from entering the duct and lessening the recirculating effect of the sealed return. Hinges for the door are soldered or bolted in place and a latch opposite hinges keeps door closed.

As the oilstove used to heat his home is in a front room and therefore does not adequately heat the adjoining bathroom, one man devised a way to pipe hot water from the stove to a radiator in the bathroom. Having a double-burner oilstove, he made a water jacket of welded sheet metal to fit between the two burner chambers and welded a pipe fitting to the top and bottom of the jacket. He welded sheet-metal baffles to the inside walls of the jacket at an angle to cause the water to swirl as it ascends, and thus become evenly heated. Then, he ran pipe from the jacket to the radiator. Note that the radiator is equipped with an expansion tank for the water. He found that this arrangement provides more than enough heat to keep the bathroom comfortable even in the coldest weather and also that it does not noticeably affect the efficiency of the oilstove, which is operated at the

Oilstove Fitted with Sheet-Metal Jacket Supplies Hot-Water Heat to Bathroom

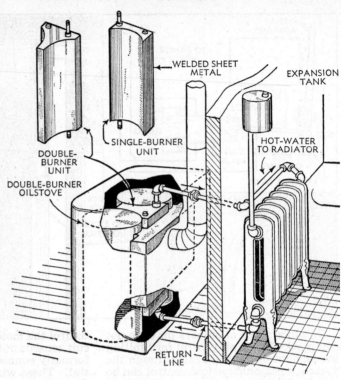

same setting as before the installation. A similar unit for a single-burner stove is made, as shown, to fit partially around the outside of the burner chamber.

Heating Small Home Effectively with a Circulating Heater

Homes of three or four rooms with a closet or small hallway located in the center of the house can be heated effectively with a heating stove as indicated, by using the closet or hallway as a heat distributor. First, a large grill is installed at ceiling height in the closet or hallway wall next to the room containing the stove. Then smaller grills, leading to adjoining rooms, are put in the other walls. In this way, heated air will pass to all rooms as indicated by arrows in the drawing, cold air returning to the heater via the floors and doorways. The reason this arrangement is an improvement is that hot air rising to the ceiling often is pocketed in one room because the door openings are usually several feet below the ceilings. The grills allow an unobstructed passage from room to room for the hot air. It may be desirable to install a false ceiling below the grills to keep the closet clean.

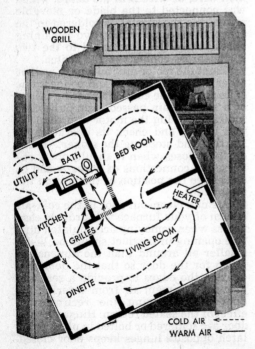

Part 5

OUTSIDE HOME MAINTENANCE,
LAWN AND GARDEN

HOME LANDSCAPING

Generally, the pyramidal type is used against narrow columns of wall space and beside entrances, while the semierect and the lower-growing prostrate forms are best under windows. Broad pyramidals are out of place along short foundations. Choose narrow columnars for narrow spaces, and under windows use varieties that will grow no higher than the sills. These should be shearable; therefore avoid using tall spruces and firs. The junipers, arborvitaes and dwarf mugo pines (all shearables) supply an abundance of form and color.

What to select: Vigorous conifers cannot be produced cheaply. Propagation is by seeds, cuttings and grafts. Young plants are set in rows close together, and so cultivated. Before crowding begins, they are lifted, the roots are pruned back, and then the trees are transplanted farther apart. This process

By Robert Stahler

IN FORM and color, evergreens are so varied that, if judiciously placed as shown in Figs. 1, 2, 4 and 5, they will beautify almost any landscape without the addition of other kinds of plants. For proper effect, the shape and size of the evergreen should conform generally to the architectural pattern against which it is to be placed. The various shapes are shown in Fig. 9. These are: A, creeping or prostrate; B, globular; C, semi-erect; D, narrow columnar; E, broad columnar; F, narrow pyramidal; G, medium pyramidal; H, broad pyramidal. The pyramidal forms may be bought in tall, medium and low-growing varieties, and are suitable either for group planting as windbreaks and screens, or as single specimens.

228

with EVERGREENS....

may be repeated four or five times. In catalogs, the symbol X means that the tree has been pruned and transplanted. Thus, the description "XXXX" means that the roots have been pruned four times and the tree transplanted each time. Such a tree will have a compact root system and top growth; it will be thrifty, in contrast to the cheaper tall, sparse specimens that were left to grow at random from their seedling stage. If price is a consideration, buy the small X'd varieties rather than the inferior taller ones. You should specify, too, B&B trees—those having balled and burlapped roots, as shown in Figs. 7 and 11.

A partial list of evergreens includes the following: Arborvitaes—perhaps the most adaptable of all. The American varieties do well on ordinary soils that are not too heavy, and are quite hardy. The Chinese varieties are beautiful, but are a risk north

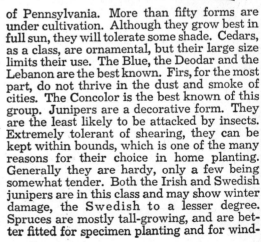

of Pennsylvania. More than fifty forms are under cultivation. Although they grow best in full sun, they will tolerate some shade. Cedars, as a class, are ornamental, but their large size limits their use. The Blue, the Deodar and the Lebanon are the best known. Firs, for the most part, do not thrive in the dust and smoke of cities. The Concolor is the best known of this group. Junipers are a decorative form. They are the least likely to be attacked by insects. Extremely tolerant of shearing, they can be kept within bounds, which is one of the many reasons for their choice in home planting. Generally they are hardy, only a few being somewhat tender. Both the Irish and Swedish junipers are in this class and may show winter damage, the Swedish to a lesser degree. Spruces are mostly tall-growing, and are better fitted for specimen planting and for wind-

(7)

(8) REFLECTED HEAT KILLS TREES PLANTED TOO CLOSE TO BUILDING

breaks. The blue color of the Colorado and Koster's (a grafted form of the Colorado) is too intense and striking for combining with other varieties in foundation or group plantings. Hemlocks are graceful trees that often attain great size, and are used mostly for this purpose. Yews are superb for low hedges. The bushy Japanese form is quite hardy, and perhaps is the best of this kind. Fig. 12 shows the characteristic appearance of several of these species.

Where to plant: Before planting, set stakes of the estimated height of the trees you will use, and allow between them the spread you will permit the trees to attain. Set the trees as in Fig. 11, tying the stakes as indicated in the circular detail. After staking, it is a good idea to provide a burlap shield around the newly planted tree, as in Fig. 6, to protect it from being uprooted by the wind. Don't plant too close to the wall of the house; reflected heat burns the foliage, causing it to drop off, Fig. 8, and the light is restricted, resulting in sparse foliage on the rear, or shaded side. Fortunately, most conifers are adaptable to various soil conditions. The common American arborvitae is sometimes found in a swampy environment, yet does well on comparatively dry garden soils. But because conifers are adaptable, they are too often placed on soils wholly unsuitable. In their native habitat, they are mostly residents of slopes, where nature is in the process of soil making. The soil is gritty; mixed into it is the decaying debris of leaves, needles and twigs, called humus. Often the roots are under great rocks, which are prime conservers of moisture. The slopes furnish perfect drainage. Here the trees grow to heights never reached in cultivation.

Preparing the soil: To plant the trees, strip the sod and work the soil deep and fine, Fig. 7. Mix humus and plant foods thoroughly into the soil down to a depth of about 12 in. Damp peat, not soaked, mixes better with the soil than when dry. B&B trees can be set in early winter in many parts of the country, even well into the North, if given the proper depth of mulch, Fig. 3. Spring is the best time to plant, but

CHARACTERISTICS OF CONIFERS

Group	Type	Av. Ht. (1) (in ft.)	Color	Form (2)
Juniper	Meyer	3	Blue-green	C
	Globe	3½	Lt. green	B
	Savin	—	Dk. green	A
	Pfitzer's	3½	Green-grey	C
	Goldenrod	3½	Golden-yellow	C
	Koster's	3	Blue-green	C
	Japanese	—	Blue-green	A
	Andora	—	Silver-green	A
	Spiny Greek	6	Blue	E
	Blue	18	Blue	H
	Chinese columnar	17	Blue-grey	D
	Pyramid	17	Grey-green	F
	Irish	15	Blue-green	D
	Swedish	20	Blue-green	D
	Tamarix		Bright green	A
Pine	Dwarf mugo (3)	4	Dark green	B
Cedar (4)	Silver	15	Silver-blue	F
	Concolor red	17	Green	F
	Red	23	Silver-green	F
Arbor-vitae	American	40	Green	G
	Pyramidal	15	Green	D
	Globe	3	Green	B
	Golden	40	Golden-yellow	D
Spruce	Koster's Blue	40	Blue	H
	Colorado Blue	60	Silver-blue	H
	Shiner (5)	—		H
	Black Hills	40	Green	H
	White	70	Green	H
	Norway	100	Green	H
Fir	Concolor	80	Green	H

(1) In cultivation; wild species may grow taller
(2) See Fig. 9
(3) These may be cut back
(4) Not true cedars
(5) A species of Colorado Blue. Always buy these balled and burlapped

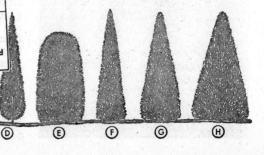

(9)

Ⓐ   Ⓑ   Ⓒ   Ⓓ   Ⓔ   Ⓕ   Ⓖ   Ⓗ

mid-summer planting is not recommended.

It is a waste of money to apply nitrogen at planting time. Phosphorus and potash in bone meal will combine with the soil with little loss by leaching, but nitrogen escapes. Moreover, the shortened root systems are inadequate to supply the moisture needs of the new growth that nitrogen forces. Four to six months can elapse before using nitrogen; if you have used leaf mold for humus, a year may well go by. Peat has almost no food value. If it is the source of humus, apply twelve pounds of dry sheep manure per 100 sq. ft. and work it in, four to six months after planting. Other forms of vegetable or animal nitrogen may be used, but avoid chemicals. To keep the food supply constant, each year apply 15 lbs. of bone meal, 2 lbs. of potash, and 12 to 15 lbs. of sheep manure. Use half of

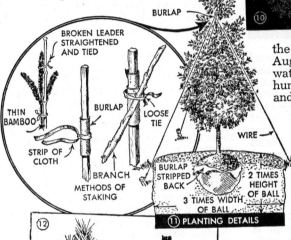

BURLAP

BROKEN LEADER STRAIGHTENED AND TIED

THIN BAMBOO

BURLAP

LOOSE TIE

STRIP OF CLOTH

BRANCH

METHODS OF STAKING

WIRE

BURLAP STRIPPED BACK

2 TIMES HEIGHT OF BALL

3 TIMES WIDTH OF BALL

⑪ PLANTING DETAILS

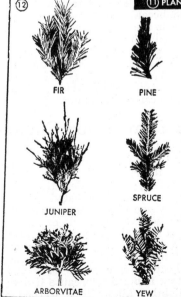

FIR

PINE

JUNIPER

SPRUCE

ARBORVITAE

YEW

the latter in early spring; half in early August. Work in these materials and water thoroughly. Using plenty of humus not only keeps the soil open and light, but also enables it to retain large quantities of moisture, which is essential for dense foliage, health and vigor.

Fall and spring care: Don't let conifers begin the winter in dry soil. Soak the ground thoroughly to root depth at least. After the first freeze, apply the winter mulch. Remember that evergreens are more or less active at all times, even in winter. If the ground freezes to an appreciable depth, the trees suffer for want of moisture exactly as they would during a summer drouth. Partial damage or complete destruction of the trees results.

In early spring, remove all but an inch of the mulch; then when the ground dries to a workable condition, apply plant foods and work them and the inch of mulch into the soil, the latter to keep the humus supply constant. Cultivate at 10-day intervals, until hot weather begins. Meantime, don't neglect the moisture supply, but, of course, do not flood the soil. Doing so will result in a soured soil. The ideal soil is evenly moist from near the top down to a considerable depth, but not soaking wet. A thorough drenching at 10 to 14-day intervals will, under normal conditions, suffice.

When hot weather sets in, apply the summer mulch, and apply nitrogenous fertilizer in early August.

Pruning: Pruning of conifers consists mostly of shearing to control height and

and fir only where they will have plenty of room to develop. Never prune the low branches of conifers, unless these are dead; they should spread from the ground up.

Insects and disease: Though conifers are a healthy group and are more or less immune to serious insect and disease attack, you should nevertheless be on the alert. In fall look for bagworm nests, which are pendant bags made of bits of leaves bound with silk and suspended by the same material. Remove and burn them. The spruce budworm cuts off the needle-like foliage and weaves it into a web shelter. The larvae of these two insects, also those of the gypsy moth, emerge in spring and attack the foliage. Control is by spraying, Fig. 13. Use a lead arsenate spray applied when the weather warms in early spring; repeat in 10 days.

Aphids or plant lice are of a different type from those found on flowering plants. Many form galls. Spray with a miscible oil in early spring before new growth begins, and only on a sunny day, temperature at 50 degrees or more, with no chance of it dropping within six hours. The oil must dry quickly, else damage will result. Oil sprays are injurious to some junipers whose needles form cup-like depressions.

In hot weather, red spider is most likely to attack. Only about $\frac{1}{50}$ in. long, they are most difficult to see, as are the webs they weave. Treat them with dusting sulphur. Use it weekly, but never within a month after using oil. Borers and beetles have little chance of affecting a healthy evergreen, but may attack a weak one.

Only a few conifers are subject to serious diseases. The white pine is seldom planted, because of white-pine blister rust. Wood rots are more often encountered in forest and other dense growth. If dead wood develops, prune it out with a sharp tool. "Cedar apples," caused by a fungus that produces soft spongy masses of yellow-orange color, may attack junipers and should be carefully cut out.

spread. Such work is easily done on dwarf mugo pine, arborvitae, juniper, yew and cypress in spring and early fall. Young specimens of fir and spruce are sometimes pruned by pinching back side branches slightly, Fig. 10. However, it is best to let someone familiar with evergreens do this work for you. Remember that you cannot control height and spread of fir and spruce as you can with ordinary shrubs. Fir and spruce will show a stubby effect if pruned, and their recovery is slow. If the leader is cut in an effort to limit height, the growth is thrown to the sides; if the sides are clipped, the strength goes to the top. A correct balance, which makes for a beautiful pyramid shape, cannot be achieved by using the knife. While any top growth can be cut back, the root system remains intact and constantly extends itself. And as it extends, it throws more strength to the top. It is advisable, therefore, to plant spruce

Preignition Caused by Hot Spot in Combustion Chamber

If your car will not run at high speeds without spitting through the carburetor, likely the trouble is caused by preignition —some part of the combustion chamber becomes sufficiently hot to ignite the fuel charge before the spark occurs at the plug. The trouble probably can be traced to carbon, a valve that does not close tightly, or a plug that operates too hot. First, be sure that the correct type of spark plug is being used. Then, before removing the cylinder head to check for a hot spot, look over the following adjustments which might cause trouble: A too-lean fuel mix-

ture or a clogged fuel line at the carburetor screen. Insufficient cooling due to lack of water in the radiator. A stoppage in the water system, such as a defective pump, or slipping fan belt. Overheated spark plugs due to leakage where they screw into the cylinder head, or a weak or worn fuel pump. If all of these are in order, remove the cylinder head and check for a carbon or metal projection that might be heated to white heat at high speed. Or look for a valve that is burning because it does not close tightly. Likely it is warped or is adjusted incorrectly at the tappet.

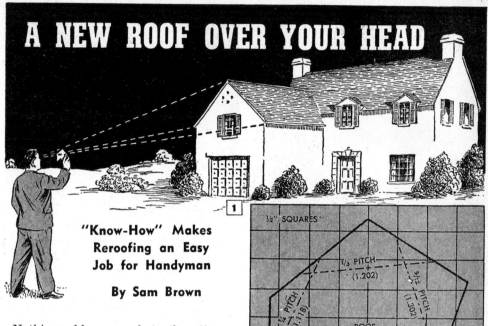

A NEW ROOF OVER YOUR HEAD

"Know-How" Makes Reroofing an Easy Job for Handyman

By Sam Brown

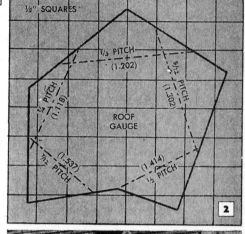

Nothing adds so much to the attractiveness of the small home as a colorful roof. Moreover, the job of reroofing with modern asphalt shingles is easily within the capabilities of any home craftsman.

Getting started demands first an estimate of the quantity of roofing necessary. This can be done by using the roof gauge shown in Fig. 2. With this in your hand, step off about 100 paces from the main gable, making certain that your selected position is directly centered with the ridge and directly at right angles to the sidewall. Then, by sighting over the various angles of the gauge, as in Fig. 1, you can readily determine the exact pitch of the roof. Say, it is ⅓ pitch. The pitch factor for this is 1.202, as shown in the same figure, and the roof surface is found by multiplying the area of the roof measured flat by the pitch factor, adding as many feet as you deem necessary for waste, duplications, hips and valleys. Here's an example: Your home is 30 by 30 ft. The area of the flat roof would be, then, 30 by 30, or 900 sq. ft. The roof is ⅓ pitch. So, 900 by 1.202 would give you 1,082 sq. ft. A dormer would make no difference except that you would add the roofing necessary to cover at the eaves where the dormer roof would overlap the main roof, 1 sq. ft. of roofing being added for every running foot of hip or valley. Working in this manner, the most irregular roofs can be quickly and easily figured. The rule applies whether

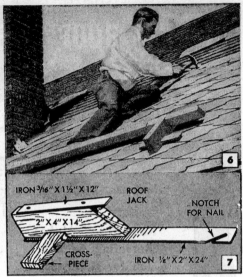

IRON ³/₁₆" X 1½" X 12"   ROOF JACK

NOTCH FOR NAIL

2" X 4" X 14"

CROSS-PIECE   IRON ⅛" X 2" X 24"

the house be four-gabled, three-gabled, gable, hip or dormer hip. Imagining your calculations run 1,150 sq. ft. of roof, you will need 11½ "squares" of roofing, the square being a unit of 100 sq. ft. Pick a good grade of roofing. Cut-out roll roofing, as shown in Fig. 4, makes an inexpensive covering which is quite practical. Other types in strip, individual and patented shingles usually cost more, but give greater protection and are obtainable in a wider variety of patterns and colors.

First of all, the old wood shingles must be given the "once over." Warped slabs should be split with a hatchet and securely nailed to the lath, using 12-gauge roofing nails. Gutter fastenings should be checked and repaired if necessary. Loose brickwork should be pointed up. The roofing job proper commences with the fitting of the metal edge strips, as shown in Fig. 3. These measure about 3 by 1 in. and are of light galvanized sheet iron. Their purpose is to give a finished edge over the old wood shingles.

They are not absolutely necessary, but are invariably used in better-class work. Over the metal edge strip, and projecting just a bit beyond the eaves, is fitted the starting strip, as shown in Fig. 4. This is usually roll roofing, regardless of what the finishing shingle is like, and it should be of a width equal to the depth of the shingles selected. No. 12-gauge 1½-in. galvanized roofing nails should be used for fastenings. These can be inserted anywhere, as the combined thickness of the old shingle roof and the new covering will never be less than ¾ inch.

If you are using cut-out roll roofing as a finish, the job proceeds as shown in Fig. 5, the first strip being placed directly over the starting strip, with each succeeding strip laid so as to expose the proper part of the strip immediately under it. Instructions on this are usually stamped on each roll. Working up to the final strip on, say, a porch roof, fit the free end of the strip neatly under the siding, as shown in Fig. 8. Plastic roof cement may be used, but it is not necessary.

234

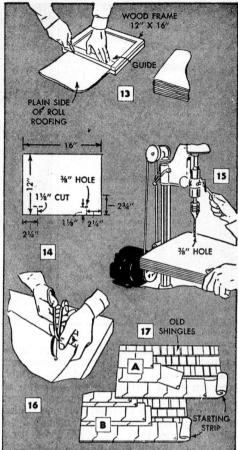

WOOD FRAME
12" X 16"

GUIDE

PLAIN SIDE
OF ROLL
ROOFING

13

16"

12"

3/8" HOLE

1 1/8" CUT

2 3/4"

1 1/8" 2 1/4"

2 1/4"

14

15

3/8" HOLE

16

17 OLD
SHINGLES

A

B

STARTING
STRIP

7/8" X 2" X 5"

AMOUNT OF HEAD LAP

STRAP IRON

12

11

Ridges and hips should be finished with individual strips measuring about 8 by 12 in., as shown in Fig. 9, although one continuous strip can be used where expense is an item. If there is a valley in any part of the roof surface, this should be covered first. Use a continuous strip, not less than 16 in. wide, fitting this in place as shown in Fig. 11. The roofing—roll or shingle—is brought to a rough fit at the valley and later trimmed with a straightedge, as shown in Fig. 10, allowing about 3 in. on either side of the joint. Fig. 7 gives the necessary details of a simple roof jack which you will find quite necessary before you are finished. This is used as shown in Fig. 6, one jack being attached at each end of any suitable length of 2 by 4-in. stock. Each jack is held by a nail, which is hammered down when the jack is moved.

Would you like to make your own asphalt shingles? Figs. 14 to 17 inclusive show how this can be done. Take roll roofing, 32 in. wide, and split it down the center to obtain two strips 16 in. wide.

18

19

20

21

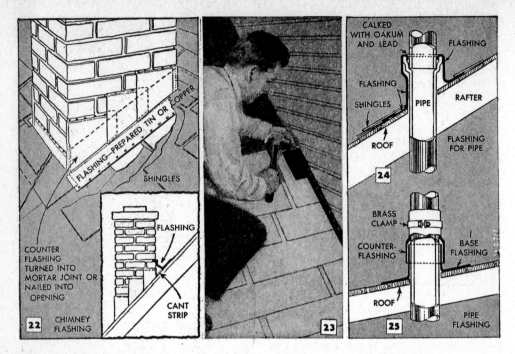

22 CHIMNEY FLASHING — FLASHING—PREPARED TIN OR COPPER — SHINGLES — COUNTER FLASHING TURNED INTO MORTAR JOINT OR NAILED INTO OPENING — FLASHING — CANT STRIP

24 CALKED WITH OAKUM AND LEAD — FLASHING — FLASHING — SHINGLES — PIPE — RAFTER — ROOF — FLASHING FOR PIPE

25 BRASS CLAMP — COUNTER-FLASHING — BASE FLASHING — ROOF — PIPE FLASHING

Each strip is readily cut into large individual shingles by using the simple box frame shown. You will find that knives and tin snips do better on this job if dipped occasionally in kerosene. If you care to go a step farther, you can make a lock-type of shingle, as indicated in Figs. 15 and 16. Fig. 17A gives one method of laying a shingle of this type, the exposure being 10 in. to the weather. Notice how the one fault of roll roofing—exposed nailing—is eliminated by covering each nail head with the locking flap. Double coverage can be obtained by laying the shingles 5 in. to the weather in this fashion or by using the ribbon course of 10 and 3-in. exposures shown in Fig. 17B. A simple lock shingle like this can be laid in many different ways. Used without the lock, these large shingles can be laid up either vertically or horizontally with a 5-in. exposure and ¾-in. channels, as shown in Fig. 20. Notice, in Figs. 18 and 21, how each succeeding course is stepped up and nailed to form a watertight joint against brickwork and abutting siding.

A little jig which comes in handy in laying many types of shingling is shown in Fig. 12. With the metal straps hooked over the previous course, you can't go wrong in allowing the exact amount of exposure, and at the same time you keep each course perfectly straight from end to end. Another useful bit of roofing equipment is shown in Fig. 11: a tri-

angular support of wood held to the roof by two nails projecting slightly from the underside of the base piece. If your choice of roofing material runs to rigid asbestos or composition shingles, it will be necessary to flash all joints with metal instead of following the simpler method possible with asphalt roofing. The necessary details on this work are shown in Figs. 22 to 25. The procedure is much the same as previously described with the exception that flashing tin or 16-oz. copper is used. Chimneys should be flashed and counterflashed for best results, as in Fig. 25, with the counterflashing either turned into the mortar seam or nailed well inside the joint. A cant strip of wood stock is sometimes fitted at the upper side of the chimney, as in Fig. 22, in order to break what would be otherwise an exceedingly sharp angle. On abutting sidewalls, metal flashing is laid up with every course of shingles, as in Fig. 23, fastening the metal securely to the siding. Vent pipes can be treated as in Figs. 24 and 25, the latter showing the usual procedure in treating a pipe which projects without break above the roof.

❧ Window screens are converted to temporary storm windows by coating them with thinned cellulose cement or clear lacquer. This fills the wire mesh but still admits light. In spring, the screens are restored to original condition with thinner.

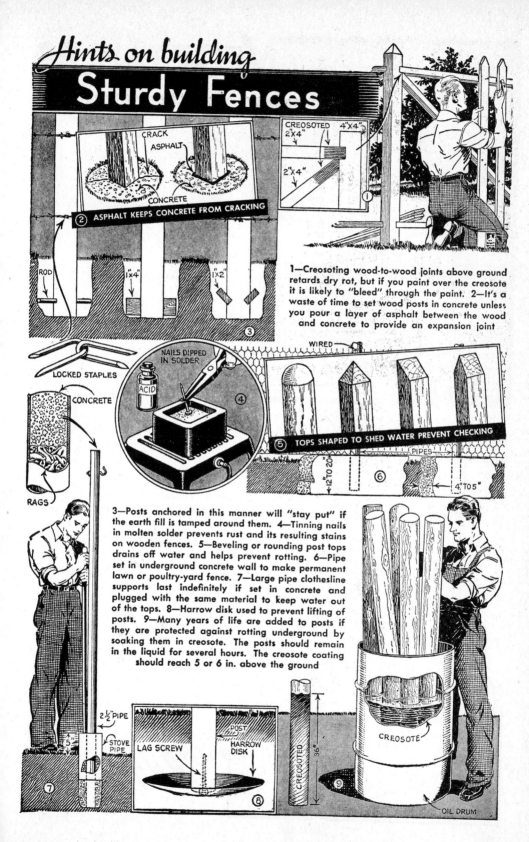

Hints on building
Sturdy Fences

CRACK
ASPHALT
CONCRETE

② ASPHALT KEEPS CONCRETE FROM CRACKING

CREOSOTED 4"X4"
2"X4"
2"X4"

①

ROD
1"X4"
1"X2"

③

1—Creosoting wood-to-wood joints above ground retards dry rot, but if you paint over the creosote it is likely to "bleed" through the paint. 2—It's a waste of time to set wood posts in concrete unless you pour a layer of asphalt between the wood and concrete to provide an expansion joint

LOCKED STAPLES

CONCRETE

NAILS DIPPED IN SOLDER
ACID

④

RAGS

WIRED

⑤ TOPS SHAPED TO SHED WATER PREVENT CHECKING

12" TO 20"
PIPES
4" TO 5"

⑥

3—Posts anchored in this manner will "stay put" if the earth fill is tamped around them. 4—Tinning nails in molten solder prevents rust and its resulting stains on wooden fences. 5—Beveling or rounding post tops drains off water and helps prevent rotting. 6—Pipe set in underground concrete wall to make permanent lawn or poultry-yard fence. 7—Large pipe clothesline supports last indefinitely if set in concrete and plugged with the same material to keep water out of the tops. 8—Harrow disk used to prevent lifting of posts. 9—Many years of life are added to posts if they are protected against rotting underground by soaking them in creosote. The posts should remain in the liquid for several hours. The creosote coating should reach 5 or 6 in. above the ground

2½" PIPE
5"
STOVE PIPE

LAG SCREW
POST
HARROW DISK

CREOSOTED
36"

CREOSOTE

⑦

⑧

⑨

OIL DRUM

Fresh VEGETABLES

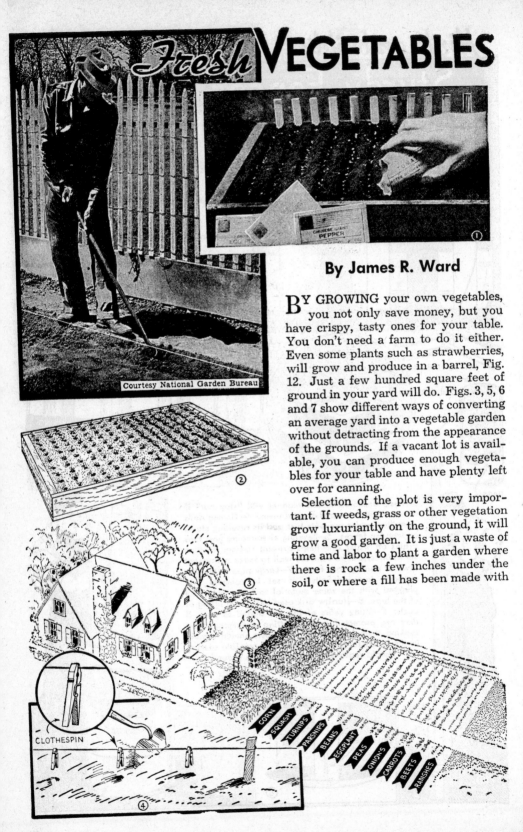

Courtesy National Garden Bureau

CLOTHESPIN

CORN SQUASH TURNIPS PARSNIPS BEANS EGGPLANT PEAS ONIONS CARROTS BEETS RADISHES

By James R. Ward

BY GROWING your own vegetables, you not only save money, but you have crispy, tasty ones for your table. You don't need a farm to do it either. Even some plants such as strawberries, will grow and produce in a barrel, Fig. 12. Just a few hundred square feet of ground in your yard will do. Figs. 3, 5, 6 and 7 show different ways of converting an average yard into a vegetable garden without detracting from the appearance of the grounds. If a vacant lot is available, you can produce enough vegetables for your table and have plenty left over for canning.

Selection of the plot is very important. If weeds, grass or other vegetation grow luxuriantly on the ground, it will grow a good garden. It is just a waste of time and labor to plant a garden where there is rock a few inches under the soil, or where a fill has been made with

Courtesy Peter Henderson & Co.

cinders, broken brick, stones, etc. The ideal soil is a dark, sandy loam. Do not locate your garden under or near large trees that will steal the moisture and plant food from the crops.

After selecting the plot, you are ready to prepare the soil. Spade or plow it 6 to 10 in. deep. If possible, turn under manure. Leaves and other dead vegetation are also good. Their value as a fertilizer is nominal but they supply humus to help retain moisture. If the ground is of a clay type, sifted coal ashes worked well into the soil will tend to loosen it. So will wood ashes. Those from soft woods add little food value but most hardwoods contain potash and lime, which are good fertilizers. When natural fertilizers are unavailable, you can use the commercial type at planting time. Before using these, it is a good idea to test the soil so that you can use the food elements needed; a few samples of the soil

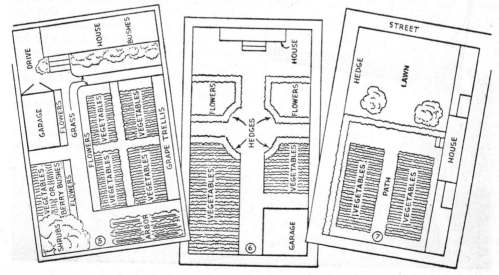

Courtesy National Garden Bureau

BEANS STARTED IN BERRY BOX

⑨ PLANTS MULCHED WITH MAGAZINES

⑩ HOLES

WATERING YOUNG PLANTS

MUSLIN

can be sent to your local seed company, or to the state agriculture college or university.

Next comes the selection of the seeds and planting. What vegetables to plant will depend on the space available. On a small plot, it is best to avoid those that take considerable space such as corn, cucumbers, etc. However, some vegetables that mature early can be resown in the same ground to have a succession of them, or they can be followed by others in the same space as indicated in the table of Fig. 15. Half the pleasure of a garden is having something to use just as early in the spring as possible. To do this, seeds are started early and then transplanted in the garden after danger of frost is past. Truck gardeners start theirs in hotbeds, but the home gardener who needs only a few of each kind can start them indoors in window boxes or flats, Fig. 1. The flats should be kept in a south window and the temperature should be maintained over 60° F. Tomatoes, cabbage, peppers, eggplant and lettuce can be started this way and then transplanted later. The seeds are sown thickly in tiny drills and transplanted to another flat in small hills after they have grown to a height of an inch or so, Fig. 2. The plants mentioned above can usually be purchased locally, but it is fun to grow them yourself. Other vegetables that do not permit transplanting in the usual way, can be started early if the seeds are sown in individual containers such as ice-cream cartons, flowerpots or berry boxes, Fig. 8. In transplanting, be careful not to disturb the root system. Cut the container away and set the entire contents in the ground. Perhaps the best way for the small gardener is to have six to twelve containers of each vegetable started indoors for early use, and then start the rest of the garden in the usual way by sowing seeds in the ground or by purchasing the seedlings.

Vegetables are divided into about four groups as to planting time. Early cabbage, kale, onion sets, peas, potatoes, spinach and radishes may be planted two weeks before the average date of the last killing frost. Beets, Swiss chard, carrots, lettuce, peas, cauliflower and sweet corn should be planted about the date of the last killing frost; while beans, parsnips, salsify, cucumbers and tomatoes should not be planted for at least a week after frost. Heat-loving plants, such as peppers, eggplant, Lima beans, etc., should not be planted until the ground is thoroughly warm.

As soon as the weather permits, work down the ground, which has already been spaded or plowed, and prepare it for planting. Use a garden rake and pulverize the soil finely. If you are using commercial fertilizer, work it into the ground as you prepare the seed beds. If you want to conserve the fertilizer, work it into the soil only where the seed rows are to be made or where seedlings are to be transplanted. In general follow the directions on your seed packets. Use a guide line to make straight seed furrows. Fig. 4 shows a good marker to get uniformity in rows of vegetables that are planted in hills.

Seedlings that have been transplanted must be protected from the sun for a few days. Fig. 11 shows a good way to do this. When transplanting seedlings wrap paper around the stems as in Fig. 13. This will keep cutworms from killing them. If your garden plot is unfenced, a coil spring to shield each transplanted seedling, as in Fig. 14, will keep dogs or cats from breaking them off. If you have only a few seedlings, a tin can buried beside each one when it is transplanted, Fig. 10, will enable you to water it easily during dry weather. Or, you can mulch each one with an old magazine or newspaper, Fig. 9, to retain the moisture in the ground. Also, mulching of entire small plots can be done by laying heavy paper between the rows and weighting it with a little soil.

3" DOWNSPOUT PERFORATED FOR WATERING

2" HOLES, SPACED 8" TO 10" APART

PAPER WRAPPING

CUSHION SPRING

YOUNG PLANT

BARREL IS SET ON LARGE STONES FOR AIR CIRCULATION

PLANTING TABLE

Kind of Vegetable	Planted	Bears Until	Replaced by
Beans, pole and lima · · Sweet Corn,	Late May	Frost	
late or main crop · · Sweet Corn,	Mid-May	Sept.	Pumpkin and vine
mid-season varieties · Sweet Corn,	Mid-May	Mid-Aug.	Squash planted in corn rows by
early varieties · · · · Tomatoes, set from	Mid-May	Early Aug.	mid June will succeed the corn
hotbed · · · · · · · ·	Late May	Frost	
Peas, late or main crop varieties · · · · ·	Apr. or May	Early Aug.	Rutabaga and late Turnips
Peas, early and mid-season varieties · · · ·	Apr. or May	Mid-July	Celery from seed-bed
Beans, dwarf or bush varieties · · · · · · ·	Mid-May	July	Cabbage and Cauliflower from seedbed
Lettuce and Endive · ·	Apr. or May	Mid-July	Beets for fall and winter use
Cabbage and Cauliflower Kohlrabi, ½ row;	Apr. or May	Aug.	Beans, dwarf or bush varieties
Swiss Chard · · · · · Carrot and Turnip,	Apr. or May	Aug.	Lettuce and Endive
early varieties · · · · Radish, Mustard and	Apr. or May	Aug.	Chinese Cabbage and Florence Fennel, from seedbed
Cress · · · · · · · · ·	Apr. or May	July	or sown in Radish
Onion Sets · · · · · · ·	Apr. or May	Aug.	row will occupy the three rows
Beets, early varieties · ·	Apr. or May	Aug.	Spinach for fall use
Spinach · · · · · · · ·	Apr. or May	Mid-June	Carrots 2/3 row; winter Radish
Eggplant and Peppers ·	Late May	Frost	
Beans, bush lima · · ·	Late May	Frost	

GLASS CUTTING

While it is true that most home-owners can have window glass cut to exact size at the store where they buy it, many times scrap glass around the home will do to reglaze a window. That's when it pays to know how to cut the glass yourself

By Ralph E. Moore

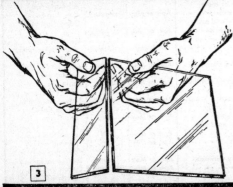

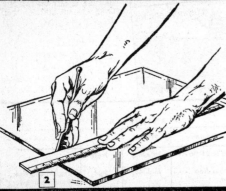

For a clean break, dip the cutter in light oil and apply kerosene to the glass before scoring

Break off scored strip 1 to 2 in. wide by placing index fingers on score and bending downward

"IF I EVER TRIED to cut a piece of glass like that I would break it in a thousand pieces." No doubt you have heard this said before and, perhaps, have even found it so. But cutting window glass is as easy as the professional glazier makes it look, and not necessarily because his cutter may have a diamond point. It is due more to the way the cutter is held and to the tricks of the trade. With a little practice anyone can become adept at using a glass cutter and score a clean break every time.

First of all, get the feel of holding the cutter properly and recognize the sound it should make when it is actually cutting. When the tool is cutting properly, it should sound similar to paper or cloth being torn. The best way to get the feel of the cutter is to practice on an old piece of glass. Never try to cut dirty glass. Grit will prevent uniform cutting of the wheel. The glass should be placed on a flat surface. A small carpet or a piece of old rug, Fig. 1, makes the best surface on which to cut glass. Fig. 2 shows the proper way to hold the cutter. Note that it is not held vertically but at a slight, backward angle and also that the notches point downward.

To make a trial cut, first apply kerosene along the line of cut. Kerosene has been found to give "bite" to the cutter. A small brush or swab on a stick is handy to apply the kerosene to the glass. Next, using a yardstick as a straightedge, dip the cutter in light oil and start the cut at the far edge of the glass. Draw the cutter toward you with a swift, continuous movement, bearing down with a steady, firm pressure. The amount of pressure required is determined by the sound of the cutter. If it skips, pressure should be increased. Remember that the cutter actually cuts the glass and does not merely scratch it. *Never go over the same cut twice.* This is an important point to remember. Besides dulling the cutting wheel, scoring the glass a second time blunts the taper on the inside of the first cut and the glass will not break cleanly. For this reason, if the cutter does

MADE EASY

skip, run it over only the spots missed.

The professional glazier classifies glass as being either window glass (single or double strength) or plate glass. In cutting window glass it is advisable to use a sharp cutter as window glass, being lighter than plate glass, will not stand great pressure.

Where it is required that a strip as narrow as 1/8 in. be cut from the edge of window glass, lay the yardstick 1/16 in. to the left of the line of cut to allow for the overhang of the cutter. Next, apply kerosene to the glass where it is to be cut, using a small brush or an oilcan, and dip the cutter in oil to lubricate the wheel. If this is not done, the wheel may "freeze" when the cut is half completed and merely slide the rest of the way. To break off the strip, use the notches provided in the cutter as shown in Fig. 5, selecting the notch that fits the thickness of the glass. Don't insert the edge of the glass all the way in the notch of the cutter. The proper distance varies with the width of the strip. In most cases, strips less than 3/16 in. break off in little pieces. When breaking off strips 1 to 2 in. wide, grip the glass as shown in Fig. 3. Place the fingers and thumb of each hand close together on each side of the cut. Then, using the index fingers as pivots, snap off the waste piece by bending the glass downward with a quick twist of the wrists. To break off pieces wider than 2 in., place the yardstick directly under the cut, as shown in Fig. 4, and press downward on each side.

The procedure for cutting plate glass is the same as that used for cutting window glass. However, a somewhat different method is used to break off narrow pieces. Where the waste strip is 1 in. wide or less, parallel-jaw pliers with paper between the jaws are used to remove the strip as in Fig. 6. Strips 1 to 4 in. wide are snapped off in a manner similar to the yardstick method, except that in the case of plate glass, it is recommended that a pencil be placed directly under the cut.

If glass is being cut for purposes other than glazing, such as a new top for a coffee table, the sharp edges of the glass may require rounding slightly. This can be done with an oilstone and water. The stone is soaked in water and then rubbed across the edge of the glass with the stone held at a 45-deg. angle. Rubbing is done with a circular motion and the stone is dipped in water occasionally as the work progresses. In polishing the edges of plate glass, the stone is held lengthwise and at right angles to the surface of the glass.

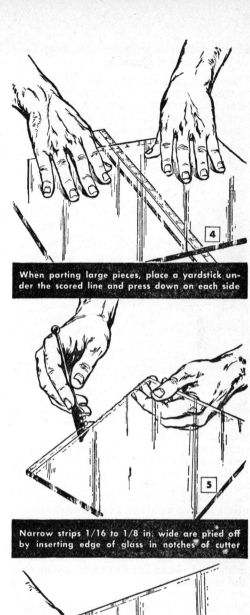

When parting large pieces, place a yardstick under the scored line and press down on each side

Narrow strips 1/16 to 1/8 in. wide are pried off by inserting edge of glass in notches of cutter

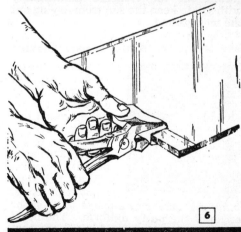

Parallel-jaw pliers provide greater leverage for removing narrow strips from edge of plate glass

Simple Irrigating System to Keep Your Garden Growing

By using this simple irrigating system to water your garden you not only save time, but you also save water, as there is less loss from evaporation when you irrigate than there is when you sprinkle

HOLES SPACED ABOUT 18" APART

2" X 4"

with a hose. Sprinkling, of course, requires your constant attention, which is not necessary when you irrigate. To install the system, all you need is a suitable length of ¾-in. pipe, which is capped at one end and provided with a fitting at the other to take a garden hose. Wood blocks support the pipe, which has ⅛-in. holes drilled in one side to direct the water into trenches between the rows. After irrigating, fill the trenches immediately with soil to keep the sun from drying out the wet ground.

Beveled Putty Knife Speeds Glazing

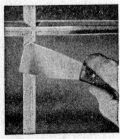

Faster, neater jobs of window glazing can be done with a putty knife ground to a 45-deg. bevel at one corner of the blade. The bevel permits scraping off just the right amount of excess putty and serves as a gauge to keep the angle of the putty uniform. The bevel also is useful when working in the corners of the pane, as it allows the knife to fit against the putty in the adjacent rabbet of the sash.

Remember These Points When Glazing Sash

Even in such an easy job as glazing a sash, simple but important details of correct procedure are often overlooked. The first thing that comes up is the condition of the sash frame. If it has weathered for some time and most, or all, of the putty has fallen out, look the frame over carefully for rotted wood, loose joints, and splintered or warped muntins, the latter in a multiple-pane sash. Remove the glass, clean away loose putty, tighten up the frame with bar clamps and secure the loose corners with ¼-in. dowels. These are driven in holes bored at right angles through the tenoned joints. Repair splintered or rotted muntins by cutting away all the old wood to the bottom of the rabbets and putting in strips of white pine as in Figs. 1 and 2. Give the frame a priming coat of paint. Putty will not bond to the bare wood. If the pane, new or old, fits tightly, score it ¹⁄₁₆ in. or so from the edges with a glass cutter and chip away the waste. The reason for this loose fit is important, as shown in the cross-section, Fig. 5. Note that the putty has been forced in between the edges of the glass and the sides of the rabbet, forming a strong bond and a waterproof joint. After the paint on the frame is thoroughly dry, replace the glass and secure each pane with glaziers' points placed as in Fig. 3. Whether you use a common putty or the new nonhardening putty it should be well worked or kneaded in the palm of the hand, Fig. 4, before being used. In puttying, start as in Fig. 6 by filling the rabbet the full length before smoothing as in Fig. 7. When you make the smoothing strokes, tilt the leading edge of the knife and apply a fairly heavy pressure to force the putty behind the edge of the glass. Allow the putty to dry before painting.

❧ To loosen a rusted screw, press a hot soldering iron against it for a few minutes.

How to Remove Glazier's Points

GLAZIERS' POINTS BENT UP

WINDOW SASH

Time and labor can be saved when removing glazier's points from a sash if the projecting ends are bent upward. When bent in this manner, the points are pried out with a screwdriver.

Sash Glazing

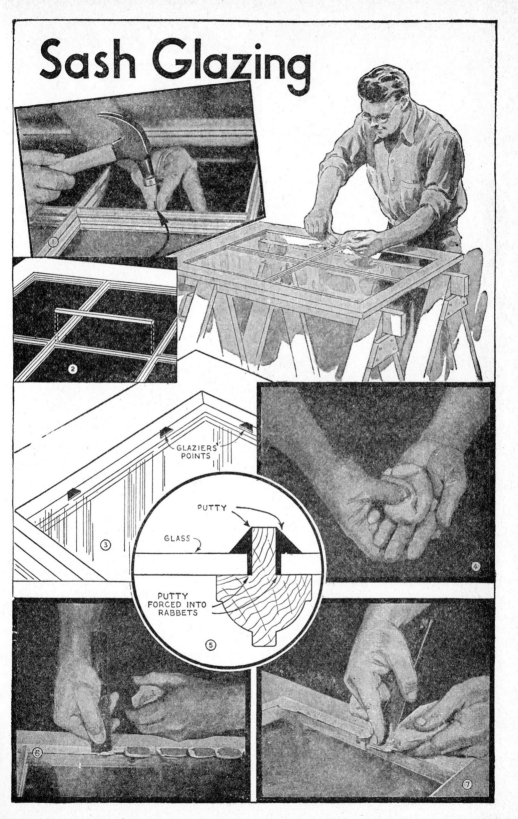

GLAZIERS' POINTS

PUTTY

GLASS

PUTTY FORCED INTO RABBETS

How to Make

Test for organic matter

Silt test

DURABLE concrete is a result of careful selection of materials, correct proportioning of ingredients, especially the cement and water, and proper treatment after pouring the concrete. For best results, there are a few tests that anyone can employ to judge materials, and equally simple rules to follow in mixing the ingredients. First is the correct selection of aggregate, which is sand and gravel. Fine sand is composed of particles ranging in size from just a bit larger than dust, to pebbles that will pass through a screen having four meshes to a linear inch. Coarse aggregate or gravel consists of particles ranging in size from ¼ in. to 1½ in. or more. The largest size of gravel to use is dependent, in many cases, on thickness of the concrete work. Generally, no particle larger than

one third the thickness of the thinnest section of the work should be used.

For concrete that will stand long wear, use aggregates made of hard, sound material. Soft or flaky aggregates will not stand much weathering, and sometimes are responsible for unsightly holes often seen in improperly puddled sidewalks. The aggregate should be well graded. That is, it should consist of particles of various sizes so proportioned that they will fit nicely together to form a uniform mass, with the smaller particles filling the spaces between the larger ones as in Fig. 9. In most cases, material direct from a sand or gravel bank is not proportioned correctly as to particle size, and usually contains too much sand. It must be washed, screened and recombined for best results. For this reason it is best to purchase your aggregate from a dealer who sells aggregate washed and correctly graded. Good concrete cannot be made with sand that contains an appreciable amount of extremely fine material (silt). Sand can be tested very easily for

CONCRETE *That Will Last*

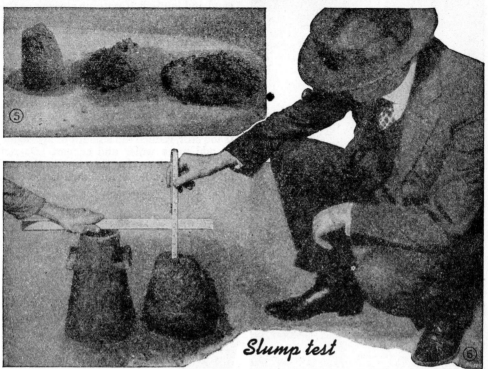

Slump test

silt content with nothing more than a quart fruit jar and a ruler, Fig. 1. Fill the jar to a depth of 2 in. and pour in enough water to fill the jar about three-quarters full. Screw on the lid and shake the jar vigorously for a minute. Then set it aside for an hour, or until the water clears. The silt, settling out of the water, will form a layer on top of the sand. If this layer is more than ⅛ in. thick, Fig. 2, the aggregate is unfit for use, and should be washed to remove the fine material.

Another thing that causes poor concrete is too much organic matter in the sand; bits of roots, pulverized leaf mold and so on. A simple test for this is shown in Fig. 3. Get a 12-oz. prescription bottle from the drug store, and fill it with sand to the 4½-oz. mark. Dissolve sodium hydroxide (caustic soda), ¼ oz., in water, 8 oz. and pour this into the bottle to the level of the 7-oz. mark. Cork the bottle and shake it for several seconds. Then let it stand for 24 hours. By examining the color of the liquid, you can judge the amount of organic matter present as indicated by bottles A, B and C in Fig. 3. If it is clear, the aggregate contains no organic material. A straw color is caused by the presence of some organic matter, but not enough to cause trouble. If the solution is dark, there is too much vegetable material and the sand should not be used for concrete. This test is useful for appraising new sand deposits as well as for checking sand you buy from a dealer or that which has been stored in the open for a long time. The test is easy to make, but caution should be exercised in handling the hydroxide solution, which is injurious to the skin, leather and clothing.

Any water that is suitable for drinking can be used for making concrete. Do not use water containing salt, as it will make reinforcing bars rust. The amount of water used in proportion to the cement is highly important. Hardening of cement is a chemical action in which the cement combines with a certain amount of water to form a permanent compound. If too much water is used, there will be small spaces or voids in the concrete after the excess water evaporates, and the concrete will not be watertight and durable. Extensive research on the amount of water to use for best results has been carried out until today the rules are fairly well fixed and easy to follow as indicated by the table in Fig. 11. When mixing concrete with special attention to the quantity of water, the amount of moisture already in the sand must be

water in the sand, spread some of it, say 2 lbs., in a shallow pan. Then mix denatured or wood alcohol thoroughly with the sand and ignite it. Continue stirring as the alcohol burns. If the sand still seems damp after the alcohol has burned, repeat the treatment. Let cool for about 10 min. Then weigh the sand again. The percentage of moisture can now be calculated by subtracting the dry weight from the wet weight and multiplying by 100.

If you have a quantity of concrete to mix, first make a trial batch. Try the proportions suggested in the table. If the batch is too stiff, reduce the amount of aggregate or add more water and cement. Do not add water alone, for that upsets the cement-water ratio. If the batch is too thin,

simply add more aggregate, but not more cement. In general, a stiff concrete is best for footings, foundations, pavements and walls, while a more plastic mixture is best for work that is of thin section. You can use the slump test, Figs. 4 and 6, to determine the consistency of concrete. First make a sheet-metal cone of 16-ga. galvanized iron. Set the cone, large end down, on a flat surface, and fill the cone about one-fourth full. Compact this by puddling with a 5/8-in. iron rod, using 25 strokes. Add concrete to fill the cone to about half its depth, again puddle with 25 strokes and finally fill the cone completely, and puddle as before. Now lift the cone straight up, leaving the concrete on the board or slab or whatever surface you used. The "slump" of the pile is the difference in inches between its height, measured as soon as the cone is removed, and the height of the cone. If the slump is from 1 to 4 in., the concrete is of the right consistency for massive construction such as pavements and floors laid on the ground. A slump of 3 to 6 in., indicates concrete suitable for posts, walls, beams, heavy slabs and tank walls. Concrete that slumps from 4 to 8 in. is best for garden furniture and vases, ordinary beams or slabs, columns and thin

taken into account. Water in the coarse aggregate does not matter because the maximum volume such aggregate can retain is low. Sand can be divided into four classes: very wet, wet, damp and dry. You can test these conditions accurately enough with your hand. Very wet sand is dripping wet, and leaves much moisture on the skin when handled. Wet sand, which is the condition usually encountered, feels wet to the touch, and leaves a small amount of moisture on the skin. Damp sand feels a little damp but leaves almost no moisture. Dry sand runs freely through the fingers. In general, the amount of water in a cubic foot of sand can be expressed as follows: Very wet sand, 3/4 gal. or 6 percent, wet sand, 1/2 gal. or 4 percent, damp sand, 1/4 gal. or 2 percent, and dry sand, none. If you want to be exact on the amount of

walls. The three slump batches pictured in Fig. 5 show stiff, medium and wet concrete mixtures.

For sidewalks, driveways and terraces, Figs. 7 and 12, the concrete can be placed directly on the ground if there is good drainage, first tamping the earth to compact it. If drainage is poor, use a 6-in. layer of clean, coarse gravel or clean cinders beneath the concrete. Compact this sub-base thoroughly. Concrete should be placed in the forms within 30 min. after mixing, Fig. 10. Puddle it thoroughly with a stick, spade or trowel, to work the coarser particles of aggregate away from the forms and the top surface and thus produce a uniform outer surface on the work.

And finally, after you have gone to the trouble of making and placing your con-

(11) WATER AND CEMENT PROPORTIONS Courtesy Portland Cement Association						
Kind of Work	Water, gals. per sack of cement			Suggested trial-batch mixtures		
	Very wet sand	Wet sand	Damp sand	Cement, sacks	Aggregates Fine cu. ft.	Coarse cu. ft.
5-gal. paste, for greatest durability						
Topping for heavy wearing surfaces and other 2-course work such as pavements, tennis courts, walks, floors	4¼	4½	4¾	1	1	1½
One-course industrial, dairy and other floors, and concrete subjected to weak acids and alkalis	3¾	4	4½	1	1¾	2
6-gal. paste, for watertight concrete exposed to moderate weather						
Watertight floors, foundations, walks, drives, tennis courts, storage tanks, septic tanks, swimming pools, reinforced structural beams, slabs, etc.	4¼	5	5½	1	2¼	3
7-gal. paste for concrete not subjected to water, weather or wear						
Foundation walls, footings, mass concrete	4¾	5½	6¼	1	2¾	4

Note: In calculating mixes, remember that 1 cu. yd. contains 27 cu. ft. Sand classed as "wet" in table is average sand.

days. In cold weather protect the work but do not moisten it. Extra attention to quality of materials, methods of mixing, etc., will assure long life for projects such as the concrete outdoor living room in Fig. 8.

Remember to tamp the earth or base under a sidewalk or driveway thoroughly; use aggregate that has been graded properly, proportion the cement, water and aggregate correctly and mix the ingredients thoroughly. Puddle the cement to bring the fine particles to the top and make a smooth, finished surface.

crete correctly, don't lose half of its strength by improper curing. Concrete that is kept moist seven days is 50 percent stronger than concrete that is permitted to dry out immediately. Keeping it damp one month boosts the strength 100 percent. To keep sidewalks, driveways, floors and the like moist, cover them with straw, leaves or earth as soon as the surface has hardened enough to prevent marring, and sprinkle occasionally with water. Cover vertical walls with burlap, canvas or old carpet, and keep moist for ten

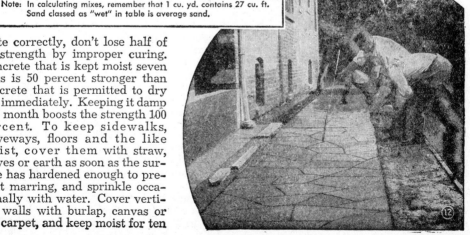

BRICK GATEPOSTS
That Will Last

By John Modroch

ATTRACTIVE entrance and gateposts improve the appearance of a homesite and, if soundly constructed of permanent materials, constitute a valuable property investment. Posts laid with brick and capped with concrete meet these requirements. They can be built by any handyman with common tools.

Footing: Always lay a brick post on a firm footing, which, in cold territories, must extend into the earth below the frost line, where it cannot be heaved up by expansion of frozen ground. To safeguard against damaging force being exerted against its sides, make the base larger than the top as shown in Fig. 1. The frost-swol-

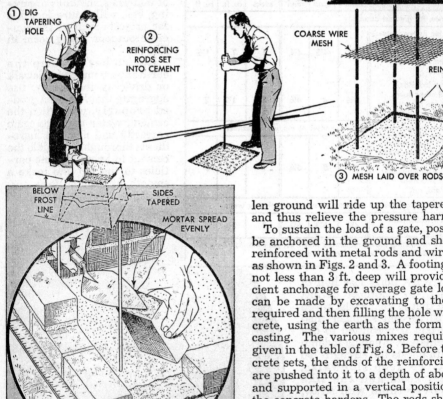

① DIG TAPERING HOLE

② REINFORCING RODS SET INTO CEMENT

COARSE WIRE MESH

REINFORCING RODS

③ MESH LAID OVER RODS

BELOW FROST LINE

SIDES TAPERED

MORTAR SPREAD EVENLY

CARPENTER'S SQUARE

④ LAY FIRST COURSE SQUARE

len ground will ride up the tapered sides and thus relieve the pressure harmlessly.

To sustain the load of a gate, posts must be anchored in the ground and should be reinforced with metal rods and wire mesh, as shown in Figs. 2 and 3. A footing that is not less than 3 ft. deep will provide sufficient anchorage for average gate loads. It can be made by excavating to the depth required and then filling the hole with concrete, using the earth as the form for the casting. The various mixes required are given in the table of Fig. 8. Before the concrete sets, the ends of the reinforcing rods are pushed into it to a depth of about 2 ft. and supported in a vertical position until the concrete hardens. The rods should be long enough to reach to within an inch of the top of the completed post. A sheet of coarse wire mesh then is placed over the rods midway between the top and bottom, as in Fig. 3. Entrance posts to which a

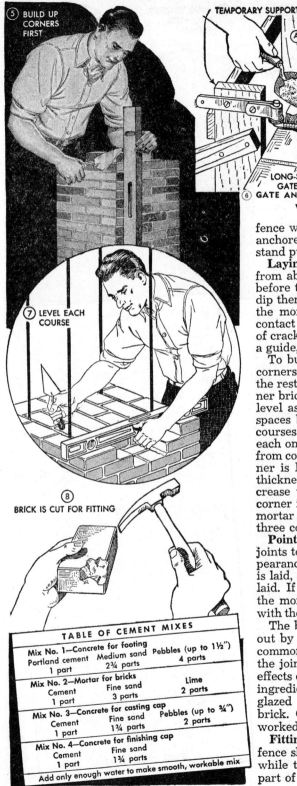

⑤ BUILD UP CORNERS FIRST

TEMPORARY SUPPORT

Ⓐ   Ⓑ   ROD →   ─ PIPE

LONG-SHANKED GATE HINGE

─ FENCE WIRE

⑥ GATE AND FENCE FITTINGS ARE EMBEDDED IN MORTAR WHILE THE BRICKWORK IS BEING LAID

⑦ LEVEL EACH COURSE

⑧ BRICK IS CUT FOR FITTING

TABLE OF CEMENT MIXES		
Mix No. 1—Concrete for footing		
Portland cement 1 part	Medium sand 2¾ parts	Pebbles (up to 1½″) 4 parts
Mix No. 2—Mortar for bricks		
Cement 1 part	Fine sand 3 parts	Lime 2 parts
Mix No. 3—Concrete for casting cap		
Cement 1 part	Fine sand 1¾ parts	Pebbles (up to ¾″) 2 parts
Mix No. 4—Concrete for finishing cap		
Cement 1 part	Fine sand 1¾ parts	
Add only enough water to make smooth, workable mix		

fence will be attached should be similarly anchored and reinforced in order to withstand pull exerted by the fencing.

Laying the brick: To prevent dry brick from absorbing moisture from the mortar before they have been completely bedded, dip them into a pail of water. Then spread the mortar evenly and bring it into full contact with the brick to avoid formation of cracks and, with a carpenter's square as a guide, lay the first course, Fig. 4.

To build a wide post plumb, lay up the corners a couple of courses in advance of the rest of the brickwork, keeping the corner brick in a plumb line with the aid of a level as shown in Fig. 5. Then fill in the spaces between the corners. To keep the courses on a true horizontal plane, check each one with a level laid across the brick from corner to corner, Fig. 7. Where a corner is low, build it up by increasing the thickness of the mortar layer. Do not decrease the thickness of the mortar if the corner is high, however, as a thin layer of mortar is weak. Instead, build up the other three corners.

Pointing up: Pointing up the mortar joints to give the brickwork a uniform appearance may be done on each course as it is laid, or later after all courses have been laid. If you intend to point up later, scrape the mortar from the surface of the joints with the point of the trowel as you proceed.

The brick pattern can be made to stand out by using white cement instead of the common dark mortar mix for pointing up the joints. A variety of color and texture effects can be achieved by mixing coloring ingredients with the mortar or by using glazed and other decoratively surfaced brick. Of course, special effects need to be worked out only in the surface courses.

Fittings: Fittings for attaching a gate or fence should be embedded in the masonry while the brick is being laid, Fig. 6. The part of a fitting that extends into the post

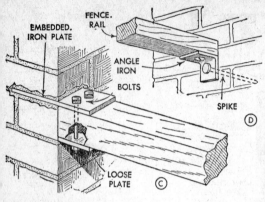

EMBEDDED. IRON PLATE

FENCE. RAIL

ANGLE IRON

BOLTS

SPIKE

D

LOOSE PLATE C

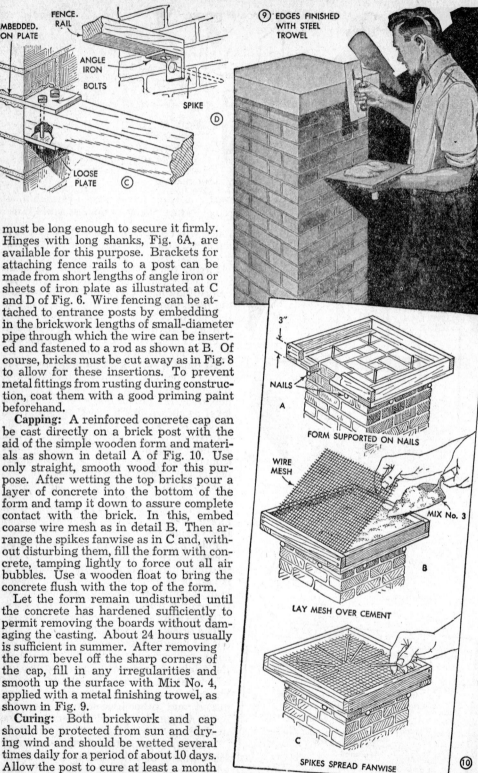

⑨ EDGES FINISHED WITH STEEL TROWEL

3″

NAILS

A

FORM SUPPORTED ON NAILS

WIRE MESH

MIX No. 3

B

LAY MESH OVER CEMENT

C

SPIKES SPREAD FANWISE

⑩

must be long enough to secure it firmly. Hinges with long shanks, Fig. 6A, are available for this purpose. Brackets for attaching fence rails to a post can be made from short lengths of angle iron or sheets of iron plate as illustrated at C and D of Fig. 6. Wire fencing can be attached to entrance posts by embedding in the brickwork lengths of small-diameter pipe through which the wire can be inserted and fastened to a rod as shown at B. Of course, bricks must be cut away as in Fig. 8 to allow for these insertions. To prevent metal fittings from rusting during construction, coat them with a good priming paint beforehand.

Capping: A reinforced concrete cap can be cast directly on a brick post with the aid of the simple wooden form and materials as shown in detail A of Fig. 10. Use only straight, smooth wood for this purpose. After wetting the top bricks pour a layer of concrete into the bottom of the form and tamp it down to assure complete contact with the brick. In this, embed coarse wire mesh as in detail B. Then arrange the spikes fanwise as in C and, without disturbing them, fill the form with concrete, tamping lightly to force out all air bubbles. Use a wooden float to bring the concrete flush with the top of the form.

Let the form remain undisturbed until the concrete has hardened sufficiently to permit removing the boards without damaging the casting. About 24 hours usually is sufficient in summer. After removing the form bevel off the sharp corners of the cap, fill in any irregularities and smooth up the surface with Mix No. 4, applied with a metal finishing trowel, as shown in Fig. 9.

Curing: Both brickwork and cap should be protected from sun and drying wind and should be wetted several times daily for a period of about 10 days. Allow the post to cure at least a month before attaching a gate or fence to it.

Novel Igloo Incinerator of Troweled Concrete Combines Both Utility and Attractiveness

GALV. FORM FOR SMOKE HOLE

EXPANDED METAL LATH

ROUGH WOODEN FORM

FIRE DOOR

STAKES RETAIN SHEET METAL OR LINOLEUM FORM

Wish you could burn rubbish in the back yard without having an old oil drum or other eyesore cluttering up the place? Then, here's just the thing for you— an attractive concrete incinerator that will do the job and always present a neat appearance. The base of the unit is poured in a sheet-metal or linoleum form. A wooden form for the igloo is made as shown, and this is covered with expanded metal lath, except over the fire-door and smoke-hole openings. Galvanized iron is used for the smoke-hole form and also to support the concrete over the fire-door frame. Then, cement is troweled over the lath to a 4-in. thickness. The wooden forms may be burned away later.

Simple Rigging Laces Canvas "Carryall" to Avoid Spilling Contents

The practice of raking leaves and grass onto a canvas or other large cloth and grabbing the four corners to carry it often results in eventually losing grip and spilling the load. To overcome this, one gardener riveted a sheet-metal strip, having a hole at each end, to one edge of his canvas and fitted two eyelets, correspondingly spaced, along the opposite edge. Then he tied a 3-ft. length of clothesline or sash cord to each eyelet.

In use, the canvas is heaped with leaves in the usual way, two sides are folded inward as shown and then the ends are brought over. Finally, the ropes are threaded through the holes in the metal strip and drawn up snugly and tied. Wrapped in this manner, the load can be carried or dragged easily without spilling.

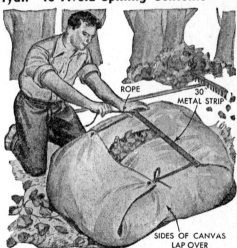

ROPE

30" METAL STRIP

SIDES OF CANVAS LAP OVER

Old Stump Removed from Lawn with Saltpeter Solution

If it is inconvenient to chop or blast that old stump from the front lawn, try using a solution of saltpeter. Bore a series of holes in the top and sides of the stump and fill them with the solution. In a short time the wood will rot away. As much saltpeter as can be dissolved in the water should be used in order to make a saturated solution.

"Water Wheel" at Side of House Is Used as Flower Garden

Built against the side of a house, an imitation water wheel, which is made of 2-in. lumber, will transform the house into an old mill. To add to the decorative effect, the wheel can be used as a novel flower garden, the "paddles" being filled with soil for plants.

❡ Pour paraffin over unused paint remaining in a can and it will not harden.

PLANTAIN

CRAB GRASS

BUTTERCUP

½" HOSE TAPED TO WHEEL

DRIVE WHEEL

ROLLER

2"

BED KNIFE

④ RAISE MOWER TO PROPER HEIGHT

WHY do all kinds of noxious weeds and unwanted grasses apparently thrive in my lawn while the good grass steadily grows more thinly sodded, spindly and sickly in color? That is the question many home owners ask themselves each year. Other pertinent associated problems are what to do with bare spots, creeping moss, washed terraces and places where grass doesn't seem to grow at all. Solutions are often found upon investigating the characteristics of the soil, condition of the grass and the method of mowing it.

Starved, close-clipped lawns provide just the right conditions for a flourishing crop of weeds. The sod, when thin, offers a place for the weed seeds to lodge, and also provides protection for the tiny but vigorous weeds during their starting period while the repeated close clippings only help to stimulate weed growth. A thinning lawn with a steadily thickening weed crop simply means that the tame grass is slowly starving. Weeds never crowd out a healthy, vigorous sod as they cannot root and survive in a heavy turf. If you give lawn grass the growing conditions it requires—ample plant food in a deep soil well supplied with organic matter and plenty of moisture, set the lawnmower so high that the mowing job looks just a bit "shaggy," the grass will win every time in the battle against weeds.

Fig. 1 shows five of the most troublesome weeds and grasses that are quick to strike root and spread in any poor sod. They can safely be called the most troublesome for several reasons. Quack grass and dandelions are familiar and unwanted aliens in any lawn but even more to be dreaded are crab grass, spurge and creeping buttercup. After these get a solid foothold, they are

CARE

KNOTWEED

SPURGE

tenacious and difficult to get rid of. Although new chemical-control methods are effective in eradicating the stands of most of them, crab grass for example, the growing and spreading habits of these weeds make it necessary to decide whether control by chemicals or uprooting and complete rebuilding of parts of the lawn are advisable. Either way, the existing grass is certain to be damaged to some extent. If single weeds are scattered here and there over the lawn, they can usually be eliminated by digging them out with a small hand trowel. But where they are growing in clusters surrounded by a fairly vigorous sod, it is usually best to dig them out with a shovel, making sure that you get all the roots, add new soil and reseed to grass, as in Figs. 5, 6 and 7. This method is very effective where the growth is so concentrated that if weeds were killed out by chemicals a resulting bare spot would necessitate patching in the end anyway. As a rule chemical control is most effective where there is only a moderate weed infestation of a fairly vigorous sod. Then you can use an over-all application of the chemical or a "spotting" procedure for individual plants or clusters. Which method is best is determined by the number of weeds and their distribution over the lawn. The common lawn bluegrasses are unusually resistant to injury by the chemical weed killers if administered as recommended by the manufacturers. It should be remembered that injury to the grass is not likely to be permanent unless unduly heavy and frequent appli-

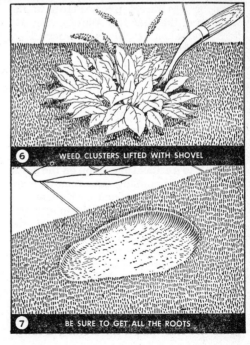

6 WEED CLUSTERS LIFTED WITH SHOVEL

7 BE SURE TO GET ALL THE ROOTS

BEFORE SEEDING TOP SOIL IS FINELY PULVERIZED BY RAKING TO DEPTH OF 1"

TOP DRESSING, ⅓ SAND, ⅓ LOAM, ⅓ HUMUS TO DEPTH OF NOT MORE THAN ½"

HEAVY MULCH WILL SMOTHER THE GRASS

⑨ SPREAD THE TOP DRESSING

mower to these heights, Figs. 2, 3, and 4, is usually very simple, although some of the older machines cannot be adjusted to a 2-in. height. In this case, a length of old garden hose bound to each wheel rim as in Fig. 4, will usually provide the necessary height.

Of course, the blades of the mower should be sharp. If not, the grass will be crushed and torn instead of being severed cleanly. The time and frequency of mowing are important also. Twice a week or once a month depends altogether on the condition of the grass and the previous mowing schedule, the rapidity of growth and the weather. If you have mowed to 1½ in., let the grass grow to at least 3 in. before you mow again. Or, if you have formerly cut it to ¾ or 1 in. high, it is better to raise the mower by stages, that is, raise it to 1½ in. and clip the grass a couple of times when it is 2 in. high, then raise to 2 in. and clip when the grass is 3 in. high. The longer the period for recovery of growth between mowings the better. Coming into the hot, dry summer months, the frequency of mowings should be determined by the height and condition of the grass and not by intervals of time. In some localities it is advisable to use a grass catcher behind the mower, as an accumulation of clippings may cause fermentation which may injure the grass. However, in most sections the clippings which dry soon provide excellent mulch.

Avoid raking a lawn too vigorously during early spring. Usually a bamboo rake is best as it gets leaves and trash without tearing the sod. After a winter of alternate freezing and thawing, an early spring rolling is helpful as it tends to firm the soil around the grass roots. However, it is best to avoid rolling when the soil is wet. A top

cations are used. The toxic effect is in more or less direct proportion to the strength of the chemical solution. Several light over-all applications at intervals of three weeks or so are generally better than one heavy dose. Some chemicals are applied dry and the lawn is immediately sprinkled so that there will be slight discoloration of the grass.

On either new or old lawns, the way the grass is mowed has much to do with the maintenance of a vigorous sod. Every time you mow the lawn you perform what amounts to a critical operation on the grass. Medium-close clipping may remove more than half the blades from each plant. As the blade or leaf aids the plant in converting to growth the food taken up by the roots, the result is a greatly weakened plant. Although the bent grasses can be clipped as close as ½ in. and in some instances even shorter, bluegrass and the various fescues should never be cut closer than 1½ in. Bent grasses will do better if clipped not less than 1 in., and the bluegrass not less than 2 in. Setting a lawn-

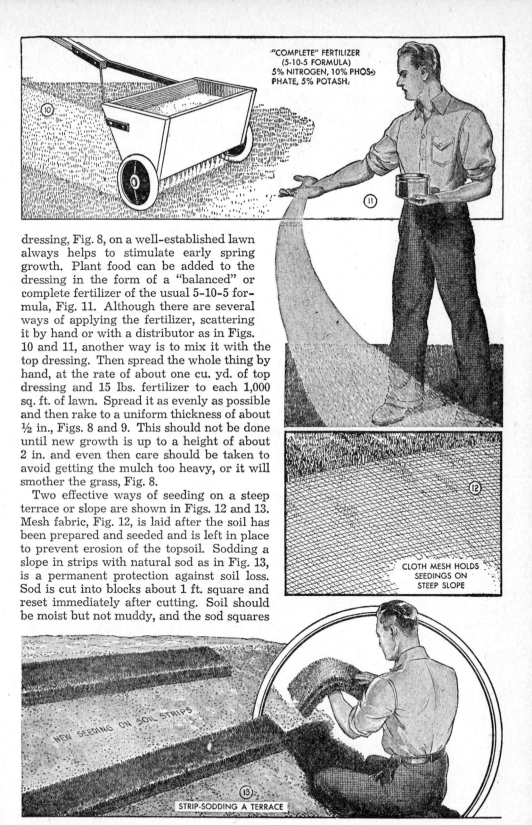

"COMPLETE" FERTILIZER
(5-10-5 FORMULA)
5% NITROGEN, 10% PHOS-
PHATE, 5% POTASH.

dressing, Fig. 8, on a well-established lawn always helps to stimulate early spring growth. Plant food can be added to the dressing in the form of a "balanced" or complete fertilizer of the usual 5-10-5 formula, Fig. 11. Although there are several ways of applying the fertilizer, scattering it by hand or with a distributor as in Figs. 10 and 11, another way is to mix it with the top dressing. Then spread the whole thing by hand, at the rate of about one cu. yd. of top dressing and 15 lbs. fertilizer to each 1,000 sq. ft. of lawn. Spread it as evenly as possible and then rake to a uniform thickness of about ½ in., Figs. 8 and 9. This should not be done until new growth is up to a height of about 2 in. and even then care should be taken to avoid getting the mulch too heavy, or it will smother the grass, Fig. 8.

Two effective ways of seeding on a steep terrace or slope are shown in Figs. 12 and 13. Mesh fabric, Fig. 12, is laid after the soil has been prepared and seeded and is left in place to prevent erosion of the topsoil. Sodding a slope in strips with natural sod as in Fig. 13, is a permanent protection against soil loss. Sod is cut into blocks about 1 ft. square and reset immediately after cutting. Soil should be moist but not muddy, and the sod squares

CLOTH MESH HOLDS
SEEDINGS ON
STEEP SLOPE

NEW SEEDING ON SOIL STRIPS

STRIP-SODDING A TERRACE

(A) VEGETABLE REFUSE, GRASS CLIPPINGS, ETC.
(B) WELL-ROTTED MANURE WITH SUPERPHOSPHATE ADDED

soil fertility. Where moss grows there is little use of reseeding unless the soil is built up either by adding new soil, or compost and plant food in readily available form. If there are scattering patches of moss in your lawn, take a dozen or more samples of soil from points uniformly spaced over the whole area and have them tested at your state experiment station or by your county advisor. The data thus obtained will enable you to rebuild the soil to the humus and plant-food requirements of a healthy and vigorous sod. In rebuilding any old lawn it is always a good idea to test the soil.

Shaded areas, Fig. 16, usually require special treatment and seeding with grasses that will make a satisfactory growth under this condition. Heavy feeding is generally the primary requirement as the grass must compete with the feeding roots of the tree. Borders around flower beds and edgings along walks are perfect lodging places for blown weed seeds. Also these edges are difficult to mow so it is best to keep them clipped with shears made for the pur-

should be tamped into firm contact with the earth. If the slope is curved and of considerable extent make sure that the strips follow the contour on the level. On a medium slope, the strips should be about 6 ft. apart; on a steep slope not more than 3 or 4 ft. apart.

Lawn clippings, weed stalks, refuse from the vegetable and flower gardens, wheat straw, and well-rotted manure can be made into a valuable humus and plant-food compost by piling it in layers, as in Fig. 14. The important detail is to keep the edges of each layer higher than it is at the center. Then each time you add more material, tramp the center and soak the pile thoroughly with water. The size of the pile should not be less than 4 by 8 ft., but a size of 6 by 10 ft. is preferable. Add 20 percent acid phosphate, bone meal, ammonium sulphate, or complete fertilizer, about a pound or two, to each layer. To hasten the fermentation or breaking-down processes of the organic matter shovel earth against the sides of the pile.

Patches of moss, Fig. 15, indicate low

PATCHES OF MOSS INDICATE LOW SOIL FERTILITY

SHADED AREAS REQUIRE LIGHT CLIPPING, HEAVY FEEDING

EDGES CLIPPED AROUND FLOWER BEDS

pose as in Fig. 17. Whenever you patch bare spots with new soil add enough soil to bring the level up to that of the surrounding turf, rake it to break up any lumps, then roll as in Fig. 18. After rolling, rake the surface lightly and scatter the seed. If the soil is fairly dry so that it does not stick to the roller, roll again to press the seed into firm contact with the earth. Then sprinkle gently, but long enough to soak the spot thoroughly. Be careful that the water does not "puddle." Keep the soil from drying out on top until the grass starts. If the patch is on a slope or the crown of a steep terrace and is more than 1 ft. square, it will be necessary to protect it from washing away with a mesh fabric or with coarse burlap.

In feeding old, established lawns on clayey soils, "spiking" the sod with the implement shown in Fig. 19 is a valuable practice. The openings made by the spiker allow air to enter the soil and also conduct water and fertilizer to the root level more rapidly. As a rule, spiking should be done in the spring; once a season is best. It should be done uniformly over the whole lawn, forcing the tool into the sod at a slight angle, and at intervals of about 6 or 8 in. Move the handle of the spiker back and forth slightly each time to enlarge the openings somewhat, but be careful not to lift or tear the sod.

(18)

CANVAS IRRIGATOR

(20)

(19)

SOD SPIKER

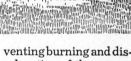

HOSE

venting burning and discoloration of the grass.

For regular watering of the lawn, anyone can make a canvas irrigator such as shown in Fig. 20. It consists of a length of heavy canvas, sewed to form a tube, with one end sewed shut. A standard coupling is fitted to the other end for attaching the tube to the garden hose. Water oozing out through the cloth will soak the ground thoroughly and gently. As soon as one area is soaked, the irrigator is moved to a new location, until the entire yard has been covered.

The one prime requirement in watering is to give the ground a thorough soaking. Frequent scanty watering will cause the feeding roots to seek the surface moisture, while prolonged drought or neglect of watering will also cause serious damage.

Dry chemical fertilizers of higher concentrations should be scattered over the lawn on a still day. If there is any wind, it will make it impossible to distribute the chemical uniformly over the ground. Those who have a large lawn to care for will find a wheeled distributor of the kind shown in Fig. 10 very convenient. It speeds the work of spreading the fertilizer over large areas uniformly. Immediately after spreading the fertilizer, the lawn should be sprinkled. Adjust the hose nozzle to give a gentle spray, as this will wash the chemical from the blades of grass and into the soil, pre-

Designs
for
Swimming

By Hi Sibley

WHETHER it's large and elaborate or small and unpretentious, there's nothing like the privacy and convenience of a swimming pool right in your own back yard. And when you can do most of the work yourself or with the help of friends and neighbors, the cost can be kept well within the limitations of the average pocketbook. The suggestions and pointers presented here cover construction ranging from simple wading pools to a large family-size swimming pool.

When building a wading pool for youngsters, locate it on high ground if possible to simplify draining and also to save excavating, Fig. 1. A simple circular-shaped wading pool is shown in Fig. 2. A novel feature of this pool is a sprinkler head which is attached to a length of pipe and screwed into a coupling on the drainpipe. The children will enjoy frolicking in the spray from the sprinkler while the pool is being filled. When the sprinkler head is not used, it is removed and the drain stopped with a pipe plug, Fig. 2. The sprinkler feature is practical only if the drainpipe outlet is easily accessible for attaching a hose. Galvanized sheet metal or heavy linoleum makes ideal forms for a circular pool. Fig. 7 shows how stakes and cross braces are used to support metal forms. As a safety precaution, do not make the depth of the pool at the center more than 12 in.

Fig. 6 details a pool of unusual construction which is suitable for youngsters learning to swim. However, it is not desirable in regions where winter temperatures drop below freezing as the 2-in. walls will not withstand movement of the ground due to frost. The excavation for this pool is furred with strips nailed to stakes driven into the earth walls. Then metal lath is stapled to the furring strips and poultry wire is used in the bottom for reinforcement. Walls are plastered with cement and the

Here is an example of how a pool built on sloping ground reduces the job of excavating. Double-formed, pool is ready to be poured

This view shows the pool poured, the forms removed and drain installed. Walls take less concrete when bottom of pool is sloped

Pool of William D. Soper, La Mesa, Calif.

Finished pool in use. Drainage is no problem of pool similarly situated. Here, drain in side carries water off for irrigation purposes. Note metal ladder which is embedded in concrete at time of pouring

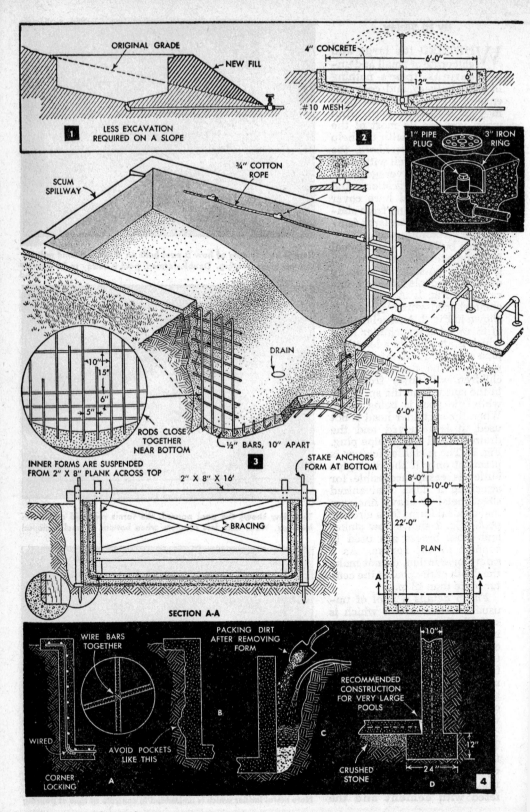

ORIGINAL GRADE

NEW FILL

1 LESS EXCAVATION
REQUIRED ON A SLOPE

4" CONCRETE

6'-0"

6"

12"

#10 MESH

2

1" PIPE
PLUG

3" IRON
RING

SCUM
SPILLWAY

¾" COTTON
ROPE

10"

15"

6"

5"

RODS CLOSE
TOGETHER
NEAR BOTTOM

½" BARS, 10" APART

DRAIN

3

STAKE ANCHORS
FORM AT BOTTOM

3'

6'-0"

8'-0"

10'-0"

22'-0"

PLAN

A   A

INNER FORMS ARE SUSPENDED
FROM 2" X 8" PLANK ACROSS TOP

2" X 8" X 16'

BRACING

SECTION A-A

WIRE BARS
TOGETHER

PACKING DIRT
AFTER REMOVING
FORM

10"

WIRED

AVOID POCKETS
LIKE THIS

B.

C.

RECOMMENDED
CONSTRUCTION
FOR VERY LARGE
POOLS

12"

CORNER
LOCKING

A

CRUSHED
STONE

24"

D

4

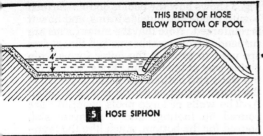

THIS BEND OF HOSE
BELOW BOTTOM OF POOL

5 HOSE SIPHON

bottom is covered with a 3-in. layer of concrete poured over a 4-in. bed of gravel and strengthened with the wire. Finally, a reinforced curbing or parapet is laid around the edge.

An inexpensive pool without plumbing is shown in Fig. 5. Measuring 12 by 20 ft., it is designed for high ground to eliminate drainage piping and has sloping walls to do away with the need for forms. Bottom and sides of the excavation are tamped well and then 2 in. of concrete is poured over the bottom. This is reinforced with 6-in. spot-welded wire mesh, on top of which an additional 2-in. layer of concrete is poured. When the bottom is firm but still soft, the walls are plastered with cement to form an integral mass which is troweled into a parapet all around the top. The bottom is troweled to slope toward a sump from which the water is siphoned with a hose to drain the pool.

Figs. 3 and 11 detail an adult-size pool, 10 by 22 ft. Note that it is complete with water filter, centrifugal pump, suction-cleaning facilities, diving board and ladder. The deep portion just off the diving board slopes upward at each end to cut material cost. However, don't skimp on the wall thickness and the reinforcement. A minimum wall thickness of 6 in. is recommended for mild climates. Pools built in regions of severe cold should be 10 in. thick to avoid cracking. Section A-A of

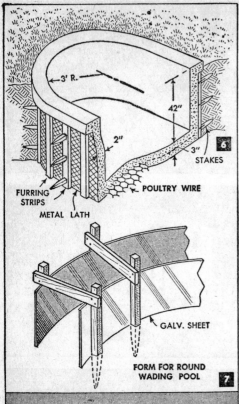

3' R.

42"

2"

3"
STAKES

FURRING STRIPS

POULTRY WIRE

METAL LATH

6

GALV. SHEET

FORM FOR ROUND WADING POOL

7

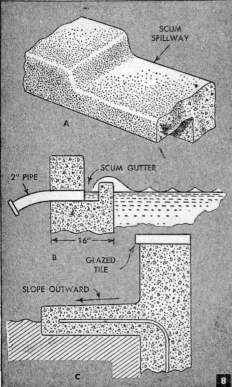

SCUM SPILLWAY

A

SCUM GUTTER

2" PIPE

16"

B

GLAZED TILE

SLOPE OUTWARD

C

8

Fig. 3 shows how the pool is double-formed —with inside and outside forms, and how it is reinforced. Note that the inner forms are suspended from crossbeams and that stakes are used to prevent the outer forms from giving way at the bottom. Rods reinforcing the walls and bottom are wired together at the lower corner as shown in Fig. 4, detail A. The walls of large pools generally are poured on footings and a separate slab poured for the bottom, much like the foundation of a house. Then a mastic is run in the joint to make it watertight as shown in Fig. 4, detail D.

Figs. 9 and 10 give suggestions for making ladders of pipe or wood, and also plans for a springboard. The metal ladder should be of galvanized or stainless steel and embedded in the concrete at the time it is poured. Spruce is the best material for the springboard. Bevel the edges and cover the end with a nonslip padding of rope matting.

Three types of parapets are shown in Fig. 8. Parapets A and B incorporate a spillway in the top of the wall for floating off leaves and litter by raising the water level. In the case of B, drainpipes are spaced about 8 ft. apart all around the pool. Detail C shows construction of a parapet which extends above ground to provide a low seat around the pool and keeps debris from blowing into the water.

The concrete for small wading pools can be mixed in a wheelbarrow, but for large pools it is best to rent a small power mixer.

3'-6"

6" MINIMUM CONCRETE

4" GRAVEL OR SAND

A recommended proportionate mix consists of portland cement, 1 part; sand, 2½ parts; and gravel, 3¼ parts. If the pool is to be plastered, the proportions should be as follows: portland cement, 1 part; and sand, 3 parts. Six gallons of water per sack of cement is about right. It is always best to pour a job complete at one time, but if this cannot be done, the joint should be roughened to assure a good bond and brushed with a soupy mixture of cement and water just before the pouring is resumed. Be sure that the concrete is well spaded in the forms with a long pole, to prevent air pockets and porous places in the finished wall. Also, avoid cave-in areas in the dirt walls, Fig. 4, detail B, which take considerably more concrete. Forms should not be removed for two or three days, after which the concrete should be cured gradually by wetting it frequently for several days. Dirt fill around the outside of the walls is packed solidly by wetting with a hose as it is shoveled in place, Fig. 4, detail C.

The nozzle from an old vacuum cleaner attached to a long pole will be found handy for cleaning the walls and bottom of a pool. Fasten it to a length of large hose and connect it to the suction-pump inlet, Fig. 11. Finish the walls and bottom of the pool with a couple coats of rubber-base paint. When cracks develop which cause serious leakage, they can be filled with asbestos roofing cement and then painted.

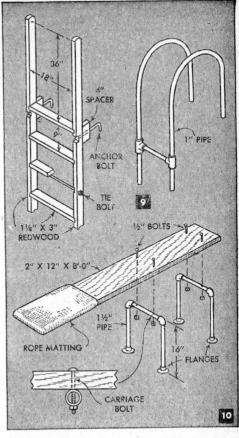

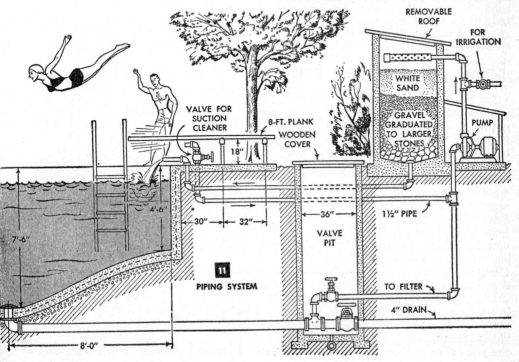

PIPING SYSTEM

265

Revolving Sprinkler Cutouts Give Novel Effect

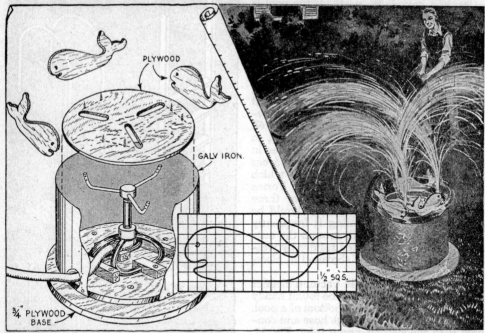

Miniature cutouts of whales that give the appearance of swimming and "blowing" in a lifelike manner make this sprinkler a novel addition to other lawn and garden ornaments. Almost any ¼-in. wood or hard-pressed board can be used for the cutouts and top, and the base disks can be cut from ¾-in. stock. After assembling the two-part base, the sprinkler head is centered on it and fastened securely with four cleats. A piece of galvanized iron or a large tin can, with the top and bottom removed, provides a shield to hide the head and a screw eye driven into the edge of the base makes a convenient method of hanging the unit on a wall when not in use. Also, the can or metal shield serves as a handy reel on which to wind the hose. You can design and use other figures besides whales.

Bricks Laid Along House Aid in Mowing Grass

Laid end to end in rows around the foundation of a house, along the sides of a sidewalk or driveway, bricks will keep grass from growing at these points where it cannot be reached with a lawnmower. The bricks eliminate almost all of the cutting which usually has to be done with hand clippers. If the bricks are laid flush with the ground, they provide a level place on which the lawnmower wheel will ride so that you can cut the grass close to them.

FOUNDATION WITHOUT BRICK   FOUNDATION WITH BRICK   WALK WITH BRICK

LAWN HOUSE NUMBERS

Nothing is more appreciated by your callers than a well-designed house number located where it is easy to see. The lawn is the ideal place, so try your hand at some of these. A jig-saw or coping saw and some ½ or ¾-in. outdoor plywood are all you need. Stakes of ½-in. pipe will make ideal supports

2" SQ'S

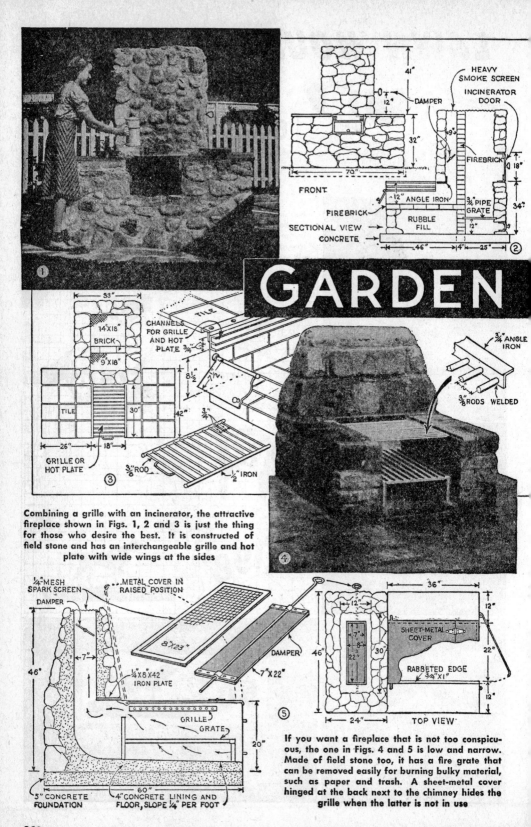

GARDEN

Combining a grille with an incinerator, the attractive fireplace shown in Figs. 1, 2 and 3 is just the thing for those who desire the best. It is constructed of field stone and has an interchangeable grille and hot plate with wide wings at the sides

If you want a fireplace that is not too conspicuous, the one in Figs. 4 and 5 is low and narrow. Made of field stone too, it has a fire grate that can be removed easily for burning bulky material, such as paper and trash. A sheet-metal cover hinged at the back next to the chimney hides the grille when the latter is not in use

SCREEN

21"

30"

17"

8"

FIREBRICK
20"

RUBBLE
FILL

36"

40"

26"

9"R.
8" 18"

ASH WELL

INCINERATOR

SECTIONAL VIEW ⑥

FRONT

⑦

FIREPLACES

PARTITION

58"

TOP VIEW

15"X18"

20"

9"

18"

HANGERS
WELDED

ASH WELL   WALL

OVEN BROILER

⑧

⑨

Figs. 6, 7 and 8 show an unusually attractive fireplace of brick that is a real asset to the garden landscape. It is built on two grade levels and has a high chimney for a good draft. Construction requires **about 500 bricks and less than a sack of cement**

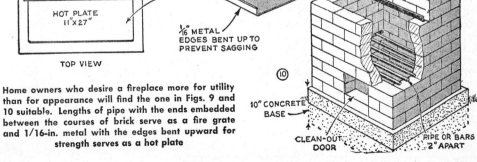

SCREEN CEMENTED IN
3½" X 13"

HOT PLATE
11" X 27"

TOP VIEW

1/16" METAL
EDGES BENT UP TO
PREVENT SAGGING

THESE BRICKS
SET ON EDGE

ANGLE–IRON
SUPPORT

⑩

10" CONCRETE
BASE

CLEAN–OUT
DOOR

PIPE OR BARS
2" APART

Home owners who desire a fireplace more for utility than for appearance will find the one in Figs. 9 and 10 suitable. Lengths of pipe with the ends embedded between the courses of brick serve as a fire grate and 1/16-in. metal with the edges bent upward for strength serves as a hot plate

Two Distinctive Gates for the Informal Garden

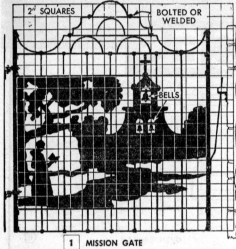

2" SQUARES — BOLTED OR WELDED — BELLS

1 MISSION GATE

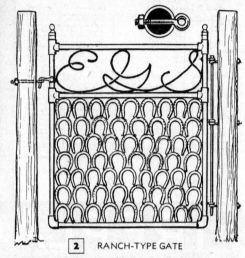

2 RANCH-TYPE GATE

Here are two unusual and interesting gates for a garden entrance or pathway to the house. The mission gate, Fig. 1, with its tinkling bells, and the ranch-type gate paneled with horseshoes, will impart a western atmosphere to your grounds. The mission gate is constructed of two ¾-in. iron bars used as end posts, to which are bolted four crosspieces made from ³⁄₁₆-in. flat iron. The seven vertical members are ⅜-in. iron rods, threaded at both ends and fastened to the top and bottom pieces with two nuts. Form the ornamenal ironwork at the top of the gate from the same material as the four crosspieces and bolt it to the end posts. The gate is pivoted on eyebolts and is fitted with a spring-type latch. Make a full-sized paper pattern for the silhouette and tape it to a piece of 26 or 28-ga. sheet metal. Then cut out the metal silhouette by using a small cold chisel and anvil. Mount the bells in position rigidly so they will ring only when the gate is moved, and solder the silhouette to the gate. After assembling, paint the gate with red lead and then finish a

dull black to contrast with brass or silver bells.

Construct the ranch-type gate, Fig. 2, from 1-in. pipe, using tees and elbows where indicated. Over-all dimensions are determined by the size of horseshoes used, which are either welded together or merely wired to poultry fencing stretched over the opening. Add a personal touch to the gate by forming "rope" initials from a single length of soft-iron wire and welding or wiring them to the upper opening of the gate. In keeping with the western theme, suspend the gate between two bark-covered posts. A ⅜-in. iron rod inserted through eyebolts in the edge of the frame and in one of the supporting posts, forms the hinge. Add a nut to the top of the rod to stop it from sliding through the eyes, and cap the tees with pipe plugs.

Easily Constructed Gate Latch

Only a ring and two door handles or short lengths of rod and flat iron are required to make this simple but effective gate latch. If door handles are used, a ring is slipped over one which is screwed to the fence post. One end of the other handle is cut off and fastened to the gate with the open end up. To close the gate, slip the ring over the open end of the handle.

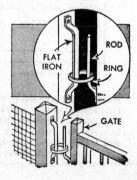

ROD
FLAT IRON
RING
GATE

EVERLASTING TREE STUMP
"Blooms" in the Rock Garden

① PAPER FORM FILLED WITH SAND

12"

8"

② CEMENT APPLIED TO FORM

WIRE MESH OVER HOLES

SMALL STONES

1½" DRAIN

③ HOW KNOT HOLES ARE FORMED

L IKE a real tree stump, this long-lasting one of cement can be "planted" in the rock garden and filled with soil for growing plants and flowers. It is formed by laying cement over a rolled-paper form and adding knot holes as a realistic touch. If you intend to make several stumps, the diameter of the paper forms can be varied. Heavy wrapping or roofing paper is best. The form is tied with twine and then filled with sand, Fig. 1, to support and keep it shaped. A disk of the same paper, cut to fit the top, is laid over the sand, and a 1½-in. layer of cement is troweled over the entire form, including the top, as in Fig. 2. The cement mixture is made of fine, sharp sand, 2 parts, portland cement, 1 part, and water to make a thick paste. After this has set a while, but before it is dry, several openings about 2½ in. in diameter are scooped out at random for knot holes, and in the top, which will be the bottom of the stump, another hole, somewhat smaller, is made for a drain, as shown in Fig. 3. When the form has set hard enough to handle, it can be turned over and wire mesh pressed into the cement around the knot holes, after which cement is troweled on to form the knots. Bark is simulated by laying on cement in small dabs and troweling them down. It is best to copy these details from a real tree. The stump now can be set out in the garden over a small mound of stones to provide good drainage, and cement applied to represent large roots. As a finish, a thin coat of cream-colored oil paint is applied to the top rim to represent wood, and the trunk is painted as natural as possible in browns and grays. The stump is filled with soil, and small plants and flowers are set out to grow. As the knot holes open into the stump, plants set in them will grow there as well as in the main trunk. If desired, a gnome or other similar garden ornament can be placed near the stump as added attraction.

Tuckaway
Picnic Furniture

By Keith Vining

The chair goes together in a jiffy. Just open up the sides, raise the seat, insert the back in the slots and push down to interlock the parts

JUST the thing for outdoor dining in your back yard or on a picnic, this novel plywood table-and-chair set comes apart so that it can be transported easily or tucked away in the fall in a minimum of space. Each chair consists of four parts, the sides being exactly alike, except for the slots. Fig. 3 gives the patterns for the parts which are cut out of $\frac{3}{8}$-in. waterproof plywood. The sides of the chair are mortise-hinged together at the front, while its seat is surface-hinged to the back to fold downward. The slots must be cut to slant inward and accommodate the chair back. Cut them slightly oversize to allow for coats of paint or varnish. To set up a chair, you merely open its sides, Fig. 1, lift up the seat, engage the back piece in the slots and then push down on the back to interlock all of the parts as in Fig. 2.

The top of the table is a piece of plywood, 36 in. square, supported by "frame" legs, one frame being made in two separate parts which slide together in a dovetail groove on the underside of the top, Fig. 4, and interlock the complete assembly. The only fastening used is a removable dowel which pins the sliding legs together. The frames are assembled with open-mortise corner joints, as detailed in Fig. 5. Note that the crossrails of the solid frame are notched to take the ends of the sliding frame. The sliding frame has a dovetail tenon cut in the top edge to match a dovetail groove in the table top. The best way to cut the groove is with a portable router, equipped with a dovetail cutter, guiding it along a straightedge placed diagonally across the plywood and clamped. After the groove is made, the top is cut exactly in half and surface-hinged. When the table is assembled, a hole is drilled through the cross joint formed by the two frames and a dowel is inserted in the hole to lock the parts together. The dowel can be tied to the legs for safekeeping.

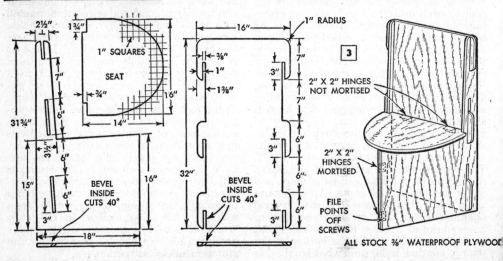

ALL STOCK $\frac{3}{8}$" WATERPROOF PLYWOOD

Although outdoor plywood is recommended for this furniture, it should be protected against moisture by finishing both sides and all edges of the parts with two coats of weather-resistant spar varnish. Sand the parts first, and as a touch of decoration, decals can be applied when the first varnish coat is dry. Then the second coat will protect the decals and keep them looking bright. Avoid making the sliding joints too snug as they should be a loose fit. Waxing will help if the parts do not slide freely

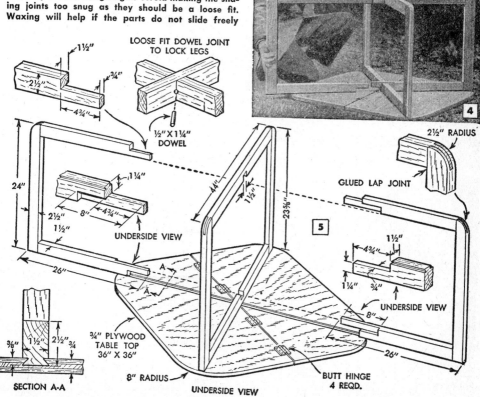

LOOSE FIT DOWEL JOINT TO LOCK LEGS

1½"

2½"

¾"

4¾"

½" X 1¼" DOWEL

4

2½" RADIUS

GLUED LAP JOINT

24"

1¼"

2½"

8"

4¾"

1½"

UNDERSIDE VIEW

44"

1½"

23⅝"

5

1½"

4¾"

1¼"

¾"

UNDERSIDE VIEW

8"

26"

A

A

26"

⅜"

1½"

2½"

¾"

SECTION A-A

¾" PLYWOOD TABLE TOP 36" X 36"

8" RADIUS

UNDERSIDE VIEW

BUTT HINGE 4 REQD.

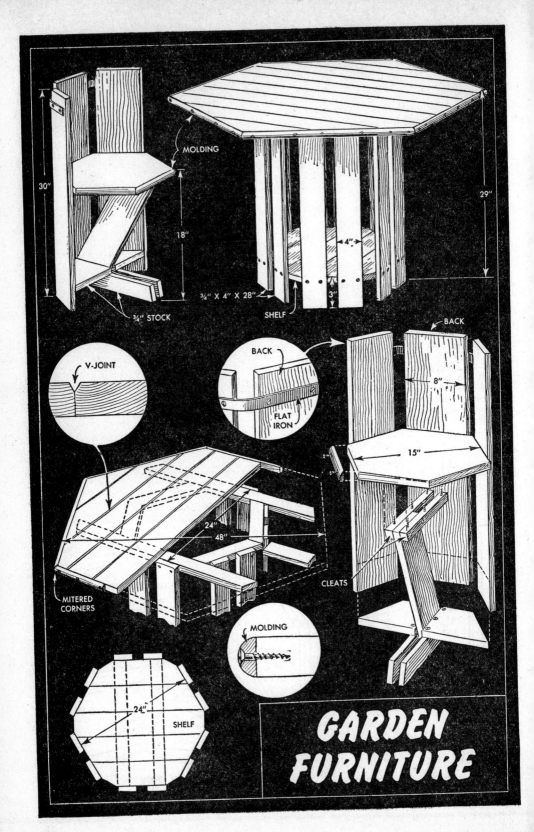

MOLDING

30"

18"

¾" STOCK

¾" X 4" X 28"

SHELF

29"

4"

3"

V-JOINT

BACK

FLAT IRON

BACK

8"

15"

CLEATS

MITERED CORNERS

24"

48"

MOLDING

24"

SHELF

GARDEN FURNITURE

Wooden Slats Replace Canvas Seat of Lawn Chair

If the canvas seats on your lawn chairs are threadbare or torn, replace them with a durable slat seat like this one. In addition to having an attractive appearance, it will withstand plenty of punishment from the elements, and unlike a canvas seat, you can use it immediately after a rain by wiping it dry. To make this slat-type seat, get two lengths of fairly heavy rope long enough to permit sufficient curvature for comfort, and then cut a number of wooden slats to the same length as the width of the canvas. Fasten the slats to the rope about 1 in. apart with a small metal clip near each end. A screw, set flush in the face side of the slat opposite the clip and turned into the rope, keeps the slat from slipping. Of course, you can paint the slats either before or after mounting them on the ropes. However, painting them before assembling

likely will result in a better looking job. Regardless of the paint requirements for the rest of the chair, give the slats at least two coats of a good outdoor paint. After the paint dries, attach the seat to the chair by looping the ends of the rope over the crosspieces of the frame and fastening them with cable clamps. Another method of doing this, which permits easy removal, is to tie the ends of the ropes to S-hooks and hook them over the crosspieces.

Rubber-Tired Wheels for Toys Formed From Can Lids and Hose

Sturdy wheels for small coaster wagons, doll buggies, scooters, etc., can be made by using compression-type can lids for wheel disks and garden hose for tires. First, shape a hardwood hub for each wheel as shown in the left-hand detail, and then dish the can lids to match the curvature of the hub. Drill a hole through the wooden

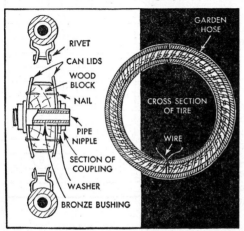

hub for the bearing assembly, which consists of a bronze bushing pressed into a pipe nipple. The latter is held in place by washers and short lengths of pipe coupling that serve as nuts for the threaded ends of the nipple. The can lids, when placed back to back, form a tire rim. The tire is made from a length of garden hose reinforced with a core of armored electrical cable. Cut the cable a little shorter than the length of hose required and pull out the wires. Next, drill a ¼-in. hole through one wall of the hose at a point one half its length. Insert a long tie wire through the cable, letting it extend about 2 ft. from each end, and pass one end of the wire through the hole in the hose. After this, push the end of the cable into the same end of the hose until it meets the hole in the hose. Do the same with the other end of the wire and cable, inserting both in the opposite end of the hose. Finally, when the ends of the hose meet, pull the tie wires taut and twist them. Mount the tire between the can lids before they are nailed to the hub and riveted as shown.

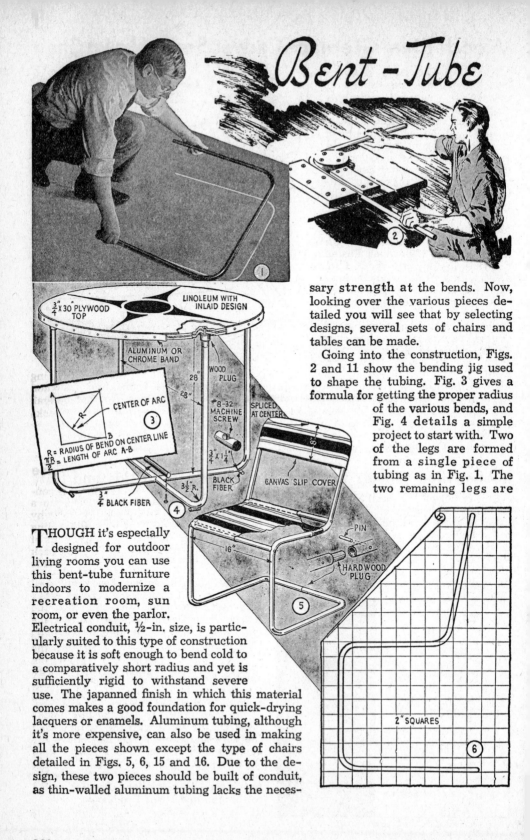

Bent-Tube

sary strength at the bends. Now, looking over the various pieces detailed you will see that by selecting designs, several sets of chairs and tables can be made.

Going into the construction, Figs. 2 and 11 show the bending jig used to shape the tubing. Fig. 3 gives a formula for getting the proper radius of the various bends, and Fig. 4 details a simple project to start with. Two of the legs are formed from a single piece of tubing as in Fig. 1. The two remaining legs are

THOUGH it's especially designed for outdoor living rooms you can use this bent-tube furniture indoors to modernize a recreation room, sun room, or even the parlor. Electrical conduit, ½-in. size, is particularly suited to this type of construction because it is soft enough to bend cold to a comparatively short radius and yet is sufficiently rigid to withstand severe use. The japanned finish in which this material comes makes a good foundation for quick-drying lacquers or enamels. Aluminum tubing, although it's more expensive, can also be used in making all the pieces shown except the type of chairs detailed in Figs. 5, 6, 15 and 16. Due to the design, these two pieces should be built of conduit, as thin-walled aluminum tubing lacks the neces-

Figure labels:
- ¾" x 30" PLYWOOD TOP
- LINOLEUM WITH INLAID DESIGN
- ALUMINUM OR CHROME BAND
- WOOD PLUG
- 28"
- 28"
- #8-32 MACHINE SCREW
- SPLICED AT CENTER
- CENTER OF ARC
- R
- B
- R = RADIUS OF BEND ON CENTER LINE
- $\frac{\pi R}{2}$ = LENGTH OF ARC A-B
- ¾" x 1¼"
- BLACK FIBER
- 3½" R.
- ¾ BLACK FIBER
- CANVAS SLIP COVER
- 8"
- 16"
- PIN
- HARDWOOD PLUG
- 2" SQUARES

FURNITURE

for Modern Gardens

bent separately and the lower ends are filed concave to fit the first member and form a neat right-angled joint. A short length of ¾-in. round black fiber is fastened over the joint with screws driven through the tubing. This holds the joint and further carries out the modern design. The four feet are of the same material. Hardwood plugs, turned to a tight fit, are driven into the top end of each leg, and screws, which hold the circular plywood top, are driven through the top into these

plugs. Linoleum, of whatever design you choose, is cemented to the top. A chrome or aluminum band around the edge finishes the job.

Now, to build the other two tables, shown in Figs. 7, 8, 9 and 19, you follow the same general procedure in bending the tubing and joining parts together. When you bend thinwalled aluminum tubing, it's best to fill the tube with sand, ramming it hard, and plug the ends as in Figs. 17 and 18. Also, it's a good idea to turn a concave groove in the edge of the bending disk on the jig,

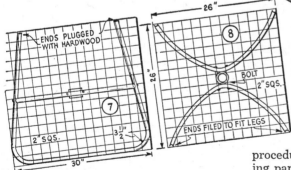

A table just suited to use in the outdoor living room for refreshments, card parties, etc. It's arranged to hold a lawn umbrella which can be anchored with a pin driven into the ground. The inlay design shown in Fig. 4 can be used on this table top, if desired

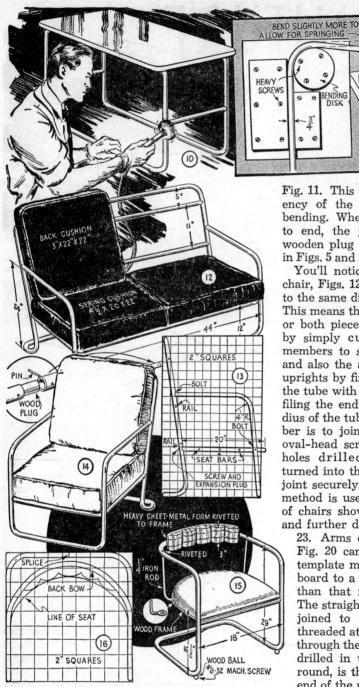

Fig. 11. This will prevent any tendency of the tube to flatten when bending. Where the tubing joins end to end, the joint is made with a wooden plug and two metal pins as in Figs. 5 and 12.

You'll notice that the settee and chair, Figs. 12 and 14, are fashioned to the same dimensions as in Fig. 13. This means that you can build either or both pieces from the same plan, by simply cutting the lengthwise members to suit. Here these parts and also the arms are joined to the uprights by first plugging the end of the tube with a hardwood plug, then filing the end concave to fit the radius of the tube the horizontal member is to join. A chromium-plated oval-head screw inserted through holes drilled in the upright and turned into the wood plug holds the joint securely. Practically the same method is used in joining the parts of chairs shown in Figs. 20 and 22 and further detailed in Figs. 21 and 23. Arms of the chair shown in Fig. 20 can be shaped around a template made by band-sawing a board to a slightly shorter radius than that required on the tube. The straight rails of this chair are joined to the legs with a rod, threaded at both ends and passing through the rail and through holes drilled in the legs. A nut, filed round, is then turned up on each end of the rod. Another way is to simply use the rod as a long rivet, peening over the projecting ends. If you countersink the hole before inserting the rod, the ends can be peened over and the excess filed

By halving the width, the settee in Fig. 12 becomes the chair shown in Fig. 14, as the end dimensions are the same. Spring-cushioned backs and seats can be made by purchasing the spring assembly ready-made, padding it lightly with cotton and sewing on a covering of cloth or artificial leather. The metal frames can be made of conduit, enameled in color, or polished aluminum tubing

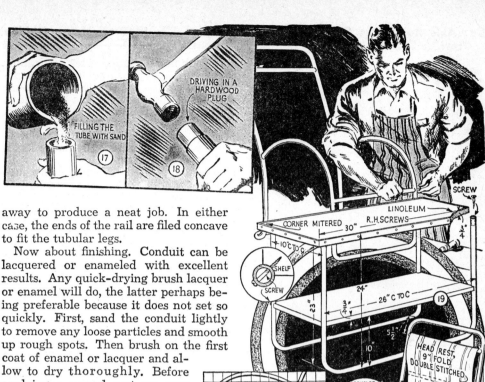

away to produce a neat job. In either case, the ends of the rail are filed concave to fit the tubular legs.

Now about finishing. Conduit can be lacquered or enameled with excellent results. Any quick-drying brush lacquer or enamel will do, the latter perhaps being preferable because it does not set so quickly. First, sand the conduit lightly to remove any loose particles and smooth up rough spots. Then brush on the first coat of enamel or lacquer and allow to dry thoroughly. Before applying a second coat, go over the first lightly with fine sandpaper. Then follow with the finish coat, carefully brushed out to avoid sagging on the rounded surfaces. Where aluminum tubing is used it may be polished highly with a buffing wheel driven by a flexible shaft as in Fig. 10. A coat of clear metal lacquer will help to preserve the high polish.

Keeping Dogs and Cats Out of Your Garden

By spraying flowers or shrubs with a dilute nicotine-sulphate solution you can keep small animals, such as dogs and cats, out of your garden. The spray is harmless to plants but it is very offensive to the animals. Commercial preparations usually contain 40 per cent of nicotine sulphate, and such preparations should be used in the proportion of 1½ teaspoonfuls to a gallon of water. Spraying should be renewed about every two weeks during ordinary weather and after a rain.

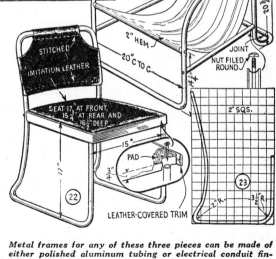

Metal frames for any of these three pieces can be made of either polished aluminum tubing or electrical conduit finished in quick-drying colored lacquer or enamel. By combining these and other designs shown, several sets of attractive porch and garden furniture can be made

Car Axle Reinforces Gate Post and Provides Sturdy Hinge

Embedded in a concrete gate post as indicated, the front axle of an old car strengthens the post and provides a rigid support on which to pivot the gate. Before using the axle, it is bent at right angles at the ends, which project beyond the post. Bolts through the kingpin holes in the axle and the sockets in the gate pivot the latter.

Implement Seat for Garden

Comfortable to sit in and easy to move about, this portable garden seat is made from a discarded implement seat. A heavy metal rod serves as the supporting standard for the seat and slips through a metal disk, which serves as a base and prevents the standard from sinking into the ground under the weight of the occupant. Two holes spaced ⅜ in. apart are drilled through the standard to take large cotter pins on each side of the disk.

❦ When painting a house in regions of intense summer heat, use a light color of paint. This will tend to make the house cooler, as light colors absorb less heat.

Compost Pile in Well House Hidden from View ⟶

If your home grounds lack a shrub or evergreen screen behind which a compost pile can be hidden, this well house will serve the purpose, and also add a decorative touch. Built as shown, with a concrete pit 38 to 40 in. below the ground, and boarded up to a height of 28 to 30 in. above ground, the house has a capacity of approximately 75 cubic feet. Besides being used for composting garden waste, the well also is handy for composting and storing manure over the fall and winter months, or for housing a bale of peat moss which, after a thorough soaking, will loosen and crumble within the pit. The roof prevents loss by leaching, and the sides deflect drying winds so that after the compost is wetted thoroughly, little moisture need be added. Compost in the well is kept at a higher temperature during winter than if piled on the open ground, thus hastening decomposition. Having one side removable as shown, permits you to work in the pit, and provides a convenient means of removing the compost. If desired, you can make one pile in half of the pit, then start another pile in the other half, separating the two with old boards. Lumber for the sides and posts should be cypress or other rot-resistant wood. All wooden parts should be given several coats of wood preservative, using one that has a brown color if possible to carry out the desired weathered appearance. It is a good idea to line the sides above the ground line with old boards as you build up the compost pile.

Garden-Hose Ring Supports Bushes

The spreading of small garden bushes may be prevented by supporting them with a ring made from garden hose. The ring is formed by inserting heavy-gauge wire and twisting the ends together. Three or four stakes are used to support the ring at the desired height. Because the hose acts as an insulator, the sun cannot heat the wire and injure the plant.

❦ Rose bouquets will stay fresh longer if the stems are cut off under water. This prevents tiny air bubbles from blocking the small openings in the stems through which the water rises to the flowers.

Imitation WELL HOUSE hides compost pile

½" ROPE

SIDES NOTCHED

4"

2½"

1½"

1"

SHINGLES

CAP

1" X 4" RIDGE

SHEATHING

1⅛" X 3" RAFTERS

2" X 4"

4" X 4"

GROUND LEVEL

56"

40"

6'4"

38"

CONCRETE

HOOK

LAG SCREW

HOW REMOVABLE SIDE IS FASTENED

1" PIPE

⅜" BOLTS

6"

PIPE DENTED TO ANCHOR IN CONCRETE SECURELY

8"

BAR-B-Q CART

By Benjamin Nielsen

PICNICS where you want 'em — that's the feature of this rolling outdoor grill, for not only can you wheel it to any spot in the back yard, but you can take it with you on camping trips. The frame of the cart is bent cold from rigid electrical conduit, then welded and equipped with rubber-tired coaster-wagon wheels. Both the firebox and ash pan of the original were made from metal salvaged from discarded auto hoods, making use of the hinged parts to provide folding windshields. However, the firebox can be formed from sheet metal and the windshields hinged with small butt hinges. Note that friction tabs are formed on the front windshield.

Draft holes are punched in the sloping sides of the firebox and corresponding holes are made in a draft regulator which, in use, remains inside the firebox and is shifted back and forth to control the draft. Note also that an opening is made in the bottom of the firebox for dumping the ashes. Ash pan and firebox are riveted together, and two notched posts support a spit at different heights above the coals.

Steak grill

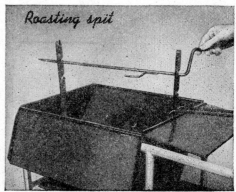

Roasting spit

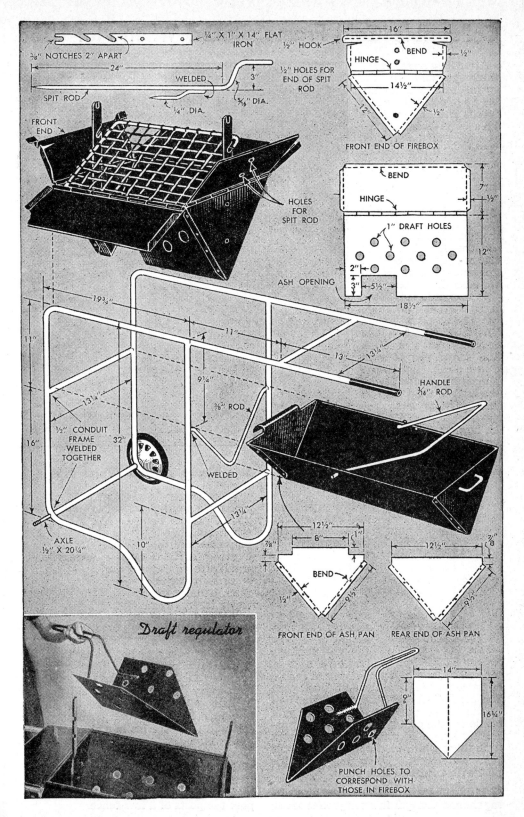

¼" X 1" X 14" FLAT IRON

⅜" NOTCHES 2" APART

24"

SPIT ROD

WELDED

3"

¼" DIA.

5⁄16" DIA.

½" HOOK

½" HOLES FOR END OF SPIT ROD

16"

BEND

HINGE

½"

14½"

12"

½"

FRONT END OF FIREBOX

FRONT END

HOLES FOR SPIT ROD

BEND

HINGE

7"

½"

1" DRAFT HOLES

2"

3"

5½"

12"

ASH OPENING

18½"

19¾"

11"

11"

13¼"

13"

13¼"

9¼"

HANDLE 3⁄16" ROD

⅜" ROD

½" CONDUIT FRAME WELDED TOGETHER

32"

WELDED

16"

13¼"

AXLE ½" X 20¼"

10"

13¼"

12½"

8"

1"

7⁄8"

BEND

½"

9½"

12½"

⅜"

9½"

Draft regulator

FRONT END OF ASH PAN

REAR END OF ASH PAN

14"

9"

16¼"

PUNCH HOLES TO CORRESPOND WITH THOSE IN FIREBOX

Collapsible Cold Frame Stored When Not Used

After they have served their purpose in the spring, most cold frames become filled with weeds and detract from the well-ordered appearance of the garden. Here's a frame that is quickly disassembled after it has served its purpose, and can be stored out of the way until needed again. The lower detail shows the method of assembly and construction. The exact size of the frame will be governed by the size of the sash that is used. In this case, it is two four-light barn sash with 10 by 12-in. glass panes. The four sides are held together with a hook and screw eye at each corner. Loose-pin hinges are used to fasten the sash to the frame as this permits easy removal. Either 2 by 4-in. lumber or bricks can be used as a base.

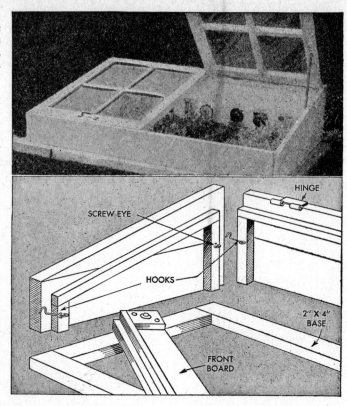

Repairing Pipe Fence Posts Rusted Off at Base

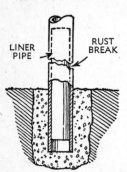

If a pipe fence post has rusted off at its base, it can be repaired to last for years. To make the repair, select a length of galvanized pipe which will fit inside the post snugly. For example, a 1½-in. pipe will fit nicely inside a 2-in. pipe. The length of pipe required should be twice the length of the embedded post. The pipe is inserted inside the lower half of the rusted post, and then the upper portion of the post is placed over the projecting length of pipe. Coat the break with thick white-lead paint to make the joint watertight. When dry, paint the post with a rubber-base paint.

❦ Fishhook leaders can be dyed by soaking them overnight in strong coffee or tea.

Salt Thaws Vertical Water Pipe

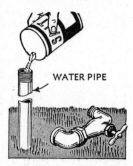

When water is piped to a poultry house, barn or other building it may freeze in the exposed portions of the pipe during a sudden cold snap. Usually the water freezes at a point just below the tap and you can save the trouble of carrying hot water from the house to thaw out the pipe by using ordinary table salt. Remove the faucet, chip away some of the ice and pour in a little salt. Then replace the faucet and turn it to the "on" position. The salt will thaw the ice in a short time, or put in more.

❦ One homeowner sank hollow building tiles in his lawn slightly below ground level and cemented them in place to support the posts of a low fence.

Portable Screened "PORCH" in the GARDEN

Open-air retreat excludes flies and mosquitoes yet provides shelter from light rains and too much sun

LARGE enough for a cot and two camp chairs, or a card table and four small chairs, this "porch" is the place to spend warm days and evenings in the garden.

Standard screen-frame material is used for all of the frames, Fig. 1, which are assembled with simple joints, Fig. 2. These can be cut with

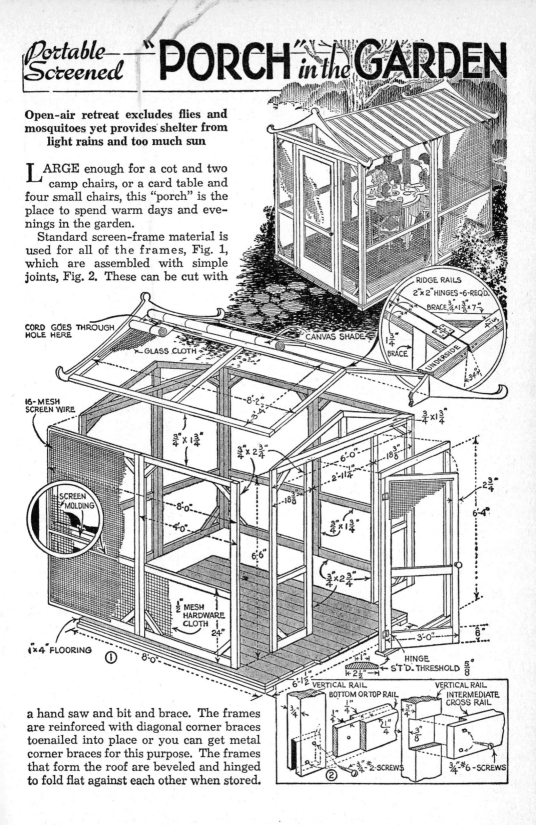

CORD GOES THROUGH HOLE HERE

RIDGE RAILS
2"x 2" HINGES -6-REQD.
BRACE 3/4 x 1 3/8 x 7"

CANVAS SHADE

GLASS CLOTH

1 1/4" BRACE

UNDERSIDE

3 1/4"

16-MESH SCREEN WIRE

8'-2"
3 1/4"

3/4" x 1 3/4"

3/4" x 2 3/4"

6'-0"
18 3/8"

2'-11 1/4"

18 3/8"

2 3/4"

6'-4"

SCREEN MOLDING

8'-0"
4'-0"

6'-6"

3/4" x 1 3/4"

3/4" x 2 3/4"

1/2" MESH HARDWARE CLOTH
24"

1"x4" FLOORING
① 8'-0"

3'-0"
6"

HINGE
ST'D. THRESHOLD 5/8"

6'-1 1/2"
1" 2 1/2"

VERTICAL RAIL
BOTTOM OR TOP RAIL

VERTICAL RAIL
INTERMEDIATE CROSS RAIL

3/4"
1/4" 1/4"
1" 1/4"

3/4"
3/8"

3/4"#2-SCREWS

3/4"#6-SCREWS

②

a hand saw and bit and brace. The frames are reinforced with diagonal corner braces toenailed into place or you can get metal corner braces for this purpose. The frames that form the roof are beveled and hinged to fold flat against each other when stored.

285

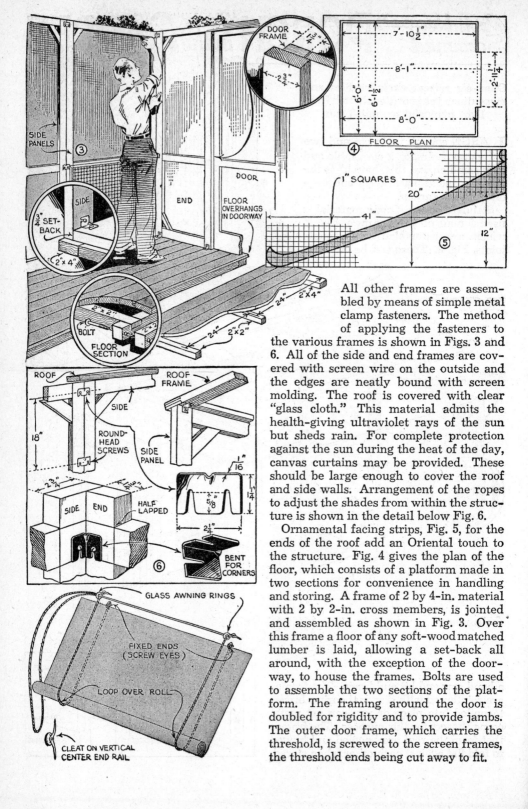

DOOR FRAME

4¼"

2¾"

SIDE PANELS

3

SIDE

¾" SET-BACK

2 x 4

2" 2"

BOLT

2" 2"

FLOOR SECTION

END

DOOR

FLOOR OVERHANGS IN DOORWAY

24" 2" x 4"

24" 2" x 2"

7'-10½"

8'-1"

6'-0"

6'-1½"

8'-0"

2'-1½"

FLOOR PLAN

4

1" SQUARES

20"

41"

12"

5

ROOF

ROOF FRAME

SIDE

18"

ROUND-HEAD SCREWS

SIDE PANEL

2¾"

SIDE

END

HALF LAPPED

1/16

1¼"

5/8

2¼"

BENT FOR CORNERS

6

GLASS AWNING RINGS

FIXED ENDS (SCREW EYES)

LOOP OVER ROLL

CLEAT ON VERTICAL CENTER END RAIL

All other frames are assembled by means of simple metal clamp fasteners. The method of applying the fasteners to the various frames is shown in Figs. 3 and 6. All of the side and end frames are covered with screen wire on the outside and the edges are neatly bound with screen molding. The roof is covered with clear "glass cloth." This material admits the health-giving ultraviolet rays of the sun but sheds rain. For complete protection against the sun during the heat of the day, canvas curtains may be provided. These should be large enough to cover the roof and side walls. Arrangement of the ropes to adjust the shades from within the structure is shown in the detail below Fig. 6.

Ornamental facing strips, Fig. 5, for the ends of the roof add an Oriental touch to the structure. Fig. 4 gives the plan of the floor, which consists of a platform made in two sections for convenience in handling and storing. A frame of 2 by 4-in. material with 2 by 2-in. cross members, is jointed and assembled as shown in Fig. 3. Over this frame a floor of any soft-wood matched lumber is laid, allowing a set-back all around, with the exception of the doorway, to house the frames. Bolts are used to assemble the two sections of the platform. The framing around the door is doubled for rigidity and to provide jambs. The outer door frame, which carries the threshold, is screwed to the screen frames, the threshold ends being cut away to fit.

Half-Lapped Trellis Cut Quickly on Table Saw

An attractive trellis of the type shown in the photo is easy to build with half-lapped joints if this miter-guide jig is used to space the notches uniformly. The notches preferably are made with a dado saw, but they also can be cut with an ordinary saw blade. The notches, of course, must be the same width as the thickness of the stock and as deep as one half its width. Standard lattice stock is used for the grillwork of the trellis which, when assembled, is framed with 1 by 2-inch pieces. First, notch a short length of stock and drive a nail into it as indicated, distance A being equal to the distance the notches are to be spaced. Then screw this strip to the miter guide on the saw table. To cut the notches with a dado saw, make the first one near the end of the strip, and using the jig with the nail as a stop pin, proceed to cut each succeeding notch. Approximately the same method is used with a saw blade, except that the notches are made by holding one side of the preceding notch against the nail and making repeated cuts until the other side of the notch contacts the nail. By adjusting the miter guide, angle cuts also can be made in this way to obtain a diamond-shaped pattern. After notching the strips, cut them to length and assemble the trellis with brads in the usual manner by driving them through the center of the half-lapped joints. Before nailing each joint, apply white lead to

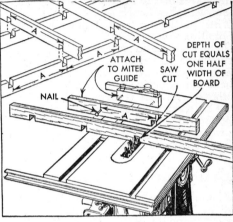

the meeting faces to prevent dry rot. The trellis is supported by two center stakes, the ends of which are preserved by dipping in creosote.

Flagstone Retaining Wall Around Tree Provides Attractive Fernery

This unusual and beautiful outdoor fernery is made from flagstones which encircle the trunk of a tree to form a retaining wall for ferns or other rock-garden plants. Build a low wall similar to the one shown in the photo, allowing the coping course on top of the wall to project a few inches. If you wish, mix a little lampblack with the mortar so that the black mortar joints will contrast with the light-colored stone. Then fill the area inside the wall with a suitable soil and plant ferns well in the background near the tree. To add variety, place small, brightly colored foliage plants around the ferns along the inner edge of the coping.

"Old Oaken Bucket" Is Container for Ice Cubes

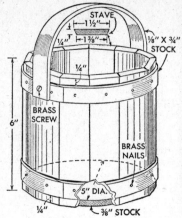

The "old oaken bucket" takes a new lease on life in the form of an ice-cube container designed especially for back-yard barbecues and picnics. Staves and hoops are of contrasting hardwoods. In this case, gumwood was used for the staves, and walnut for the hoops and handle. The bottom can be any scrap stock. The edges along the length of the staves are mitered to obtain the correct inside width. In assembling, nail the staves first to the bottom, using headless brads.

When putting on the last stave, it may be found to be a trifle wide. This is due to a slight variance in mitering the staves. It should be planed to fit. The strips for the hoops and the handle must be steamed to bend in a circular shape. A wash boiler or other vessel that is large enough to hold the strips may be used. Pour water in the bottom to a depth of about 1 in. Lay in several pieces of waste wood and place the three strips across them. The supporting pieces of wood should be high enough to raise the strips above the water. Put on the cover and steam the strips until they are flexible enough to be bent around a form. A No. 10 tin can makes a good form for this purpose. Bend the strips around the can and clamp. Miter the ends of the hoops for a smooth fit and secure to the staves with small brass-plate nails. A liner of pottery or glass is needed. In this case, it was a beater bowl.

Ball-Bearing Weather Vane Will Spin in a Light Breeze

Here's a weather vane that needs only a slight breeze to set it turning and in a strong wind it will spin like a top. Start by constructing the fan, which is cut from a square piece of sheet metal. Note that a small triangular piece is trimmed off each corner. A wooden spool is placed between the front and back of the fan to serve as a hub that slides over the bolt on the bicycle hub. A 4-in. metal disk is bolted to the back of the fan to complete this assembly. The arm and tail piece are assembled next, except for drilling the hole through which the unit is fastened to the post. The hub is fastened to the arm with two U-bolts and a tin-can cover is made to slip over the hub. When the unit is finished, determine the point of balance on the arm and drill it to receive a metal bushing. Fasten the weather vane to a post with a lag screw and washer.

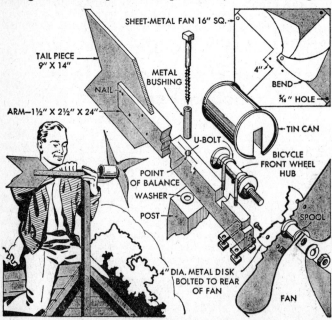

Portable Barbecue Pit Has Motor-Driven Spits

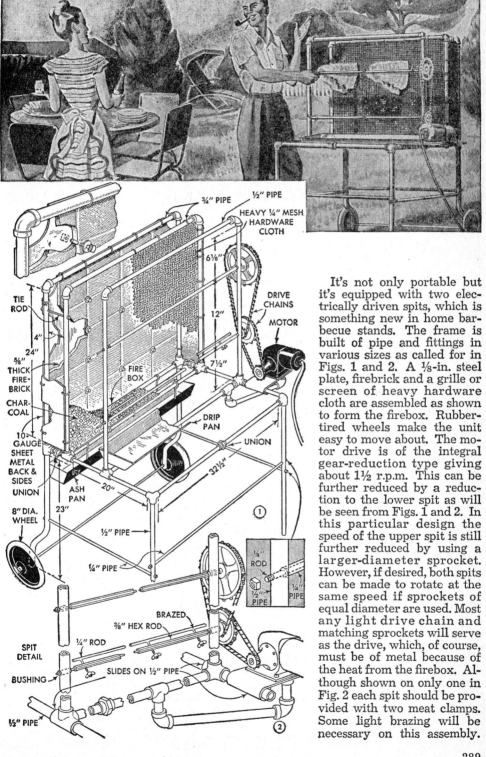

It's not only portable but it's equipped with two electrically driven spits, which is something new in home barbecue stands. The frame is built of pipe and fittings in various sizes as called for in Figs. 1 and 2. A ⅛-in. steel plate, firebrick and a grille or screen of heavy hardware cloth are assembled as shown to form the firebox. Rubber-tired wheels make the unit easy to move about. The motor drive is of the integral gear-reduction type giving about 1½ r.p.m. This can be further reduced by a reduction to the lower spit as will be seen from Figs. 1 and 2. In this particular design the speed of the upper spit is still further reduced by using a larger-diameter sprocket. However, if desired, both spits can be made to rotate at the same speed if sprockets of equal diameter are used. Most any light drive chain and matching sprockets will serve as the drive, which, of course, must be of metal because of the heat from the firebox. Although shown on only one in Fig. 2 each spit should be provided with two meat clamps. Some light brazing will be necessary on this assembly.

289

MOLDED BIRDS
for the Lawn

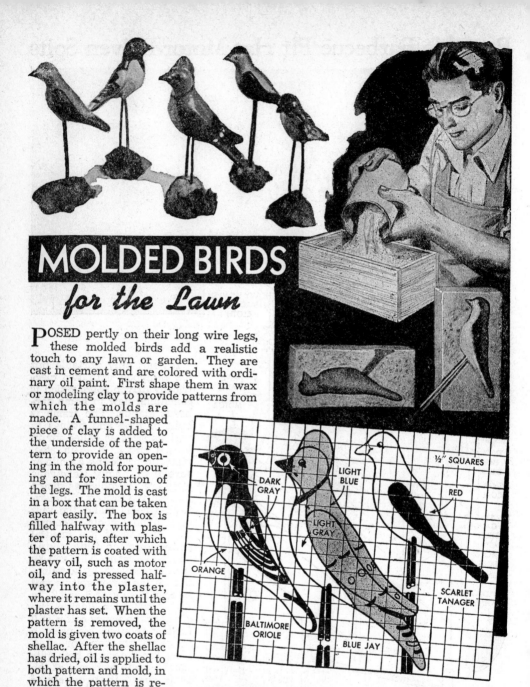

½" SQUARES

DARK GRAY

LIGHT BLUE

LIGHT GRAY

RED

ORANGE

BALTIMORE ORIOLE

BLUE JAY

SCARLET TANAGER

POSED pertly on their long wire legs, these molded birds add a realistic touch to any lawn or garden. They are cast in cement and are colored with ordinary oil paint. First shape them in wax or modeling clay to provide patterns from which the molds are made. A funnel-shaped piece of clay is added to the underside of the pattern to provide an opening in the mold for pouring and for insertion of the legs. The mold is cast in a box that can be taken apart easily. The box is filled halfway with plaster of paris, after which the pattern is coated with heavy oil, such as motor oil, and is pressed halfway into the plaster, where it remains until the plaster has set. When the pattern is removed, the mold is given two coats of shellac. After the shellac has dried, oil is applied to both pattern and mold, in which the pattern is replaced. Then more plaster is poured to fill the box. When dry, remove the box, separate the mold and then apply shellac to the upper half. Be sure that both halves of the mold are oiled thoroughly before pouring each casting.

Now, mix together portland cement, **3** parts, plaster of paris, 2 parts, and fine sand, 1 part, adding just enough water to form a mixture that can be poured. When pouring the cement, rock the mold gently to remove air bubbles. Finally, insert two lengths of wire for legs and let the mixture set for 15 min., or until hard. Then remove the casting and submerge it in water for 24 hrs. After a thorough drying, the casting is painted and later coated with spar varnish for luster. The three models shown in the cross-hatched pattern will enable you to make many different species simply by changing the markings and coloring.

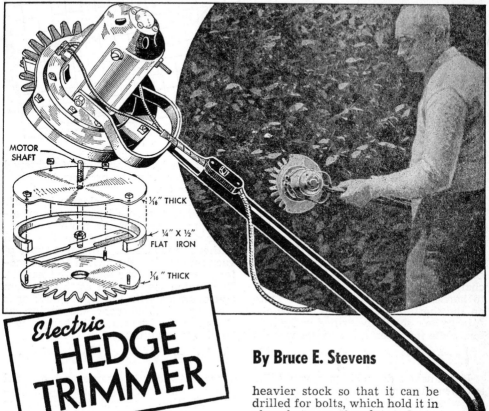

MOTOR SHAFT

1/16" THICK

1/4" X 1/2" FLAT IRON

1/16" THICK

Electric
HEDGE TRIMMER

By Bruce E. Stevens

IMPROVISED from an old vacuum cleaner, this electric hedge trimmer is fast, efficient and easy to handle. Also, it can be used not only on privets and similar shrubbery, but on weed patches and in other places that cannot easily be clipped by a lawn mower. To convert a vacuum cleaner into a hedge trimmer of this kind, first remove the sweeper housing, including the suction fan. The assembly usually can be taken off merely by removing a few bolts that secure it to the motor housing. Next, substitute a new housing as shown in the illustration. This consists of top and bottom plates, with a flat metal segment between them which forms the side. On the trimmer shown in the illustration, sheet aluminum was used for the plates and spacer in order to assure light weight. However, 1/16-in. sheet iron or other similar material can be used for the plates, but the spacer must be of heavier stock so that it can be drilled for bolts, which hold it in place between the plates. Over-all sizes of the plates are not given as they are determined by the particular type of vacuum cleaner you use. The lower plate is serrated nearly halfway along its edge to form teeth between which twigs of shrubbery enter to be cut off by a rotating knife. The width and depth of the teeth and the slots are given in the cross-hatched pattern.

For the knife, you can grind down an old file of suitable size. Dimensions of the knife shown are correct only when the bottom plate is the size given in the pattern. For a plate of a different size, the length of the knife must be varied accordingly, although its thickness need not exceed 1/8 in. In general, the knife should be long enough to extend to within about 1/8 in. of the tip of the teeth, and the center hole should fit the motor shaft snugly. To drill a hole in a file, it is necessary first to remove the temper. This is done by heating the file to a dull red and then allowing it to cool gradually. After removing the temper and

291

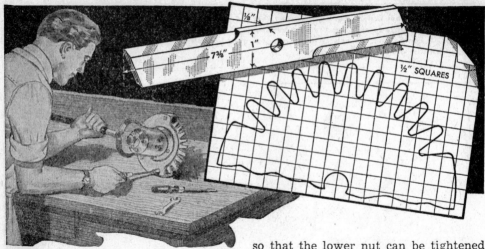

drilling the hole, the file should be ground to a knife edge on opposite sides as shown, so that the cutting edge is toward the bottom plate, taking into consideration the direction in which the blade will move on the motor shaft. Also, it is important to balance the knife to avoid vibration. When the knife is completed, it should be heated to a cherry red and quenched in oil or water to harden it. Two nuts hold the knife on the shaft, one above and one below. A large hole should be drilled in the bottom plate for inserting a socket wrench so that the lower nut can be tightened whenever needed to prevent the knife from slipping.

The original vacuum-cleaner handle is retained because its length counterbalances the weight of the motor and enables the operator to guide the head without much effort. On some types of vacuum cleaners the switch for the motor is located at the end of the handle. The switch may be left at this location and operated with the right hand; or it may be mounted near the motor, as shown in the illustration, where it will be visible at all times.

Installing a Narrow Door in a Wide Opening

If you have a door that you would like to use in an opening that is several inches too wide, you can do an attractive job without plastering, which usually leaves a patched effect. If it is necessary to center the door in the opening, install extra studs and attach the door frame to them in the usual manner. Then bridge the

PLYWOOD EXTENDS UNDER SIDE TRIM

BLOCKING

EXTRA STUD

¼" PLYWOOD

space between the frame and original edges of the opening with ¼-in. plywood, letting it extend back under the full width of the trim as shown in the circular detail. It will be necessary to block out from the sides of the extra studs a distance equal to the thickness of the lath and plaster. If it is not necessary to center the door in the opening, the frame can be set against one side of the opening, thus making it necessary to install only one extra stud. If this is done, the space between the extra stud and the side of the opening is bridged with plywood as before. Plywood also is placed over the plaster an equal distance on the other side to balance the appearance of the door. The plywood should extend under the trim.

Bottle of Soapy Water Is Handy When Going on a Picnic

Before going on a picnic dissolve a little soap in a bottle of water and take it along to wash the children's hands. A few paper towels or some pieces of cloth cut about 15 in. square complete the washing kit and save regular towels.

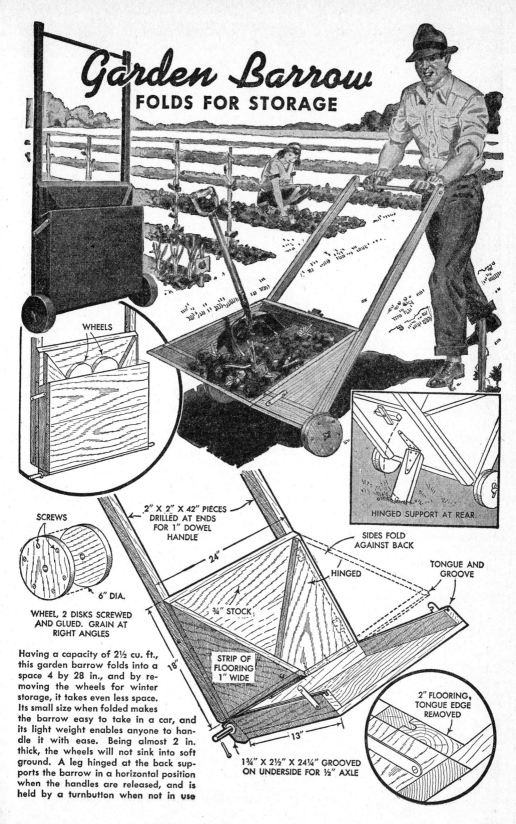

Garden Barrow
FOLDS FOR STORAGE

WHEELS

SCREWS

6" DIA.

WHEEL, 2 DISKS SCREWED AND GLUED. GRAIN AT RIGHT ANGLES

2" X 2" X 42" PIECES DRILLED AT ENDS FOR 1" DOWEL HANDLE

24"

¾" STOCK

18"

STRIP OF FLOORING 1" WIDE

13"

SIDES FOLD AGAINST BACK

HINGED

TONGUE AND GROOVE

HINGED SUPPORT AT REAR

2" FLOORING, TONGUE EDGE REMOVED

1¾" X 2½" X 24¼" GROOVED ON UNDERSIDE FOR ½" AXLE

Having a capacity of 2½ cu. ft., this garden barrow folds into a space 4 by 28 in., and by removing the wheels for winter storage, it takes even less space. Its small size when folded makes the barrow easy to take in a car, and its light weight enables anyone to handle it with ease. Being almost 2 in. thick, the wheels will not sink into soft ground. A leg hinged at the back supports the barrow in a horizontal position when the handles are released, and is held by a turnbutton when not in use

SLAT HOUSES
aid in starting seedlings

BUILT from rough framing stock and sided and roofed with spaced wooden lath or lattice stock, the slat house provides a means of controlling plant shade. Spaced slats give just the right amount of shade to tender seedlings and transplants. During the day each plant is alternately shaded and exposed to direct sunlight at regular intervals. This tends to lower the temperature both of the air and seedbed and also prevents too rapid evaporation of moisture. A slat house can be made an at-tractive feature of the garden if some thought is given to selecting a design which fits in with the plan of the grounds. While the type pictured at the lower right on the next page is wholly utilitarian, others shown are more ornate architecturally. The design detailed in Figs. 1 to 4 inclusive has been selected as an all-around type suitable for most home grounds. The plan, Fig. 4, includes the potting bench, Fig. 2, and the framing is detailed in Fig. 3. Frame and slats should be stained.

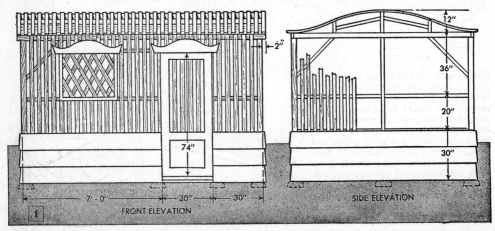

FRONT ELEVATION

SIDE ELEVATION

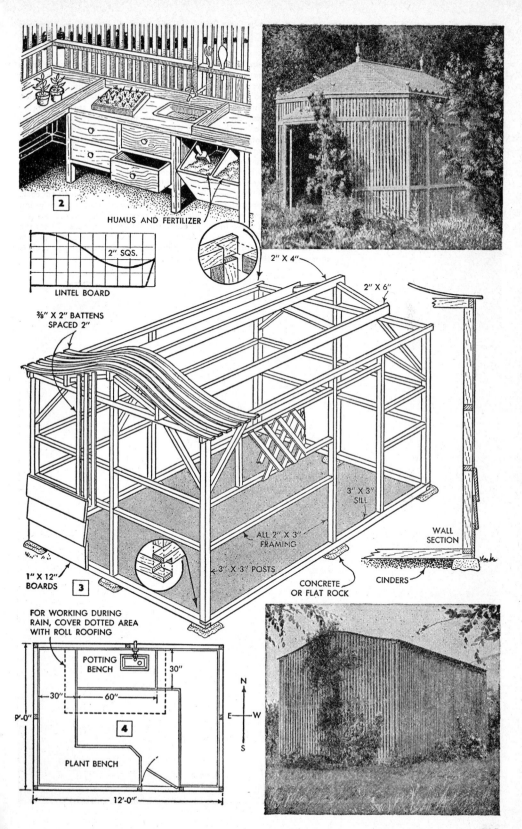

2

HUMUS AND FERTILIZER

LINTEL BOARD

2" SQS.

3/8" X 2" BATTENS
SPACED 2"

2" X 4"

2" X 6"

3" X 3"
SILL

ALL 2" X 3"
FRAMING

3" X 3" POSTS

WALL
SECTION

CONCRETE
OR FLAT ROCK

CINDERS

1" X 12"
BOARDS

3

FOR WORKING DURING
RAIN, COVER DOTTED AREA
WITH ROLL ROOFING

POTTING
BENCH

30"

30"

60"

9'-0"

N

E   W

S

4

PLANT BENCH

12'-0"

LAWN-SPRINKLER SHUTOFF

This novel lawn-sprinkler shutoff automatically waters your lawn during early morning hours when sprinkling is not restricted, or during a hot dry spell when you are away from home over a week end. The device can be regulated to open and close a valve alternately and repeat a slow cycle continuously. It can also be set to turn on the sprinkler during the night, or it can be adjusted to shut off the water after it has been turned on manually. The shutoff operates by action of water dripping from pet cocks into pails hanging from the ends of a crossarm attached to a quick-acting-type steam cock. To set the device so that it turns a sprinkler on and off at intervals, open each pet cock to drip at the desired rate. With the steam cock closed and the sill faucet open, water will drip from the right-hand pet cock and into the pail. Weight of the water will cause the pail to lower and, in turn, to open the steam cock. This starts the sprinkler and at the same time starts water dripping from the other pet cock. Simultaneously, water in the lowered pail escapes through a valve in the bottom, and the cycle repeats. To set the device to turn off the sprinkler, the right-hand pet cock is closed. To turn the sprinkler on for continuous operation, the right-hand pet cock is opened and the other one is closed.

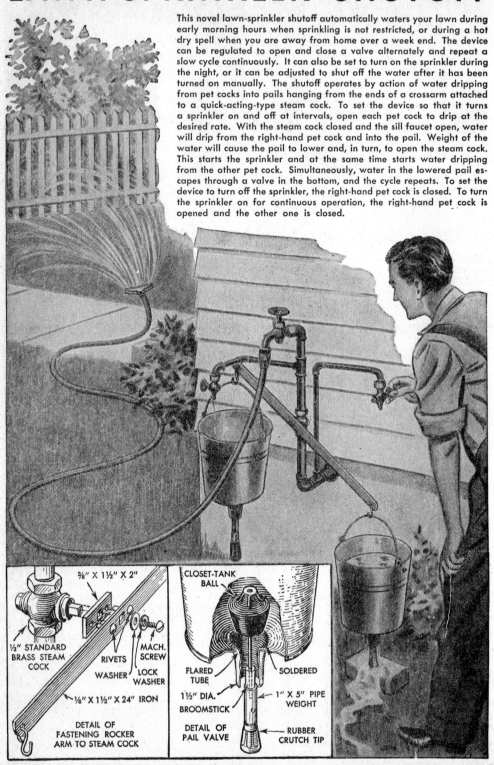

DETAIL OF FASTENING ROCKER ARM TO STEAM COCK

⅜" X 1½" X 2"

½" STANDARD BRASS STEAM COCK

RIVETS

WASHER

MACH. SCREW

LOCK WASHER

⅛" X 1½" X 24" IRON

DETAIL OF PAIL VALVE

CLOSET-TANK BALL

FLARED TUBE

1½" DIA. BROOMSTICK

SOLDERED

1" X 5" PIPE WEIGHT

RUBBER CRUTCH TIP

Motorize Your
LAWN MOWER

⅛" X 1" X 1" STEEL ANGLE, 4 OR 5 AS REQUIRED

ENDS OF KNIVES CUT FLUSH WITH SPIDER

HUB SAWED OUT

6" DIA. V-PULLEY

THESE RIVETS REMOVED

RATCHET PAWLS REVERSED

① ② ③

⅜₆" HOLES

24"

¾"

¾"

10"

8½"

13½"

5½"

9"

¼" X 1" FLAT IRON 2 REQUIRED RIGHT AND LEFT HAND

A

B

C

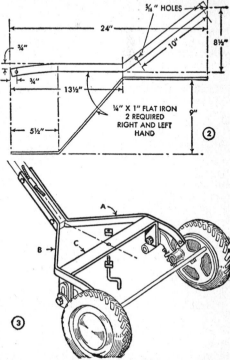

By Sherman Butler

IT'S easy to take the "push" out of a hand-power lawn mower with a ⅝ or ¾-hp. gasoline engine and a few pieces of flat iron. These small, compact engines can be mounted on almost all hand lawn mowers of 18-in. cut or wider. Due to the relatively higher speed and steady forward movement over the ground the grass is cut more cleanly and uniformly. Moreover, the mower will handle taller and heavier growth than can be cut by hand power alone. In this particular type of drive the motor is belted directly to the cutting reel so there's no need to bother about "differential" or a clutch with a complicated throw-out mechanism. Needed differential is taken care of by slippage of the drive wheels induced by a light downward pressure on the handle as you steer the mower in the direction desired. Declutching is accomplished simply by bearing down on the handle when you want to stop or make a sharp turn. This, in turn, raises the drive wheels and shifts the weight to the roller, allowing the mower to be turned in any direction or pulled backward to clear a fence, shrub or other obstruction.

intended merely as a rough guide to the size. Different types of mowers will require some variation. Measure the mower at hand to determine the dimensions required before cutting material.

Connect Fig. 3 with the details in Figs. 4 and 5 and you will readily see how the additional parts of the engine support are fitted on the mower frame. Note that the engine sub-base, made from a steel plate, is hinged on the mower shrub bar as in Fig. 5, and rests on the end of the belt-tightener screw, Fig. 4. This simple arrangement allows easy adjustment of the belt tension. With these parts made and fitted, reassemble the mower with the ratchet pawls reversed in the drive pinions. Be sure to slip the V-belt over the reel pulley first. Bolt the engine and fuel tank in position as in Fig. 4, making sure that the pulleys align properly. Size of the engine drive pulley will depend on the average speed of the engine and you can easily calculate the required diameter of the pulley once the speed of the engine is known. By installing a throttle control on the handle as in the photo, Fig. 1, the engine speed usually can be controlled so that the mower is driven at a comfortable walking pace.

The first thing to do when installing the power drive is to disassemble the mower, removing the reel and the handle. Save the wood section of the handle assembly. Usually, because of the nature of the installation, it will be necessary to make a new yoke, Fig. 2. When removing the reel be careful not to lose or damage any part of the bearings. Fig. 1 shows the method of attaching a pulley to the end of the reel. Diameter of the pulley may have to be varied to suit the mower at hand. The four-blade reel shown in Fig. 1 is not standard as some mowers are fitted with five blades. Ends of the blades projecting beyond the spider are cut off flush and the rivets removed as shown. Steel angles are attached to the spider with stove bolts which pass through the rivet holes. Although a standard metal V-pulley can be used as in Fig. 1, it may be necessary to cut the hub to obtain a free fit between the spider and the inner end of the reel-shaft bearing housing. A pulley also can be turned from ¾-in. hardwood or waterproof plywood of the same thickness. Use lock washers on all bolts in this assembly.

Fig. 3 shows the flat-iron parts which are made and attached to the mower frame. The two parts of the handle yoke, A and B in Fig. 3, are detailed in Fig. 2. However, the dimensions and the bends indicated are

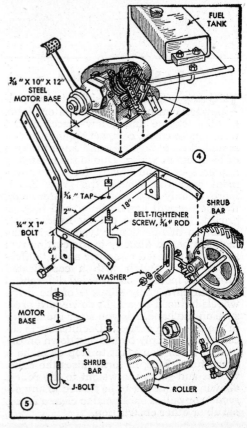

MOW'EM DOWN

WITH THIS
ROTARY CUTTER

By Benj. Nielsen

POWERED by a 1½-hp. air-cooled engine, the rotating blades on this powerful mower cut everything from dandelions to the tallest and toughest weeds. An outstanding feature of this machine is that the front wheel may be set to either side of the cutting path to avoid rolling down uncut grass. This insures clean cutting with no ridges left standing. Also note that the center of gravity of the engine is well back of the rear wheels to secure a nice balance.

The engine platform and guard for the cutter blades are cut and bent from a piece of No. 10-ga. sheet steel to the dimensions given in the upper right-hand detail of Fig. 2. Then a band of flat iron is welded around the edge of the guard. Two lengths of 1½ by 1½-in. angle iron are welded to the top of the guard and the bottom of the platform to give additional strength and

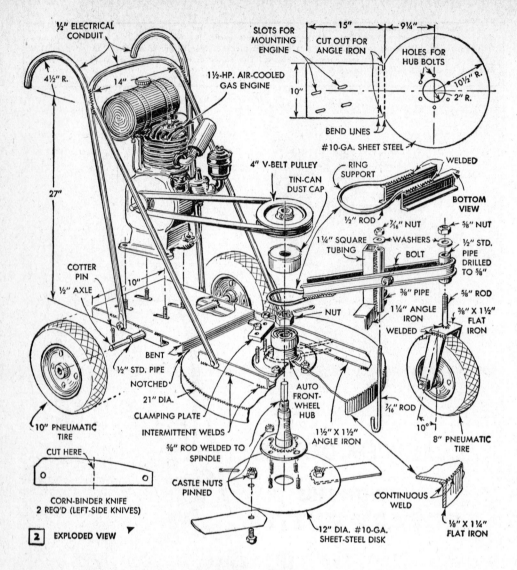

½" ELECTRICAL CONDUIT

4½" R.

14"

1½-HP. AIR-COOLED GAS ENGINE

27"

SLOTS FOR MOUNTING ENGINE

CUT OUT FOR ANGLE IRON

15"

9¼"

10"

HOLES FOR HUB BOLTS

10½" R.

2" R.

BEND LINES

#10-GA. SHEET STEEL

4" V-BELT PULLEY

RING SUPPORT

WELDED

TIN-CAN DUST CAP

BOTTOM VIEW

½" ROD

7/16" NUT

WASHERS

5/8" NUT

1¼" SQUARE TUBING

BOLT

½" STD. PIPE DRILLED TO 5/8"

COTTER PIN

½" AXLE

10"

3/8" PIPE

5/8" ROD

1¼" ANGLE IRON

3/8" X 1½" FLAT IRON

WELDED

NUT

BENT

½" STD. PIPE

NOTCHED

21" DIA.

CLAMPING PLATE

INTERMITTENT WELDS

AUTO FRONT-WHEEL HUB

7/16" ROD

10°

8" PNEUMATIC TIRE

10" PNEUMATIC TIRE

CUT HERE

5/8" ROD WELDED TO SPINDLE

1½" X 1½" ANGLE IRON

CORN-BINDER KNIFE 2 REQ'D (LEFT-SIDE KNIVES)

CASTLE NUTS PINNED

CONTINUOUS WELD

⅛" X 1¼" FLAT IRON

2 EXPLODED VIEW ▼

12" DIA. #10-GA. SHEET-STEEL DISK

furnish mounting surfaces for the handle and the rear-wheel sleeve bearing. The cutter assembly consists of a cut-down spindle and hub from the front wheel of an auto. A short piece of rod is welded to the spindle and threaded for a castle nut. This rod also serves as a shaft for the driven pulley, center detail. As shown in the lower left-hand detail, the cutter blades are made from two corn-binder knives and are bolted to a 12-in. disk of No. 10-ga. sheet metal. After these parts are completed, the disk is bolted to the spindle, the hub is bolted to the guard and a V-belt pulley and tin-can dust cap are fitted for a trial assembly. The parts should turn freely and be in line, Fig. 1.

The front-wheel assembly, which consists of an adjustable arm, a clamping plate that bolts to the auto hub, and a fork, are illustrated in the right-hand center detail of Fig. 2. The height of the arm, and consequently the height of the cutting blades from the grass, is adjusted by means of a J-bolt and sleeve that fit between the two sides of the arm. In addition, the arm furnishes a means of lateral adjustment so the wheel can be set to either side of the cutting path. The rear wheels ride on an axle that turns in a pipe-sleeve bearing welded to the platform angle iron. When slotting holes for the engine mounting, notice that these holes are off center and at an angle so the centers on the driving and driven pulleys will line up correctly. To complete the mower, form the handle and brace of ½-in. rigid electrical conduit.

Garden Lounging Chair Has Barrel-Stave Seat

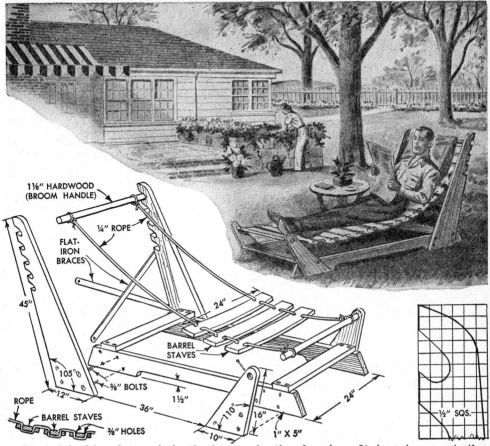

1⅛" HARDWOOD (BROOM HANDLE)

¼" ROPE

FLAT-IRON BRACES

45"

24"

BARREL STAVES

105°

⅜" BOLTS

1½"

ROPE

12"

36"

BARREL STAVES

⅜" HOLES

110°

16"

10"

1" X 5"

24"

½" SQS.

A good-looking lawn chair that's as comfortable as it is easy to build, is made by suspending a barrel-stave seat from a wooden frame. The notches in the back uprights permit the seat to be adjusted to suit the individual requirements of the user. The chair is constructed as shown in the drawing, ¾-in. pine or similar wood being suitable for the frame. The squared pattern will aid in cutting the notches accurately. After sawing the barrel staves to length, drill ⅜-in. holes near each end and string staves 1 in. apart on 2 lengths ¼-in. manila rope.

Multiple Lawn Sprinkler on Rollers Moved Without Damaging Sod

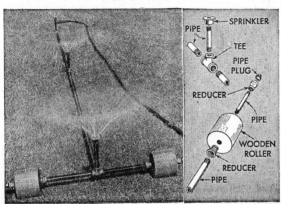

SPRINKLER

PIPE

TEE

PIPE PLUG

REDUCER

PIPE

WOODEN ROLLER

REDUCER

PIPE

This multiple lawn sprinkler permits the watering of large areas at one time. The unit is assembled from pieces of pipe and standard fittings, and the rollers are turned from wooden blocks. Outlets are spaced at intervals along the length of pipe so that the spray will cover the largest possible area. Any of the various types of stationary and rotary sprinkler heads or spray nozzles may be attached to the outlets. The rollers are held on the axles by pipe reducers and a pipe plug is inserted in the end of each outside reducer. Assemble all fittings with pipe compound.

Attention to WINDOWS

¹⁄₁₆" STEEL PLATE IN SLOT

NAILS ①

¹⁄₃₂" RABBET

UPPER SASH ②

STOPS

BEVEL CUTS

SILL ③

GROOVE ⅜" DEEP

⅛" FELT ④

Although often neglected, windows need attention just as frequently as the rest of your home if they are to last and keep out rain and cold air. If a sash frame has rotted at the lower corner so that the tenon is weakened or has broken, it can be repaired as indicated in Fig. 1. To do this, remove the sash and make a diagonal saw cut as deeply as possible at the corner. Then draw the parts together tightly with clamps and insert a triangular piece of sheet metal in the saw cut and nail it in place, cutting the projecting ends off flush with the wood. Fig. 2 shows how to repair a loose, rattling sash. Remove the two outer stop strips and replace them with new ones, making them about ¹⁄₃₂ in. wider than the originals. Rabbet one face of each strip so that it will fit the groove in the window frame. Then place the strips with the offset face next to the sash frame and drive them in place. Another way of tightening loose sash and also of weatherstripping them is to cement narrow strips of thin felt to their sides where they contact the stop strips. Put the felt on the inner sides of the sash where it is less likely to get wet. Still another method is to use a few thumbtacks instead of felt. This latter method prevents rattling, but does not seal the windows against drafts. Moisture collecting in the corners formed where the inner and outer window-stop strips meet the sill often is a cause of rotting at these points. The damage can be avoided by cutting a short bevel across the inside corner of each strip as shown in Fig. 3, so that water can drain away quickly. If you have noticed cold air coming in around the check rail of an old window, this can be prevented by cutting a groove about ⅜ in. deep in the rail of the upper sash and inserting a strip of felt in the groove, as in Fig. 4. The felt should project about ⅛ in. from the groove. When the window is closed and locked, the felt strip will prevent any leakage of air or rattling at this point. A combination of this felt strip and those in Fig. 2 will make any window airtight, but still movable.

Putty Colored before Applying Eliminates Painting

When reglazing a window sash and time is a factor, you can save yourself the job of painting the putty later by coloring it before applying. If the window trim is white, simply add a little white lead or paint and knead it into the putty until the mixture is uniform in color and workable.

PUTTY MIXED WITH PAINT

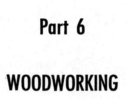

Part 6

WOODWORKING

KNOW WOOD *for* BETTER

3—Steam bending is easy with:
(a) Mahogany   (c) Birch
(b) White Pine   (d) White Oak

1—This arch will last. It is:
(a) Hard Maple   (c) Redwood
(b) White Pine   (d) Red Gum

2—The end grain shows this wood has been:
(a) Slash-sawed   (c) Flat-cut
(b) Quarter-sawed   (d) Plain-sawed

4—Careful! This wood splits:
(a) Beech   (c) Sycamore
(b) Ash   (d) Poplar

5—Excellent for white inlays:
(a) White Pine   (c) Holly
(b) Poplar   (d) Prima Vera

6—This mallet head is one of the hardest woods. It is:
(a) Harewood   (c) Cocobola
(b) Chestnut   (d) Amaranth

ANSWERS:
1—(c)
2—(b)
3—(d)
4—(a)
5—(c)
6—(c)
7—(c)
8—(a)
9—(a)
10—(b)
11—(b)

7—This shutter will be very durable against all kinds of weather:
(a) Hickory   (c) Cypress
(b) Spruce   (d) Basswood

8—It's easy to see this is:
(a) Bird's-eye Maple   (c) Flake Figure
(b) Sycamore Burl   (d) Feather Crotch

9—Excellent for boat planking:
(a) Mahogany   (c) Fir
(b) Ash   (d) Red Oak

Do You Know Your WOODS?
TRY THIS SIMPLE CRAFT QUIZ

10—Best wood for paint:
(a) Orientalwood   (c) Maple
(b) White Pine   (d) Lacewood

11—This is most likely to happen when wood is:
(a) Green   (c) Heartwood
(b) Flat-cut   (d) Edge-grain

CRAFTING

KNOWING wood not only adds to the enjoyment of crafting but also helps in making any project a success. Naturally, the crafter is chiefly interested in how the wood will look when finished, but other important features should not be neglected.

Stability: "Will it stay put?" is an important consideration in all forms of woodcrafting. All woods shrink in seasoning, which causes distortion or warp, the four principal types being shown in Fig. 4. Some woods warp more than others, as indicated in Table No. 1, and can be made more stable by proper use. The common method of testing a board for warp is shown in Fig. 1. Sticks placed at either end of the board reveal cup and also show any twist or wind. The top edge of one stick should be light and the other dark to provide maximum vision. Just what makes a board warp is often illustrated by means of a fan made from a strip of thin paper about 6 in. wide by 2 ft. long. Brush marks are drawn across the fan to represent boards sawed from a tree, Fig. 3. Shrinkage in wood always occurs along the annual rings, so that if the fan is cut on either side, it will immediately shrink just like a split log would do. What happens to the original straight boards is shown by the

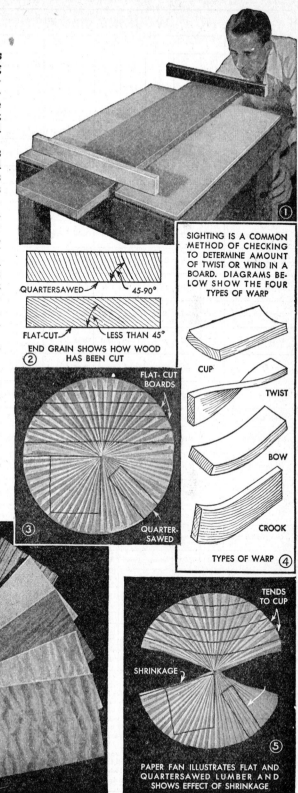

QUARTERSAWED — 45-90°

FLAT-CUT — LESS THAN 45°

END GRAIN SHOWS HOW WOOD HAS BEEN CUT ②

FLAT-CUT BOARDS

③ QUARTER-SAWED

SIGHTING IS A COMMON METHOD OF CHECKING TO DETERMINE AMOUNT OF TWIST OR WIND IN A BOARD. DIAGRAMS BELOW SHOW THE FOUR TYPES OF WARP

CUP

TWIST

BOW

CROOK

TYPES OF WARP ④

TENDS TO CUP

SHRINKAGE

⑤

PAPER FAN ILLUSTRATES FLAT AND QUARTERSAWED LUMBER AND SHOWS EFFECT OF SHRINKAGE

⑥

Table No. 1 — WORKING PROPERTIES OF COMMON WOODS

Name of Wood	Weight Per Cubic Foot (1)	Hardness	Strength (2)	Stability (3)	Gluing	Nailing (4)	Steam Bending	Planing and Jointing (5)	Turning (6)	Sanding (7)	Shaping	Mortising (8)	Remarks
Ash	35	Med.	Med.	Best	Fair	Good	Good	Good 10-25	Fair	Best 2/0	Best	Fair	Tough—Hard to work with hand tools
Basswood	24	Soft	Weak	Good	Best	Best	Poor	Good 20-30	Poor	Poor 4/0	Poor	Fair	Excellent for toys, drafting boards, corestock
Beech	39	Hard	Med.	Poor	Poor	Poor	Good	Fair 10-20	Fair	Good 4/0	Fair	Best	Not durable outside. Hard on tools because of mineral deposits in cells
Birch	40	Hard	Strong	Good	Fair	Poor	Good	Good 15-20	Good	Fair 4/0	Best	Best	Excellent for furniture, turning, dowels, handles
Butternut	25	Soft	Weak	Best	Good	Fair	Poor	Good 10-25	Good	Fair 4/0	Fair	Fair	Furniture—Perfect for walnut imitation
Cherry	36	Med.	Med.	Good	Best	Fair	Poor	Best 10-25	Best	Best 4/0	Best	Best	Furniture, boat trim, novelties
Chestnut	27	Soft	Weak	Best	Best	Good	Fair	Good 15-20	Best	Best 3/0	Good	Good	Stains badly in contact with wet iron. Very dusty in all machining operations
Cottonwood	27	Soft	Weak	Fair	Best	Best	Poor	Poor 5-20	Poor	Poor 4/0	Poor	Fair	Excellent for boxes and other nailing jobs. Wears very well for a soft wood
Cypress	29	Soft	Med.	Good	Fair	Fair	Poor	Good 15-25	Poor	Fair 2/0	Poor	Poor	Tends to splinter. Most durable of American woods for outdoor and soil exposure
Elm (Southern)	34	Med.	Med.	Poor	Fair	Best	Good	Poor 15-20	Poor	Good 2/0	Poor	Good	Very durable under paint. A good furniture wood despite difficulties in machining
Gum (Red)	33	Med.	Med.	Poor	Best	Good	Fair	Fair 10-20	Best	Fair 4/0	Fair	Fair	One of the most used furniture woods for imitations of walnut and mahogany
Hickory	42	Hard	Strong	Good	Good	Poor	Good	Good 10-25	Good	Best 2/0	Fair	Best	Excellent for furniture and long a favorite for steam bending, tool handles, wheels
Magnolia	30	Soft	Weak	Fair	Best	Best	Best	Good 5-15	Fair	Good 4/0	Good	Poor	Excellent for steam bending, although little used as such. Often marketed as poplar
Mahogany	35	Med.	Med.	Best	Best	Good	Poor	Good 5-25	Best	Good 4/0	Best	Best	One of the best furniture woods
Mahogany (Phil.)	33	Med.	Med.	Best	Best	Good	Poor	Good 5-25	Good	Poor 3/0	Fair	Fair	Generally coarser and softer than true mahogany. Furniture, boat planking, trim
(9) Maple (Hard)	41	Hard	Strong	Good	Fair	Poor	Fair	Fair 15-20	Good	Good 4/0	Best	Best	Fine furniture, flooring, turnings, bowling pins. One of the best hardwoods
Maple (Soft)	31	Med.	Med.	Fair	Good	Fair	Fair	Poor 10-15	Fair	Good 4/0	Fair	Poor	Same uses as hard maple but an inferior wood. Difficult to machine smooth
Oak (Red)	39	Hard	Strong	Best	Good	Good	Best	Best 10-25	Good	Best 2/0	Fair	Best	Substitute for white oak in cheaper work
Oak (White)	40	Hard	Strong	Best	Good	Good	Best	Best 10-20	Good	Best 2/0	Good	Best	Interior trim, floors, furniture. One of the most used American woods
Pine (White)	25	Soft	Weak	Good	Best	Best	Poor	Good 10-25	Good	Fair 2/0	Good	Fair	Best all around soft wood. Excellent for paint
Pine (Yellow)	38	Hard	Strong	Fair	Fair	Poor	Poor	Good 10-25	Poor	Fair 2/0	Good	Good	Main uses—House construction, trim, floors
Poplar	29	Soft	Weak	Good	Best	Best	Fair	Good 5-20	Good	Poor 4/0	Poor	Fair	Excellent for carvings, toys, corestock
Redwood	29	Soft	Med.	Best	Best	Good	Poor	Good 10-25	Fair	Poor 2/0	Good	Poor	Excellent for outdoor furniture, window sills, etc.
Sycamore	35	Med.	Med.	Poor	Good	Best	Poor	Poor 5-15	Good	Poor 3/0	Poor	Best	Interior trim, furniture. Difficult to machine, but excellent appearance
Walnut	36	Med.	Strong	Best	Best	Fair	Good	Good 15-20	Best	Best 4/0	Good	Best	Has every good feature for furniture and cabinet work

NOTES

Data in this chart is largely from extensive tests made by U. S. Forest Products Laboratory, with some additions.

1. Pounds per cubic foot, dry. All woods vary in weight, even in the same tree from trunk to top. A variation of 10% over or under average should be allowed.
2. Composite strength value. Woods rated weak are strong enough for all average work.
3. Rated on unrestrained warp. Most woods are quite stable if properly seasoned and cared for.
4. Rated on ability to take nails near end without splitting.
5. All flat grain stock, shallow cut. Rating is average from runs at 15, 20 and 25-degree cutting angles. Bottom figure is best knife angle for smooth cutting.
6. Rated on smooth cutting and ability to hold detail. Not much difference between best and good.
7. Rated on freedom from fuzz. Bottom figure is coarsest abrasive grit which can be used without scratching.
8. Rated on smoothness of cut. Work speed decreases with hardness of wood and this factor might be of more importance than smoothness in production work.
9. Sugar, white or hard maple. Should be distinguished from silver, red, big-leaf or soft maple, which is an inferior machining wood although often marketed simply as "maple."

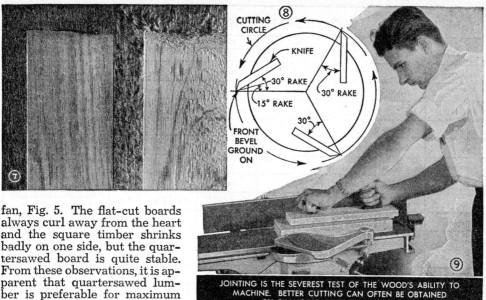

JOINTING IS THE SEVEREST TEST OF THE WOOD'S ABILITY TO MACHINE. BETTER CUTTING CAN OFTEN BE OBTAINED BY CHANGING RAKE ANGLE OF KNIVES

fan, Fig. 5. The flat-cut boards always curl away from the heart and the square timber shrinks badly on one side, but the quartersawed board is quite stable. From these observations, it is apparent that quartersawed lumber is preferable for maximum stability. Also, if the board is cupped, it is certain that the rounded side is the heart side. Fig. 2 shows how the end grain indicates the type of sawing. Quartersawed lumber also is known as radial-cut, edge-grain, rift-grain and comb-grain. Flat-cut lumber is variously named slash-grain, bastard-grain, plain-sawed and tangential cut.

The right side: When using flat-cut lumber, keep the heart side toward the outside surface of the work. Then, if the board does cup, it will show rounded on the face, which is much better than a hollow and much stronger structurally. An exception is painted wood used outdoors. Paint holds better on the bark side and there is less danger of the grain shelling out.

Moisture content: Wood for furniture will be stable if the moisture content is from 6 to 8 percent. This is obtained automatically if the wood is stored for three or four weeks in the same atmosphere at which it will be used. Lumber from commercial dry kilns has a moisture content of about 8 percent. Lumber air-dried outdoors will have a moisture content of about 20 percent, and should not be used for furniture until it has seasoned three or four weeks indoors. Sometimes it is a good idea to check the moisture content of wood before using it. Weigh a small sample exactly and then put it in the kitchen oven. Check the weight at intervals until the wood ceases to lose weight. Ascertain the weight difference and divide by the bone dry weight to get the moisture content. For example, if the test piece weighs 10 oz. at the start and 8 oz. oven dry, the difference is 2 oz., representing moisture, or 25 per-

cent moisture content. The test can be done in a half hour by splitting the sample into thin strips to hasten drying.

Machining: Some woods machine much better than others. Note in Fig. 7 how walnut takes a smooth jointer cut, while soft maple is very rough. Suitability of various woods for machining is indicated in Table No. 1. Jointing, Fig. 9, is the most important test. Other than the wood itself, the method of machining affects the finished work. This can be observed in jointing, where much better work often can be done by changing the rake angle of the knives. Most small jointers have the knives fixed at about 30 degrees rake. This is excellent for knife efficiency, but the sharp angle tends to tear the grain of many woods. For production work in these woods it is advisable to reduce the rake angle by using shims or grinding a front bevel as shown in Fig. 8. Other useful characteristics of woods are given in the table. The "hardness" column lists woods according to whether they are physically hard or soft. Generally, the botanist's classification of hardwoods (broad-leaved trees) indicates a physically hard wood, but there are several exceptions, including such hardwoods as basswood, poplar, cottonwood and aspen, all of which are quite soft. Exceptions in reverse also will be found. Yellow pine, for example, although botanically a softwood (coniferous or needle-leaved trees), is actually harder than many hardwoods. If the wood is hard, it is always heavy without exception; if the wood is hard, it generally is strong.

Table No. 2 — WOODS-FINISHING DATA

Note: NGR = Non-Grain-Raising (Applies to stain)

	Natural Color	Usual Grain Figure	Stain Type (1)	Stain Color	Filler Wt. (2)	Filler Color	Bleach	Paint	Natural Finish	Remarks
Alder (Red)	Pink to Brown	Plain or Figured	Wiping or Water	Red or Brown	None		Yes	Yes	Yes	Principal hardwood of Pacific coast. Like red gum
Amaranth (Purpleheart)	Purple	Mild Stripe or Mottle	None		None or 6	Match Wood	No	No	Yes. Pref.	Usually finished natural to retain purple color
Ash (U.S.A.)	White to Brown	Plain or Fiddleback	Any	Any	15	White or Brown	Yes	Yes. Fill First	Yes	White filler used for frosted finish (3)
Basswood	Cream	Very Mild	NGR	Red or Brown	None		Not Nec.	Yes	No	Fuzzy grain. Usually muddy under oil stain
Birch	Cream	Mild	Any	Walnut or Mahogany	8	Natural or Brown	Yes	Yes. Interior	Yes	Used extensively for walnut and mahogany
Butternut	Heart: Amber Sap: Cream	Like Walnut	Water	Walnut or Oak	14	Medium Brown	Yes	No	Yes	Good for amber walnut without bleaching
Cedar (Aromatic Red)	Heart: Red Sap: Cream	Knotty	None		None		No	No	Yes. Pref.	Red wiping stain can be used to blend sap wood
Cherry	Red to Brown	Good	Water	Red or Black	6-8	Red to Black	No	No	Yes	Takes excellent finish. Good for brown mahogany
Chestnut	Gray-Brown	Heavy Grain	Oil or Wiping	Red or Brown	15	Red or Brown	No	Yes	Yes	Large pores. Good for novelty finishes (3)
Cypress	Heart: Brown Sap: Cream	Plain or Figured	Water, Oil or Wiping	Red or Brown	None		No	Yes (6)	Yes	Good for sand blast (4) If water stained, see (5)
Ebony	Dark Brown to Black	Plain or Stripe	NGR	Dark Red or Brown	None or 3	Brown or Black	No	No	Yes	Oily. Gaboon ebony is blackest
Elm (Southern)	Brown to Cream	Heavy Grain	Water	Red or Brown	12	Dark Brown	No	Yes	Yes	Cross-grained. Sometimes hard to get even color
Fir (Douglas)	Cream to Red	Plain or Wild	Wiping or Oil	Brown	None		No	Yes (7)	No	Good for sand blast (4) Not pleasing stained
Gum (Red)	Heart: Br. Red Sap: Cream	Plain or Figured	Any	Red or Brown	None or 3	Match Wood	Yes	Yes	Yes	Most used wood for walnut and mahogany imitations
Hickory	White to Cream	Usually Straight	Water	Red or Brown	15	Brown	Yes	No	Yes	Good walnut or mahogany —blond finishes
Holly	Silver White	Mild	Water	Amber	None		Not Nec.	Yes	Yes	One of the whitest woods. Usually finished natural
Magnolia or Poplar	White to Yellow	Mild	Oil or Water	Red or Brown	None		No	Yes	No	Usually painted. Makes fair satinwood imitation
Lacewood (Silky Oak)	Medium Brown	Flake	Water	Oak or Lt. Walnut	12	Dark Brown	Fairly Well	No	Yes	Excellent cabinet wood. Very decorative
Mahogany	Brown to Red-Brown	Stripe	Water	Red or Brown	12	Red to Black	Yes	No	Yes	Best known cabinet wood. Excellent for finish
Mahogany (Philippine)	Brown to Red-Brown	Stripe	Water or Wiping	Red or Brown	18	Red to Black	Yes	No	Yes	NGR stain preferable to minimize grain-raising
Maple	Cream	Varied	Water and Wiping	Maple	None		Yes	No	Yes	Use NGR stain and tone with wiping stain after sealer
Oak (English Brown)	Deep Brown	Plain, Flake or Swirl	NGR	Brown	15	Brown to Black	Yes	No	Yes	One of the best cabinet woods. Also "Pollard Oak"
Oak (Red)	Red-Brown	Plain or Flake	NGR	Green Toner (8)	15	Brown	Yes	Yes	No	Bad grain-raising with water stain, hence NGR stain preferable. Good for novelty finishes (3)
Oak (White)	White to Light Brown	Plain or Flake	NGR	Brown	15	Brown	Yes	Yes	Yes	
Orientalwood	Light Brown	Stripe Crossfire	Water	Amber or Brown	12	Brown	No	No	Yes	Good walnut effects
Pine (White)	White to Cream	Mild	Water (5) or Oil	Brown Only	None		No	Yes	No	Best for painting
Prima Vera	Yellow-White	Stripe Crossfire	Water	Amber	12	Natural or Dark	Yes	No	Yes	Also "White Mahogany". Excellent "blond" color
Redwood	Red	Mild St. Grain	Red only for toning		None		No	Yes	Yes	Excellent exterior wood. Best painted
Rosewood (Brazil)	Red-Brown	Varied	NGR	Red	15	Dark Red or Black	No	No	Yes	Oily. Wash off with lacquer thinner before staining or finishing
Rosewood (East Indies)	Red-Purple	Stripe	NGR	Dark Red	12	Dark Red	No	No	Yes	
Sapeli	Medium Brown	Stripe	Water	Red or Brown	10	Dark Brown	No	No	Yes	Very similar to striped mahogany
Sycamore	White to Pink	Flake	Water	Amber or Brown	None		Seldom	Yes	Yes	Good for natural finish
Walnut	Heart: Brown Sap: Cream	Varied	Water	Walnut	14	Brown to Black	Yes	No	Yes	Obtainable in all figures
Zebrawood	Tan with Brown Stripe	Heavy Stripe	Water	Light Oak	12	Natural	No	No	Yes	Very pronounced grain. Good for modern effects

NOTES

1. Where water stain is indicated, NGR (non-grain-raising) stain can also be used. "Oil" means penetrating oil stain; "wiping" means wiping oil stain.
2. Pounds of filler paste per gallon of thinner.
3. All coarse-grain woods are good for novelty finishes, using contrasting filler, usually white.
4. Woods with alternate hard and soft streaks can be sand-blasted or burned with torch to cut out soft wood.
5. Water stains take better on resinous woods if wood is first sponged with 4 oz. sal soda and 1 oz. washing soda to gallon of water.
6. Add 1 pt. benzol per gal. of paint for better penetration (primer only).
7. Special sealers available to kill grain.
8. For brown tones, first spray weak green stain to kill red color of wood.

Finishing: Finishing often is the prime characteristic in selecting a cabinet wood. When you have a wood that machines and finishes nicely, then you have a top-notch cabinet wood. Information given in Table No. 2 will help in selecting a wood for finish, and is a fair guide as to how the wood should be finished. Finishing is closely related to the natural beauty of the wood, necessitating some knowledge of grain and "figures" for suitable selections. Figures in wood constitute a whole subject in themselves, and the few samples shown in Figs. 10 to 16 can be taken only as typical examples. Perhaps the best way to become acquainted with figures and also the many different kinds of woods is to purchase a set of wood samples, Fig. 6. A set of fifty samples is an inexpensive and worthwhile investment, and it is surprising how quickly identification and general knowledge of various woods can be learned by "leafing" through such a set. The samples are small wood blocks packaged in a neat box and should be kept in a clean, dry place.

Grading of wood: A knowledge of wood grading is useful. For example, if you want a poplar board for painting, you would order "stained saps," (fifth-grade lumber), and the finished job would be practically as good as if made from "firsts and seconds." Essential grading data is given in Table No. 3. This table is not complete nor absolutely accurate, but it can be taken as a general guide. There are actually ten grades of lumber. Of these, eighth and ninth grade mahogany is the only one of interest to the crafter. This grade comprises wood of firsts and seconds quality but in short lengths. It should be noted in the table that numbered gradings are not comparable between different woods. For example, fifth grade poplar is a much better wood for a paint job than fifth grade chestnut. Grading rules for softwoods are much different than for hardwoods, and the differences should be carefully noted from the table.

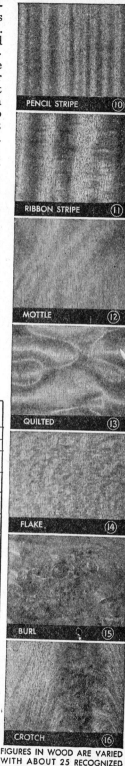

PENCIL STRIPE ⑩

RIBBON STRIPE ⑪

MOTTLE ⑫

QUILTED ⑬

FLAKE ⑭

BURL ⑮

CROTCH ⑯

FIGURES IN WOOD ARE VARIED WITH ABOUT 25 RECOGNIZED STYLES, A FEW OF WHICH ARE SHOWN ABOVE

Table No. 3 GRADING OF WOODS (Condensed)

Hardwoods	General Grading—Indicates let-down in quality					
	1st Grade	2nd Grade	3rd Grade	4th Grade	5th Grade	6th Grade
Ash, Beech, Birch, Hard Maple, Red Alder	Firsts and Seconds		Selects	No. 1 Common	No. 2 Common	Sound Wormy
Cherry	Firsts and Seconds		Selects	No. 1 Common	No. 2 Common	No. 3A Common
Chestnut	Firsts and Seconds		Selects	No. 1 Common	Sound Wormy	No. 2 Common
Cottonwood, Red Gum	Firsts and Seconds		Selects	No. 1 Common	No. 2 Common	No. 3A Common
Elm, Hickory	Firsts and Seconds		No. 1 Common	No. 2 Common	No. 3A Common	No. 3B Common
Mahogany	Firsts and Seconds		Selects	No. 1 Common	No. 2 Common	No. 3 Common
Red Oak, White Oak Locust, Sycamore	Firsts and Seconds		Selects	No. 1 Common	No. 2 Common	Sound Wormy
Poplar	Firsts and Seconds		Saps	Selects	Stained Saps	No. 1 Common
Walnut, Butternut	Firsts and Seconds		Selects	No. 1 Common	No. 2 Common	No. 3 Common

Firsts—About 91% clear both sides.   Selects—90% clear one side.
Seconds—About 83% clear both sides.   No. 1 Common—About 75% clear face.
Firsts and Seconds—Best commercial   No. 2 Common—About 66% clear face.
  grade. Not less than 20% firsts.   Sound Wormy—No. 1 common but with wormholes.

Softwoods	1st Grade	2nd Grade	3rd Grade	4th Grade	5th Grade	6th Grade
Boards	A Select	B Select	C Select	D Select	No. 1 Common	No. 2 Common
Dimension Stock	No. 1 Common	No. 2 Common	No. 3 Common			

A Select—Clear and suitable for natural finish. B Select—Allows a few small defects but suitable for natural finish. C Select—Allows a few defects which can be covered by paint. D Select—Allows any number of defects, which can be concealed by paint. No. 1 Common—Sound and tight-knotted wood

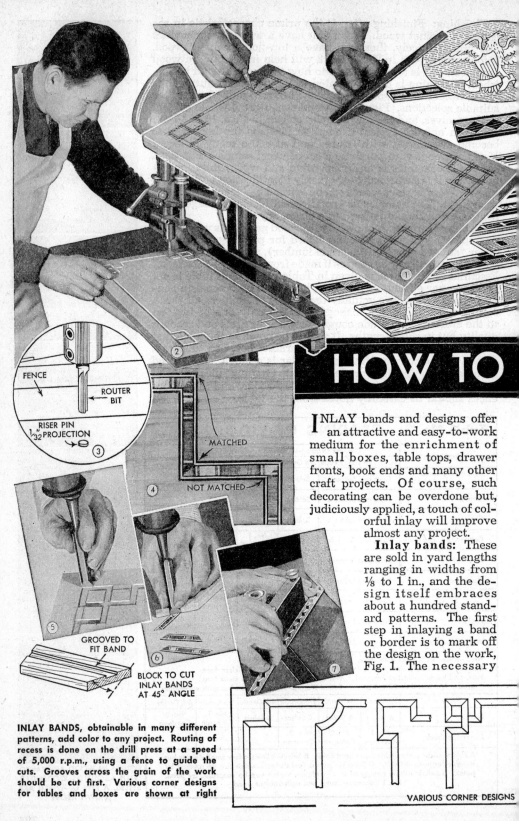

FENCE

ROUTER BIT

RISER PIN
1/32" PROJECTION

③

MATCHED

④

NOT MATCHED

⑤

GROOVED TO FIT BAND

⑥

BLOCK TO CUT INLAY BANDS AT 45° ANGLE

⑦

INLAY bands and designs offer an attractive and easy-to-work medium for the enrichment of small boxes, table tops, drawer fronts, book ends and many other craft projects. Of course, such decorating can be overdone but, judiciously applied, a touch of colorful inlay will improve almost any project.

Inlay bands: These are sold in yard lengths ranging in widths from ⅛ to 1 in., and the design itself embraces about a hundred standard patterns. The first step in inlaying a band or border is to mark off the design on the work, Fig. 1. The necessary

INLAY BANDS, obtainable in many different patterns, add color to any project. Routing of recess is done on the drill press at a speed of 5,000 r.p.m., using a fence to guide the cuts. Grooves across the grain of the work should be cut first. Various corner designs for tables and boxes are shown at right

VARIOUS CORNER DESIGNS

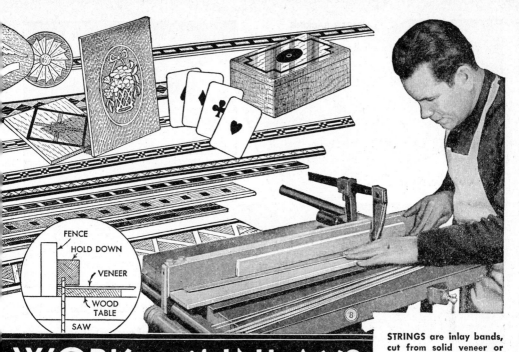

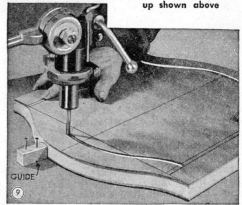

WORK *with* INLAYS

recessing then is done with a single or double-flute router bit of the same diameter as the width of the band. Cuts across the grain should be run in first, after which with-the-grain cuts at the same fence setting can be made, Fig. 2. This method of working will avoid tearing the wood at the end of the cut. The depth of the recess should be a little less than the thickness of the inlay band. If the work is slightly warped, it is advisable to work over a riser pin, as shown in Fig. 3, to assure a groove of uniform depth. The drill speed should be no less than 5,000 r.p.m. After routing, it is necessary to clean the corners with a sharp chisel as in Fig. 5. The inlay band itself can be cut with chisel and guide block, Fig. 6, or the miters can be rough-cut and then sanded smooth, Fig. 7.

Miter joints should be matched

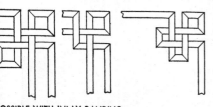

OSSIBLE WITH INLAY BANDING

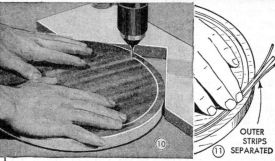

CURVES are routed by using a guide pin or, if the work is circular, a V-block or pivot pin

OUTER STRIPS SEPARATED

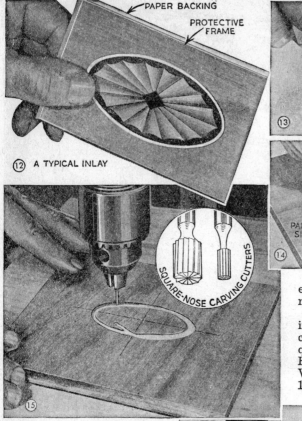

PAPER BACKING

PROTECTIVE FRAME

⑫ A TYPICAL INLAY

⑬

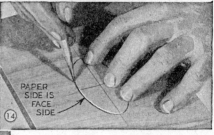

PAPER SIDE IS FACE SIDE

⑭

SQUARE-NOSE CARVING CUTTERS

⑮

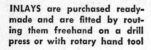

INLAYS are purchased ready-made and are fitted by routing them freehand on a drill press or with rotary hand tool

(see Fig. 4). If you use the chisel method of cutting, trimming to the exact miter line, perfect matching, Fig. 4, will be obtained by simply turning one of the pieces over. If the miter is not correct, it should be sanded down until the design comes to the proper repeat position for matching. Some borders permit mismatching; others expose a mismatch like the proverbial sore thumb.

Strings: Strings are inlay bands cut from solid veneer, celluloid or thin plastic. The method of cutting shown in Fig. 8 permits ripping of strings as narrow as $\frac{1}{16}$ in. with perfect accuracy. The application is the same as for ornamental banding. Another method of making strings is to use veneer of a thickness

equal to the width of the banding required.

Banding of curves: The average inlay banding will take moderate curves. Cutting the recess requires a pin guide as shown in Fig. 9 or, if the work is circular, a V-shaped guide or pivot pin, Fig. 10. Curves should not be attempted with banding over $\frac{5}{16}$ in. wide. Fitting on abrupt turns is easier if the banding is heated. If this does not turn the trick, the banding can be wetted to permit peeling the outer strips free as in Fig. 11. In this condition, the various separated strips will slide past each other, permitting abrupt turns.

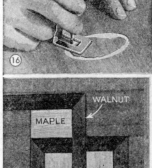

⑯

WALNUT

MAPLE

⑰

SOLID CORNERS, built up from lumber stock, have many advantages in production work. The design is completed with veneer strings

⑱

312

Inlays: This word in itself indicates a built-up pattern design as shown in Fig. 12. The design is surrounded with a protecting veneer frame, and the whole thing is backed with paper, the paper side being the face side. Bandsaw around the design and then trim to the joint line with a knife, as in Fig. 13. Using the inlay as a pattern, mark around it onto the work, Fig. 14. Note that the paper side is up. Cut the recess freehand, using a square-nose carving cutter mounted in a drill press, Fig. 15, or a rotary hand tool, Fig. 16. The carving cutter does not

⑲

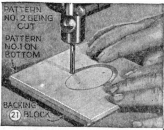

PATTERN NO. 2 BEING CUT
PATTERN NO. 1 ON BOTTOM
INLAY
BACKING BLOCK
⑳ PATTERN NO. 1 BEING SANDED
㉑ BLOCK

DOUBLE PATTERNS provide a good working method of inlaying the same design in production work, such as the box shown above

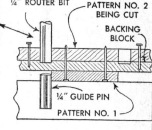

¼″ ROUTER BIT
PATTERN NO. 2 BEING CUT
BACKING BLOCK
¼″ GUIDE PIN
PATTERN NO. 1

Fit inlay on 3/16-in. plywood and saw; then sand pattern, taking off a little of the inlay to assure pattern of exact size

Fit pattern on underside of backing block and rout pattern No. 2, using ¼-in. router bit and ¼-in. guide pin. Rout in 2 bites

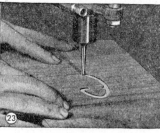

㉒ ¾″ GUIDE PIN
㉓

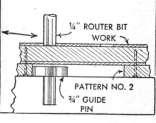

¼″ ROUTER BIT
WORK
PATTERN NO. 2
¾″ GUIDE PIN

Center pattern No. 2 on underside of work. Be sure face side is up. Fit ¾-in. guide pin. Do not change setup of router bit

Rout the recess, cutting to a depth a little less than thickness of inlay. This part is easy since pattern supplies positive control

kick like a single or double-flute router bit, and it is quite simple to trim the recess exactly to the pencil line. Freehand cutting of this kind is recommended for all jobs where a single inlay is to be fitted; other methods using patterns are best for production work, as will be described later.

Solid corners: A type of inlay border using a solid built-up corner is illustrated in Fig. 17. The work is built up in a thickness of about 1 in., which, when ripped on

㉔

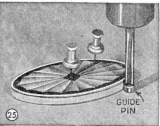

㉕ GUIDE PIN

Leave pattern in place and rout out freehand the wood in center of recess. Go around the outside again to assure a full cut

Other inlays of same pattern are shaved to exact size by using pattern No. 1 with ¼-in. guide pin and ¼-in. router bit

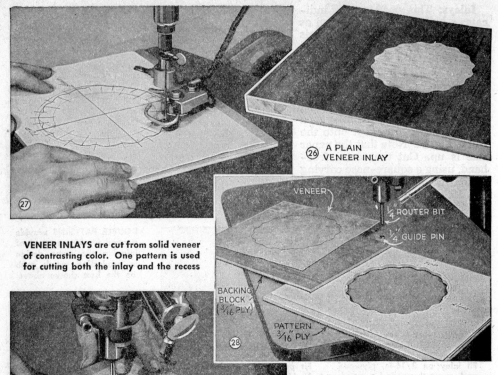

VENEER INLAYS are cut from solid veneer of contrasting color. One pattern is used for cutting both the inlay and the recess

VENEER

¼ ROUTER BIT

¼ GUIDE PIN

BACKING BLOCK (³⁄₁₆" PLY)

(28)

PATTERN ³⁄₁₆" PLY

(27)

(29)

the band saw, Fig. 18, supplies several corner pieces. Joining strips are plain veneer, ripped to the required width.

Double patterns: This method is useful when the same stock design is to be inlaid several times, such as production work on a box like the one shown in Fig. 19. Start by sawing and sanding a pattern of the same size as the inlay, Fig. 20. Follow the successive operations as described in the captions of Figs. 20 to 25. A ¼-in. double-flute router bit is used in these operations and is the best size for average work. Two guide pins are used, one being the same diameter as the router bit; the other, three times the diameter of the bit, less about .005 in. These should be turned from metal and must be exact. The fitting hole in the table must be exactly under the router bit

and a tight fit for the pins. Keep in mind which side of each pattern is the face and work accordingly. In the popular oval designs, it is not at once apparent that the design has a right and left side. This feature is at once apparent when working an inlay like the inlay letter B shown in Fig. 30. Work all symmetrical designs the same way.

Veneer inlays: Single or production work on plain veneer inlays, Fig. 26, is best done with a pattern, the pattern serving as a guide for both inlay and recess. With slight variations, this is the same as the system already described. The pattern is scrollsawed as in Fig. 27, using a fine blade to get a smooth, regular outline. No particular dimensions need be followed, except it should be remembered that the inlay will be smaller than the pattern by the size of the router bit. Fig. 28 shows the setup for cutting the veneer, using ¼-in. router bit and ¼-in. guide pin. Fig. 29 shows the veneer being cut. The pattern must be kept tight against the pin to avoid cutting the veneer undersize. As a visual guide, it is good practice to center and mark the design with pencil on the veneer before starting the routing operation. After the veneer inlay has been cut, the same pattern is fitted on the underside of the work, and the recess is cut, using the same

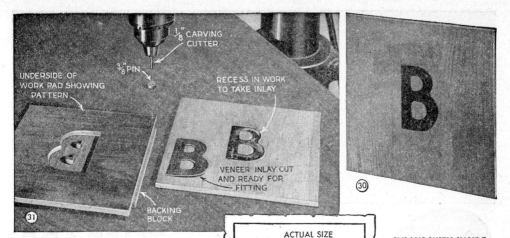

UNDERSIDE OF WORK PAD SHOWING PATTERN

¼" CARVING CUTTER

³⁄₈" PIN

RECESS IN WORK TO TAKE INLAY

VENEER INLAY CUT AND READY FOR FITTING

BACKING BLOCK

㉛

㉚

ACTUAL SIZE OF INLAY

⅛"

EDGES OF PATTERN

㉜ PAPER PATTERN

INLAYS WITH INSIDE CUTS are worked with a single pattern. The work is limited by the size of the inside cuts which cannot be smaller than about ½ in. For single pieces, use the freehand method of cutting

router bit but with the ¾-in. minus guide pin. Cutting the recess is the simpler of the two operations since the pattern in this case supplies a positive guide so that overcutting is impossible. Go around the work twice to make sure that you are out to the full limits of the pattern.

Inside cuts: These, such as the letter B, Fig. 30, are worked the same as solid veneer inlays except that the pattern is a bit more complicated. The design should be drawn actual size, after which the actual lines of the pattern are set off outside the inlay, Fig. 32. The setup recommended is the ⅛-in. router bit. This requires a ⅛-in. guide pin for cutting the inlay, and a ⅜-in. (minus) pin for cutting the recess. Fig. 31 shows the work finished and the pattern turned over. It will be apparent that the size of the work is limited by the inside cuts, which must be large enough to permit taking-off and still leave wood enough for handling and mounting. Do not destroy the paper design when doing work of this kind since it will be needed in properly positioning the inside parts of the pattern. Obviously, this method is useful only for production work; if the job is a single piece it can be inlaid much quicker by using the freehand method of cutting the recess.

Finishing: Use cold resin or hot glue for mounting, applying glue to recess only. Avoid using any kind of glue which stains. Banding will usually stick without clamping; inlay designs should be clamped under a board with paper between. Allow the glue to dry thoroughly, then sand the inlay flush, finishing with no coarser than 4/0 paper. The best finish is French polish. The fastest and clearest finish is clear lacquer or varnish, about three coats, without filler. If filler is used, it should be natural. If a very dark filler is used, the inlay

must be protected with masking tape or by giving it a coat of shellac. If this is not done, the inlay will pick up some color from the filler and lose brilliancy. However, some types of inlays, such as Holly banding or other close-grain wood, will wipe clean with just the right amount of contrast. The use of stain on the ground work should be avoided. This positively requires masking the inlay and even then there is danger of the stain striking into the edges of the inlay and spoiling the effect.

Scored Line Aids in Sanding Work on a Disk Sander

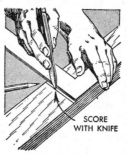

SCORE WITH KNIFE

Sanding work accurately to line on a disk sander is easy if you follow a stunt used by pattern makers. First the line of cut (sanding line) is scored with the point of a knife, after which a chisel-edge pencil is run in the score to make it readily visible. The scoring establishes a definite parting line to which you can sand more accurately than is possible when sanding to a pencil line.

Cutting THREADS

By Sam Brown

THREADS in wood have a wide application, and the job of cutting them is quite simple. A lathe with a lead screw is almost a necessity, but work can be done with hand-screw boxes and by hand chasing.

Woods to use: Proper selection of wood is important. Excellent woods for this purpose are white birch, hard maple, beech, persimmon, apple, cherry, ironwood, hickory and dogwood. Walnut and mahogany rate second choice because their coarse-grain structure tears slightly. However both are workable. Among imported hardwoods there are many, such as lemonwood, ebony, cocobola, lignum vitae, etc., all so tough they can be turned with an ordinary threading tool. For most work the logical choice is white (paper) birch or hard maple, both common domestic hardwoods. A distinction should be made be-

② TANGENT CUTTER CUTS COMPLETE THREAD IN ONE PASS

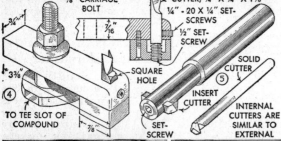

⅜" CARRIAGE BOLT

CUTTER, ¼" X ¼" X 1⅛"

¼" - 20 X ¼" SET-SCREWS

⁷⁄₁₆"

½" SET-SCREW

SOLID CUTTER

SQUARE HOLE

⑤ INSERT CUTTER

INTERNAL CUTTERS ARE SIMILAR TO EXTERNAL

④ TO TEE SLOT OF COMPOUND

3⅜"

⅞"

SET-SCREW

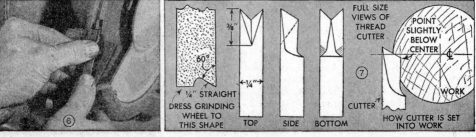

⑥

⅜"

60°

¼" STRAIGHT
DRESS GRINDING
WHEEL TO
THIS SHAPE

←¼"→

TOP   SIDE   BOTTOM

FULL SIZE
VIEWS OF
THREAD
CUTTER

⑦

CUTTER

POINT
SLIGHTLY
BELOW
CENTER

WORK

HOW CUTTER IS SET
INTO WORK

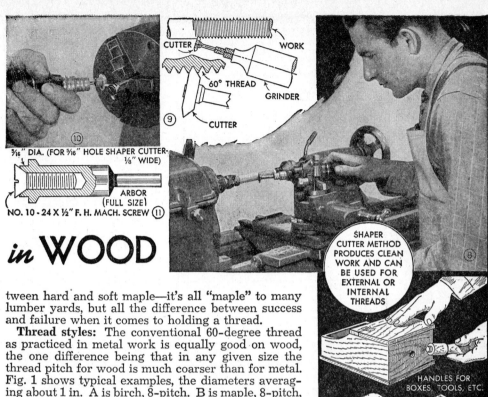

⁵⁄₁₆″ DIA. (FOR ⁵⁄₁₆″ HOLE SHAPER CUTTER-⅛″ WIDE)

ARBOR (FULL SIZE)

NO. 10 - 24 X ½″ F. H. MACH. SCREW ⑪

CUTTER   WORK

60° THREAD

GRINDER

⑨   CUTTER

⑩

SHAPER CUTTER METHOD PRODUCES CLEAN WORK AND CAN BE USED FOR EXTERNAL OR INTERNAL THREADS

HANDLES FOR BOXES, TOOLS, ETC.

LATHE CHUCKS FOR THREADING DIRECT ON SPINDLE NOSE

BED LEGS

SCREW-TOP BOXES

A FEW OF THE MANY APPLICATIONS OF WOOD THREADS IN CRAFT AND CABINET WORK

SPIRAL THREADS FOR LAMP STEMS

ADJUSTABLE CANDLE STAND AND ASH TRAY

SPLIT

MOLDINGS AND HANDLES

in WOOD

tween hard and soft maple—it's all "maple" to many lumber yards, but all the difference between success and failure when it comes to holding a thread.

Thread styles: The conventional 60-degree thread as practiced in metal work is equally good on wood, the one difference being that in any given size the thread pitch for wood is much coarser than for metal. Fig. 1 shows typical examples, the diameters averaging about 1 in. A is birch, 8-pitch. B is maple, 8-pitch, but a double thread as differing from A. C is cherry, 4-pitch, and D is lemonwood, 4-pitch. E is walnut, 4-pitch, with flats somewhat wider than normal in order to eliminate grain chipping as much as possible. F is a 4-pitch spiral thread, excellent for decorative use and subject to very little chipping. G is birch, 4-pitch, cut with a screw box.

Tangent cutter: The tangent cutter shown in Figs. 2 and 3 is the best for cutting V-threads. It cuts a clean thread as coarse as 4-pitch in one pass. The cutter is V-shaped and can be compared to twin thin, sharp chisels standing on end. It is held in a special holder, Fig. 4, and is presented to the work in a tangent position, Fig. 7. The same style cutter for internal threads is of similar shape as can be seen by comparing Figs. 4 and 5. If you grind the external cutter first you will have no trouble with the internal. The cutter is made from ¼-in. high-speed steel. It is necessary to use a 60-degree edged wheel or shape this same angle on a square-edge wheel as shown in Fig. 7. Fig. 6 shows how the blank is held against the wheel to cut the vee, which is the most important part of the grind. In use, set the cutter for a full depth-of-thread bite, and run the lathe between 50 and 100 r.p.m. If desired, the cut can be made in two passes. "Hairline" feeding should not be practiced, since this cutter needs a definite "bite" to do good work.

Shaper method: The shaper or milling method of thread cutting is pictured in Figs. 8 to 11 inclusive. The hand grinder or tool-post grinder used should be angled slightly to the axis of the work so that the tool will be in the clear, Fig. 9, the cutter being ground so that it will cut a 60-degree thread with grinder in

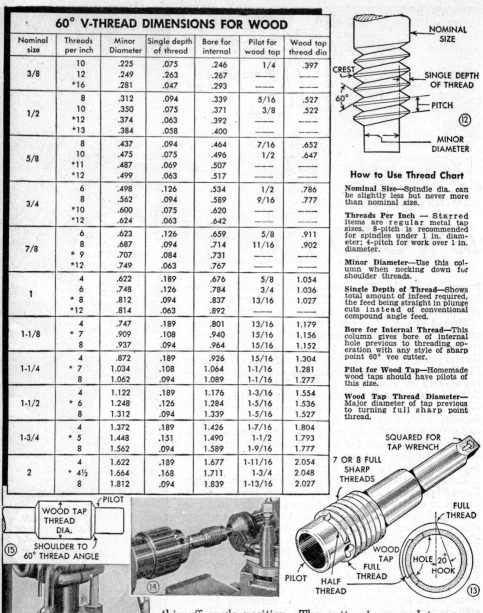

60° V-THREAD DIMENSIONS FOR WOOD

Nominal size	Threads per inch	Minor Diameter	Single depth of thread	Bore for internal	Pilot for wood tap	Wood tap thread dia
3/8	10	.225	.075	.246	1/4	.397
	12	.249	.263	.267	----	----
	*16	.281	.047	.293	----	----
1/2	8	.312	.094	.339	5/16	.527
	10	.350	.075	.371	3/8	.522
	*12	.374	.063	.392	----	----
	*13	.384	.058	.400	----	----
5/8	8	.437	.094	.464	7/16	.652
	10	.475	.075	.496	1/2	.647
	*11	.487	.069	.507	----	----
	*12	.499	.063	.517	----	----
3/4	6	.498	.126	.534	1/2	.786
	8	.562	.094	.589	9/16	.777
	*10	.600	.075	.620	----	----
	*12	.624	.063	.642	----	----
7/8	6	.623	.126	.659	5/8	.911
	8	.687	.094	.714	11/16	.902
	* 9	.707	.084	.731	----	----
	*12	.749	.063	.767	----	----
1	4	.622	.189	.676	5/8	1.054
	6	.748	.126	.784	3/4	1.036
	* 8	.812	.094	.837	13/16	1.027
	*12	.814	.063	.892	----	----
1-1/8	4	.747	.189	.801	13/16	1.179
	* 7	.909	.108	.940	15/16	1.156
	8	.937	.094	.964	15/16	1.152
1-1/4	4	.872	.189	.926	15/16	1.304
	* 7	1.034	.108	1.064	1-1/16	1.281
	8	1.062	.094	1.089	1-1/16	1.277
1-1/2	4	1.122	.189	1.176	1-3/16	1.554
	* 6	1.248	.126	1.284	1-5/16	1.536
	8	1.312	.094	1.339	1-5/16	1.527
1-3/4	4	1.372	.189	1.426	1-7/16	1.804
	* 5	1.448	.151	1.490	1-1/2	1.793
	8	1.562	.094	1.589	1-9/16	1.777
2	4	1.622	.189	1.677	1-11/16	2.054
	* 4½	1.664	.168	1.711	1-3/4	2.048
	8	1.812	.094	1.839	1-13/16	2.027

How to Use Thread Chart

Nominal Size—Spindle dia. can be slightly less but never more than nominal size.

Threads Per Inch — Starred items are regular metal tap sizes. 8-pitch is recommended for spindles under 1 in. diameter; 4-pitch for work over 1 in. diameter.

Minor Diameter—Use this column when necking down for shoulder threads.

Single Depth of Thread—Shows total amount of infeed required, the feed being straight in plunge cuts instead of conventional compound angle feed.

Bore for Internal Thread—This column gives bore of internal hole previous to threading operation with any style of sharp point 60° vee cutter.

Pilot for Wood Tap—Homemade wood taps should have pilots of this size.

Wood Tap Thread Diameter—Major diameter of tap previous to turning full sharp point thread.

this off-angle position. The cutter is ground to proper profile shape while rotating in the lathe, Fig. 10, and then is backed off for clearance on the bench grinder. The tool isn't quite rugged enough to wade right into a 4-pitch thread or even an 8-pitch one. Two methods can be followed. Either set the cutter for a full thread and then turn the lathe slowly by hand with the thread feed engaged, or set the cutter for a light bite and run the lathe at 50 to 100 r.p.m. The direction of the lathe rotation is immaterial. With a heavy-duty tool-post grinder, the full thread can be cut in one pass with the lathe running.

V-thread dimensions: Follow the chart at left of Fig. 12 as a guide to thread sizes, especially when working mating parts. As a general rule, wood threads fit looser than metal threads to compensate for wood shrinkage or swelling.

Internal threads: Internal threads can be cut by tapping or by modifications of the methods already described. A tap for wood is shown in Figs. 13 and 14. It should be turned on the lathe, using any grade of mild tool steel; no hardening is needed. The blank should be shouldered at 60 degrees, Fig. 15, which will automatically establish the half thread needed for the first cutting point. The lathe can be turned by hand to further dress the half thread and remove surplus metal. The actual cutting points are made by spotting flats on the thread by grinding, and then drilling holes through the hollow pilot at a 20-degree hook angle as shown in Figs. 13 and 16. In addition to making the cutting points, the holes provide for chip disposal, hence should be made as large as possible without cutting into the crest of the next thread. The tap is used much the same as a metal tap, boring a hole for the pilot and then turning the tap in with a tap wrench, Fig. 18. As slight tearing of the wood may occur at entry and exit, it is advisable to clamp a block of wood on the work, Fig. 19, if the thread opening is a "show" surface. Wood taps of this kind do excellent work across the grain, but usually fail on end-grain threading. Fortunately, this condition seldom hampers actual work since end-grain threading usually indicates work of a size and shape that can be threaded in the lathe. However, where tapping of the end grain is necessary, a fair thread sometimes can be obtained by using a threaded block, Fig. 20, as a strain-lessening guide for the tap. The operation of cutting an internal thread with a tangent cutter is shown in Fig. 17, the cutter shape being very similar to the external cutter except that the top need not be raked back quite

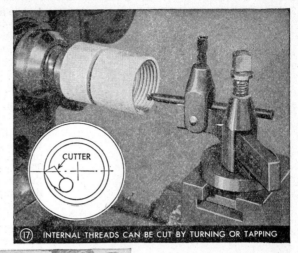

⑰ INTERNAL THREADS CAN BE CUT BY TURNING OR TAPPING

so much. Internally, the tangent cutter works best if the cut is taken in three or four equal bites.

Hand chasing: Lacking a lathe with lead screw, threads can be cut with hand-chasing tools. The metal for chasing tools should be good chisel stock, from ⅛ to ¼ in. thick, depending on the coarseness of the thread. The cutting point is a series of from four to eight teeth ground to the proper shape and back-beveled about 35 degrees, Fig. 21. The simplest grinding method is

㉔ HAND CHASING IS NOT DIFFICULT IF DONE AT SLOW SPEED

SCREW BOXES CUT CLEAN THREADS AND CAN BE USED TO ADVANTAGE WHEN A LATHE IS NOT AVAILABLE

to use an edged wheel, working the profile shape to that of a paper pattern stuck to the chisel and then backing off the heel for clearance. The operation of hand-chasing is shown in Fig. 24. The lathe must run at slow speed, not over 300 r.p.m. At speeds higher than this, it is very difficult to time the travel of the chisel, which obviously must be the same as the thread pitch. The tool should be angled down to bring the cutting points to the work centerline as shown in Figs. 23 and 24, while providing 10 to 15 degrees negative rake. The first bite is made by gently touching the chaser to the work and then moving it along toward the headstock at a speed proportionate to the pitch. This travel is aided by the fact that several teeth are in contact with the work. Repeated passes then are made over the work, concentrating on the deepening of the first five or six threads. It is good practice to have the work ten or twelve threads overlength, so that the starting threads, which may be imperfect, can be cut off. Internal threads are chased with a tool like the one in Fig. 22 in much the same manner, the tool rest being at right angles across the work opening and the chaser projected into the hole.

Screw boxes: Screw boxes in sizes from ¼ to 2 in. diameter spindle thread can be purchased at a nominal cost. The cutting principle of the screw box, Fig. 25, is similar to the tangent cutter as used on the lathe, the only difference being that the cutter turns around the work while being held in the screw-box frame. No particular skill is needed in using a screw box. Use firm pressure in starting the thread, after which the rear portion of the box, which is threaded, provides a positive guide for the following threads.

Cutting threads to a shoulder: One of the most important applications of wood threads is the shouldered thread found in tool handles, screw-top boxes and screw-on furniture legs. A simple practice suitable for some classes of work is to use an insert thread, Fig. 26, instead of cutting the thread in solid wood. The insert thread

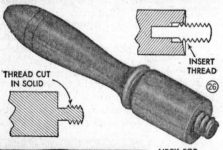

THREAD CUT IN SOLID

INSERT THREAD

NECK FOR CLEARANCE

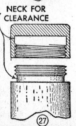

CUTTING THREADS TO A SHOULDER

TOP, FIRST STAGE

FULL SIZE 42°

FULL SIZE

FINISHED SHAPE OF SIDE

60° CUTTER

CUTTER   WORK

SPIRAL CUTTER

OTHER TYPES OF CUTTERS

can be tenoned, but also is quite practical if the whole thread is used as a dowel joint. Working in this manner, a length of thread stock can be made up and cut off as needed for various jobs. Cutting the thread in the solid is required for screw-top boxes, and the operation is quite simple if the thread shoulder is necked down to provide a space for disengagement of the lathe thread feed, as shown in Fig. 27. In making boxes, the lid is turned first, followed by the body, Figs. 28 and 29, after which the lid is screwed to the body for finishing cuts as in Fig. 30.

Other types of cutters: Two additional cutter shapes for use on the lathe are shown in Figs. 31 and 32. Fig. 31 is a good shape for a V-thread scraping tool. This cutter is presented radially to the work like a hand chisel, and should be fed in at the rate of about .010 in. per cut. The V-cut at the top of the cutter is run in last when grinding and can be cut on the corner of a square-edge wheel. The compound angle thus obtained will result in an actual cutting edge of 60 degrees despite the initial grind of 42 degrees. The box thread, Fig. 29, was cut with this cutter, and it is particularly useful for close-in, delicate work. Fig. 32 shows a spiral cutter worked on a ¼-in., high-speed steel blank for a 4-pitch spiral thread. This cutter is used in conventional scraping position, the grind at top providing about 15 degrees negative rake. Because of the rounded surfaces there is no tearing. Properly shaped, the cutter will cut both external and internal threads. These cutters are scrapers and for best results, spindle speed should be as high as nature of work and mechanism of engaging thread feed allows.

Spring Fixture Steadies T-Square on Drawing Board

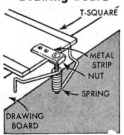

This spring attachment steadies a T-square and is especially helpful when lettering instruments are being used with the square. A piece of metal with edges bent down to accommodate the nut is screwed to the edge of the square and drilled to take a bolt, which is turned in tightly. Spring wire, such as can be obtained from an old spring-type clothespin, shaped as shown and turned onto the bolt, completes the unit. Simply remove the screws to take the unit off the square.

You Can Get at Almost Any Screw with This Multi-Blade Driver

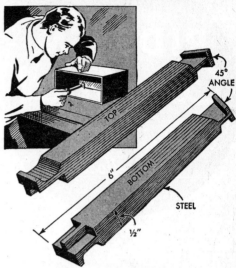

A mechanic who did a lot of assembly work designed this screwdriver, which has a number of blades each ground at a different angle, so that he could get at screws located in places difficult to reach with an ordinary screwdriver. The driver is made from a piece of ½-in. steel 6 in. long. If the angles of some of the blades shown are not suitable to your particular kind of work, they can be ground to suit.

Hasp Screws "Locked" in Place by Using Screen Staples

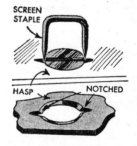

Many door hasps that are fitted with padlock loops have exposed screw heads, which can be unscrewed and the hasp removed, making the lock ineffective. One way to prevent this is to file V-notches in opposite sides of the screw holes in the hasp. Then when the screws are driven in place the slots in their heads are turned to register with the notches, after which screen staples are driven into the wood through the openings filed in the hasp as shown. Once the staples are driven home it is impossible to turn out the screw.

❡ When drilling tubular rivets from metal the rivet will be less apt to spin with the drill if you hold the metal at a 45° angle and drill straight down. The rivet will fall out easily.

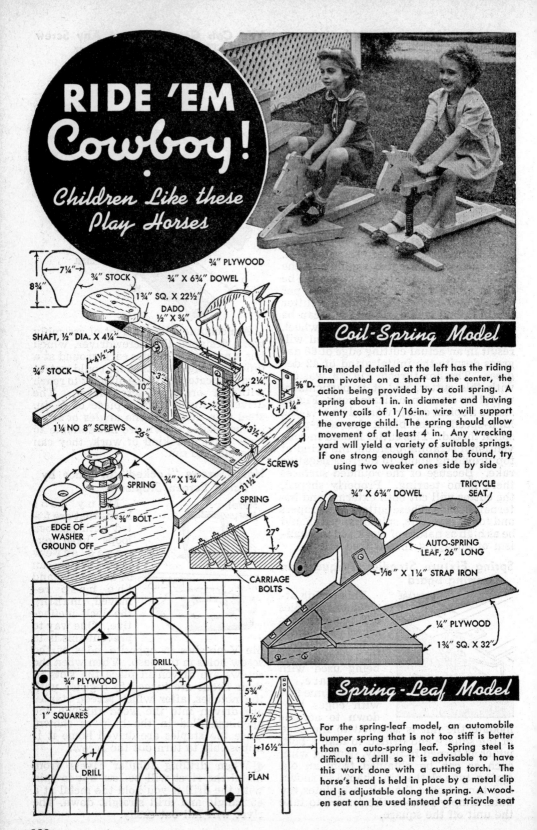

RIDE 'EM Cowboy!
Children Like these Play Horses

7¼"
8¾"

¾" STOCK
¾" X 6¾" DOWEL
¾" PLYWOOD

1¾" SQ. X 22½"
DADO ½" X ¾"

SHAFT, ½" DIA. X 4¼"

¾" STOCK
4½"
3"
10"
1¼ NO 8" SCREWS
26"
7"
2" 2¼"
3/8"D.
1¼"
3½"
21½"
¾" X 1¾"
SCREWS

SPRING
3/8" BOLT
EDGE OF WASHER GROUND OFF

SPRING
27°

CARRIAGE BOLTS

¾" PLYWOOD
1" SQUARES
DRILL
DRILL

5¾"
7½"
16½"
PLAN

¾" X 6¾" DOWEL
TRICYCLE SEAT
AUTO-SPRING LEAF, 26" LONG
1/16" X 1¼" STRAP IRON
¼" PLYWOOD
1¾" SQ. X 32"

Coil-Spring Model

The model detailed at the left has the riding arm pivoted on a shaft at the center, the action being provided by a coil spring. A spring about 1 in. in diameter and having twenty coils of 1/16-in. wire will support the average child. The spring should allow movement of at least 4 in. Any wrecking yard will yield a variety of suitable springs. If one strong enough cannot be found, try using two weaker ones side by side

Spring-Leaf Model

For the spring-leaf model, an automobile bumper spring that is not too stiff is better than an auto-spring leaf. Spring steel is difficult to drill so it is advisable to have this work done with a cutting torch. The horse's head is held in place by a metal clip and is adjustable along the spring. A wooden seat can be used instead of a tricycle seat

Decorative Fittings

IN YOUR CLOSET

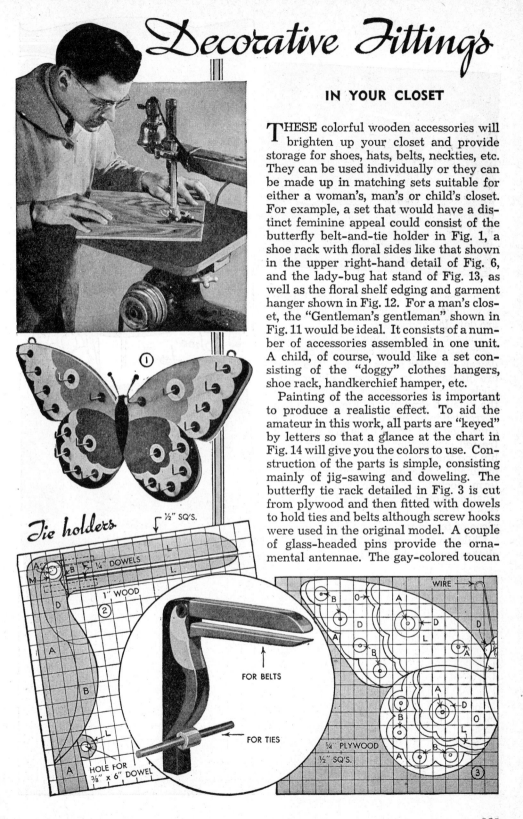

THESE colorful wooden accessories will brighten up your closet and provide storage for shoes, hats, belts, neckties, etc. They can be used individually or they can be made up in matching sets suitable for either a woman's, man's or child's closet. For example, a set that would have a distinct feminine appeal could consist of the butterfly belt-and-tie holder in Fig. 1, a shoe rack with floral sides like that shown in the upper right-hand detail of Fig. 6, and the lady-bug hat stand of Fig. 13, as well as the floral shelf edging and garment hanger shown in Fig. 12. For a man's closet, the "Gentleman's gentleman" shown in Fig. 11 would be ideal. It consists of a number of accessories assembled in one unit. A child, of course, would like a set consisting of the "doggy" clothes hangers, shoe rack, handkerchief hamper, etc.

Painting of the accessories is important to produce a realistic effect. To aid the amateur in this work, all parts are "keyed" by letters so that a glance at the chart in Fig. 14 will give you the colors to use. Construction of the parts is simple, consisting mainly of jig-sawing and doweling. The butterfly tie rack detailed in Fig. 3 is cut from plywood and then fitted with dowels to hold ties and belts although screw hooks were used in the original model. A couple of glass-headed pins provide the ornamental antennae. The gay-colored toucan

Tie holders

½" SQ'S.

¼" DOWELS

1" WOOD

FOR BELTS

FOR TIES

HOLE FOR ⅜" x 6" DOWEL

WIRE

¼" PLYWOOD

½" SQ'S.

tie holder in Fig. 2 has a jig-sawed body to which the two parts of the long beak are doweled and glued.

The shoe holders shown in Figs. 4 and 5 consist of two sides connected by long dowels on which shoes are set. The sides are jig-sawed to represent either fish, birds, animals or flowers as indicated in the detailed drawings of Fig. 6. The fish is grooved to outline the tail and fins. The dove, dog and floral ends are similarly treated, except that the dove's wing, dog's hip and the floral center of the flower are outlined by attaching separate pieces to form pockets in which brushes and small cans of polish are stored. In addition to this, the dog's ear is a removable piece of felt to use as a polishing cloth.

Children will appreciate the "doggy" clothes hangers detailed in Fig. 7. Each

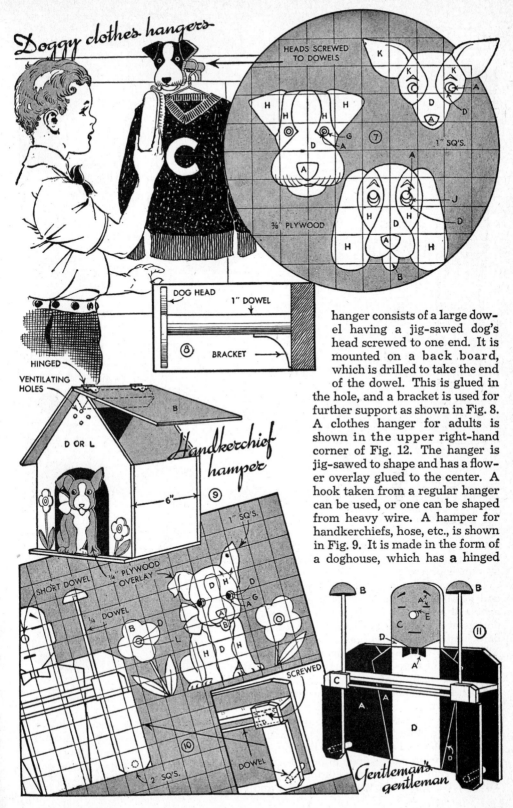

Doggy clothes hangers

HEADS SCREWED TO DOWELS

K

K   K

A

D

D

A

1" SQ'S.

H   H   H

H   H

D

A

G
D
A

⑦

J

H   H

D

A   D

3/8" PLYWOOD

H   H

A

B

DOG HEAD   1" DOWEL

⑧   BRACKET

HINGED
VENTILATING HOLES

B

D OR L

Handkerchief hamper

6"

⑨

SHORT DOWEL   1/4" PLYWOOD OVERLAY   1" SQ'S.

D H H   D
A G
A

1/4 DOWEL

B   D

L

H   D   H

⑩   SCREWED   2' SQ'S.   DOWEL

B   B

A
C   E

D

A

C

A   A

D

D   ⑪

Gentleman's gentleman

hanger consists of a large dowel having a jig-sawed dog's head screwed to one end. It is mounted on a back board, which is drilled to take the end of the dowel. This is glued in the hole, and a bracket is used for further support as shown in Fig. 8. A clothes hanger for adults is shown in the upper right-hand corner of Fig. 12. The hanger is jig-sawed to shape and has a flower overlay glued to the center. A hook taken from a regular hanger can be used, or one can be shaped from heavy wire. A hamper for handkerchiefs, hose, etc., is shown in Fig. 9. It is made in the form of a doghouse, which has a hinged

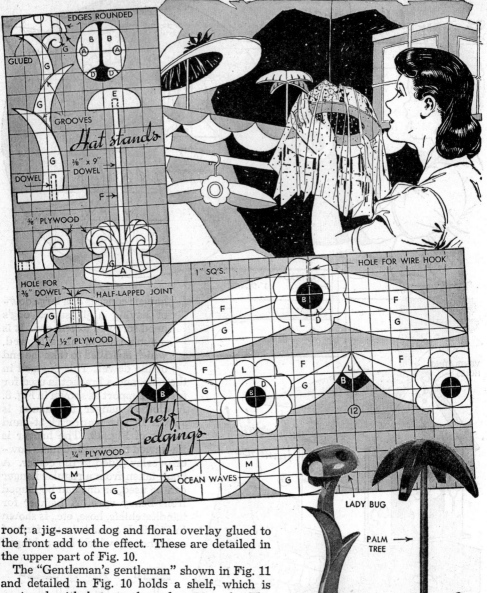

EDGES ROUNDED

GLUED

GROOVES

Hat stands

³⁄₈" × 9" DOWEL

DOWEL

³⁄₈" PLYWOOD

HOLE FOR ³⁄₈" DOWEL

HALF-LAPPED JOINT

½" PLYWOOD

1" SQ'S.

HOLE FOR WIRE HOOK

Shelf edgings

¼" PLYWOOD

OCEAN WAVES

⑫

LADY BUG

PALM TREE

⑬

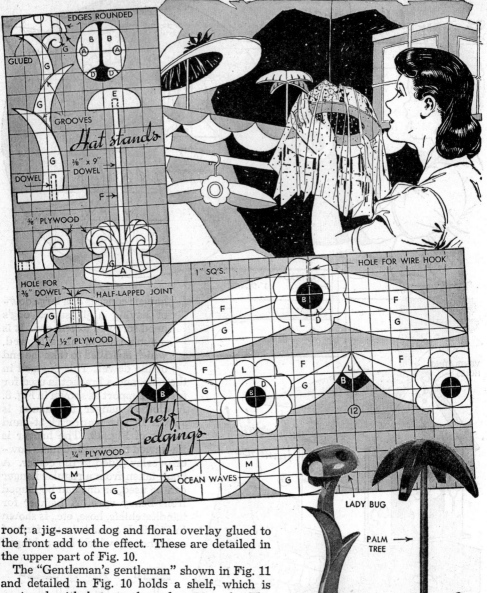

⑭ COLOR KEY

Black · · A	Brown · · H
Red · · · B	Amber · · J
Flesh · · C	Tan · · · K
White · · D	Yellow · · L
Pink · · · E	Blue · · M
Lt. green · F	Silver · · N
Green · · G	Orange · O

roof; a jig-sawed dog and floral overlay glued to the front add to the effect. These are detailed in the upper part of Fig. 10.

The "Gentleman's gentleman" shown in Fig. 11 and detailed in Fig. 10 holds a shelf, which is equipped with hat stands and a tie rack. The dowels at his elbows are convenient for hanging belts, umbrellas and scarves.

Edging to decorate the shelves is shown in the lower part of Fig. 12. It is jig-sawed from thin wood, and can be cut from one long piece, or it can be made in short sections to utilize scrap wood. The hat stands shown in Fig. 13 and detailed in the upper part of Fig. 12 complete the accessories. The one on the right is made in the form of a palm tree. The top is made in two sections and glued together and a dowel forms the trunk, which is glued in the base and top. The stand on the left consists of a standard sawed to represent a plant stalk topped by a large lady bug. The latter is turned or whittled to shape and glued in place.

table to shoulder the hauch, as in Fig. 37. Then make the cheek cuts, as in Fig. 38. In cutting the mortise, tilt the drill table for the hauch, checking by holding the tenon in place against the fence. Make the angle cuts first, as in Fig. 39, then level the table and cut the rest of the mortise.

Door Clamped to Tool Chest to Support It for Planing

Often called to fit doors and windows where he would not have the facilities of his shop, one carpenter avoided the usual difficulty of supporting them on edge for planing by simply clamping the

work to the opened lid of his tool chest. A large C-clamp with blocks placed under the jaws to protect the work surfaces will hold the assembly together.

Spring Catch Holds Drawer Closed

To prevent small children from opening drawers, fit this simple spring catch on one side of each drawer as shown in the detail. This type of catch requires no locking device, does not mar the cabinet in any way and is invisible when the drawer is closed. Bend it from a strip of spring brass and mortise into the drawer side as shown, then attach with small flat-headed screws. As the drawer is closed, the hump bent in one end of the catch bears against the bottom of the drawer runner above.

The spring can be adjusted so that a considerable pull will be required to open the drawer.

Clamp Prevents Pinching of Saw When Cutting Plywood Panels

When cutting a large panel of plywood, the severed edges can be prevented from pinching the saw by using a large paper clamp. After you have sawed into the panel a sufficient distance, the clamp is slipped over the edge of the panel so that it grips the wood on both sides of the saw cut, as shown in the detail.

Honing on Leather Makes Woodworking Tools Keen

An excellent leather hone to get keen edges on woodworking tools can be made from scraps of dry oak-tanned sole leather, obtained from a shoe-repair shop. Cut the pieces roughly to $\frac{5}{8}$ by $2\frac{1}{2}$ in. and assemble enough of them to make up a block 5 to 8 in. long. After the smooth (hair) side has been trimmed or sanded, all surfaces are coated with a good grade of hot hide glue and clamped together under moderate pressure. When the glue has dried, smooth both sides of the block on garnet cloth, scrape the surfaces slightly to remove clinging grit grains and apply several coats of saddle soap to both sides; soak for an hour in neat's-foot oil. One side of the hone should be treated with a cream-thick mixture of finest silicon carbide or aluminum oxide, flour and lard oil, well rubbed in. Leave the other side plain or rub it with jeweler's rouge. Use the hone exactly as you would an oilstone except that you strop the tool from its edge.

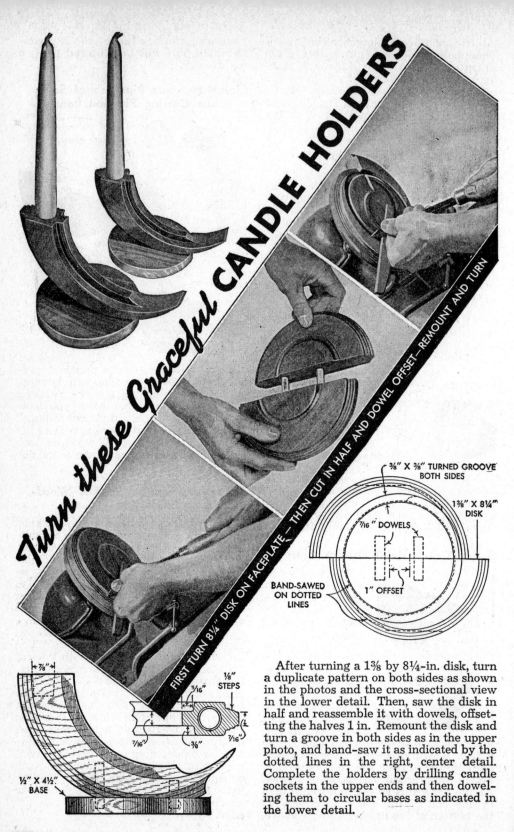

Turn these Graceful CANDLE HOLDERS

FIRST TURN 8¼" DISK ON FACEPLATE — THEN CUT IN HALF AND DOWEL OFFSET— REMOUNT AND TURN

⅜" X ⅜" TURNED GROOVE BOTH SIDES

1⅜" X 8¼" DISK

7/16" DOWELS

1" OFFSET

BAND-SAWED ON DOTTED LINES

⅛" STEPS

5/16"

7⅞"

7/16"   ⅜"   7/16"

½" X 4½" BASE

After turning a 1⅜ by 8¼-in. disk, turn a duplicate pattern on both sides as shown in the photos and the cross-sectional view in the lower detail. Then, saw the disk in half and reassemble it with dowels, offsetting the halves 1 in. Remount the disk and turn a groove in both sides as in the upper photo, and band-saw it as indicated by the dotted lines in the right, center detail. Complete the holders by drilling candle sockets in the upper ends and then doweling them to circular bases as indicated in the lower detail.

Strip Moldings Cut Safely with this Shaper Jig

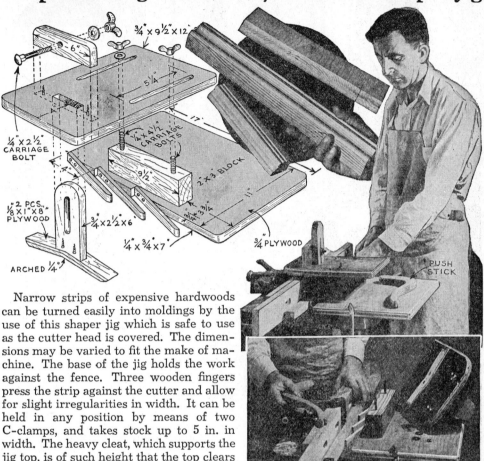

Narrow strips of expensive hardwoods can be turned easily into moldings by the use of this shaper jig which is safe to use as the cutter head is covered. The dimensions may be varied to fit the make of machine. The base of the jig holds the work against the fence. Three wooden fingers press the strip against the cutter and allow for slight irregularities in width. It can be held in any position by means of two C-clamps, and takes stock up to 5 in. in width. The heavy cleat, which supports the jig top, is of such height that the top clears the fence. The top has slots to receive the cleat bolts and to make adjustments. A rectangular hole takes the slotted hold-down slide, and a cleat behind it locks the slide by means of a bolt and wing nut. The wooden spring on the hold-down, added to give positive pressure against the table, is made of two thicknesses of ⅛-in. three-ply hardwood, curved up into the slide arch with two screws. To use the jig, loosen the three clamp bolts and adjust the base with the fingers ¹⁄₁₆ in. less than the strip width, from the fence. Set the top with the hold-down near the fence, and clamp. Then lock the hold-down. Feed the stock from right to left, and if it is not long enough to grasp easily on the far end, for pulling through in finishing the cut, use a long push stick.

Length of Endless Belt Measured Accurately by Rolling It on the Floor

One of the best methods of measuring an endless belt to find its length is as follows: Place the belt on a floor or other smooth surface. Then mark both the belt and floor. Roll the belt across the floor as indicated by A*1, A*2 and A*3 until the mark comes to the floor again, taking care that there is no slip between the belt and floor as it is rolled. The distance between A*1 and A*3 will be the exact length of the belt.

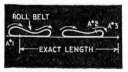

¶Keep a three-minute egg timer near the phone to check long-distance calls; invert it as soon as the connection is made.

Part 1.
LAMINATIONS and SEGMENTS

It's Fun Making BUILT-UP

By Sam Brown

BUILT-UP work has both utilitarian and artistic value in making lamps, boxes and similar turned work, such as those pictured in Fig. 1. The construction permits the use of average-size lumber on large turnings, and the work, if well glued, actually is stronger and more stable in many instances than solid wood. Being built up from many pieces of wood, work of this kind offers countless possibilities for pattern and color effects.

Classes of work: Built-up turnings can be classified in three main groups: Laminated, Segmental, and Post Blocked. Laminated, or bread-and-butter construction, is the simplest. In segment work, the turning ring is made from pie-shaped wedges of wood. Post blocked work features a central stem or post, with various layers of contrasting wood built around it.

Selection of wood: Wood is selected primarily for color value. The table in Fig. 4 gives a typical selection of light, medium and dark woods, scaled in order from lightest to darkest. Two-color pattern effects

Laminations

"BREAD-AND-BUTTER" CONSTRUCTION IS THE SIMPLEST METHOD OF MAKING BUILT-UP TURNINGS

CENTER CUT OUT TO SIMPLIFY TURNING

GRAIN IS CRISS-CROSSED ON ALTERNATE LAYERS

④ **SELECTION OF WOOD FOR COLOR**

	WOOD	COLOR	HARDNESS
LIGHT	HOLLY	VERY WHITE	MEDIUM
	BASSWOOD	VERY WHITE	VERY SOFT
	MAPLE	WHITE-PINK	HARD
	WHITE PINE	WHITE-YELLOW	SOFT
	BIRCH	WHITE-BROWN	MEDIUM
MEDIUM	GREENHEART	GREEN-YELLOW	HARD
	BUTTERNUT	LIGHT BROWN	SOFT
	MAHOGANY	RED-BROWN	MEDIUM
	RED GUM	RED-BROWN	MEDIUM
DARK	CHERRY	RED	MEDIUM
	WALNUT	BROWN	MEDIUM
	PURPLEHEART	PURPLE	MEDIUM
	ROSEWOOD (EAST INDIAN)	PURPLE-BROWN	HARD

TURNINGS

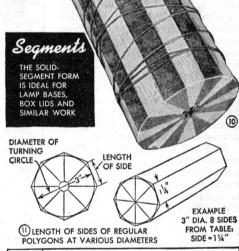

DIAMETER OF TURNING CIRCLE

LENGTH OF SIDE

3″

1¼″

EXAMPLE
3″ DIA. 8 SIDES
FROM TABLE:
SIDE = 1¼″

⑪ LENGTH OF SIDES OF REGULAR POLYGONS AT VARIOUS DIAMETERS

usually are based on a white wood, such as holly or maple, combined with dark wood, such as gum, cherry or walnut. The wood should be of even color, sound, free from sap or mineral streaks. Hardness also should be considered, as best results are obtained when the woods used in the build-up possess approximately the same degree of hardness. Any hardwood will turn well alongside any medium hardwood. Any medium wood can be combined with any softwood. Softwoods should not be combined with hardwoods except in the case of thin spacers for laminated work. In all other instances the use of softwood alongside hardwood will cause the work to turn out-of-round, and sanding will develop positive flats.

Laminations: The build-up for this type of work is made from solid rings or squares of wood glued together face to face, as shown in Fig. 2. The only principle that need be observed is that the grain in alternate layers should be at right angles, Figs. 3 and 5, in order to equalize shrinkage-and-warping strains. The grain of thin ⅛-in. spacers need not be considered. Turning time is saved if the individual rings are cut to the approximate circular shape inside and out before assembly.

Segments: Many novel pattern effects are possible by using segments, some of the most complex build-ups being quite simple. Fig. 6 is a typical example. While this appears to be a complex bit of work, it really is easy to do. First, a cylinder is made up from maple and walnut wedges,

DIA. OF TURNING CIRCLE	NUMBER OF SIDES								
	8	10	12	14	16	18	20	24	30
2	27/32	21/32	17/32	15/32	13/32	3/8	5/16	9/32	7/32
2½	1 1/16	13/16	11/16	19/32	1/2	15/32	13/32	11/32	9/32
3	1¼	1	13/16	11/16	19/32	17/32	1/2	13/32	5/32
3½	1 15/32	1 5/32	15/16	13/16	23/32	5/8	9/16	15/32	3/8
4	1 21/32	1 5/16	1 3/32	15/16	13/16	23/32	21/32	17/32	7/16
4½	1 7/8	1 15/32	1 7/32	1 1/32	29/32	13/16	23/32	19/32	1/2
5	2 3/32	1 5/8	1 11/32	1 5/32	1	29/32	13/16	21/32	17/32
6	2½	1 15/16	1 5/8	1 3/8	1 7/32	1 1/16	31/32	25/32	21/32
7	2 29/32	2 9/32	1 7/8	1 19/32	1 13/32	1¼	1 1/8	15/16	3/4
8	3 5/16	2 5/8	2 5/32	1 27/32	1 19/32	1 7/16	1 9/16	1 1/16	27/32
9	3 3/4	2 15/16	2 7/16	2 1/16	1 13/16	1 19/32	1 7/16	1 3/16	31/32
10	4 5/32	3¼	2 11/16	2 9/32	2	1 25/32	1 19/32	1 5/16	1 1/16
12	5	3 29/32	3 7/32	2 3/4	2 13/32	2 1/8	1 29/32	1 19/32	1 9/32
14	5 13/16	4 9/16	3 3/4	3 7/32	2 25/32	2 15/32	2 7/32	1 27/32	1½
16	6 5/8	5 7/32	4 9/32	3 21/32	3 3/16	2 27/32	2 17/32	2 1/8	1 11/16

SIDES	MITER GAGE AND TILT-TABLE ANGLES FOR REGULAR POLYGONS	
	MITER GAGE	TILT TABLE
6	60	30
8	67.5	22.5
10	72	18
12	75	15
14	77.15	12.85
16	78.75	11.25
18	80	10
20	81	9
24	82.5	7.5
30	84	6

TURN WORK OVER FOR ALTERNATE CUTS

MITERED SEGMENTS (TAKE MITER-GAGE ANGLE FROM TABLE)

BEVEL RIPS

BEVELED SEGMENTS (TAKE TILT ANGLE FROM TABLE)

CROSSCUT

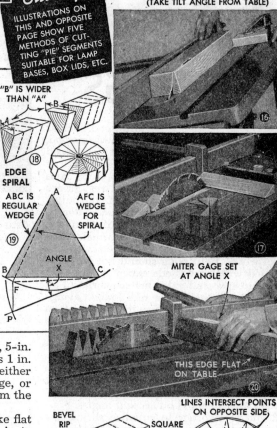

Cutting

ILLUSTRATIONS ON THIS AND OPPOSITE PAGE SHOW FIVE METHODS OF CUTTING "PIE" SEGMENTS SUITABLE FOR LAMP BASES, BOX LIDS, ETC.

"B" IS WIDER THAN "A"

EDGE SPIRAL

ABC IS REGULAR WEDGE

AFC IS WEDGE FOR SPIRAL

ANGLE X

MITER GAGE SET AT ANGLE X

THIS EDGE FLAT ON TABLE

BEVEL RIP

SQUARE CROSS CUTS

LINES INTERSECT POINTS ON OPPOSITE SIDE

CROSS CUT

TWO WAYS OF CUTTING RIGHT-ANGLE SEGMENTS

FACE SPIRAL— ALL REGULAR POLYGONS CAN BE BUILT FROM RIGHT-ANGLE TRIANGLES

as shown in Fig. 10. The cylinder is rough-turned, Fig. 8, and slices are then cut off on the circular saw, as shown in Fig. 9. These slices can be stacked and glued in checkerboard style, as indicated in the foreground, Fig. 9, or succeeding rings can be rotated slightly to break the joints, as illustrated by the lamp, Fig. 6. The plain cylinder itself produces the effect shown by the box in Fig. 7. In all cases, the cylinder can be turned to any desired shape without affecting the arrangement of the pattern.

Size and cutting angles: First consideration in making a built-up segment turning must be given to the size and shape of the wedges required. The matter of size is simplified by the table in Fig. 11. Just run down the left-hand column until you find the required diameter of work, and then, under the number of sides, you will find the side length in inches of the segments. For example, 5-in. diameter, 16 sides, requires segments 1 in. wide. The matter of cutting requires either swinging the circular-saw miter gage, or tilting the table, taking the angle from the table in Fig. 13.

Cutting: The simplest way to make flat assemblies for bases and box lids is to swing the miter gage, Fig. 12. Fig. 14 shows how the pie-shape wedges are cut without waste by alternately turning the work over. Segments cut in this manner will show the grain running round-and-round. Following out the example, (5-in. diameter, 16 sides) the base of each segment will measure 1 in., and the direct miter-gage setting will be at 78¾ degrees (from table, Fig. 13). The width of the work will, of course, be one-half the diameter (2½ in.). Another

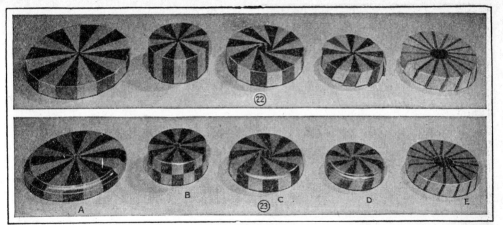

way of cutting is to bevel-rip the work at the required angle, taking the tilt setting from Fig. 13. Fig. 15 shows this method of cutting. Note in this instance that the grain of the wood runs up-and-down. If wedges are ripped from wide stock in this manner, a stop block should be used as in Fig. 16, to gage the set-over. Fig. 17 shows the long strips being crosscut into shorter lengths.

Spirals: Segment work can be assembled to show a spiral on either the edge or face. The edge spiral, Fig. 18, is cut by using an angular miter-gage setting when cutting off short lengths from a long, bevel-ripped wedge. Fig. 20 shows the operation, a good effect being obtained with a spiral angle of 15 to 25 degrees. Since angle cutting changes the width of the wedge, as can be seen in Fig. 18, the original wedge shape must be altered to suit. The easiest way to determine the size is to make a simple drawing, Fig. 19. Lay out a triangle ABC of the size and shape required for a straight assembly, or cut out a standard wedge and trace around it. Then from point C lay out the spiral angle of from 15 to 25 degrees, as indicated by angle X. With center C and radius CB, strike an arc intersecting the angle line at P. Project P to the circle of the triangle at F. AFC is the size wedge required for the spiral assembly. If you prefer trial-and-error methods instead of the layout, simply rip the wedges about 1/16 in. narrower than normal. In our previous example (5-in. diameter, 16 sides) make the base of the wedge 15/16 in. instead of 1 in. Then, angle a line across the wedge so that the line will be 1 in. long. This angle will be the cutoff line, and the miter gage can be set accordingly. All this is harder to describe than do—you will find it quite sim-

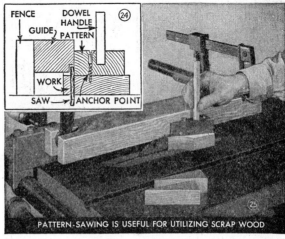

PATTERN-SAWING IS USEFUL FOR UTILIZING SCRAP WOOD

ple when you start doing the actual work.

The face spiral, Fig. 21, shows a spiral design on the face of the work. This spiral is based on right-angle triangles, and all regular polygons can be built from the right-angle triangle. The simplest way to determine the shape is to lay out a full-size circle of the diameter required, dividing this into the number of pieces desired. Erect lines at right angles to the sides of the polygon to arrive at the shape of wedges required. You will notice that the right-angle lines, if projected across the circle, will intersect points on the opposite side, thereby simplifying the layout.

Pattern sawing: Sawing wedges with the use of a pattern can be employed to advantage in utilizing scrap pieces of wood. A pattern of the required wedge is first made up in hardwood and fitted with a handle and anchor points. It can be seen, Figs. 24 and 25, that if the pattern is fixed to a scrap piece of wood, the work can be cut to the same exact shape as the pattern by guiding the pattern along the wooden guide. This technique is much slower than

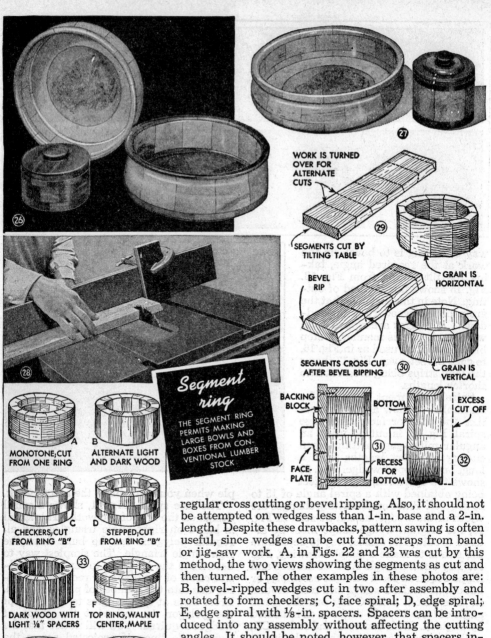

WORK IS TURNED OVER FOR ALTERNATE CUTS

SEGMENTS CUT BY TILTING TABLE

BEVEL RIP

GRAIN IS HORIZONTAL

SEGMENTS CROSS CUT AFTER BEVEL RIPPING

GRAIN IS VERTICAL

BACKING BLOCK

BOTTOM

EXCESS CUT OFF

FACE-PLATE

RECESS FOR BOTTOM

Segment ring

THE SEGMENT RING PERMITS MAKING LARGE BOWLS AND BOXES FROM CONVENTIONAL LUMBER STOCK

A MONOTONE; CUT FROM ONE RING

B ALTERNATE LIGHT AND DARK WOOD

C CHECKERS; CUT FROM RING "B"

D STEPPED; CUT FROM RING "B"

E DARK WOOD WITH LIGHT ⅛" SPACERS

F TOP RING, WALNUT CENTER, MAPLE

G ⅛" SOLID SPACERS BETWEEN RINGS

H SPIRAL IN LIGHT AND DARK WOOD

I LAMINATED FROM RINGS "B" AND "H"

J RIGHT AND LEFT-HAND SPIRALS

regular cross cutting or bevel ripping. Also, it should not be attempted on wedges less than 1-in. base and a 2-in. length. Despite these drawbacks, pattern sawing is often useful, since wedges can be cut from scraps from band or jig-saw work. A, in Figs. 22 and 23 was cut by this method, the two views showing the segments as cut and then turned. The other examples in these photos are: B, bevel-ripped wedges cut in two after assembly and rotated to form checkers; C, face spiral; D, edge spiral; E, edge spiral with ⅛-in. spacers. Spacers can be introduced into any assembly without affecting the cutting angles. It should be noted, however, that spacers increase the size of the work and also increase the size of the opening.

Segment rings: Very often it is desired to make the segment build-up a ring instead of the solid "pie" previously described. In this event the work is cut from flat stock. The cutting angles are the same as before since the segments are simply the outside portion of a full pie-shaped wedge. Segments of this kind usually are cut by tilting the saw table, as shown in Figs. 28 and 29, the grain in the assembly running round-and-round. Also, segments can be cut by straight cross cutting after bevel-ripping, Fig. 30, in which case the grain in the assembly is vertical. The simplest method of turning

PENCIL MARKS

First: Backing block faced and guide lines marked

Second: The segment ring is glued on the backing block

Third: Recess of largest possible inside diameter cut to take bowl bottom

Fourth: Bowl bottom turned to fit recess in segment ring

Fifth: Ring glued to bottom and a ¾-in. ring marked off

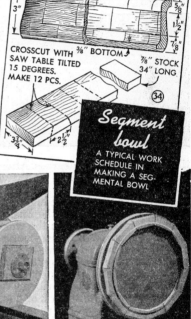

9″ — 3″ — 5/8″ — 1½″ — 7/8″

CROSSCUT WITH SAW TABLE TILTED 15 DEGREES. MAKE 12 PCS.

⅜″ BOTTOM

7/8″ STOCK 34″ LONG

3¾″ — 2½″

(34)

Segment bowl

A TYPICAL WORK SCHEDULE IN MAKING A SEGMENTAL BOWL

Sixth: Work is cut through with saw while on faceplate, lathe being turned off

Seventh: Base segment ring is faced off square; inside is rough-turned if desired

the assembly is to make the work a little longer than required to take the screws from a backing block, Fig. 31. Mounted on this block, the recess for the bottom of the bowl or box can be cut. After fitting the bottom, the work can be rechucked, turned, and the excess material cut off, Fig. 32. Figs. 26 and 27 are examples of segment-ring work, while Fig. 33 shows various ways in which the segment ring can be manipulated to form pattern effects.

Segment bowl: A typical schedule of operations in making a segment bowl is shown by the photos on this page and in Fig. 34, which gives the dimensions of the bowl. The construction style is a three-layer monotone cut from a single 12-piece segment ring. Referring to Table Fig. 11, it can be seen that a 12-side polygon to turn 9 in. diameter should have sides 2⁷⁄₁₆ in. long. Since the exact bowl size is not critical, the segments can be cut a little oversize, 2½ inches. The segments are cut by tilting the saw table, taking the tilt angle from Table Fig. 13, which shows that a 12-side polygon requires a

Eighth: Carefully centered, the segment ring is reglued, being sure to break joints

Ninth: Other rings are cut and glued in the same manner to give the final build-up

The long spiral

SPIRAL-TURNED WORK
CAN BE PRODUCED
FROM STRAIGHT
LUMBER BY USING
THE BUILT-UP METHOD
SHOWN HERE

WORK
DIA.

SET
MITER
GAGE
AT THIS
ANGLE

42

MAXIMUM SPIRAL
IS ABOUT ⅔ DIA.
OF WORK

LENGTH OF WORK

40

41

tilt table setting of 15 degrees. After cutting, the segments are glued up by wrapping with twine or soft wire. The photos and captions take up the schedule at this point and carry it through to the final stages of the build-up, after which the work can be turned to shape. After completing the first step, the segment ring must be centered on the block before gluing it.

The long spiral: Some peculiarities arise when the edge spiral previously described is built up in lengths over 3 or 4 in. Basically the work is the same as the short-edge spiral, the wedge shape being determined in the same manner, Fig. 19. Fig. 36 shows the wedge strips being cut to length at the required spiral angle. Assembly is made by gluing and bradding pairs together, Fig. 38, and then assembling the pairs to form the complete build-up, which gives the rather odd-looking shape shown in Fig. 39. Extra length should be allowed so that the work can be turned without running into the brad fastenings, Figs. 35 and 37. Fig. 40 shows the finished work and Fig. 41 indicates how slices can be cut from the original cylinder and stacked checkerboard style. The long spiral has limitations and works out best with a moderate spiral angle. The maximum angle is about two-thirds the diameter of the turning and can be determined by making a simple drawing of the work, as shown in Fig. 42.

Quick Method of Fitting Paper Accurately in Drawers

Fitting clean paper into drawer bottoms is simplified if the drawer is taken out and inverted. On most drawers the outline of the space to be fitted is apparent on the bottom, so that if the paper is folded to fit this outline, it will fit the drawer exactly. If the paper has a pattern, it must be placed with the pattern down against the bottom of the drawer while being folded so that the pattern side will be up when the paper is in place.

Chopping-bowl COOKIE JAR

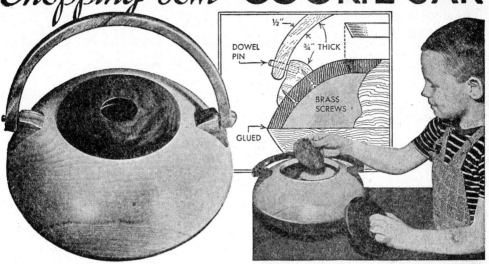

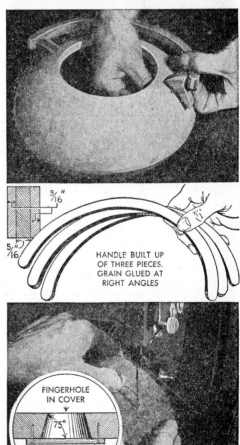

HANDLE BUILT UP OF THREE PIECES. GRAIN GLUED AT RIGHT ANGLES

FINGERHOLE IN COVER

75°

3/16" DISK

TWO maple chopping bowls are used to make this novel cookie jar. About all you have to do is to replace the bottom of one with a cover, and add a handle. Scroll-sawing out the bottom is done with the table tilted 10 degrees to seat a walnut disk which you bevel at the same angle. A good way to cut down the edges of the bowls evenly so that a tight-fitting joint will be had when both are placed together, is to fasten several sheets of sandpaper side by side, to a flat bench top upon which you can rub each bowl back and forth until perfectly flat. Try to sand down each one the same amount so that the two will match flush. In gluing the bowls together, warping can be checked if you place them with the grain at right angles to each other. Watch to see that they do not shift and then weight them with a heavy object until dry. The handle, which can be built up of three separate pieces of solid walnut stock or simply cut from a piece of ¾-in. plywood, is attached to ears of maple which you fasten with screws from the inside. Apply paste wood filler to the walnut parts, let flatten and wipe off across grain. After 24 hrs. give the complete jar two coats of shellac followed by two of wax or varnish. Leave the inside surface of the bowls bare.

❡Large turnings made from solid stock will be more likely to retain their original shape if they are seasoned a few days after rough-turning to approximate shape.

It's Fun Making
BUILT-UP TURNINGS
Part Two

POST-BLOCKING gets its name from the fact that the work is built around a central stem or post. In its artistic form, built-up work of this kind does not differ greatly from conventional post-blocking used to build up wood for large spindle turnings, except that the woods in the build-up are selected for color contrast.

Mechanics of post-blocking: Mechanical operations involved are simple and should be learned by making a planned design before doing any creative work. A good practice piece is the lamp shown in Fig. 43. Dimensions of the project are given in Fig. 49, which also shows how the various layers of wood must be arranged around a central core. The first operation is to make the core. In this instance, the hole through core center for the lamp cord was run in after turning, as shown in Fig. 44. However, if suitable drills are not available, the core should be grooved centrally and glued up in halves to form a square as in Fig. 45. Notice that the groove is stopped short of the end of work to provide solid stock for centering. After the work has been turned, it is a simple matter to drill from the ends into the groove. Fig. 46 shows an optional but worthy point in the build-up. Here the core is centered and

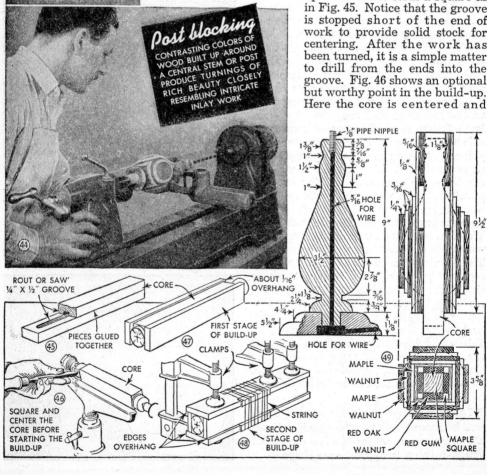

Post blocking
CONTRASTING COLORS OF WOOD BUILT UP AROUND A CENTRAL STEM OR POST PRODUCE TURNINGS OF RICH BEAUTY CLOSELY RESEMBLING INTRICATE INLAY WORK

¼" PIPE NIPPLE

1⅜"
⅜"
⁷⁄₁₆"
1"
⅝"
1½"
1"

⁵⁄₁₆" HOLE FOR WIRE

9"

3½"

2⅞"

3"/16
3¾"

1⅛"

HOLE FOR WIRE

⁵⁄₁₆
1⅛"

⅛"

³⁄₁₆"
¼"

9½"

CORE

ROUT OR SAW ¼" X ½" GROOVE
CORE
ABOUT ¹⁄₁₆" OVERHANG
2¼"
1⅛"
4¾"
5½"
FIRST STAGE OF BUILD-UP
PIECES GLUED TOGETHER
45
CLAMPS
47
CORE
46
SQUARE AND CENTER THE CORE BEFORE STARTING THE BUILD-UP
EDGES OVERHANG
STRING
SECOND STAGE OF BUILD-UP
48

49
MAPLE
WALNUT
MAPLE
WALNUT
RED OAK
WALNUT
RED GUM
MAPLE SQUARE
3⅝"

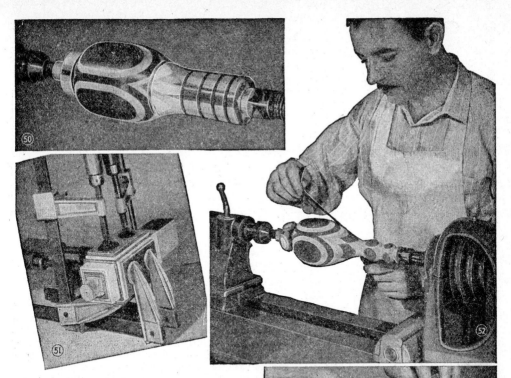

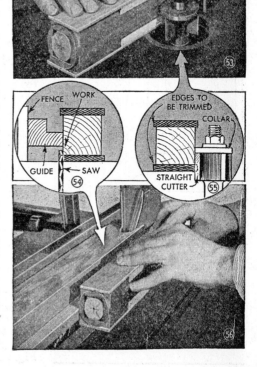

checked carefully before any layers of wood are glued to it. Exact centering of the work is important to avoid a lopsided figure. Fig. 47 shows the first set of blocks glued in place, with the edge slightly overhanging the core. After the glue has dried, the overhangs are dressed off flush to permit addition of the second pair of blocks, Fig. 48. In the same operation, the $\frac{5}{16}$-in. maple squares are tied into openings previously cut along the edges of the wood. After the glue has dried, the edges are again dressed flush to form a level surface for the third pair of blocks, continuing this procedure, a pair of blocks at a time, until the build-up is complete. Exceptions are the two outer layers. Since these do not overlap, they can be glued face to face at any time, and the double blocks can be fitted to all four faces in one gluing operation as shown in Fig. 51.

Throughout the build-up it is permissible to use small brads to hold the blocks in position so they will not slide when clamping pressure is applied. Needless to say, the brads should come in portions of the work well inside the turning. Any kind of glue can be used provided it holds tightly and permits a reasonable length of time to position and clamp the blocks. Turning the complete assembly follows standard practice. Fig. 50 shows sizing cuts run in, while Fig. 52 shows the work being finish-sanded.

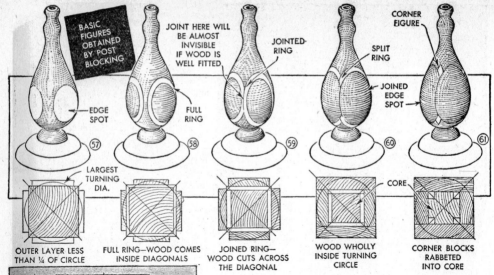

BASIC FIGURES OBTAINED BY POST BLOCKING

EDGE SPOT

JOINT HERE WILL BE ALMOST INVISIBLE IF WOOD IS WELL FITTED

FULL RING

JOINTED· RING

CORNER FIGURE

SPLIT RING

JOINED EDGE SPOT

JOINED EDGE SPOT

⑤⑦ ⑤⑧ ⑤⑨ ⑥⓪ ⑥①

LARGEST TURNING DIA.

CORE

OUTER LAYER LESS THAN ¼ OF CIRCLE

FULL RING—WOOD COMES INSIDE DIAGONALS

JOINED RING— WOOD CUTS ACROSS THE DIAGONAL

WOOD WHOLLY INSIDE TURNING CIRCLE

CORNER BLOCKS RABBETED INTO CORE

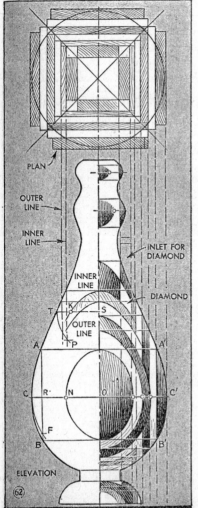

PLAN

OUTER LINE

INNER LINE

INNER LINE

INLET FOR DIAMOND

DIAMOND

OUTER LINE

T K S

A P A'

C R N O C'

F

B B'

ELEVATION

⑥②

LAYOUT FOR POST-BLOCKED TURNING

Dressing overhangs: It will be apparent that dressing the overhanging edges is the principal mechanical operation involved. Two good methods are shown in Figs. 53 to 56 inclusive, one using a shaper and the other a circular saw. The shaper method requires a straight cutter and guide collar of the same diameter. The work is guided along the collar, the cutter trimming the overhang exactly flush. The saw method requires a wood guide clamped to the regular fence. The guide is located exactly flush with face of saw, Fig. 54. When the work is pushed along the guide as in Fig. 56, the overhanging edge is sawed off flush. In each case, trimming should be followed by a very light jointer cut or a hand rub on a sheet of sandpaper over a perfectly flat surface, such as the saw table.

Basic figures: The six basic figures in post-blocking are shown in Figs. 57 to 61 inclusive, each example showing the build-up for a single figure, except Fig. 60 which illustrates both the split ring and joined-edge spot. The rules governing these figures are simple: Edge spots and full rings must come inside the diagonals of the turning square. The joined ring cuts the diagonal, the split ring is wholly inside the largest turning circle and the corner figures lie on the diagonals. Any shape of post-blocked work will show one or more of these basic figures. Projects can be planned to include as many of the basic figures as desired.

Layout for original designs: Creative work requires some sort of advance drawing in order to determine how the build-up will look when turned. This can be very elementary, or complete right down to the finished shape, as shown in Fig. 62. In all cases, start with the contour outline of the project, and above it draw the largest turning diameter and the diagonals of the turning square. The contour and plan are then sliced off layer by layer to form the basic figures. To determine the full shape of any figure, consider the edge spots shown in Fig. 62. The edge blocks cut the contour at points

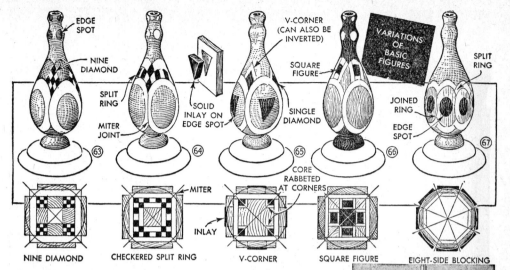

NINE DIAMOND   CHECKERED SPLIT RING   V-CORNER   SQUARE FIGURE   EIGHT-SIDE BLOCKING

A and B, marking the height of the edge spot. To obtain the width, draw line CC across the widest part of the turning. With center O and radius OC, describe an arc cutting line AB at point F. RF, then, is the half width of the edge spot, and is transferred with dividers to line CC, establishing the point N. With the limits of the figure thus set, it is easy to sketch in the approximate shape of the edge spot. Very exact work can be done by drawing additional guide lines across the turning. A second example in Fig. 62 shows the development of the split ring shape. The top limits of the ring will be marked by lines drawn from the plan intersecting the contour of the turning. Now, imagine you want to determine the width on line TS. With dividers at S and radius ST, describe an arc cutting the vertical line at P. Measure from P to TS and set off this dimension from S to establish point K. If you are not familiar with this type of drawing, you will find the layout a bit confusing at first, but actually it is not difficult, especially if you make the sample project first to use as visual evidence.

Variations of basic figures: Figs. 63 to 67 inclusive show variations of basic figures. In Fig. 63, the single diamond of the original design is enlarged and laminated to form a nine diamond. In Fig. 64, the split ring is laminated instead of being solid wood. Fig. 65 illustrates the use of solid inlays and the development of the V-corner. Fig. 66 shows the square figure, and Fig. 67 shows how basic figures look in an eight-side block. In most of these examples the design variation is pictured as being stopped inside the turning instead of running right through. This usually is good practice since intricate corner figures, etc., often show as mere slivers of wood if

LAMP SHOWING SOLID INLAY ON EDGE SLOT, SINGLE DIAMOND AND CHECKERED JOINED RING

EIGHT-SIDED BLOCKING WITH FOUR PIECES OF JOINED RING LAMINATED WALNUT AND MAPLE

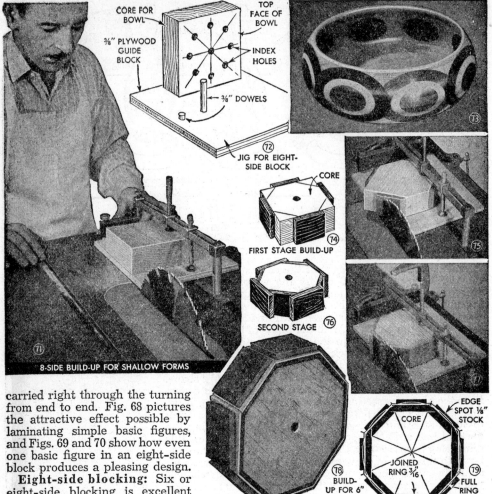

CORE FOR BOWL

³⁄₈" PLYWOOD GUIDE BLOCK

TOP FACE OF BOWL

INDEX HOLES

³⁄₈" DOWELS

72 JIG FOR EIGHT-SIDE BLOCK

73

CORE

74 FIRST STAGE BUILD-UP

75

76 SECOND STAGE

77

71 8-SIDE BUILD-UP FOR SHALLOW FORMS

78 BUILD-UP FOR 6" BOWL

CORE

JOINED RING ³⁄₁₆"

EDGE SPOT ⅛" STOCK

FULL RING ³⁄₃₂" STOCK

79

carried right through the turning from end to end. Fig. 68 pictures the attractive effect possible by laminating simple basic figures, and Figs. 69 and 70 show how even one basic figure in an eight-side block produces a pleasing design.

Eight-side blocking: Six or eight-side blocking is excellent for shallow forms such as bowls or boxes. Fig. 73 is an example of an eight-side block. The shallowness of the project permits a difference in working which is both simple and accurate. Start by cutting the square core a little oversize. Center the work in the lathe and use the dividing head to set off eight holes on the top face of the core, as in Fig. 72. Make a plywood guide block as shown, with dowel pivot and index pin to fit the holes in the work. Now, fit the work on the guide block and fasten this to the circular saw miter gage. Rotate the work four square to trim the core to net size, as shown in Fig. 71. Fit the first set of blocks in place, Fig. 74, then trim the corners of the core as in Fig. 75, which also trims the first set of blocks at the same time. Glue the second set of blocks, Fig. 76, then trim the first set to net thickness, Fig. 77, which also trims the ends of the second set of blocks. Proceed in the same manner until the build-up is

complete as in Fig. 78. Fig. 79 shows a plan of the build-up. It will be noted that the basic figures are the same as for a four-block. Very thin stock must be used to keep the full rings inside the diagonals. Turning follows standard practice, the work being inspected frequently to note how the figure is developing.

Removing Spots From Wallpaper

Almost any grease can be removed from a papered or plastered wall with a paste made by mixing powdered China clay, 2 or 3 oz., with enough carbon tetrachloride to form a thick paste. With a table knife spread a layer of the paste over the spot to be removed, let it dry and then dust it off. Some spots may require a couple of applications.

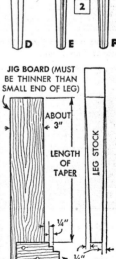

CUTTING TAPERED LEGS

Simple wooden jigs to guide the work make it easy to duplicate tapered legs in quantity with saw, jointer or shaper. Includes straight and spade-foot types

By Sam Brown

CHARACTERISTIC of the Adam and Hepplewhite influence in period-furniture design, the square tapered leg in any of its variations lends itself to mass-production in the home shop by using a few simple jigs. Power tools are required, but the straight-taper leg can be cut completely on just a circular saw. A shaper or jointer is needed to produce the popular spade-foot leg.

Design variations: Various leg styles are pictured in Fig. 2. Style A is a straight taper with a decorative groove at the top and an inlaid or painted band near the bottom. B shows the spade foot commonly used for period pieces, and C is somewhat similar but with the spade rolled into the taper without a break of line. Leg style D is a straight taper on two sides only, a style often used because it represents less work and the slight splayed effect is quite attractive. E is a straight taper with outside corner rounded, very popular for modern furniture, and F shows another edge treatment, with all edges beveled. In period pieces, the legs often are ornately carved, fluted or inlaid on the show faces, but for modern pieces the only decoration in popular use is the banded style pictured at A.

Cutting the straight taper: Whenever practical, the taper should be sawed in preference to jointer and shaper methods. The best

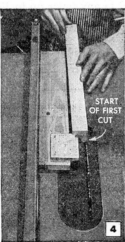

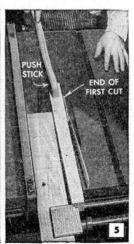

JIG BOARD (MUST BE THINNER THAN SMALL END OF LEG)

ABOUT 3"

LENGTH OF TAPER

LEG STOCK

¼"

¼"

NOTCHED BLOCK

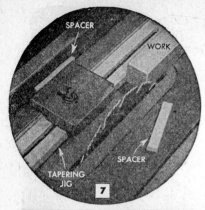

SPACER
WORK
SPACER
TAPERING JIG

7

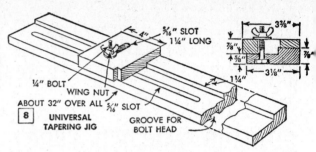

4"
⁵⁄₁₆" SLOT
1¼" LONG
3⅜"
⅞"
⁵⁄₈"
¼" BOLT
WING NUT
ABOUT 32" OVER ALL
⁵⁄₁₆" SLOT
1¼"
3⅛"
⅞"

8   UNIVERSAL
TAPERING JIG
GROOVE FOR
BOLT HEAD

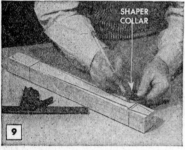

SHAPER COLLAR

9

Draw outline of leg in pencil on adjacent faces and use shaper collar to mark curve

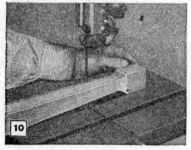

10

To save wear on the cutting edges of the shaper knife, remove waste wood first

STOP

11

Either a jointer or shaper can be used to cut the taper. Infeed table or fence, as the case may be, is offset a distance equal to the amount of taper you desire

blade to use for this is a combination one, hollow ground, sometimes called a planer saw. Such a blade produces an exceptionally smooth cut, requiring only light sanding. Fig. 6 shows a typical straight-taper leg design, calling for a ¼-in. taper on each face on all four sides. Fig. 6 also shows a simple jig which is used in conjunction with a circular saw. The jig board should be as long as the tapered part of the leg, plus 3 or 4 in. to accommodate the notched block. Notice that the depth of the notches in the block must equal the taper, in this case, ¼ in.

How the jig is used: With work dressed to net size and perfectly square, the saw-fence setting is made to equal the combined width of jig board and work, as shown in Fig. 3. Then the work is placed in the first notch of the jig and pushed into the saw, Fig. 4. Note that feed pressure is on the work, not the jig. The end of the cut is shown in Fig. 5. Two adjacent sides are cut with the work in the first notch. Then, without disturbing the fence setting, the two remaining sides are cut with the work in the second notch. To compensate for the waste removed from two sides, retack a block equal to the thickness of the waste so that the work will ride horizontally in cutting each taper. A push stick must be used for feeding near the end of the cut, Fig. 5.

Universal jig: While the jig board is practical, some workers prefer a more permanent device, such as the one shown in Fig. 8. Here, only one notch is used, the sliding block being arranged so that it can be adjusted to any taper up to ½ in. (about 1⅛-in. taper if the cut is made on one side only). This jig is set with spacing blocks placed between the jig and

CUTTING TAPER WITH SPADE FOOT   12

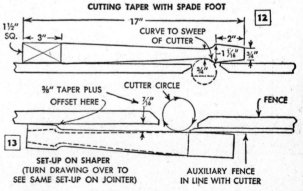

1½"
SQ.
3"
17"
CURVE TO SWEEP
OF CUTTER
2"
1¹¹⁄₁₆"
¾"
¾"

⅜" TAPER PLUS
OFFSET HERE
CUTTER CIRCLE
⁷⁄₁₆"
FENCE

13

SET-UP ON SHAPER
(TURN DRAWING OVER TO
SEE SAME SET-UP ON JOINTER)
AUXILIARY FENCE
IN LINE WITH CUTTER

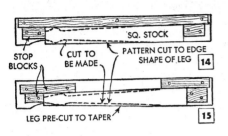

STOP BLOCKS | CUT TO BE MADE | SQ. STOCK | PATTERN CUT TO EDGE SHAPE OF LEG | **14**

LEG PRE-CUT TO TAPER | **15**

CUTTER | WORK | COLLAR PATTERN

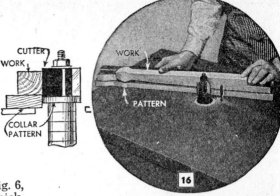

WORK | PATTERN | **16**

17

saw fence. In the example shown in Fig. 6, the spacer blocks would be ¼ in. thick. The saw-fence setting is made as before. Offsetting the block for the first cuts is made with one spacer block, as shown in Fig. 7. The final cuts are set with two spacer blocks as in Fig. 1.

The spade foot: It is not possible to make the long taper of this style of leg on a circular saw, hence the cut must be made by a jointer or shaper. Start by laying out the shape of the leg for a master pattern, Fig. 12, and make the curve at the bottom equal the radius of the shaper collar or jointer cutterhead, Fig. 9. Rough-bandsaw some of the surplus wood on all four sides, but leave the spade portion at full thickness, Fig. 10. Next, set up the shaper or jointer for tapering. This setup requires that the infeed table or fence must be offset from the cutter a distance equal to the taper desired, in this case, ⅜ in., Fig. 11. Also, because the shape of the leg holds the work out from the fence, as shown in Fig. 13, this extra distance must be added to the offset. The out-feed end of the shaper fence is fitted with an auxiliary fence and this should be pushed up as close to the cutterhead as possible in order to minimize the slight bite at the beginning of the cut. The out-feed fence of the shaper or the jointer table must be exactly in line with the cutting circle of the knives. Fig. 18

shows the start of the cut and Fig. 19 shows the cut near completion. All four sides are run with the same setup. The short taper comprising the foot is sawed with a modification of the step-block idea. The taper required is ⅜ in. on each side, hence the step-block has ⅜-in. steps. The proper position of the work in relation to the saw for the first cut is obtained by using a straightedge across the saw blade, aligning the pencil mark on the leg with the straightedge. Then the step block is nailed to the jig board at this setting. The first pair of adjacent sides is cut as before with the work in the first notch; the remaining pair requires that the work nest in the second notch, Fig. 20, to cut the taper.

18

Auxiliary fence minimizes slight "bite" of cutter at start of cut

STOP | **19**

Here taper cut is nearing completion. Note use of handscrew as a stop block

⅜" STEPS | **20**

Taper of foot is cut on saw, using a modification of stepped block

345

VENEERING

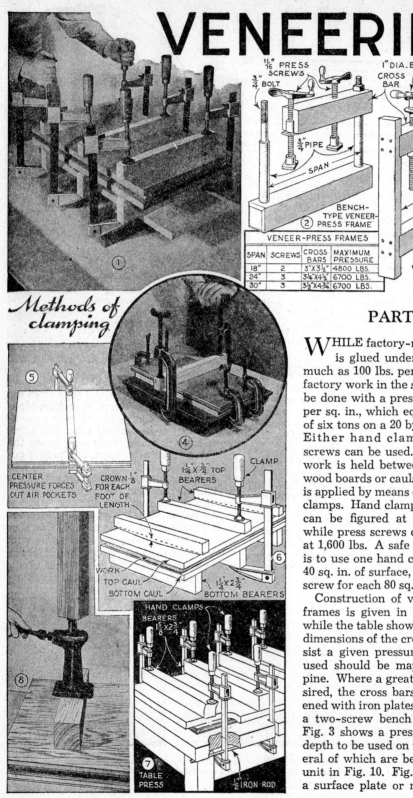

1¹⁄₁₆" PRESS SCREWS			I" DIA. BENCH SCREWS
³⁄₄" BOLT		CROSS BAR	
³⁄₄" PIPE			
SPAN			SPAN
			CROSS BAR

BENCH-TYPE VENEER-PRESS FRAME (2)

FLOOR-TYPE VENEER-PRESS FRAME (3)

VENEER-PRESS FRAMES

SPAN	SCREWS	CROSS BARS	MAXIMUM PRESSURE
18"	2	3"X3½"	4800 LBS.
24"	3	3¼"X4½"	6700 LBS.
30"	3	3½"X4¾"	6700 LBS.

Methods of clamping

(5) CENTER PRESSURE FORCES OUT AIR POCKETS

CROWN ¹⁄₈" FOR EACH FOOT OF LENGTH

(4)

CLAMP

1¼ X ³⁄₄" TOP BEARERS

WORK
TOP CAUL
BOTTOM CAUL
BOTTOM BEARERS

1¼ X 2¾"

(6)

(8)

HAND CLAMPS

BEARERS 1⁵⁄₈ X 2³⁄₄"

(7) TABLE PRESS

½" IRON ROD

PART I

WHILE factory-made plywood is glued under pressures as much as 100 lbs. per sq. in., satisfactory work in the small shop can be done with a pressure of 20 lbs. per sq. in., which equals a weight of six tons on a 20 by 30-in. panel. Either hand clamps or press screws can be used. In Fig. 1 the work is held between ³⁄₄-in. plywood boards or cauls and pressure is applied by means of bearers and clamps. Hand clamps of any kind can be figured at 800 lbs. each while press screws can be figured at 1,600 lbs. A safe rule to follow is to use one hand clamp for each 40 sq. in. of surface, and one press screw for each 80 sq. in. of surface.

Construction of veneer-press frames is given in the drawings, while the table shows the required dimensions of the cross bars to resist a given pressure. The wood used should be maple or yellow pine. Where a greater span is desired, the cross bars can be stiffened with iron plates. Fig. 2 shows a two-screw bench frame, while Fig. 3 shows a press of sufficient depth to be used on the floor, several of which are being used as a unit in Fig. 10. Fig. 4 shows how a surface plate or machine-table

Increases Scope of Craftwork

CORE MADE UP BY LAYERS OF HEAVY VENEER

FACE VENEER

VENEER CORE

BACK VENEER

CORE MADE FROM NARROW WOOD STRIPS

CROSSBAND

FACE VENEER

CROSSBAND

LUMBER CORE

BACK VENEER

CORE MADE FROM LUMBER STRIPS ON EDGE

CROSSBAND

FACE VENEER

CROSSBAND

LUMBER CORE

BACK VENEER

CROSSBAND

⑨ *Veneer construction*

⑩

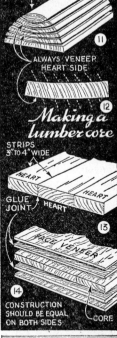

LOG SHRINKS LIKE THIS

⑪

ALWAYS VENEER HEART SIDE

⑫

Making a lumber core

STRIPS 3" TO 4" WIDE

HEART

HEART

GLUE JOINT

HEART

⑬

FACE VENEER

⑭

CONSTRUCTION SHOULD BE EQUAL ON BOTH SIDES

CORE

top can be used as a base for clamping. The standard set-up for clamping with bearers is given in Fig. 6. Note that the top bearers are not straight but are slightly curved on the underside. How the bearer method of clamping is used in making a permanent table press is given in Fig. 7. Excellent work can be done by using an automobile jack, Fig. 8, pushing against a heavy ceiling joist. After applying pressure in the center, the edges of the work are held by means of hand clamps. In any method of clamping, center pressure must be applied first, Fig. 5. This forces air pockets and excess glue to the edges of the work.

Veneer construction: Three of the commonest methods of constructing veneer panels are shown in Fig. 9. All are known as plywood. The center portion of the panel is the core. Lumber core plywood has a core of solid lumber strips. These are covered by a veneer called the crossband, and the crossbands are then faced with the face and back veneers. In all forms of construction, the grain of each layer is at right angles to the grain of the layer under it.

Making a lumber core: Plywood with either a veneer or lumber core can be purchased and needs only the application of face and back veneers to complete it. If the worker should wish to make his own core, the principles of core construction are illustrated in Figs. 11 to 14. Fig. 11 shows how lumber shrinks—always bowing out on the heart side. As a sheet of veneer has a tendency to pull the work hollow, it follows that where one face only of the core is to be veneered, the veneer should be applied on the heart side. This side is distinguished readily by inspecting the end grain, Fig. 12. To further eliminate warping, the lumber is usually ripped into narrow strips 3 to 4 in. wide, reversing every other piece end for end so that the heart side is alternately up and down, Fig. 13. Lumber cores always should be cross-banded, the best lumber for both cores and crossbands

⑮

Flattening veneers

coat is essential, and is always applied to the core, not to the veneer.

Flattening veneers: Veneers are normally flat, and if kept between boards will stay that way. Intricate graining in burls and butts, however, tends to warp the veneer, and the piece must be straightened before it can be applied. Various preparations are available for this purpose, and can be applied by brush, dip, or spray, Fig. 16. When the surface wetness has dried, the veneer is placed between boards, Fig. 17, for overnight drying. A good glue size for flattening can be made by mixing, by weight, casein glue, 1 part, water, 4 parts, and then adding slowly alcohol, 2½ parts and glycerine, 1½ parts.

Assembling a panel: A panel with one-piece faces on a veneer core is shown in Fig. 18. The face and back veneers can be cut with a knife, saw, or heavy scissors, Fig. 19, and should be about ¼ in. larger all around than the core. Glue is brushed on one side of the

Assembling a panel

being poplar. Veneer cores need not be crossbanded as the top layer of veneer is itself a crossband. Face veneers should be applied with the right side out whenever possible. The right or "tight" side can be determined by rubbing the surface of the veneer with the fingers, as in Fig. 15, the right side having a slightly smoother grain.

Concerning glue: Casein glue is used for most homecraft veneering. It is in dry powder form and requires only mixing with water to make it ready for use. Cold resin glue is also excellent. Both types should be applied with a brush having fairly stiff bristles. An even

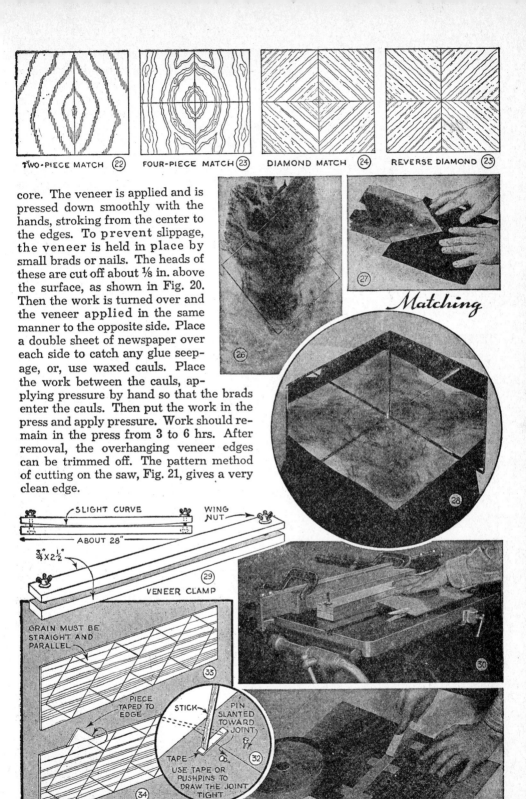

TWO-PIECE MATCH ㉒   FOUR-PIECE MATCH ㉓   DIAMOND MATCH ㉔   REVERSE DIAMOND ㉕

core. The veneer is applied and is pressed down smoothly with the hands, stroking from the center to the edges. To prevent slippage, the veneer is held in place by small brads or nails. The heads of these are cut off about ⅛ in. above the surface, as shown in Fig. 20. Then the work is turned over and the veneer applied in the same manner to the opposite side. Place a double sheet of newspaper over each side to catch any glue seepage, or, use waxed cauls. Place the work between the cauls, applying pressure by hand so that the brads enter the cauls. Then put the work in the press and apply pressure. Work should remain in the press from 3 to 6 hrs. After removal, the overhanging veneer edges can be trimmed off. The pattern method of cutting on the saw, Fig. 21, gives a very clean edge.

Matching

SLIGHT CURVE   WING NUT

ABOUT 28"

¾"x2½"

VENEER CLAMP ㉙

GRAIN MUST BE STRAIGHT AND PARALLEL

PIECE TAPED TO EDGE

STICK   PIN SLANTED TOWARD JOINT

TAPE

USE TAPE OR PUSHPINS TO DRAW THE JOINT TIGHT

CUTTING DIAMOND PATTERN FROM SINGLE PIECE OF VENEER

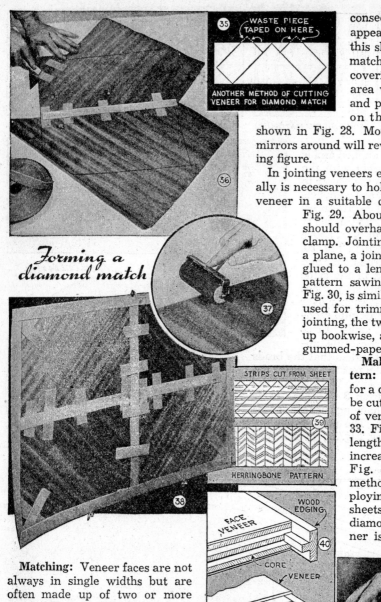

Forming a diamond match

Treatment of edges

consecutive sheets. The appearance of any area on this sheet in a four-piece match can be observed by covering two edges of the area with paper, Fig. 27, and placing the mirrors on the other edges, as shown in Fig. 28. Moving the paper and mirrors around will reveal the most pleasing figure.

In jointing veneers edge to edge, it usually is necessary to hold the two sheets of veneer in a suitable clamp, as shown in Fig. 29. About $1/8$ in. of veneer should overhang the edge of the clamp. Jointing can be done with a plane, a jointer, with sandpaper glued to a length of wood, or by pattern sawing. Pattern sawing, Fig. 30, is similar to the procedure used for trimming edges. After jointing, the two sheets are opened up bookwise, and assembled with gummed-paper, Figs. 31 and 32.

Making a diamond pattern: How the four pieces for a diamond pattern can be cut from a single sheet of veneer is given in Fig. 33. Fig. 34 shows how the length of the panel can be increased by patching. Fig. 35 shows another method of cutting, employing two consecutive sheets. The assembly of a diamond cut in this manner is shown in Fig. 36.

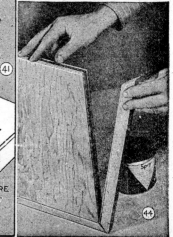

Matching: Veneer faces are not always in single widths but are often made up of two or more pieces. Frequently the various pieces are matched to form pleasing figures, a few examples of which are shown in Figs. 22 to 25. The two-piece match requires two identical consecutive sheets of veneer, while the four-piece match requires four identical pieces. Diamond patterns can be cut from either consecutive sheets or from a single sheet. In developing four-piece figures, a pair of small mirrors can be used to advantage. Fig. 26 shows one sheet of four

VENEERING
Increases Scope
of CRAFTWORK

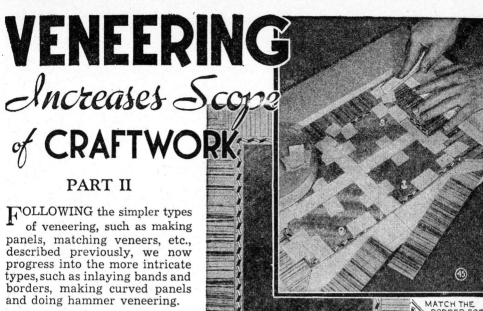

(45)

MATCH THE
BORDER FOR
PERFECT
CORNERS

(47)

SAW

(46)

PART II

FOLLOWING the simpler types of veneering, such as making panels, matching veneers, etc., described previously, we now progress into the more intricate types, such as inlaying bands and borders, making curved panels and doing hammer veneering.

Inlay bands and borders: Inlay bands are available in a variety of widths and patterns in lengths of about 40 in. Usually, the banding is taped together with the veneers

Inlay bands and borders

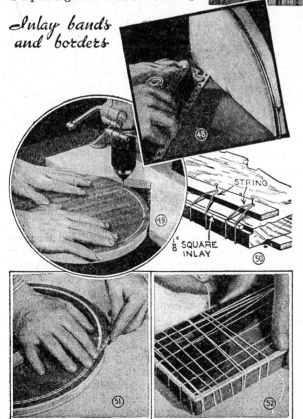

(48)

(49)

STRING

⅛" SQUARE INLAY

(50)

(51)

(52)

previous to gluing. Fig. 45 shows a typical panel comprising a mahogany diamond with banding and border being assembled. The work is done on a full-size paper pattern. Push pins or dabs of glue can be used to hold the various pieces in place. Both the banding and border should be matched at the mitered corners. This is done by matching two pieces together as in Fig. 47, and then mitering. Holding the two pieces in the same position, the joint is cleaned up by sanding as in Fig. 48. The border strips are cut across the grain from a suitable piece of veneer. Then adjacent strips are placed together so that the grain matches, after which the corner is mitered and sanded as before. Fig. 46 shows the finished panel after gluing and cleaning up.

Very narrow bandings are often laid in a groove routed in the veneered surface, Fig. 49. Glue is applied to the banding, which is then pressed into the groove, as in Fig. 51. It should fit tightly and

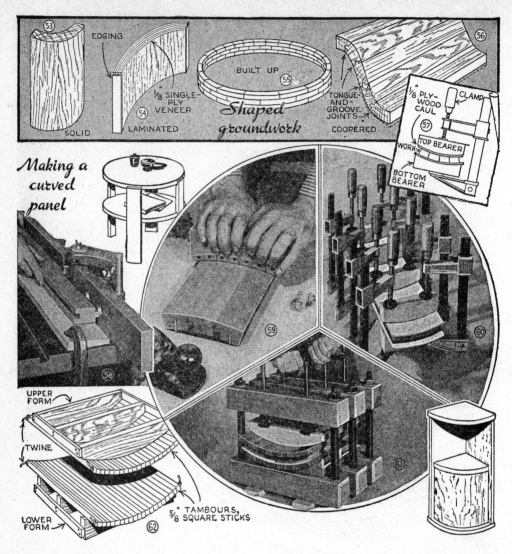

53 EDGING
54 ⅛ SINGLE-PLY VENEER
SOLID
LAMINATED
55 BUILT UP
Shaped groundwork
56 TONGUE-AND-GROOVE JOINTS
COOPERED
⅛" PLYWOOD CAUL CLAMP
57 TOP BEARER
WORK
BOTTOM BEARER

Making a curved panel

58
59
60
61
UPPER FORM
TWINE
LOWER FORM
62 ⅝" TAMBOURS, SQUARE STICKS

should project slightly above the surface so that it can be sanded flush after the glue has dried. Lengths of square inlay, commonly called strings, frequently are inlaid at the edges of a veneered surface. They can be held in place by wrapping with string, Fig. 52, or, if the work is large, by using the method shown in Fig. 50.

Shaped groundwork: Curved surfaces over which veneer is to be laid can be made by using one of the four methods shown in Figs. 53 to 56 inclusive. Small work usually can be cut from solid stock, as in Fig. 53. Laminating, Fig. 54, is ideal for large work. The built-up or bread-and-butter groundwork is made easily and has the advantage that scrap cuttings can be cleaned up and used as cauls. Coopered

curves, Fig. 56, are a standard method of working, excellent in structural soundness but demanding considerable handwork in shaping the surface.

Making a curved panel: The groundwork is made first, using soft wood such as poplar or white pine. Construction will depend on the nature of the work. In the case of a table leg curved across the face, a coopered groundwork would be suitable. A full-size paper pattern is made to show the number of pieces required and the angle at the joints. The pieces are then cut on a shaper, Fig. 58, and assembled with glue. Handwork with sandpaper tacked to shaped blocks, as shown in Fig. 59, is the most practical method of securing a finished surface, although roughing can be done with a variety of other tools. The work can now be veneered. Both cross-banding and veneer are used in first-class work, but good results can be obtained with veneer only. A simple method of clamping the veneer in place is shown in Figs. 57 and 60. Thin cauls of ⅛-in. plywood are used, together with a number of curved bearers. The general application is the same as a flat panel, both sides being veneered in one pressing.

Another example of curved work, a paneled door, is shown in Figs. 61 and 62. This features a laminated groundwork, and is one of the best methods of handling the job. Two pressings are required, one in the assembly of the groundwork and the other in the application of the veneer. Fig. 62 shows the method of working. Three or more lower bearers are band-sawed to the required curve and are held together with wood strips to make a form. The upper form is made in the same manner. Tambours, which are ⅝-in. square sticks held loosely together with twine, are used in place of cauls. The five or more layers of single-ply ⅛-in. poplar or basswood

veneer for the core are glued up, glue being spread on both sides of each piece. The pieces are assembled with the grain in all pieces running the same way, and a nail is driven through the complete thickness at the center of each end. A folded piece of newspaper is placed on each side of the work to catch surplus glue, and

Veneering around a corner

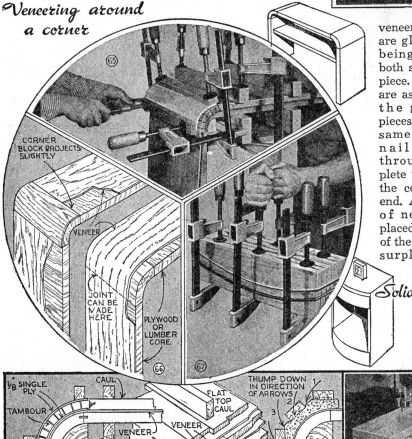

CORNER BLOCK PROJECTS SLIGHTLY

VENEER

JOINT CAN BE MADE HERE

PLYWOOD OR LUMBER CORE

Solid cauls

⅛ SINGLE PLY

CAUL

TAMBOUR

VENEER

BOTTOM BEARER

CORNER BLOCK

SHAPED CAUL

CAUL

FLAT TOP CAUL

VENEER

THUMP DOWN IN DIRECTION OF ARROWS

FLAT BOTTOM CAUL

CORNER BLOCK

SANDBAG

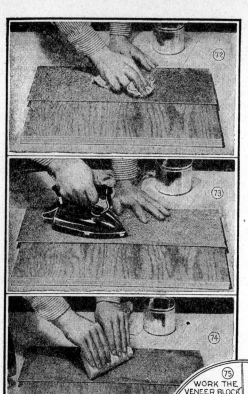

working, only the flat panels are veneered, as shown in the left-hand detail of Fig. 66. If the grain of the veneer runs crosswise, a very good job can be done in this way. In better work, the veneer runs right around the curve, or is jointed once at the lower edge, as indicated by the dotted line in the right-hand detail. Fig. 65 shows the veneer being fitted around the curve, and Fig. 68 shows the work in cross section. As one side only is being veneered, the corner blocks on the underside need not extend across the work, but are only of such length as to accommodate the clamps. Fig. 69 shows another method of working. In this case, both sides of the work are being veneered, the two shaped cauls extending completely across the work. A simple way of making shaped cauls of this kind is to band-saw the work in short lengths and then face the curve with a layer of ⅛-in. single-ply veneer. This breaks the joints and also levels the sawed surface. As many short lengths as are required can be made quickly and faced in this manner, although if more than three short pieces are used to make one caul, the joints should be doweled to obtain the required stiffness.

A sandbag offers a simple and practical method of working. This is thumped down around the curve, as shown in Fig. 70, and is then topped with bearers and clamped.

Solid cauls: The groundwork for shaped drawer fronts and similar work is usually

WORK THE VENEER BLOCK OR HAMMER IN ZIG-ZAG STROKES

VENEER BLOCK

¾"x3"x6"

VENEER HAMMER

1/16 BRASS

Hammer veneering

over the paper is placed a sheet of ⅛-in. single-ply veneer. Tambours are then fitted in place, followed by the forms, after which the work is ready for the veneer press, as shown in Fig. 61. After the work has dried, hardwood edgings are fitted, as shown in Fig. 54, and the panel is then veneered, using the same method as before.

Veneering around a corner: The round corner is widely used in modern furniture construction, a typical example being the bench shown below Fig. 64. The groundwork is prepared by turning and cove cutting, as shown in Figs. 63 and 64, after which the curved pieces are tenoned or doweled to flat panels. The work is then ready for veneering. In a simple method of

made by the built-up method. If the pad is made sufficiently large, the scrap pieces obtained by band-sawing, Fig. 71, can be used as cauls when applying the veneer, as shown in Fig. 67. A layer of felt or blotting paper should be used between the cauls and veneer to equalize the pressure. The same method can be used when the groundwork is cut from solid stock.

Hammer veneering: Hammer veneering can be done on both flat and curved surfaces, and differs from veneering as previously described in that it is done with hot animal glue. The veneer hammer is not a hammer at all, but simply a block of wood or other device, as shown in Figs. 76 and 77, used to press the veneer in place. In the typical example shown in the photos, two pieces of veneer are fitted together to form a flat panel The groundwork and veneer are first brushed with glue. It is immaterial whether or not the glue chills after application. One of the veneer pieces is then fitted in place, and it is quite likely that the glue will be tacky enough to hold it in position. After sponging the veneer with water to prevent burning, Fig. 72, the chilled glue is again made liquid by the application of a moderately warm iron, as shown in Fig. 73. The veneer is then immediately pressed in place with the hammer, Fig. 74, working with zig-zag strokes as in Fig. 75, so that all surplus glue is squeezed out. The second piece of veneer is similarly glued, allowing a 1-in. overlap. The joint is then cut with a sharp chisel or knife, using considerable pressure so that one stroke will cut through both thicknesses, Fig. 78. A light touch with the iron will then soften the glue enough so that the veneer can be peeled back to remove the waste piece, as in Fig. 79, after which the whole surface is damped and hammered.

Ear Syringe Applies Liquid Glue

For rapid application of liquid glue, an ear syringe can be used to advantage. The tip is cut as shown in the upper left-hand detail so that it will fit into narrow joints and corners better than a brush and do a neater job. After use the syringe should be washed thoroughly in order to keep it efficient.

ENLARGED END VIEWS
EAR SYRINGE

Column Clamp Made from Cord and Screen-Door Spring

The next time you are building up a column or half column and there are no suitable clamps at hand, try some screen-door springs. Use as many as necessary and tie them around the work with strong cords as shown. Clamps of this type exert uniform pressure on all joints of the column regardless of its contour.

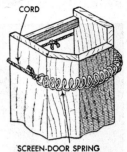
CORD
SCREEN-DOOR SPRING

Jar Lid Used as Picture Frame

Two-piece lids that are used to seal fruit jars will make clever frames and pictures. The lid part is placed with the white side out and decorated with a decal, and the sealing ring is used as the frame. Hang the picture with a ring and short length of ribbon. This type of decoration will be found especially attractive for a child's room or for an otherwise bare wall.

Closet-Door Shoe Rack

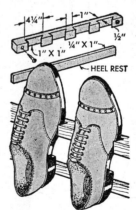
4¼" — 1"
½"
¼" X 1"
1" X 1"
HEEL REST

Only two strips of wood are needed to make this shoe rack, which can be fastened to the inside of a closet door. Size of the rack, and the number of shoes that it will hold are determined by the width of the door. Dimensions given for the top piece are for average-size men's shoes. The bottom piece merely serves as a buffer strip to keep heels from marring the door finish.

❧ Sash pulls always should be provided on the lower sash of a window for raising it, because if it is lifted by the top rail, the joint between the rail and stiles may break.

Distinctive FLOWER

By Milt Evans

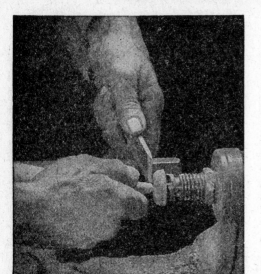

When the turning is completed it is cut free of the waste in the manner shown above. The skew is held with the left hand and the work is caught as it falls

CONTRASTING mahogany and maple combine to make this little vase for artificial flowers a striking and unusual ornament. To make it, cut a 3⅝-in. mahogany turning square 8½ in. long, and plane off the corners 45 deg. Mount the block in a lathe so that it is offset 5⁄16 in. at the tailstock center, as in Fig. 3, detail A, and extend the quill of the tailstock to the limit to give working clearance. Bore inward from the end, using a narrow skew chisel to hollow the inside to correspond with the shape indicated by the dotted lines in the profile view, Fig. 2. To guide the direction of the chisel, mark a line around the turning block 6⅞ in. from the tailstock end. Then lay a straightedge on the top of the block in the position shown in Fig. 4, and align the chisel with the straightedge by sighting along the edge of the chisel. When the chisel enters far enough to reduce the core to the point of breaking off, remove the turning from the lathe and break out the waste core by hand.

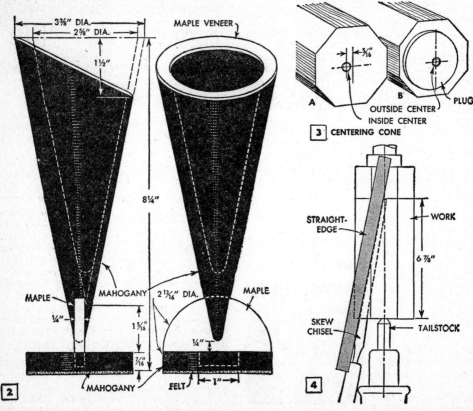

VASE

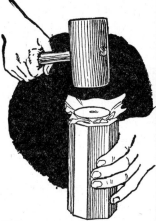

To provide a center for turning the outside of the vase, plug the open end with a tapered plug, Fig. 5. This plug is glued in place with paper between the parts so that it can be removed easily. Next, mark the true center of the block at the tailstock end, Fig. 3, detail B, and remount the work in the lathe for turning the outside. When cutting the tapered end free from the waste part, hold the skew chisel with the left hand and the work with the right hand to catch it when severed, Fig. 1. Finally, bore a hole in the wooden plug for inserting a chisel to pry it out.

Rest the thick side at the top of the turning on a 1½-in.-thick block and scribe around the cone with a compass set 1½ in., as in Fig. 6. Then, using this line as a guide, roughly saw the slanted end, finishing it smooth on a sanding disk. Glue a piece of maple veneer to the rim and carefully trim it flush with the sides after the glue dries. The base of the vase consists of a disk of mahogany and a semicircular disk of maple tenoned and glued to it. The base is attached to the vase by slotting the end to fit over the maple piece. The slot can be cut by supporting the work level, and sawing with a bandsaw or a scrollsaw, gradually widening the slot by trimming the sides.

Before staining and filling the mahogany, apply a coat of shellac to the maple parts to prevent them from absorbing stain. If the work is to be lacquered, give it a coat of sealer first. If you want the vase to hold cut flowers, the inside can be lined with a metal cone. A suitable cone is made by rolling a piece of sheet metal and soldering the seam to make it watertight. Complete the vase by gluing felt to the bottom.

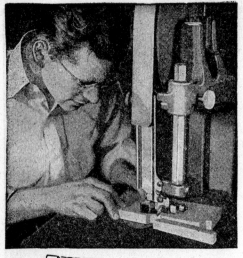

Six Styles in

By W. T. Warde

ATTRACTIVE book ends like these make ideal gifts, as the design can be suited to the recipient's tastes—even to his initial. For instance, instead of the spaniel you can use a likeness of another dog—a bulldog is particularly effective. The horsehead book ends are made of three laminations, the long curve of neck and mane being cut first, after which the pieces are glued together and the head and inside of the neck cut as one piece. In the spaniel

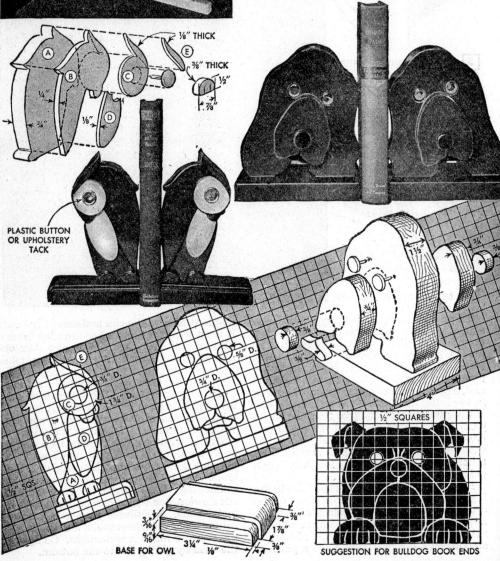

⅛" THICK

⅜" THICK

¼"

¾"

⅛"

½"

⅞"

PLASTIC BUTTON OR UPHOLSTERY TACK

1½"

¾"

⅜"

¾"

¾"

⅜"

⅜"

E

¾" D.

1¾" D.

⅝" D.

¾" D.

½" SQS.

BASE FOR OWL

3"⁄16

9⁄16"

3¼"

⅛"

⅜"

1⅞"

⅜"

⅜"

½" SQUARES

SUGGESTION FOR BULLDOG BOOK ENDS

BAND-SAWED BOOK ENDS

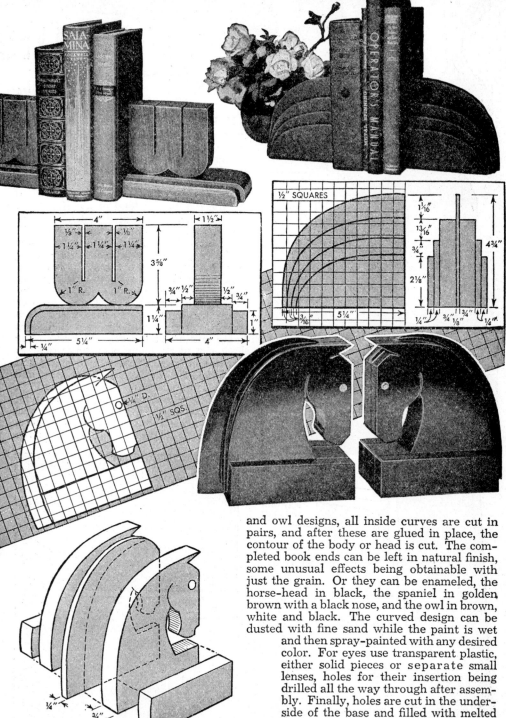

and owl designs, all inside curves are cut in pairs, and after these are glued in place, the contour of the body or head is cut. The completed book ends can be left in natural finish, some unusual effects being obtainable with just the grain. Or they can be enameled, the horse-head in black, the spaniel in golden brown with a black nose, and the owl in brown, white and black. The curved design can be dusted with fine sand while the paint is wet and then spray-painted with any desired color. For eyes use transparent plastic, either solid pieces or separate small lenses, holes for their insertion being drilled all the way through after assembly. Finally, holes are cut in the underside of the base and filled with melted lead to add weight, the bottom then being covered with felt.

More SPEED on CUTOUTS

by Sam Brown

BOX JIG

IN PRODUCING novelty cutouts for profit, the owner of a small shop must make every possible use of production methods in order to turn out work that can be sold at competitive prices.

Pad sawing: This is a popular method of producing several figures at one time by the familiar method of making a pad of the work. Band-saw work should be about 3 in. thick, and scrollsaw about 1½ in. Even where the machine has greater capacity, there is little to gain in exceeding these thicknesses. Simplest method of assembling the pad is by nailing, locating the nails in the portions of the work that will be waste stock as in Fig. 7. Two or more figures on a panel as in Fig. 3 often saves lumber, and in all cases eliminates some cutting of the original blank. For long-run work, many operators prefer to use holding jigs. The box jig in Figs. 1 and 2 is ideal for work that has at least one uncut square corner. The clamp jig, Figs. 4 and 6 can be used for any figure having one uncut edge. In making jigs of this kind, the base block is left in-the-square, being cut to shape at the same time as the

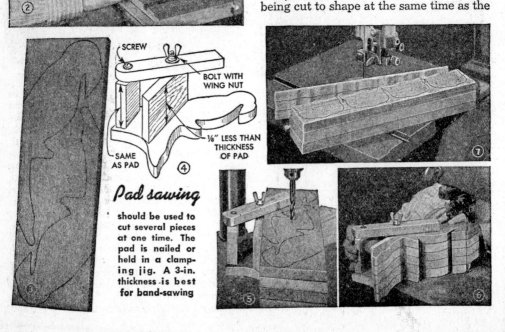

SCREW

BOLT WITH WING NUT

SAME AS PAD

⅛" LESS THAN THICKNESS OF PAD

Pad sawing

should be used to cut several pieces at one time. The pad is nailed or held in a clamping jig. A 3-in. thickness is best for band-sawing

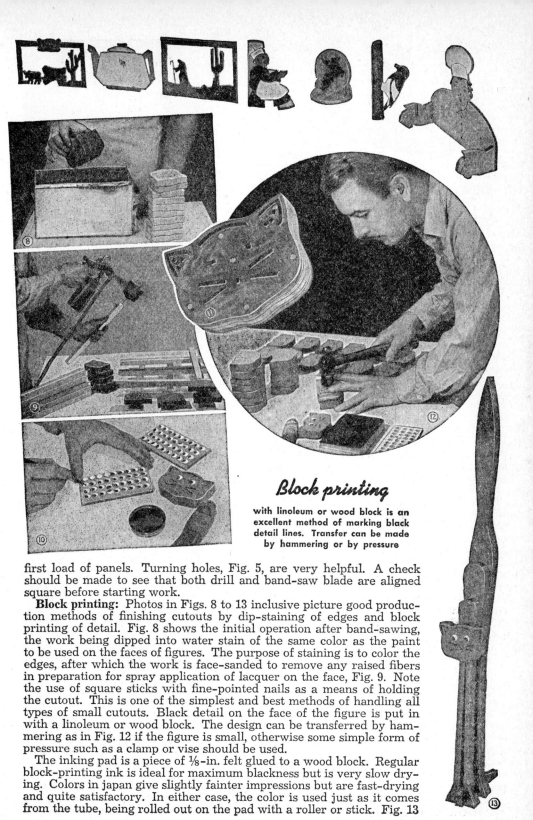

Block printing

with linoleum or wood block is an excellent method of marking black detail lines. Transfer can be made by hammering or by pressure

first load of panels. Turning holes, Fig. 5, are very helpful. A check should be made to see that both drill and band-saw blade are aligned square before starting work.

Block printing: Photos in Figs. 8 to 13 inclusive picture good production methods of finishing cutouts by dip-staining of edges and block printing of detail. Fig. 8 shows the initial operation after band-sawing, the work being dipped into water stain of the same color as the paint to be used on the faces of figures. The purpose of staining is to color the edges, after which the work is face-sanded to remove any raised fibers in preparation for spray application of lacquer on the face, Fig. 9. Note the use of square sticks with fine-pointed nails as a means of holding the cutout. This is one of the simplest and best methods of handling all types of small cutouts. Black detail on the face of the figure is put in with a linoleum or wood block. The design can be transferred by hammering as in Fig. 12 if the figure is small, otherwise some simple form of pressure such as a clamp or vise should be used.

The inking pad is a piece of ⅛-in. felt glued to a wood block. Regular block-printing ink is ideal for maximum blackness but is very slow drying. Colors in japan give slightly fainter impressions but are fast-drying and quite satisfactory. In either case, the color is used just as it comes from the tube, being rolled out on the pad with a roller or stick. Fig. 13

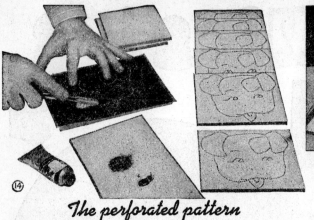

The perforated pattern

is ideal for transferring outline or pattern for hand painting. Best medium for the pattern is celluloid obtained from old photo negatives. The paint should be thick color in japan, applied sparingly

shows the finished cutout, painted thumbtacks being used for eyes. The body of the figure is not a cutout, strictly speaking, but is formed with the use of a pattern on the shaper. Note again the use of stain as a means of coloring the edges of the cat's face. This method is fast and clean, and can be used to advantage on any type of cutout. The slight grain raising of water stain is not objectionable since it helps to conceal band-saw marks, but non-grain-raising stain can be used if desired.

Perforated patterns: The perforated pattern is an excellent method of transferring designs for hand painting. Best material for the pattern is thin celluloid such as old photograph negatives. The original pencil drawing of the design is rubber-cemented to the celluloid, after which the design is perforated by drilling with a $\frac{1}{32}$ to $\frac{1}{16}$-in. drill as in Fig. 15. The finished pattern is shown in Fig. 16. In use, the pattern is held firmly against the work while color is applied by means of a toothbrush, as indicated in Fig. 14. Use colors in japan at tube thickness and keep the brush almost dry. Do not attempt to use any type of paint or ink that is the least bit fluid. Advantages of this method are that the pattern need not be cleaned and can be used continuously for as many times as desired, it can be turned over if opposite side of cutout is to be painted, and the design takes equally well on coated or bare wood panels.

Waxed-paper transfers: This is a good method of transferring the design for short-run work. The paper used can be made by brush-coating with hot paraffin wax, but is best purchased as it is inexpensive. This paper is not the familiar waxed wrapping paper, but is a special product made for transferring designs. A pencil sketch is made first, using a soft lead pencil. The wax paper is rubbed over this, Fig. 17, and then is stripped off as in Fig. 18. Rubbing the waxed paper over the work, Fig. 19, completes the transfer. This method gives eight to ten clean impressions on smooth coated stock. The design takes poorly on bare wood, hence painting of the panels before cutting is essential.

WAX PAPER RUBBED OVER PENCIL SKETCH

PAPER PICKS UP DESIGN

RUBBING TRANSFERS DESIGN TO WORK

Wax-paper transfers

are used for transferring designs. The paper lifts the design from a pencil sketch and is then rubbed onto work

Hand painting: Many cutout designs consist only of a solid base color with black lines for detail. On short-run work it is advantageous to freehand the detail. Transfer methods previously described can be used for guide lines, and the painting medium should be colors in oil or japan.

Silk-screen stencils: Best of all production methods of painting is the silk screen stencil. This method is quite simple, and gets beautiful effects when carefully done. Briefly, the stencil

Silk-Screen Stencils

offer the best production method of painting. Sample illustrated shows paint-filled screen

work are first painted black, as in Figs. 20 and 21, and the stencil is blocked off to leave a black margin around the cutout. The silk screen method allows many manipulations, multiple color work, photographic screens, etc. Every serious worker in cutouts should give this method a trial.

Metal stencils: Metal stencils are widely used on both short and long runs. The stencil can be made from tin, brass, zinc or other metal about .012 in. thick (28-gage). Cutting of stencil is done

Metal Stencils

can be cut out on the scrollsaw and are excellent for general work. Magnet method of holding shown at right is used extensively in industrial painting of cutouts

material is a silk cloth, running about 140-mesh per inch. The silk is tacked drum tight on a wooden frame, and the areas which are not to print are blocked out with a special filler. Fig. 22 pictures the set-up for stenciling the letter "E," the area around the letter being blocked out. Paint is poured on the screen and wiped from one end to the other by means of a rubber squeegee. The action of the squeegee forces paint through the silk and thus transfers the design. A typical set-up with silk screen stencil is shown in Fig. 23. The edges and face of

SPRAY WHITE UNDERCOAT (LACQUER)

to minimum, and directing gun at right angles to the work at all times. "Blow-unders" can be eliminated entirely by using some method to actually "glue" the stencil to the work. The wax paper previously mentioned is fairly good; plain paper with dabs of wax, rubber cement or other sticky substance often can be used, or the stencil can often be held down by small weights or pins. Best of all is duplex stencil paper. This is a rubber-coated pa-

on a scrollsaw, with the metal held between plywood sheets. It is preferable to have two or more stencils of the same figure. Simplest working method is a wooden frame into which the stencil fits, Fig. 24, the work being held by hand behind the stencil, which will run seven or eight pieces before the paint starts to pile up. The dirty stencil then is thrown into a pan of lacquer thinner, and the second stencil is picked out of the thinner, brushed off and blown dry ready for use. One of the neatest methods of holding the metal stencil is shown in Fig. 26 and employs a magnet. The wood cutout is placed against the magnet and is topped by the stencil. The magnet then holds everything in place for painting. Any ordinary magnet of fair size will hold small cutouts of ¼-in. plywood. For larger or thicker work, several magnets can be grouped together. "Magnetic chucks" of this kind, both plain and electro, can be purchased in any size and have the advantage of increased power plus off-on switch control. Whatever method is used, the metal stencil should have tabs or other locating device to position the work, Fig. 25. Obviously, if the magnet method is used, the stencil must be tin, iron or steel and not brass, copper or zinc.

Paper stencils: Plain paper stencils in several variations have many uses in cutout painting. If paper stencils are used, it is advantageous to cut fifty or more stencils at one time by clinch-nailing the paper sheets between plywood as in Fig. 29. Tightly nailed and cut on the scrollsaw, edges will be sharp and clean. Used stencils are thrown away when dirty. The principal disadvantage of the paper stencil is the difficulty encountered in getting it to lie flat on the work. Unless firmly held, the spray gun blast will blow under the edges of the stencil. This can be minimized by using a round spray, reducing air pressure

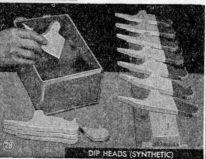

DIP HEADS (SYNTHETIC)

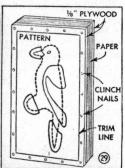

⅛" PLYWOOD

PATTERN

PAPER

CLINCH NAILS

TRIM LINE

FIT STENCIL IN PLACE

Gummed - paper stencils

provide perfect adhesion to the work and are excellent for use on long- or short-run jobs

per with strip-off backing. To use the stencil, simply strip off the backing and roll the stencil onto the work, as shown in Fig. 30. This paper has an advantage in that it leaves no deposit whatever on the work. The same stencil can be used for several pieces of work. The complete painting schedule for the figure used to illustrate stenciling methods is shown in Figs. 27 and 28. The work is first sprayed with white undercoat and then white lacquer enamel, after which the head of the figure is painted red by dipping, Fig. 28, using a synthetic to avoid stripping the lacquer undercoat. The work is now ready for the black detail, using any of the stencil methods described. If both sides of the figure are to be painted by using gummed stencils, one half of the pad should be turned over when cutting so that the cement will be on the proper side when the stencil is reversed.

By Dick Hutchinson

A Book for Your Surplus Stamps

STAMP collectors who find it hard to keep surplus and duplicate stamps filed in an orderly manner will welcome this book, Figs. 1 and 2, which provides plenty of space to keep the spare issues. The cover for the book is made from ¼-in. chestnut, but any wood with an attractive grain will do equally well. Dimensions for the covers are given in the upper detail of Fig. 3. No. 22-ga. soft copper is used for the hinges, lower left-hand detail, which are hammered on the face side. The bends for the hinge pins are formed around a No. 20 brad. A method of page assembly for the pockets and hinges is shown in the lower right-hand detail. Note how the page hinges are spaced, center left-hand detail, so the pages will fold over.

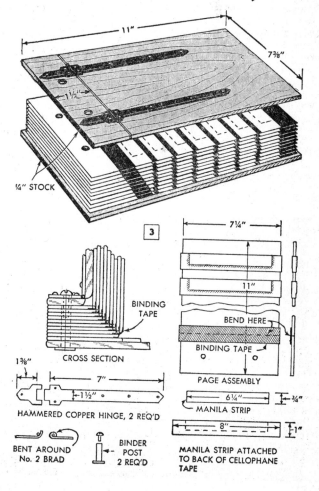

11"

7⅜"

1½"

¼" STOCK

3

BINDING TAPE

CROSS SECTION

1⅜"

7"

1½"

HAMMERED COPPER HINGE, 2 REQ'D

BENT AROUND No. 2 BRAD

BINDER POST 2 REQ'D

7¼"

11"

BEND HERE

BINDING TAPE

PAGE ASSEMBLY

6¼"

¾"

MANILA STRIP

8"

1"

MANILA STRIP ATTACHED TO BACK OF CELLOPHANE TAPE

Turned Candlesticks in New

These modern candlesticks, in novel "climbing spiral" design, offer something new in one-evening projects for the wood-turning hobbyist

By E. M. Love

A FEW HOURS of fun with your wood-turning lathe can result in these attractive candlesticks, Fig. 1, that will please even the most discriminating person. While they are not a true climbing-spiral design, they do give that impression, and when made of contrasting woods, such as mahogany and maple or birch, they will add a decorative touch to any home.

Mark and cut the cone sections for both candlesticks from a block of hardwood as shown in the detail, and sand the top face of each one. Locate the center on the bottom of each piece by drawing intersecting lines from the corners. Rough out the sections by removing waste from the corners with a chisel. Then mount one of the upper sections in the lathe on a screw center, Fig. 3. Set the tool rest at a 30-deg. angle and use it as a guide in turning the diameter. When this piece has been turned to size, bore the candle socket, Fig. 4, and sand the part to a smooth finish. Duplicate this procedure on the upper section of the other candlestick, and drill the tops of both sections to take 1/8-in. dowels which are used to attach a cylinder. Next, fashion each of the two middle sections of the candlesticks

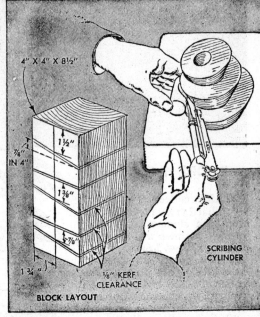

4" X 4" X 8½"

7/8" IN 4"

1½"

1¾"

7/8"

SCRIBING CYLINDER

1¾"

1/8" KERF CLEARANCE

BLOCK LAYOUT

in the same manner, but counterbore the top to fit the bottom of the upper cone. Follow with the lower sections, which also are counterbored. Then, screw the cone sections together and stain them.

The dimensions of the decorative cylinders are given in the detail. Turn them as in Fig. 2, cut them apart and dress the ends on a sander. Then, scribe each cylinder as indicated to fit against the corresponding cone section, and shape with a half-round

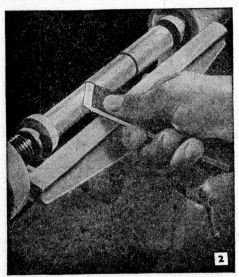

2

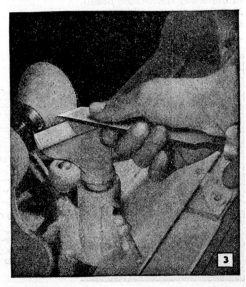

3

Styling ★ ★

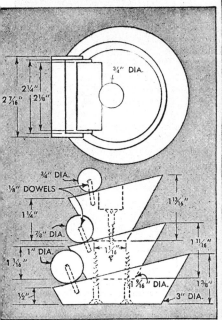

file. Drill each one for attaching with dowels. Sand or scrape the cone sections at the points where the cylinders contact the sides of the cones in order to remove the stain and filler. Before gluing the cylinders in place, notch each top one at the point where it overhangs the candle socket, Fig. 5. When the glue sets, varnish or lacquer the candlesticks.

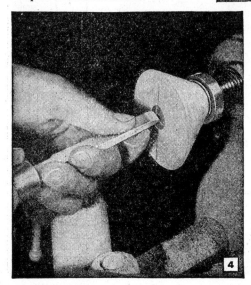

Novelty MATCH BOXES

for the Kitchen

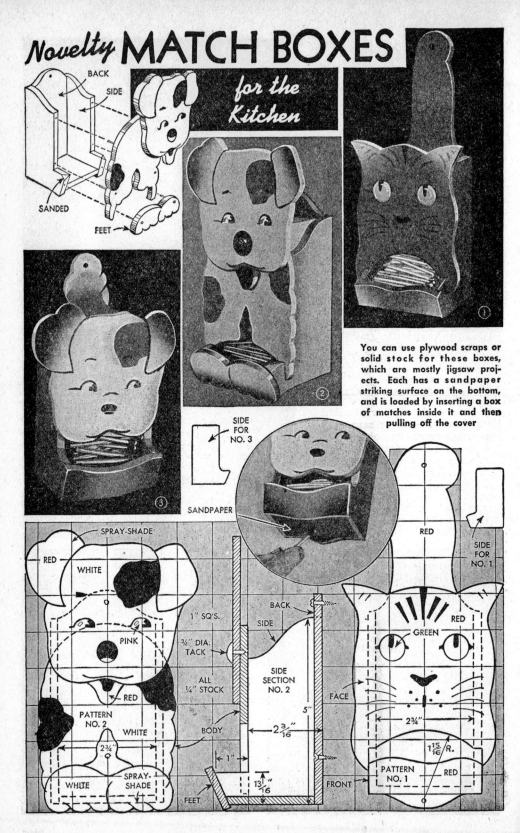

BACK

SIDE

SANDED

FEET

You can use plywood scraps or solid stock for these boxes, which are mostly jigsaw projects. Each has a sandpaper striking surface on the bottom, and is loaded by inserting a box of matches inside it and then pulling off the cover

SIDE FOR NO. 3

SANDPAPER

SPRAY-SHADE

RED

WHITE

PINK

RED

PATTERN NO. 2

WHITE

2¾"

WHITE

SPRAY-SHADE

FEET

1" SQ'S.

¾" DIA. TACK

ALL ¼" STOCK

BACK

SIDE

SIDE SECTION NO. 2

BODY

2 3/16"

1"

5"

13/16"

FRONT

RED

SIDE FOR NO. 1

GREEN

RED

FACE

2¾"

1 15/16" R.

PATTERN NO. 1

RED

CARVED DESK SET
Has Decorative Inlays

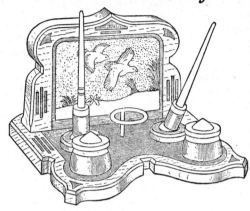

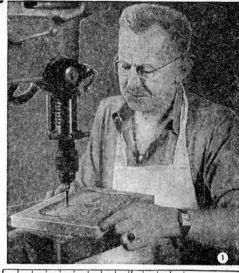

By Carmen J. Gentile

WITH the exception of a few small items, such as the ivory used for initials, this desk set is built of either holly or birch and inlaid with walnut. Although carving the panel that forms the background may seem difficult, if done with care the result will be satisfactory. The back panel, which can be a starting point, is inlaid and sawed to shape. Fig. 1 shows the panel being routed to the dimensions indicated in Fig. 4. The inlay for the carved part is ½ in. thick, while the smaller inlays are ⅛ in. for both panel and base.

After the walnut has been glued in and the panel cut to the dimensions indicated in Fig. 4, plane and sand the surfaces and chamfer the edges. In the same

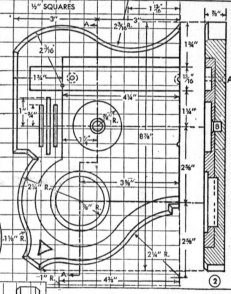

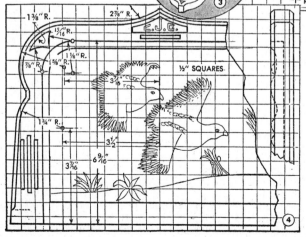

manner, the inlays for the base are cut and finished, Figs. 2 and 3. The larger inlay for the base, however, is only ⅜ in. thick instead of ½ in. as in the case of the panel. Referring to Fig. 2, the recesses for the penholders are ¼ in., as is the groove that receives the back panel. Holes are drilled and countersunk, detail A, for three No. 12, 1-in. flathead wood screws to hold the panel. The spring compartments, detail B and Fig. 6, are approximately ¾ in. deep and the recesses for the inkwells ½ in. deep. Note that the ink

cessed and glued into each cap To hold the caps when ink is being used, a wire ring, Fig. 8, is bent as shown to set in the base.

The birds carved on the back panel are bobwhites in flight. Draw the design to size on paper and transfer it to the panel with carbon paper. Then cut the relief with a gouge or small chisel. After the panel has been carved, the initials shown in the top inlay can be cut from a strip of ivory and glued in the piece of walnut.

Just before assembly, give the penholders and collars a coat of shellac which is rubbed down with fine steel wool. Assemble the holders as shown in Fig. 6. Then glue and clamp them to the base. The back panel then is glued and screwed to the base, after which the covers for the ink bottles are glued and clamped. When the adhesive has hardened, all surfaces are smoothed with fine sandpaper, except for the carving which can be high lighted with steel wool to give an antiqued effect.

To finish the set, apply a coat of boiled linseed oil to the walnut parts, masking off

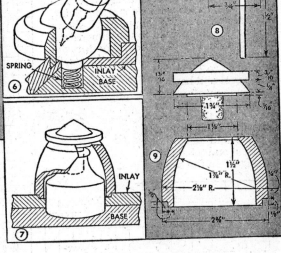

bottles used are those which contain India ink.

The walnut collars for the penholders, upper left-hand detail of Fig. 5, are turned on a lathe, using a template to check the curvature of the rings into which the balls fit. When making the holly-ball penholders, first drill ⅜-in. holes for the pens, plug them with dowels and glue on waste stock with paper between the pieces of wood. Then turn the ball to the dimensions indicated in the lower details of Fig. 5. The complete assembly is shown in Fig. 6. The buttons on which the balls ride also are dimensioned in the lower left-hand detail of Fig. 5. Shown in the upper right-hand detail of Fig. 5, the pens are about ⅜ in. in diameter sanded down to fit the holders. The ink-bottle covers and caps, Figs. 7 and 9, are built of walnut and holly or birch respectively. A cork is re-

the holly or birch. Let the oil stand for ½ hour and wipe with a cloth dampened in turpentine. Then, using thin shellac, brush all surfaces except the inside of the carved panel. Rub down the shellac with fine steel wool and apply a light second coat of linseed oil to the panel, working it in well. Let the set dry for about 24 hours and finish with two coats of furniture wax. To prevent scratching the desk, felt should be glued to the base. The metal ring or ferrule for the penholder and the wire cork holder are added after the set is finished.

Strip-Cut DRAWER PULLS

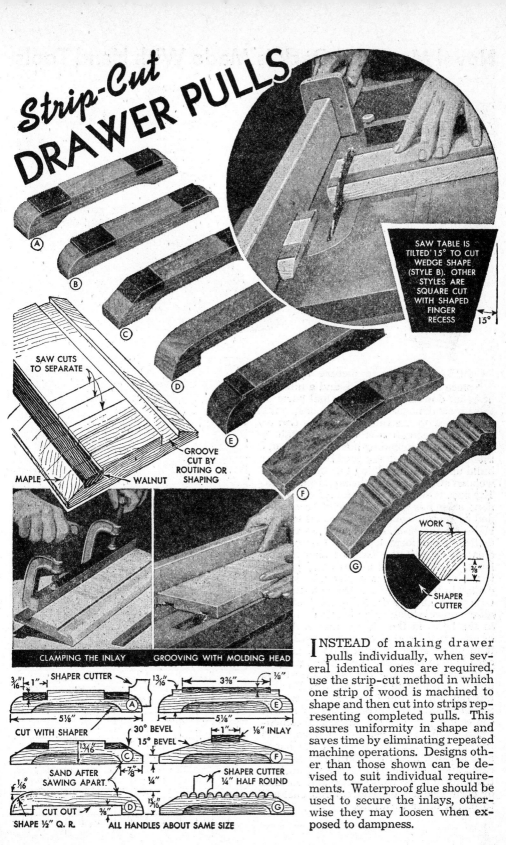

SAW TABLE IS TILTED 15° TO CUT WEDGE SHAPE (STYLE B). OTHER STYLES ARE SQUARE CUT WITH SHAPED FINGER RECESS

15°

SAW CUTS TO SEPARATE

GROOVE CUT BY ROUTING OR SHAPING

MAPLE   WALNUT

WORK

3/8"

SHAPER CUTTER

CLAMPING THE INLAY   GROOVING WITH MOLDING HEAD

3/16" 1"   SHAPER CUTTER   13/16"   3 3/8"   1/8"

Ⓐ   Ⓔ

5 1/8"   5 1/8"

CUT WITH SHAPER

30° BEVEL   1"   1/8" INLAY

15° BEVEL

13/16"   Ⓒ   Ⓕ

SAND AFTER SAWING APART.   7/8"   1/4"

1/16"   SHAPER CUTTER 1/4" HALF ROUND

1/16"   CUT OUT   3/8"   13/16"

SHAPE 1/2" Q. R.   ALL HANDLES ABOUT SAME SIZE   Ⓓ   Ⓖ

INSTEAD of making drawer pulls individually, when several identical ones are required, use the strip-cut method in which one strip of wood is machined to shape and then cut into strips representing completed pulls. This assures uniformity in shape and saves time by eliminating repeated machine operations. Designs other than those shown can be devised to suit individual requirements. Waterproof glue should be used to secure the inlays, otherwise they may loosen when exposed to dampness.

371

Novel Magazine Rack Is Made With Hand Tools

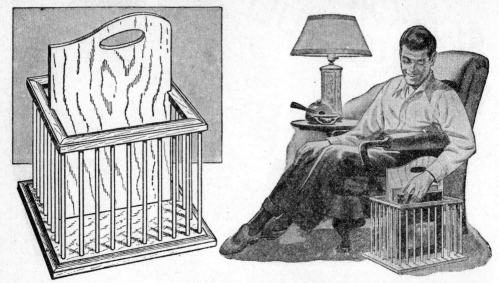

A BREADBOARD, a picture frame, a piece of ½-in. plywood, and a number of ¼-in. dowels are the principal parts of this unusual magazine rack. The design fits in nicely with the furnishings of a den or basement recreation room. Although a breadboard or kneading board from an old kitchen cabinet makes a good base, you can build up a base by gluing together several wooden strips to make the required width. The base is detailed with molded edges but if no shaper is available it can be simplified by merely rounding the edges evenly. Holes for the ¼-in. dowels are spaced and drilled to a uniform depth in the base as indicated. Groove the base as shown. Top frame of the rack is a hardwood picture frame of the dimensions given. Holes are drilled in the back of this frame to register with those already drilled in the base. Cut all the dowels to an equal length and insert in the holes in the picture frame. A spot of glue on the end of each dowel will hold it in place. Next, place a drop of glue in each hole in the base. Then invert the picture frame over the base and insert the dowels one by one into the holes. Finally, tap the top of the frame lightly with a mallet to seat the dowels in the holes. Cut the center panel to the shape and dimensions given in the squared pattern, sand the top edge and the edges of the handhole smooth, notch the top frame as indicated and glue the part in place. Finish in the natural color with shellac and varnish or clear lacquer, or with colored enamels to match other furniture.

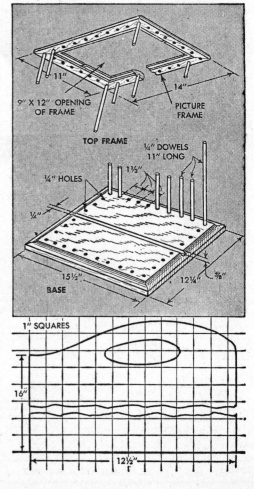

9″ X 12″ OPENING OF FRAME

11″

14″

PICTURE FRAME

TOP FRAME

¼″ DOWELS 11″ LONG

¼″ HOLES

1½″

¼″

15½″

12¼″

⅜″

BASE

1″ SQUARES

16″

12½″

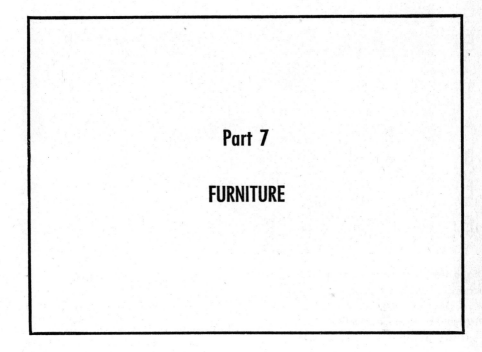

Part 7

FURNITURE

Diagonal slice from hardwood log produces beautiful grain effect to give this graceful coffee table a distinctive and exclusive touch. Legs are half-lapped and interlock

By W. J. LaFleur

IF IT'S the unusual you crave in occasional furniture, this coffee table should really intrigue you. Its novel construction calls for a top sliced diagonally from a log. Cut in this manner, the top assumes the natural contour of the log and the grain is enhanced by the annual-growth rings which take on a beautiful pattern.

The original table top was cut from an 18-in. cherry log, 4 ft. long. The log should be fairly round, thoroughly seasoned and the bark should be removed. To mark the log for cutting, make a wooden frame from stock 1⅜ in. wide, measuring 18 by 29⅛ in., inside measurement. The frame is placed over the log as in Fig. 3 and is tacked temporarily in place. Then a pencil is run around both sides of the frame to mark the log and the space between the lines is chalked. Fig. 1 shows how the log can be supported at an angle with a ladder and braced for sawing. Work carefully with a crosscut saw and try to make both cuts parallel. The saw will produce a rough surface which must be planed flat on the side selected for the underside of the top. Then ¾₁₆-in. grooves are run on

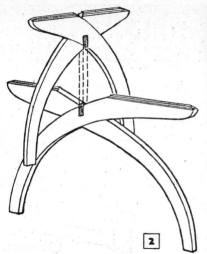

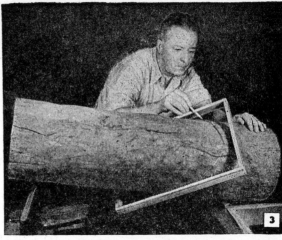

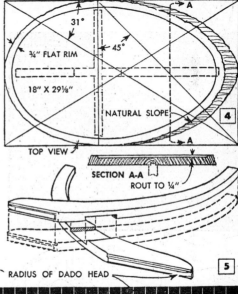

the underside for the leg tenons, locating them according to Fig. 4. Each groove can be cut on a bench saw by cutting a wooden strip to slide in one of the saw-table grooves and tacking it to the underside of the work parallel with the line of cut. A ¾-in. rim is marked around the top surface and the area inside the rim is routed ¼ in. deep. This can be done with a router bit in a drill press, or with a portable router. After sanding smooth, a sealer should be applied to both sides of the top to seal the end grain and to retard checking. Fig. 6 details the leg patterns. Although the point of half lap is indicated by dotted lines, it is best to determine this by placing one corresponding leg on top of the other, as in Fig. 5, and marking directly. The assembled pairs of legs are notched to fit together as in Fig. 2 and then the top is glued to the leg tenons.

31°

45°

¾″ FLAT RIM

18″ X 29⅛″

NATURAL SLOPE

TOP VIEW

SECTION A-A

ROUT TO ¼″

RADIUS OF DADO HEAD

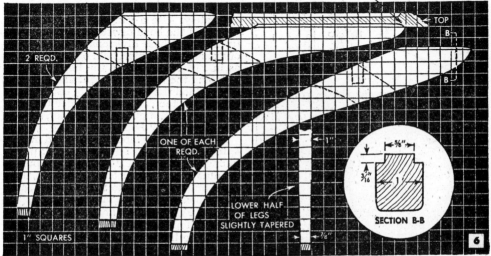

2 REQD.

ONE OF EACH REQD.

LOWER HALF OF LEGS SLIGHTLY TAPERED

1″ SQUARES

TOP

⅝″

3/16″

1″

SECTION B-B

1″

7/8″

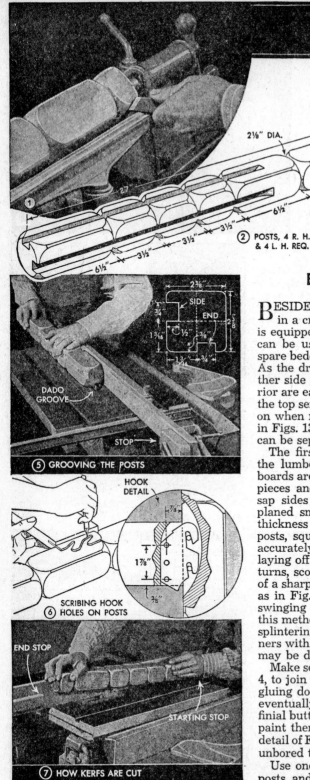

BUNKS and

By Edwin M. Love

B ESIDES saving considerable floor space in a crowded room, this bunk-bed unit is equipped with a mammoth drawer that can be used for storage, whether this is spare bedding or a fleet of model airplanes. As the drawer can be pulled out from either side of the bunk all parts of the interior are easily accessible. A plank fitted to the top serves as a handy platform to stand on when making the upper bed, as shown in Figs. 13, 15 and 16. The beds, however, can be separated and used as twin beds.

The first step in construction is to cut the lumber roughly to size. If the wide boards are warped, rip them into narrower pieces and glue together with heart and sap sides alternating. They then can be planed smooth without too much loss of thickness and will remain flat. To turn the posts, square the pieces and center them accurately. Use a gauge stick, Fig. 3, for laying off the bead divisions. As the work turns, score these divisions with the point of a sharp skew chisel held on the tool rest as in Fig. 1, and shape the bead ends by swinging the tool to the right and left. By this method the bead ends are cut without splintering the corners. Chamfer the corners with a light cut on the jointer, or this may be done by hand.

Make separator blocks as detailed in Fig. 4, to join the upper and lower bunk posts, gluing dowels in their ends. If the bunks eventually are to be used as twin beds, turn finial buttons to go into the post holes, and paint them to match the beds. See upper detail of Fig. 10. Disks are sufficient for the unbored tops of the upper bunk posts.

Use one blade of a dado saw to slit the posts and bed-rail ends to take the rail

STORAGE SPACE *in One Unit*

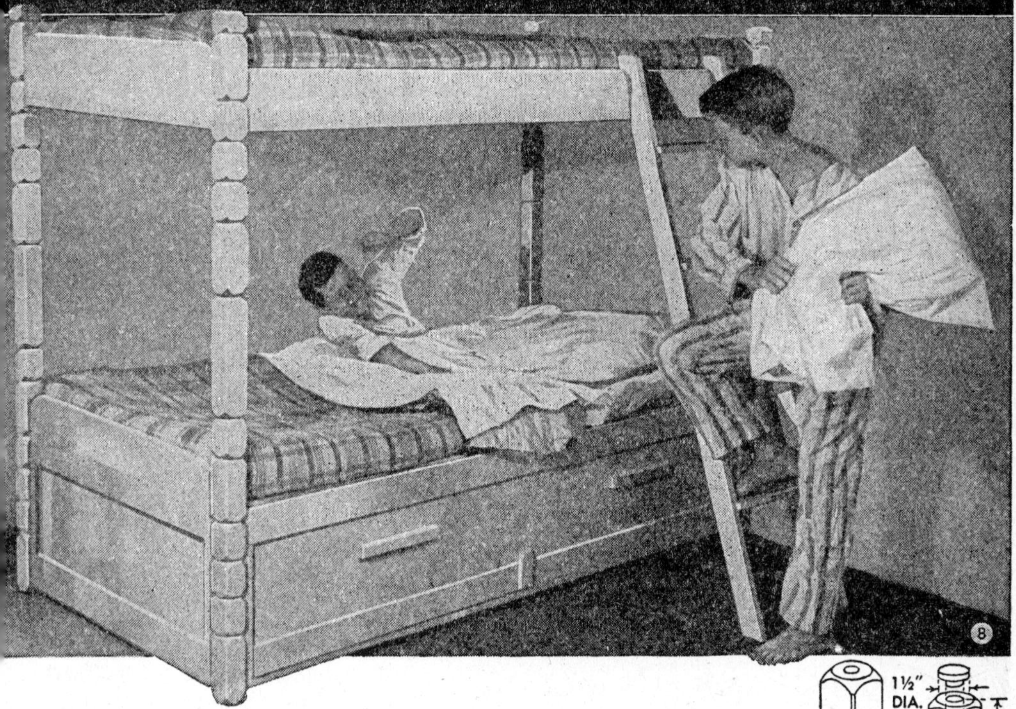

Here's the logical solution to the frequent problem of getting more space in the growing boys' bedroom. Consisting of two separate beds, which can be used individually instead of in bunk formation, this unit is provided with a mammoth drawer that can be pulled out at either side for easy access to its contents

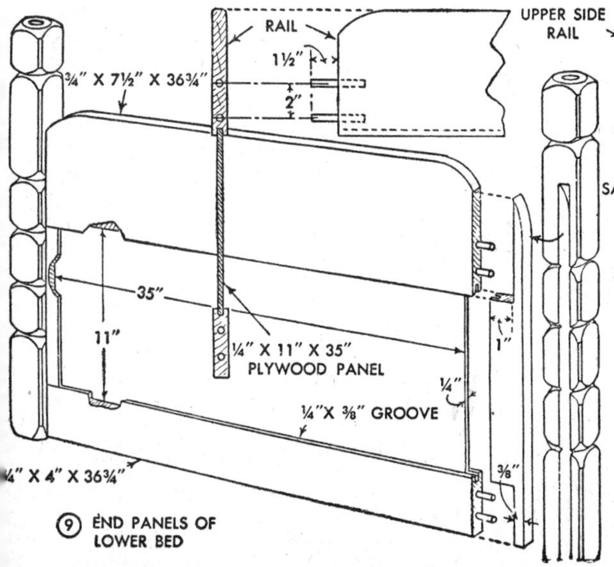

⑨ END PANELS OF LOWER BED

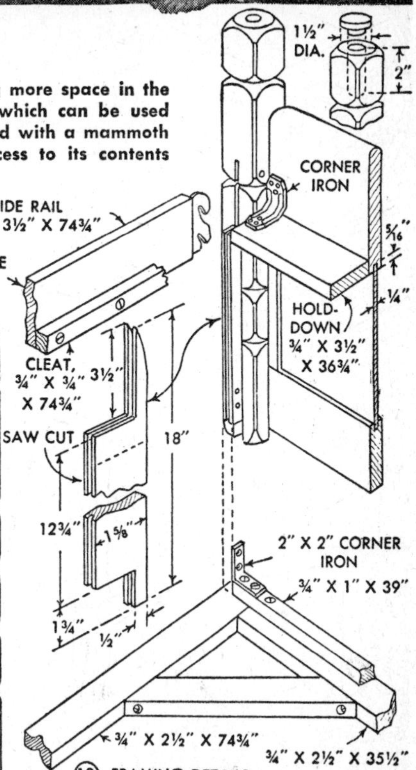

¾" X 7½" X 36¾"

RAIL

1½"

2"

UPPER SIDE RAIL

SIDE RAIL
¾" X 3½" X 74¾"

35"

¼" X 11" X 35"
PLYWOOD PANEL

11"

¼" X ⅜" GROOVE

¼" X 4" X 36¾"

1"

¼"

⅜"

CLEAT,
¾" X ¾" X 3½"
X 74¾"

SAW CUT

12¾"

1⅝"

1¾"

½"

18"

1½"
DIA.

2"

CORNER IRON

HOLD-DOWN
¾" X 3½"
X 36¾"

5/16"
¼"

¼"

2" X 2" CORNER IRON
¾" X 1" X 39"

⑩ FRAMING DETAILS OF LOWER BED

¾" X 2½" X 74¾"

¾" X 2½" X 35½"

hooks. Install the hooks in the rails and secure the pins with wooden wedges to prevent them from dropping out. Use one rail end fitted with a hook as a template for scribing the pin locations on a post as in Fig. 6, taking a pattern from this for the rest. Center the pins where the hooks will bear against them and draw the rail ends tight when the rail is ⅛ in. above level. The joints will be rigid when the rails are driven down to position. Then determine the length of the saw kerfs in the posts, and set start and stop blocks on the circular saw to correspond, as shown in Fig. 7.

Next mount a ¾-in. dado head and groove the posts ½ in. deep to receive the panel stiles as shown in Figs. 2 and 5. Make the stiles, rounding the ends to fit the grooves or chiseling the groove ends square, as preferred. The exact position of the grooves is shown in the detail of Fig. 5. Kerf the ends of the drawer stiles to receive the ends of the hooks that project below the rails.

Bore dowel holes in the end rails and use them as patterns for locating the post dowel holes. As-

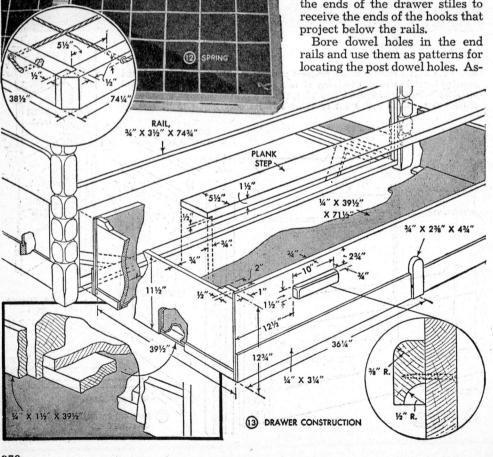

⑫ SPRING

RAIL, ¾" X 3½" X 74¾"

PLANK STEP

⑬ DRAWER CONSTRUCTION

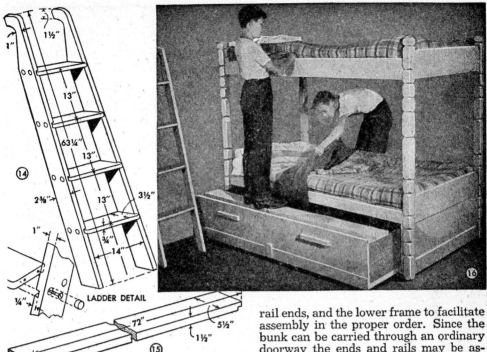

LADDER DETAIL

72"

5½"

1½"

⑮

PLANK STEP

½"   ¾"

semble the rails and stiles with the end panels and when the glue is dry assemble with the posts as in Fig. 9. Clean up the ends and attach the side rails. Build the lower frame to fit, screwing in the corner braces as in Fig. 10 and reinforcing all joints with corrugated fasteners driven into the underside. Wax the upper side of the frame. To support the frame make six blocks of suitable thickness, nailing one under each corner, set well back, and one at the center of each drawer rail. Add the drawer guides, which are flush with the sides of the drawer, since this can be pulled from either side. The four corner irons screwed to the guides and inner surfaces of the drawer stiles prevent the frame from dropping if the bunk is lifted. The corner irons are not intended to take the weight of the drawer, for which purpose the blocks, already mentioned, are provided.

Build the drawer with the sides rabbeted into the fronts and the bottom rabbeted into the front and sides as in Fig. 13. Hardwood strips nailed to the ends and across the center take the wear and provide clearance for easy sliding of the drawer. Use plywood to make overlays for the drawer fronts. A wooden overlay shaped to match the post turning is placed at the center. Both sides are made exactly alike.

Before taking the bunk apart, number the four corners of the drawer, the bed and

rail ends, and the lower frame to facilitate assembly in the proper order. Since the bunk can be carried through an ordinary doorway the ends and rails may be assembled by means of dowels, making a rigid housing for the drawer and eliminating the bother of fitting rail hooks. The upper bunk ends are assembled with two posts and a wide rail, and are put together with the rails like any ordinary bed.

Glue and screw cleats inside the rails near the lower edges to carry the springs. Rope springs, Fig. 12, are quite satisfactory, although they tend to sag like hammocks when the ropes stretch, and the ropes cannot be drawn too tightly or the sides bow in unduly. If tight and flat springs are desired, stiffen the sides by nailing a 1 by 6-in. board lengthwise under each edge, setting it in ¾ in. to allow for the rail cleats. The rope is laced through holes drilled in the spring frames as shown in Fig. 11, the ends of the rope being knotted. Details of frame corner construction and sizes are given in the circular insert of Fig. 12.

A simple four-step ladder is shown in Figs. 8 and 14. Gain the ends of the steps into the sides of the ladder and secure them with screws having heads sunk in counterbored holes. Glue plugs into the holes and dress them flush when dry.

❧ If you will cover the corners of your wire bed springs with adhesive tape, the sheets will not catch and tear.

❧ Remove grease and grime from mahogany furniture with a cloth wrung out in lukewarm water to which a little pure soap has been added. Dry with a soft cloth, wiping lightly with grain of wood.

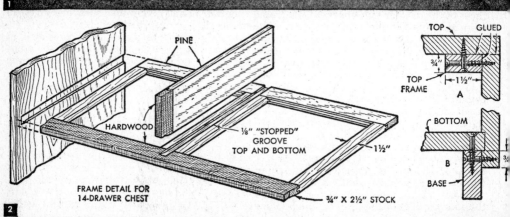

TOP

GLUED

¾"

TOP
FRAME

1½"

A

BOTTOM

B

BASE

PINE

HARDWOOD

⅛" "STOPPED"
GROOVE
TOP AND BOTTOM

1½"

FRAME DETAIL FOR
14-DRAWER CHEST

¾" X 2½" STOCK

HER OWN CHEST OF DRAWERS

By Wallace W. Buffmire

FOR the little girl in your home—or the small boy, for that matter —chests of drawers, such as the two shown here, will do much to improve the appearance of the bedroom and also serve as an incentive for the youngster to keep her clothes and possessions in a neat and orderly manner. Either chest may complement and serve to expand a suite that you have already. There is ample space in both for all your youngster's linen with possibly a drawer or so left over for a collection of childish treasures. The chest with two doors, Fig. 1, has a top drawer that is shallower and a bottom drawer that is deeper than the other five. All extend the full width of the chest. If you want to store blankets and bulky clothing, drawers like these are best. The other chest, Fig. 5, has fourteen drawers of equal size. Where many individual compartments are required, this chest would be the better choice. Selection of the one you prefer to build may be governed by these factors. The chests look best when made of hardwoods, such as walnut or maple, and stained. Or they can be made of the semi-hardwoods such as poplar or gum and then painted. The originals were made of maple and given a blond or bleached finish.

Construction of the closed chest is given in Fig. 3. The doors are glued up from solid stock and splined top and bottom as in Fig. 4 to prevent warping. Drawer construction is of the usual type. However, in this case narrow strips were nailed to the sides near the lower edge. The strips help avoid binding by preventing the entire side from coming in contact with the chest. Notice that the chest top overhangs an amount equal to the thickness of the doors so they are flush. If available, use long piano hinges to hang the doors. These will help prevent warping also. Friction catches are used in the top edge to hold the doors closed.

The sides, top and bottom are made of built-up sections joined as shown in Fig. 3. The back is plywood rabbeted to the sides. Blind grooves are cut in the sides for the frames which are

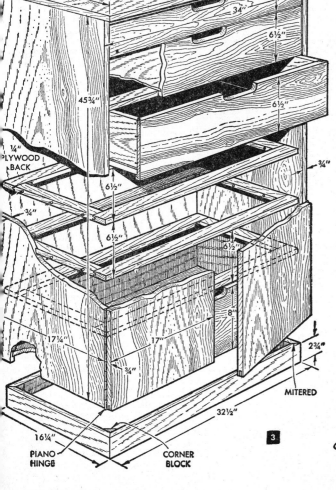

18" 34" 3¾" 6½" 6½" 6½" 45¾" ¼" PLYWOOD BACK 6½" ¾" ¾" 6½" 6½" 8" 17¼" 17" ¾" 2¾" MITERED 32½" 16¼" PIANO HINGE CORNER BLOCK

3

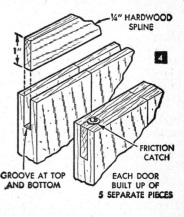

¼" HARDWOOD SPLINE 1" **4** FRICTION CATCH GROOVE AT TOP AND BOTTOM EACH DOOR BUILT UP OF 5 SEPARATE PIECES

DRAWER PULL
14 REQ'D

SECTIONAL
VIEW

cut at the front corners to fit. Tongue-and-groove joints are used in assembling the frames. These are glued and screwed in place. The base has mitered joints reinforced with corner blocks and sets inside the cabinet. It is attached as indicated in detail B of Fig. 2. Detail A shows how the top is fastened to the sides and frame. After the cabinet is assembled, you may find that several thumbtacks in the frame where the drawers slide will make them work more smoothly. Also, the runners can be waxed occasionally. Although not shown, handles for the doors add to the beauty of the chest. These are round pieces planed to have one flat side and they are screwed to the doors.

In many ways, the construction of the 14-drawer chest is similar to that of the other chest. The sides, top, back and base are built in a similar manner. The overall dimensions vary, however. The spacing for the frames of the 14-drawer chest is equal since all drawers are the same size. Fig. 2 gives details of the frame assembly. Note that the front of the frame and the divider

can be hardwood while the remainder is pine or some other less expensive wood. This will reduce the cost of construction to some extent. The same type of construction can be used for the door chest. Fig. 6 gives the dimensions and method of assembly for the drawers. Plywood is used for the bottom, and the sides, front and back are made from solid stock. The front overlaps the frame on all sides. The drawer pulls are cut from 1-in.-square stock. In this chest the top is flush with the sides and does not overlap as in the previous case.

Many effects may be obtained in finishing the chests. If they are made of a semi-soft wood, spraying with a bone-white lacquer gives an excellent finish that is very popular. As a further touch, they may be decorated with decals. If hardwood is used, some light-toned finish is best. Maple can be bleached to a blond color that is almost white, while walnut will bleach to a russet or straw color. After the bleaching has been done and the bleach neutralized, spray with clear gloss lacquer. If the wood is maple a water-white lacquer is used.

All-Purpose KNEEHOLE DESK

By Willard Allphin

Hᴇʀᴇ is the desk you've been waiting for—a big roomy one, good looking, with built-in typewriter slide, and designed to harmonize with both modern and traditional furniture. What's more, it is very easy to make. Ends, front and top are plywood, hardwood faced, which can be had in oak, birch, walnut, mahogany, etc. The rest of the desk is made of solid hardwood stock with inner shelves, partitions and other unexposed parts being made of soft and less expensive wood. Both end compartments of the desk are assembled as separate units. Cut out the three corner posts of each unit first.

Finished in limed oak, bleached mahogany, blond or rich walnut, this stunning desk will harmonize with most furniture. Featuring a built-in typewriter slide and the latest "island" base, the desk has four roomy drawers and a 24 by 48-in. working surface. Clean lines make construction easy

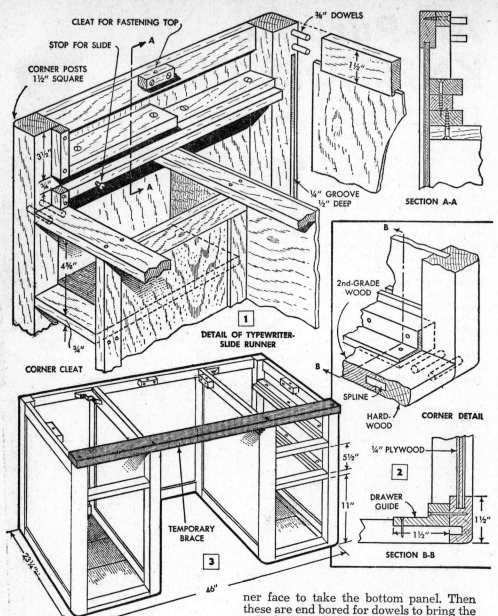

CLEAT FOR FASTENING TOP

STOP FOR SLIDE

CORNER POSTS
1½" SQUARE

3½"

¾"

4⅝"

¾"

CORNER CLEAT

⅜" DOWELS

1½"

¼" GROOVE
½" DEEP

1

DETAIL OF TYPEWRITER-
SLIDE RUNNER

SECTION A-A

2nd-GRADE
WOOD

B

B

SPLINE

HARD-
WOOD

CORNER DETAIL

¼" PLYWOOD

2

DRAWER
GUIDE

1½"

1½"

SECTION B-B

TEMPORARY
BRACE

23¼"

3

46"

5½"

11"

These are 1½-in. square stock and are grooved lengthwise for ¼-in. plywood. Note that the grooves are run ¼ in. in from the outside edge and that they are stopped 1 in. from each end for dowel joints. The rear posts of each unit are grooved on one face only, whereas the others are grooved on two adjacent faces. All end rails are edge-grooved for the plywood panels, the lower ones also being grooved on the in-

ner face to take the bottom panel. Then these are end bored for dowels to bring the rails flush with the outer face of the corner posts. The bottom panel of each unit is made up of soft wood and the front edge is faced with a hardwood rail. The bottom panel of the right-hand unit differs from the other in that a shallow groove is run along each edge for an L-shaped drawer guide, as detailed in Fig. 2. The outer corners of all posts and the lower edge of all bottom rails are rounded ½ in. The panels of the kneehole are made the same size as the end panels, except that the edge which butts against the front panel is edged with

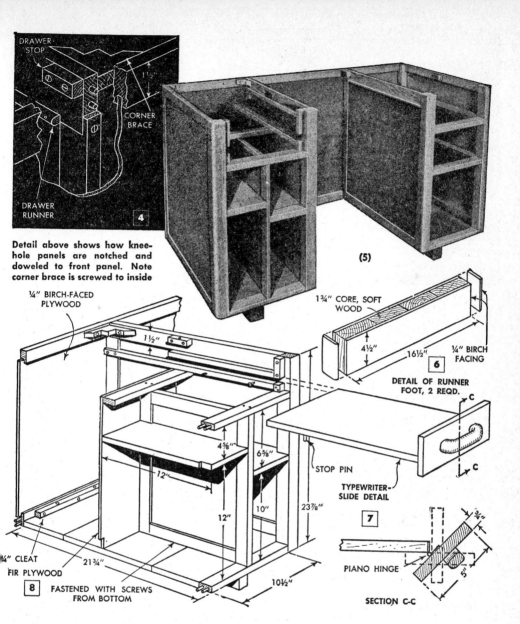

DRAWER STOP

$1\frac{1}{2}''$

CORNER BRACE

DRAWER RUNNER

4

Detail above shows how kneehole panels are notched and
doweled to front panel. Note
corner brace is screwed to inside

$\frac{1}{4}''$ BIRCH-FACED
PLYWOOD

$1\frac{1}{2}''$

(5)

$1\frac{3}{4}''$ CORE, SOFT
WOOD

$4\frac{1}{2}''$

$16\frac{1}{2}''$

$\frac{1}{4}''$ BIRCH
FACING

6

DETAIL OF RUNNER
FOOT, 2 REQD.

C

$4\frac{5}{8}''$

$6\frac{5}{8}''$

STOP PIN

$12''$

$12''$

$10''$

$23\frac{7}{8}''$

C

TYPEWRITER-
SLIDE DETAIL

7

$\frac{1}{4}''$ CLEAT

FIR PLYWOOD

$21\frac{3}{4}''$

8 FASTENED WITH SCREWS
FROM BOTTOM

$10\frac{1}{2}''$

PIANO HINGE

$\frac{3}{4}''$

$\frac{5}{8}''$

SECTION C-C

a $\frac{3}{4}$-in. member notched to fit over the
lower rail, Fig. 3. Fig. 4 shows how a notch
is formed at the top, after which the piece
is doweled to both rails at the top and
bottom.

Start assembling the parts by gluing and
clamping together the rear ends of the
units. Follow this by gluing and clamping
the outer end panels to them. When this is
done, place a brace diagonally from post to
post and nail temporarily to hold the assembly square while the glue is drying.
Next, put in the dustproof bottom panels
and then add the kneehole panels. Finally,
glue and clamp both assembled units to the
front plywood panel. In doing this, fit the
dowel joints of the kneehole panel first.
When dry, spring out the corner posts to
engage the dowels in the ends of the rails.
Your desk should now look like Fig. 3.
Note that a temporary wooden brace is
placed across the two units to hold the assembly square.

Fig. 8 details the book compartments for
the left-hand unit, and you'll notice that
these do not extend the full depth of the
unit. Here, the shelves are edge-faced with
hardwood as before, the facing strips being
fastened to the posts with screws driven
from the underside and at an angle. Figs.

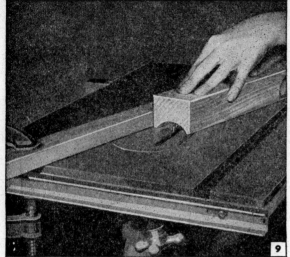

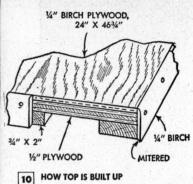

Here is how the thickness of the top is obtained. Two thicknesses of plywood, plus ¾ by 2-in. battens, form core which is faced around the edge with ¼-in. hardwood

¼" BIRCH PLYWOOD, 24" X 46¾"

¾" X 2"

½" PLYWOOD

¼" BIRCH

MITERED

1 and 8 show how the guide is installed for the typewriter slide which folds up to represent a drawer when not in use. Section A-A shows how three strips placed on top of one another form a channel for the slide. Construction of this varies slightly when installing it on the opposite side, as shown in Fig. 8. Fig. 7 details the slide itself and how the front is hinged.

Next come the bases. These are of the popular "island" type and are built up as in Fig. 6. A core of softwood is faced with ¼-in. hardwood and then counterbored holes are made through the core for attaching the base to the bottom and in the center of each unit. At this point the desk should look like Fig. 5. This brings you to the construction of the top, Fig. 10, which is built up of two panels of plywood, one being of ½-in. fir plywood, and the other ¼-in. hardwood faced. These are glued together and backed with five ¾ by 2-in. strips, which run lengthwise to add thickness and provide a gluing surface for a ¼-in. edging.

The drawers are detailed in Figs. 11, 12 and 13. The center drawer has no handle. Grooves cut in the side of the drawer, ride over runners which are bradded to the sides of the kneehole panels. Fig. 9 shows a method of cutting the pencil tray by repeatedly passing the work across a rotating saw blade at an angle.

PENCIL TRAY

4"

9"

4" SQ.

3½"

¼" DRAWER-RUNNER GROOVE

18"

11

20"

1⅛"

5"

1½"

12

DRAWER HANDLE, 4 REQD.

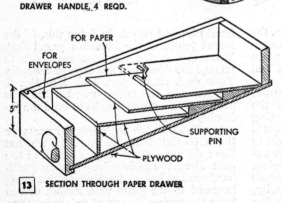

FOR PAPER

FOR ENVELOPES

5"

SUPPORTING PIN

PLYWOOD

13 SECTION THROUGH PAPER DRAWER

BACHELOR CHEST
built with hand tools

Low, four-drawer chest of Colonial design has a pull-out leaf under the top to provide a handy place for writing

By W. W. Buffmire

IDEAL for the man who does occasional writing, but whose room will not accommodate both a chest and a desk, the attractive chest shown in Fig. 1 combines both. If the chest appeals without the desk feature, the pull-out shelf can be omitted and the overall height increased to a full-size chest.

For economy, rip the front rails of the six drawer frames of finished stock and the inner members of less expensive material such as birch or gum. From Fig. 3 you will see that the bottom frame differs from the others by being of thicker stock, wider and fitted with a dust panel. Dovetails formed on the ends of the top frame to engage similar cuts in the chest sides as in Fig. 2, lock the assembly together at the top. At the base, the sides are fastened even with the bottom edge of the lower frame, using screws and glue, the screw

TOP FRAME

SIDE OF CHEST

TWO TOP FRAMES SPACED ¾" APART FOR PULL-OUT SHELF BOARD

30½"

3/4" X 2"

DRAWER GUIDE

15½"

2" X 2" STOCK

6"

¼" DUST BOTTOM

¼" BACK-PANEL GROOVE

heads being concealed later by the base and its molding. All the frames, with the exception of the two top ones, include a center crossrail to which a narrow strip is nailed to register with a grooved one fastened to the underside of the drawer bottom. If you prefer, a rabbet can be cut along the rear edge of the lower frame instead of a groove as indicated. Keep the dust panel close to the top of the frame so it will not interfere in attaching the base with screws, which are driven from the inside. The screw holes should be drilled before the frame is assembled. Use two 1/4-in. dowels at each joint, glue and clamp flat.

As the sides of the chest are 16 in. wide, you will have to build these up in width from three or four separate pieces. Take care in planing the abutting edges straight and true and in locating the dowel holes in the edges to bring the surfaces flush. The use of dowels will assure sound construction, but a glued butt joint will be satisfactory provided the edges have been jointed properly. Fig. 6 gives the spacing of the frames. All the frames are fastened to one side of the chest first, and then to the other side. Notice from Fig. 8 that short dowels and screws are used in addition to glue to hold the frames, three screws being driven through each end from the inside as shown in Fig. 9. Before fastening the two top frames to the sides, be sure to provide holes in the top frame for the screws that hold the top in place; also bore holes in the second frame to permit insertion of a screwdriver to reach the screws. This is shown in the detail to the right of Fig. 4. Leave about a 7/8-in. space between the top

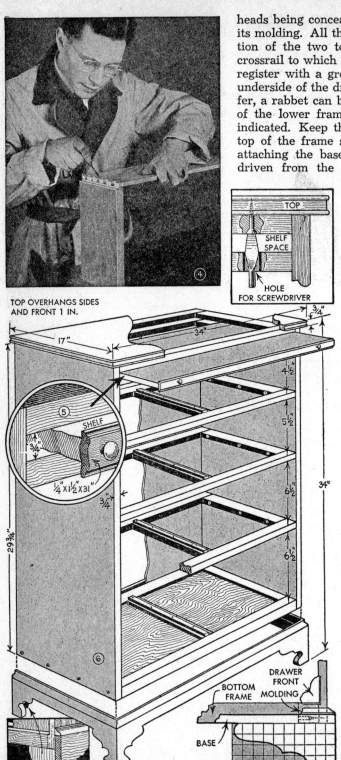

TOP OVERHANGS SIDES AND FRONT 1 IN.

TOP

SHELF SPACE

HOLE FOR SCREWDRIVER

17"

34"

3/4"
3/4"

4 1/2"

5 1/2"

34"

6 1/2"

6 1/2"

29 3/4"

SHELF

3/4"

1/4" X 1 1/2" X 31"

3/4"

BRACE

BOTTOM FRAME

DRAWER FRONT MOLDING

BASE

1/2" SQS.

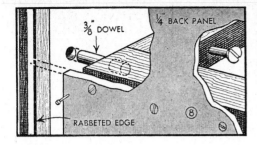

frames to allow ample clearance for the finish and for thumbtacks, which are pressed in place at each end to make the shelf slide easier. Cut the back plywood panel squarely so that when it is fitted snugly in the rabbets and screwed to each frame, it will automatically square up the assembly.

The base pieces, which are mitered to overlap the sides and front of the chest, are scrollsawed at the ends according to the pattern given in Fig. 7. The chest is set down inside the base ¾ in., and is attached with screws from the inside through holes provided for them in the lower frame. At the back the cross grain of the leg is reinforced with a brace as indicated in the detail to the left of Fig. 7, while each front leg is fitted with a triangular corner block. Complete the base by attaching the molding to it with small finishing nails, setting the heads below the surface and filling with plastic wood.

Drawer fronts are rabbeted as shown in Fig. 10 to overlap the openings ¼ in. If you feel capable of cutting a dovetail drawer joint, this may be used instead of rabbets as in Fig. 4. As in the case of the frames, only choice stock is used for the fronts. With this type of drawer, ample clearance can be allowed to prevent binding as the extra-loose fit of the drawer will not be seen. The bottom, which is set in grooves run in the front and sides, is left long enough to extend under the drawer back. The writing shelf is built up like a drawing board,

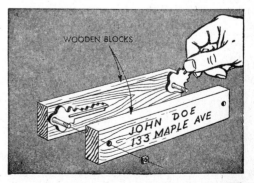

that is, with strips doweled across the ends to check warping. Saw kerfs cut lengthwise on the underside of the shelf about 1 in. apart and ⅜ in. deep, before the end strips are added, also will help keep it from warping. The facing strip along the front edge of the shelf is cut to overlap the opening about ¼ in. all around as shown in Fig. 5, after which a small brass knob is fitted at each end. Metal drawer pulls of the type shown on the original chest are standard and can be obtained in either antique finish or polished brass.

Wooden Key Container Floats

Made of balsa wood, this container or holder is ideal for boat and tackle-box keys because it won't sink if accidentally dropped into the water. The two blocks that form the sides of the holder should be large enough to provide buoyancy and float the weight of the metal. Brass screws, which will not rust and are resistant to the action of salt water, are used to hold the keys in place. Your name and address can be burned, cut or stamped into the wood as a means of identification.

Auxiliary Table Top Increases Playing Surface

Where to play when the gang comes in for an evening of cards is solved in a hurry when you have this auxiliary top, which is designed to set over an ordinary card table. Hinged at the center, it takes up little storage space in a closet, and when open, it forms a large-size playing surface which seats eight persons comfortably. Construction consists of adding trough-like compartments around the edge of an octagon-shape centerpiece. The whole thing can be assembled as one unit and later sawed in half, or each half can be made up separately. Start by laying out and sawing the eight-sided centerpiece. The compartments are added to the edge of this by first fitting and nailing ½ by 3-in. pieces all around, mitering them where they meet at the corners. Next, the 3-in. pieces forming the bottom of the trough are nailed to the lower edge of the previous piece, mitering it as before. This is followed by fitting the outside piece, and then the trough is divided into compartments by inserting partitions at the eight points. A continuous (piano) hinge makes the neatest job, although two or three butt hinges will do. Complete the job by gluing felt to both top and bottom. Finish with enamel or varnish to match your furniture.

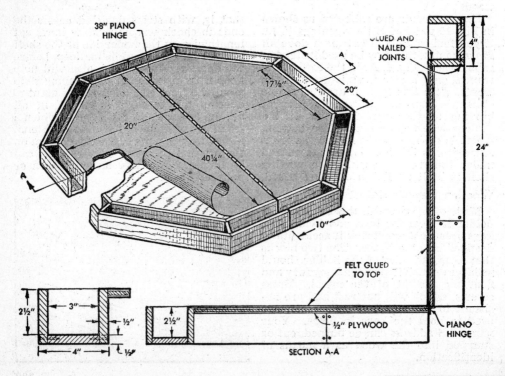

SECTION A-A

Before

After

Restoring
ANTIQUE FURNITURE

By Robert Clarence Stahler

PART I—Making Repairs and Removing Old Finish

Have you a piece of antique furniture that you would like to use in your home, but have kept hidden away because it needed restoring? Or, if you have none on hand, but would like an antique piece or two in your home, inquire among your friends or at used-furniture stores. From such sources, you can often pick up a piece for practically nothing that needs only minor repairing and finishing to restore its original beauty. With a few common hand tools, some shellac and varnish, any good craftsman can do this. If possible, before beginning work, inspect a genuine old piece that has never been refinished. Probably you will find minute marks and scars all over it, and the finish will have

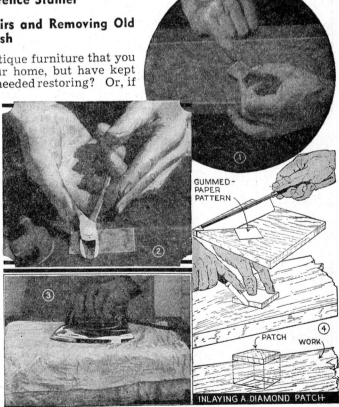

GUMMED-PAPER PATTERN

PATCH WORK

INLAYING A DIAMOND PATCH

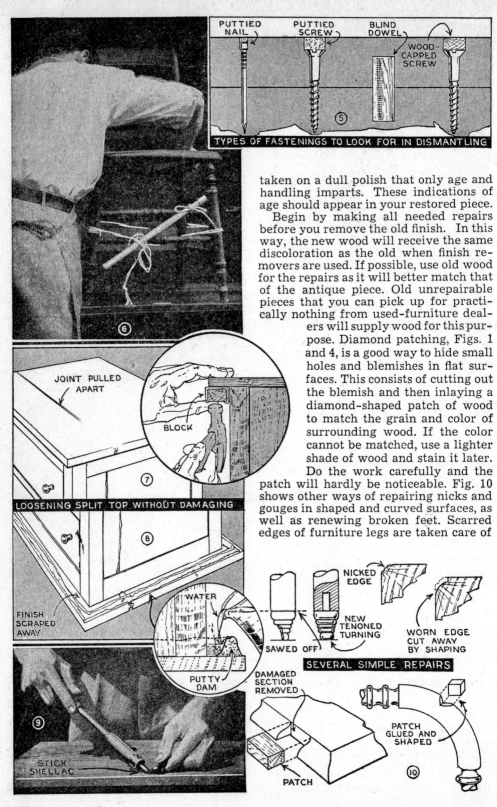

TYPES OF FASTENINGS TO LOOK FOR IN DISMANTLING

taken on a dull polish that only age and handling imparts. These indications of age should appear in your restored piece.

Begin by making all needed repairs before you remove the old finish. In this way, the new wood will receive the same discoloration as the old when finish removers are used. If possible, use old wood for the repairs as it will better match that of the antique piece. Old unrepairable pieces that you can pick up for practically nothing from used-furniture dealers will supply wood for this purpose. Diamond patching, Figs. 1 and 4, is a good way to hide small holes and blemishes in flat surfaces. This consists of cutting out the blemish and then inlaying a diamond-shaped patch of wood to match the grain and color of surrounding wood. If the color cannot be matched, use a lighter shade of wood and stain it later. Do the work carefully and the patch will hardly be noticeable. Fig. 10 shows other ways of repairing nicks and gouges in shaped and curved surfaces, as well as renewing broken feet. Scarred edges of furniture legs are taken care of

JOINT PULLED APART

BLOCK

LOOSENING SPLIT TOP WITHOUT DAMAGING

FINISH SCRAPED AWAY

WATER

PUTTY DAM

STICK SHELLAC

NICKED EDGE

NEW TENONED TURNING

SAWED OFF

WORN EDGE CUT AWAY BY SHAPING

SEVERAL SIMPLE REPAIRS

DAMAGED SECTION REMOVED

PATCH

PATCH GLUED AND SHAPED

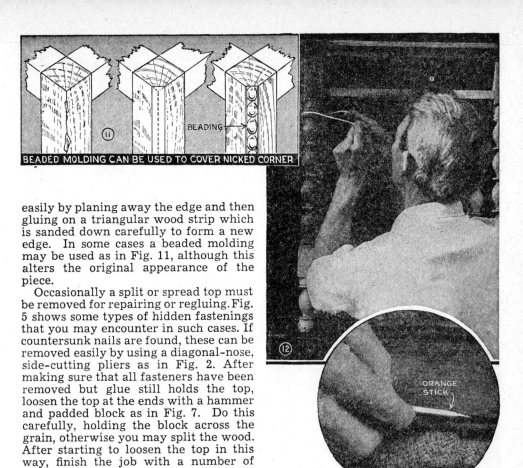

BEADING

BEADED MOLDING CAN BE USED TO COVER NICKED CORNER

(12)

ORANGE STICK

(13)

easily by planing away the edge and then gluing on a triangular wood strip which is sanded down carefully to form a new edge. In some cases a beaded molding may be used as in Fig. 11, although this alters the original appearance of the piece.

Occasionally a split or spread top must be removed for repairing or regluing. Fig. 5 shows some types of hidden fastenings that you may encounter in such cases. If countersunk nails are found, these can be removed easily by using a diagonal-nose, side-cutting pliers as in Fig. 2. After making sure that all fasteners have been removed but glue still holds the top, loosen the top at the ends with a hammer and padded block as in Fig. 7. Do this carefully, holding the block across the grain, otherwise you may split the wood. After starting to loosen the top in this way, finish the job with a number of wedges driven progressively underneath it. However, if this method fails to loosen the top, you will have to soften the glue with water, as in Fig. 8. Invert the furniture piece and make a putty dam around the overhanging top to retain the water.

Wobbly pieces will have to be taken apart. Less resistance will be had if the pieces are stored in a hot, dry place for a few days—in an attic in summer or over a hot-air register in winter. This causes the wood to shrink and loosens the tight joints. Before reassembling the work, remove every trace of old glue. A cloth dipped in hot water is effective to clean the rung and stretcher holes of chairs. Use only the best glue, such as the new resin glue, and be sure to return the various parts to their original positions. Use plenty of clamps with pads under the jaws, to hold the parts tightly until the glue dries. If you lack these, rope tourniquets, Fig. 6, can be used on chairs if they are set on a flat surface, while an improvised clamp as in Fig. 16 will take care of flat work. In using this clamp, first put the work in it, holding it down with a C-clamp. Locate and screw the

wedge blocks to the cross members, allowing clearance to start the wedges. Then remove the work, apply glue to the joints, replace it in the clamp and pull up the joints tightly by driving the wedges between the work and the wedge blocks. All wet glue that oozes from the joints must be removed carefully as stain will not penetrate it after it dries.

If you are working on a drop-leaf table, the top or leaves are likely to be warped, Fig. 14. The usual cure by soaking them in water and then clamping them flat to dry is only a temporary cure as the warp eventually reappears. A more permanent method is shown in Fig. 15. The leaf is clamped in a frame and steamed slowly, using a hot iron and a damp cloth as when pressing a garment, Fig. 3, alternately wetting the cloth and ironing it dry on the wood. While doing this the clamps are slowly tightened at intervals until the leaf is straight. It may take an hour of steaming to do this. When the leaf is flat, release the clamps a trifle, which permits the expanded wood to contract upon drying without danger of splitting, which might occur if the clamps were left tight. When dry, strips are screwed across the underside.

After all repairs have been made, except those in which stick shellac or plastic wood must be used as in Fig. 9, the old finish is removed with

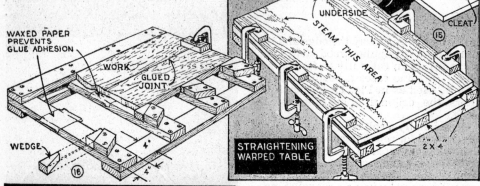

The old finish is wiped off after softening it with varnish remover

the best grade of paint-and-varnish remover. Clean burlap is excellent for wiping off the loosened finish, Fig. 17. When as much as possible has been removed, apply clean remover to loosen the remaining traces. Then while the wood is still wet, wash off all traces of varnish remover with turpentine. However, naphtha or benzine can be used if sufficient ventilation is provided to carry off the fumes. It is important that all traces of varnish

remover must be eliminated before any finish is applied; new finish will not dry over traces of remover even if this is dry. After thorough cleaning, the pieces are set in a warm, airy location but not in direct sunlight where they might warp. If some of the wood has a muddy tint or is too dark to match adjacent pieces, it may have to be lightly bleached. Bleaching solutions or powders can be obtained at a paint store or you can use a saturated solution of oxalic-acid crystals (poisonous) dissolved in water for moderate bleaching. It is often difficult to remove all traces of light colored enamels from open-grained wood, but after washing with turpentine, naphtha or benzine, proper filling to be described later, will cover these traces of enamel. Ink stains can usually be removed by means of a commercial ink-remover and mildew stains will usually fade under a bleach, but if they remain, you may have to resort to scraping.

Thoroughly cleaned work, when dry, is ready for sanding with No. 4/0 garnet paper, which should be rubbed with the grain. Crosswise strokes cause objectionable scratches. On turnings you can use narrow strips of fine emery cloth drawn back and forth in boot-black fashion as shown in Fig. 12, while steel wool is best for carvings. Also, to get into crevices, an orange stick, Fig. 13, flattened at one end will be handy.

Restoring Antique Furniture

By R. C. Stahler

PART II—Finishing Methods

Apply water stains evenly with a full-bodied brush, avoiding sloppy places and "rivers," which are likely to streak the wood

After you have made all major repairs on your antique piece and sanded it smooth, you are ready for finishing. First comes staining which is very important as you can ruin the appearance of an otherwise beautiful piece by improper use and application of stain. Mix and apply stains in natural light. Acid, spirit and penetrating stains are difficult to apply evenly. Colors in oil, used in oil stains, are not permanent, and in time will fade out. Oil stain is popular because it is easy to apply. Dye, or water stain, is the best and is as permanent as the wood itself. It must, however, be applied evenly with a full-bodied brush, Fig. 18. First, be sure that the piece requires staining. Unless you have had to do some bleaching, mahogany, cherry and maple usually do not require staining. Pine is best finished in its natural color.

Dry, sanded wood usually lacks color, but its approximate tone will be revealed if you brush water lightly over the entire piece. If stain is not needed all over, moisten a small area around defects, which you will fill with colored plastic wood or stick shellac. Match colors to the moistened area. When dry, sand the work and finish by rubbing with No. 00 steel wool.

Parts that have been repaired must now be tinted, Fig. 19. Moisten and test color as you did before making shellac and plastic-wood repairs. Dilute the stain, test on similar scraps of wood until color is right, then apply. Use a medicine dropper to proportion small amounts. Do not sand the stained wood until after the sealer coat is applied. If the piece is to to have an all-over stain coat, let the stained repair parts dry first. Woods of more or less uniform grain will take stain without showing much variation of color. Fancy butt, burl and crotch woods, however, reveal a wide color range. Therefore, repaired parts and all-

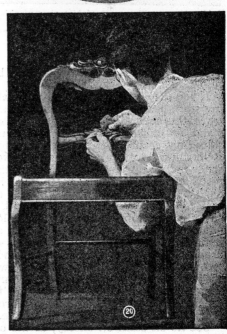

Bring yellow wax to a brown color with a level teaspoonful of dry burnt umber per pound of wax

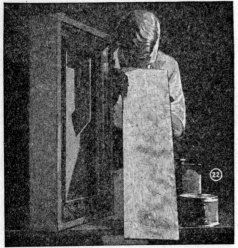
A clean board with a coat of high-gloss varnish is used for testing dry-dull varnish for brush marks. If marks show after 10 min., thin the varnish with a little turpentine

over stains for such wood should be tested on pieces of similar grain.

If you suspect that a reddish penetrating stain has been used previously, test by coating several spots with shellac. Let stand for a week or more. If a pink 'bleeding" occurs, then use a penetrating stain. On walnut, stain to a much darker shade to conceal possible bleeding. If the piece is maple or pine, nothing can be done as there is no suitable bleach or sealer. When staining is necessary the color to use is determined by the color of the wood. The sapwood of walnut, or butternut — often miscalled walnut — usually has a warm color. These woods are found in light to medium-brown shades. Black walnut may be a dark brown to almost black. If necessary to use this darker wood for light colored repairs, it may be bleached, then tinted. Use no oil stain on cherry, as the oil

has a too darkening effect. A light brownish-red tone is best. Between a light and dark colored honey shade is about right for maple. Curls will come out much darker, which makes this wood so desirable. Do not stain mahogany too dark, and avoid a too reddish shade. Brown with a hint of red should be your choice. When the stain is thoroughly dry, it must be sealed in.

Usually either shellac, shellac-wax or a varnish finish is best for an antique piece. Shellac dries dust-proof in a few minutes, and thoroughly hard in a few hours. White shellac, colored to a very light brown is best. Mix dry burnt umber, 1 tablespoonful, in denatured alcohol, 3 tablespoonfuls. Let stand 12 hrs., shaking it occasionally. Stir this color into white shellac until you get a light brown shade. For a sealer coat, reduce with denatured alcohol, 4 parts, and apply evenly. When dry, sand down the raised grain with No. 7/0 garnet paper. Rub to final smoothness with No. 00 steel wool and brush the dust out of the open pores.

Filling the wood is next. This is necessary usually on mahogany, walnut, etc. However,. as pine, maple and cherry are close grained, generally no filler is needed. Buy a filler slightly darker than the stain you are using. Thin with turpentine to a cream consistency. Use a stiff, stubby brush, and stroke with the grain. Do only a small area at a time. Use clean cloths to rub it off across the grain as indicated on the facing page, Fig. 23. Be sure to get all off, as this material dries hard. A cloth over an orange stick is useful to remove filler from panel crevices, carvings, etc., Fig. 20. Linseed oil and colors in oil are part of filler ingredients. These will act as a stain and will further darken the wood unless the sealer coat is applied as herein advised, before filling. Fillers applied over oil stains will require more time for drying than ones applied over water stains. In any event, be sure that the filler in the pores is thoroughly dry before sanding. If it isn't, the filler will come out when sanding. While filling, watch for dull spots to appear and work the filler into the pores with a pad of burlap, or the palm of your hand, using a circular, twisting motion.

When the filler is dry, sand lightly, then coat the piece with shellac cut one half with denatured alcohol. Use this same reduction for successive coats. Two to four coats may be required. Between each coat, sand down the laps, then lightly sand the entire piece. Do not begin rubbing with No. 00 wool until a good gloss is obtained. After rubbing the shellac down, inspect the piece for "high" or glossy spots. Cut these down with wads of discarded worn steel wool, then use the worn wool to again go over the entire piece. By now very little shellac will be left on the piece, which means better wearing qualities and a soft dull finish.

For a shellac-wax finish, proceed as above through the sealing, filling, and sanding stage, then apply one coat consisting of equal parts of shellac and alcohol. Let dry, rub down with No. 00 steel wool. The object now is to have a

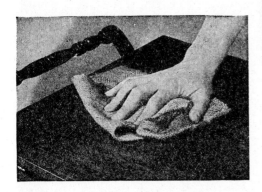

very thin film of shellac on the wood. Coat the piece with brown wax, applied lightly particularly on carvings. Yellow wax can be used if it is colored with dry burnt umber, Fig. 21. Instead of waiting the usual 20 min., before polishing with a non-scratching cloth, delay at least 24 hrs. Two or three waxings may be necessary. Shellac and shellac-wax finishes wear well on picture and mirror frames, chairs, corner shelves, and other furniture not subjected to warm food dishes, beverages, perfume, etc. Such pieces are better finished with varnish. An excellent finish, one that closely resembles the dull sheen of old original finishes, is had by using a flat varnish which gives a dull finish upon drying. Coat a clean board with high-gloss varnish and then use this for testing dry-dull varnish for brush marks, Fig. 22. Proceed through the sealing, filling and sanding process as for shellac, but cut the varnish sealer coat only one half with turpentine. After sanding, apply enough coats of high-grade floor varnish to produce a high gloss. Sand between coats with No. 7/0 garnet paper, well worn but clean. Inspect the paper frequently for "glazing,"

When filling wood, watch for dull spots to appear and work the filler into the wood pores with a pad of clean burlap

particularly when sanding after filling, for glazed paper will surely scratch. After three or four days drying, cut down the high gloss with No. 00 steel wool, and apply dry-dull varnish. One coat is usually sufficient, but give two if necessary.

❧ Rather than take the time to plane the edges of plywood panels before abutting them, obtain a perfectly matched joint in just a few minutes by laying the panels edge-to-edge on a flat surface and running a power handsaw through the joint.

Secret Drawer in Buffet

Located behind the top drawer of a buffet, a concealed compartment will hold your guest silver and keep it safe from intruders. The hidden drawer is formed by cutting off part of the original drawer and fitting it with a front. The remaining portion is fitted with a back and a pivoted stop to prevent spilling the contents of the drawer if pulled out too far.

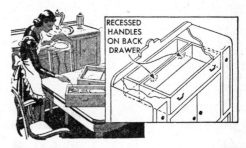

RECESSED HANDLES ON BACK DRAWER

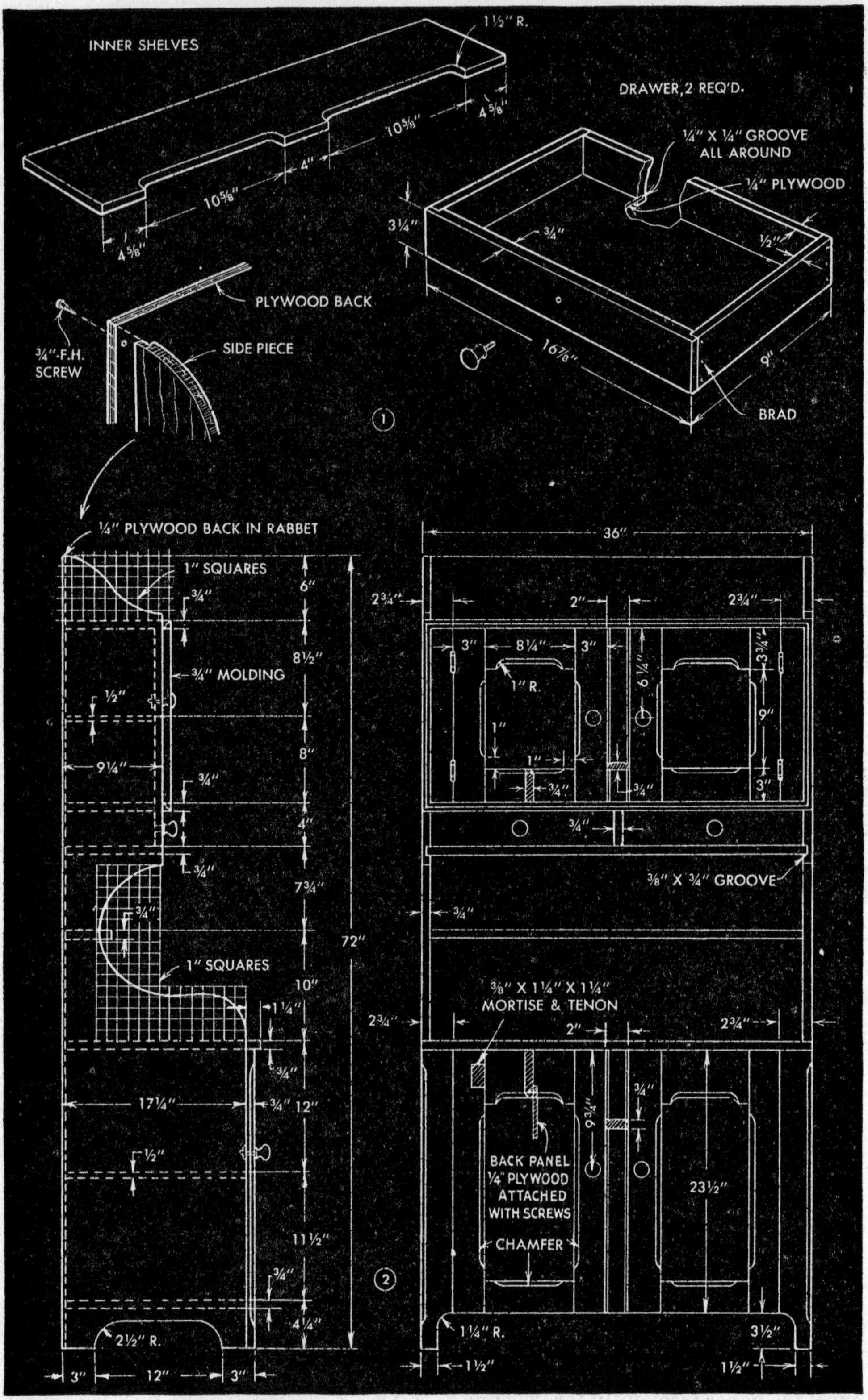

INNER SHELVES
1½" R.
DRAWER, 2 REQ'D.
10⅝"
4⅝"
4"
10⅝"
4⅝"
¼" X ¼" GROOVE ALL AROUND
¼" PLYWOOD
3¼"
¾"
½"
PLYWOOD BACK
¾"-F.H. SCREW
SIDE PIECE
16⅞"
9"
BRAD
1
¼" PLYWOOD BACK IN RABBET
1" SQUARES
6"
¾"
8½"
¾" MOLDING
½"
8"
9¼"
¾"
4"
¾"
7¾"
¾"
72"
1" SQUARES
10"
1¼"
¾"
17¼"
¾" 12"
½"
11½"
¾"
4¼"
2½" R.
3"
12"
3"
2
36"
2¾"
2"
2¾"
3"
8¼"
3"
6¼"
3¾"
1" R.
9"
1"
1"
¾"
¾"
3"
¾"
⅜" X ¾" GROOVE
¾"
⅜" X 1¼" X 1¼" MORTISE & TENON
2¾"
2"
2¾"
¾"
9¾"
BACK PANEL ¼" PLYWOOD ATTACHED WITH SCREWS
23½"
CHAMFER
1¼" R.
3½"
1½"
1½"

PENNSYLVANIA DUTCH CUPBOARD

By NORBERT ENGELS

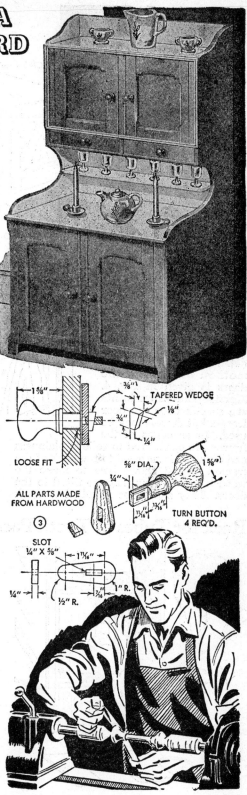

IF your taste in furniture leans toward the plain and simple lines of colonial days, here's a charming old cupboard that typifies the simplicity of early American craftsmanship. It's the type of furniture that challenges the skill of the craftsman who works with hand tools mainly and who takes special pride in producing an expert job of finishing.

Begin by building up two panels of solid stock for the sides of the cupboard. This is done by jointing four or five narrow boards, using either tongue-and-groove joints or plain butt joints doweled and glued. A saving in stock may be had by running only two of the boards the full length and using shorter lengths for the lower half. In arranging the pieces keep in mind that right and left-hand side members are required. You may find it more convenient to cut the rabbet for the plywood back if it is done before the boards are glued together. The scroll cuts likewise may be roughed out beforehand and later dressed down with a spokeshave or file, although they can be done afterward with a keyhole saw. Except for one shelf, which is set in a dado as shown in Fig. 2, the eight shelves simply are butted against the side members and glue-blocked. Note that the ½-in. shelves, Fig. 1, are cut out along the front edge, and that the desk shelf, Fig. 4, is notched at the front corners to project 1¼ in. and fit flush with the surface of the sides. The plywood back will add rigidity to the whole assembly, and it's a good idea when attaching it to do so while the framework is still clamped.

Next, the facing strips to which the lower doors are hinged are fitted to the front corners of the assembly. These are chamfered on the outer edge and are cut out at the bottom to form a part of the leg. Finally, the opening is divided equally with a beaded upright, which is fastened at the top to a nailing block and at the bottom by driving nails up through the lower shelf. The upper compartment is fitted the same way except that the pieces are set in flush with the sides and the shelves. A small molding like the one shown in the sectional detail A-A in Fig. 4 is mitered at the corners and glued and bradded to the facing edges of the opening. The two-drawer

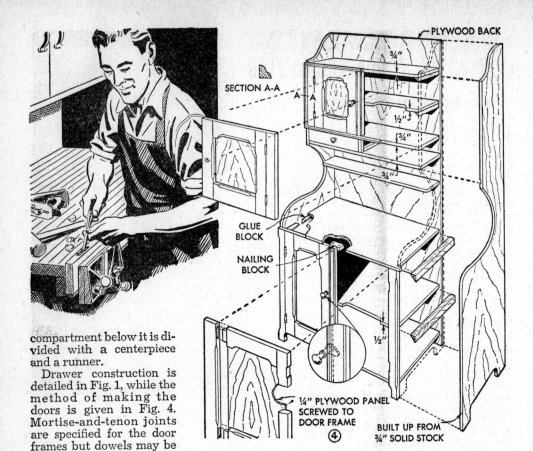

SECTION A-A

PLYWOOD BACK

¾"

½"

¾"

¾"

GLUE
BLOCK

NAILING
BLOCK

½"

¼" PLYWOOD PANEL
SCREWED TO
DOOR FRAME
④

BUILT UP FROM
¾" SOLID STOCK

compartment below it is divided with a centerpiece and a runner.

Drawer construction is detailed in Fig. 1, while the method of making the doors is given in Fig. 4. Mortise-and-tenon joints are specified for the door frames but dowels may be used. Inner edges of the frames are chamfered to relieve plainness and plywood is screwed to the back of the frames. Fig. 3 shows how to make the wooden turnbuttons that are fitted to the doors. They should be installed to work freely and latch against the back of the beaded uprights. A natural or a varnish finish is applied to the exterior of the cupboard, but the interior may be painted a pastel shade of bluish-green.

Rack for Tubes of Tooth Paste Attached to Cabinet Shelf

If you wish to keep tooth-paste tubes and other similar containers out of sight, a simple holder like the one shown may be screwed to the underside of one of the shelves in the bathroom cabinet. Any piece of nonrusting sheet metal will do for the holder and it can be made any size desired, depending on the number of tubes to be kept in the rack.

Repairs for Desk Drawers

If the joints of a drawer have become loose, it will be difficult to open and close it. In such a case, the remedy is to renail and glue the drawer so that it will slide easily. If swelling or warping is the cause of the trouble, the high spots should be sanded and waxed. It may be necessary to plane high spots.

REST YOUR FEET

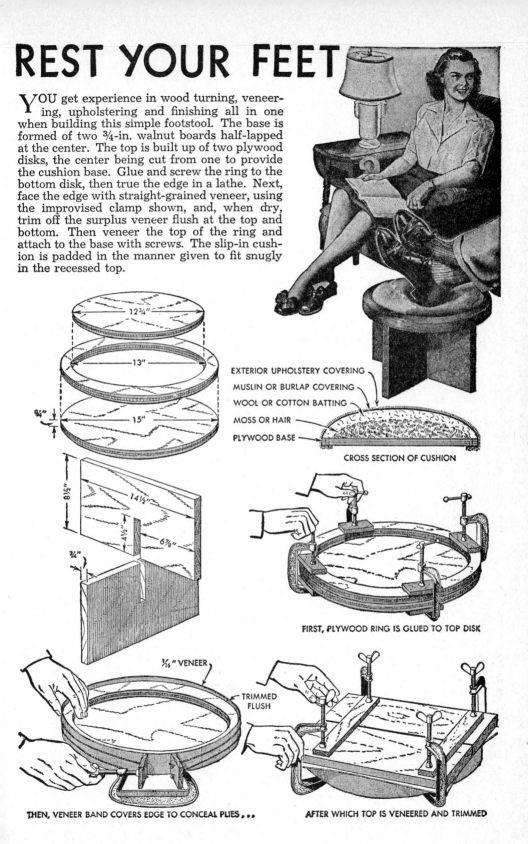

YOU get experience in wood turning, veneering, upholstering and finishing all in one when building this simple footstool. The base is formed of two ¾-in. walnut boards half-lapped at the center. The top is built up of two plywood disks, the center being cut from one to provide the cushion base. Glue and screw the ring to the bottom disk, then true the edge in a lathe. Next, face the edge with straight-grained veneer, using the improvised clamp shown, and, when dry, trim off the surplus veneer flush at the top and bottom. Then veneer the top of the ring and attach to the base with screws. The slip-in cushion is padded in the manner given to fit snugly in the recessed top.

12¾"

13"

¾"

15"

EXTERIOR UPHOLSTERY COVERING
MUSLIN OR BURLAP COVERING
WOOL OR COTTON BATTING
MOSS OR HAIR
PLYWOOD BASE

CROSS SECTION OF CUSHION

8½"

14½"

4½"

6⅞"

¾"

FIRST, PLYWOOD RING IS GLUED TO TOP DISK

1/16" VENEER

TRIMMED FLUSH

THEN, VENEER BAND COVERS EDGE TO CONCEAL PLIES ...

AFTER WHICH TOP IS VENEERED AND TRIMMED

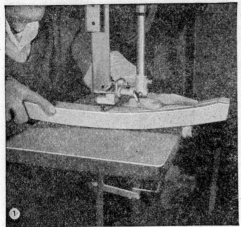

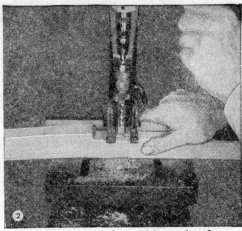

In bandsawing the first and second cuts care should be taken to keep the blade just outside the dimension line. This will allow for finishing to exact size

In making mortise-and-tenon joints a close fit assures strength equal to that of the wood itself. Be sure that the square chisel is tight in the holder

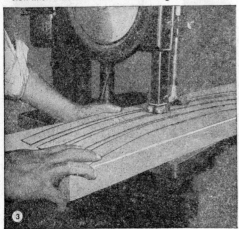

The back posts or legs are rough-sawed from a single piece of solid stock. This piece should be uniform in grain otherwise defects may show in the work

A small sanding drum mounted in the drill press is just the thing for smoothing the curved surfaces of the rough-sawed legs and rails to finish size

Use a sheet-metal or cardboard template to mark the parts for the second bandsaw cuts. Saw cut should be kept outside the line in the waste wood

The hole forming the curved offset in the back leg is drilled before bandsawing. Select a bit of the same radius as the curve indicated in the details

OCCASIONAL CHAIR in Sheraton styling

By Henry E. Belden

THERE'S just enough handwork on this fine chair to give it the professional touch of the individual craftsman. Fine cabinet wood such as mahogany or walnut should be used. If more than one chair is desired, simply duplicate the parts. Important steps in the construction procedure are shown in Figs. 1 to 6 inclusive. First, full-size patterns of the back posts are cut from heavy paper or thin cardboard for transferring to the work. You'll note in Fig. 9 that the right and left-hand patterns are duplicates; one will serve to lay out both posts by merely turning it over. Saw cuts "A" are made first, then the waste is tacked back on, the second pattern traced and cut "B" is made. Edge "C" is straight. Before making cut "B" it is a good idea to drill a ⅜-in. hole as shown in Fig. 6. This assures a well-rounded notch.

The posts now are ready for mortising, which can be done by hand or with a drill press and mortising attachment as in Fig. 2. Use a ⅜-in. hollow chisel and adjust the fence so that the cut will be in the center of the wood and parallel with the edge. The seat-rail mortises also are cut with the ⅜-in. hollow chisel. Use the scraps left from bandsawing to block up the work so the face of the mortise will be square with the chisel. The front legs are somewhat longer than the back ones, which gives a slight rake to the back and seat. Next cut the mortises for the stretchers. It will be necessary to block up the work so the chisel will cut at right angles to a center line and parallel with the floor line of the assembled chair. The mortise should be cut parallel with the straight or outside edge of the back post, this edge being held against the fence. The mortise for the lower cross rail is cut with the straight or outside edge of the leg resting directly on the drill-press table so that the chisel is at right angles to this surface.

Each chair requires two side rails made from 2-in. stock in accordance with the pattern in Fig. 9. The tenons on the side rails measure ⅜ in. wide, ⁷⁄₁₆ in. deep and 1½ in. long. The mortises on the front legs, Fig. 9, should be cut before the legs are tapered. Start each mortise ¼ in. from the top of the leg and 3⅞ in. from the bottom. Before cutting the lower mortise be sure you have selected the correct face of the leg.

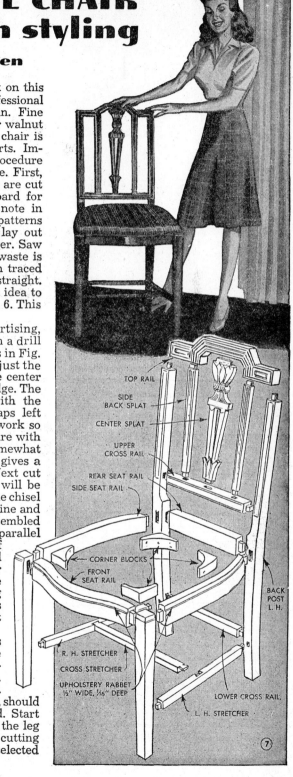

TOP RAIL

SIDE BACK SPLAT

CENTER SPLAT

UPPER CROSS RAIL

REAR SEAT RAIL

SIDE SEAT RAIL

CORNER BLOCKS

FRONT SEAT RAIL

BACK POST L. H.

R. H. STRETCHER

CROSS STRETCHER

UPHOLSTERY RABBET ½" WIDE, ¹⁄₁₆" DEEP

LOWER CROSS RAIL

L. H. STRETCHER

⑦

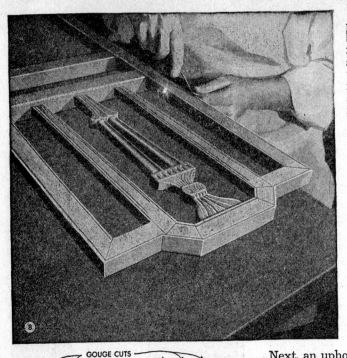

The front legs are tapered on the circular saw by the "notched-stick" method. Take a piece of stock slightly longer than the leg and nail a block near one end. This block should have two step-like notches cut in it. The first one is ⅜ in. and the second ¾ in., both measured from the inside face of the stick. Place the lower end of the untapered leg in the first notch with the stick next to the ripping fence. After the first cut is completed turn the leg completely over so the saw engages the opposite edge and place the lower end of the leg in the second notch. In each instance the fence should be adjusted so that the saw engages the leg at a point 2¹⁄₁₆ in. below the upper end, as in Fig. 9.

Next, an upholstery rabbet is cut in the seat rails and across the front legs, Fig. 7, making it slightly deeper on the legs. The front legs now can be glued to the front seat

GOUGE CUTS
V-CUTS

SECTION, SIDE SPLAT   SECTION, TOP RAIL

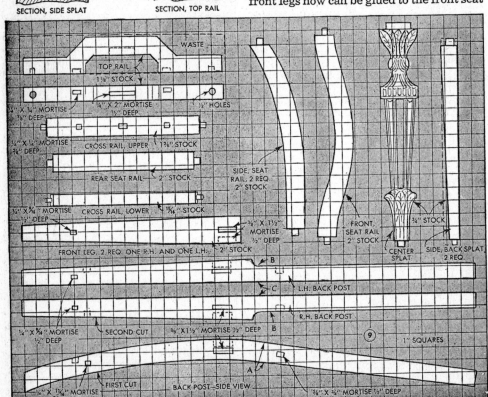

rail and the back posts glued to the lower cross rail, the seat rail and the upper cross rail. It's a good idea first to try assembly without glue. Do not glue any other parts at this time. Two side back splats are required, which are tapered, as shown by the dotted lines in Fig. 9, to leave a ¼-in. shoulder around the tenon at the lower end of the splat. The back-splat pattern, Figs. 9 and 11, is traced on a piece ¾ by 3 by 16¹³⁄₁₆ in., then sawed to shape. In carving the splat, work from the sectional views in Fig. 11.

The top rail, Figs. 7 and 9, is cut from 1⅛-in. stock. The offset over the center splat is cut out first, then ½-in. dowel holes are drilled 1 in. from each end and mortises are cut for the splats, after which the sawing can be completed. Do not cut this to exact length until after assembly. After drilling the top of the posts for dowels, the parts are ready for gluing and clamping to the rest of the back. When the glue has hardened, the back assembly is clamped to a bench so that the back may be fluted as in Fig. 8, making the cuts as indicated in the sectional views. Use a very shallow veining to simulate the mitered effect in the top rail. After the stretchers, Fig. 12, have been fitted, assemble the chair in clamps for a trial fit as in Fig. 10. Then apply glue and clamp the parts together. Corner blocks glued and screwed in the seat complete construction.

To finish, coat the wood with an oil stain. Allow to dry for 24 hours, then seal with a coat of thinned white shellac or prepared sealer. Next fill the grain with a paste filler colored a shade darker than the stain and thinned with turpentine to the consistency of thin varnish. The filler should be well rubbed in and wiped off across grain with a coarse cloth. The wiping is done when the filler begins to flatten. If one coat does not fill the pores completely apply a second coat. The "heel" of the hand is good to pack the filler level with the surface before wiping. Let dry for 36 hours, after which any rough spots should be sanded lightly. Follow with a full-bodied coat of white shellac and when dry rub with fine steel wool. Finish with several coats of paste wax rubbed to a fine gloss. A hair-bristle brush will polish the carved surfaces. The simplest upholstery job is a foam or sponge-rubber cushion supported on a bottom of ⅜-in. plywood. This is covered with a layer of muslin and tapestry in whatever pattern you wish. The edges of the top covering are nailed in the upholstery rabbet and the job is finished with upholstery gimp applied to the edge of the seat to conceal the tacks and provide a neat finish to the raw edges of the covering on all sides.

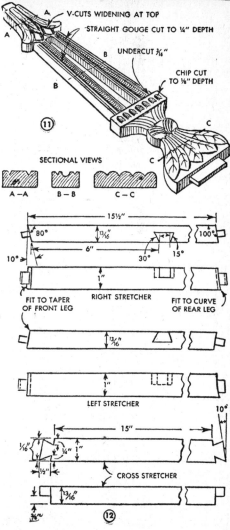

½"

BACK

BEVELED EDGES

¾"

SIDE PANEL

CENTER LINE OF CABINET

½"

GRAIN

1" SQUARES

DOWEL JOINT

4" R.

38"

10"

½" COVED MOLDING

SIDE PANEL

GRAIN

SHELVES

34¾"

6" 3½" 4" 3" 4"

DOVETAIL JOI

¾"

36"

1"

18"

COVED MOLDING

¾"

4"

DRAWER GUIDES

GUIDE STRIPS

37¼"

2¼" 6"

WALNUT FRONTS

DOOR STOP

¼" PLYWOOD

17"

36"

¾"

7½"

TURNED ROSETTE

1¼"

7¾"

2" DIA.

LEG 4 REQ'D

½" SQUARES

A fine, rugged piece of Early American furniture to lend authentic setting to your pewter or silver collection. Cabinet base provides storage galore for silverware, linen and china. Its plainness makes it simple to duplicate with ordinary tools

By W. W. Buffmire

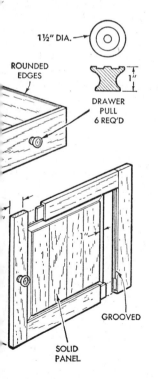

1½" DIA.

ROUNDED EDGES

DRAWER PULL 6 REQ'D

1"

GROOVED

SOLID PANEL

Reproduce this WELSH DRESSER *for your best china*

To be traditionally authentic this quaint old piece should be reproduced in American black walnut, although it can be copied in maple or birch and finished to match other Early American pieces that you may have. A study of the pull-apart view on the opposite page will acquaint you with the way the whole job goes together. Start by gluing edgewise two or more ¾-in. pieces to build up wide panels for the top and ends of the lower unit. Except for the plywood panel covering the back of the cabinet, solid stock is used throughout, although the bottom could be of plywood, too, as the front edge of it is faced with a scrolled apron. The bottom is set 1¼ in. up from the lower edge of the ends and the turned legs are glued and screwed in the corners formed by the apron across the front. The bottom, however, is not assembled until the three drawer frames are made ready, then the whole unit is clamped together at one time. Note in the detail that the top frame is fitted to the ends in dovetail mortises, while the other two are simply doweled and glued in blind holes.

The ½-in. shelves of the upper unit can be doweled or set in grooves cut in the sides. The scrollwork around the face of the unit fits flush in the notched shelves and the back of the unit is paneled vertically with ½-in. pieces of varying widths. Drawers and doors are assembled as shown, the latter being held shut with spring-type friction catches.

TWIN

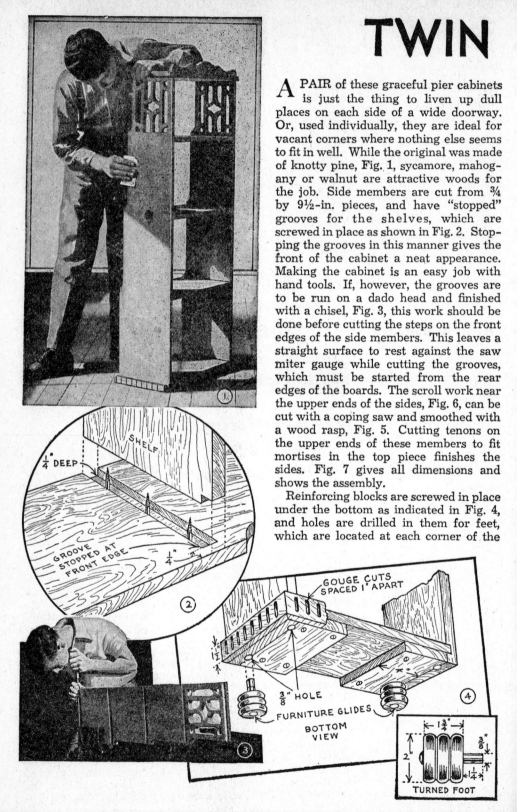

A PAIR of these graceful pier cabinets is just the thing to liven up dull places on each side of a wide doorway. Or, used individually, they are ideal for vacant corners where nothing else seems to fit in well. While the original was made of knotty pine, Fig. 1, sycamore, mahogany or walnut are attractive woods for the job. Side members are cut from ¾ by 9½-in. pieces, and have "stopped" grooves for the shelves, which are screwed in place as shown in Fig. 2. Stopping the grooves in this manner gives the front of the cabinet a neat appearance. Making the cabinet is an easy job with hand tools. If, however, the grooves are to be run on a dado head and finished with a chisel, Fig. 3, this work should be done before cutting the steps on the front edges of the side members. This leaves a straight surface to rest against the saw miter gauge while cutting the grooves, which must be started from the rear edges of the boards. The scroll work near the upper ends of the sides, Fig. 6, can be cut with a coping saw and smoothed with a wood rasp, Fig. 5. Cutting tenons on the upper ends of these members to fit mortises in the top piece finishes the sides. Fig. 7 gives all dimensions and shows the assembly.

Reinforcing blocks are screwed in place under the bottom as indicated in Fig. 4, and holes are drilled in them for feet, which are located at each corner of the

SHELF

¼" DEEP

GROOVE STOPPED AT FRONT EDGE

¼"

②

GOUGE CUTS SPACED 1" APART

1½"

⅜" HOLE

FURNITURE GLIDES

BOTTOM VIEW

③

④

1¾"

2"

⅜"

1¼"

TURNED FOOT

PIER CABINETS
balance wide doorway

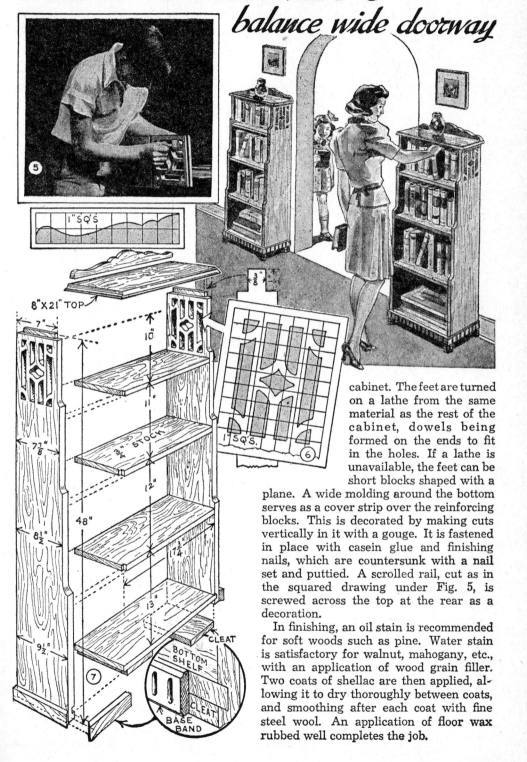

cabinet. The feet are turned on a lathe from the same material as the rest of the cabinet, dowels being formed on the ends to fit in the holes. If a lathe is unavailable, the feet can be short blocks shaped with a plane. A wide molding around the bottom serves as a cover strip over the reinforcing blocks. This is decorated by making cuts vertically in it with a gouge. It is fastened in place with casein glue and finishing nails, which are countersunk with a nail set and puttied. A scrolled rail, cut as in the squared drawing under Fig. 5, is screwed across the top at the rear as a decoration.

In finishing, an oil stain is recommended for soft woods such as pine. Water stain is satisfactory for walnut, mahogany, etc., with an application of wood grain filler. Two coats of shellac are then applied, allowing it to dry thoroughly between coats, and smoothing after each coat with fine steel wool. An application of floor wax rubbed well completes the job.

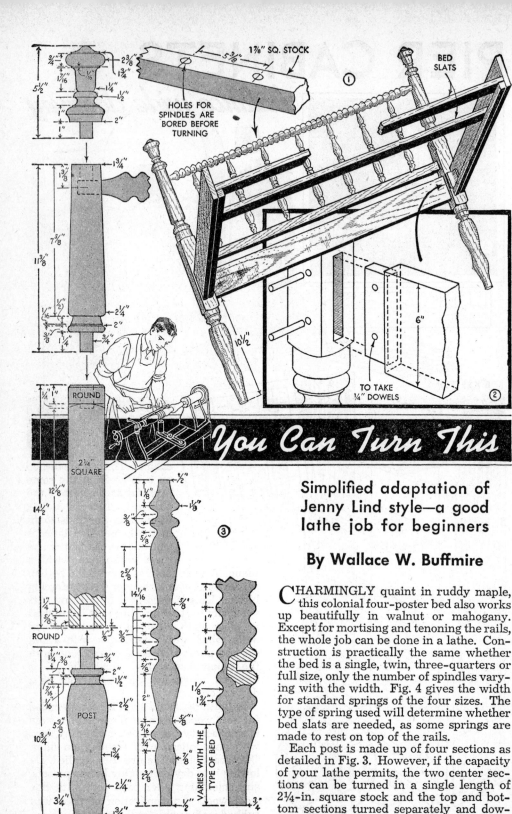

1⅞" SQ. STOCK

HOLES FOR SPINDLES ARE BORED BEFORE TURNING

BED SLATS

TO TAKE ¼" DOWELS

ROUND

2¼" SQUARE

ROUND

POST

SPINDLE

STRETCHER

VARIES WITH THE TYPE OF BED

You Can Turn This

Simplified adaptation of Jenny Lind style—a good lathe job for beginners

By Wallace W. Buffmire

CHARMINGLY quaint in ruddy maple, this colonial four-poster bed also works up beautifully in walnut or mahogany. Except for mortising and tenoning the rails, the whole job can be done in a lathe. Construction is practically the same whether the bed is a single, twin, three-quarters or full size, only the number of spindles varying with the width. Fig. 4 gives the width for standard springs of the four sizes. The type of spring used will determine whether bed slats are needed, as some springs are made to rest on top of the rails.

Each post is made up of four sections as detailed in Fig. 3. However, if the capacity of your lathe permits, the two center sections can be turned in a single length of 2¼-in. square stock and the top and bottom sections turned separately and doweled to it. Solid turning squares are best

COLONIAL BED

While the chart at the right gives both inside and overall widths of five standard-size beds, it's best to measure the spring which you plan to use

BED WIDTHS	
Single	A—3'-2"
	B—3'-0"
Twin	A—3'-5"
	B—3'-3"
Three quarter (small)	A—3'-8"
	B—3'-6"
Three quarter (large)	A—4'-2"
	B—4'-0"
Full	A—4'-8"
	B—4'-6"

(Overall length 6'-10")

④

for the posts, but where these cannot be had, built-up stock will do, providing the pieces are properly jointed and a good resin-type glue is used. It is best to bore the holes for the stretcher tenons while the work is square, especially so in the case of the stretcher itself, Fig. 1. In turning each post, as well as all other duplicate parts, try to match each one as closely as possible, using calipers frequently to check the work at respective points. A jig consisting of a wooden strip having brad points projecting from one side and spaced to correspond with the drawing, will serve as a master pattern to use in marking off duplicate turnings lengthwise. If the posts are made in four sections, care must be used in centering the holes in the ends of the square sections, so that adjoining parts will be in alignment. Fig. 2 details how the end rails are crosspegged in mortises cut in the posts. The narrow rail above it is about 1½ in. wide, and is pegged in the same way. In the case of the two front posts, the holes for the pegs should be made blind so that the dowels will not show on the face of the post.

Both head and foot are exactly alike. In assembling each one, glue the spindles to the stretcher and narrow rail first, then glue this to the posts as a unit at the same time the end rail is fitted. There are various type bed-rail fasteners available, one of which is shown in Fig. 6. In fitting them, locate the socket part on the posts to bring the top of the spring about 18 in. above the floor. The spring should be at hand in determining this as it will make a difference if the spring sets inside the rails.

The finish to apply depends upon the effect desired and the kind of wood used. Whether stained or left natural, walnut and

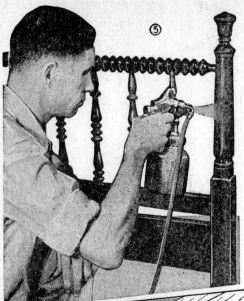

mahogany require a paste filler to fill the pores of the wood, over which a thin sealer coat of shellac is applied, then lightly sanded and followed with several coats of high-grade varnish. Filling and wiping all turnings can be done conveniently while they are in the lathe. In fact, if a French polish of shellac and oil is desired, the turned work can be completely finished in the lathe. In following this method, you must be careful to see that tenons are kept free of shellac to assure good glue joints. If spraying equipment is available, a satin-sheen, lacquer finish can be applied. Here the work is filled as before and a coat or two of lacquer sanding sealer is applied as in Fig. 5. Because of the light body of a clear lacquer finish, it is important that the pores be filled perfectly flush. If upon close examination they are not completely filled, apply a second coat of filler. When the sealer coat is dry, it is sanded lightly with 7-0 paper, then dusted and sprayed with several coats of gloss lacquer, thinned 50 percent with lacquer thinner. Undercoats of gloss lacquer are preferred in building up a good body, as they contribute to a clearer finish. A fairly good imitation of a hand-rubbed finish is obtained by using a flat lacquer as a final top coat. This dries with a soft, satin luster, requiring no rubbing. "Orange peel" texture in the finish, which results when the gun is held too far from the work, or when the air pressure is too low, can be corrected to some extent by spraying the final top coat lightly with plain lacquer thinner.

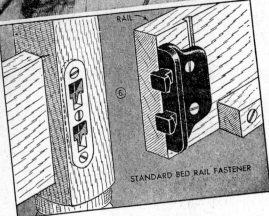

RAIL

STANDARD BED RAIL FASTENER

Barbs in Chisel Ferrule Embed to Hold Handle Securely

If you are annoyed by having the ferrules of a set of wood chisels become loose on the handles, you can correct the trouble by peening or notching the inner edges of the ferrules with a cold chisel as indicated. Tiny prongs or barbs formed by this procedure became embedded in the wood when the handles were forced into place to hold them securely.

Window Streaks Located Easily

When washing windows it is a good idea to dry them on the outside by stroking the cloth up and down, and on the inside by stroking the cloth horizontally. Then, if there are any streaks you can tell at a glance whether or not they are outside or inside the window.

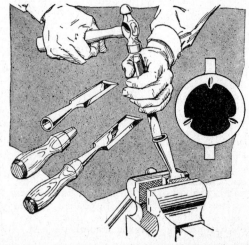

18th Century CLOCK CASE
has electric works

Y OU can adapt a small electric clock to harmonize with period furnishings by removing the works and putting them in a case like this one, which will look well on a mantelpiece or table. Or the works of an alarm clock may be used if desired. Wood for the case should match other furnishings in the room where it is to be used. For instance, in a paneled room, such as a library, pine is a good choice. If the clock is to be used in the living room, hardwood is preferable.

The case is assembled as shown in Fig. 1. Notice that the sides are butted against the bottom, where they are held by screws and a triangular cleat. Top edges of the sides, and ends of the top piece, however, should be mitered and glued, then secured by a similar cleat. All pieces are rabbeted so that the back panel, of ¼-in. plywood, will seat flush with the edges. On the bottom and top pieces, the rabbet is routed out to leave the ends intact, the small remaining fillet being chiseled square, so that there

TO FIT WORKS

SLOT FOR DOOR CATCH

DOOR STOP

MITERED

¾" R.

¼"

½"

½"

HALF ROUND

½"

1¾"

① ¼" PLYWOOD

¼" X ¼" RABBET

②

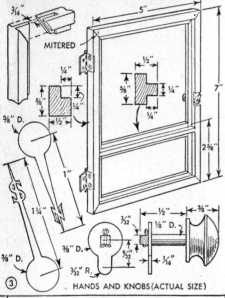

MITERED

5"

7"

½"

⅝"

¼"

¼"

¼"

½"

⅝"

2⅝"

1"

1¼"

⅜" D.

⅜" D.

⅜" D.

3/32" R.

3/32"

⅛" D.

½"

⅜"

9/32"

1/16"

③

HANDS AND KNOBS (ACTUAL SIZE)

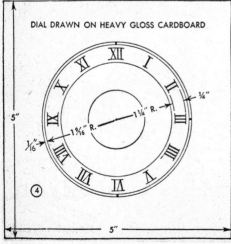

DIAL DRAWN ON HEAVY GLOSS CARDBOARD

XII XI X IX VIII VII VI V IIII III II I

¼"

1¼" R.

1 5/16" R.

1/16"

5"

④

5"

will be no gap at the corners after the back panel is screwed in place. Then wide molding is nailed along the sides and front to cover the joints, and half-round molding is bradded on the front edges, after which the nail holes are filled. As a frame for the works, cleats are nailed in the case, and a door stop is placed in line with and below the frame to space a door.

The door frame is shown in Fig. 3. Members are rabbeted as indicated in the sectional details to take pieces of glass, and the corners are mitered and joined by tongues and grooves as shown in the upper detail. Then a hole is drilled for a knob shaft, and the edge of the frame is recessed for a catch, which can be cut from thin sheet metal to the dimensions shown in the lower right-hand details. The shaft is a short length of metal rod, one end of which is filed to fit a square hole in the catch and drilled to take a cotter pin. A wooden knob then is forced over the rod. The door frame is mounted in the case by hinges and a slot is sawed to engage the catch, Fig. 1.

You may want to remove the face and hands of your clock and substitute others more in harmony with the period design of the case. The hands shown in the left-hand corner of Fig. 3 are appropriate, and a suitable dial, with Roman numerals, can be made as shown in Fig. 4. It is inked onto a square of stiff, glossy cardboard and antiqued by staining it with weak coffee, which gives it a slightly yellow cast. The hands are sawed from brass or other light sheet metal.

Now pieces of glass are installed in the door frame and held in place by strips of molding. The upper piece can be left clear, or flower designs can be painted in the corners to harmonize with the lower panel, on which a scrolled design should be applied in gold-bronze paint. Any ornate pattern will be appropriate for the lower panel, the one shown in Fig. 2 being merely a suggestion. It can be drawn on the rear surface of the glass with a stub pen, which will serve better than a brush for tracing the fine lines. When the gold paint is thoroughly dry, the entire surface is coated with flat black paint, after which a coat of varnish is applied to protect the paint.

Replacing Woven Cane Webbing in Furniture

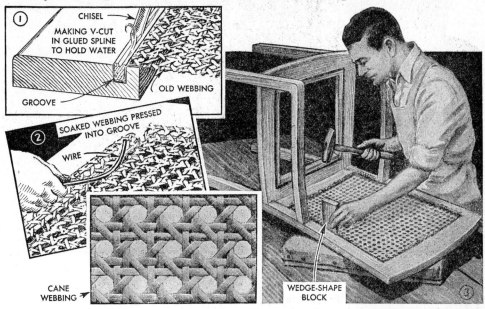

1. CHISEL — MAKING V-CUT IN GLUED SPLINE TO HOLD WATER — GROOVE — OLD WEBBING

2. SOAKED WEBBING PRESSED INTO GROOVE — WIRE

CANE WEBBING

WEDGE-SHAPE BLOCK

3.

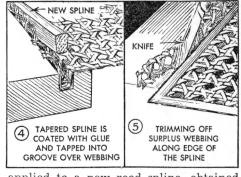

4. TAPERED SPLINE IS COATED WITH GLUE AND TAPPED INTO GROOVE OVER WEBBING

NEW SPLINE

5. TRIMMING OFF SURPLUS WEBBING ALONG EDGE OF THE SPLINE — KNIFE

On furniture fitted with prefabricated cane webbing—not the hand-woven caning—it is sometimes necessary to replace the webbing, which may seem quite a difficult job, but is really quite simple if the cane spline that holds the old webbing in place is removed properly. Usually this can be done by softening the glue with water. With a V-shaped chisel cut a groove in the surface of the spline, Fig. 1, to retain water, which is applied and left to soak overnight. It is best to have the spline in a horizontal position so that the water will not run out of the V-cuts. Water may have to be applied several times before it has soaked through and softened the glue, allowing no time between applications for the spline to dry out. When ready to remove the spline, pick it up at the end with a sharp-pointed tool and then pull it out, after which the webbing comes out easily. A new piece of webbing, which is available in four different sizes of weaving, can be obtained from upholstering supply houses. To match the old webbing, send a piece along with your order. The new piece must be soaked in water for an hour or so before using it so that when it dries and shrinks after installing, it will be drum tight. Also, soaking is necessary to permit bending the edges into the groove, which can be done by means of a piece of heavy wire shaped as shown in Fig. 2. After pressing the edges into the grooves, so that the webbing is reasonably taut, glue is applied to a new reed spline, obtained at the same time you get the webbing. These come in various widths, so be sure to duplicate the old one. You will notice that it is tapered. After applying a sufficient amount of glue, the narrow edge of the spline is tapped into the groove over the webbing as shown in Fig. 4. A small block to take the hammer blows as in Fig. 3, will prevent marring the spline. The ends should be mitered at the corners so that they will butt together snugly. After the glue has dried, you cut off the ragged edge of the webbing on one edge of the spline with a sharp knife, as in Fig. 5. When the webbing has dried out thoroughly, go on with finishing.

¶ When using pine cones and branches of trees for indoor decorating, they can be painted white easily with liquid shoe cleaner, which gives them an attractive dull finish that dries rapidly.

Upholster It Yourself!

By Charles E. Troutt

UPHOLSTERING old living-room furniture to renew it and give it many additional years of service requires only a few inexpensive tools. You can cut the new covering without worrying about it fitting, as the original material, if removed carefully, will provide a perfect pattern. Other than the covering selected, there will be little new material needed, the old springs, stuffing, webbing and burlap being reused to cut down cost. In some cases, however, additional stuffing such as hair, moss, fiber, etc., may be required. In all cases, a small amount of layer cotton will be needed. These items are available from upholsterer's supply houses and most large department stores and mail order houses.

For upholstering furniture successfully, the following tools will be needed: A pair of scissors, ice pick (used as a regulator for shifting filling in stitched edges), tack hammer, a dozen upholsterer's pins, one 7-in. curved upholsterer's needle and one smaller curved needle (size from 3 to 5 in.). If the piece of furniture to be recovered has a web base, you will also need a webbing stretcher, which can be purchased or made easily in your own shop. These tools are shown in Fig. 3.

Removing old cover material: As this will be used as a pattern for cutting the new cover, it should be removed carefully. A screwdriver and wooden mallet or hammer are satisfactory for this purpose. In removing tacks, place the screwdriver under the material, next to the frame and against the tack as in Fig. 4. A few light taps with the mallet, and the tack is out. Do not pry the tacks out by twisting the screwdriver, as this will damage the wood. Label each piece of the old cover as it is removed and make any notes which might help you in fitting the new cover. On some pieces of upholstered furniture, it is necessary that

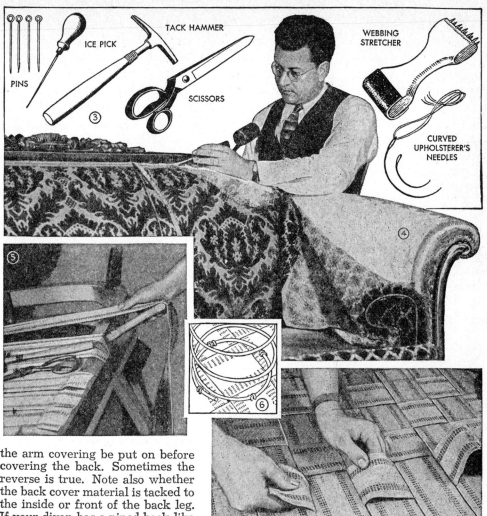

PINS
ICE PICK
TACK HAMMER
SCISSORS
③
WEBBING STRETCHER
CURVED UPHOLSTERER'S NEEDLES
④
⑤
⑥
⑦

the arm covering be put on before covering the back. Sometimes the reverse is true. Note also whether the back cover material is tacked to the inside or front of the back leg. If your divan has a piped back like the one at the top of the opposite page, the position of these pipes should be marked on both the top and bottom rails as the cover is taken off. The burlap or other spring covering should be removed also, as in most cases it is necessary to straighten and retie the springs. After all cover material and filling have been removed, the frame should be examined for loose joints and repaired, using glue, new dowels, corrugated fasteners, hardwood corner blocks or other means to strengthen it. Any exposed wooden parts such as legs or top back rail in need of refinishing should be done at this time.

Repairing web base: If your furniture has bar springs (springs mounted on metal bars), examine these for loose nails. Bent bars should be removed, straightened and renailed. If the piece has a web base, check for sagged webbing. In case this needs repairing, first remove the tacks from one end of a piece of webbing. Then, pin a piece of this material to the loose end, making the lap the length of the piece turned over on the old webbing as in Fig. 1. This extra piece (about 12 in. long) is pinned to the old webbing to facilitate the use of a webbing stretcher as shown in Fig. 2. If the webbing is too frayed for the pins to hold sufficiently, it may be necessary to clamp two hardwood blocks over the joint and draw them up tightly with a C-clamp. Stretch one piece at a time and tack with four or five tacks (6-oz. size). Remove the extra piece of webbing, fold back the end of the piece you have stretched and tack with an additional six or eight larger tacks (12-oz. size). If new jute webbing is not available, a heavy cotton webbing will be entirely satisfactory in the event you pre-

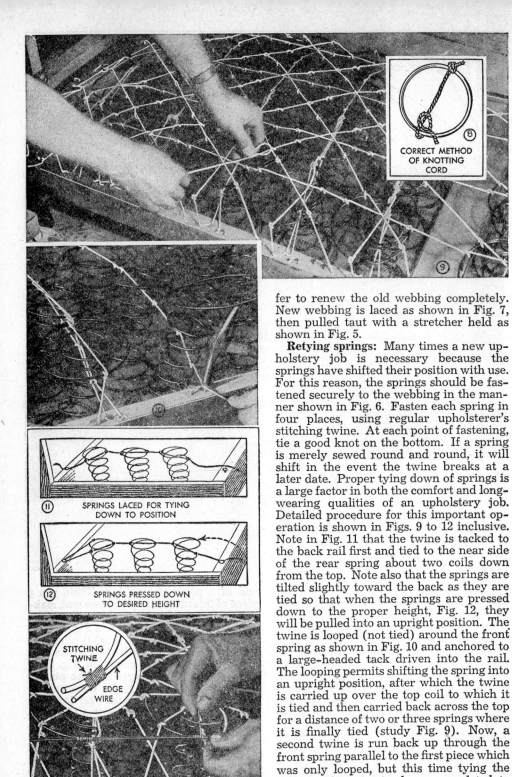

CORRECT METHOD OF KNOTTING CORD

SPRINGS LACED FOR TYING DOWN TO POSITION

SPRINGS PRESSED DOWN TO DESIRED HEIGHT

STITCHING TWINE

EDGE WIRE

fer to renew the old webbing completely. New webbing is laced as shown in Fig. 7, then pulled taut with a stretcher held as shown in Fig. 5.

Retying springs: Many times a new upholstery job is necessary because the springs have shifted their position with use. For this reason, the springs should be fastened securely to the webbing in the manner shown in Fig. 6. Fasten each spring in four places, using regular upholsterer's stitching twine. At each point of fastening, tie a good knot on the bottom. If a spring is merely sewed round and round, it will shift in the event the twine breaks at a later date. Proper tying down of springs is a large factor in both the comfort and long-wearing qualities of an upholstery job. Detailed procedure for this important operation is shown in Figs. 9 to 12 inclusive. Note in Fig. 11 that the twine is tacked to the back rail first and tied to the near side of the rear spring about two coils down from the top. Note also that the springs are tilted slightly toward the back as they are tied so that when the springs are pressed down to the proper height, Fig. 12, they will be pulled into an upright position. The twine is looped (not tied) around the front spring as shown in Fig. 10 and anchored to a large-headed tack driven into the rail. The looping permits shifting the spring into an upright position, after which the twine is carried up over the top coil to which it is tied and then carried back across the top for a distance of two or three springs where it is finally tied (study Fig. 9). Now, a second twine is run back up through the front spring parallel to the first piece which was only looped, but this time tying the spring. This step is shown completed to the left in Fig. 10. The proper method of knotting the twine is shown in Fig. 8.

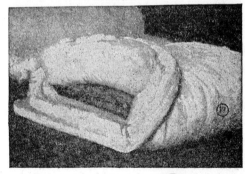

WELT TOP BORDER

A B C

⑮ CORRECT WAY TO SEW WELT CORD TO CUSHION TOP
AND BORDER

⑯

⑰

Each row of springs is tied from back to front first, then from side to side and finally, diagonally as in Fig. 9. Note that the twine is tied to every piece of twine which it crosses between springs, in addition to being tied at every point where a spring is touched. Tying the edge wire to the front row of springs with stitching twine is done as shown in Fig. 13. Springs in the back are treated in the same manner as those in the seat, except for the edge wire, which is omitted.

You are now ready to cover the springs with burlap. If there are any holes in the old piece, they can be patched with material from a burlap bag. In the event the burlap is not in condition to use again, it can be replaced with Osnaburg or denim, which are entirely satisfactory as substitutes. Cover the bottom springs first. Next,

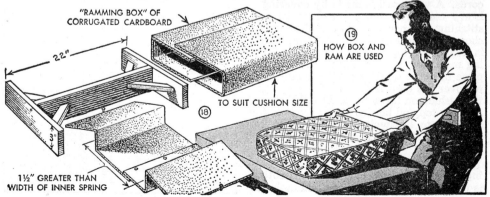

"RAMMING BOX" OF
CORRUGATED CARDBOARD

22"

3"

1½" GREATER THAN
WIDTH OF INNER SPRING

⑱

TO SUIT CUSHION SIZE

⑲
HOW BOX AND
RAM ARE USED

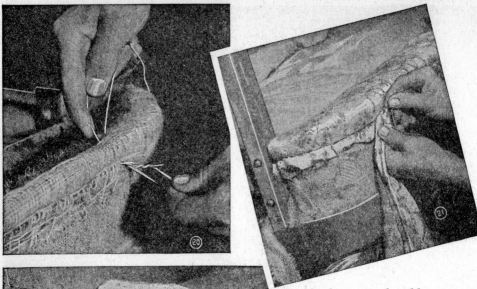

cover the back springs, tacking the cover to the bottom rail first, then to the top rail, beginning near the center as in Fig. 14.

Re-covering the cushions: At this point, the cushions should be re-covered, as they will be used later to determine the amount of stuffing needed for the arms and back, which are filled out to the cushions. By using the old cushion covers for patterns, cutting new ones is a simple procedure. You will, of course, have to use new welt cords. A welt cord is made by covering a heavy cord with top cover material and stitching on a machine close to the cord as shown at A in Fig. 15. A half foot, which is standard equipment on most home sewing machines, is used in the stitching. A piece of material 1⅜ in. wide is sufficient to cover the cord and allow for sewing to the cushion on three sides. Detail B shows how the top and border pieces are held for stitching to the welt which conceals the raw edges when the cover is turned inside out as at C.

Some new cotton is necessary in covering the spring units, Fig. 16, as old cotton is usually packed and lumpy. Smooth out

the lumps in the old cotton and tear off even with the edge of the spring unit. Then, wrap the unit in a layer of new cotton, letting this layer project over the edge as in Fig. 17. One layer of new cotton is sufficient where old cotton is also used. To slip this unit into the cushion cover without displacing the cotton layer requires a stuffing jig like the one shown in Fig. 18. This jig consists of a ram and a box in which the cotton-covered spring unit is placed, after which the cushion cover is pulled over it. The ram is used as in Fig. 19 to hold the filling in place while the box is being withdrawn. The open end, which should be at the back of the cushion, is hand sewn.

Stitching the roll edge: If you like, the old roll edge can be used. Any soft spots should be regulated by inserting an ice pick through the burlap and shifting

Kind of Furniture	No. of Cushions	36-in. Fabric	50 to 54-in. Fabric
	APPROXIMATE YARDAGE OF COVER MATERIAL REQUIRED		
Wing chair	1	9 yards	5 yards
Wing chair	None	7 "	4 "
Club chair	1	7½ "	5 "
Club chair	None	5½ "	4 "
Wooden arm chair	None	2 "	1½ "
Arm chair (seat only)	None	⅞ "	⅞ "
Boudoir chair	1	5½ "	3 "
Boudoir chair	None	4 "	2½ "
Loveseat	2	12 "	7½ "
Loveseat	None	10 "	6¼ "
Divan (69 to 84-in. back)	3	16 "	9½ "
Divan (60 to 84-in. back)	None	10 "	7 "
3 piece suite	5	32 "	19 "

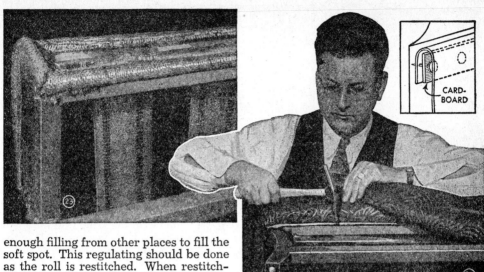

enough filling from other places to fill the soft spot. This regulating should be done as the roll is restitched. When restitching, start the needle in the front edge pointing up and permit it to go behind the edge wire. In returning the needle, go in front of the edge wire as in Fig. 20. Wind the twine around the needle as shown and pull tight. Repeat this operation until you have covered the entire front edge. If your job differs from this, replace the front edge as it was originally.

Putting on the top front band: The top front band consists of three pieces of the new material with a welt cord sewed between them. The center piece of the front band should be the same width as the center cushion and should match the pattern in the cushion material. Use your old cover for a pattern.

Before attaching this band to the divan or chair as the case may be, sew it to a piece of under-cover material large enough to cover the seat springs. Cut this piece amply large, as it can be trimmed after tacking. Under-cover material, which will be directly under the cushions, can be of denim. Or, you can use service velour or sateen, if desired. Pin the completed front band to the burlap to hold it in place. Then, stitch the back edge of the burlap at the point where the denim is joined, catching under the springs wherever possible. Use a curved needle and stitching twine. Put an even layer of cotton under this band, tear-

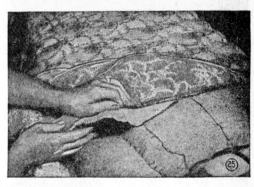

ing it off even with the front edge. Pull the band down over this filling and hand stitch beneath the roll. A completely sewed top band is shown in Fig. 21.

Making the bottom front band: Also made in three pieces, the bottom front band has a welt cord sewed between each piece and along the top edge. This front band should be cut from the cover material so that the design will appear to continue down from the top band. Hand stitch this to the top band as in Fig. 21, running it straight and using a blind stitch, which is made by first inserting the needle through the top band, then through the inside of the welt cord on the bottom band.

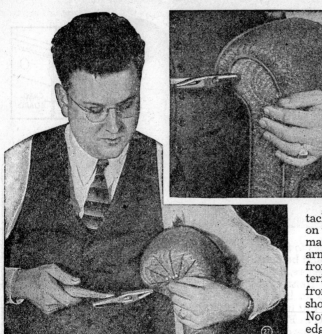

sign is in the center. Tack the cover to the bottom rail (over the top of the seat cover), using only a few tacks. These tacks may have to be removed to make the pattern run straight. Put plenty of filling on the inside and over the top to give a nicely rounded arm, stitching the filling to the burlap in the same manner as the filling was stitched to the bottom. Large tacks will hold the filling in place on top of the arm. Pull the cover material up over the inside of the arm, tack it to the bottom of the front post and then pull the material tightly over the post at the front edge and tack. Fig. 26 shows an arm properly filled. Note the roll around the inside edge of the post. Now tack the cover to the front edge of the post and pull the material tightly toward the back of the arm and tack. Mold the filling to the proper shape by patting with the palm of your hand, bearing in mind that the filling always should follow the contour of the arm. Begin this patting process at the front and tack the cover under the arm as you go. Tack to the back post on the side or edge. This operation will depend on the manner in which your divan or chair was upholstered originally. Pull the cover around the inside of the front post, splitting where necessary to make a smooth fit, and tack to the front of the post as in Fig. 27. Pleat the material as you go around the top curve. The back covering of the divan is usually put on before putting on the outside arm covers.

When pulled tight, the stitch will not show on the surface. After this second band is attached at the top, turn the divan over on its back and place a layer of cotton all the way across under the band. Then pull the cover material down smoothly over this layer of cotton and tack underneath the bottom rail. If there is a finished bottom rail, tack the band to the top of the mold-ing, cover the edge with gimp and fasten either with gimp tacks or antique nails.

When the front bands are finished, cover the seat of the divan with a thin layer of the old filling (hair, moss or fiber), stitch-ing this to the burlap spring cover with three rows of long stitches to hold it in place. After this is done, cover the filling with a layer of cotton as in Fig. 22. Note that the under-cover material is turned back. Draw the under-cover material over the filling evenly and tack to the back and side rails. Do not use too much filling as the seat should always be lower than the front edge, otherwise you will be able to see under the front cushions.

Covering the arms: Put the cushions in place before covering the arms, as these are stuffed out to meet the cushions. Fur-niture having wide, flat arms such as shown in Fig. 23, should have the edges built up with roll edges to improve the appearance and make the piece more comfortable. Cut the cover material for the arms, using the old pieces for patterns. If new cover ma-terial is of a floral design, be sure the de-

Covering the back: Ordinarily, the back is in three pieces to match the design of the cushions and front bands, a welt cord being sewed between each of the panels. Turn the divan on its back and put in a layer of stuffing, stitching it to the burlap as you did before. It is necessary to have more filling in the back than was used in the seat, and it is also necessary that you take closer stitches. The back should be stuffed out far enough to reach the cushions. Cov-er this stuffing with a layer of cotton, let-ting the cotton stick up far enough to pull over the top of the back rail. Tack the cov-er to the bottom rail first and proceed in the same manner as you did with the arms, tacking to the back side of the top rail and to the back posts. If the piece has a piped

back, it will be stuffed in the manner shown in Fig. 25, stuffing one pipe at a time and hand stitching it to the burlap.

Putting on the outside arm covers: The outside arm covers come next. First, the material is tacked to the rail directly under the arm, Fig. 24, using a cardboard strip to give a straight edge here when the material is drawn down and tacked under the bottom rail. Finally, re-cover the front post panels and nail them on with 1¼-in. brads, cutting the heads off before driving them in as in Fig. 28. Pull the cover material over the headless nails by sticking an upholsterer's pin into the material and lifting.

Putting on the outside back: Gimp tacks can be used to apply the outside back cover or it may be blind-sewed, using the same stitch as was used in attaching the second front band. Covering the bottom with cambric completes the job.

Spiral Pins Hold Tidy Sets on Your Upholstered Furniture

Fastening a tidy securely to an upholstered chair is no problem if you use a pin that has been bent spirally so that it can be turned into the fabric. Pins with colored heads add a decorative effect; and a pair of pliers is used to bend the pin around a nail, thus making a coil, as indicated in the detail. The turns of the spiral part of the pin can be stretched to space them as desired after the pin has been bent to shape.

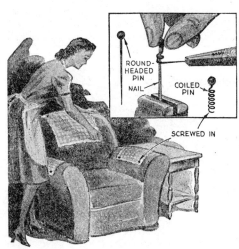

ROUND-HEADED PIN

NAIL

COILED PIN

SCREWED IN

¶ To prevent leather upholstery from sticking to your clothing wash it with gasoline and allow to dry. Then mix lacquer and lacquer thinner in equal parts and apply over the leather.

Tongs Close Tear in Upholstery and Grip It for Sewing

To close a tear in upholstery and hold it for sewing, one w o r k m a n employs a pair of tongs made from stout spring wire. These have small hooks formed on the ends to engage the fabric at either side of the tear so that the latter can be closed. The sliding loop on the tongs is then pushed down to hold them securely.

Torn Upholstery Mended Easily with Aid of Barbless Hooks

Torn upholstery can be pulled together for mending with needle and thread by stringing a number of barbless fishhooks on a stout line, attaching one hook permanently at either end. By engaging the hooks in the fabric in the arrangement indicated, and drawing the line taut, the fabric will be pulled together for easy sewing.

Fixing Loose Furniture Casters

When the casters in furniture work loose, they can be made to fit tightly again by filling the caster hole and reboring it. Select a dowel or whittle a plug that is a tight fit in the worn hole. Coat the plug well with glue and drive it home, then saw it off flush with the bottom of the leg. When reboring the hole, use a bit of slightly less diameter than the caster pin. The latter is coated with soap before it is driven into place.

Stains Removed from Upholstery

Many stains on upholstery can be removed with a solution consisting of oxalic acid granules, 1 teaspoon, dissolved in water, 1 pt. Wet the stain repeatedly and, for the last step, make a paste of the acid using fuller's earth. Spread this over the spot and, when dry, brush it off. On some fabrics it may be necessary to repeat the paste treatment at least once.

¶ A wet chamois will remove dog hair from upholstery without damaging the cloth.

Easy-To-Make

It's actually a 5-gal. paint pail fitted with a padded seat and tailored inside and out with a gay-colored slip cover. Seat lifts off for storing shoes inside

By Peter R. Ruppe

UTILIZING a common 5-gal. pail for its framework, this vanity stool is both lightweight and sturdy, simple to make and provides a convenient storage compartment for shoes, hats, etc. Select a pail having straight sides—one in which paint comes will do—remove the handle if it has one, and clean the inside thoroughly by scraping or burning out the old paint.

A tacking strip or ring is fitted inside the pail about 2 in. down from the top and is fastened with flathead screws from the outside as in Fig. 2. The ring need not be in one piece—it can be of several segments

1

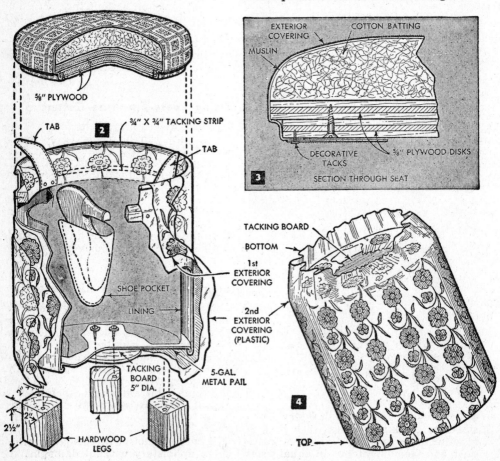

⅝" PLYWOOD

TAB

2

¾" X ¾" TACKING STRIP

TAB

SHOE POCKET

LINING

TACKING BOARD 5" DIA.

5-GAL. METAL PAIL

2"

2"

2½"

HARDWOOD LEGS

EXTERIOR COVERING

COTTON BATTING

MUSLIN

DECORATIVE TACKS

⅝" PLYWOOD DISKS

3   SECTION THROUGH SEAT

TACKING BOARD

BOTTOM

1st EXTERIOR COVERING

2nd EXTERIOR COVERING (PLASTIC)

4

TOP

VANITY STOOL

as it is hidden from view. Next, the bottom of the pail is drilled for screws to attach the three stub legs. These can be made of fancy hardwood and varnished, or cut from pine and painted. Two 1-in. screws are used to attach each leg. Holes are drilled in the bottom also for fastening a ⅜ by 5-in. wood disk to serve as a tacking surface for the outer covering. This is located in the center of the pail. The rabbeted edge of the seat board is formed by two ⅝-in.-plywood disks screwed together, one being the same diameter as the pail and the other about ¼ in. smaller, Fig. 3.

You're now ready to tackle the upholstering. The inside lining is applied first. This can be of a material contrasting with that used on the outside. Make a tubular-shaped bag of it to fit the inside diameter of the tacking ring. If the stool is to be used for shoe storage, pockets should be sewed to the lining before it is tacked in place at the top. The outside covering is likewise sewed in a tubular shape to be pulled snugly over the pail. Fold the upper edge of it under and tack it neatly to the wood ring, forming small pleats where necessary to eliminate wrinkles. After the top edge is tacked, the fabric is pulled down smoothly and tacked to the wood disk at the bottom. Although optional, the outside covering of the stool can be protected from soiling by covering it with any of the transparent plastic materials, tacking it the same as before. See Fig. 4. Finally, two strong tabs of cloth are tacked to opposite sides of the wood ring to provide handles for carrying

the stool. These should be long enough to extend out from under the seat as shown in Fig. 1. This leaves the seat to be padded as indicated in the cross-sectional view in Fig. 3. Cotton batting is first applied generously and is held in place with a muslin cover. Several thicknesses of foam rubber, available in sheet form, could be used in place of the cotton. The outer covering is brought around and tacked neatly to the under edge and finished with a circular piece. Where the material covers the rabbeted edge it should be tacked to the underside of the top disk.

Attractive Four-Piece Picture Frame Can Be Dismantled in a Jiffy

Just four parts make up this novel picture frame, a slotted wood base, two pieces of glass and a slotted wood clip. The whole thing goes together without a fastening of any kind. The slot in the base has a 10-deg. rake to give the glass a slight backward slant. The photo is sandwiched between the two pieces of glass and held together at the top by the slotted clip. The base dimensions given will accommodate a 5 by 7 photo, although it can be made to take almost any size picture.

SLOTTED CLIP

PHOTO

GLASS

BASE
¾×2¾×5   10° ANGLE

BED HEADBOARD

Pad it with

DINING CHAIR   PIANO BENCH   FOOTSTOOL   VANITY SEAT

Photos courtesy United States Rubber Co.

First, the old chair seat is removed. Usually a screw on the underside holds each corner. Then seat board is stripped of old padding and all tacks are removed

Using the seat board as a pattern, place it on the rubber and mark around it. Then cut with scissors as above. With foam rubber in place, outer fabric is pulled firmly and tacked to seat board as below

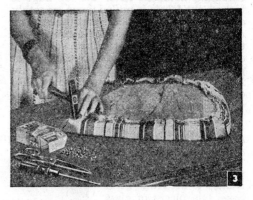

THANKS TO FOAM RUBBER, home upholstering takes on the ultimate in simplicity. This new cushioning material eliminates the use of cotton or other loose-type padding over springs or seat boards—you simply cut the rubber to fit the particular job and cover it with the finish fabric. That's all there is to it. Furthermore, foam-rubber padding retains its shape. It cannot mat or shift like regular loose padding and its resiliency keeps the outer fabric smooth and free from wrinkles, and produces an

exceptionally soft, comfortable cushion. Foam rubber, of pure latex, is marketed in sheet form and is available in the following sizes: 36 by 62 in., 17 by 21 in., and 16 by 16 in., the latter size being suitable for padding the seat of a dining chair. It can be had in ½, ¾ and 1-in. thicknesses and three densities, soft, medium and firm. The 36 by 62-in. sheet also is sold in ¼-in. thickness.

Generally used for padding chair seats, foam rubber can be used wherever a cushioned surface is desired. You can use it to pad the headboard of a bed or the bench of

426

FOAM RUBBER

EXERCISE BOARD

WINDOW SEAT

BREAKFAST NOOK

LAWN FURNITURE

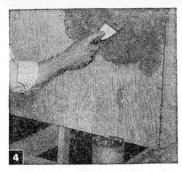

Above, foam rubber is held in place on vertical surfaces with linoleum cement. Abutting edges of sheets are held with 1-in. adhesive tape as shown below. This permits small pieces to be used

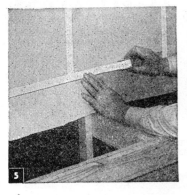

Here foam rubber is being applied to the back board of a breakfast-nook seat. The cement-coated surface is allowed to become tacky, then the individual sheets of rubber are pressed in place, butting the edges. This makes it convenient to apply the covering

By Wayne C. Leckey

a breakfast nook, and to cushion the top of a footstool or vanity bench. It can be used as filling in a removable pad for a piano bench, window seat or lawn furniture. These are just a few of the many practical purposes to which foam rubber can be adapted.

The simplicity of padding a dining chair is pictured in Figs. 1, 2 and 3. First, remove the old seat and strip it of the padding. Then, using the original seat board as a pattern, lay it on the rubber, trace around it and cut to shape with a pair of scissors. Finally, apply the new covering by pulling it over the foam-rubber padding and tacking to the bottom of the seat board. In applying foam rubber to a vertical surface, such as the bench of a breakfast nook, coat the surface with linoleum cement to hold the sheets in position, Fig. 4. Then, when the cement is tacky, press the rubber onto it as in Fig. 6. The joints of all the pieces are held together with adhesive tape as shown in Fig. 5. Taping also permits small pieces to be utilized.

427

FRONT VIEW

24"
7"
1⅝" R.
12"
16⅝"
3¾"
6¾"
8"
¾"
¼"
2"

ROUNDED

HARD-PRESSED BOARD

24"

24"

CORNER CLEAT

1" X 1¼"

1" X 2"

As dogs usually select a spot that is free from drafts when they want to rest, this simple bed is designed for their comfort and protection where they are trained to sleep on a porch or in the house near a window. Note that hard-pressed board is used almost entirely in constructing the bed, which has a raised bottom, instead of separate legs, to provide air space underneath

A BED for your DOG

HOLES, 1¾" C TO C

DOWEL

26"

20"

8" R.

1¾"

¾" HARDWOOD

1½"

8"

DOWELS EXTEND 3" BELOW BOTTOM TO FORM LEGS

CORNERS CAPPED WITH METAL

DOWELS ENTER RAILING ⅜"

½" X 8" DOWELS

Although this bed, the sides of which consist of dowels, was built for a cocker spaniel, dimensions given can be altered to provide plenty of room for a larger dog. When boring the holes for the dowels in the bottom and in the railing, tack or clamp the pieces together and bore both at the same time to assure the holes being in line. Note that four dowels are cut 3 in. longer than the others to serve as legs

Part 8

THE HOME WORKSHOP

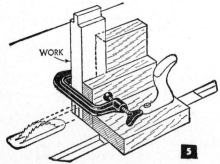

POWER-TOOL

Part I

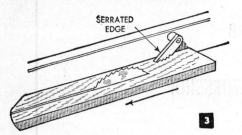

SERRATED EDGE

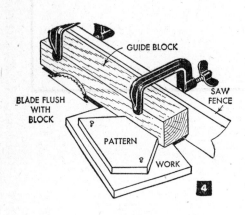

GUIDE BLOCK

SAW FENCE

BLADE FLUSH WITH BLOCK

PATTERN

WORK

1—When making duplicate angle cuts keep the miter gauge set at 90 deg. and use angle blocks to guide the stock. This saves much time in production work, especially where the angles vary from lot to lot

2—It's easy to get the correct depth of cut when you have a stepped depth gauge. Each step is simply a rabbet cut in the sloping face of a hardwood block

3—If you are making a number of duplicate ripping cuts in thin stock it's a good idea to fit an anti-kick-back pawl on the rip fence. File a serrated edge on a length of ⅛ x ½-in. flat iron and bolt to the fence with a spacer between. Pawl should be free to rise as the end of the work passes underneath it

4—Pattern sawing is easy to do if you clamp a wood guide piece to the saw fence at such a height that the work will slide under it. Outer surface of the blade should be flush with the face of the wood guide

5—Tenoning goes much faster with a jig that rides in the table groove and supports the work in a vertical position. Two saw blades are placed on the arbor with a spacer between equal to the width of the tenon. In this way you can make the cuts in one pass

6—Improvised clamps attached to a crosscut guide enable you to make some unusual cuts on the shaper. Here's a safe way of holding a disk for cutting flutes around the edge. It's a handy jig for making decorative rosettes of the type having a molded edge

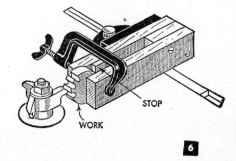

WORK

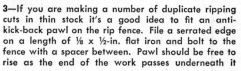

STOP

WORK

SHORT CUTS

By Kenneth Murray

7—To square large pieces of hard-pressed board on the circular saw, clamp a straightedge to the work so that it projects over one edge and rides against the ripping fence, thus acting as a guide for the squaring cut. Repeat the operation on the four edges

8—A good serviceable hold-down for small pieces can be made from a broken C-clamp. Use the screw part of the clamp as shown and weld a threaded section of rod to it so that it will screw into the crosscut guide in a hole already drilled and tapped for it

9—Another clamp, which is simply a wood cam operated by a handle, can be attached to the crosscut guide by means of a bolt and metal angle. The clamp is handy on shaper when cutting across the grain

10—For sanding small duplicate parts in the lathe make a quick-acting chuck by fitting a length of rubber hose into a turned wood holder. It is not necessary to stop the lathe when changing work

11—A "right-left" miter gauge is a real timesaver for you can miter both ends of a single piece without changing the gauge. The drawing shows how to make it and how it works. Use hardwood for all the parts

12—Ripping duplicate narrow strips on the circular saw is a ticklish business. It can be dangerous, too, unless you take proper precautions. Of course, any careful workman will use a push stick, but another and faster way is to screw a block to the crosscut guide and let it push the strip safely past the saw blade

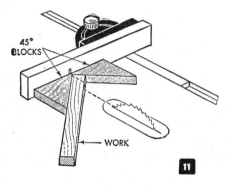

45°
BLOCKS

← WORK

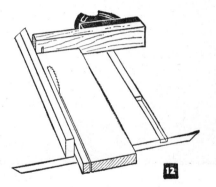

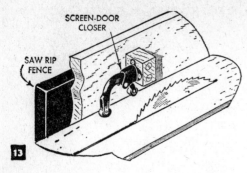

SCREEN-DOOR CLOSER

SAW RIP FENCE

13

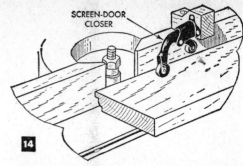

SCREEN-DOOR CLOSER

14

13—A screen-door closer of the snap-action "over-center" type makes a good hold-down when cutting thin stock on the circular saw. It prevents the stock being lifted by the blade and thrown forward and also aids in holding material firmly against the fence

14—This same type of door closer also will serve as a hold-down when molding straight work on the shaper. Moreover, it bears right at the point where you ordinarily have to place your fingers when the shaper cutter is working on the lower corner of the stock

15—Mount a sandpaper disk and another of ⅛-in. plywood on the shaper spindle with a spacer between and you have a good setup for rounding corners. As wood disk guides stock it should be smaller than the sandpaper disk. Wear goggles for this operation

16—A high-speed hand grinder clamped to the jigsaw blade guide gives you a router suitable for light routing and veining operations. The guide gives the necessary depth adjustment. On some operations it's better to move the work rather than the router

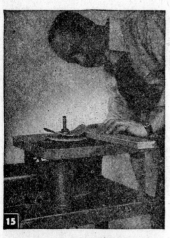

15

16

17

18

19

20

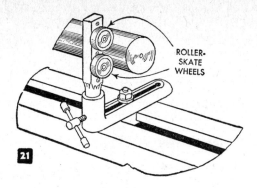

ROLLER-SKATE WHEELS

21

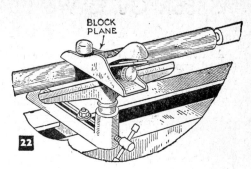

BLOCK PLANE

22

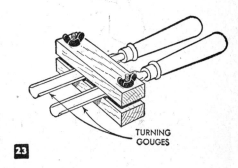

TURNING GOUGES

23

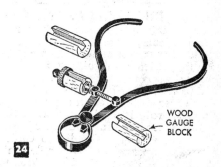

WOOD GAUGE BLOCK

24

17—Using a metal corner brace, a small C-clamp and a hand grinder you can quickly improvise a high-speed router that can be guided anywhere over the surface of the work. It's especially suitable for cutting shallow recesses for inlay designs of irregular shape

18—The problem of supporting small turning squares in a steady rest is overcome by cutting several plywood disks which slip over the square as shown. Supported in this way the work rides smoothly in the rest. It's easy to make disks for different sized squares

19—A pattern knife, for pattern turning in the lathe, can be made up easily by sliding several shaper cutters over a bolt. Supported in a slide rest, the cutting edges are fed slowly into the work with the cross-feed. Work should be rotated at high speed

20—When you have to turn large-diameter work on the outer end of the lathe spindle, there's no use bothering to construct a makeshift tool rest if you have a floor drill press. Just bolt the lathe tool rest to the drill-press table and you have a solid support for the turning tool with universal adjustments

21—A rolling back rest is usually necessary when turning long spindles in the wood lathe. Two discarded roller-skate wheels bolted to a short length of hardwood will do the trick. Support this improvised rolling rest in the regular tool-rest holder as shown

22—If you require a fine finish on cylindrical turnings, particularly if these are of softwood, try using a block plane as illustrated. Plane should be held at a slight angle with the axis of the work to obtain a shearing cut. It leaves a clear, glass-smooth finish

23—To rough-size a cylindrical turning to a given diameter, clamp two turning gouges between hardwood blocks with both cutting edges projecting the same distance. Then merely slide the block along the tool rest, which has been located parallel with work axis

24—You can check a number of diameters quickly with a single caliper if you first take time to make hardwood gauge blocks for each setting. These act as stops for each predetermined setting. Of course, settings should be carefully checked before using caliper

25—To lay out spiral turnings to almost any pitch an inked "wheel" taken from an ordinary typewriter eraser works fine. The wheel is fitted in a simple holder made from dowel rod. It is held freehand against the work which is supported between centers in the lathe and rotated slowly by hand. Angle of the wheel with the work determines the pitch of the spiral

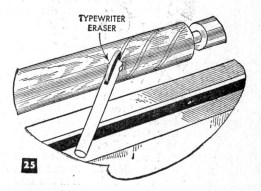

TYPEWRITER ERASER

25

Spools Guide Workbench Drawer and Serve as Support

A drawer that rides smoothly on thread spools and an angle-iron track can be installed in a bench or worktable with little effort. For support, two spools are required. One is cut in two with

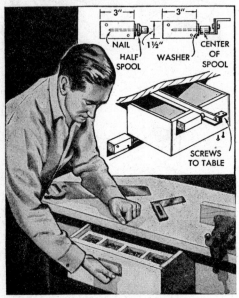

halves pivoted on nails at the sides of the drawer opening in the bench apron so that the lower edge slides on them. The back of the drawer is cut out for a track, which is a length of angle iron attached beneath the bench top by means of corner brackets as indicated. Flanges or ends are cut off a second spool, which then is pivoted to a hardwood block screwed to the back of the drawer so the spool will ride on the track.

Wooden Plugs Cut on Bandsaw by Using Simple Jig

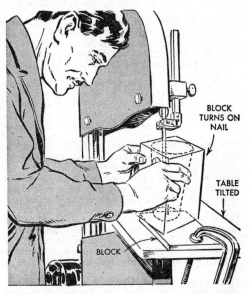

Jig Guides Drill in End Grain

When building bookcase shelves and similar projects where it is necessary to drive the screws in end grain, a sheet-metal jig will aid in guiding the pilot drill for the screw starter holes. The jig is bent to fit over the board and has a hole of the proper size drilled in the center of the top. A rule is used to mark off the holes and, since it is 1 in. from the edge of

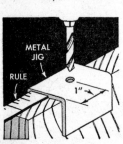

the jig to center of the hole, this must be added to the dimension on the rule to get the correct distance. If the jig has a tendency to "creep," a clamp will hold it. Be sure the clamp is on securely.

❰ To glue doweled joints, lay the dowel on a worktable and roll it under a coarse wood rasp before applying the adhesive. This roughens the surface of the wood so that glue will adhere better and a stronger bond will result. Care must be taken when rolling the dowel not to reduce its diameter so that it is too loose a fit in the joint.

Instead of shaping them on a lathe, one craftsman found that with the aid of this jig a number of large, tapered wooden plugs could be cut on a bandsaw more easily. A nail is driven through a piece of wood near one edge and the block is centered on this. The board then is clamped to the bandsaw table which is tilted to get the correct taper. The plug is cut by rotating the block on the nail. Note that the nail is near the edge of the board so the bottom of the plug will clear it when being cut.

Lighter Fluid Helps Loosen Bolts

A bottle of cigarette lighter fluid kept on the workbench will be handy in loosening rusted or tight bolts and nuts, especially the small ones on electrical appliances that have been "burned on" by the heat. Usually a few drops will loosen most threads.

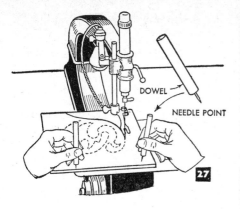

DOWEL

NEEDLE POINT

27

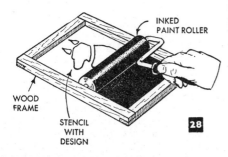

INKED
PAINT ROLLER

WOOD
FRAME

STENCIL
WITH
DESIGN

28

26

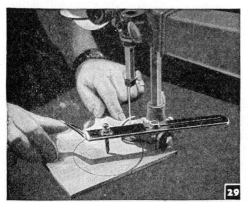

29

30

POWER-TOOL
SHORT CUTS

PART II

By Kenneth Murray

As explained previously in Part I of this story, simple jigs and fixtures for power tools enable owners of small job shops and home workshops to adapt their machines to a variety of uses. Also, by using suitable jigs, it is possible to do production work on machines not originally intended for such work.

Jigsaw: The crosscut gauge for use on a jigsaw in Fig. 26, and the pivot fixture in Fig. 29 for cutting disks are two good examples. The gauge is one from a circular saw and is turned upside down and used on a jigsaw table as pictured. The pivot fixture is merely a length of flat iron having a point at one end and a slot at the other to straddle a machine screw on the blade-guide assembly. The slot also permits adjustment of the pivot to cut disks of various radii. A pointed stove bolt serves as the pivot. It is important that the pivot be at right angles to the blade teeth so that the latter will not draw to one side.

When cutting intricate scrolls in thin stock, the needle-pointed jigs shown in Fig. 27 will aid in maneuvering the work over a jigsaw table. When duplicating a design on several pieces of work, time can be saved by making a mimeograph stencil of the design, then cementing it to the underside of a light wood frame and using it to transfer the design out-

435

31

line to the work as indicated in Fig. 28.

Fig. 30 shows a fixture on a jigsaw motor for making starting holes when cutting inside designs. In this case, the fixture was made from a hole cutter by removing the cutter arm and then inserting the cutter-arm holder tightly in the cone pulley on the motor.

Drill press: Likely, few inexperienced operators realize the versatility of this machine when jigs and fixtures are used in connection with it. As an example, lack of a drill-press vise need not be a handicap if a lathe chuck is at hand. It makes a good substitute as shown in Fig. 31, and can be bolted to the table when used on special setups. As a timesaver when laying out equally spaced holes to be drilled, the jig shown in Fig. 32 is hard to beat. It is nothing more than a "lazy tongs" having the pivot holes along one side enlarged to take short pencils. A drill press not having a tilting scale can be set accurately by using angle blocks as shown in Fig. 33.

The problem of cutting round tenons on irregularly shaped work is solved by using a hole cutter in a drill press as shown in Fig. 34. Shoulders are cut after the tenon has been formed. If you have experienced difficulty in holding small round work to drill the end, a cam-locking vise like the one shown in Fig. 35 will help. Pulling the handle causes the wood cam to wedge the work tightly against two blocks screwed to a base.

32

33

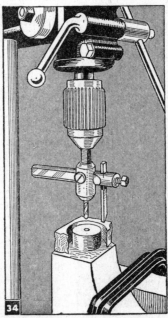

34

35

In Fig. 36 the operator, lacking an indexing head for drilling, moved the drill press up to his lathe and used the indexing head on the latter. The jig pictured in Fig. 37 takes all the worry out of drilling holes in mitered frames for starting nails or screws. If you have a job that requires sanding the inner surfaces of rings it can be done quickly on a drill press using a strip of abrasive cloth held in a split dowel, Fig. 38. A wide strip cut from inner tube and snapped around the drill-press table, Fig. 39, provides a non-slip surface for flat work. A mandrel for a variety of cleaning and polishing operations is shown in Fig. 40. It consists of a wood cylinder wrapped with steel wool in the roll form. The cylinder is mounted on a steel arbor and is grooved lengthwise to hold one end of the steel-wool roll, which then is wound onto the cylinder in a direction opposite to that of rotation. No other fastening is required as the wool will quickly mat itself together in use. Always wear goggles when operating this polisher.

Bandsaws: Although bandsaws usually are limited to sawing irregular outside shapes in wood and metal, there are several simple jigs and fixtures that can be made to increase the versatility of these saws. The jig for splitting a dowel, Fig. 41, is just one of many. It is merely a straightedge to which the dowel to be split is nailed at one end. In use, the straightedge is pushed along a fence. Such a jig is

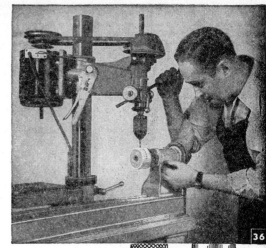

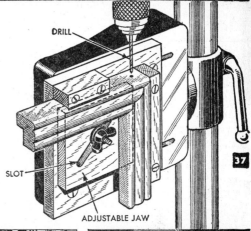

DRILL

SLOT

ADJUSTABLE JAW

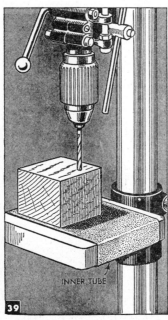

INNER TUBE

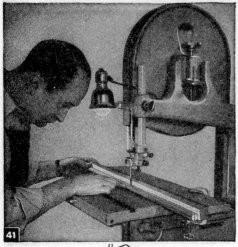

`41`

handy for flattening one side of long dowels, which later are cut into short lengths for making doweled-and-glued joints.

The pivot point shown in Fig. 42 simplifies the job of cutting true disks on a bandsaw. The point is soldered near one end of a piece of brass, which is bent at right angles to slip into the blade slot in the table. A wedge holds the brass piece in place. For cutting duplicate pieces to length, a setup like the one shown in Fig. 43 makes a production machine of your bandsaw. The backing block serves as a crosscut guide. If your bandsaw is equipped with a ripping fence, it can be used to center turning squares quickly and accurately. Make a long V-block to slide along the fence and run the saw blade in from one end as shown in Fig. 44. Then place the work in the block and push the assembly against the blade just enough to score the work.

If a bandsaw does not have a ripping fence, one can be improvised for some kinds of work by simply turning the crosscut gauge upside down and using it as shown in Fig. 45. A C-clamp will keep the gauge in position. The step gauge in Fig. 46 is handy when you have varied short lengths of work to cut off. It also is useful in cutting dowels to short lengths when using them in assembly work.

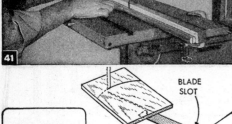

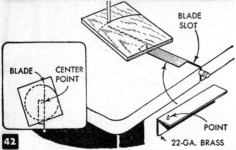

BLADE SLOT

BLADE   CENTER POINT

POINT

22-GA. BRASS

`42`

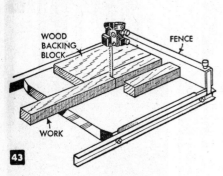

WOOD BACKING BLOCK   FENCE

WORK

`43`

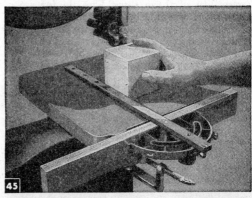

`45`

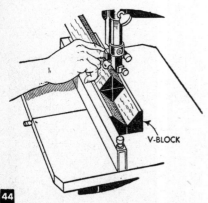

V-BLOCK

`44`

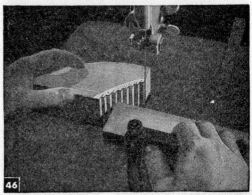

`46`

A place for everything and everything in its place. An old adage and one that you can practice in your workshop with the tool chest described below. You can build it yourself. It has a spacious drawer for storing planes and other large tools, nine drawers for small tools, and plenty of room inside the lid for hanging saws, a level and a square.

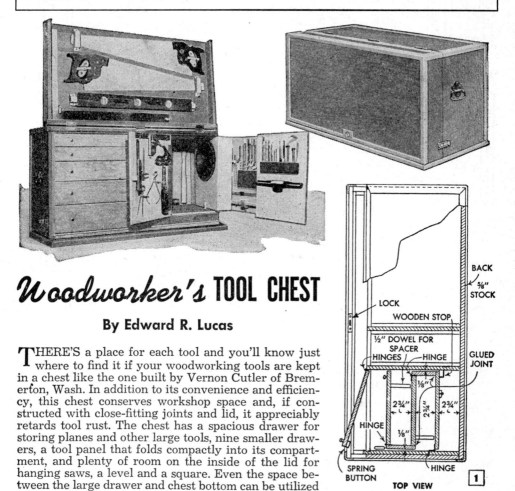

Woodworker's TOOL CHEST

By Edward R. Lucas

THERE'S a place for each tool and you'll know just where to find it if your woodworking tools are kept in a chest like the one built by Vernon Cutler of Bremerton, Wash. In addition to its convenience and efficiency, this chest conserves workshop space and, if constructed with close-fitting joints and lid, it appreciably retards tool rust. The chest has a spacious drawer for storing planes and other large tools, nine smaller drawers, a tool panel that folds compactly into its compartment, and plenty of room on the inside of the lid for hanging saws, a level and a square. Even the space between the large drawer and chest bottom can be utilized

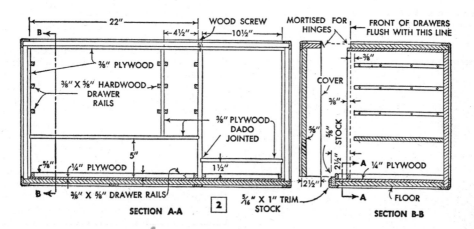

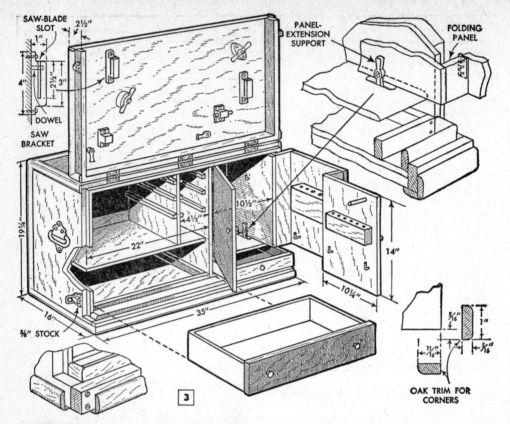

SAW-BLADE SLOT

DOWEL

SAW BRACKET

SAW-BLADE SLOT

PANEL-EXTENSION SUPPORT

FOLDING PANEL

5⁄8" STOCK

OAK TRIM FOR CORNERS

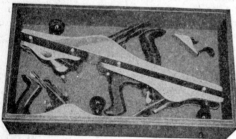

Above, roomy bottom drawer provides ample storage space for planes or other large tools. Below, drawer inserts permit the number of compartments to be increased without the installation of extra drawers

for storing blueprints, magazine plans and pamphlets.

The outer shell of the chest is of cedar with all corners and edges protected by oak trim. The top and sides are lined with 3⁄8-in. plywood panels and the bottom with 1⁄4-in. plywood. These liners extend 3⁄8 in. beyond the front edges of the top and sides to form a rabbet for the lid, Fig. 1 and Fig. 2, section B-B. Two 5⁄16 by 1-in. oak cleats are fastened across the bottom of the chest to give additional support. The vertical partitions and hardwood drawer runners are inserted as in Fig. 1 and Fig. 2, section A-A. All drawer fronts and the door for the tool-panel compartment should fit flush with the chest sides.

The tool panels are hinged and fitted as in Fig. 1, leaving at least 1⁄8-in. clearance between each wall of the compartment and the panels when they are folded. Note the wooden stop and the dowel spacers for the panels. The extension support, upper right-hand detail, Fig. 3, holds the tool panels in the open position. The lid is constructed in the same way as the rest of the chest, and is mortise-hinged to the chest top. Fig. 3 shows fixtures for mounting tools on inside of lid.

Knurled Handle Holds Tool Bits When Grinding

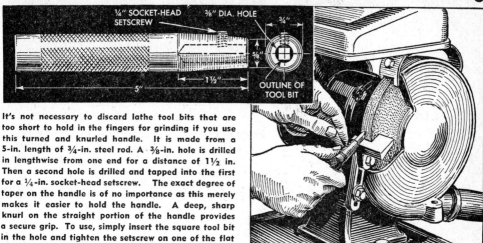

It's not necessary to discard lathe tool bits that are too short to hold in the fingers for grinding if you use this turned and knurled handle. It is made from a 5-in. length of ¾-in. steel rod. A ⅜-in. hole is drilled in lengthwise from one end for a distance of 1½ in. Then a second hole is drilled and tapped into the first for a ¼-in. socket-head setscrew. The exact degree of taper on the handle is of no importance as this merely makes it easier to hold the handle. A deep, sharp knurl on the straight portion of the handle provides a secure grip. To use, simply insert the square tool bit in the hole and tighten the setscrew on one of the flat sides of the tool.

Sturdy Sawhorse Is Small Enough to Be Hauled in Your Car

Small and light enough in weight to be carried in a passenger car, this sturdy sawhorse has many uses. The lower shelf provides a handy tray to keep tools and small parts conveniently at hand, and the sawhorse is low and strong enough to be used as a support to stand on when working in places above your head. When used for this purpose, the shelf serves as a step to reach the top member. The dimension for the width of this member can be varied, and for that reason is indicated by a blank arrow. If it is made about 6 in. wide it will provide a place to lay saws and similar tools as well as a flat working surface.

Brushes Held in Released Position Simplify Electric-Motor Assembly

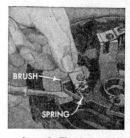

Assembly of some induction motors or generators is facilitated if the brushes are wedged in a released position so they will slide over the commutator without trouble when the bell, or end cap, is replaced. Each brush is pushed back in its holder to the point where the pressure of the spring will bear against the side of the brush. Then, after the motor is completely assembled, the brushes are pushed down with a screwdriver, inserted through the opening in the cap, until the spring returns to its normal position.

Try This When Grinding Bolts

Before reshaping a bolt head on a grinder, one auto mechanic turns a nut halfway up the threads. The nut absorbs sufficient heat to permit him to hold the lower end of the bolt comfortably with his fingers.

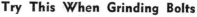

BRAZING TORCHES USE

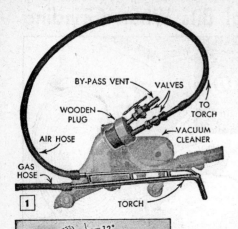

A vacuum cleaner supplies air for operating these simple gas torches, which are designed in two sizes to cover the widest range of light brazing, silver soldering, soft soldering, annealing and hardening

CONNECTED to any source of illuminating gas and supplied with air from a vacuum cleaner, these torches give sufficient heat to handle any ordinary brazing job. Silver soldering, soft soldering, annealing, hardening and tempering also can be done with either size. The torches will not operate on acetylene gas or "bottled" gas.

Both torches are very similar in construction, the only essential difference being in the size of copper tubing used to conduct air and gas to the tips. Figs. 4 and 5 detail the construction. It is impractical to bend tubing to the sharp radius required to form the torch tip, so to save time simply cut an 82-deg. notch in the tube as in Fig. 2. Be careful not to cut into the wall of the tubing at the bottom of the notch. Leave the wall full thickness at this point. Then bend to the position shown by the dotted lines in Fig. 2, and silver solder the joint as in Fig. 3, using a gasoline blowtorch. Place the work on a couple of bricks while heating the joint. The air tubes can be bent by hand to the required radius. Drill a hole just back of the joint in the gas tube for insertion of the air tube. It is important that the air tube project into the tip of the large torch the distance shown in Fig. 5 and that it be exactly centered in the larger gas tube. Wedge it in place before silver soldering the joint at the point where it is inserted

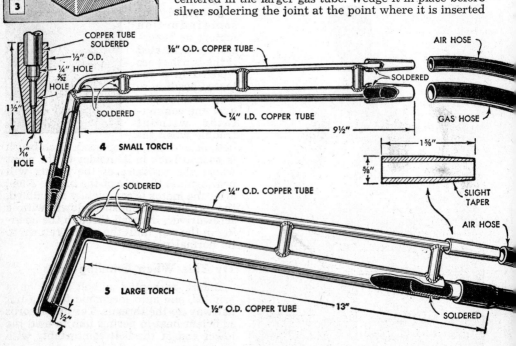

ILLUMINATING GAS

By Edward J. Thatcher

in the gas tube. Joint should be gas-tight.

The three spacers along the length of each torch between the air and gas tubes are short lengths of tubing, silver soldered to both tubes to hold them securely in position. The small torch, Fig. 4, has a separate tip counterbored in four steps as shown in the sectional view. This tip is silver soldered to the gas tube after the latter has been formed.

The air and gas tubes on both the large and small torches are fitted with tapered sleeves turned from thick-walled brass or copper tubing. These are silver soldered to the tubes as in Figs. 4 and 5. Note that one sleeve fits inside the gas tube, Fig. 5. Tapered ends of the sleeves make it easier to connect the lengths of rubber hose which bring gas and air to the torch.

The vacuum cleaner is used without any alteration except for the removal of the dust bag. A wooden plug is turned to fit into the outlet for the dust bag as in Figs. 1 and 8. The tapered end of the plug is covered with felt to prevent air leaks. Two air outlets, each consisting of a pipe nipple, a short length of pipe threaded at one end, and a valve, are turned into holes drilled in the outer end of the plug as in Fig. 8. One serves as a by-pass for excess air. The air hose from the torch is connected to the other. Where more than one torch is to

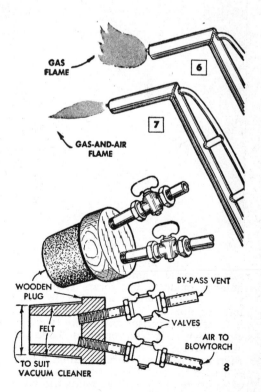

GAS FLAME

6

GAS-AND-AIR FLAME

7

WOODEN PLUG

FELT

TO SUIT VACUUM CLEANER

BY-PASS VENT

VALVES

AIR TO BLOWTORCH

8

be operated from the same vacuum cleaner, make an air regulator from a gallon can as in Fig. 9. The sliding door in the regulator provides a means of controlling the volume of air supplied to the torches, by-passing the excess through the opening cut in the can.

To use the torches, connect the respective lines to the gas and air, close the air valve at the cleaner and open the by-pass valve. Turn the gas on and light it at the tip, Fig. 6. Turn down until a fairly small flame is produced. Then slowly turn on the air, with the by-pass valve on the cleaner open. Close the by-pass valve slowly, stopping when the pointed flame turns blue as in Fig. 7. Too much air will reduce the heat of the flame and may cause it to "pop" out. It will take some experi-

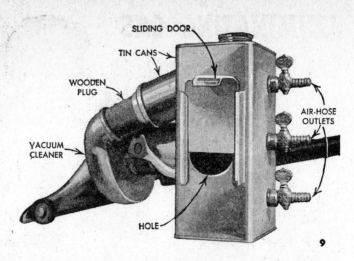

menting to produce the proper flame, as the air pressures are likely to vary with different cleaners.

With proper adjustment, the smaller torch gives a fine, needle-point flame ideal for a close work where the heat must be concentrated in a small area.

Holder Supports Boring Tool Close to Work

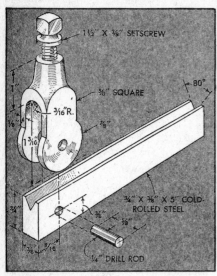

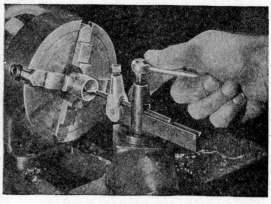

For boring and threading work of small internal diameter, this boring tool holder, made from scrap steel, will prove a worthwhile addition to your lathe equipment. To slot the yoke, drill a hole near the center and make two saw cuts down to it from one end. Then the slot is brought to finish size and the circular part rounded by hand filing. A hole is drilled through the slot to take a piece of ¼-in. drill rod, which holds the yoke

to the shank. The tapered end is turned to size and, while the yoke is still in the chuck, the hole for the setscrew is drilled and tapped. An ordinary setscrew can be used, or you can make up one to fit. The shank of the holder is grooved in a shaper to hold the boring tool, and a hole is drilled in one end for the drill rod, which is a press fit.

❡ When chipping carbon off a cylinder block or piston, always wear safety goggles to protect your eyes.

❡ Clean holes with a minimum of tearing in using an ordinary twist drill can be obtained by sharpening the drill to an included angle of 135 degrees and operating the drill at a fairly high speed.

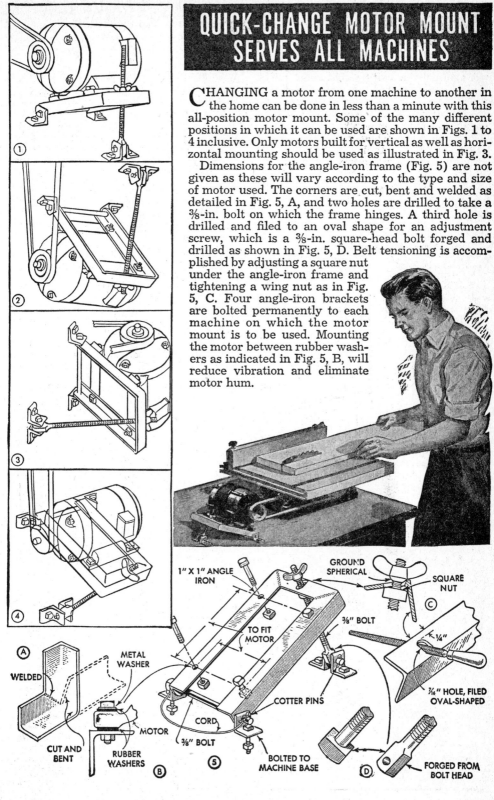

QUICK-CHANGE MOTOR MOUNT SERVES ALL MACHINES

CHANGING a motor from one machine to another in the home can be done in less than a minute with this all-position motor mount. Some of the many different positions in which it can be used are shown in Figs. 1 to 4 inclusive. Only motors built for vertical as well as horizontal mounting should be used as illustrated in Fig. 3.

Dimensions for the angle-iron frame (Fig. 5) are not given as these will vary according to the type and size of motor used. The corners are cut, bent and welded as detailed in Fig. 5, A, and two holes are drilled to take a ⅜-in. bolt on which the frame hinges. A third hole is drilled and filed to an oval shape for an adjustment screw, which is a ⅜-in. square-head bolt forged and drilled as shown in Fig. 5, D. Belt tensioning is accomplished by adjusting a square nut under the angle-iron frame and tightening a wing nut as in Fig. 5, C. Four angle-iron brackets are bolted permanently to each machine on which the motor mount is to be used. Mounting the motor between rubber washers as indicated in Fig. 5, B, will reduce vibration and eliminate motor hum.

445

Tool Rack Hanging from Ceiling Saves Space in Workshop

To save space in his basement workshop, one craftsman devised a rack that would hold all his tool boxes and swing up against the ceiling, between joists, where it was out of the way. The boxes were pivoted to the sides of the rack by means of pipe which was capped at both ends to keep it from slipping out of place. When not in use, a hook holds the rack in place, but when tools are needed, the rack swings down against the wall.

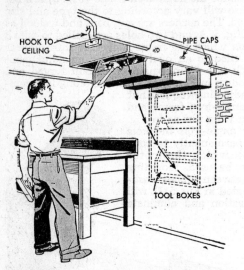

Plywood Panel on Jigsaw Table Increases Life of Blades

When using fine blades in a jigsaw for cutting thin stock, a false table will elevate the work and bring it into contact with an unused part of the blade, resulting in a longer cutting life. In many cases this will double the life of the blade. A

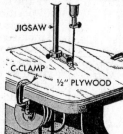

piece of ½-in. plywood makes an ideal table and C-clamps are used to hold it in place. For a neat-looking job, the wood is cut and sanded to the exact shape of the jigsaw table.

Attaching Wire to Sheet Metal

To make good electrical contact between a wire and sheet metal, cut the metal lengthwise a short distance and wrap the ends around the wire in opposite directions, as indicated in detail A. For larger sheets, make a slit in one corner and bend the metal down and over the wire, detail B. If the wire is insulated, the insulation should be removed.

Level Equipped with Adjustment Measures Angles Accurately

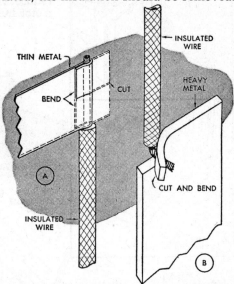

←Measuring the angle or pitch of an object with an ordinary level is difficult because it is hard to hold the level steady while taking a reading with a rule. With this adjustment, which is removable, the job is easy. A recess or slot is cut in one end and a vertical hole is drilled to take a headless bolt. A nut fits into the recess and permits adjustment of the bolt. When the level is not used, the bolt is removed. A tin shield holds nut in place.

BENDING BRAKES
for Your Sheet-Metal Jobs

By Sam Brown

THESE bending brakes will simplify sheet-metal fabrication. Two designs are described, both capable of bending 24-ga. galvanized iron the width of the brake, or heavier metal when the bend is not at full 12-in. capacity. Design No. 2, Fig. 8, while more difficult to make, is somewhat superior in that it offers stronger construction and also permits partial (tab) and reverse bends which are not possible with No. 1 design.

Design No. 1: Both designs are of the folding-leaf variety, and the general features of construction are grasped easily from Fig. 3. The essential feature is that the center of hinge pin must line up exactly with the meeting edges of folding leaf and table. This is diagramed in Fig. 4. The working of the brake is shown in Fig. 1, the metal being clamped under the forming bar and then bent by pulling up on the folding leaf. The forming bar should be notched for easy removal. It is positioned exactly for duplicate work by means of two sliding

1

BENDING METAL TILE—ONE OF MANY JOBS POSSIBLE WITH BRAKE

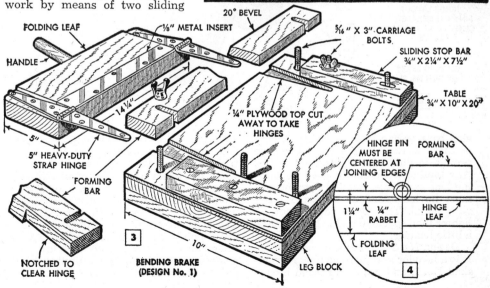

2 SAMPLE BENDS

FOLDING LEAF

HANDLE

20° BEVEL

⅛" METAL INSERT

14¼"

5"

5" HEAVY-DUTY STRAP HINGE

FORMING BAR

NOTCHED TO CLEAR HINGE

¼" PLYWOOD TOP CUT AWAY TO TAKE HINGES

⁵⁄₁₆" X 3" CARRIAGE BOLTS

SLIDING STOP BAR ¾" X 2¼" X 7½"

TABLE ¾" X 10" X 20"

HINGE PIN MUST BE CENTERED AT JOINING EDGES

FORMING BAR

1¼"   ¼" RABBET

HINGE LEAF

FOLDING LEAF

3

4

BENDING BRAKE (DESIGN No. 1)

10"

LEG BLOCK

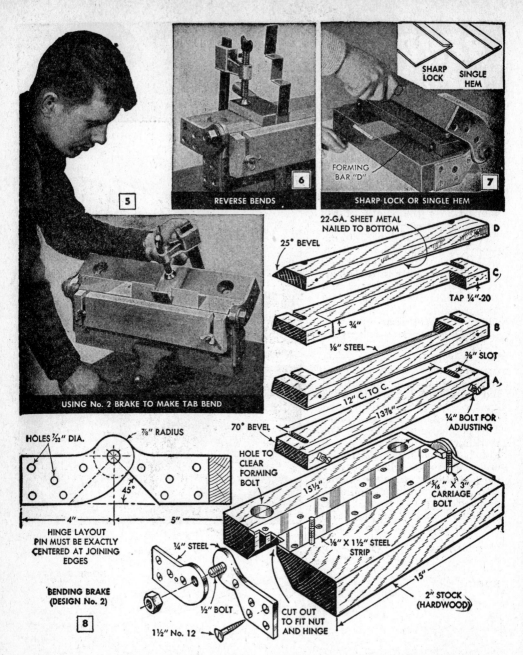

5

6 REVERSE BENDS

SHARP LOCK / SINGLE HEM

7 SHARP LOCK OR SINGLE HEM

FORMING BAR "D"

USING No. 2 BRAKE TO MAKE TAB BEND

22-GA. SHEET METAL NAILED TO BOTTOM — D

25° BEVEL

C

TAP ¼"-20

¾"

⅛" STEEL — B

⅜" SLOT

12" C. TO C.

13⅞"

¼" BOLT FOR ADJUSTING

A

70° BEVEL

HOLE TO CLEAR FORMING BOLT

HOLES ⅞" DIA.

⅞" RADIUS

45°

4"

5"

HINGE LAYOUT
PIN MUST BE EXACTLY
CENTERED AT JOINING
EDGES

BENDING BRAKE
(DESIGN No. 2)

8

¼" STEEL

½" BOLT

1½" No. 12

CUT OUT
TO FIT NUT
AND HINGE

15½"

⅛" X 1½" STEEL
STRIP

5/16" X 3"
CARRIAGE
BOLT

15"

2" STOCK
(HARDWOOD)

stop bars, as can be seen in Fig. 3. One of these works along a fixed block to provide a guide for right-angle bends. Any kind of wood can be used for folding leaf and table, but the forming bar must be hardwood or softwood faced with metal. The hinge should not be lighter than specified and is better made a little heavier.

Design No. 2: This is shown in Fig. 8. It is a heavier and more compact design than No. 1, and requires special hinges cut from ¼-in. steel, as shown. The 45-deg. cut on the underside of leaf and table weakens the construction somewhat, but offers an arrangement that is essential for reverse bends. The four styles of forming bars shown in Fig. 8, will handle all ordinary work. Care should be taken in assembly to get the pivot points in exact alignment. This design also works out nicely with hinges made from ¾-in. plywood, pinning the bolt to the table member and providing

a brass bushing in the other to prevent wear.

Tab and reverse bends: Tab and reverse bends are worked on No. 2 brake by mounting the brake on edge in a vise and folding the leaf all the way back. A block of wood is clamped to the folding leaf and becomes the forming member. Fig. 5 shows the operation on a tab bend; Fig. 6 shows the same setup for reverse bends. Neither can be done on the No. 1 brake.

Standard operations: The sharp lock, Fig. 7, is made by using the brake in a normal position with a style D forming bar. This bend is used frequently for fastening two pieces of metal together. If the bend is at full capacity (12 in. long), it is best to form it to a flange with the stronger A or B bar and then complete the lock with the sharp-edge D bar. The single sharp lock when pressed tightly together in a vise or by hammering becomes the single hem or bend, as shown. If the single bend is hemmed again, it makes a double hem. At full capacity on a narrow hem less than ¼ in. wide, this bend offers the ultimate strength and accuracy test for your brake —a poorly made brake will fail in this double-hem operation.

Large return bends or channels are made with the standard forming bar (style A), and offer no difficulties. Smaller channels are made with the B bar, which permits working as small as ⅛-in. cross section. This operation is shown in Fig. 9. The B bar is used also for bending small closed forms, as shown in Fig. 10. As can be seen, the brake does not fully close the form on the final bend, but it is close enough so that a little springing by hand will complete it. Style C bar offers another way of working small closed forms, as shown in Fig. 11. Complete closure is possible with

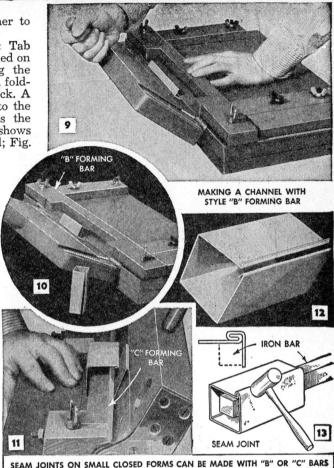

"B" FORMING BAR

MAKING A CHANNEL WITH STYLE "B" FORMING BAR

"C" FORMING BAR

IRON BAR

SEAM JOINT

SEAM JOINTS ON SMALL CLOSED FORMS CAN BE MADE WITH "B" OR "C" BARS

this bar, but the work must be resprung to remove it from the bar. When the closed form has a seam joint, Fig. 12, the final bend, as in Fig. 11, is really a reverse bend and is best worked by the method shown in Fig. 5. However, the reverse caused by the narrow flange is slight and does not materially affect the bending operation. Fig. 13 shows how the seam joint is closed by hammering. This is not an easy joint to make and should be practiced before you attempt it on finished work.

Box bends: One of the most used forms of sheet-metal work is the simple square box. Like its companion in wood, it can be made a dozen different ways. Simplest way is to cut out the corners and then bend the work over a forming block, Fig. 14, or over

flange which can be riveted or soldered to the sides (a sample is shown in Fig. 2), and this style is made easily by first forming the tabs, working as shown in Fig. 5, and then bending the sides over a forming block.

Work capacity: Work capacity of both brakes described is about 12 in. No. 2 design will work satisfactorily up to about 18-24 in. No. 1 brake will not handle metal thicker than 24 ga. (usual furnace-pipe weight as obtained at tin shops); No. 2 brake will work 22-ga. material. Both will handle much thicker metal if the bend is short. Dimensions given are working specifications and can be varied.

14

MAKING A BOX WITH USE OF FORMING BLOCK

a special style A forming bar, Fig. 15. For the latter operation, the forming bar has notches cut to accommodate the flanges previously turned up. The notches (saw kerfs) do not affect the bend, and one bar can be notched many times to suit different sizes of work. The simple style of box shown, while easy to bend, presents a fair amount of work in soldering the corners. Some shapes in this style (such as lids), if shallow, are often strong enough not to require soldering. Most larger boxes make use of some kind of inside or outside

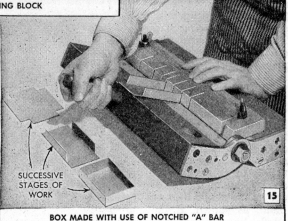

SUCCESSIVE STAGES OF WORK

15

BOX MADE WITH USE OF NOTCHED "A" BAR

Absorbent Cotton Stuffed in Covered Box Cleans Drawing Pencil

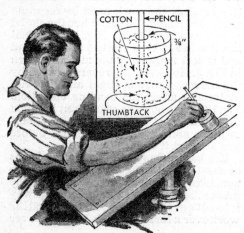

COTTON · PENCIL · 3/8" · THUMBTACK

Finding a way to clean the point of a pencil after sharpening it is always a problem for the draftsman. One solution is to fill a small, covered box with absorbent cotton. Cut a hole in the top large enough for the pencil. To clean the point, insert it in the hole and rotate in the cotton. This will remove powdered lead.

"Manicure" for Small Commutators

Emery boards, which are strips of fine sandpaper bonded together to form a resilient blade shaped like a nail file, are well suited to the job of cleaning, smoothing and polishing the commutators of small generators and motors. Because of the low cost, a new one can be used for each job.

DRILL-PRESS CLAMPS

By Will Thomas

These clamps are so designed that they drop into the slots in the drill-press table and can be tightened in a jiffy. They are especially handy when doing close work because it's never necessary to remove nuts and washers from bolts that project under the table. As you see in Fig. 1, the individual clamps can be set in various positions to hold work which is irregular in shape. Fig. 2 details one unit, and you can make as many as you need by simply duplicating parts and operations. To make duplicate clamps, chuck 1½-in. round cold-rolled stock off-center as in Fig. 4, carrying the outer end of the piece on the tail center. Turn to the dimensions given in Fig. 2 and you have four cam shapes as in Fig. 4. Saw these apart, then drill and tap for the clamping bolts, Fig. 3. The rectangular-shaped nuts, Fig. 2, are cut from ³⁄₁₆-in. flat steel and finished by filing. Be sure that the nuts slip through the table slots. Drill and tap nuts exactly in the center so that strain is equalized when the bolts are tightened.

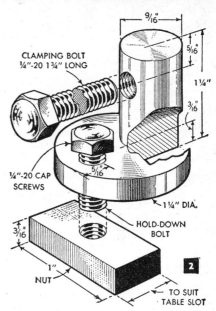

CLAMPING BOLT
¼"-20 1¾" LONG

¼"-20 CAP SCREWS

HOLD-DOWN BOLT

NUT

TO SUIT TABLE SLOT

$\frac{9}{16}$"

$\frac{5}{16}$"

1¼"

$\frac{3}{16}$"

$\frac{5}{16}$"

1¼" DIA.

$\frac{3}{16}$"

1"

2

Clamps also can be used on a milling machine or lathe faceplate to hold irregular-shaped work

451

DRILLING

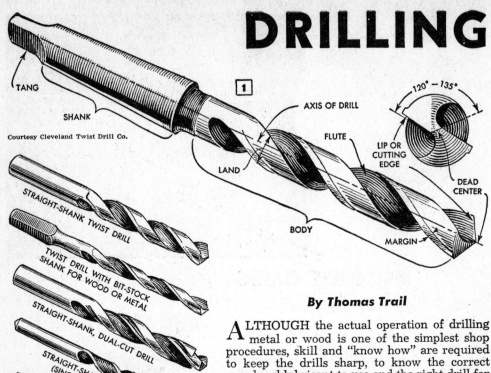

TANG

SHANK

Courtesy Cleveland Twist Drill Co.

AXIS OF DRILL

FLUTE

LAND

LIP OR
CUTTING
EDGE

BODY

120° – 135°

DEAD
CENTER

MARGIN

STRAIGHT-SHANK TWIST DRILL

TWIST DRILL WITH BIT-STOCK
SHANK FOR WOOD OR METAL

STRAIGHT-SHANK, DUAL-CUT DRILL

STRAIGHT-SHANK BOBBIN BIT
(SINGLE FLUTED DRILL)

TAPER-SHANK, OIL-TUBE DRILL

STRAIGHT-SHANK, STRAIGHT-FLUTED
DRILL FOR WOOD OR SOFT METAL

2 TYPES OF DRILLS

By Thomas Trail

ALTHOUGH the actual operation of drilling
metal or wood is one of the simplest shop
procedures, skill and "know how" are required
to keep the drills sharp, to know the correct
speed and lubricant to use and the right drill for
the job at hand. The principal parts of a drill are
shown in Fig. 1. The dead center should be on
the exact center of the drill axis and the cutting
edges must be equal both in length and in angle.
The margin is a narrow, raised rib with a cutting edge being the full diameter of the drill. In
operation, the rib accurately sizes the hole and
reduces friction. The shank is the end of the drill
that is held by a drill-press chuck or a taper
socket. The drill shown has a tapered shank with
a tang on the end which engages a slot in the
small end of the tapered socket to give a positive drive. Drills also are made with a straight

3 CAUSES AND CURES FOR COMMON DRILL TROUBLES

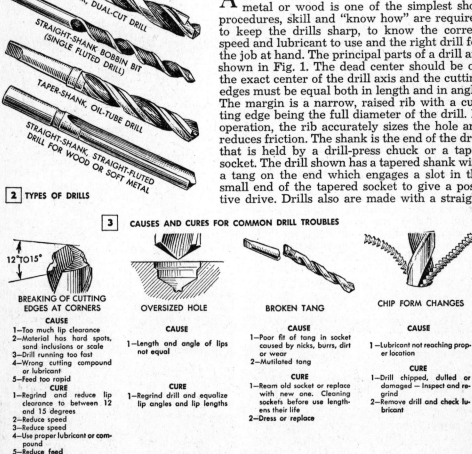

12° TO 15°

BREAKING OF CUTTING EDGES AT CORNERS

CAUSE
1—Too much lip clearance
2—Material has hard spots,
   sand inclusions or scale
3—Drill running too fast
4—Wrong cutting compound
   or lubricant
5—Feed too rapid

CURE
1—Regrind and reduce lip
   clearance to between .12
   and 15 degrees
2—Reduce speed
3—Reduce speed
4—Use proper lubricant or compound
5—Reduce feed

OVERSIZED HOLE

CAUSE
1—Length and angle of lips
   not equal

CURE
1—Regrind drill and equalize
   lip angles and lip lengths

BROKEN TANG

CAUSE
1—Poor fit of tang in socket
   caused by nicks, burrs, dirt
   or wear
2—Mutilated tang

CURE
1—Ream old socket or replace
   with new one. Cleaning
   sockets before use length-
   ens their life
2—Dress or replace

CHIP FORM CHANGES

CAUSE
1—Lubricant not reaching proper location

CURE
1—Drill chipped, dulled or
   damaged — Inspect and regrind
2—Remove drill and check lubricant

DATA

shank and a bit-stock shank, as in Fig. 2. The diameter of a drill decreases slightly from the cutting point in order to prevent binding in the drilled hole. Sizes are designated in four classifications. Number drills range from No. 80 to No. 1 (.0135 in. to .228 in.); letter drills from A to Z (.234 in. to .413 in.); fractional drills rise from ¼4 in. upward by 64ths, and metric drills are listed from .5 mm. to 10 mm. by .1 mm., larger than 10 mm. by .5mm.

Normally, the cutting edges of a new drill gradually wear away with use and require sharpening. A dull drill will not cut properly and may be damaged by excessive heat generated by friction at the cutting point. Drills should be sharpened on a medium-grit grinding wheel. To prevent a drill from overheating and losing its temper while grinding, it should be dipped frequently in water while being sharpened. Cold water should not be used for this purpose, however, as it may cause cracking or distortion of the drill bit.

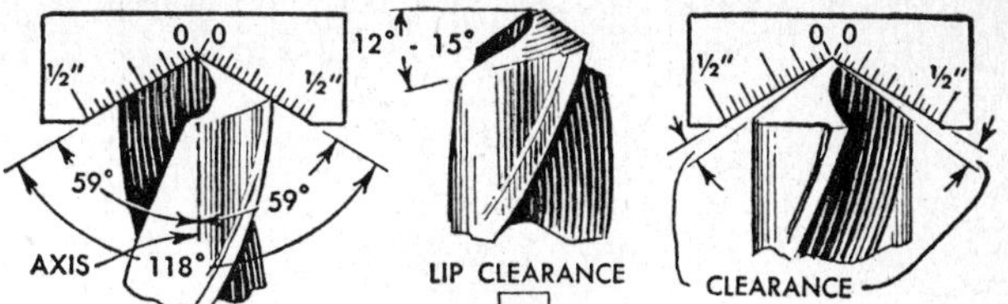

Most drilling trouble is due to faulty grinding of the cutting-edge clearance and angle. The two cutting edges of a drill must be made equal both in length and angle, and the angle must be such as to produce best results in the material to be drilled, Figs. 3 and 4. For average drilling, an angle of 59 deg. at the cutting edges has been found most satisfactory and new drills are ground to this angle unless made for special purposes. A drill gauge, Fig. 4, is used to check the angle of the cutting edge when grinding.

If either the lengths or angles of the cutting edges are ground unequally, the drill will drift and form an oversize, stepped hole. This will happen even though lip clearance is correct for the angle at which each lip is ground. The clearance, as shown in the center and right-hand details in Fig. 4, allows the drill to penetrate the material being drilled. For average work the clearance angle back of the cutting edges

BOTH LIPS MUST BE OF EQUAL LENGTH AND HAVE THE SAME ANGLE TO THE AXIS

4

LIP CLEARANCE

ANGLE AT PERIPHERY OF DRILL GRADUALLY INCREASES TOWARD BACK OF LIPS

CLEARANCE

CLEARANCE ANGLE AT BACK OF LIPS

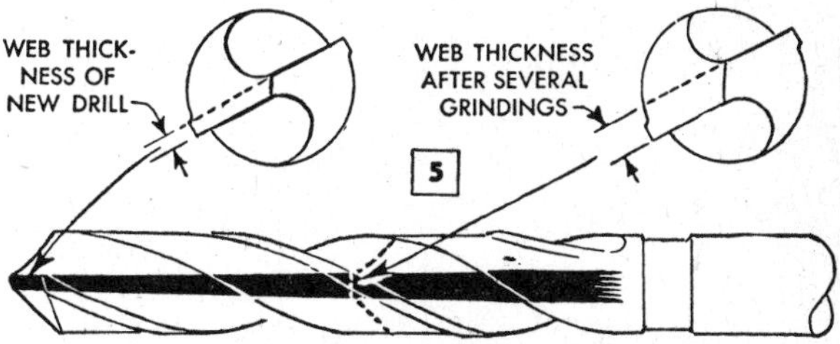

WEB THICKNESS OF NEW DRILL

WEB THICKNESS AFTER SEVERAL GRINDINGS

5

WEB THICKNESS INCREASES TOWARD SHANK OF DRILL

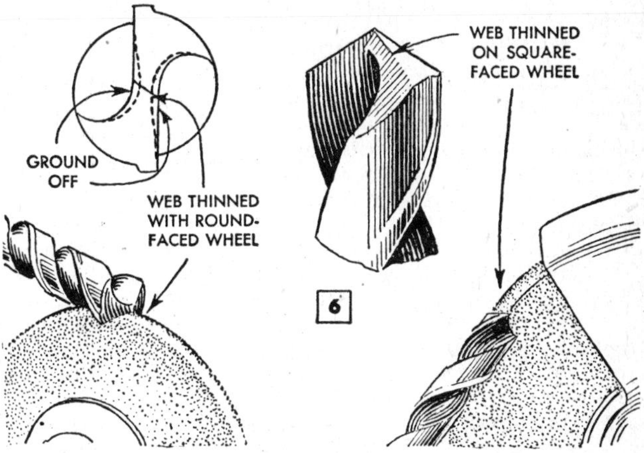

GROUND OFF

WEB THINNED WITH ROUND-FACED WHEEL

WEB THINNED ON SQUARE-FACED WHEEL

6

should be between 8 and 12 deg., but it is sometimes increased to 15 deg. where heavy feeds are taken in soft materials. When cutting-edge clearances have been ground uniformly to the proper angle, the angle subtended by the dead-center line and each cutting edge should be at least 120 deg., and not more than 135 deg., as shown in Fig. 1. Excessive clearance will weaken the cutting edges and cause them to break down. Insufficient clearance will prevent the drill from properly penetrating the material and may result in splitting the drill. After grinding, the drill point should be checked carefully to assure accuracy of the cutting-edge lengths and angles, the clearance angles and the location of the dead center.

Although with practice the mechanic can do an accurate job of drill grinding

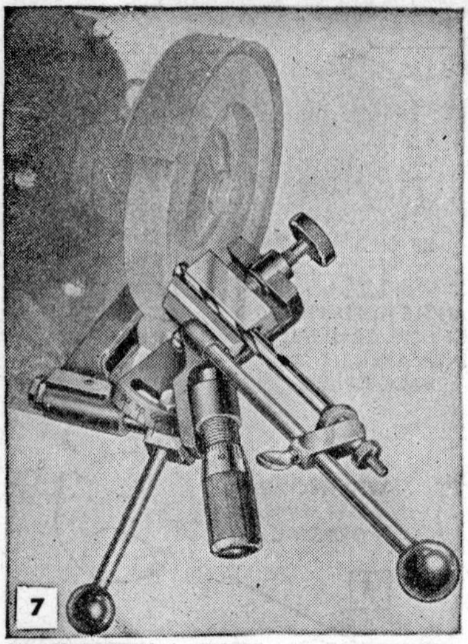
7

Atlas Press Co. photo

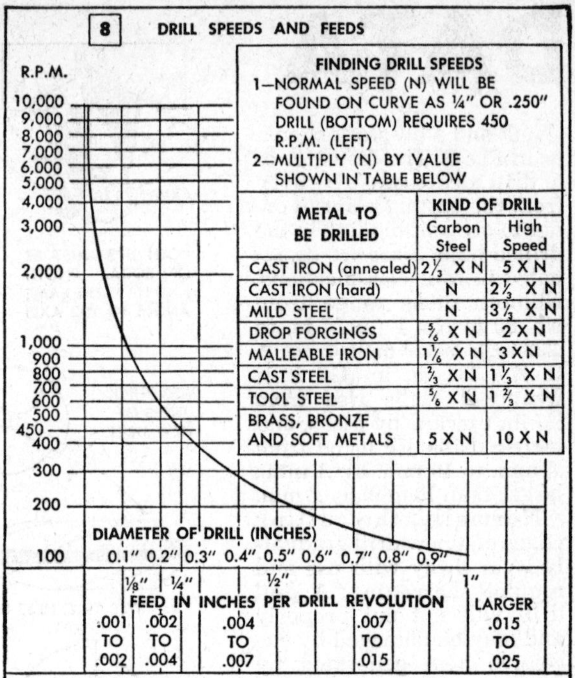
8
DRILL SPEEDS AND FEEDS
R.P.M.
10,000
9,000
8,000
7,000
6,000
5,000
4,000
3,000
2,000
1,000
900
800
700
600
500
450
400
300
200
100
DIAMETER OF DRILL (INCHES)
0.1" 0.2" 0.3" 0.4" 0.5" 0.6" 0.7" 0.8" 0.9"
1/8" 1/4" 1/2" 1"
FEED IN INCHES PER DRILL REVOLUTION
.001 TO .002
.002 TO .004
.004 TO .007
.007 TO .015
LARGER .015 TO .025

FINDING DRILL SPEEDS

1—NORMAL SPEED (N) WILL BE FOUND ON CURVE AS 1/4" OR .250" DRILL (BOTTOM) REQUIRES 450 R.P.M. (LEFT)

2—MULTIPLY (N) BY VALUE SHOWN IN TABLE BELOW

METAL TO BE DRILLED	KIND OF DRILL	
	Carbon Steel	High Speed
CAST IRON (annealed)	2 1/3 X N	5 X N
CAST IRON (hard)	N	2 1/3 X N
MILD STEEL	N	3 1/3 X N
DROP FORGINGS	5/6 X N	2 X N
MALLEABLE IRON	1 1/6 X N	3 X N
CAST STEEL	2/3 X N	1 1/3 X N
TOOL STEEL	5/6 X N	1 2/3 X N
BRASS, BRONZE AND SOFT METALS	5 X N	10 X N

LUBRICANTS

Cast Iron—None
Mild Steel—Lard Oil
Drop Forgings—Lard Oil
Malleable Iron—Soda Water
Tool Steel—Lard Oil
Cast Steel—Lard Oil
Brass and Bronze—Dry or Paraffin Oil
Wrought Iron—Lard Oil
Aluminum—Kerosene

by hand, use of an automatic grinding attachment, Fig. 7, is recommended. This will produce an accurately ground drill point and will save excess grinding.

When drilling hard material it is sometimes desirable to use a heavy feed pressure. To prevent the drill from chipping, a narrow flat is ground on the leading side of each cutting edge. Care must be taken not to give the edge a negative rake, however, as this would cause heating and possible breakage. This type of drill point also is used when drilling soft materials, such as brass, where a normal point may tend to dig in. Note from Fig. 5 that the web increases in thickness from the cutting point to the shank to give the drill greater rigidity. As a result, the web becomes thicker at the point after a number of sharpenings and must be thinned by grinding to maintain ease of penetration of the drill point. Fig. 6 shows two methods of reducing the thickness of the web at the point. The best way is to use a round-faced grinding wheel, the radius of the wheel face being less than that of the flutes. Another method is to grind a bevel on the trailing edge of the heel as in the upper right-hand detail of Fig. 6, using a square-faced wheel. Except for cast iron, which is drilled dry, most metals require use of a lubricant for best results. Lubricant serves a threefold purpose. It dissipates heat rapidly, lubricates the drill at the cutting edges and aids in the formation of uniform chips. This results in smooth, clean work with a minimum of wear on the drill.

The chart, Fig. 8, makes it easy to figure proper drill speeds and feeds in all common drilling operations. It also lists the correct lubricants used on various types of metals.

Work to be drilled should be clamped securely to the drill-press table and the drill should be held firmly by the chuck or taper socket. When using taper-shank drills, see that the shank and the inside of the socket are smooth and free from grit, and that the drill tang is not damaged. Use a block of wood to drive the drill shank tightly in the socket. In removing the drill from the socket, place a piece of wood under the drill point to prevent it from striking the drill-press table or the work, and use a drift of the correct size to drive out the drill. When drills are used at the bench, keep them in a metal stand especially made for the purpose. Drills not in use should never be stored loose in a drawer or chest or together with other tools as they are likely to become nicked or otherwise damaged. Stored drills should be oiled to prevent rusting.

Testing Gear Compound for Grit

Whether or not gear grease contains grit can be determined by placing a small amount of the grease between two clean pieces of glass. These are rubbed together until a thin film of grease remains and then held up to the light. Any foreign particles will be apparent.

WORK BENCHES
you can build

By W. CLYDE LAMMEY

FOR the average craftsman, who wants a general utility bench that is solid and has plenty of drawer space for tools, a cabinet type of bench, made of maple, as illustrated in Figs. 1 to 3 incl., will fill the bill. The ends are first made up, and are joined to the rails with ⅜-in. machine bolts. The rails are fitted with dowel guides, no glue is used and the nuts on the machine bolts are mortised into the rails. Holes for the nuts are centered at least 4 in. from the ends. The drawer runners are screwed to the end upright. For guides, 2½-in. strips of ½-in. stock are nailed to the runners. Front and back rails are absent as the

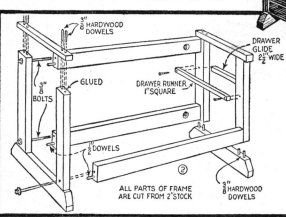

drawer fronts overlap the space ordinarily taken up by the rail. The corner construction of the drawers is shown in the detail of Fig. 3 and also in Fig. 5. The top is built up from several separate pieces doweled and glued together, and then planed and sanded smooth on both

Arms on Sawhorse Top Support Wide Work

Often needing a bench-like surface to support wide work on jobs away from his shop, one carpenter pivoted a couple of arms to the top of one of his sawhorses. When needed, these could be swung around to support the work, and when not in use were moved around parallel to the top of the sawhorse where they were held by nails dropped through holes in the ends. When the arms were swung to this position, the sawhorse was ready for use in the regular way.

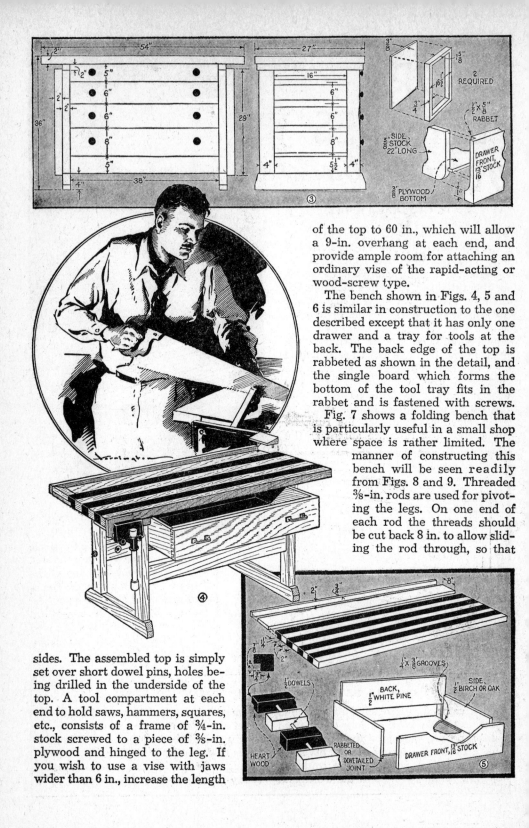

of the top to 60 in., which will allow a 9-in. overhang at each end, and provide ample room for attaching an ordinary vise of the rapid-acting or wood-screw type.

The bench shown in Figs. 4, 5 and 6 is similar in construction to the one described except that it has only one drawer and a tray for tools at the back. The back edge of the top is rabbeted as shown in the detail, and the single board which forms the bottom of the tool tray fits in the rabbet and is fastened with screws.

Fig. 7 shows a folding bench that is particularly useful in a small shop where space is rather limited. The manner of constructing this bench will be seen readily from Figs. 8 and 9. Threaded ⅜-in. rods are used for pivoting the legs. On one end of each rod the threads should be cut back 8 in. to allow sliding the rod through, so that

sides. The assembled top is simply set over short dowel pins, holes being drilled in the underside of the top. A tool compartment at each end to hold saws, hammers, squares, etc., consists of a frame of ¾-in. stock screwed to a piece of ⅜-in. plywood and hinged to the leg. If you wish to use a vise with jaws wider than 6 in., increase the length

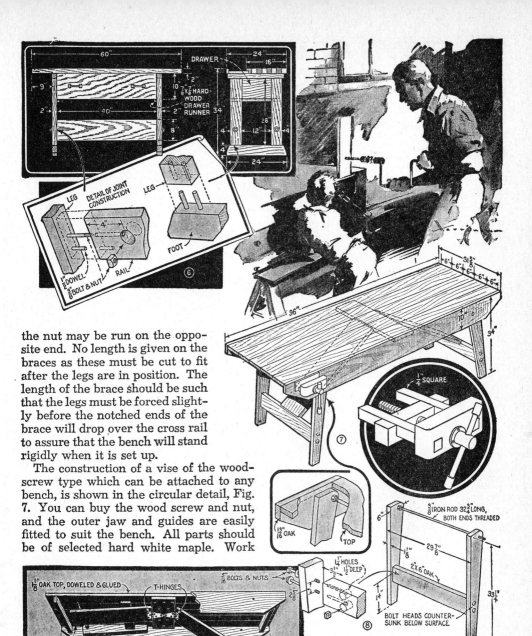

the nut may be run on the opposite end. No length is given on the braces as these must be cut to fit after the legs are in position. The length of the brace should be such that the legs must be forced slightly before the notched ends of the brace will drop over the cross rail to assure that the bench will stand rigidly when it is set up.

The construction of a vise of the woodscrew type which can be attached to any bench, is shown in the circular detail, Fig. 7. You can buy the wood screw and nut, and the outer jaw and guides are easily fitted to suit the bench. All parts should be of selected hard white maple. Work benches should always be shellacked to preserve the wood and to prevent absorption of moisture. This will help to keep them in good condition. And, after making a work bench of which you may be proud, a little care in using it will prevent much unnecessary damage from sharp-edged tools.

THE TRICKS OF USING
COLD CHISELS

By C. A. Crowley

CUTTING bar stock, shearing heavy metal, roughing down large pieces of metal, cutting oil grooves and keyways, and many other operations can be done quickly and accurately with cold chisels, if a few simple rules are observed in using them. Cold chisels are bars of steel, tempered and sharpened at one end, and of such size that they can be driven with a hammer for removing or cutting metal. The flat chisel, double and

CAPE CHISEL

FLAT CHISEL

FACETS
FLAT CHISEL 65°-70°
DOUBLE-FACET CAPE 65°-70°
SINGLE-FACET CAPE
FACET 65°-70°
ROUND-NOSE CHISEL
FACET 65°-70°
DIAMOND-POINT CHISEL

To remove a large section of metal, first chip a number of grooves with a cape chisel, then remove metal between grooves with a flat chisel

CHISEL IS HELD FLUSH WITH TOP OF VISE JAWS

SINGLE-FACET CHISEL

DOUBLE-FACET CHISEL
CHIP

CHISEL HELD AT ANGLE
TOP VIEW

Heavy sheet metal is sheared by clamping it in a vise so line to be cut is flush with the jaws, and using a flat chisel held at an angle to the work

single-facet cape chisels, round-nose and diamond-point chisels illustrated in Fig. 2 are the five main types. While there are variations of each of these designed for special purposes, these five styles usually are sufficient for most jobs.

Whether it is divided between one or two facets, the cutting angle should be kept about 65° or 70° for average work, as

shown in Fig. 2. The edge of the flat chisel should not be more than ¾ in. wide because on iron and steel this will take all the driving power that can be applied with the usual shop hammer. When a heavy chip is to be removed, such as in cutting a keyway, a cape chisel is used. Round-nose chisels can be used for cutting oil grooves, filleting corners, etc. The diamond-point chisel is useful in trimming out sharp corners. To chip, or remove surplus metal from a broad, flat piece, chip grooves in the work with a cape chisel and remove the material between the grooves with a flat chisel, as shown in Fig. 1. The grooves should be spaced slightly closer together than the width of the flat chisel. The work is placed in the vise at about elbow height, and in such a manner that the blows are struck at right angles to the jaws to prevent the work from slipping. The chisel is

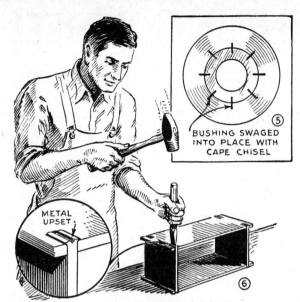

⑤ BUSHING SWAGED INTO PLACE WITH CAPE CHISEL

METAL UPSET

⑥

fastening together small assembled parts where the pieces fit closely and need only a little upsetting of the metal to keep them from slipping apart. With a little care, hand knurling on small cylindrical pieces can be done. Place the work in a V-block and use a sharp flat chisel, making grooves around the work parallel to its length.

In order to do good work, chisels must be kept sharp. Some of the newer chisels on the market are made of alloys which are tough enough to stand hard use but still are soft enough to be filed sharp. Better results are obtained, however, by grinding chisels to sharpen them.

held firmly enough to guide it, but still loosely enough to prevent the shock of the hammer blow from imparting a sting to the hand through the chisel. As illustrated in Fig. 3, chisels should be held so that the lower facet or surface lies flat on the work. Too steep an angle will tear and gouge the metal. It helps to keep the eyes focused on the cut rather than the head of the chisel. When working with metals other than cast iron, chisels should be lubricated every few blows. Any good grade of cutting oil will be found satisfactory.

Heavy sheet metal can be trimmed or sheared to shape quickly as shown in Fig. 4. The line along which the cut is to be made is placed flush with the jaws of the vise. A flat chisel is used, the edge being held at an angle to the work to produce a shearing action. Holes in sheet metal can also be cut with cold chisels. The metal stock is placed on a flat surface and a narrow chisel is applied so that the cut conforms closely to the guide line. When trimming off large projections, such as bolt or rivet heads, a cape chisel is used. Always make the first cut down from the center, and then chip off the rest. This method will remove them easily and avoid damaging the surface of the work.

In cutting oil grooves or keyways, chip both ways toward the center of the desired keyway or groove to prevent the ends from breaking out. Swaging, as illustrated in Figs. 5 and 6, is best done with a flat or cape chisel. This procedure is useful for

Nail Started in High Work By Using Hammer Claws

When nailing braces across the uprights of a high scaffold, one carpenter found that he could not reach high enough to hold a nail so that it could be struck, as no ladder was available. To avoid having to go after one, the nail was placed point out between the claws of a hammer, as shown, and started in the wood. Then the hammer was disengaged and the nail was driven in.

Wedge Fastens Handle to Head

WOOD SCREW

SCREW HAMMERED FLAT

A serviceable wedge to hold a hammer or hatchet head on its handle can be made from an ordinary wood screw. Before being driven into the handle, the screw is flattened so that it has a triangular shape. The teeth which are formed by the flattened threads serve to hold the wedge in place.

GRINDING WHEEL

By Sam Brown

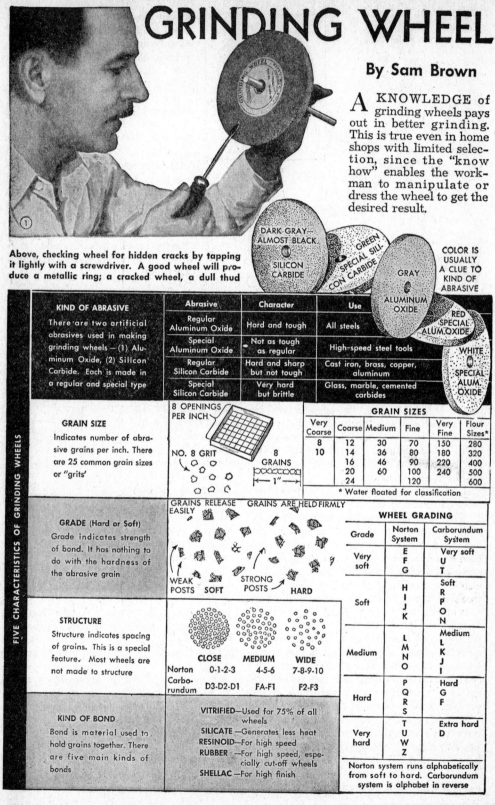

A KNOWLEDGE of grinding wheels pays out in better grinding. This is true even in home shops with limited selection, since the "know how" enables the workman to manipulate or dress the wheel to get the desired result.

Above, checking wheel for hidden cracks by tapping it lightly with a screwdriver. A good wheel will produce a metallic ring; a cracked wheel, a dull thud

DARK GRAY—ALMOST BLACK SILICON CARBIDE

GREEN SPECIAL SILICON CARBIDE

GRAY ALUMINUM OXIDE

COLOR IS USUALLY A CLUE TO KIND OF ABRASIVE

RED SPECIAL ALUM. OXIDE

WHITE SPECIAL ALUM. OXIDE

FIVE CHARACTERISTICS OF GRINDING WHEELS

KIND OF ABRASIVE

There are two artificial abrasives used in making grinding wheels — (1) Aluminum Oxide, (2) Silicon Carbide. Each is made in a regular and special type

Abrasive	Character	Use
Regular Aluminum Oxide	Hard and tough	All steels
Special Aluminum Oxide	Not as tough as regular	High-speed steel tools
Regular Silicon Carbide	Hard and sharp but not tough	Cast iron, brass, copper, aluminum
Special Silicon Carbide	Very hard but brittle	Glass, marble, cemented carbides

GRAIN SIZE

Indicates number of abrasive grains per inch. There are 25 common grain sizes or "grits"

8 OPENINGS PER INCH
NO. 8 GRIT
8 GRAINS
1"

GRAIN SIZES					
Very Coarse	Coarse	Medium	Fine	Very Fine	Flour Sizes*
8	12	30	70	150	280
10	14	36	80	180	320
	16	46	90	220	400
	20	60	100	240	500
	24		120		600

* Water floated for classification

GRADE (Hard or Soft)

Grade indicates strength of bond. It has nothing to do with the hardness of the abrasive grain

GRAINS RELEASE EASILY
GRAINS ARE HELD FIRMLY
WEAK POSTS **SOFT**
STRONG POSTS **HARD**

WHEEL GRADING		
Grade	Norton System	Carborundum System
Very soft	E F G	Very soft U T
Soft	H I J K	Soft R P O N
Medium	L M N O	Medium L K J I
Hard	P Q R S	Hard G F
Very hard	T U W Z	Extra hard D

STRUCTURE

Structure indicates spacing of grains. This is a special feature. Most wheels are not made to structure

	CLOSE	MEDIUM	WIDE
Norton	0-1-2-3	4-5-6	7-8-9-10
Carborundum	D3-D2-D1	FA-F1	F2-F3

KIND OF BOND

Bond is material used to hold grains together. There are five main kinds of bonds

VITRIFIED—Used for 75% of all wheels
SILICATE—Generates less heat
RESINOID—For high speed
RUBBER—For high speed, especially cut-off wheels
SHELLAC—For high finish

Norton system runs alphabetically from soft to hard. Carborundum system is alphabet in reverse

460

SELECTION and CARE

Anatomy: What you might call the "bare bones" of grinding wheels is pictured in the tabular diagram shown below Fig. 1. The two types of abrasive grains—aluminum oxide and silicon carbide—are sold under various trade names, such as Aloxite, Alundum and Borolon for aluminum oxide, and Carborundum, Crystolon and Carsilon for silicon carbide. Color is a good means of identification, silicon carbide wheels being almost black, while aluminum oxide wheels run from light to medium gray. A white wheel indicates aluminum oxide with a special porous bond and with the grain itself treated so that it is not as tough as regular. Red wheels are aluminum oxide with regular vitrified bond and the same treated grain used in the white wheel. A green wheel is a very hard type of silicon carbide. The nature of other physical characteristics—grain size, grade, structure and bond—should be plain enough from the diagram. Fig. 3 shows a few shapes in which wheels are made.

Selecting the abrasive: When the material to be ground is hard and tough, the right abrasive to use, Fig. 2, is hard, tough aluminum oxide. If the work is extremely hard, such as glass or cemented carbides, it must be ground with silicon carbide. In addition to being very hard, silicon carbide grains have sharp corners, which make the wheel ideal for grinding soft metals and nonmetallic materials. As long as the material being ground is not tough, silicon carbide does excellent work. When you get up to metals with a tensile strength of 50,000 lbs. per square inch or more, the silicon carbide wheel begins to wear away fast without doing much cutting because the brittle grains break down against the tougher material. Hence, the general rule that all high tensile strength materials (this includes all of the steels) can be ground best with aluminum oxide. On the other hand, aluminum oxide is not so good for low tensile strength materials such as brass, plastic, wood, etc. These materials are not tough enough to fracture the tough grain and each grain simply wears to a dull, noncutting edge with resultant loading, glazing and burning.

The special types of aluminum oxide feature a grain somewhat less tough than regular. These wheels are excellent for grinding carbon and high-speed steel tools because the ready fracturing of the grain keeps the wheel continually sharp, fast-cutting and cool. The obvious drawback is rapid

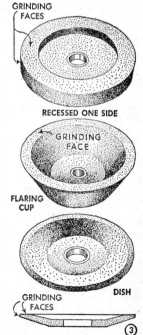

STRAIGHT WHEEL

RECESSED ONE SIDE

FLARING CUP

DISH

461

Learn These Simple Rules ...

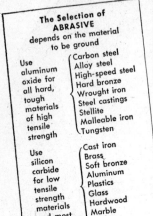

The Selection of ABRASIVE
depends on the material to be ground

Use aluminum oxide for all hard, tough materials of high tensile strength
- Carbon steel
- Alloy steel
- High-speed steel
- Hard bronze
- Wrought iron
- Steel castings
- Stellite
- Malleable iron
- Tungsten

Use silicon carbide for low tensile strength materials and most non-metallics
- Cast iron
- Brass
- Soft bronze
- Aluminum
- Plastics
- Glass
- Hardwood
- Marble
- Rubber

The Selection of GRAIN SIZE*

Soft materials require coarse grain; hard materials require fine grain

Rapid removal of stock requires coarse grain

A fine finish requires fine grain

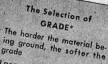

The Selection of GRADE*

The harder the material being ground, the softer the grade

Large area of contact requires a soft wheel. (See drawing)

High wheel speed and low work speed require a soft wheel

* Both grit and grade can be controlled to a considerable extent by proper dressing of wheel and work manipulation

REQUIRES MEDIUM WHEEL — SMALL AREA OF CONTACT

④

LARGE AREA CONTACT — REQUIRES VERY SOFT WHEEL

REQUIRES SOFT WHEEL — WORK — MEDIUM CONTACT AREA

wheel wear. Special (green) silicon carbide is the only abrasive other than the diamond hard enough to cut cemented carbides.

Selection of grit and grade: Follow the simple rules given in the table below Fig. 1. The key to selecting grade is: The harder the material, the softer the grade. Hard, dense materials resist the penetration of the abrasive grains and cause them to break down quickly. When the bond is weak (soft grade), it releases the dulled grains quickly, exposing new, sharp grains. The second rule—contact area—can be explained by the fact that a wide contact area, Fig. 4, spreads the stress over a considerable number of grains. The bond, therefore, must be weak (soft) so that the lessened force against each grain can break it loose when it becomes dull. When the contact area is small, as in cylindrical grinding, all of the stress comes on a very few grains. In this case, a hard grade (strong bond posts) is needed to hold the grains so that they will not be torn away before doing their share of cutting.

Wheel recommendations: Specific recommendations can be used to advantage whenever the wheel specified is available. The table below Fig. 4 gives a condensed version of tabular matter supplied by all manufacturers of grinding wheels. Obviously, very complete hairsplitting tables are useless to the

Material or Operation	Abrasive	Grit Rough	Grit Finish	Grade
Aluminum	S. C. ①	30 ②	40	Soft
Brass	S. C.	36	60	Soft to Med.
Cast Iron	S. C.	30	46	Soft to Med.
Chisels (wood)	A. O.	—	60	Medium
Copper	S. C.	36	60	Soft to Med.
Cork	S. C. ①	36·	46	Soft
Duralumin	A. O. ①	30	46	Soft
Drills (H.S.S.)	A.O.(wht.)	—	60	Medium
Glass	S.C.(green)	80	220	Medium
Grinding (general)	A. O.	46	60	Medium
Mal. Iron (annealed)	A. O.	30	46	Hard
Mal. Iron (not annealed)	S. C.	30	46·	Hard
Plastic	S. C.	46	120	Medium
Rubber (soft)	S. C.	24	46	Soft
③ Rubber (hard)	S. C.	36	46	Soft
Saws (gumming)	A. O.	—	60	Medium
Steel (soft)	A. O.	46	60	Medium
Steel (carbon)	A. O.①	46	60	Medium
Steel (hi-speed)	A. O.①	46	60	Soft
Welds (smoothing)	A. O.	24	46	Med. to Hard
Wood (hard)	S. C.	24 ②	30	Soft
Wrought Iron	A. O.	30	46	Med. to Hard

GENERAL RECOMMENDATIONS*

1 White or red aluminum oxide also used

2 Tends to load if fine grit is used

3 Resinoid bond preferable

* All wheels vitrified bond. Structure is not considered

METAL CHIPS EMBEDDED IN WHEEL **LOADED WHEEL**

⑤

GRAINS WORN DOWN LEVEL WITH BOND **GLAZED WHEEL**

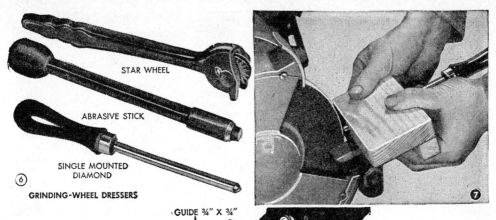

STAR WHEEL

ABRASIVE STICK

SINGLE MOUNTED DIAMOND

6 **GRINDING-WHEEL DRESSERS**

7

GUIDE ¾" X ¾"

¼" X 1½" STOVE BOLT AND WING NUT

NUT

8 HOLDING FIXTURE FOR DIAMOND DRESSER

¾" X 3" X 4" BLOCK

Dressing removes the outer dulled layer of abrasive grains and exposes new sharp grains. Truing is precision dressing so that the wheel runs perfectly true. Proper manipulation of the dressing tool can alter the wheel's cutting action within reasonable limits

9 5-15° DRAG ANGLE

ON OR BELOW CENTER

CORRECT POSITION OF DIAMOND TOOL

CHUCK IS STATIONARY

SET SCREW

CUT IS ALWAYS VERY LIGHT, NOT OVER .001 INCH

RAPID TRAVERSE FOR FREE-CUTTING WHEEL. SLOW TRAVERSE FOR SMOOTH FINISH

WHEEL IN TOOL POST GRINDER **11** ROUND BAR HOLDS DRESSER

10

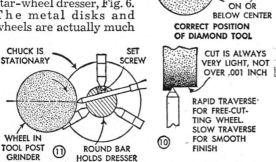

12

average worker because he does not have the wheels. The best system of selection is to know why a certain wheel should be used, and then manipulate such wheels as are available to get the desired result.

Dressing and truing: When a wheel becomes loaded or glazed, Fig. 5, it is necessary to press some hard object against it while rotating to restore the cutting edges. Simplest device for this is the star-wheel dresser, Fig. 6. The metal disks and wheels are actually much softer than the grinding wheel, but by using firm pressure the faulty abrasive grains can be torn loose. This dresser is worked freehand, but always supported on the tool rest. It should not spark. Sparking is an indication that the grinding wheel is cutting the dresser and therefore, the dressing tool should be pressed harder against the wheel. The stick-type dresser is inexpensive and efficient. It is a very coarse, silicon carbide abrasive, which readily cuts the finer grain of the grinding wheel. Best of all is the diamond, especially for precision dressing (truing). It should be used only for precision work. If dressing requires removal of embedded metal chips or heavy shaping, the star-wheel or stick dresser should be used first, and can then be followed by the diamond. Use a simple jig like the one shown in Fig. 8 to hold the diamond dresser. Always contact the wheel on or below center and always at a drag angle, as in Figs. 7 and 9. Fig. 11 indicates how the dresser can be held when dressing the wheel of a tool-post grinder. Fig. 12 pictures the dressing of a recessed wheel mounted and used on the lathe.

An important feature of dia-

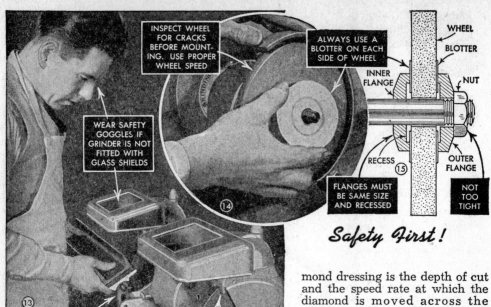

INSPECT WHEEL FOR CRACKS BEFORE MOUNT-ING. USE PROPER WHEEL SPEED

ALWAYS USE A BLOTTER ON EACH SIDE OF WHEEL

WHEEL

BLOTTER

INNER FLANGE

NUT

WEAR SAFETY GOGGLES IF GRINDER IS NOT FITTED WITH GLASS SHIELDS

RECESS

OUTER FLANGE

15

FLANGES MUST BE SAME SIZE AND RECESSED

NOT TOO TIGHT

14

Safety First!

SUPPORT WORK ON TOOL REST WHEN POSSIBLE. KEEP REST CLOSE TO GRINDING WHEEL

KEEP CHIP CATCHER CLOSE TO WHEEL

13

Trouble Shooting

FAULT	CAUSE	CORRECTION
WHEEL LOADING (Metal chips embedded in wheel)	Wrong wheel	Use coarser grain or open structure wheel
	Faulty dressing	Dress with rapid traverse
	Faulty operation	Use slower wheel speed and faster work speed or traverse
WHEEL GLAZING (Slick, shiny appearance —does not cut)	Wrong wheel	Use coarser grit, softer grade
	Faulty dressing	Use faster traverse with deeper penetration
	Faulty operation	Use more pressure. Increase work speed
WHEEL DOES NOT CUT (Glazes and burns)	Wheel is too hard	Use coarser grit and softer grade
		Open up wheel by fast dressing
		Decrease wheel speed, wheel diameter and width
		Increase work speed and pressure
RAPID WHEEL WEAR	Wheel is too soft	Use harder wheel
		Dress with slow traverse and very little penetration
		Increase wheel speed, wheel diameter and width
		Decrease work speed and pressure
ROUGH WORK	Wrong wheel	Check abrasive, grit and grade
	Wheel out of round	Dress wheel
	Machine fault	Check bearings and wheel mounting

mond dressing is the depth of cut and the speed rate at which the diamond is moved across the wheel. In all cases the cut must be very light, not over .001 in., as shown in Fig. 10. A fast traverse opens up the wheel, making it, in effect, a coarser grain and a softer grade than it actually is. A slow traverse makes the wheel, in effect, finer grain and harder grade. For open dressing you use a maximum depth of cut, and the diamond is pushed just once, and quickly, across the wheel. When dressing the wheel for fine finishing, the depth of cut is held to a minimum, and the traverse is made slowly and repeatedly until the cut sparks out. By applying these rules, a wheel can be made coarser or finer, harder or softer.

Wheel safety: A lot has been said about wheel safety, and, while we pass over this quickly, simply by referring you to Figs. 13, 14 and 15, it is of prime importance and should not be neglected. Always check a new wheel for cracks by striking it with a screwdriver as in Fig. 1.

Trouble-shooting: Some of the common faults encountered in grinding are listed in the table shown below Fig. 13. Observe how the work and wheel can be manipulated for hard or soft effect. This can be used to advantage in making one or two wheels do a wide variety of work.

Letter Press of Pipe Fittings for the Home Shop

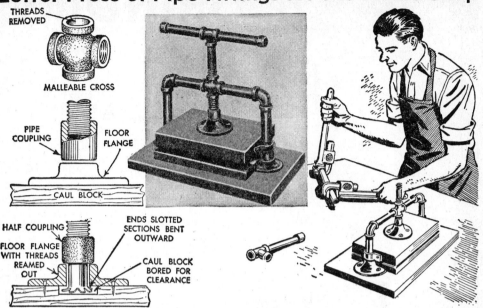

THREADS REMOVED

MALLEABLE CROSS

PIPE COUPLING — FLOOR FLANGE

CAUL BLOCK

HALF COUPLING

FLOOR FLANGE WITH THREADS REAMED OUT

ENDS SLOTTED SECTIONS BENT OUTWARD

CAUL BLOCK BORED FOR CLEARANCE

There's nothing quite so handy in the home workshop as a letter press when it comes to veneer work and other small gluing jobs. Commercial presses are expensive, but you can have this sturdy press in your shop just for the cost of a few pipe fittings. The fittings needed are three floor flanges; two elbows; six nipples, or seven if you use the method of mounting the spindle on the caul block shown in the lower left-hand detail; two pipe caps; two tees, or one tee and a cross; and a length of threaded pipe for a spindle. To make the press, fashion the base, caul block and base block of thick hardwood. Screw the flanges and base block to the base and assemble the frame. If a cross is used to take the spindle, the threads must be removed from the top opening. These may be bored out on a lathe, or you can take the cross to a local plumbing shop and have the threads reamed out. If a tee is used instead of a cross, drill a hole through the top of the tee to permit insertion of the spindle. The caul block is guided between the vertical nipples of the frame by means of pipe straps fastened to the ends of the block. A pipe coupling is turned on the lower end of the spindle to press down on a floor flange fastened to the top of the caul block. If this method is used, the caul block will have to be raised by hand. However, if you wish the spindle to raise the caul block, have the threads of the flange reamed out and turn a nipple into the bottom of the spindle coupling. The lower end of the nipple is slotted and the sections bent outward to hold it to the flange. The caul block must be recessed to clear the pipe-nipple sections. The handle is made from two nipples, two pipe caps and a tee.

Scalloped Boards Made Easily by Drilling Holes and Sawing Apart

Here is an easy way to make identical, evenly spaced scallops in boards for decorative molding and window valances. First, a line is scribed lengthwise along the center of a board. Equidistant points are marked along this line, and then a series of holes is drilled through the board at the points marked. The size of the holes determines the width of the scallops. After the holes are drilled, the board is sawed in half along the scribed line. This will result in two identically scalloped boards.

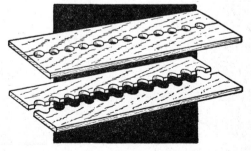

TOOL GRINDING

By W. C. Lammey

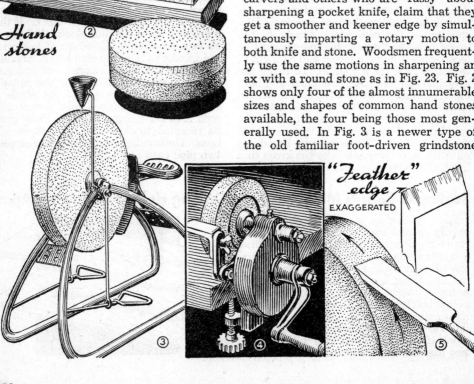

FREEHAND grinding of small tools, holding them against, or moving them over a stone with the fingers without the aid of a clamp, can be done by anyone after a little practice. In this work, you depend largely on the sensitivity of your fingertips. Of course, what you can see is important, but it's really the sense of touch that counts. By it you control pressure on the grinding surface, degree of bevel, straightness of the edge and, on certain tools, the amount of metal removed. Much depends on how the tool is held.

To produce a smooth razor-sharp edge, three or more operations must be delicately coordinated. Sharpening a pocket knife, Fig. 1, is an example. If you hold the knife lightly in one hand and the stone in the other as shown, you can even close your eyes and still know just how much pressure is being applied, whether the blade is riding flat on the grinding surface or at the proper angle, and whether the stroke is taking in the full length of the edge. Some carvers and others who are "fussy" about sharpening a pocket knife, claim that they get a smoother and keener edge by simultaneously imparting a rotary motion to both knife and stone. Woodsmen frequently use the same motions in sharpening an ax with a round stone as in Fig. 23. Fig. 2 shows only four of the almost innumerable sizes and shapes of common hand stones available, the four being those most generally used. In Fig. 3 is a newer type of the old familiar foot-driven grindstone

Hand stones

"*Feather*" *edge*
EXAGGERATED

—FREEHAND

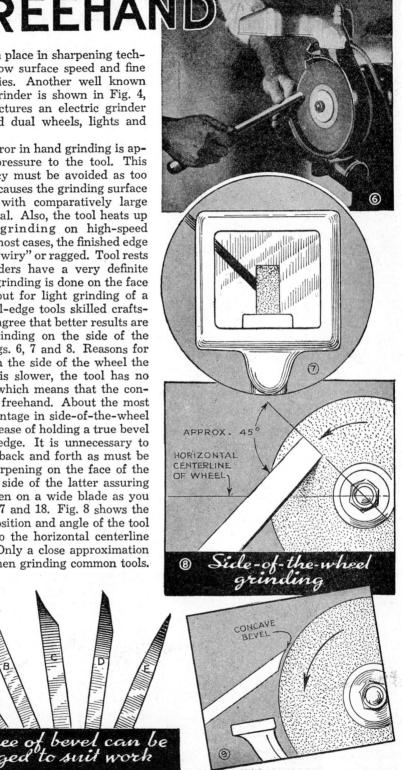

which still has a place in sharpening technique due to slow surface speed and fine cutting properties. Another well known type of hand grinder is shown in Fig. 4, while Fig. 6 pictures an electric grinder with high-speed dual wheels, lights and eye shields.

A common error in hand grinding is applying undue pressure to the tool. This natural tendency must be avoided as too much pressure causes the grinding surface to be clogged with comparatively large particles of metal. Also, the tool heats up rapidly when grinding on high-speed wheels and, in most cases, the finished edge will be unduly "wiry" or ragged. Tool rests on power grinders have a very definite purpose when grinding is done on the face of the wheel, but for light grinding of a variety of small-edge tools skilled craftsmen generally agree that better results are obtained by grinding on the side of the wheel as in Figs. 6, 7 and 8. Reasons for this are that on the side of the wheel the cutting action is slower, the tool has no rigid support, which means that the control is entirely freehand. About the most important advantage in side-of-the-wheel grinding is the ease of holding a true bevel and a square edge. It is unnecessary to move the tool back and forth as must be done when sharpening on the face of the wheel, the flat side of the latter assuring a true edge even on a wide blade as you see from Figs. 7 and 18. Fig. 8 shows the approximate position and angle of the tool with relation to the horizontal centerline of the wheel. Only a close approximation is necessary when grinding common tools.

APPROX. 45°

HORIZONTAL CENTERLINE OF WHEEL

⑧ Side-of-the-wheel grinding

CONCAVE BEVEL

⑩ Degree of bevel can be changed to suit work

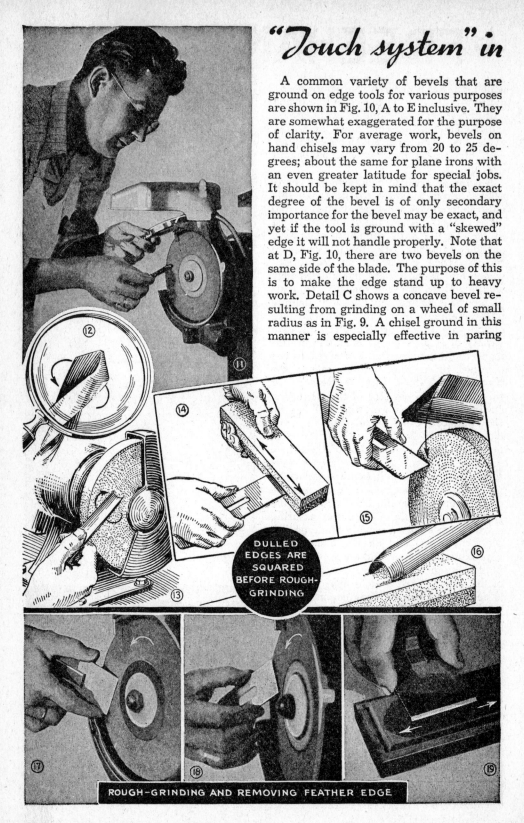

A common variety of bevels that are ground on edge tools for various purposes are shown in Fig. 10, A to E inclusive. They are somewhat exaggerated for the purpose of clarity. For average work, bevels on hand chisels may vary from 20 to 25 degrees; about the same for plane irons with an even greater latitude for special jobs. It should be kept in mind that the exact degree of the bevel is of only secondary importance for the bevel may be exact, and yet if the tool is ground with a "skewed" edge it will not handle properly. Note that at D, Fig. 10, there are two bevels on the same side of the blade. The purpose of this is to make the edge stand up to heavy work. Detail C shows a concave bevel resulting from grinding on a wheel of small radius as in Fig. 9. A chisel ground in this manner is especially effective in paring

DULLED EDGES ARE SQUARED BEFORE ROUGH-GRINDING

ROUGH-GRINDING AND REMOVING FEATHER EDGE

hand grinding

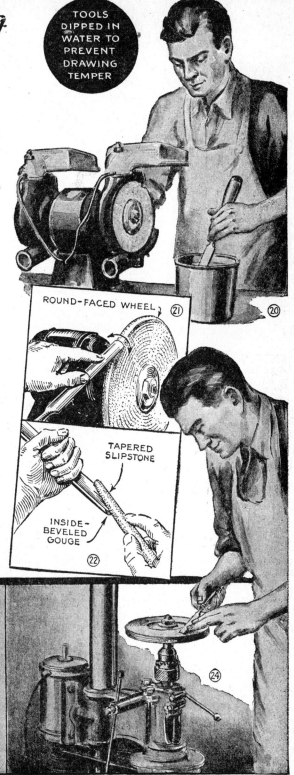

cuts but the edge will not stand prying. "Feathering" of the edge results when you grind with the wheel running away from the tool as in Fig. 5. Sometimes this is necessary, especially on grindstones, but care should be taken to avoid feathering as much as possible.

Now for a grinding job that's tricky but entirely practical. Only a few craftsmen and small shops have available a precision grinder attachment for sharpening twist drills. So the job must be done freehand. Take the drill bit between the thumb and index finger, allowing the middle finger and third finger to rest lightly on the body of the drill. Then bring one cutting lip up to the side of the wheel. Now, right here is the first critical point in the whole business. The correct angle depends on touching the lip to the wheel in just the right position. To do this stand so that your sighting eye is directly over the work as in Fig. 11. A reading glass will help by magnifying the point of the drill. As soon as the lip touches the wheel with no light showing, turn the body of the drill slowly to the right, Fig. 12, simultaneously drop your elbow slightly and at the same time pivot your hand to the right at the wrist. That's all. And after you have duplicated these movements in grinding the

ROUND-FACED WHEEL

TAPERED SLIPSTONE

INSIDE-BEVELED GOUGE

grinding on the side of the wheel. When grinding any tool on a wheel don't forget to dip the edge in water frequently to prevent heating, Fig. 20.

If a floor or bench grinder is not available, Fig. 24 shows how you can rig a drill press for the work. While the picture shows a pedestal-type drill press with the head inverted, the job can be done in almost any drill press simply by gripping the grinding-stone mandrel in the chuck. There will be sufficient clearance on most drill presses so that you can hold practically all hand tools on the rotating stone. A grinding wheel, a flanged adapter to fit ½-in. shafting and a 2-in.

HONED CUTTING EDGES STAY SHARP LONGER

second lip, check with a drill gauge. You'll probably be surprised at the accuracy of the job. If it's a little inaccurate, just a slight touch to the wheel will correct it. Although one can hardly expect to equal the work of the precision jig, a drill bit ground in this fashion will serve very well where the job does not require reamerlike accuracy.

Grinding a gouge, Fig. 13, is done in much the same way as grinding a drill. First, true up the edge as in Fig. 16. Gouges with an inside bevel should be ground on either a round-faced wheel as in Fig. 21 or a tapered slipstone as in Fig. 22. A plane iron requires several steps as in Figs. 14 and 15 and 17 to 19 inclusive, first squaring the edge as in Fig. 14 and then beveling the corners as in Fig. 15. Unless the iron is badly nicked, omit the step shown in Fig. 17, where the nick is removed somewhat more quickly by feathering the edge then removing the feather by grinding against the wheel as in Fig. 18. Fig. 19 is the finish step to remove the wire edge. Some users prefer a slightly rounded cutting edge on a jack plane for rough work. This is formed easily by rocking the blade slightly while

finishes the job

length of the latter are all you need. Finally, most tools used for the finer work should be finished by honing or stropping, either of which can be done in a number of ways. As an example, craftsmen in wood and pattern shops sometimes strop hand tools on a moving leather belt as in Fig. 27, a handy and quick method that does the job nicely. A length of leather belting glued to a wood block, Fig. 25, with the hair side up and coated with polishing rouge rubbed in with the palm as in Fig. 28 does very well. A length of leather belting 2 in. wide, or an old razor strop, Fig. 30, is just the thing for stropping a pocket knife or any similarly bladed tool. Some even strop edge tools on the palm of the hand but most craftsmen who are particular about keen edges on chisels, plane irons and turning tools make a leather-faced honing wheel as in Figs. 31 and 32. To make a honing wheel, first turn a hardwood disk to the desired size, drilling it centrally to slip over the spindle of your grinder or buffing head. Then cover the

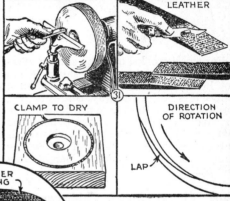

TURN A WOOD DISK

SKIVE ENDS OF LEATHER

CLAMP TO DRY

DIRECTION OF ROTATION

LAP

LEATHER FACING

GLUE

outer edge with a strip of leather, which is skived as indicated in Fig. 31, and glued in place, using a specially made wood clamp to hold it until the glue dries. Next, cut a leather facing, coat one side of the wood disk with glue and clamp the facing to it. Be sure the wheel is balanced carefully to avoid vibration. Such a wheel is most efficient for honing to a smooth edge after grinding and for touching up the edge between grindings. As shown in Fig. 26, the tool should be held with the heel of the bevel raised slightly so that only the extreme edge contacts the leather. In using the wheel, first coat it with polishing rouge as in Fig. 29. Fig. 33 shows how to hold the tools, and the direction of rotation.

LEATHER-FACED HONING WHEEL GIVES KEEN EDGE

Sawhorse Fits Under Workbench to Conserve Shop Space

For small workshops, the sliding sawhorse illustrated is a space saver. When not in use it fits under the workbench where it is out of the way. Slides for the top member of the horse are fastened to the inside of the legs of the bench. The distance between the two sawhorses is determined by the length of the workbench, and any convenient height may be used.

Tape "Clamp" Mends Chinaware

Instead of cementing one piece at a time when repairing broken china, the whole mending job can be done at once if cellulose tape is used to hold each piece in place while the cement dries. It is best to fit all the pieces together first, using the tape only. In this way the job can be done more quickly and, since all the cementing is done at one time, the risk of having a last piece that does not fit is avoided.

Washer an Aid in Adjusting Drill

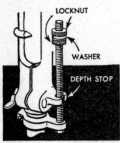

The depth stops on some drill presses are made adjustable by means of a locknut arrangement similar to the one which is shown here. If a flat washer is placed between the two nuts, it will facilitate changing the adjustment as the "lock" will break more easily. Keep the washer covered with a light film of grease to aid in loosening the adjustment.

Grooved Jaws Hold Small Work

Bolts, small rods and other round work sometimes is hard to hold in a vise if the jaws are smooth. Or, if the vise is tightened enough to hold such work, the screws or rods may be flattened. To avoid this, one craftsman filed vertical and horizontal grooves in the jaws and found that he could hold small work easily.

Short Nipples Can Be Threaded in Vise with Pipe Clamp

When making plumbing repairs in your basement, you may find it difficult to clamp short pieces of pipe, an inch or so long, in a vise for threading. But by using a longer piece of pipe you can make and thread short nipples. Detail A shows how the pipe is threaded at both ends and cut off at one end for a nipple of the correct length. Then a coupling is screwed on the threaded end of the longer piece and the short length is fastened to it, as in detail B. The unthreaded end of the nipple can be finished now by using a die of the right size and the collar that is to be used is one size larger so it will slip over the coupling. For example, a ½-in. die will require a ¾-in. collar.

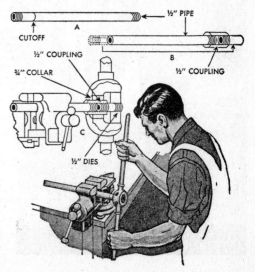

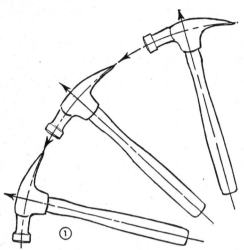

HINTS ON
Hammering
by W. Clyde Lammey

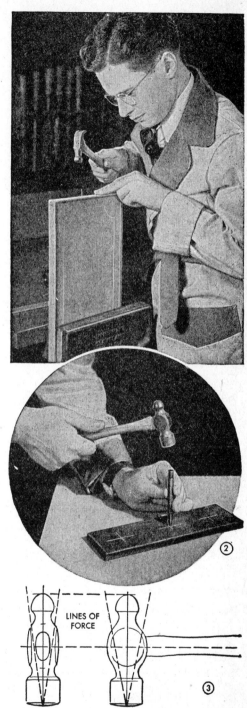

SKILLFUL handling of a hammer results from the trained coordination of eye and hand. Muscular action alone can build up and control the force of the blow, which will lack direction unless you can clearly see the object to be struck. Thus, any hammering operation compares quite closely with the technique of throwing a ball.

Fig. 5 details and names parts of the head of an ordinary "nail" hammer. This is important to know when you buy one. Examine the head of a top-quality hammer and you will see that the poll and face are ground to a true curve, the cheeks are sized equally, the eye is slightly tapered and the claws are finished and ground to identical shape. And along the handle of a well-balanced tool is a point where the hammer hangs and "feels" just right when you grasp the handle in your hand.

Fig. 2 shows the accepted manner of holding a hammer when doing any work requiring a degree of precision. The thumb extended along the handle as shown aids in control, gives a surer grip and is less tiring in most hammering operations. On nearly all hammers the handle is shaped to give the most comfortable grip when

LINES OF FORCE

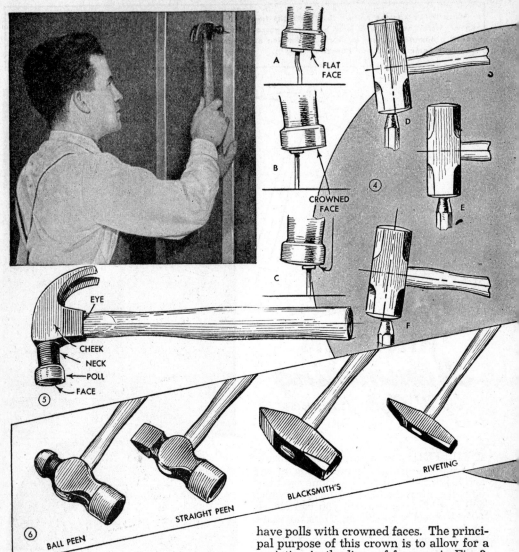

A — FLAT FACE

B

CROWNED FACE

C

D

E

F

④

EYE

CHEEK

NECK

POLL

FACE

⑤

⑥ BALL PEEN

STRAIGHT PEEN

BLACKSMITH'S

RIVETING

grasped approximately at the point indicated. The common types of hammers, hatchets and sledges used by craftsmen in a variety of work are shown in Fig. 6.

Fig. 1 shows in a simplified manner how the forces acting on the head of a hammer are similar to those acting on a weight swinging at one end of a length of cord. Head of the hammer may be compared to the weight while the handle supplants the cord. Rigidity of the hammer handle enables the operator to control and direct the force of the blow. In giving a hammer the proper swing, your arm pivots at the shoulder, elbow and wrist. It is difficult to make an effective stroke without movement of the arm at these three points.

With certain exceptions all hammers have polls with crowned faces. The principal purpose of this crown is to allow for a variation in the lines of force as in Fig. 3. Detail A of Fig. 4 shows what usually happens when you try to drive a nail with a hammer having a poll face either worn or ground flat, or where the surface of the face is otherwise irregular. Generally the nail will bend or the hammer head will glance off the head of the nail. Details B and C show, in somewhat exaggerated form, how a crowned face helps to prevent this. Due to the curve of the poll face the centerline or axis of the hammer can angle as much as 5 degrees or more with the centerline of the nail and still the blow will be fully effective. Likewise it will be seen from details D and F of Fig. 4 that the angle can vary about the same amount in another direction; that is, the angle of the handle can vary 5 degrees or more above or below the theoretical perpendicular, as

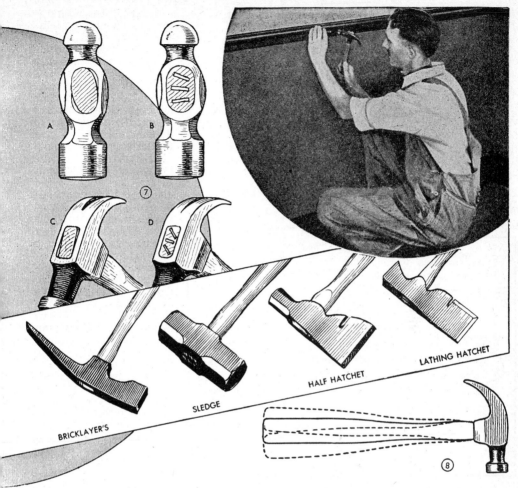

SLEDGE

BRICKLAYER'S

HALF HATCHET

LATHING HATCHET

shown in E in Fig. 4, and still the blow will be delivered with full force. Therefore, it's important that the poll face of any hammer used for these purposes be ground to a regular curve without pits or irregularities.

As indicated in Figs. 7 and 8 there's a trick in fitting a hammer handle. First, it's important to trim the handle to a close fit in the eye. In some hammers the eye is slightly tapered. The purpose of this is to prevent the handle from pulling out when wedged in place. The error of fit shown in details A and C in Fig. 7 should be avoided as it may result in the irregularity diagrammed in Fig. 8. When properly fitted the handle will wedge into the head as shown at B and D, Fig. 7, and will be true with the head both vertically and horizontally. If available, metal wedges should be used to tighten the handle in the head.

Airtight Seal of Paraffin Preserves Oil Paint in Partially Filled Cans

Ordinary methods of resealing partially used cans of oil paint usually fail to preserve the paint for long periods of time. However, one man found that covering the paint with an airtight seal of paraffin keeps it in perfect condition. To do this, melt the paraffin in a can which is placed in a saucepan filled with water. This is done because paraffin melted directly over the fire may burst into flame. After the paraffin has melted, pour a 1/8-in. layer over the paint. When this cools, pour a thinner second layer, tilting the can slightly all around so that the wax forms a tight seal against the sides of the can.

◖A few drops of gun oil will prevent garment slide fasteners from sticking.

Bench Stop with Clamping-Bar Members Has "Gripping" Action When Holding Work

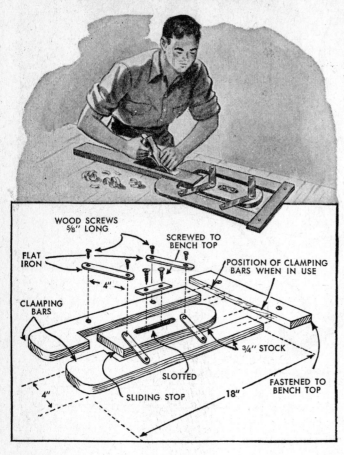

WOOD SCREWS 5/8" LONG

SCREWED TO BENCH TOP

FLAT IRON

POSITION OF CLAMPING BARS WHEN IN USE

4"

CLAMPING BARS

3/4" STOCK

SLOTTED

FASTENED TO BENCH TOP

4"

SLIDING STOP

18"

Made from two clamping bars, a sliding member or stop and a fixed piece, this bench stop adjusts itself automatically to various widths, and holds the work in a vise-like grip. Only a few general dimensions are given; the others can be determined by the size of the work to be handled. Remember that the length of the flat-iron pieces to which the clamping bars pivot, will determine the width of boards that the stop will take. After the bars and sliding member have been cut out of 3/4-in. hardwood stock, assemble them as shown in the detail, fastening the pivots to the bars and the stop with wood screws 5/8 in. long. Then fasten the fixed piece in place and determine the position of the sliding stop. When this is located, screw it in place using flat-headed wood screws and a length of flat iron drilled for the screws. Since the unit is fastened to the work bench by only four screws, it is removed easily if additional space is required.

Filing Home-Workshop Publications

TAPE

Colored cellulose tape attached to the backs of home-workshop magazines provides an excellent means of keeping them in order on the bookshelf. After arranging the issues in order as to month and year, fasten a strip of colored tape diagonally across their backs and then cut the tape between each magazine. When you wish to return a magazine to its proper position on the shelf, merely insert it between the other publications so that the diagonal line appears unbroken. Use different colors of tape and reverse the direction of the diagonals for other magazines.

Soldering-Iron Cleaner Is Handy When Kept in Floor Flange

Steel wool or cotton waste packed into a floor flange provides a handy cleaner for a soldering iron. In most cases the flange will be heavy enough to prevent skidding around. However, if more weight is required, the flange can be screwed to a wood block. If soldering is always done in the same place, the flange can be screwed to the bench top within easy reach of the working area.

WASTE BURLAP OR STEEL WOOL

FLOOR FLANGE

¶ To loosen a rusted screw, press a hot soldering iron against it briefly.

TO DRIVE A SCREW

Little tricks and proper procedure will make screws hold effectively

By
W. Clyde Lammey

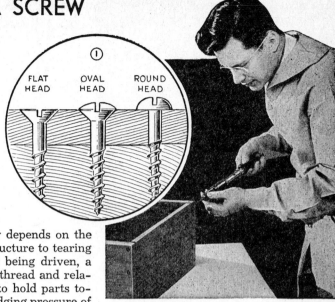

UNLIKE glue or bolts as a means of joining parts made of wood, the holding power of a screw depends on the resistance of the wood structure to tearing or pulling strains. When being driven, a wood screw taps its own thread and relatively little of its power to hold parts together depends on the wedging pressure of the wood fibers, as is true with a nail.

In joining any wooden pieces it is necessary first to consider the type, size, number and length of the screws to be used. Fig. 1 shows the three types in most common use, any one style being made in a variety of sizes and lengths. After selecting the desired length, you take into account whether the assembly requires that the threaded section of the screw is to be driven into end grain, edge grain or flat grain, Figs. 2 and 3. Edge and flat grain are about equal in respect to the holding power of screws in most common woods with the exception of knots or other defects at the point where the screw is to be driven. When screws are driven into end grain, the smaller diameter of the counterbore or body hole for the screw, is really a pilot hole and should be drilled only deep enough to start the threads, Fig. 2. In the common softer woods the threads will cut their way into end grain without the ne-

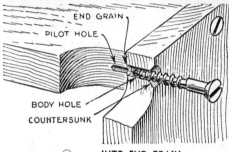

(2) . . . **INTO END GRAIN**

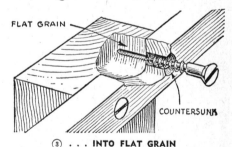

(3) . . . **INTO FLAT GRAIN**

Cement to Hold Tool Handles Securely

Cement to hold tools in their handles can be prepared by mixing rosin, 4 oz., beeswax, 1 oz., and fine brick dust, 1 oz. Grind the rosin and brick dust to as fine a powder as possible with a mortar and pestle. Then melt the mixture, stir it thoroughly and fill the hole in the handle. While the mixture is still molten, force the tool into the handle. To give added firmness, it is a good idea to roughen the tool shank with a file before forcing it in place. The melted cement may be poured into molds and be kept for use as required.

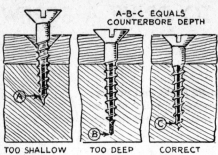

A-B-C EQUALS
COUNTERBORE DEPTH

TOO SHALLOW   TOO DEEP   CORRECT

④ USE THE RIGHT COUNTERBORE

Counterboring

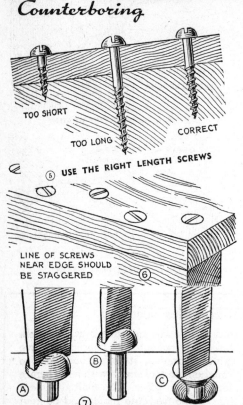

TOO SHORT

TOO LONG

CORRECT

⑤ USE THE RIGHT LENGTH SCREWS

LINE OF SCREWS
NEAR EDGE SHOULD
BE STAGGERED ⑥

Ⓐ   Ⓑ   Ⓒ

⑦

SCREW-DRIVER BITS OF PROPER WIDTH SAVE TIME

cessity of counterboring for a greater length of the threaded section. The only exceptions to this are the very hard, close-grained woods such as "rock" maple. In end grain the wood fibers lie parallel or nearly so to the axis of the screw and those directly in the path of the screw are either severed or forced aside. When driving screws into flat grain of hard close-grained woods, the small diameter of the counterbore should be just slightly less in depth than the length of the threaded section of the screw as in detail C of Fig. 4. If the counterbore is too shallow in hardwood as in detail A, the undue twisting strain necessary to drive the screw may break it. On the other hand if the counterbore is too large or too deep as in detail B, the threads may pull loose before the countersunk head of the screw is seated flush. In hardwood, the diameter of the counterbore should be the same or a trifle larger than the body of the screw measured at the bottom of the threads, while in softwoods the diameter of the counterbore should be smaller in most cases.

To say that a screw is too long does not imply that its effectiveness is lessened, but means that there is little point in using a screw longer than necessary. An example is shown in the center detail in Fig. 5. In the detail at the left the screw is obviously too short to hold the parts together while a screw of the proper length as in the extreme right-hand detail, will result in a joint of maximum strength. When you drive a line of flat-head screws near the edge of the stock it's generally best to stagger them as in Fig. 6. Using a screwdriver bit of the proper width is also important. See Fig. 7. In detail A the wide bit is likely to twist out of the slot. Details B and C show bits of the correct size and

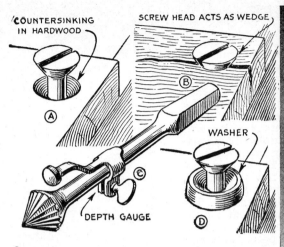

COUNTERSINKING IN HARDWOOD

SCREW HEAD ACTS AS WEDGE

(A) (B)

WASHER

(C)

DEPTH GAUGE (D)

⑧ **COUNTERSINK HOLES FOR FLAT-HEAD SCREWS**

width for the size and type of screw. Countersinking flat-head screws to the proper depth in hardwoods is shown in detail A of Fig. 8. Countersinking to a diameter less than the head of the screw as in detail B sometimes results in splitting the wood. Use a depth gauge on the countersink as in detail C. A metal countersunk washer of the kind shown in detail D may be used with either a flat or oval-head screw to prevent splitting where the screw must be driven close to the edge of thin stock.

Grinding reverse bevels on the screwdriver bit as in Fig. 9 will help to give larger bits a better "bite." Fig. 10 shows one way of filing the screw slot to prevent the screw being turned out. Sometimes this is desirable, as on door hasps. Another kink that helps when driving screws into very hard woods or hard fiber is shown in the right-hand detail of Fig. 10. Filing a V-slot along the length of the screw causes the threads to cut through the hard material much like a tap. When driving a large number of screws of the same size you will find that a short piece of tubing slipped over the head of the screw prevents the screwdriver bit from sliding out of the slot. Using a little soap on screw threads should also be kept in mind as this helps to reduce friction.

❡Copper, brass and pewter may be cleaned successfully by applying a paste made with equal parts of flour, vinegar and salt. Let the paste stay on for about an hour, then rub it off, and wash the metal with warm water before polishing.

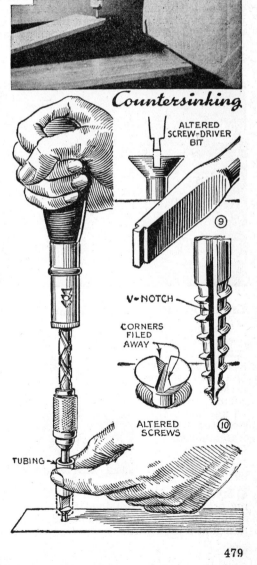

Countersinking

ALTERED SCREW-DRIVER BIT

⑨

V-NOTCH

CORNERS FILED AWAY

TUBING

ALTERED SCREWS ⑩

Small Clamps from Hinges

Hinges need not serve only as hinges. They can be put to work as efficient clamps. Ideal for holding small work in position for soldering and light brazing, they are especially useful where the nature of the work requires a clamp having narrow jaws and a deep throat. Modelmakers will find these clamps just the thing for holding odd-shaped work, as the ends of the jaws can be bent and shaped to fit the exact contour of the parts to be glued or soldered. The four examples show various applications of hinges for clamping small work.

Strap hinges make the best clamps. The drawing below shows a typical clamp and also a few of the many different types of jaws that can be formed. A wing nut, washer and stove bolt provide clamping pressure. The bolt is placed in a hole drilled in the hinge leaf and the head is backed with a nut. A slot formed in the other leaf engages the end of the bolt and permits opening the clamp jaws. The amount the jaws can be opened is determined by the length of the slot. A small coil spring placed over the bolt between the leaves of the hinge will provide a clamp with self-opening jaws. When a clamp is used to hold parts to be brazed, the parts should be clamped to an asbestos pad.

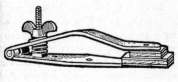

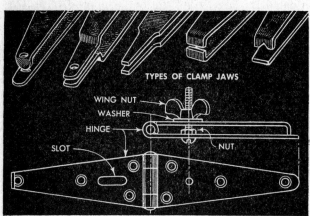

TYPES OF CLAMP JAWS

WING NUT
WASHER
HINGE
SLOT
NUT

Easier Operation of Tin Shears

Tin shears will operate easier if graphite is blown around the screw that joins the halves. Care should be taken to see that the powder penetrates thoroughly. Graphite will not pick up dust easily.

GRAPHITE

❡ Steel rods and tubing for metal-working projects can be obtained cheaply by dismantling old metal bedsteads obtained at a junk yard.

Comb Rack Files Shop Data

A handy card index for shop data can be made easily from 2 coarse-toothed combs and a block of wood. Drill 2 holes in each of the combs and fasten them with round-headed screws and washers to opposite sides of the block. Then insert the reference material between teeth of combs.

❡ To preserve plans, glue to cheesecloth and coat with clear shellac.

Soldering, like any workshop operation, must be done right. Almost any home craftsman can get practical hints from the following article. It gives the three general requirements for soldering light work: a correctly-tinned iron heated to the proper temperature; the right flux for the job, and a clean surface. There's your beginning. Read on.

Solder it RIGHT

By Wm. Riederich

SOLDERING is something like painting—at some time or other nearly everyone finds it necessary or desirable to do the job himself and save both time and money. But in making the average soldered joint the procedure is so simple that there is a tendency to slight some of the details essential to good work. Correctly made, a soldered joint is durable. Take as an example gutter and downspouts, the parts of a building which are exposed to the most severe weathering. If you examine old gutters which have long since eroded to the point where they no longer serve their purpose you will see that in nearly every instance the soldered joints are still sound. The same will be found true of many other kinds of work, parts of which have been joined by soldering.

There are three general requirements for good soldering on average light work. They are, a correctly-tinned iron heated to the proper temperature, the right flux for the job, and a clean surface. Tools required for the ordinary job are a soldering iron or bit, as it is often called, a suitable means of heating the iron or the work quickly and efficiently, a coarse file, sandpaper and a wire brush, a damp cloth and clamps to hold the parts to be joined firmly in place. Of course, if the work is of such a nature that it can be dipped, you will need a ladle of sufficient size. If you use an electrically heated iron exclusively then that disposes of the heating problem.

A new iron must be tinned and where the iron is in continuous use frequent retinning is necessary. The chief purpose of tinning is to prevent the formation of copper oxides on the bevels of the tip. Oxides act as an insulator, interfering with rapid heat transfer from the iron to the work. Also an untinned bit won't "take" the solder properly. To tin a new iron or retin one that has been in use, first heat it to a temperature of 500 to 700 deg. F., and clean with a wire brush.

The soldering iron must be cleaned before tinning. Use a coarse file but be careful not to remove more copper than necessary

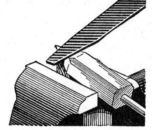

Heat the iron with a blowtorch and watch that it does not get too hot. Always place the iron in the special rack as indicated

Apply flux to the tip, then coat the four bevels with solder. Build up sufficient solder so that it can be spread out evenly

Finally, wipe and twist the tip on a damp cloth to spread patches that remain on the surface. Reheat if necessary

Here's what happens when the iron is too cold. The solder won't flow, but only softens to a waxlike consistency on the surface

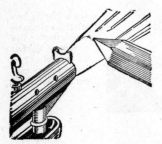

But when the iron is heated to just the right temperature the solder flows or "draws" smoothly into joint without piling up

Don't hold the tip of the iron in the blowtorch flame this way. Direct flame will overheat the iron and remove the tinning

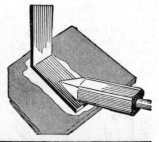

Trick of sweat-soldering one small part securely to another is easy if you proceed correctly in the preparation of the work

TABLE I
MELTING POINT OF VARIOUS SOLDER ALLOYS

Tin	Lead	Antimony	Melting Point °F.
0	100	0	618.8
10	90	0	577.4
20	80	0	532.8
30	70	0	491.0
31	67	2	370.4
38	60	2	370.4
40	60	0	446.0
49.25	50	.75	365.0
50	50	0	401.0
60	40	0	368.0
66	34	0	356.0
70	30	0	365.0
80	20	0	388.4
90	10	0	419.0
100	0	0	450.0
0	0	100	1166.

Sometimes it will help to rub the beveled tip on a block of sal ammoniac or ammonium chloride. Usually, however, it is only necessary to apply a rosin flux to the cleaned tip and flow on solder until the entire tip of the iron is covered. Finally, wipe and twist the tip on a damp cloth to spread the solder in a uniform coating.

The purpose of a flux is in most cases twofold—to help clean the work and to prevent the formation of oxides which interfere with the flow of solder. There is no all-purpose flux. Different metals require different fluxes. See Table II. Two commonly used fluxes are those made from rosin and from muriatic acid (hydrochloric acid) which has been "cut" with zinc, forming zinc chloride. Most fluxes are available ready to use in both liquid and paste forms. For light work you use the handy wire solder with acid core. The acid flux is contained in the hollow wire so no separate flux is necessary. Solder is also supplied in solid-wire form without the flux and in convenient bars. It comes in varying proportions of lead and tin, and in lead-tin-antimony and lead-tin-bismuth alloys. These are all commonly known as "soft" solders. A 50-50 solder, 50 percent tin and 50 percent lead, is good for average light work, although these proportions do not give maximum strength. Where the greatest holding power and resistance to bending or flexing is called for, a 60-40 solder, 60 percent tin and 40 percent lead, is generally used. Some alloys contain 67 percent tin and 33 percent lead. On the other hand, for special jobs such as soldering pewter, a solder composed of 1 part lead, 1 part tin and 3 parts bismuth is quite commonly used. The melting point of this alloy is only 240 deg. F. See Table I.

Cleaning of work to be soldered is done with sandpaper or emery cloth, steel wool, files or a wire brush. A power-driven wire wheel speeds up the job of cleaning where the size or shape of the work allows its use. Tinsmiths use reduced solutions of muriatic acid to clean galvanized sheet metal. Hydrochloric acid is an excellent cleaner on some metals, but it is necessary to give the work a thorough washing in a strong solution of soda water immediately after soldering to remove all traces of the acid and stop its corrosive action. Small, irregular-shaped parts, difficult to clean by brushing or by other means, can be dipped in hydrochloric acid. Suspend these on a wire and don't get the acid on your hands or clothing. Avoid breathing the acid fumes at any time. Some metals and certain types of work won't stand the acid bath. Don't use it to clean electrical work.

The requirements of the soldering operation are just as simple as actually doing the job. The first of these essentials is that the parts to be soldered shall be heated as nearly as possible to a temperature equal to the melting point of the solder. This assures the strongest bond. On large parts to be joined which contain considerable metal or where the cross sections of the parts are thicker than ordinary, preheating usually is necessary. This ordinarily is done with a blowtorch. Where work must be preheated it is necessary that it be held together with clamps during the heating period, also for a time after soldering until the work cools well below the melting point of the solder. Work soldered in this way should not be subjected to any strain during the cooling period. Where seams, butt joints, corner joints, and curved work are to be joined by soldering, parts must always be carefully fitted beforehand and provision made for holding the assembly in place while soldering. Galvanized sheet-metal parts should always be held together with clamps or by other means. Where you have an intricate assembly requiring soldering several joints in close proximity, use damp or wet cloths to protect the joints already soldered. When using a torch to heat large work preparatory to soldering, heat all the area about the joint but avoid playing the flame directly on the meeting surfaces or on the solder as it is applied. When doing such a job, flux the work first then heat until the flux boils. Apply the solder immediately. When it melts and flows into the joint, withdraw the heat and allow the work to cool to room temperature before removing the clamps or other fasteners that hold the parts together.

Soldering with an iron is much the same as with the torch except that the iron is used to heat the work and melt the solder in a more or less simultaneous operation. A suitable flux is applied to the work which is then heated by applying the iron to the surface. After a preliminary heating, solder is flowed into the joint. On some types of work such as a common butt joint, flowing the solder onto the iron as it moves slowly along the joint will often give the smoothest job. If the temperature is right the molten solder will flow off the iron onto the work in just the right amount.

Making a lap joint on two flat surfaces is done by a method known as "sweat-soldering." First the edges are fluxed and tinned. The tinned surfaces are then placed together and heat applied. Where an acid flux is used wash the work immediately with a solution made by dissolving ½ lb. baking soda in a gallon of water. This will remove all remaining traces of acid and stop any corrosive action on the metal.

When soldering small parts such as a wire splice, hold the iron under the work. The solder will "draw" into the joint neatly

Small parts can be rustproofed by tinning in a bath of molten solder. Attach a wire to work and hold in solder until heated

To repair a cracked tube, wrap it with wire, closely spaced, then heat and run solder until spaces between wires are filled

Wash parts to remove the flux. A shallow porcelain-enameled pan is generally the best. Always do a good job of washing

TABLE II
SOLDERING FLUXES USED FOR VARIOUS METALS

Metal	Flux
Iron	Ammonium chloride or zinc chloride
Steel	Ammonium chloride or zinc chloride
Copper	Ammonium chloride or zinc chloride
Brass	Ammonium chloride or zinc chloride
Bronze	Ammonium chloride or zinc chloride
Gun metal	Ammonium chloride or zinc chloride
Nickel	Ammonium chloride or zinc chloride
Lead	Rosin or tallow
Steel (Tinned)	Zinc chloride or rosin
Galvanized steel	Hydrochloric acid
Zinc	Hydrochloric acid
Pewter	Tallow
Silver	Chloride of zinc
Gold	Chloride of zinc
Cast iron	Chloride of zinc with tallow added
Stainless steel	Muriatic acid

Battery Cable Is Repaired Easily with Copper Wire and Solder

FRAYED CABLE

WOUND TOGETHER

COPPER-WIRE WRAP

SOLDERED AND TAPED

If battery cables become frayed or broken, they can be repaired by winding the ends together and wrapping the exposed area with bare copper wire of a medium gauge. Following this, flow solder onto the joint and then wrap with friction tape.

Hinge Serves as Secret Lock on Workbench Drawer

This simple drawer lock defies detection mainly because it is hidden and also because the nail which operates the lock appears to be one of those used to fasten the bench top to the legs. As the detail shows, the lock, consisting of a strap hinge with a nail release pin attached to one leaf, is recessed into the underside of the bench over the drawer. One leaf of the hinge is screwed flush in the recess and the other leaf is left free to swing downward to form a stop, which prevents the drawer from being pulled out. The nail release pin is attached loosely to the hinge with wire and a washer. Should the nail become detached from the hinge, a shallow notch cut in the top of the drawer in line with the hinge at the time the lock is installed, will provide clearance so that the drawer can be withdrawn. Several decoy nails should be driven where shown.

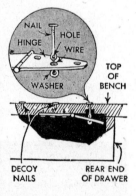

NAIL

HINGE

HOLE

WIRE

WASHER

TOP OF BENCH

DECOY NAILS

REAR END OF DRAWER

Extension Lamp for Workbench Supported by Coat Hanger

Suspended by a bracket bent from a coat hanger, an ordinary drop-cord lamp will provide ample light at any point on your workbench top. A cork, which has been drilled slightly smaller than the drop cord and grooved around the side, is slipped over the cord. Then, a wire coat hanger is bent around the cork, as shown, and is hung from a nail or hook driven into the wall above the bench. Several nails or hooks placed at intervals along the wall permit the light to be moved as needed. The light is adjusted to the desired height by pulling the cord through the cork.

Foil Grip on End of Rasp or File Protects Your Hands

Wrapped tightly around the end of a file or wood rasp, a strip of lead foil serves as a comfortable hand grip when using the tool for long periods of time. It is unnecessary to tie or wire the foil in place as the soft metal presses firmly into the file teeth, which hold it in place when the grip of your hand is released.

LEAD FOIL

How much do you know about sandpaper? How can it be more useful to you? Do you know what kind of particles make up the abrasive on sandpaper? How the grits and grains are numbered? What makes grit papers lose their cutting power? How to sand irregular surfaces? This article answers and illustrates all the things you want to know about sanding. It also will show you many new sanding techniques to improve your floors and beautify your furniture. Here it is, for smoother sanding.

WOOD DOWEL

¾" STRIPS EMERY CLOTH 6" LONG

① SLOT, 1½" DEEP

LIGHT CANVAS

SHOE-LACE

BRICK

②

③ 3" 2" 5"

2 PIECES INNER TUBE CEMENTED TO BLOCK

④ SANDPAPER

⑤ TURPENTINE

SMOOTH SANDING

By R. F. Yates

AMATEUR mechanics often fail to obtain the full value from their coated abrasives because they do their sandpapering by rule-of-thumb methods. It is possible, however, to get more value from each piece of abrasive and turn out smoother work. Abrasive papers are coated with particles of garnet, quartz, flint or aluminum oxide. These abrasives come in standard 9 by 11-in. sheets and in belts, disks, cones, drums and strips for special purposes. Grits are numbered from 8/0 to 4, the finer grains—those from 8/0 to 2/0—having softer, more flexible paper backing. Medium grit papers used in preliminary treatment of cabinet woods range from 1/0 to 2, and very coarse papers for removing paint or for fast cutting range from 2½ to 4. There is a choice of grit for every purpose and for every type of wood; the closer the grain and the harder the wood, the finer the abrasive must be for the finishing operation.

Grit papers lose their cutting power when the abrasive particles become dull and when wood dust packs between them. By turning the sanding block at a 90-degree angle or by reversing it as soon as the paper becomes dull, a new cutting edge will be brought into use, thus adding

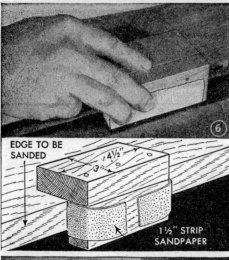

EDGE TO BE SANDED

3½" · 4½"

1½" STRIP SANDPAPER

(6)

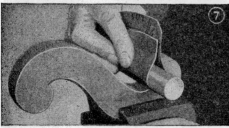

(7)

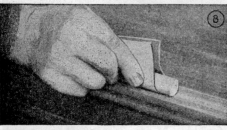

(8)

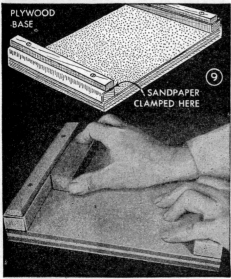

PLYWOOD BASE

SANDPAPER CLAMPED HERE

(9)

as much as 50 percent to the life of the paper. Packing of wood dust between the abrasive particles cannot be prevented but can be minimized by occasionally brushing the abrasive with a stiff brush, as in Fig. 4. Wood dust also plugs the pores of the wood and, unless it is removed, it might spoil the finish coat. To prevent this, the wood should be brushed thoroughly, then wiped off with a clean cloth moistened with turpentine, as in Fig. 5.

Where irregular surfaces are to be sanded, the little gadget illustrated in Fig. 1 will be useful. The tool is placed in the chuck of a drill press with the cutting side of the abrasive facing the direction of rotation. Fine emery cloth will last longer in this operation than paper-backed abrasives. In straight sanding, the line of movement should be with the grain. Equal pressure should be applied on all points, and the abrasive must not be twisted or it will cause cross-grain scratches that cannot be removed easily. By using blocks around which the paper is wrapped, greater pressure can be applied than with the fingers alone, and there will be less chance of grooving the wood, especially with coarse, fast-cutting papers. Such a block can be made from an ordinary brick or piece of wood covered with light canvas, as in Fig. 2. A softer block and finer paper should be used for re-working the first heavy sanding. A blackboard eraser or slab of cork makes an ideal block, or one can be made from a piece of wood to which pieces of inner tube or sponge rubber are glued, as in Fig. 3.

The sanding block shown in Fig. 6 will help to keep the edges of cabinets and tabletops square without the rounding often noticed in the work of inexperienced workmen. After a perfectly square surface is produced, a few light strokes with fine paper will take off the sharp knife edge. Wrapping the paper around a wood dowel, as in Figs. 7 and 8, will enable the craftsman to reach all curved surfaces, especially if the paper is first soaked in turpentine to make it more flexible. Where small pieces are to be sanded by hand and kept square, the sanding board shown in Fig. 9 will help a great deal. Often two edges may be sanded simultaneously with this arrangement.

Improperly treated end grain may ruin an otherwise beautifully finished piece of furniture. Therefore these ends must be sanded to an almost glazed surface, otherwise they will absorb more than their share of the stain or varnish. Some woods require sponging and re-sanding with fine paper to bring out the proper accentuation of grain effects. In such cases, water is applied to the wood with a soft cloth after the first sanding with fine-grit paper. The

wood should be thoroughly dried before re-sanding, and only very light pressure used with papers of 2/0, 3/0 or 4/0 grits.

The amateur finisher should not overlook the usefulness of steel wool. This comes in grits of 2, 1, 0, and 000. The 000 wool leaves a hardwood surface with a satin sheen that cannot be achieved with grit papers. Of course the same rules apply in using wool as in sanding to avoid cross-grain scratching.

Varnish sanding between coats was formerly pretty much a fine art. However, with wet sandpapers it is possible to achieve pleasing effects without a great deal of experience. Wet-sanding papers come in extremely fine grits from 8/0 to 6/00, are extremely tough, and are impervious to water. To make them more flexible, such papers are soaked in water before they are applied, as in Fig. 10. The varnished surfaces to be sanded are also kept moistened by water applied with a sprinkler bottle, as in Fig. 11.

The water modifies the cutting action of the paper and prevents the scratches that would result with dry paper.

After using this paper, the varnished surface should be carefully sponged off and wiped as dry as possible with a chamois to avoid leaving lint on the surface. These papers work so well that they often may be used instead of the felt pad and pumice usually employed for the finish coat. However, since they cut much faster than pumice, the workman must be careful not to carry the operation beyond the point needed for the type of finish he seeks.

Adjustable Holder for Grinding Produces Accurate Work

FLAT IRON

To do more accurate grinding, one mechanic made this adjustable holder for round work. The flat-iron bracket is bolted to the bench, and the holder, which also is of flat iron, is fastened to the bracket with a bolt, wing nut and washer. The V-cut in the holder supports the work.

Easy Way to Sand Narrow Slots

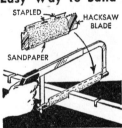

STAPLED
HACKSAW BLADE
SANDPAPER

Narrow slots are easily sanded with sandpaper which is fastened around a hacksaw blade. The blade is removed from the saw and the paper is stapled over it so that the teeth point toward the stapled part. When used, the blade is inserted in the reverse position so the teeth will not cut the paper.

If you can see traces of a white line on the tool edge when held up to a light, the tool is dull and requires sharpening

UTILITY FILE

SCYTHESTONE

KNIFE SHARPENERS

1

COMBINATION BENCH STONE

GOUGE SLIP

ROUND-EDGE SLIP

AUGER BIT STONE

SOFT ARKANSAS POCKET STONE

STICKS

¼" PLYWOOD

FELT GLUED TO LID

⅛" PLYWOOD

LID

OPENING TO SUIT SIZE OF STONE

STONE MINUS ³⁄₁₆"

½"

BOTTOM

NAIL AND GLUE

2 STONE BOX

9"

LEATHER STROP **3**

2½"

LEATHER

HONE TOOLS

By Sam Brown

UNLESS there are nicks in the cutting edge, it's not necessary to grind a tool each time to sharpen it. Once ground, any tool can be kept razor sharp for many hours of use by frequent, light honing. The right stone to use in honing depends upon the type of tool and its purpose. Grass and bread knives cut best if honed on a coarse stone, while most other tools require honing on a medium or fine stone to prevent the edge from tearing the work and to hold up under cutting pressure.

Artificial abrasives, aluminum oxide and silicon carbide, are gradually replacing natural or mined stones for honing tools. Aluminum oxide is of the same physical structure as natural corundum and is often called "India." In this country, Arkansas is about the only natural oilstone

5 NATURAL STONES

HARD ARKANSAS — finest grit of all natural stones. Excellent for all delicate cutting edges

SOFT ARKANSAS — softer and more porous than hard Arkansas but cuts considerably faster

LILY-WHITE WASHITA—a soft but fast-cutting stone with good bite. Best for carpenters

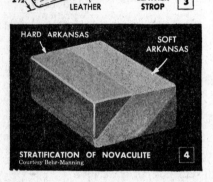

HARD ARKANSAS

SOFT ARKANSAS

STRATIFICATION OF NOVACULITE **4**
Courtesy Behr-Manning

HALF-AND-HALF MIXTURE OF NO. 20 MOTOR OIL AND KEROSENE

6

7

Above, new stone should be soaked in oil before using and then always used with oil to prevent wearing unevenly

Right, if continued use produces hollow in the stone, rub the stone on smooth glass, using silicon carbide and water

WITH THE RIGHT STONE

of commercial importance. This stone is mineral novaculite, and is largely composed of silica. The stratification of novaculite, Fig. 4, runs from hard Arkansas to soft and then grades off to the still softer and more porous lily-white Washita, Fig. 5. First-grade Washita is the same as lily-white, but is not graded for color.

The bench oilstone: The conventional combination coarse-fine oilstone is widely used in sharpening most straightedge tools in the home shop, although Fig. 1 shows several other shapes which are recommended for honing special tools. The combination oilstone usually consists of either aluminum oxide or silicon carbide. Artificial stones are graded coarse, medium and fine—150, 240 or 320 abrasive grains per inch. Natural stones are not graded by grit

size, but by the variety of stone itself. Hard Arkansas, for example, is of both hard and fine texture, whereas soft Arkansas is soft and coarse. The soft stones cut faster but produce a coarse edge. Certain species of fine sandstone, such as Queer Creek and Hindustan, possess this feature to a marked degree and are used extensively for sharpening scythes and other tools requiring a coarse edge.

The bench oilstone should be kept in a box such as shown in Fig. 2. If the stone has not been preoiled, it should be soaked overnight in a mixture of oil, 1 part, and kerosene, 1 part, Fig. 6. In use, the stone should be worn down uniformly to prevent the formation of a hollow. However, should the stone become hollowed, it should be rubbed flat on a piece of glass, Fig. 7, using

8 ARTIFICIAL STONES

9 TYPES OF GRITS

SILICON CARBIDE
Hardest abrasive made. Cuts fast with light pressure, but breaks down under a heavy pressure

ALUMINUM OXIDE
Physically the same as natural corundum, hence often called "India." It is fast-cutting oilstone

COARSE-FINE
All oilstones can be obtained in a combination of two stones. Coarse-fine is most widely used

MEDIUM
The standard grits in artificial oilstones are: coarse, medium and fine. Combination type is best

Tips on Sharpening a Variety of Tools

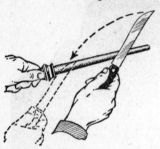

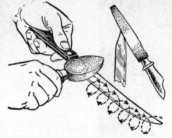

KNIFE (first method)

This type of sharpener is coarse-fine, cuts fast with little pressure and requires no oil. Start the initial stroke as shown, pulling the knife down smartly from heel to tip. Repeat on other side

KNIFE (second method)

Stone is fine-grit silicon carbide, excellent for sharpening stainless steel. Honing is done dry or with water lubricant. Use little circular strokes, as indicated, working stone on one side, then on other

GOUGE

Use flat side of round-edge slip or surface of bench stone. Apply oil, then hold gouge steady and move stone up and down, at same time slowly rotating gouge. Clear view of bevel is had at all times

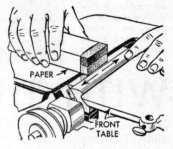

GOUGE (continued)

Wire edge from previous operation is removed by honing with round-edge. Use oil, hold stone flat on tool. Hollow stone is used to hone gouge having outside bevel to help keep proper bevel

DRAWKNIFE

Use a scythestone or a flat stone of coarse grit. Stroke up or down or round and round. Watch bevel by sighting and use stone dry or wet. Same technique is used to sharpen blade of scythe or sickle

JOINTER

Hone jointer knives by wrapping bench stone in paper to prevent marking table. Wedge pulley to hold cutterhead steady. Use oil and hone lightly. Use coarse side of stone first if blades are dull

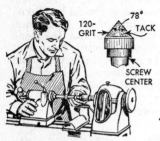

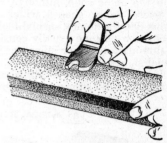

MORTISING CHISEL

If you are unable to obtain a stone of the correct cone shape for sharpening a mortising chisel, turn a wooden cone and cover it with silicon-carbide paper. Apply oil and run lathe at slow speed

LATHE TOOL BITS

Although having blunt edges, lathe bits will stand up much longer if honed to a medium or fine edge. If tool is carbide tipped, use silicon-carbide stone. Mount stone in chuck of jigsaw

SHAPER CUTTERS

Use coarse, then fine side of bench stone. Hone only on flat side of cutter. Give bevel a light paring stroke with sharpening stick to remove wire edge. Molding cutters are honed the same

CLEARANCE

CHISEL IS FLAT ON STONE

1. Chisel has been newly ground on 60-grit wheel, so honing starts on coarse side of stone. Apply a few drops of light oil beforehand

2. Hold chisel with heel slightly above stone, as shown in the side view. Stroke chisel back and forth using medium pressure

3. Alternate operations **2** and **3** until edge shows sharp with minimum of burr or wire edge. Repeat same steps on fine side of stone

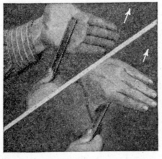

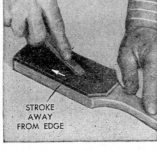

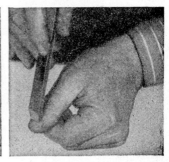

STROKE AWAY FROM EDGE

4. To remove final burr or wire edge, hone the chisel on palm of hand, stroking away from edge. This bends and breaks wire edge

5. Velvety smoothness, provided previous steps have been done properly, is obtained by stropping chisel on smooth piece of leather

6. Test on your thumbnail — if chisel is sharp, it will bite in; if not, it will slide off. Make this test also at end of step **3**

80-grit silicon-carbide grains and water as a lubricant. Silica sand also can be used to dress a hollowed stone.

Using the oilstone: There are no stroking rules in honing other than the obvious one of having the tool in contact with the stone at the proper angle. It is advisable, however, to hone against the edge of the tool whenever possible to hold burring to a minimum. Always use oil but avoid charging the stone with anything heavy or gummy. A kerosene-and-oil mixture is excellent. Being fairly thin, the mixture floats away any metal particles and prevents them from becoming embedded in the stone. It also permits smooth stroking and reduces friction. After a stone has been used, it should be wiped dry with a clean cloth. Never let oil containing metal particles dry on it, as this will form a glaze.

Kinds of edges: When magnified, any edge will show as a series of sharp "mountain peaks," and the relative size of the peaks classes the edge as coarse, medium or fine. When a chisel is ground on a 60-grit wheel, the edge may be sharp but it is very coarse. Honing on the coarse side of an oilstone gives an ordinary coarse edge, which then can be brought to any degree of fineness by honing on the fine side.

Honing suggestions: The photos in Fig. 10 show the general procedure in honing a chisel and the steps also apply equally as well to plane irons and similar tools. To construct a strop, Fig. 3, glue the leather to a wooden block with the hair side up. Hints on the opposite page cover honing operations for a variety of tools.

Household Lye Distinguishes Aluminum Stock From Similar Metals

When you wish to determine if a piece of metal actually is aluminum or another type of metal with a similar appearance, try this easy test. First make a 40-percent solution of household lye in water, being sure to use a glass container. Then, file or cut a few chips from the stock in question and drop them into the solution. If the chips produce a vigorous reaction and disappear in a few seconds, the metal is aluminum. When using this solution, be careful not to get it on your hands or clothing. Also, flush the drain thoroughly after disposing of the solution.

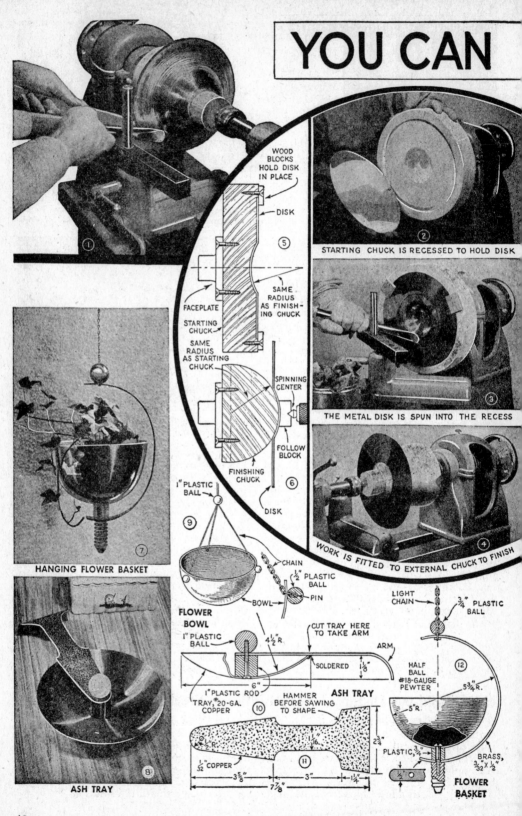

YOU CAN

①

② STARTING CHUCK IS RECESSED TO HOLD DISK

③ THE METAL DISK IS SPUN INTO THE RECESS

④ WORK IS FITTED TO EXTERNAL CHUCK TO FINISH

⑤ WOOD BLOCKS HOLD DISK IN PLACE — DISK

FACEPLATE

STARTING CHUCK

SAME RADIUS AS STARTING CHUCK

SAME RADIUS AS FINISHING CHUCK

SPINNING CENTER

FOLLOW BLOCK

FINISHING CHUCK

⑥ DISK

⑦ HANGING FLOWER BASKET

⑧ ASH TRAY

⑨ 1" PLASTIC BALL

FLOWER BOWL

CHAIN

½" PLASTIC BALL

PIN

BOWL

1" PLASTIC BALL

1" PLASTIC ROD

4½"R.

CUT TRAY HERE TO TAKE ARM

SOLDERED

ARM

1⅛"

6"

TRAY, #20-GA. COPPER

ASH TRAY

⑩ HAMMER BEFORE SAWING TO SHAPE

½₂"R.

½₂" COPPER

⑪

3⅝"

16"

3"

1¼"

2¾"

7⅞"

LIGHT CHAIN

¾" PLASTIC BALL

⑫

HALF BALL #18-GAUGE PEWTER

5¾"R.

5"R.

PLASTIC, ¾"

½"

BRASS, ³⁄₃₂" X ½"

FLOWER BASKET

SPIN IT

CLOCK DIAL

DINNER GONG

TRAY

DISK
SCREW
CHUCK

WHERE A CENTER
HOLE IS PERMISSIBLE,
THE DISK FOR THE
BALL SHAPE CAN
BE SCREWED
DIRECT TO
CHUCK

½" BRASS
BALL

PIN

CORD

BELL
16-GA.
BRASS

½" BRASS
BALL

³⁄₃₂" x ½"
BRASS

3"

6"

BASE
4"x4½"

½"
¼"

4"

DINNER GONG

CLOCK
HANDS

PLASTIC
CYLINDER

SMALL
ELECTRIC
CLOCK

SPUN DIAL
3⅜" DIA.
20-GA.COPPER

4½"R

CEMENTED
JOINT

3⅞"

2½"

ELECTRIC CLOCK

Attractive and Useful Articles in Pewter and Copper That Anyone Can Spin on a Lathe

REQUIRING only a wood-turning lathe and a few added accessories, metal spinning opens a field of interesting, smart projects for the craftsman. Pewter of about 18 gauge should be the first choice of the beginner as it spins easily without annealing, and can be polished to a beautiful mirror finish.

The ball shape: A half ball of polished metal or a smaller portion of it has numerous applications. Typical is the flower bowl, Fig. 9, the hanging flower basket shown in Figs. 7 and 12, the ash tray, Figs. 8, 10 and 11, and the clock dial, Figs. 13 and 18. In many projects featuring this shape, a hole is required in the center of the metal. This is a fortunate feature as it permits the disk to be fastened directly to the chuck, Fig. 16, without the need of preliminary spinning on a starting chuck. Where the work has no center hole, the disk is started on a starting chuck, as in Figs. 2, 3, and 5. After the metal has been spun into the starting chuck, it is mounted on the finishing chuck to complete the spinning, Figs. 4 and 6.

The bell shape: This is very similar to the half-ball shape and requires a starting chuck unless the work specifies a center hole large enough to take a suitable screw. The dinner gong, Fig. 14, is an example of the bell shape. Fig. 17 shows the construction. This project uses a fairly heavy metal (16 gauge) in order to give a mellow tone to the bell when struck with a felt mallet.

Shallow tray shape: The shallow tray or plate shape is probably featured more than any other in spun projects. The various terms applied to the tray shape are given at the top of Fig. 21, which also gives the dimensions of the ash tray and nut bowl shown in the photos, Figs. 19 and 20. This shape can be spun on either an internal or external chuck. An internal chuck indicates that the metal is to be spun into the chuck; an external chuck indicates that the metal is to be spun over the chuck. Fig. 22 shows an internal chuck with recessed rim to take a round metal blank. Fig. 23 shows the preferable method, using a square sheet

ASH TRAY

NUT BOWL

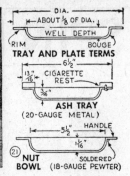

DIA.
ABOUT ⅛ OF DIA.
WELL DEPTH
RIM   BOUGE
TRAY AND PLATE TERMS

6½"
13/16" CIGARETTE REST
¾"
ASH TRAY
(20-GAUGE METAL)

5½"   HANDLE
1/16"
NUT BOWL (18-GAUGE PEWTER)   SOLDERED

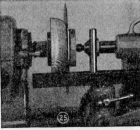

½" SQ'S.
2¾" R.
HANDLE
#18-GAUGE PEWTER

SPINNING SHALLOW TRAY SHAPE ON INTERNAL CHUCK

SPINNING SHALLOW TRAY SHAPE ON EXTERNAL CHUCK

of metal screw-fastened to the sides of the chuck. The advantage of this mounting is that the face of the metal is completely clear. In any case, spinning is simply a matter of forcing the metal into the chuck shape, as shown in Fig. 24. The stroking action of the spinning tool should be from rim to center. Attention should be concentrated on getting the sharp turn at the rim down to the chuck surface. The rim will tend to lift during the spinning operation and should be hammered flat with a rawhide mallet.

In spinning the tray shape with the use of a standard external chuck, the metal disk is held in place by means of a follow block, which should be about ⅛ in. less in diameter than the flat bottom of the tray. Pressure of the spinning center on the follow block holds the disk securely for spinning. The starting set-up is shown in Fig. 25. The spinning action is aimed at getting a small section of the metal down to the chuck sur-

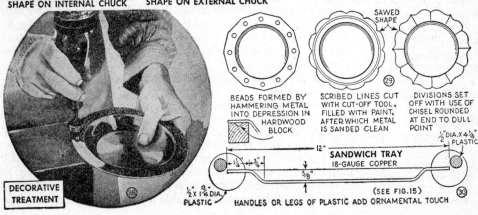

DECORATIVE TREATMENT

SAWED SHAPE

BEADS FORMED BY HAMMERING METAL INTO DEPRESSION IN HARDWOOD BLOCK

SCRIBED LINES CUT WITH CUT-OFF TOOL, FILLED WITH PAINT, AFTER WHICH METAL IS SANDED CLEAN

DIVISIONS SET OFF WITH USE OF CHISEL ROUNDED AT END TO DULL POINT

½" DIA. X 4¼" PLASTIC

12"
1¼" ¾"
5/8"
SANDWICH TRAY
18-GAUGE COPPER

½" & 1/16" DIA.
PLASTIC
(SEE FIG.15)
HANDLES OR LEGS OF PLASTIC ADD ORNAMENTAL TOUCH

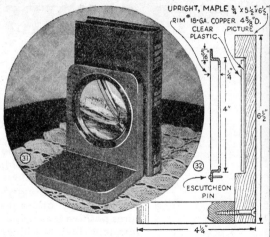

UPRIGHT, MAPLE ¾"×5½"×6½"
RIM #18-GA. COPPER 4⅝"D.
CLEAR PICTURE
PLASTIC
5/16"
¼"
4"
6½"
ESCUTCHEON
PIN
◄───── 4¼" ─────►

face while keeping the rest of the metal in a straight V-shape. The natural tendency of the metal to form a bell shape should be counteracted by stroking the metal not yet down to the chuck surface, at the same time, backing the spinning tool with a broomstick sharpened to a chisel point. The technique is shown in Fig. 1. After obtaining the V-shape in this manner, the flat tool takes another "bite" in forcing another short section of metal down to the chuck surface. Every time this is done the disk will start to "bell" and must be straightened to the required V-shape. After the metal is all down to the chuck surface, the rim can be trimmed, as shown in Fig. 26. The project shown as an example is the nut bowl, Fig. 20. This requires handles, which are soldered in place with pewter solder melted with a blow pipe, Fig. 27. Excessive heat must be avoided since the melting temperature of pewter is very close to the heat necessary to melt the special solder. Well done, soldered joints in pewter can be filed and polished to make a perfectly invisible joint.

Decorative treatment: Plates and trays can be decorated by hammering after spinning, Fig. 28, or by any of the simple methods shown in Fig. 29. The use of handles or legs of plastic adds an ornamental touch, as can be seen in the sandwich tray, Fig. 15. The dimensions of this tray are given in Fig. 30.

Metal-covered forms: In some projects, notably bases for lamps and candlesticks, the metal can be spun permanently over the chuck. This has an advantage in that narrow, neck shapes can be formed without resorting to complicated sectional

chucks. The base and top of the lamp stem shown in Fig. 33 illustrate the idea.

Metal rims: Metal rims for use on clocks, picture frames, etc., are spun easily by using the same technique as in spinning a shallow tray on an internal chuck. It can be seen that the rim used in the nautical book ends, Figs. 31 and 32, is simply a shallow tray with the center cut out.

General features of spinning: All chucks should be made from hard maple—the use of a softer wood will result in the grain of the wood printing on the metal. A good speed for all spinning operations is 1,000 r.p.m. The metal disk must be kept lubricated at all times. A half-and-half mixture of soft soap and soft grease is satisfactory. Although pewter is the most satisfactory, copper has excellent decorative value and is easy to spin as long as it remains soft. However, action of the spinning tool causes it to harden and become brittle. When this occurs, the metal blank should be removed from the lathe and annealed by heating over a gas ring to a dull red and then quenching in water. 20 gauge is a good all-around thickness for spun projects in copper. The same gauge in aluminum spins readily and has the advantage of requiring no annealing throughout the spinning process.

─────────

❡ The life of a sanding sleeve can be increased by reversing it on the drum. Worn and clogged abrasive grains take on new life with this reversal of rotation.

TWO POWER SANDERS

★

One model combines three sanders in one machine driven by a single motor. The other, a 6-in. belt sander, employs standard shaft hangers for bearings, and features positive tension adjustment. Both machines can be built at nominal cost from scrap parts

By
R. Barsamian

HERE ARE TWO homemade sanders that will handle practically every sanding job in the home shop. One is a combination band, disk and drum sander, while the other is a conventional 6-in. belt sander. Both can be made inexpensively, using standard parts along with odds and ends.

Band Sander: Figs. 1 and 2 picture and detail the construction of the combination sander. The framework is assembled from pieces of channel iron, the upright being 3-in. channel welded to a 6-in. channel base. Note that the upright is located 2 in. from one edge of the base and that a 3 by 8-in. opening is cut in the base to permit belting and driving the machine from below. The dimensions given for the frame accommodate a 45-in. standard belt. If a longer one is used, the upright must be lengthened. Holes are drilled in the top surface of the base for mounting two ball-bearing pillow blocks. These carry the drive pulley and double-end shaft which drive the sanding belt and the disk. The arm, which carries the upper bearings, also is a length of 3-in. channel iron with the web cut out at one end, as shown, and the flanges spread apart to fit over the flanges of the channel upright. The arm is drilled and pivoted to the upright with a ½-in. bolt, after first being drilled for two bronze-bushed pillow-block bearings and a tensional rod. In drilling the mounting holes for the pillow blocks, extra care must be taken to assure perfect alignment of both upper and lower bearings. This is important, as there is no provision for adjustment of sanding-belt trackage other than the use of shims under the pillow blocks. It is also important that the holes for the tensional rod in both base and arm be aligned accurately to avoid the necessity of shimming the pillow blocks. The hole for the rod in the arm must be elongated slightly with a round file to provide clearance. The rod, which is threaded at each end, is anchored to the base by two nuts and a lock washer. A washer and nut on the upper end provide a shoulder for the end of a ⅜-in. i.d. compression spring which bears against

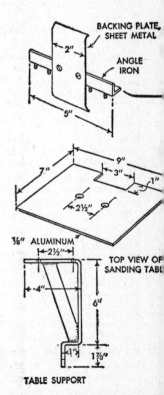

BACKING PLATE, SHEET METAL

2"

ANGLE IRON

5"

9"
3"
1"
7"
2½"

TOP VIEW OF SANDING TABLE

⅛" ALUMINUM
2½"
4"
6"
1"
1⁷⁄₈"

TABLE SUPPORT

FILL ALL NEEDS

the underside of the arm. The location of
the nut and washer must suit the spring
used and tension desired. The end of the
rod is capped with a handwheel, which is
tightened or loosened to regulate belt tension. The flanges of the channel-iron base
are drilled for three studs on which the
swivel blocks and table bracket are mounted. Two of the studs are formed by a single
rod, one end being threaded before tack-
welding the rod in position.

The idler and driving drums for the belt
sander are turned to size and balanced
right on their shafts. This is done by drilling a ½-in. hole in the end grain of hardwood blocks and pinning each block to its
shaft with a nail driven crosswise through
an undersize hole in both drum and shaft.
Note that the drums are crowned ⅟₁₆ in.
The sanding-belt table, which can be either
metal or wood, is supported by a 90-deg.
bracket bent and welded from 1¼-in. flat
iron. This bracket is mounted on the
threaded base stud. Note that the table is

1

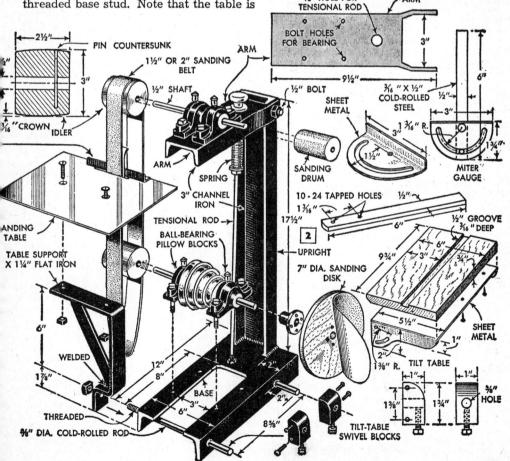

2

497

3

gauge or a home-made one as detailed. The front edge of the wooden table is beveled 45 deg. The sanding disk is a piece of plywood faced with sandpaper and mounted on the shaft by means of a small faceplate. A regular metal sanding disk can be purchased if you wish. Likewise, a commercial unit can be used for the drum on the idler shaft.

Belt Sander: This sander uses standard ½-in. shaft hangers and a 6-in. endless sanding belt. The base parts of the hangers are bolted to the ends of a metal framework that is shaped and braced as shown in Fig. 4. The top part, to which a wooden table is bolted, is bent from one piece of angle iron by drilling a small hole at the point of bend and then cutting out a 90 deg. segment or gusset as indicated in the detail. Weld or bolt mitered corners and two rear legs to frame. The front leg pivots to permit mounting and removing sanding belt.

To balance the idler and driving drums, pin and turn them on their shafts. Belt tension and tracking adjustment are provided by a piece of angle iron drilled and tapped at each end for a ¼-in. adjusting screw and locknut. This piece

notched at the rear edge to take a backing-plate fixture for the belt. This fixture is installed after belt is on drums.

The sanding disk features a tilting table which accommodates a miter gauge. Swivel blocks for the table are cut from 1-in.-square bar stock, drilled to fit over the studs on the base. The top edges of the blocks are rounded to give proper clearance. Note that setscrews are provided to lock the blocks to the studs and that two small machine screws are fitted in tapped holes in the outer faces of the blocks. These screws are for the one-piece trunnion fixture which is bent from sheet metal and faced with a hardwood table, the latter being grooved to take a commercial miter

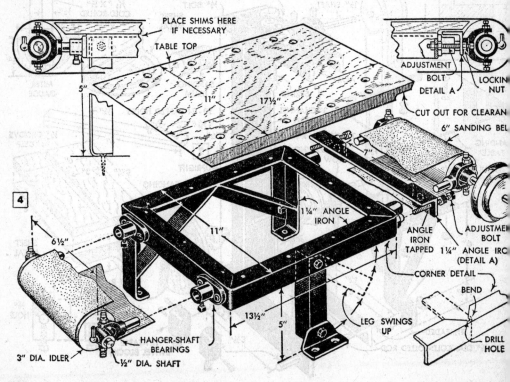

4

PLACE SHIMS HERE IF NECESSARY

TABLE TOP

ADJUSTMENT BOLT

LOCKIN NUT

DETAIL A

CUT OUT FOR CLEARAN

6" SANDING BEL

5"

11"

17½"

7"

1¼" ANGLE IRON

11"

ANGLE IRON TAPPED 1¼" ANGLE IRC (DETAIL A)

ADJUSTME BOLT

CORNER DETAIL

BEND

6½"

13½"

5"

LEG SWINGS UP

DRILL HOLE

HANGER-SHAFT BEARINGS

3" DIA. IDLER

½" DIA. SHAFT

also is drilled at each end to slip loosely over the post of each hanger. It may be necessary to cut out a 7-in. section of the angle iron to give clearance for the driving drum. Belt tension and trackage are maintained simply by turning in or backing out the adjusting screws, as the ends of the screws bear against the frame and force the hangers inward or outward. You may find it necessary to rabbet the underside of the wooden table to provide clearance for the tension fixture. Also, shims may be required between the frame and wooden table to bring the surface flush with the sanding drums. While the sander is shown without a fence in Figs. 3 and 5, one can be made by clamping angle-iron supports to the rear legs of the machine and fastening a hardwood fence to them to overhang and clear the sanding belt.

Note that the pillow-block bearings of the band sander, Fig. 2, and the shaft-hanger bearings of the belt sander, Fig. 4, are fitted with either oil cups or grease fittings. A ¼-hp. motor is sufficient to operate the band sander. However, the belt sander should be driven by a motor of at least ⅓ or ½ hp., especially when coarse sanding belts are used.

Vise Equipped With Hardwood Die Serves as Sheet-Metal Brake

Sheet metal of light gauge can be formed without marring its surface by using a brake which consists of a block of hardwood cut into two parts so that the pieces come together at the desired angle. The metal is placed between the two parts of the block and a vise is used to force the pieces together. Because of the natural "spring back" tendency of most metals, cut the block apart at an angle greater than the bend required so the metal will be bent slightly more than the desired angle. Also, flatten the corners of the block which rest against the vise jaws to keep the block from slipping when pressure is applied.

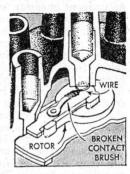

Hairpin Makes Emergency Repair For Broken Rotor Contact Brush

Motorists caught on the road with a broken distributor-rotor brush will profit by remembering this simple emergency repair. It can be made with any bit of wire, even a hairpin, by twisting the wire around the remaining part of the brush and forming the free end of the wire into an eye. The eye is bent upward to make contact with the center terminal of the distributor cap. While this is only a temporary repair, it will permit driving to a garage.

SHEET METAL

WIRE

ROTOR

BROKEN CONTACT BRUSH

SHOP "FLOOR LAMPS" By A. Maxwell

ALTHOUGH the human eye is adaptable to varying light conditions, it's better to provide a good source of illumination when working in a shop or around machinery where accuracy and precision are essential. The two shop floor lamps described here are designed to give the kind of light that will avoid eyestrain and to direct it where needed. In addition, by using special bulbs now on the market, the lamp shown in Fig. 1 will do multiple duty by serving as a source of infra-red, ultraviolet and photographic light. The baby spotlight, Fig. 2, also performs well in the photographic studio.

Of the two lamps, the one with the gooseneck adjustment is easier to make because it requires fewer parts, and in some respects it is more versatile, due to the fact that many different types of bulbs can be used with it. The base should be heavy and compact. The cast-iron standard or base taken from an old floor lamp will serve—the heavier the better. Probably it will be necessary to bore and tap the hole in the base to fit the threads on the ½-in. pipe that serves as the lower half of the upright. The upper half, which serves as the sliding member, is a length of ⁷⁄₁₆-in. rod approximately 36 in. long, as is the pipe. The diameters of these two pieces do not have to be held exactly, but they should be sufficiently rigid and not fit together too loosely. Drill and tap the pipe for the thumbscrew that adjusts the height of the lamp.

A metal block that serves as a swiveling member for the gooseneck fits on top of the rod and is locked in position with a headless setscrew. First, machine the outside dimensions and then drill and

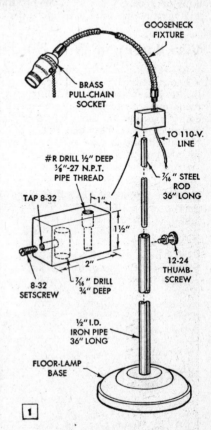

GOOSENECK FIXTURE

BRASS PULL-CHAIN SOCKET

#R DRILL ½" DEEP ⅛"-27 N.P.T. PIPE THREAD

TAP 8-32

1"

1½"

TO 110-V. LINE

⁷⁄₁₆" STEEL ROD 36" LONG

2"

8-32 SETSCREW

⁷⁄₁₆" DRILL ¾" DEEP

12-24 THUMB-SCREW

½" I.D. IRON PIPE 36" LONG

FLOOR-LAMP BASE

1

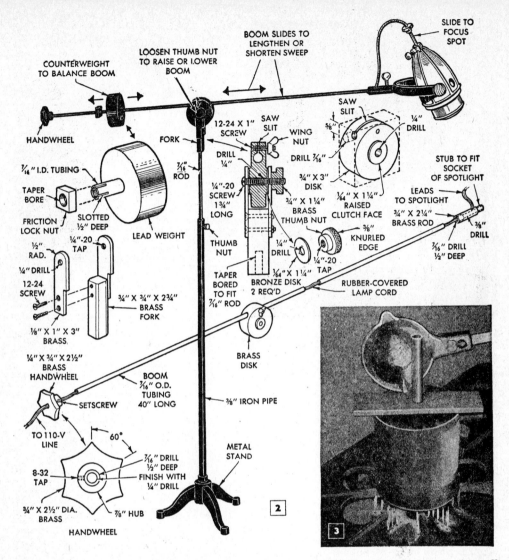

COUNTERWEIGHT TO BALANCE BOOM

LOOSEN THUMB NUT TO RAISE OR LOWER BOOM

BOOM SLIDES TO LENGTHEN OR SHORTEN SWEEP

SLIDE TO FOCUS SPOT

HANDWHEEL

FORK

7/16" ROD

12-24 X 1" SCREW

SAW SLIT

WING NUT

DRILL 1/4"

1/4"-20 SCREW 1 3/4" LONG

3/4" X 3" DISK

3/4" X 1 1/4" BRASS THUMB NUT

SAW SLIT

5/8"

DRILL 7/16"

1/64" X 1 1/4" RAISED CLUTCH FACE

1/4" DRILL

STUB TO FIT SOCKET OF SPOTLIGHT

LEADS TO SPOTLIGHT

3/4" X 2 1/4" BRASS ROD

3/8" DRILL

7/16" I.D. TUBING

TAPER BORE

FRICTION LOCK NUT

SLOTTED 1/2" DEEP

LEAD WEIGHT

THUMB NUT

TAPER BORED TO FIT 7/16" ROD

1/4" DRILL

BRONZE DISK 2 REQ'D

3/8" KNURLED EDGE

1/4"-20 TAP

7/16" DRILL 1/2" DEEP

1/2" RAD.

1/4"-20 TAP

1/4" DRILL

12-24 SCREW

3/4" X 3/4" X 2 3/4" BRASS FORK

1/64" X 1 1/4"

RUBBER-COVERED LAMP CORD

1/8" X 1" X 3" BRASS

1/4" X 3/4" X 2 1/2" BRASS HANDWHEEL

SETSCREW

BOOM 7/16" O.D. TUBING 40" LONG

BRASS DISK

3/8" IRON PIPE

TO 110-V LINE

8-32 TAP

3/4" X 2 1/2" DIA. BRASS

60°

7/16" DRILL 1/2" DEEP FINISH WITH 1/4" DRILL

7/8" HUB

METAL STAND

HANDWHEEL

2

3

tap the holes as indicated in the center left-hand detail of Fig. 1. The tolerance between the rod and the block should be small so that any vibration transmitted from machinery will not affect the lamp. When selecting a gooseneck fixture for the lamp, be sure to get one that is long enough to provide the range of adjustment that you want. It should be possible to set the lamp near a machine and direct the light almost on the work. A brass pull-chain socket is used because it's easy to reach the chain when turning the light on and off. However, any type of socket that has a built-in switch will serve equally well. No reflector is needed for this lamp since the bulbs that are used have an inside coating that serves this purpose. For ordinary service in the shop, a 200-watt flood or spotlight, as com-

monly used for photographic work, will fulfill most requirements. For specialized purposes, such as drying paint in a hurry, an infrared bulb is used. And, of course, with an ultraviolet light in the socket, you have a health-giving sun lamp.

The second lamp, the focusing baby spot, Fig. 4, has a smooth, universal manipulation that is obtained by careful workmanship and fitting of each part. It has a large range of adjustment and is especially handy for reaching hard-to-get-at places where the lamp must be set at some distance from the work. Also, the focusing feature makes it possible to cover a wide area or to concentrate the light in one spot, whichever is required. The effectiveness of the lamp is indicated by Figs. 5 and 6. In Fig. 5 the mechanic is outside the beam of

light, which spreads an even illumination over the motor, while in Fig. 6 an ordinary bulb is suspended from the hood, directing its light into the mechanic's eyes as well as on the work.

The spotlight and mounting fork are purchased as an integral unit and, if obtainable, should be made of aluminum because of its light weight. The lighter the holder, the smaller the counterweight and the greater the ease with which the lamp can be manipulated. A heavier stand is needed than that shown in Fig. 1, and the three-legged type illustrated in Fig. 2 is recommended. Construction of the two upright members is similar to that given for the first lamp and they can be made of materials at hand if sufficiently sturdy. The boom is made of $7/16$-in. outside dia. tubing instead of rod and is about 40 in. long.

With the exception of the counterweight, the remaining parts, which control the adjustments, can be turned in a lathe. The counterweight is made of lead and should weigh about one third more than the spot. Casting it requires the use of a tin can in which the guide sleeve, $7/16$-in. inside dia. tubing, is carefully centered. To prepare the tin can for pouring, bore a press-fit hole in the bottom and steady the sleeve with a wooden brace, Fig. 3. Unless you have a large ladle, it will be necessary to pour the metal in batches. To prevent chilling between pourings, set the can over a low flame but be careful not to melt the bottom. After the lead has set, remove as much of the can as is possible with tin snips; mount the weight in a lathe and true it up. Then shorten and slot the sleeve,

fitting it with a friction lock nut as indicated in the upper left-hand detail, Fig. 2. The fork and disk that serve as the pivoting member for the boom are dimensioned in the upper right-hand and center left-hand details. Construction of the handwheel is shown in the lower left-hand detail. The spotlight may come equipped with a fork that will not fit the boom, and in this case it will be necessary to add a brass-rod bushing, as shown in the lower boom detail. When assembling the unit, run the light cord from the spot through the boom tubing and out the handwheel.

Fence and Table Extension Improve Bandsaw

By Edward R. Lucas

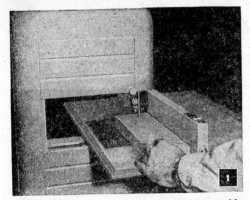

The photos above and below show the bandsaw-table extension being used for straight and bevel cuts

An enlarged working area and provision for a long rip fence are advantages of this bandsaw-table extension. The fence is shown in use in Fig. 1, and Fig. 2 shows the table tilted for a bevel cut. Because sizes of bandsaw tables and throats vary, no over-all dimensions are given; the extension must be made to suit the saw being used. Fig. 3 shows how the parts are cut and assembled. The table extension consists of a piece of plywood having edges faced with solid stock. These are tongue-and-groove joints glued flush with the surface of the plywood. The opening for the bandsaw table is jigsawed for a snug fit. Four cleats are screwed around the opening on the underside and holes are drilled in them for ¼-in. bolts. Matching holes are drilled and tapped in the sides of the bandsaw table, and the extension is attached to the table with bolts through these holes. Next, add the beveled guide rails for the rip fence and cut the slot for the saw blade, being sure that it is aligned with the slot in the metal table. The rip fence is detailed in Fig. 3. Note that the guide blocks are grooved to fit the guide rails and attached to the end pieces by half-lapped joints. Then one end piece is screwed to the fence and the other is hinged and drilled for a hanger bolt and wing nut for clamping the fence in place. The lower right-hand detail shows how the fence is assembled.

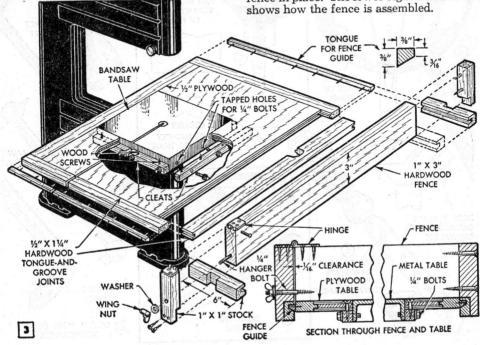

SECTION THROUGH FENCE AND TABLE

Your
SCREW DRIVERS

1. STANDARD WING-TYPE BLADE
2. SQUARE BLADE
3. CABINET-TYPE BLADE

4. A. RIGHT B. WRONG C.
RELIEVED BACK OF POINT

TOO NARROW BLADE MARS EDGE OF SLOT
TOO WIDE BLADE SCRAPES EDGES OF HOLE

6. CORRECT BLADE SLIGHTLY NARROWER THAN SLOT

SIDES OF BLADE GROUND FLAT TO REMOVE SET OF TEETH

5. PIECE OF HACK-SAW BLADE WITH TEETH TOWARD HANDLE

7. A B END

8. SPLIT-TYPE DRIVER

SCREW-DRIVER BIT

RATCHET OFFSET

DOUBLE-END OFFSET

4-WAY OFFSET

PHILLIPS OFFSET

9. SPECIAL TYPES OF SCREWDRIVERS

Selecting the Right Screw Driver

Although few hand tools are used more universally than a screw driver, this simple tool often is misused and generally abused. Mutilated screw-head slots, broken screw shanks, marred work around a screw, inability to loosen and tighten a screw are results of using a screw driver of the wrong size or type, or one with blade tip ground incorrectly.

Like other widely used tools, there are several types of screw drivers, each designed for a special purpose. The three common types are shown in Figs. 1, 2 and 3. The wing-blade types are preferred for screws set flush with the surfaces, while the wingless or cabinet styles are used when screws are to be driven into counterbored holes. But regardless of style no screw driver will handle a screw properly unless it is shaped and ground to fit the slot correctly. Detail A in the magnified view of Fig. 4 shows how a screw-driver blade should appear when ground for ordinary work, while detail B shows an incorrectly shaped blade— one that will slip out of a screw slot as soon as a little pressure is applied. For fine or delicate work, some mechanics prefer to relieve the blade back of the point as shown in detail C.

When selecting a driver for a job always use one having a blade a trifle narrower and thinner than the length and width of the screw slot as shown in the two lower details of Fig. 6. The two upper details show what happens if the blade is too narrow or too wide. It is always a good idea to have a 3-in. length of hacksaw blade, set into a small handle, for cleaning slightly misshaped screw slots or for reshaping those that have been slightly mutilated. Such a saw is shown in Fig. 5. The set of the teeth should be removed by grinding.

For screws that have been driven too tightly to remove with a straight-blade driver, the two types shown in Fig. 7 will do the job. The one in detail A is an ordinary screw driver bent at right angle near the tip, while the one in detail B is ground from flat steel. Both should be hardened before they are put into use. Fig. 8 shows a split type of driver that holds the screw for starting it in deeply counterbored holes or other hard-to-reach places. On jobs that require driving or loosening a large number of screws, much time can be saved by using a spiral ratchet screw driver like the one shown in the photo. Then there are the special types, some of which are shown in Fig. 9. These are used on jobs where straight-shank screw drivers are unsuitable.

Adapter Chucks Spark Plug in Drill Press for Cleaning of Exterior

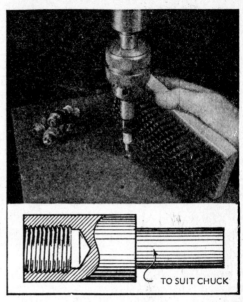

TO SUIT CHUCK

After cleaning the inside of a spark plug, one mechanic chucks it in a drill press and gives the outside of the plug a quick and thorough cleaning by rotating it against a wire brush. He uses several adapters, like the one shown, to fit various sizes of plugs. The shank is turned to suit the chuck and a blind hole is drilled and tapped in the other end to take the threaded base of the spark plug. When the outside of a plug is clean, he applies a little black lacquer to the steel shell, which makes the plug look like new. In using the wire brush be careful that the porcelain insulator is not damaged.

Increasing Blowtorch Efficiency

As the performance of a blowtorch depends on the maintenance of the proper generating temperature, it can be improved by insulating the nozzle with asbestos paper. Wrap two or three layers of this paper around  the nozzle, covering about 1 in. of the end, and fasten it with wire. In addition to insulating, the asbestos paper will permit the torch to be relighted without preheating if the flame is extinguished accidentally.

Wall Cabinet Contains Stepped Drill Rack

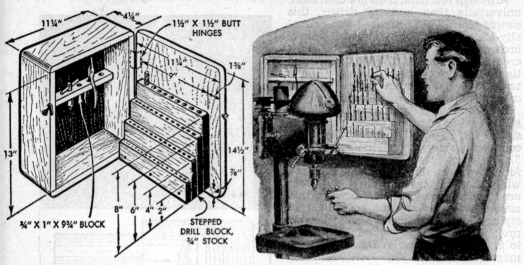

Mounted within easy reach of the drill press, this handy wall cabinet keeps an entire set of drills available for immediate selection. Both cabinet and drill rack are made of ¾-in. white pine, the rack consisting of four blocks of wood of increasing width fastened to the inside of the cabinet door. A shelf across the back of the cabinet holds wrenches, micrometer and other necessary tools. The drills are stored upright in blind holes drilled in a row along the top edge of each block, each hole being made with a drill of the next size larger than the one the hole is to retain. After the blocks have been drilled, the holes are labeled appropriately and the blocks are nailed and glued together as shown. Then they are attached to the cabinet door in the same manner. The door is hung on butt hinges and is held closed with a hook or with a hasp and padlock.

Collet Chuck Is Compressed by Knurled Cap Instead of Draw Rod

Here's a collet chuck that differs from the draw-in type in that a knurled cap instead of the draw rod usually employed compresses the collet. It also has the feature of admitting larger collets. The lathe spindle, part A, first is fitted with a hardened and ground taper sleeve, part E. Next, part B is machined and threaded to fit the lathe spindle, after which the part is drawn up tightly against the shoulder of the spindle with a spanner wrench. The outer end of part B has a fine thread for a knurled cap, part C. Note that the hole in the cap is beveled on the inside to match the taper on the front end of the collet, Fig. 1. Pressure at this point, when the cap is tightened, causes the collet to grip the work. A pin, part F, pressed into part E, prevents the collet, D, from turning. If a lathe does not have a hollow spindle, the chuck can be adapted for use by lengthening part B and using the short collet shown in Fig. 2. In this case, of course, only short work could be held in the chuck.

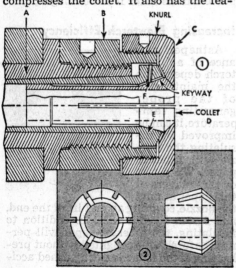

❑ To remove rust from the flutes of an auger bit use a small rope which is coated with glue or shellac and sprinkled with fine emery.

From SEWING MACHINE to JIG SAW

By GUST M. LARSON

THAT old sewing machine long relegated to the attic can be converted into an excellent motor-driven jig saw at practically no cost. All you have to do is strip the machine of its shuttle mechanism, located on the underside of the base, and install the blade-tension device shown at the right. Thickness of the stock that the saw will handle depends upon the stroke of the machine at hand, although it is possible to increase the stroke of most machines simply by raising the needle bar in the head. Drive is by a ½ or ⅓-hp. motor mounted on a hinged base to bring it in line with the pulley on the handwheel. A small insect sprayer, attached by brackets to the cover plate, is operated by the needle bar to provide an efficient sawdust blower.

The machine can be left on its original stand, or you can set the head and base flush in the top of a sturdy bench. In either case, a board must be installed, as shown in the cutaway view, so that the tensioner can be screwed to it, directly below and in line with the needle bar. The tension device consists of a floor flange threaded to a slotted tube in which slides a spring-loaded shaft. The tension of the spring is adjusted by a nut at the end to suit the blade being used. A cross pin keeps the shaft from turning in the tube, and a collar and setscrew, soldered to the upper end of the shaft, form a blade clamp. The needle clamp will hold jeweler's blades but will require enlarging for saber-type blades.

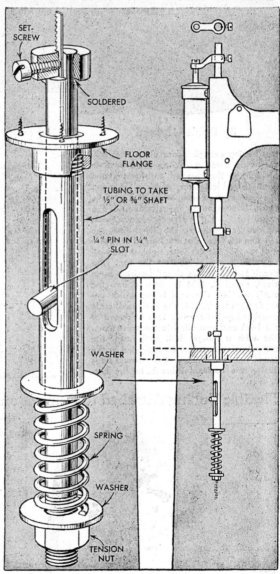

SET-SCREW

SOLDERED

FLOOR FLANGE

TUBING TO TAKE ½" OR ⅝" SHAFT

¼" PIN IN ¼" SLOT

WASHER

SPRING

WASHER

TENSION NUT

Folding Workbench in the Garage Saves Space

By Daniel Hyland

Not having enough space elsewhere, one craftsman made a folding workbench in his garage that proved satisfactory and when folded left plenty of room for a car. The back of the bench, which is 2 by 8-in. stock, is screwed to the studding and a brace for the top is screwed to the back. As can be seen from the illustration, the top and the front legs are hinged in such a manner that the top folds against the wall and the legs fold against the top. The bench is held in the closed position by a cleat, detail A, that is screwed into the studding. The diagonal brace which extends from the back to the horizontal cross member bracing the two legs is hinged at the back and connected to the cross member with a hanger bolt and hasp, the latter having been cut as indicated in the lower right-hand detail. Squarehead bolts fasten the horizontal brace to the legs

Flexible Tubing Attached to Drum Is an Aid When Filling Containers

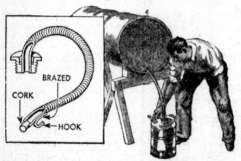

It won't be necessary to look high and low for a funnel when filling small containers with oil if you attach this flexible tubing to the drum. Get a plug that will fit the hole in the drum and drill it to take the tubing. Then braze the tubing to the plug and braze a wire hook to the nozzle end. When not in use, the tube is hooked over the top of the drum.

¶Hardened glue can be softened by placing a few drops of vinegar in the container.

INDEX